Approaches to
Social
Research

FOURTH EDITION

Royce A. Singleton, Jr.
College of the Holy Cross

Bruce C. Straits
University of California, Santa Barbara

New York ■ Oxford
Oxford University Press
2005

Oxford University Press

Oxford   New York
Auckland   Bangkok   Buenos Aires   Cape Town   Chennai
Dar es Salaam   Delhi   Hong Kong   Istanbul   Karachi   Kolkata
Kuala Lumpur   Madrid   Melbourne   Mexico City   Mumbai   Nairobi
São Paulo   Shanghai   Taipei   Tokyo   Toronto

Published by Oxford University Press, Inc.
198 Madison Avenue, New York, New York, 10016
www.oup.com

Oxford is a registered trademark of Oxford University Press

Library of Congress Cataloging-in-Publication Data

Singleton, Royce.
    Approaches to social research / Royce A. Singleton, Jr., Bruce C. Straits.—4th ed.
      p. cm.
    Includes bibliographical references and index.
    ISBN 0-19-514794-4
    1. Social sciences—Research. 2. Social sciences—Methodology. I. Straits, Bruce C. II.
Title.
H62.S4776 2004
300′.72—dc22   2004043396

Printing number: 9 8 7 6 5 4 3 2 1

Printed in the United States of America
on acid-free paper

To Nancy and Cathy

Contents

I / RESEARCH DESIGN   41

Chapter 3 / Elements of Research Design   43

Chapter 4 / Measurement   76

Chapter 5 / Sampling   111

II / METHODS OF DATA COLLECTION   153

Chapter 6 / Experimentation   155

Chapter 7 / Experimental Designs   187

III / DATA PROCESSING, ANALYSIS, AND INTERPRETATION 443

Chapter 14 / Data Processing and Elementary Data Analysis 445

Chapter 15 / Multivariate Analysis 483

Preface

To the Student

Of all the courses we teach, none is more important than research methods. Methodology is the heart of the social sciences; more than anything else, it is what distinguishes social science from journalism and social commentary, from the humanities and natural sciences. Understanding social research methods, therefore, should give you a better sense of sociology and related disciplines and of exactly what it is that social scientists do. To facilitate your understanding, in this book we have described an abundance of actual research studies that cover the full range of social science disciplines.

Besides deepening your understanding of social science, a knowledge of social research is essential for making informed decisions about our daily lives. Social scientific methods and findings influence us in numerous ways. Many government social programs are shaped and evaluated by social research; businesses constantly rely on consumer research for key marketing and management decisions; the popular press daily reports research findings on the most personal aspects of peoples' lives—from altruism to zero population growth. One of the goals of this book is to help you understand the logic and limitations of social research so that you can evaluate it effectively.

Finally, the study of social research methods should sharpen your powers of critical thinking and evaluation and enable you to become a more intelligent gatherer of information. Social research consists of activities and ways of thinking in which everyone frequently and profitably can engage. Realizing that most readers will not become social scientists, we have linked many topics to familiar subjects and frames of reference so that you can see how broadly social research may be applied.

The book is organized in three sections. After describing the scientific foundations of social research in chapter 2, the organization generally follows the process of conducting research. Part I introduces the basic terminology of social research (chapter 3) and then examines two key considerations in planning or designing a study: measurement (chapter 4) and sampling (chapter 5). Part II, on data collection, examines the four basic approaches to social research: experiments, surveys, field research, and the use of available data. The four main chapters (6, 8, 10, and 11) describe the distinctive process of executing a study with each approach; two other chapters (7 and 9) discuss technical features of experiments and surveys; and the last two chapters in this section present strategies for combining methods and approaches (chapter 12) and for applying research methods to the evaluation of social programs and interventions (chapter 13). Part III deals broadly with the interpretation phase of research. Here we discuss data processing and elementary data analysis (chapter 14) and more advanced, multivariate analysis (chapter 15), as well as research ethics (chapter 16) and the writing of research reports (chapter 17).

The book has several special features. Key terms are in boldface type when they first appear in the text and are also listed at the end of each chapter. If you are unsure of the meaning of a term introduced earlier in the text, you can always refer to the comprehensive glossary in the back of the book. Each chapter also contains an integrative summary of main points as well as review questions and problems to help test your memory and mastery of material. Finally, boxes are inserted in each of the main chapters to complement and expand the text; these present interesting research examples, provide additional aids to learning, or discuss the historical, social, and political contexts of research.

To the Instructor

Research methods texts differ in various ways. Some books, emphasizing the "how to" of the subject, try to provide students with the skills necessary to conduct their own research; others, emphasizing the "wherefore," try to make students more intelligent consumers of research findings. Still other texts, like this one, try to achieve a balance between the "how to" and "wherefore" of research. Some books are filled with hypothetical examples that idealize research procedures and outcomes; others use a few examples from the author's narrow research interests. By contrast, recognizing the broad audience for social research methods, we discuss hundreds of actual studies drawn from sociology, social psychology, communications, demography, history, education, and political science. Many of these studies are classics; others are very recent; all are carefully chosen to heighten students' interest.

Most methods books these days make much of the distinction between "qualitative" and "quantitative" research; a few endorse the postmodernist critique of sociology as a science. We assume, however, that all social research—whether based on so-called qualitative or quantitative methods—is driven by the same search for understanding, operates from similar epistemological bases, and addresses similar methodological concerns regarding reliability, validity, and generalizability. Major differences among research methods reside in general research strategies. Therefore, this book focuses on the four basic approaches to social research: experimentation, survey research, field research, and the use of available data. We discuss the advantages and disadvantages of each, treat the approaches as complementary rather than mutually exclusive, and ultimately advocate a multiple-methods strategy.

Focusing on overall approaches to conducting social research has several pedagogical advantages. First, it enables the reader to see each approach not as a method of data collection per se, divorced from research design and analysis, but as a fundamental choice that affects the entire research process. Other books tend to separate issues of design and data collection, or discuss certain design issues only in relation to specific approaches. For example, sampling techniques are described as survey methods, or measurement is described merely in terms of self-report questionnaire items. However, because measurement and sampling must be addressed in all research, we discuss these issues in relation to each basic approach. Second, the reader's sense of both the logic and the mechanics of doing research is enhanced by understanding the unique process of executing a study with each approach. Unlike the present text, other methods texts disregard the field administration phase of survey research, limiting the discussion to sampling and/or questionnaire design. Similarly, other texts discuss experiments merely in terms of experimental design without describing the basic parts or staging of experiments. A focus on the basic approaches, we believe, gives the reader a better sense of the integrity of social research and a greater appreciation both for its power and its limitations.

We feel strongly that social research methods is the most challenging and important course we teach. The challenges lie in doing justice to the complexities of research, in going beyond the simplest techniques to provide enough information for readers to become intelligent consumers of research, in developing an understanding not only of each individual stage of research but of the interrelatedness of all phases, and in presenting information about the "nuts and bolts" of research (e.g., how to draw a sample and how to code data) while not losing sight of the logic of inquiry or the overall research process. Much of what researchers do is informed by their understanding of the entire research process, so that elements of research design are dictated by a knowledge of the means of data collection and analysis. Thus, we precode questionnaires to facilitate data processing, and in anticipation of multivariate analysis, we include seemingly irrelevant background items in a questionnaire. Getting students to comprehend the overall process is perhaps our greatest challenge, and we believe that this challenge is best met by focusing on basic approaches to social research.

Aside from our emphasis on the four major approaches, we cover essentially the same topics in most other methods texts in approximately the same sequence. We tell students what makes social research scientific, discuss the relation between theory and research, introduce basic terminology, and then provide chapters on measurement, sampling, the major methods of data collection (i.e., the four approaches), data analysis, ethics, and report writing. Unlikes some other texts, we also provide extended treatments of experimental designs, survey pretesting and field administration, multiple methods (triangulation), and evaluation research.

Because we subsume methods of data collection under the four approaches, we do not have separate chapters on quasi-experimental research, which we discuss in relation to experimental design (chapter 7) and evaluation research (chapter 13); on observational methods, which we cover in our discussion of field research (chapter 10); and on historical document research and content analysis, which we include in the general strategy of using available data (chapter 11). Rather than present largely outdated material, we have chosen not to devote a full chapter to index and scale construction. Instead, we discuss technical aspects of scaling relatively briefly in connection with multiple methods (chapter 12).

Advanced topics are included but may be skipped without any loss of continuity. This provides considerable flexibility in using the text, allowing instructors to adopt it either for a one- or two-term course, for a lower- or upper-level undergraduate course, or for a graduate course. One can skip chapter 2 and go directly from chapter 1 to chapter 3. Other advanced chapters are 7 and 9, in which we dis-

cuss technical design issues related to experimentation and survey research, respectively. For instructors who want to examine the logic of experimental design,
chapter 7 introduces sources of invalidity and basic true, factorial, and quasi-
experimental designs. For instructors who emphasize survey research and have students collect data, we have found chapter 9 on survey instrumentation to be very
effective in preparing students to design their own questionnaires. Another option
for undergraduate courses is to assign chapters 7 and 9, but omit the more technical end-sections on quasi-experimental designs and survey pretesting, respectively.
Chapter 12, on multiple methods; chapter 13, on evaluation research; and especially
chapter 15, on multivariate analysis, also are advanced. Instructors teaching one-
term courses may easily skip all or portions of the more advanced chapters.

To further serve instructor's needs, we have prepared a comprehensive instructor's manual. Each chapter in the manual contains (1) lecture, discussion, and exercise ideas; (2) answers to questions in the text; and (3) test items. We are particularly
interested in hearing about how instructors complement the text through additional
readings, lectures, and assignments. We also welcome comments and suggestions for
further improving the book and helping to make it better serve your needs. Just write
to Royce A. Singleton, Jr., Department of Sociology and Anthropology, Holy Cross
College, Worcester, MA, 01610, or to Bruce C. Straits, Department of Sociology,
University of California, Santa Barbara, CA, 93106, or send a message to either of
our e-mail addresses: rsinglet@holycross.edu or straits@soc.ucsb.edu.

The Fourth Edition

To those familiar with earlier editions of *Approaches to Social Research*, the foregoing message to instructors may suggest few changes from the third edition. But
while we have retained the same overall organization and pedagogical emphases,
we have made substantial revisions. We eliminated the chapter on logic, folding
some of this material into a new section on logical reasoning in chapter 2 on science. To provide more continuity in the discussion of basic design issues in chapters 3 through 5 and an updated example of data analysis in chapters 14 and 15, we
introduced a recent study by Beckett Broh on the relation between extracurricular
involvement and academic achievement. Readers now learn about this study as they
are introduced to the language of social research, measurement, and sampling, and
to data processing and analysis. The two data analysis chapters also have been thoroughly revised. In chapter 14, all figures and tables report current GSS data, and
outmoded discussions of data processing have been replaced with material on online data sets and documentation; chapter 15 contains an expanded discussion of
elaboration and findings from the aforementioned Broh study. Both chapters reflect
our belief that discussions of data analysis in a research methods textbook should
emphasize the consumption rather than production of statistical analysis.

Besides these major revisions, we made numerous small editorial changes,
prompted by student feedback, reviewer comments, and our own teaching experiences, to clarify the presentation. Many other changes update information, such as
new professional codes of ethics, new developments in online literature searches,
and changes in the General Social Survey, which we use extensively to illustrate

survey procedures and questions. We also have included many new and updated research examples, such as Calvin Morrill's study of conflict management in corporations, David Harding and Christopher Jencks' analysis of changes in attitudes toward premarital sex, and Maria Krysan and Reynolds Farley's study of blacks' residential preferences.

In addition, the fourth edition includes several new sections within chapters:

- To illustrate better the scientific process, chapter 2 contains a new section on Emile Durkheim's *Suicide.*
- As an alternative to the exclusive coverage of between-subject experimental designs in previous editions, chapter 7 introduces "Within-Subject Designs."
- Given the expanding use of Internet surveys, chapter 8 now contains a separate discussion of "Self-Administered Electronic Surveys."
- To provide more information on "qualitative" interviewing and and how it complements direct observation in field research, chapter 10 now has an extended discussion and example of "Field Interviewing."
- Discussed only briefly in previous editions, the ethics of "Data Collection and Analysis" now leads the discussion of research ethics in chapter 16.

We trust that these changes have improved the book, providing an ever-more accessible introduction that presents the latest developments in methodology.

Acknowledgments

Approaches to Social Research has unfolded over a period of more than 25 years. During that time we have benefited greatly from the comments of numerous persons. Although it is impossible at this point to list everyone to whom we are indebted, several persons deserve special mention. Ron McAllister of Elizabethtown College initiated the project and coauthored the first edition. Margaret Miller Clark, another former coauthor, also made major contributions to the first edition. Many of our students and colleagues at Holy Cross and UCSB have provided inspiration and ideas. As we prepared to revise the third edition, we received helpful suggestions from a number of instructors and scholars. Ed Hackett of Arizona State University, Megan Sweeney of Rutgers University, and Michael Turner of Northeastern University reviewed the entire book. Some revisions were based on thoughtful feedback on individual chapters from Mark Hallahan of Holy Cross (experimentation and experimental design); Dave Hummon of Holy Cross (nature of science); David Snow of UC Irvine (field research); Peter Rossi, emeritus of the University of Massachusetts (evaluation research); and Tom W. Smith of the National Opinion Research Center (data analysis). Holy Cross librarian Patty Porcaro brought us up-to-date on developments in on-line literature searches. Beckett Broh graciously consented to the use of her study and kindly provided additional details about herself and her research. Finally, we benefited from the talents of Robert Singleton and Katherine Singleton Blehar. We gratefully acknowledge Rob's assistance in creating examples and writing the sections on using the Internet and library. A graphic designer, Kate created the covers for the third and fourth editions.

1

✓

Introduction

Social research consists of the process of formulating and seeking answers to questions about the social world. Consider some of the questions investigated in studies reported in this book.

- As a student, you probably have received numerous comments on your papers and examinations over the years. Those instructors who regularly commented on your work no doubt assumed that their feedback would improve your performance. But is this really an effective way for an instructor to spend his or her time? Ellis Page (1958) questioned whether teacher comments made a difference in student performance and, if so, what sort of comments would be most effective.
- Some recent studies indicate that high school athletes generally receive higher grades and test scores than do nonathletes. Beckett Broh (2002) asked why. Does this finding validate the conventional wisdom that sports participation teaches characteristics such as discipline, perseverance, and a strong work ethic, which promote academic achievement? Or does sports participation benefit athletes' social networks, placing them in a peer group of academically oriented high achievers or helping to establish relations among parents and teachers that facilitate and encourage achievement?
- Bibb Latané and John Darley (1970) speculated about why thirty-eight people in Queens, New York, watching the brutal attack of a woman from their apartment windows, failed to come to her aid in time to save her life. Was it the general apathy of people in modern, urban environments, as many experts claimed? Or was there something about the situation that inhibited people from helping? Why do bystanders sometimes fail to aid people immediately in a crisis situation?
- As the number of homeless people on the streets of U.S. cities increased visibly in the early 1980s, interest in the problem of homelessness grew. Peter Rossi (1989) asked, What is the extent of the problem—that is, how many homeless individuals are there—and what forces increased the number of homeless in the 1980s? David Snow and Leon Anderson (1993) wondered how the homeless lived. What were their daily lives like? What sort of material, interpersonal, and psychological strategies and routines did they fashion to facilitate their survival?
- In the 1970s and 1980s there was considerable debate over the proper police response to misdemeanor domestic assaults. Should police end the dispute by asking one of the parties to leave the premises? Should they attempt to mediate to de-escalate the conflict? Or should they arrest the assailant? Feminists pressed for more arrests. But Lawrence Sherman and Richard Berk (1984) wondered if this was the best policy. More generally, they pondered the effects of punish-

ment on behavior. Will punishment, such as an arrest, deter an individual from
repeating the crime? Or will punishment make individuals more likely to commit crimes?

- The famous witchcraft hysteria that swept through Salem, Massachusetts, in
  1692 has interested writers, historians, and other social scientists for many
  years. Kai Erikson (1966) wondered if this crime wave was consistent with sociologist Emile Durkheim's theory on the relationship between deviance and
  social order. Did the community response to deviance demonstrate shared values and enhance community solidarity?

To answer such questions, social scientists have devised basic guidelines, principles, and techniques. The purpose of this book is to introduce you to these "methods" as they are applied in the social sciences. As you will see, however, the research process is much more broadly applicable. The methods of social research can
be applied to investigate any curiosity, and our understanding of them can make us
smarter consumers, better informed voters, and better students. Let's begin by considering the value of studying research methods.

Why Study Research Methods?

The "why study" question may be asked more often about research methods than
about any other area of study in the social sciences. Often we hear students say, "I
don't intend to go to graduate school. And I don't intend to do research. Why do I
need to study ('suffer through') methods?" The irony in such a statement is that,
beyond providing a foundation of knowledge for those who do go on to become social scientists, the study of research methods may provide more immediate and useful information than any other single course of study. A knowledge of methods can
benefit you as both a consumer and a producer of research evidence.

Consuming Research Evidence

You may be a consumer of research in several positions: as a student reading research reports and journal articles to satisfy your curiosity or to meet course requirements and write term papers; as a social worker, educator, librarian, journalist, manager, or other professional keeping up to date in your field and acquiring
knowledge to guide you in making decisions; or as an average citizen attempting to
deal with the varied claims that are purported to be based on research. To make intelligent decisions about much day-to-day information, you must be able to understand and evaluate it. It is unfortunately true that much research evidence reported
in professional journals as well as in newspapers and on television either is itself in
error or is misinterpreted. Let us consider some of the kinds of misinformation to
which you are likely to be exposed.

Some time ago the following headline appeared in a local newspaper: "Beware
Crosswalk Safety Lines—They're Dangerous." The accompanying article reported
a study on safety in crosswalks that showed that more pedestrian accidents occur in
marked crosswalks than in unmarked crosswalks by a ratio of six to one. Marked

crosswalks refer to painted crosswalks without a guard, stop sign, or traffic light. Unmarked crosswalks refer to intersections with no painted crosswalk, stop sign, traffic light, or other controlling device. The article went on to point out how shocked traffic engineers had been by this finding, to speculate about factors that might contribute to a pedestrian's apparent false sense of security and carelessness in marked crosswalks, and to mention the major policy implication of phasing out unnecessary crosswalks. Very interesting—yet are these conclusions warranted? A knowledge of social research methods will sensitize you to a major problem with this type of study that casts serious doubt on the conclusions. The problem is that statistical associations, such as that between marked crosswalks and pedestrian accidents, do not always imply that one factor has caused the other. Marking crosswalks, in other words, may not cause more accidents. In fact, a more plausible interpretation of the reported six-to-one accident ratio is that more accidents occur in marked crosswalks because pedestrians use them much more often and because they appear at intersections where the traffic is heaviest. If this is the reason for the greater number of accidents in marked crosswalks, then of course it makes no sense to consider phasing out "unnecessary crosswalks" or to speculate about pedestrians' lack of vigilance.

A knowledge of research methods also can make you aware of the mischievous use of research evidence by advertisers. For example, how seriously should we take the TV pitch that "75 percent of doctors interviewed prescribed drug X for relief of arthritic pain?" Among the questions that a careful researcher could raise about this "fact" are these:

1. How many doctors were interviewed? (The 75-percent statistic could be based on as few as four interviews.)
2. What were the doctors asked about their prescription of drug X? (If they were asked, "Have you ever prescribed drug X?," they may be just as likely to have prescribed drugs A, B, C, and D, as well as X.)
3. Who interviewed the doctors? (If the manufacturers of drug X did the interviewing, then they may have influenced, wittingly or unwittingly, the doctors to favor their product.)

Advertisers are not the only source of misleading information. Another culprit is self-selected opinion surveys. To make money, attract new customers, and increase reader or viewer involvement, the media frequently conduct mail-in and call-in polls (Crossen, 1994:123). For example, in April 1993 *Parade Magazine* invited its readers to voice their opinions about crime in America by calling a 900 number (*Parade Magazine*, 1993). In all, 15,028 readers took up the invitation, paying a nominal fee to call in. Some 38 percent ("more than a third of Americans," according to *Parade*) said that they did not feel safe in their homes, 35 percent did not think the police were doing a good job, 81 percent did not have faith in the legal system, and 85 percent supported the death penalty. Although *Parade* noted that the results were based on a call-in survey, the magazine also implied that the results were representative of U.S. public opinion. But how representative is this sample? Because it was not randomly selected, the sample is not representative of any population other than the 15,028 callers. As a source of information about public opinion, therefore, it is worthless. Indeed, social scientists have derived the acronym SLOP to describe self-selected listener or reader opinion polls. It seems plausible that *Parade's* callers would tend to be more concerned about the problem of crime than the average U.S. resident. On at least two issues, data from random samples of the U.S. adult population support this conclusion: In 1992, 11 percent, compared with 38 percent in the *Parade* poll, did not feel safe and secure in their homes (Warr, 1995:305); and in 1993, 72 percent, as opposed to 85 percent in the *Parade* survey, supported the death penalty (Davis, Smith, and Marsden, 2002).

Because social science findings are reported in the media every day, we can scarcely avoid being consumers of social research evidence. Yet, as the above examples illustrate, we cannot assume automatically that conclusions based on statistical evidence from purported scientific studies are credible. It is therefore important to be able to make judgments about the quality of the data and the limits of the conclusions that might be drawn. As every good social scientist knows, research findings must be interpreted and applied with great care. Whether you are in a position where you need to know the policy implications of research findings or you are simply an ordinary citizen wanting to be better informed about such findings, the study of research methods can help you develop the ability to understand and evaluate the validity and limits of social scientific knowledge.

Producing Research Evidence

In addition to being consumers, we are gatherers and producers of research evidence. We manufacture evidence every time we seek out others' opinions about some issue, attempt to estimate the prevailing opinion within a particular group, or draw conclusions about persons and events on the basis of our own observations. As a producer of information, you will find in this introduction to social research principles and techniques that can be applied at levels of sophistication ranging from casual observation to the conduct of small-scale research projects.

Suppose you are trying to decide whether to take a particular course from professor X or professor Y. Gathering evidence to help you decide, you solicit opinions about the professors from fellow students. A knowledge of research principles not only could increase your awareness of the limitations in this approach but also could facilitate the collection of more trustworthy information. Research principles suggest, for example, that the trustworthiness of your information will depend on (1) the number of opinions solicited, (2) the consistency of those opinions, (3) whether your informants' opinions are formed and solicited independently of one another, and (4) how you pose the question when asking for opinions about professors X and Y.

At a slightly less mundane level, a knowledge of research techniques is essential for the nonscientist who needs to acquire reliable information about a particular group. This occurs more often than you might think. For example, politicians often need to find out what their constituents think about an important legislative issue; corporate executives may need information about their clients' or employees' reactions to proposed policy changes; journalists may want to know something about the makeup of their newspaper's or magazine's readership or may want to determine a community's attitude toward certain services or policies as part of a story they are preparing; students may want to collect data about student body behaviors or opinions as part of a term project or student newspaper article. None of these endeavors needs to entail the kind of massive research effort that would require expert researchers and statisticians. Yet each endeavor calls for the systematic collection of information, which is precisely what research methods is all about.

Methodological Approaches to the Social World

As our opening set of questions reveals, the topics of social research range broadly. In fact, whether a topic or research question is a legitimate object of social research hinges on two obvious criteria. First, the topic must concern *social* phenomena. This means that the research subject involves people—how they act, think, and feel, and how they interact with one another. It looks also at the groups that people form, from bowling clubs to leagues of nations, at relations within and among such groups, and at how the groups adapt to changes in society. Second, because social research is *scientific*, it must be possible to address the topic or answer the question by making appropriate observations. In chapter 2, on the nature of science, we distinguish scientific from nonscientific questions, as we discuss the similarities among all fields of scientific inquiry. Then, in the remainder of the book, we concern ourselves with research as it is practiced in such fields as anthropology, communications, economics, education, history, political science, psychology, and sociology.

Among these disciplines there are four principal research strategies for understanding the social world: experiments, surveys, field research, and the use of available data. Each discipline tends to favor one particular strategy. For example, psychologists typically conduct experiments, sociologists most often do survey research, anthropologists characteristically conduct field research, and historians tend to make use of available data. However, all four strategies are important to the world of social research, because any of the four can be used to study most social science topics. In fact, one of the early tasks of researchers is to decide which approach or approaches to take.

A discussion of the four basic strategies or approaches to social research comprises the central core of this book (see chapters 6–11). As each strategy is discussed, you will see that each has certain strengths and weaknesses that make the researcher favor one or another in different situations. Sometimes one strategy may not be feasible for ethical reasons (see chapter 16). Sometimes an approach will be ruled out because of constraints of time, personnel, space, or some other resource. Furthermore, many researchers argue, as we do in chapter 12, that it is best, whenever feasible, to study a given problem with a variety of methods so that the weaknesses of one strategy may be canceled out by the strengths of another. But it is often possible to study a social science topic using any one of the four basic research strategies. To demonstrate this we will consider the topic of altruism.

Some Preliminary Research Questions

Although altruism has been most intensively investigated during the past forty years, its study is almost as old as social science itself. The man who coined the word "sociology," Auguste Comte, also introduced the term "altruism" over 150 years ago. Comte thought of altruism as a sympathetic instinct or motive, in contrast to the egoistic motive of self-interest. Today, popular usage of the term still resembles his original concept. Here, for example, is one dictionary definition:

> **al-tru-ism** (al'troo iz em), *n*: 1. The principle or practice of unselfish concern for the welfare of others (opposed to *egoism*). (*Random House Webster's College Dictionary*, 1991).

Let us suppose that you are interested in the subject of altruism. As a social scientist, your special interest is in understanding altruism as a social phenomenon: What are the patterns of altruism? When, where, and how is it likely to occur? Why are people altruistic? These are the sort of grand questions that motivate all scientific inquiry. To begin your study of altruism, however, you would need to formulate questions that narrow the topic, reducing these original grand questions to manageable proportions. For example, instead of asking, What explains altruism? suppose you ask, What social norms motivate altruism? What situational features determine when one person is likely to help another? Will familiarity with the setting increase the likelihood that someone will help another in an emergency? How does a person's emotional mood influence his or her willingness to help? What is the family background of committed altruists? These are narrow, specific, and consequently *answerable* research questions.

There are, of course, a limitless variety of interesting and worthwhile questions that might be investigated. In chapters 2 and 3 we will consider the form of scientifically meaningful questions. Researchable questions derive from various sources: the researcher's personal values and goals, intuition, observation of dramatic events, and the state of current scientific knowledge. Eventually, your questions would be refined on the basis of a thorough review of the relevant social science literature. Here is where you would establish the theoretical and practical relevance of the research question. Here also is where you would begin to grapple with several preliminary methodological issues that will shape your study.

One of the most important issues involves the process of definition. As it turns out, dictionary definitions are not very satisfactory for research purposes. A dictionary would not be very helpful in distinguishing between altruism and similar concepts such as "empathy" or "helping," nor would it tell you how and where to observe instances of altruism. Your literature review would thus be important in revealing how other researchers have defined altruism conceptually and identified it empirically. Suppose, for example, that your review turned up the following reference:

> Piliavin, Jane Allyn and Hon-Wen Charng. 1990. Altruism: A review of recent theory and research. *Annual Review of Sociology*, Vol. 16, pp. 27–65

Reading this review article, you would find, according to Piliavin and Charng, that social scientific definitions of altruism generally differ in their relative emphasis on two factors: motives or intentions and costs to the actor. Taking these factors into account, you could define altruism as "a voluntary act intended to benefit another person that incurs some cost to the actor." Notice how much more precise this definition is than the dictionary definition.

Still, conceptual clarification is not enough. Altruism is not a commodity sold in packages at a hardware store or mined as a natural resource in remote places. Your review of prior research, therefore, should indicate how to define the phenomenon of interest not only with abstract concepts but also with concrete observations. To do this is to *operationalize* the concept. You could imagine ways of operationalizing altruism by identifying observable altruistic acts. Suppose, for example, that you decide that donating blood is one such act. This operational definition (one of the very many possible operationalizations) corresponds well to our conceptual definition above, yet it is empirical. Donating blood is

1. "a voluntary act" (people are rarely, if ever, forced to give blood)
2. "intended to benefit another person" (since the ultimate goal of donating blood is to help others)
3. "that incurs some cost to the actor" (the time and effort to give blood).

There are problems with this operational definition (e.g., the donor may decide to give blood because it is a requirement for joining a sorority), as there are whenever we operationalize concepts. But this example should give you a sense of how the researcher moves from abstract definitions to specific, concrete observations, a process that we will consider in detail in chapter 4.

Having posed a researchable (i.e., answerable) question and considered ways of observing the phenomenon, you are in a position to select an overall research strategy. Remember, however, that while any social science topic is researchable, not every approach is reasonable or feasible in every situation. Available resources, the kind of information sought, and one's discipline and training, among other factors, will affect which particular methods you decide to use. Putting such considerations aside, let us see how we might investigate altruism using each of the four basic approaches highlighted in this book: experiments, surveys, field research, and available data research. Each of these, it will be seen, can be used to investigate the topic of altruism and to answer the general question, What explains altruism?

An Experimental Answer

For several reasons that we will discuss in chapter 6, **experiments** frequently offer the best approach for investigating the causes of phenomena. In an experiment the researcher systematically manipulates some feature of the environment and then observes whether a systematic change follows in the behavior under study. Suppose that we are interested in determining if "mood" affects altruism. More specifically, will the experience of success or good fortune increase a person's willingness to help others? To study this question experimentally, we must create a situation wherein some persons will experience good fortune and others will not, after which all persons are presented with the opportunity to help someone else. If those who experienced good fortune are more likely to help than those who did not, the "hypothesis" that good mood promotes altruism will be supported. In fact, this hypothesis has been supported in several experimental studies. Let us consider an early study by social psychologists Alice Isen and Paula Levin (1972).

To induce a good mood or feeling, Isen and Levin set up public telephone booths so that users would find "lost" change unexpectedly in the coin return slot. To do this, one of the experimenters entered the booth, made an incomplete call, ostensibly took her dime from the return slot, and then left. (Of course, pay phones cost a lot more than a dime today.) In actuality, the dime was left for half of the experimental trials. In this way half of the persons using the booth afterward received an unexpected dime when they checked the coin return, while half did not.

After the telephone booth had been "stocked" and subjects had made their calls, subjects were presented with the opportunity to help someone in the following manner. As the subject left the booth, an accomplice of the experimenter, who had stationed herself nearby, started walking in the same direction as the subject and, while walking slightly ahead of him or her, dropped a manila folder full of papers in the subject's path. "Helping" occurred if the subject helped pick up the papers. The results of the experiment clearly supported the hypothesis that feeling good leads to helping. Subjects who found a dime helped in fourteen of sixteen cases, whereas only one subject in twenty-five who did not find a dime stopped to help.

The essential feature of the Isen and Levin study that illustrates the experimental approach is that a potential influence on altruism—mood—was isolated and systematically varied from subject to subject while all other factors that might influence altruism were "held constant," or remained the same for all subjects. For example, the same experimenter used the same telephone booth with the same accomplice and the same procedures. But what purpose does it serve to hold these features of the experiment constant? Why was it necessary to include a comparison group of subjects who did not receive a dime? How did the experimenters decide which subjects to let find the dime, and why is this such an essential part of the experiment? More generally, why go to the trouble of contriving and conducting an experiment when there are lots of naturally occurring acts of altruism that can be studied? In chapter 6 we examine the logic of the experimental approach and various mechanisms for staging experiments, as well as the advantages and disadvantages of this form of research. In chapter 7 we look at different types of experimental designs.

An Answer from Survey Research

A second approach to studying altruism that might be taken is the **survey**. Survey research involves the administration of questionnaires or interviews to relatively large groups of people. One purpose of surveys is to describe the frequency of certain characteristics among groups or populations. For example, a survey might tell you how many people at your college, or in your organization, have voluntarily given blood, have done volunteer work for a charitable organization, or have contributed money to charities. Such information can be related to various other characteristics of respondents, such as their gender, age, marital status, religion, and occupation, thereby enabling the survey researcher to understand as well as describe the incidence of altruism.

Richard Titmuss's (1971) cross-national study of blood donating provides one example of the use of survey research in the study of altruism. As part of this study, Titmuss collected information via a questionnaire from over 3800 blood donors in England and Wales. Britain offers an excellent milieu for studying blood donating as an altruistic act since, unlike the United States at the time of this study, where donors often were paid or insured for their blood needs in return for their blood, donors in Britain are prohibited by law from receiving any tangible reward. To study the characteristics and motives of blood donors, Titmuss asked donors at several collection points to fill out a two-page questionnaire as they waited to give blood. The questionnaire requested information on the respondent's age, gender, marital status, family size, occupation, income, number of blood donations given, whether the respondent and close relatives had received a blood transfusion, and the respondent's reasons for giving blood. One finding was that the donor population closely resembled the general population in terms of age, sex, and marital status when age-related incapacity and childbearing were taken into account. This is a particularly interesting finding when compared with the United States, where those under the age of 30, singles, and males are vastly overrepresented among donors.

While questionnaires and interviews often are used in conjunction with other forms of research, a key feature of survey studies is that information is collected from part of a group (e.g., 3800 actual donors) to make generalizations about the whole group (all donors in England and Wales). However, such generalizations are hazardous unless careful procedures are followed in deciding who is to be included in the study. Furthermore, collecting data from very many people may exceed the budgets for most research. In chapter 5 we discuss sampling techniques for choosing respondents that are designed to increase accuracy and reduce costs.

Many questions can be raised about survey research in general and the Titmuss study in particular. Why did Titmuss choose to use written questionnaires rather than face-to-face interviews? How did he decide which questions to ask, how best to word the questions, and in what order to ask them? These are the kinds of issues we address in chapters 8 and 9.

An Answer from Field Research

Field research is essentially a matter of immersing oneself in a naturally occurring (rather than a "staged") set of events in order to gain firsthand knowledge of the situation. Anthropologists who live in remote communities for long periods to study the culture of the inhabitants are engaged in this form of research, as are other social scientists who voluntarily become members of organizations and groups or take jobs for the sake of conducting social research. In such settings, the field researcher seeks to understand the world as his or her subjects see it and to collect information without unduly influencing its shape and content.

Field research on altruism seldom has been conducted, although there are numerous settings where this approach could be applied. For example, one could work in a blood donor center or join the Red Cross, Salvation Army, or some other emergency relief organization. One also might observe altruistic actions in the wake of a community disaster, as Louis Zurcher (1968) did when he joined a volunteer work crew after a tornado ripped through Topeka, Kansas, in June of 1966. Zurcher's field study provides interesting insights into the kind of responses communities make to disasters.

Thirty-six hours after the tornado struck, Zurcher became a member of a spontaneously formed work crew that spent three days removing fallen tree limbs and trees from houses. Crew members were Topeka residents who lived outside of the tornado's direct path and whose homes had not been seriously damaged. According to Zurcher, his own and others' attraction to the crew came from an urge to do something to fight back at the tornado's destructive force. Unlike other crew members, however, Zurcher decided to use the occasion for data-gathering purposes— to observe and record the group processes. He was particularly interested in how the crew created a set of temporary disaster roles that allowed individuals to reassert their coping abilities and helped the community to restore its cohesiveness when the usual work and community activities were disrupted by the calamity. His account describes the development of the crew from a bunch of co-acting individuals to a cohesive group with a well-defined division of labor and "a sense of group history, loyalty, and humor."

To analyze this setting, Zurcher relied heavily on his direct observations as a participant in the work crew and to a lesser extent on interviews with crew members after the group dissolved. The crucial feature of his research was a running log of observations recorded at the end of each day. But how did Zurcher decide what aspects of this extraordinarily complex social situation to observe and record? Deciding what to record and when and how to record one's observations are basic problems for field researchers. While Zurcher's study was impromptu, most field researchers also face problems of selecting an appropriate setting or group for study and then of gaining entry to and getting along with others in the setting. In chapter 10 we discuss such issues in detail; we also consider the special techniques that field researchers have developed for handling, organizing, and analyzing their observations.

An Answer from Available Data

The final approach to studying the social world discussed in this volume is the use of **available data**—that is, data that have been generated for purposes other than those for which the researcher is using them. Prominent among such data sources would be written records, from letters and diaries to newspapers and government documents; but available data also would include nonverbal physical evidence such as paintings, clothing, tools, and other artifacts. Even tombstones could be considered data in this sense, since they are created for one purpose (to mark graves) but could be used for others (e.g., to study the diffusion of sculptural styles over several generations). How might altruism be studied with this approach?

In one of the earliest empirical studies of altruism, sociologist Pitirim Sorokin (1950) used two interesting data sources. The first consisted of 500 letters describing individuals who had performed good deeds. The letters were recommendations that had been sent to a 1940s radio program that rewarded "good neighbors" with an orchid and a citation on the program. The second data source consisted of biographies of Catholic saints as compiled in Butler's twelve-volume *The Lives of the Saints*.

Sorokin's analysis of these letters and biographies revealed the kinds of acts regarded as altruistic as well as numerous characteristics of people who had acted altruistically. Among other things, he found that the "good neighbors" and saints often were societal deviants whose level of moral conduct rose above or conflicted with the official law and government, that a catastrophic event frequently precipitated their altruism, and that they usually had experienced a happy childhood in a strong, well-integrated family.

Obviously, it requires a great deal of imagination and ingenuity just to think of and uncover the kinds of information analyzed by Sorokin. Simply finding appropriate available data is a major problem encountered with this approach. But once the data are in hand, still other problems arise. The most fundamental of these is how to codify the data in a systematic fashion; other issues include what to do when there is insufficient information about cases or when information is not comparable from one case to another. Then there is the issue of the authenticity of the information. How accurate is the biographer's information? How much has the biographer embellished and glorified the life of his or her subject? These and other issues raised by the use of available data are discussed in chapter 11.

Conclusions

Our goal in this introduction has been to demonstrate the value of studying research methods and to describe the general nature of social research. Social research helps us to understand the social world by producing scientifically valid answers to questions. You may seek "answers" from social research in your student and professional lives, and you inevitably will be exposed to various answers through the media. Media reports of social scientific studies, however, sometimes distort the facts and sometimes draw erroneous or misleading conclusions. Moreover, there is inevitably some degree of uncertainty and error in social research. Studying research methods will cultivate your skepticism about research evidence. But it is a healthy skepticism, because enhancing your ability to understand and evaluate how research findings are arrived at will enable you to identify whether they are based on more or less sound methods of inquiry and whether they warrant strong or weak conclusions.

Exploring how social scientists have investigated the topic of altruism introduced an important theme of this book. That is, while social scientists have developed a variety of approaches to social research, no one approach is inherently superior to another and all approaches may be understood within the framework of scientific inquiry and the quest for understanding. To be sure, the four most basic approaches differ in many ways, and each has its distinctive strengths and weaknesses. Yet, we believe that all approaches must address the same central methodological issues and are subject to the same underlying logic of inference. That the sources of error vary from one approach to another only underscores the value in combining approaches and using them in complementary ways to validate knowledge.

An Overview of the Book

In the second chapter we describe the scientific foundations of social research. As we explain the form of scientific explanations and the general process of scientific inquiry, we assume the essential unity of all the sciences, drawing examples from physics, chemistry, and biology as well as sociology. This does not mean that there is a unified method or "cookbook" for conducting scientific research. It means, rather, that all scientific disciplines abide by the same epistemic requirements for judging the credibility of theories and evidence.

The remainder of *Approaches to Social Research* is divided into three sections that roughly follow the stages in conducting research, from the formulation of a problem or question to data collection to analysis and interpretation. The first section covers the major ingredients of the overall research plan. Focusing on problem formulation, chapter 3 introduces the basic language of social research and also outlines the various purposes of conducting social research and the overall research process. Chapter 4 describes how social scientists operationalize concepts and evaluate the quality of operational definitions. Chapter 5 describes the scientific principles and methods of selecting a representative set of cases. The goal of social research is to answer questions about the social world by producing *valid* empirical evidence. Accordingly, each chapter in this section addresses a key issue in determining the validity of social scientific evidence: the validity of causal inferences (chapter 3), the validity of operationalizations of concepts (chapter 4), and the generalizability of findings (chapter 5). As we discuss these issues, we draw upon the second study mentioned at the beginning of the chapter: Broh's analysis of the impact of sports participation on academic achievement.

Each of the three validity issues is addressed again in the second section of the book with respect to the four basic approaches to social research. Four chapters outline the essential features, variants, steps in conducting, and distinctive advantages and disadvantages of each approach: experiments (chapter 6), surveys (chapter 8), field research (chapter 10), and research using available data (chapter 11). Two chapters elaborate on special technical features of experiments and surveys. Chapter 7 outlines a framework for analyzing the validity of causal conclusions and various experimental designs that serve as ideal models for establishing causal relationships. Chapter 9 describes the elements of designing a questionnaire. Chapter 12 examines how two or more of the four basic approaches to social research may be combined effectively to strengthen the validity of research findings. Finally, the concluding chapter of this section examines the special features and problems of conducting evaluation studies, a burgeoning area of social research aimed at assessing social intervention programs and policies.

Throughout this section we use several studies to illustrate the process and problems of conducting social research. Thus, here is where you will read about the other studies mentioned at the beginning of this chapter: Page's experiment on teacher comments and Latane and Darley's experiments on bystander intervention in emergencies (chapter 6), Snow and Anderson's field research on homelessness (chapter 10), Erikson's analysis of the Salem witch hysteria (chapter 11), and Sherman and Berk's analysis of the impact of arrests in cases of domestic assault (chapters 12 and 13).

The third section deals broadly with the processing, analysis, and interpretation of data. Chapter 14 outlines the steps in processing data for quantitative analysis and describes elementary statistical analyses. Chapter 15 considers various statistical techniques for analyzing causal relationships. One important framework for the conduct and interpretation of social research, which we cover in chapter 16, is research ethics: the ethics of data collection, the treatment of human subjects, and responsibility to society. And, since almost all social research ultimately becomes known and is interpreted by others through the reading of reports, books, and articles, in the final chapter (17) we examine the writing of research.

Key Terms

experiment	*field research*
survey	*available data*

Review Questions and Problems

1. From the standpoint of the consumer of research evidence, why is it important to study research methods?

2. Briefly describe and contrast each of the four major research strategies for understanding the social world: experiments, surveys, field research, and the use of available data.

3. Find a story or article in the media (e.g., newspaper, magazine, television) that reports the findings of a social scientific study or of a contention (e.g., an advertising claim) purportedly based on social scientific evidence.

2

✓

The Nature of Science

That sociology (as well as the other social sciences—anthropology, economics, political science, and psychology) claims to be scientific will not come as news to students of research methods. Yet, we have found that some students reject this claim altogether, while others believe that regardless of how scientific sociology purports to be, it differs substantially from other "true" sciences. Apparently, students' (and other educated persons') image of sociology does not fit recollections of high school courses in biology, chemistry, or physics, with their accumulated facts, abstract formulas, and laboratory experiments. Nor does it seem consistent with what students know about the theoretical genius of such well-known scientists as Albert Einstein and Sir Isaac Newton or about scientific discoveries with great practical significance like the Salk vaccine or laser beam. These impressions, however, miss the essential character of science. Science is not really about collections of facts and formulas, precise instrumentation, white lab coats and test tubes, ingenious people, or remarkable discoveries and inventions. It is something much more general than any of these things—something that unifies sociology and the other social sciences with the natural sciences.

Obviously, what unites the sciences is not specific research techniques; a book on chemical synthesis would be of no use to someone doing sociological research. What unites science are its objectives, its presuppositions, its general methodology, and its logic. That is what we focus on in this chapter—the epistemological foundations of science that transcend specific subject matters, guiding the efforts of researchers in many different disciplines.

Understanding the nature of science should clarify the objectives and general logic of social research. But such understanding also is important in a broader sense. Misconceptions undoubtedly underlie many of the fears and concerns about modern science. People who identify scientific discovery with modern technology often see science as harmful and destructive; others doubt its relevance for solving the most intractable human problems. At a time when people entertain such views, it is especially important, as the late Isaac Asimov (1980) pointed out, that the public's reactions toward science "not be based on ignorant emotion alone."

> Of the millions who watch sports events, a vanishingly small percentage can play any of the games they watch with anything approaching professional skill, yet virtually all understand the rules well enough to appreciate what they see. The public must then, in the same way, understand science if it is to react intelligently. They must at least be capable of following the game, even if they can't play it.

The Aim of Science

The word "science" comes from the Latin *scientia*, which means "knowledge." Contemporary science has been characterized falsely by some as a *profound* body of knowledge, profound in that it is not trivial and not comprehensible to the average person (Mazur, 1968). What is profound, however, is a matter of perspective and judgment. Today's seemingly trivial finding may be tomorrow's major scientific breakthrough. Research that the layperson sees as trifling and irrelevant, which the scientist may pursue purely from intellectual curiosity, may help to solve important practical problems. Who would have thought, for example, that discoveries about the mating behavior of certain insects would provide a basis for pest control, that learning principles derived from studying the bar-pressing behavior of animals in boxes could be used to help the mentally retarded, or that research on ant "trails" would provide clues to the chemistry of communication? The practical implications of scientific knowledge, as these examples suggest, often are difficult to foresee. It is clear, therefore, that qualities like profundity, relevance, and significance are of little use in differentiating science from nonscience.

The aim of science is to produce knowledge, to understand and explain some aspect of the world around us. But accumulated knowledge per se does not distinguish science from mythology. What, then, makes an endeavor scientific? Basically, it is a matter of *how* and *why* knowledge is accepted by the scientific community. Two interrelated sets of criteria determine acceptance or rejection. One set of criteria pertains to the form or logical structure of knowledge, the other to the evidence on which it is based. In discussing the nature of science, therefore, we distinguish among the laws, principles, and theories that constitute the *product* of science and the methods and logic of inquiry that comprise the *process* through which scientific knowledge is created, tested, and refined.

Although the analogy is imperfect, it may help in following our discussion to think of a factory or industrial plant in which certain raw materials are processed to create a finished product. One of the differences between industry and science lies in what is processed: Industries manufacture material things; science processes *ideas*. Of course, science has made possible innumerable technological advances, whose material fruits, perhaps because of their visibility, are often seen as the essential end-product of science. But these practical results are mere by-products of scientific inquiry. The real goal of science is to achieve understanding; the basic product is ideas.[1] We will see the form that these ideas take as we first consider science as a product. Then we will turn our attention to the science process.

Science as Product

Scientific disciplines differ in terms of their objects of study. Physics is concerned with matter and energy, biology is concerned with the life processes of plants and animals, psychology is concerned with human and animal behavior, and sociology is concerned with properties and processes of social groupings. As a consequence, each of these disciplines has developed its own unique concepts, laws, and theories.

Yet, in spite of such differences, all scientific knowledge, regardless of the field of study, shares certain defining characteristics, the first of which is the type of questions that may be addressed.

Scientific versus Nonscientific Questions

Whether a question can be approached scientifically depends on whether it can be subjected to verifiable observations. That is, it must be possible for the scientist to make observations—which others also are capable of making—that can answer the question. This means that philosophical questions about essence, existence, or morality are beyond the realm of science. Answers to some philosophical questions do become the fundamental postulates, or assumptions, of science, but these cannot be investigated scientifically. Thus, scientists can only assume that the world exists, that empirically verifiable knowledge is possible, that we can know the world through our senses, and that there is an order to the world.[2] Having made such assumptions, what scientists try to do is describe and explain the order that they assume to exist.

It would be proper for a social scientist to ask such questions as: Why do some persons read pornographic literature or view pornographic films? Why is one type of organization more efficient than another? Are sibling relationships related to adult sexual preference? But it would *not* be within the realm of science to ask: Is pornography morally wrong? Should efficiency be valued over morale? Is homosexuality contrary to God's will? The difference between these two sets of questions is that the former deal with how and why regular patterns of events occur, whereas the latter ask what is desirable. Questions of morality, existence, or ultimate causality are certainly worth asking and speculating about, but they fall within the purview of philosophy and religion. They are not scientific because they cannot be framed in such a way that *observations* can be made to answer them.

Both philosophers and scientists ask about the "why" of things. But to the scientist, as psychologists Michael Doherty and Kenneth Shemberg (1978:6) note, "the 'why' is just shorthand for, What is the relationship between . . . or, Under what conditions. . . ." When we can use these phrases, "then the question could be a legitimate scientific question, provided the other terms in the question meet the test of observability." Thus, we can observe whether people read pornographic literature or view pornographic films, and we can try to determine, through observation, the "conditions" (e.g., personal characteristics, relationships with parents and others, occupation) under which this is likely to occur. Likewise, we can determine what the relationship is between type of organization and efficiency, assuming we can decide how to distinguish different forms of organization and can decide on the pattern of observations that represents "efficiency." No such appeals to objective evidence, however, will enable us to decide if purveyors of pornography should be legally prosecuted or left alone, or to decide the relative importance of efficiency and morale.[3]

In short, scientific questions are questions that can be answered by making observations that identify the conditions under which certain events occur. Still, to qualify as scientific knowledge, the *answers* to such questions must take a particular form, a form that meets the requirements of description, explanation, prediction, and understanding.

Knowledge as Description

Scientific knowledge is by definition verifiable. For verification to be possible, explanations and findings must be communicated clearly to others. Consequently, scientists make a great fuss about language: Observations must be precisely and reliably reported; terms must be carefully defined, with clear referents; and the phenomena to which each scientific discipline addresses itself must be organized and classified in a meaningful way. Thus, description is the first step in producing scientific knowledge. We must describe objects and events before we can understand and explain the relationships among them. In order to describe, each discipline develops its own special language or set of concepts.

Concepts are abstractions communicated by words or other signs that refer to common properties among phenomena. The term "weight," for example, symbolizes a conception of a property of all physical objects. Likewise, the sociological term "status" is an abstraction that points to a property of a social structure or group. The first rule about the scientific use of concepts is one word, one concept. Sociologist George Zito (1975:21) noted that in everyday language, one word may stand for many different things; "mass," for example, may mean the quality of size and weight, the main part, a Christian religious ceremony, and the like. To the physicist, however, "it means only the quantity of matter in a body as measured in relation to its inertia." Because everyday language is so vague and full of multiple meanings, scientists find it necessary to restrict or redefine the meaning of common words or to invent new terms (sometimes called constructs), thereby creating highly technical vocabularies.

Scientists' second rule about concepts is that there must be agreed-on ways of tying concepts to tangible objects and events. This extends the first rule by stating that concepts must be defined directly or indirectly in terms of precise, reliable observations. It would be scientifically unacceptable to describe something as "heavy," not only because this term has many different connotations (i.e., refers to more than one concept) but also because as a symbol for any single concept, its referent is imprecise. If you used the term "heavy" to describe the weight of an object, some people may agree with your description and some may not. But if you use a scale and describe the weight as 50 pounds, others can agree readily on the accuracy of your description. By the same token, many concepts (e.g., "energy," "electron," "wavelength") that are not simply and directly observable in the sense of "weight" are scientifically acceptable because they imply characteristics that are observable. For example, physicists cannot directly observe or measure the movement of molecules postulated by the kinetic theory of gases; however, by using a pressure gauge, they can measure the pressure that this movement implies. Linking concepts to observable events, called measurement, is something about which we will have a great deal more to say in chapter 4.

One additional feature of language, in both conventional and scientific usage, is that it tends to determine what we see in the world. Because what we know about objective reality is represented and communicated with words, words make some distinctions more salient than others. Research has shown, for example, that people have better recognition memory for colors that they can label with familiar words (Lucy and Shweder, 1979). Furthermore, implicit in the use of all concepts are assumptions about their relative importance for describing and explaining the world around us. Scientists develop special concepts because they are useful for understanding. For instance, the existence of the term "social class" reflects its utility for explaining sociological concerns like social order and social change. This implies a third rule about language usage in science: Concepts are judged by their usefulness. Scientists are not dogmatic about concepts. Once a concept has outlived its usefulness, or the explanation in which it is embedded has been superseded by a better explanation, it is discarded. Thus, the history of science, to paraphrase an unknown philosopher, is a graveyard of concepts.

Knowledge as Explanation and Prediction

Explanations, according to sociologist Gwynn Nettler (1970), are attempts to satisfy curiosity. Depending on the type of question and the needs of the interrogator, curiosity may be satisfied in several ways: by labeling (as when the appropriate term is given in response to a child's question about what something is), by defining or giving examples (as when new terms are clarified with familiar terms and images), by evoking empathy (as when people offer motives or other "good reasons" for their conduct), by appealing to authority (as, for example, when something is attributed to "God's will"), or by citing a general empirical rule (as, for example, when we say that this book falls when dropped because it is denser than air, and all objects denser than air fall when dropped). Only this last form of explanation is capable of meeting the twin objectives of scientific knowledge—to *explain* the past and present and to *predict* the future.

The "empirical rules" with which scientific explanations are built consist of abstract statements, or propositions, that relate changes in one general class of events to changes in another class of events under certain conditions. Consider, for example, the following two propositions, the first a part of the Ideal Gas Law from chemistry, the second a generalization from social psychology known as the social facilitation effect:

1. If the volume of a gas is constant, then an increase in temperature will be followed by an increase in pressure (Reynolds, 1971:5).
2. If a task is simple or well learned, then an individual will perform it better in the presence of others than in isolation.

According to each of these propositions, a change in one set of events (temperature of a gas, absence or presence of others) is followed by a change in another set of events (pressure of the gas, performance of an individual) under specified conditions (constant volume, simple or well-learned task). The propositions are abstract in two senses. First, since they may refer to past, present, or future changes, they make no reference to historical time. Second, each proposition pertains to a *general* class of events: gases of a constant volume in one instance and individuals performing simple tasks in the other. The second proposition would be less abstract if it made reference only to males, and still less abstract if it applied only to males with high self-esteem. Level of abstractness is important because the ideal in science is to develop the most general understanding: to establish propositions capable of explaining and predicting the widest possible range of events.

Scientists use various terms to denote propositions such as the Ideal Gas Law and social facilitation effect. They may be called **empirical generalizations** when they are derived from observations or **hypotheses** when they have been proposed but not tested. To the extent that the propositions have been repeatedly verified and are widely accepted, they may become known as scientific **laws**. In any case, as scientific explanations, they describe, explain, and predict particular phenomena. The terms contained within the propositions are the concepts that describe—organize and classify—the phenomena to be explained. Thus the Ideal Gas Law classifies gases according to their volume, temperature, and pressure; the social facilitation effect organizes individual behavior in terms of the concepts of task simplicity, presence or absence of others, and level of performance. Furthermore, each proposition explains and predicts by identifying the conditions (e.g., constant volume, increase in temperature) under which particular events occur (increase in pressure).

Scientific explanation does not end here, however. For although specific events are explained by empirical laws, the regularities expressed by these laws themselves require explanation. The Ideal Gas Law raises the question of *why* increases in temperature invariably increase the pressure of gases under constant volume. Similarly, with respect to the social facilitation effect, why should the presence of others facilitate one's performance on simple tasks?

To answer such questions, and generally to explain empirical generalizations or laws, science introduces theories. **Theory** is one of the most elusive and misunderstood terms in science. It does not mean, as it is popularly understood, "idle speculation or conjecture." A scientific theory consists of a set of interconnected propositions that have the same form as laws but are more general or abstract. Notice how the following set of propositions, called the kinetic theory of gases, explains the Ideal Gas Law by showing how it follows from the "conception of a gas as a collection of molecules in constant motion" (adapted from Reynolds, 1971:8):

> As the temperature increases, the kinetic energy of the gas molecules increases.
> As the kinetic energy increases, there is an increase in the velocity of the motion of the molecules.
> As the molecules travel faster, but are prevented from traveling further by a vessel of constant volume, they strike the inside surface of the vessel more often and with more force.
> As the molecules strike the sides of the vessel more frequently, the pressure on the walls of the vessel increases.
> Therefore, assuming a constant volume, as the temperature increases, the pressure increases.

Scientific theories may be stated in various ways. The above set of propositions is arranged in a logical network that shows how the law may be deduced from the theory. In chemistry and physics, theories often take the form of mathematical formulas. For example, the formula $PV = nRT$ represents the Ideal Gas Law. Aside from economics, theories in the social sciences usually are stated less formally. What is most critical, from the standpoint of science, is not how the theory is presented, but that it is logically consistent and empirically testable.

Still, it is possible to have several logically coherent theories that explain a given empirical regularity and that make the same or similar testable predictions. This is true of the social facilitation effect, for which no established theoretical explanation exists, even though several theories have been proposed. One theory holds that an audience enhances performance on simple tasks because the mere physical presence of others increases one's physiological arousal. According to another theory, enhanced performance occurs when persons believe that the other persons present are judging or evaluating their behavior. Scientific research often is directed toward testing such alternative theories, but ultimately one theory is judged superior to other competing theories to the extent that it (1) involves the fewest number of statements and assumptions, (2) explains the broadest range of phenomena, and (3) makes the most accurate predictions.

Knowledge as Understanding

Finally, many scientists maintain that, in addition to making testable predictions, scientific laws and theories must provide a sense of understanding. Although there is no consensus on the meaning or necessity of the "understanding" criterion, social scientists generally agree that this sense is gained by describing the causal process that connects events (Reynolds, 1971). A theory often meets this criterion in explaining a law or empirical generalization. The connection between temperature and pressure in the Ideal Gas Law, for example, seems more understandable once we know the underlying process, described by the kinetic theory, by which temperature causes an increase in kinetic energy, which causes an increase in the velocity of molecules, and so on. Similarly, a law or hypothesis is thought to be scientifically meaningful when it describes a **causal relationship**—that is, a relationship in which a change in one event forces, produces, or brings about a change in another. In fact, unless a true causal relationship is identified, generalizations cannot meet the dual requirement of explanation and prediction. We can see this by examining some scientifically inadequate generalizations.

Many so-called "scientific" generalizations purport to explain but have no readily observable consequences and hence cannot predict. Standard examples abound in Freudian psychology. For instance, Freud suggested that all dreams represent the fulfillment or attempted fulfillment of a wish and that all persons have a death wish (Hall and Lindzey, 1970). The problem with these generalizations is that they too readily "explain" things after the fact. We can always find some wish with which to interpret or explain a dream, once it has occurred. Similarly, every suicide or accident can be attributed to a death wish. This is like placing your bet after the race is over. Once an event has occurred, any number of plausible, intuitively appealing explanations can be offered. The trick is also to indicate what to expect under given conditions. Without this kind of objective testability, it is impossible to tell if one event has caused the other; such post hoc generalizations thus give us a false sense of understanding.

It is also possible to predict an event on the basis of empirical generalizations without understanding the connection between generalization and prediction. Astronomical predictions of the movement of the stars were quite accurate long before satisfactory explanations for the movement existed. Today, the healing powers of aspirin are put to use even though the reason for aspirin's effectiveness is not well understood; election outcomes can be predicted accurately while their explanation remains unsatisfactory; and, more mundanely, people continue to use a variety of time-tested, reliable, yet seemingly inexplicable predictors of weather changes. It is a folk wisdom, for example, that the leaves of trees show their light green undersides when a storm is imminent. Generalizations such as these, unlike those that "explain" but do not predict, can be tested and are useful in certain contexts. However, their utility is limited. Once we have an adequate theory that describes the causal process connecting events, we get not only a better sense of understanding but more accurate and more useful predictions.

Many examples from the history of science show how identifying causal processes enhances the utility of knowledge. One of the more interesting cases is the discovery of the cause and cure of rickets (Loomis, 1970). Rickets is a disease resulting in the softening and bending of growing bones. It is caused by a deficiency of solar ultraviolet radiation, which is necessary for synthesis of a calcifying hormone released into the bloodstream by the skin. Without this hormone (calciferol), an insufficient amount of calcium is deposited in growing bones, causing the crippling deformities of rickets. Either adequate sunlight or the ingestion of minute amounts of calciferol will prevent and cure rickets. Before the causal process underlying rickets was understood, however, scientists could, in a sense, predict its occurrence. They noted, for example, seasonal variations in rickets—that is, its rise during the "darker" winter months. They observed its greater prevalence in cities than in rural districts and in northern industrial nations as opposed to northern nonindustrialized nations. Identifying such patterns eventually led to the conclusion that sunlight had the power to prevent and cure rickets. But it was not until the sun's role in the production of calciferol was understood—until the complete causal process was identified—that rickets could be eradicated completely, even in areas where the sun's ultraviolet radiation is absent.

Thus, explanation in social science generally boils down to a search for causes. Knowing when and how to infer causality is a prerequisite for most social research. One of our goals, therefore, is to enhance this ability, which we will begin to do in chapter 3 when we discuss criteria used to establish causality.

Tentative Knowledge

Psychologist B. F. Skinner (1953:11) argued that "science is unique in showing a cumulative progress," which enables each succeeding generation of scientists to begin a little further along. Thus, "our contemporary writers, artists, and philosophers are not appreciably more effective than those of the golden age of Greece, yet the average high school student understands much more of nature than the greatest of Greek scientists."

To the extent that this is true, it is due largely to the *tentative* nature of scientific knowledge. Scientists never achieve complete understanding, nor do they assume access to indubitable truths. One reason is that every answer leads to new questions, every new fact, law, or theory presents new problems, so that no matter what the present state of scientific knowledge, there is always more to know. When or where this progression ends is impossible to tell; however, it is clear that science has barely scratched a very large surface.

Aside from the vast amount that there is to know, the primitive scientific knowledge that we now possess is assumed to be tentative and uncertain for another, more definitive reason. Unlike mathematics or logic, where the "truth" of statements is either assumed or rests on other statements that are assumed to be true, science bases the "truth" of its statements upon observable evidence. And such evidence is always open to change through reinterpretation or to possible contradiction by new evidence. In other words, at some point a scientific proposition is accepted because it describes or interprets a recurring, observable event. But just because an event has occurred on several occasions, there is no guarantee that it will continue to occur. This can be seen from the following parable from Garvin McCain and Erwin Segal (1977:70):

> Once upon a time there lived a very intelligent turkey. He lived in a pen and was attended by a kind and thoughtful master. All of his desires were taken care of and he had nothing to do but think of the wonders and regularities of the world. He noticed some regularities—for example, that mornings always began with the sky getting light, followed by the clop, clop, clop of his master's friendly footsteps. These in turn were always followed by the appearance of delicious food and water within his pen. Other things varied: sometimes it rained and sometimes it snowed; sometimes it was warm and sometimes cold; but amid the variability footsteps were always followed by food. This sequence was so consistent it became the basis of his philosophy concerning the goodness of the world. One day, after more than 100 confirmations of the turkey's theories, he listened for the clop, clop, clop, heard it, and had his head chopped off.

Since it is apparent that regularity does not guarantee certainty, scientific propositions, which are based on such regularity, cannot be proven. "Knowledge," therefore, "is understood to be the best understanding that we have been able to produce thus far, not a statement of what is ultimately real" (Polkinghorne, 1983:2). Theories are accepted by the scientific community as more or less reasonable and credible according to the accuracy of their predictions and the frequency with which they have been supported by empirical evidence. Let us now examine how such evidence is processed.

Science as Process

The word "process" signifies a series of operations or actions that bring about an end result. In industry the longer phrase "manufacturing process" describes the sequence of steps through which raw materials are transformed into a finished prod-

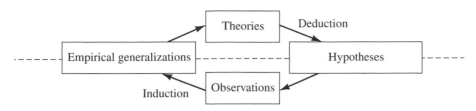

FIGURE 2.1. The scientific process.

uct. Of course, this process differs according to what is manufactured; furthermore, technological advances, shifting consumer demands, and the like lead to periodic changes in the sequence and in its products. But in a given industry for long periods of time the process is repeated over and over again along the same line from beginning to end. In science, by contrast, change is built into the process. The product itself—knowledge—is never "finished," but is constantly remodeled to fit the facts. Furthermore, the sequence of steps followed in one scientific investigation is seldom repeated precisely in another, and the end of one investigation often marks the beginning of another. In short, while the industrial process typically follows a linear progression from raw materials to completed goods, the most characteristic feature of the scientific process is its cyclical nature.

According to John Kemeny (1959:85), the great physicist Albert Einstein, whose own scientific contributions were theoretical, repeatedly emphasized that science "must start with facts and end with facts, no matter what theoretical structures it builds in between." In other words, at some point scientists are observers recording facts; next they try to describe and explain what they see; then they make predictions on the basis of their theories, which they check against their observations (i.e., the facts) again. This chain of events is diagrammed in Figure 2.1. Where we begin in this chain is arbitrary. But at some point, theories generate predictions or hypotheses, hypotheses are checked against observations, the observations produce generalizations, and the generalizations support, contradict, or suggest modifications in the theory.

The horizontal line in the diagram bisecting empirical generalizations and predictions separates the world of theory from the world of research. The development of theory, as we have seen, is the goal of science. Research supports this goal through systematic observation that generates the facts from which theories are inferred and tested. In the remainder of the text, we are concerned almost exclusively with the research side of science. The important point to remember, however, is that science is a process involving the continuous interaction of theory and research. (To see the interesting turns that scientific inquiry can take, read Box 2.1.)

Durkheim's Study of Suicide

French sociologist Emile Durkheim's classic study *Suicide* (1951), first published in 1897, nicely illustrates the interplay between theory and research. Durkheim lacked many of the tools of contemporary data analysis, and his evaluation of evi-

BOX 2.1

The Serendipity Pattern in Science

Scientific inquiry, for the most part, works within the framework of a theory. Hypotheses are derived, researches are planned, and observations are made and interpreted in order to test and elaborate theories. Occasionally, however, unanticipated findings occur that cannot be interpreted meaningfully in terms of prevailing theories and that give rise to new theories. Robert Merton (1957) refers to such discoveries as the **serendipity pattern**. In the history of science, there are many cases of scientific discoveries in which chance, or serendipity, played a part. One of these is Pasteur's discovery of immunization.

> Pasteur's researches on fowl cholera were interrupted by the vacation, and when he resumed he encountered an unexpected obstacle. Nearly all the cultures had become sterile. He attempted to revive them by sub-inoculation into broth and injection into fowls. Most of the sub-cultures failed to grow and the birds were not affected, so he was about to discard everything and start afresh when he had the inspiration of re-inoculating the same fowls with a fresh culture. His colleague Duclaux relates: "To the surprise of all, and perhaps even of Pasteur, who was not expecting such success, nearly all these fowls withstood the inoculation, although fresh fowls succumbed after the usual incubation period." This resulted in the recognition of the principle of immunization with attenuated pathogens. (Beveridge, 1957:27)

Social science has had its share of serendipitous findings also. The well-known "Hawthorne effect," which refers to the impact that a worker's awareness of being under study has on his or her performance, was an unanticipated finding of a series of studies carried out between 1927 and 1932 at the Western Electric Hawthorne plant in Chicago (Roethlisberger and Dickson, 1939). In one of the studies, six women with the task of assembling telephone relays were placed in a special test room for observation. The idea of the study was to determine the effects of various changes in working conditions (e.g., method of payment, number and length of rest pauses, length of working day) on productivity, as measured by the number of relays completed. Over an extended period of time, numerous changes, each lasting several weeks, were introduced while the women's output was recorded. To the researchers' surprise, however, the changes were not related systematically to output. Instead, the women's output rate rose slowly and steadily throughout the study, even when working conditions introduced early in the study were reintroduced later. After questioning the women, the researchers concluded that their increased productivity was a response to the special attention given to them as participants in what was considered an important experiment. The fun of the test room and the interest of management simply had made it easier to produce at a higher rate. This was an important result in the history of social research, for it indicated that subjects' awareness of being under study could affect the very actions that an investigator wishes to observe. Experiments, in particular, must take into account such effects, as we discuss in chapter 6. (Interestingly, most scholars still trace the discovery of this effect to the Hawthorne study, even though the conclusions eventually were shown to be unsupported by the evidence [see Carey, 1967].)

dence has been criticized on several grounds (Douglas, 1967; Pope, 1976; Stark and Bainbridge, 1996). Yet his book is widely regarded as a model of social research, as he mined a vast array of official statistics to test extant theories and develop his own highly influential theory of suicide.

Suicide was one of the most widely studied social problems of the nineteenth century (Giddens, 1965:4). Although early philosophical treatments focused on the moral implications of the act, it became the subject of intense empirical study when European nations began to routinely collect statistics on suicide in the late eighteenth century. Before Durkheim wrote, several studies had collected and published data relating suicide rates to such factors as occupation, urbanization, religion, rate of social change, race, and climate. Durkheim relied extensively on these works as data sources, especially a study by the Italian physician Henry Morselli, who himself built upon the work of German scholar Adolf Wagner. While Durkheim examined many of the same relationships as Wagner and Morselli, his work gained prominence for its coherent sociological theory of suicide that accounted for a broad range of established findings.

In the Introduction to *Suicide*, Durkheim highlights an interesting pattern in the suicide rates among different European countries: While the general mortality rate was quite similar from one country to another, suicide rates varied considerably. Moreover, the suicide rate for each country tended to be quite stable over time. For example, from 1866 to 1870 the suicide rates in Italy, France, and Denmark were 30, 135, and 277 per million, respectively; and from 1871 to 1875 the rates in these same countries were 35, 150, and 258 per million (Durkheim, 1951:50). Finally, he notes the steady rise in suicide rates, a point of concern which many writers attributed to the passing of the traditional social order typified by rural and village life and the growth of large industrialized cities. *Suicide* represents an attempt to explain this stability and variation in suicide rates. For Durkheim, these were social facts that required sociological explanation.

To begin, Durkheim considered existing theories of suicide based on nonsocial factors such as insanity, alcoholism, and climate. In each case, he challenged the theory dialectically and empirically. First he argued against the theory on purely logical grounds; then he presented data to test his reasoning. For example, he reasoned that if suicide were the result of insanity, the same groups with high rates of insanity ought to have high rates of suicide. Contrariwise, available statistics showed that while women outnumbered men in insane asylums, men were far more likely to commit suicide; Jews had the highest rates of insanity but lowest rates of suicide; and there was no correlation between the rates of insanity and suicide among ten European countries. Thus here Durkheim moved from theories to hypotheses to observation, as depicted in the right side of Figure 2.1.

After rejecting nonsocial explanations of suicide, Durkheim turned to social factors. He first noted that Catholic countries like Spain, Portugal, and Italy had lower rates of suicide than Protestant countries such as Germany, England, and Denmark. Knowing that other systematic differences among these countries—for example, their level of industrialization—could account for the differences in suicide rates, Durkheim next compared Catholic with Protestant areas within the same country, first Germany and then Switzerland. In each case, he found that Catholic areas had lower suicide rates than Protestant areas. From such data, he theorized that Protestantism allows "greater freedom to individual thought" and "has fewer beliefs and practices" than Catholicism, so that individuals feel less of a bond with others. More generally, the weaker the integration of the religious community, the more likely that an individual will commit suicide. And so, in this part of his analysis, Durkheim moved from observation to generalization, as shown on the left side of Figure 2.1.

Having introduced the concept of social integration to explain Catholic–Protestant differences, Durkheim proceeded to show how this concept also could account for other variations in suicide. Statistics from France indicated that unmarried persons were more likely to commit suicide than married persons and that childless persons were more likely to kill themselves than people who have children. Other data revealed that the suicide rate declined during periods of political crises. Each of these findings may be explained, Durkheim argued, by the theory that "suicide varies inversely with the degree of integration of the social groups of which the individual forms a part" (p. 209). Married persons experience more intense interpersonal attachments, hence integration, than do single persons, and the same is true of those with children as compared with those without children. Furthermore, social upheavals such as revolutions and wars tend to "rouse collective sentiments, stimulate partisan spirit and patriotism, political and national faith, alike, and concentrating activity toward a single end, at least temporarily cause a stronger integration of society" (p. 208).

The end result of this scientific study is a theory based in fact or observation. The theory is abstract enough to account for several empirical generalizations that relate suicide to religion, marital status, family size, and social change. Durkheim called this the theory of egoistic suicide, because the cause of suicide springs from "excessive individualism" or lack of social integration. Although he went on in *Suicide* to develop a more comprehensive theory that included a fourfold typology of causes, the theory of egoistic suicide, synthesized as follows by Whitney Pope (1976:23), has received the greatest attention:

> The higher the rate of social interaction, the stronger the collective sentiments.
> The stronger the collective sentiments, the stronger social integration.
> The stronger social integration, the more individuals act in the service of social interests.
> The more individuals act in the service of social interests, the more meaning they find in life and the lower the suicide rate.

While our description of *Suicide* shows how it encapsulates the scientific process, a single study such as this should be seen as part of a continuous, unending cycle of inquiry. For just as Durkheim built on the work of Wagner, Morselli, and others, numerous studies since Durkheim have questioned, refined, and tested his insights. Scholars have offered several methodological criticisms, one of which, called the ecological fallacy, we take up in chapter 3; have reinterpreted and refined his theory, especially the pivotal concept of social integration; and have repeatedly tested all of his hypotheses. Subsequent research most strongly supports the hypothesis about the family, as a large group of studies have shown that divorce rates and nonmarried status are positively related with suicide rates (see Breault, 1994). Several studies have failed to find Catholic–Protestant differences in suicide; however, other recent studies have supported the integrative effects of religion in terms of a negative relationship between church participation rates and suicide (see Breault, 1994).

The thread running through all of this work, beyond the interplay between theory and observation, is a mode of inquiry that distinguishes scientific research from other forms of research. Some people refer to this as "the scientific method." But this unfortunate phrase implies a definitive, orderly procedure that simply does not exist in science. What characterizes scientific research is a commonly understood logic of justification and a set of standards that all scientists follow in generating and assessing the evidence upon which their theories are based.

Logical Reasoning

Scientists are expected to follow the principles of logical reasoning. This does not mean that logic can tell scientists how to think or reason; rather, once an act of reasoning has taken place and is communicated, logic provides the criteria for evaluating the validity or correctness of the reasoning. Durkheim began his study with a collection of facts or observations on suicide and with the idea that social facts warranted a sociological explanation. Using his imagination, he identified several empirical generalizations and then came up with the theory of egoistic suicide. There are no logical rules that Durkheim could have followed to devise his theory; however, once he had formulated the theory, it became possible for others to assess its logical consistency and to logically deduce its testable predictions.

When people reason, they make inferences; that is, they draw conclusions based on information or evidence. The two main types of logical reasoning, inductive and deductive, differ in terms of the strength or certainty with which the evidence supports the conclusion. In **deductive reasoning**, the conclusion is absolutely certain if the evidence is true. In **inductive reasoning**, the conclusion is uncertain even if the evidence is true, because its content goes beyond the evidence.

Consider the following examples of each type of reasoning:

Inductive: Hubert, Walter, and Joan, who are union members, are Democrats.
Therefore, all union members are Democrats.
Deductive: All union members are Democrats.
Joan belongs to the union.
Therefore, Joan is a Democrat.

Notice that the first conclusion goes beyond the information at hand. Therefore, we cannot know for certain that the conclusion is true; we can only judge how probable it is, based on the evidence. For even if the evidence is true, it is always possible that new information will show that some union members are *not* Democrats. (Remember the parable of the turkey.) By contrast, according to the rules of deductive logic, the second conclusion—"Joan is a Democrat"—must be true *if* the statement about union members being Democrats is true and *if* we have accurately identified Joan as a union member.

It is sometimes said that induction moves from specific instances to general principles, whereas deduction moves from the general to the specific.[4] Thus, in our example of induction, we observe that specific union members are Democrats and infer from this the general conclusion that they *all* are. In the example of deduction, we began with the general proposition that *all* union members are Democrats and deduced that a particular union member is a Democrat.

Scientists reason inductively when they infer empirical generalizations from specific observations. This describes Durkheim's thinking when he inferred that Protestants were more likely to commit suicide than Catholics based on the fact that predominantly Protestant countries had higher suicide rates than predominantly Catholic countries. It also describes the formulation of his theory to account for generalizations relating suicide rates to religion, marital and family status, and political crises. In the scientific process depicted in Figure 2.1, inductive reasoning is a "bottom-up" process, moving from specific observations to empirical generalizations to theories.

Scientists reason deductively when they show how a hypothesis explains or predicts specific facts. Thus, deductive reasoning represents a "top-down" process in Figure 2.1, proceeding from general principles to specific observations or facts. The following set of propositions shows how, by deduction, Durkheim's hypothesis explains the fact that the suicide rate is lower among Catholics than among Protestants:

> If one group is more socially integrated than another, then its suicide rate will be
>   lower. (HYPOTHESIS)
> Catholics are more socially integrated than Protestants.
> Therefore, the suicide rate is lower among Catholics than among Protestants.
>   (FACT)

Each type of reasoning is evaluated according to different rules and criteria. Inductive inferences are analyzed in terms of the *degree* to which the evidence supports the conclusion. The degree of support, moreover, can be increased or decreased by adding information or evidence. For example, the above inductive inference that "all union members are Democrats" becomes more probable when we increase the number of observed cases or individuals who are both union members and Democrats. The inference also is strengthened to the extent that the observed cases are dissimilar, but weakened when they are similar to one another. For example, if the observed individuals are of different ages, live in different cities, and are employed in different industries, we would be more confident in the conclusion than if the individuals were all over 40 years old, lived in Detroit, and worked in the automotive industry. The more diverse sample eliminates the possibility that the inference applies only to union members of a certain age, or residence, or occupation. Similarly, Durkheim increased the strength of his generalization regarding religion and suicide by showing that suicide rates were not only higher in Protestant than in Catholic countries, but also higher in Protestant than in Catholic areas of Germany and Switzerland.

Scientists have devised logical rules for evaluating the soundness of many forms of inductive reasoning. Indeed, social science methodology is basically a system of logical rules and procedures for conducting research and evaluating knowledge claims. We introduce logical principles throughout the book as we discuss, for example, the criteria for inferring cause-and-effect relationships (chapter 3), the means of determining the reliability and validity of social measurements (chapter 4), and the bases for estimating population characteristics from sample statistics (chapter 5).

Unlike inductive inferences, which may vary in strength or probability, deductions are either valid or invalid. A conclusion logically follows from a general proposition or it does not; a hypothesis is logically consistent with the facts, as is Durkheim's hypothesis, or it is not. Checking for deductive validity or sound logical reasoning is an essential first step in evaluating hypotheses and theories; however, when a hypothesis or theory is logically consistent with the facts, this does not mean that it is necessarily true. For, logically, some other hypothesis might explain the facts just as well. Sociologist Arthur Stinchcombe (1968:18) points out, for example, that explanations other than Durkheim's social integration theory can account for the higher suicide rate of Protestants. This observation "might be explained by their occupations, by the lesser emphasis on the sin of suicide in Protestant theology, by the fact that confessors are available to every Catholic in times of trouble and crisis, and so forth."

Ultimately, Durkheim strengthened the support for his hypothesis in several ways: by replicating the findings with different data sets, as when he reproduced the Protestant–Catholic difference within different countries; by testing a wide variety of predictions, as when he showed a higher incidence of suicide among single than among married persons and a reduction in suicides during periods of parliamentary crisis; and by eliminating major alternative explanations, as when he presented results that discounted the mental illness explanation. In science, though, the verification of a hypothesis is really never complete. For no matter how strong the evidence, it is always possible for the evidence to be true and the hypothesis false. It is also possible for the evidence itself to be in error. To avoid these possibilities, scientists must (1) repeatedly conduct research to build up a large and diversified "body of confirming evidence, or to find disconfirming evidence if there is any," and (2) take all steps necessary to ensure accurate, unbiased evidence (Salmon, 1973:116). In the ensuing chapters we point out these steps. For now, we describe three key principles to which scientists adhere in gathering and evaluating evidence: empiricism, objectivity, and control.

Empiricism

As we noted earlier, scientists limit themselves to problems and issues that can be resolved by making observations. This means that scientific inquiry is based on empiricism. **Empiricism** is a way of knowing or understanding the world that relies directly or indirectly on what we experience through our senses: sight, hearing, taste, smell, and touch. In other words, information or data are acceptable in science only insofar as they can be observed or "sensed" in some way under specifiable conditions by people possessing the normal sensory apparatus, intelligence, and skills. Claire Selltiz, Lawrence Wrightsman, and Stuart Cook (1976:22), for example, point out that whereas people can see a baseball, they cannot see a neutron. "But people can see neutrons indirectly, by observing photographic representations of paths neutrons leave. Under no normal conditions can people regularly observe ghosts. Nor do ghosts leave any other observable or tangible manifestations. Thus, we can have scientific theories about baseballs and neutrons but not about ghosts." To say that science is based on empiricism, therefore, is to say that the only admissible evidence for or against a scientific hypothesis or theory must be observable, directly or indirectly, through some tangible manifestation.

This statement implies that appeals to authority, tradition, revelation, intuition, or other nonempirical ways of knowing, which may be acceptable in other endeavors (such as theology and philosophy), cannot be used as scientific evidence. Scientists do not accept a statement or generalization about the world simply because an authority or expert says it is true, or because tradition and common sense say it is so, or because it seems intuitively plausible. As Jeffrey Katzer, Kenneth Cook, and Wayne Crouch (1991:17) say:

> Evidence is paramount. If the results of well-conducted studies disagree with the authorities, then the authorities may very well be wrong. The proper method for an expert to appeal this verdict is to conduct another study. Or, if two research reports disagree, then additional studies need to be conducted to resolve the issue. The point is that knowledge about the world is best obtained by carefully looking at the world, not by looking at someone's idea of the world.

It should be noted that the terms "observable" and "empirical" have broader meaning in science than in philosophy. To the philosopher, observable applies to properties like "red," "round," "hot," which can be perceived directly by the senses. To the scientist, observables are anything that can be related to the results of perceived measurements. For example, a temperature of 98.6 degrees Fahrenheit is considered observable to the scientist because it can be related to the height of a column of mercury in a thermometer. It is not an observable to the philosopher, however, because there is no direct sensory perception of such a magnitude. One cannot feel or "see" temperature directly; one can only see a pointer reading on a thermometer (Carnap, 1966). Thus, empiricism in science often takes the form of *indirect* observation, whereby instruments are employed that aid and extend the scientist's ability to observe. What passes for empirical observation in the social sciences also extends to records of observations made by others, such as the official statistics on suicide used by Durkheim.

Objectivity

Empirical evidence is assumed to exist outside of scientists themselves. Therefore, it is sometimes held that scientists are, or should be, objective. However, in the usual sense of the term (to mean observation that is free from emotion, conjecture, or personal bias), **objectivity** is rarely, if ever, possible. Social psychologists have demonstrated that we do not see the world simply "as is." Rather, we learn to see. The light waves impinging on our eyes must be interpreted by our minds, and our interpretations depend on the sum total of our past learning and present experiences—including everything from our culture and language to our beliefs and expectations. Clearly, then, our observation—or more properly, our interpretation—of the world is inevitably distorted to some extent by factors not under our conscious control. For this reason, scientists agree that objectivity, in the sense of observation free from bias, is a practical impossibility.

Fortunately, scientists assign a limited and far more useful meaning to the term "objective." To the scientist, it merely means agreement on the results of a given observation. In other words, it must be possible for two or more independent observers working under the same conditions to agree that they are observing the same thing or event. The technical term for this is **intersubjective testability**. Doherty and Shemberg (1978:5) provide the following example of its application in social research:

> If you were to send two observers into a classroom and instruct them to rate a child on "hostility," you may well expect to get two very different ratings. The term *hostility* is open to many different interpretations. So the observations would not be very objective. On the other hand, suppose you instructed the observers to count the number of times that a particular child punched or hit other children, defined what you meant by punched or hit, maybe showed the observers a training film to sharpen the definition, and *then* turned them loose to make the observation. You would very likely get very high agreement among the observers. That's objectivity.

Because of the requirement of objectivity, scientists are supposed to describe their research in detail, outlining their logic and methods of observation in such a way that other scientists may evaluate and repeat the investigation. In this way, others can decide for themselves whether a researcher's subjectivity has distorted the conclusions. In fact, ultimately "objectivity is the product of a community of thinkers, each offering unsparing criticisms of . . . claims that the others make. For no one scientist engaged in this process of criticism is infallible, and each has his [or her] own peculiar intellectual or emotional bias" (Nagel, 1967).

Although it does not diminish his contribution, some analysts now contend that Durkheim's presentation and interpretation of evidence was biased. For example, Rodney Stark and William Sims Bainbridge (1996) strongly imply that Durkheim knowingly disregarded discordant data, including higher Catholic than Protestant suicide rates in some German states, and that he was grossly misinformed about England, a Protestant nation that, in fact, had one of the lowest suicide rates in Europe. Because Durkheim's didactic intent was to legitimize sociology as a scientific discipline, the subject of which was a distinct social reality, he also proposed a less-than-complete and hardly dispassionate explanation of the fluctuations in the suicide rate. For by restricting his attention to social causes, he ignored the full range of factors that contribute to this complex phenomenon (Phillips, Ruth, and Mac-Namara, 1994). Of course, Durkheim might well deny such biases and argue that nonsocial causes of suicide simply were not empirically supported. The important point is that the determination of objectivity and the acceptance of scientific knowledge ultimately depend on the judgment of the scientific community. (For an example of how the public nature of science contributes to its objectivity, see Box 2.2.)

Control

Even before scientists publish their findings, it is assumed that they have used procedures that eliminate, as far as possible, sources of bias and error that may distort their results. As we have said, the influence of certain biases is unavoidable, for language itself can structure our perceptions of the world. Biases even enter into the selection of problems for study and the preference for certain research strategies. However, there are many ways in which scientists, during the course of research, attempt to control for and minimize bias in order to maximize the trustworthiness of their observations. The use of control procedures that rule out biases and confounding explanations of the events being studied is the principal way in which scientific inquiry differs from casual observation. In fact, the principle of **control** lies behind virtually every procedure and technique introduced in the remainder of this book. To get a glimpse of how scientists apply this principle, let us examine some applications from medical research.

Until the twentieth century nearly all medications had little, if any, beneficial pharmacological effect on the treated (Shapiro, 1960). Whatever positive effect they seemed to have was probably due to the power of suggestion or to the fact that people improve naturally from many ailments irrespective of the medical treatment they receive. If most prescriptions were pharmacologically ineffective, however, why did so many people believe they were beneficial? The answer probably rests with the faulty evidence on which such beliefs were based. For example, it was widely held at one time that cold saltwater baths were beneficial to people suffering from high fevers. This belief appears to have been based on repeated observations of improvement in the condition of people subjected to this treatment. But this evidence is insufficient to establish the validity of the cure, because it is possible that people who did *not* take cold saltwater baths showed similar improvement. Without comparing the course of the disease in patients receiving the treatment with its course in a control group who did not receive it, there was no rational basis for deciding whether the observed improvement could be attributed to the treatment (Nagel, 1967).

Yet even this kind of comparison may be inadequate for testing the efficacy of a new treatment or drug. When a treatment group is compared with a group that has received no treatment at all, there is still no control for the psychological effect of merely receiving some form of medication. A substantial part of medical practice appears to be based on the physician's and the patient's faith in the power of drugs to cure. It has been observed, for example, that persons given an inert substance such as a saline solution or sugar pill, called a placebo, often react as favorably as persons given real medication. It is obviously important, therefore, to control for such placebo effects. One way that this is often done in medical research is through the use of "double-blind" investigations.

BOX 2.2

A Case of Scientific Fraud

The importance of the public nature of science, and the way this contributes to its objectivity, can be seen in the evaluation and reanalysis of some studies by the late British psychologist Cyril Burt (Kamin, 1974; Dorfman, 1978; Lewontin, Rose, and Kamin, 1984). For several decades—from the 1930s to the 1960s—Burt was a very influential figure in scientific research on intelligence and its genetic basis. His research on identical twins reared apart was a principal source of support for the theory that intelligence is determined primarily by heredity. Burt's data were very compelling to hereditarians for several reasons (Lewontin, Rose, and Kamin, 1984:101). Because identical twins have identical genes, one way to demonstrate the hereditary basis of a trait like intelligence is to study twins who do not share the same environment. If they resemble one another closely on a trait, the resemblance is logically attributable to that which they have in common: their identical genes. Not only did Burt report a very high correlation between the IQs of twins reared apart, supporting the heredity argument, but his data were supposedly based on the largest sample of separated twins ever studied. Furthermore, in contrast to the environmental similarity of separated identical twins that is almost always found, the environments of the separated twins in Burt's study were reported to be very dissimilar. This last point is crucial to the heredity argument as it eliminates the possibility that similar environments rather than genetic identity accounts for the high correlation in IQ scores.

Beginning in the early 1970s, Burt's published studies underwent a close scrutiny that revealed several highly implausible and inconsistent results. For example, it was noted that each time Burt reported his data on separated twins, the number of twin pairs went up, from twenty-one in the first full report in 1955, to "over 30" in 1958, to a final report of fifty-three in 1966, while the reported correlation between IQs—.771—remained the same. Moreover, this remarkable tendency for IQ correlations to remain the same to the third decimal as sample size increased was also true of Burt's published statistics on nonseparated identical twins and on other types of relatives. When a long-awaited and carefully researched biography of Burt appeared in 1979, the question of his fraudulence was beyond doubt. The evidence uncovered in the book indicated that Burt had collected no data during the period when the twin studies were reported and that he had, in fact, fabricated the figures.

In science, fortunately, fraud is extremely rare. This is ensured because of science's public nature. Due to Burt's preeminence, scientists accepted his findings uncritically for many years, especially hereditarians who were eager to see their theories supported. This demonstrates the subjective element involved in judging the work of others. But these intersubjective judgments also provide a basis for correction and revision. And so, eventually the public scrutiny of Burt's work led to the rejection of his data as scientific evidence.

In a double-blind study, several doctors are asked to prescribe and administer the drug being tested to their patients. The doctors receive the drug from the researcher in individual vials that are identified by number and contain only enough of the drug for one patient. Half of the vials contain the actual drug and half contain a placebo. Since neither doctors nor patients know which they are receiving, their beliefs about the drug cannot influence its effectiveness. Thus, in this type of study any difference observed between those receiving the drug and those receiving the placebo could not be attributed to either the doctors' or the patients' expectations about the drug.

Still, even if a double-blind procedure were used, there may be other problems of interpretation. One of the most important of these problems stems from the simple fact that people are different; they react differently to various treatments and drugs, so that most medications are not 100 percent effective. Therefore, if the patients used for testing tend to be people for whom a drug just happens not to work, the researcher may underestimate its effectiveness; and if the patients tend to be people for whom the drug does work, the researcher may overestimate its effectiveness. Fortunately, social researchers have devised methods—random selection procedures, discussed in chapters 5 and 6—that control for this problem by enabling one to estimate the likelihood of its occurring.

Research findings are often open to a variety of interpretations. The idea of control is to employ procedures that effectively rule out all explanations except the one in which the researcher is interested. In medical research this takes the form of placebo groups and double-blind techniques designed to rule out the possibility of doctors' and patients' expectations contributing to the effectiveness of a treatment. In social research, as you will see, the application of the concept of control takes many forms. Durkheim was one of the first sociologists to control for alternative interpretations through data analysis. As we mentioned, he repeated his analysis of the relation between religion and suicide rates, first examining suicide rates among countries with varying proportions of Protestants and Catholics and then considering areas with varying Protestant and Catholic populations within particular countries. By analyzing the relation between religion and suicide *within* countries, he controlled for some of the factors that varied *among* countries. In the case of Switzerland, he took advantage of the fact that both French- and German-speaking areas contained some cantons that were largely Catholic and others that were largely Protestant. This allowed "him to hold constant the effect of language as well as of nationality ('race') while examining the effect of religion on suicide" (Selvin, 1965:114).

Other control procedures in social research include (1) using several independent observers, not only to check for inter-observer agreement (i.e., objectivity) but also to cancel out the personal biases of any particular observer, (2) withholding information from subjects, who may respond differently if they knew specifically what the researcher were investigating, and (3) employing instruments like tape recorders and counters or systematic observational methods that eliminate errors of omission and commission on the part of human observers. As we turn our attention exclusively to *social* research, we not only will introduce you to such techniques but also will help you to identify the sources of error and bias for which the techniques are intended to control.

Science: Ideal versus Reality

Thus far we have presented a somewhat idealized view of science. It is a view depicted by many philosophers who have analyzed the logic of the scientific process. Teachers of social research, however, sometimes ignore this "philosophical" model or even debunk it, reasoning that it gives students an unrealistic impression of what social scientists actually do. But to disregard the picture of science outlined here is to fail to acknowledge a crucial fact: This model of knowledge and inquiry unifies and guides the activities of all scientists even if their work falls short of the ideal. Still, we would be remiss if we did not point out some of the more important realities of science, especially as practiced in the social sciences.

The first reality is that theoretical knowledge is not well developed in the social sciences. There are those who claim that, at best, the social sciences have established only a few low-level principles and certainly nothing comparable to the Ideal Gas Law examined earlier. As a consequence, social scientific theories tend to be stated less formally than the logical deductions used in this chapter or the mathematical equations often found in the natural sciences. Also, while we have defined "scientific theory" as a set of interrelated propositions from which testable hypotheses can be deduced, the term has a much looser meaning in the social sciences. In these fields, theory may refer to all sorts of speculative ideas offered as explanations for phenomena, and it is very common to see the terms "theory" and "hypothesis" used interchangeably.

It is also important to dispose of a popular misconception of scientific theory that the ideal view of science may serve to perpetuate. That is, theories do not have to make precisely accurate predictions to be judged as scientifically useful. Scientific predictions are seldom, if ever, exactly confirmed. There is always some degree of error. How much error depends on the level of development of both theory and research technology, which explains why theoretical predictions in the physical sciences, more advanced in both areas, are generally so much more accurate than in the social sciences. But this lesser degree of accuracy does not make social science theory any less scientific. In all sciences, decisions between rival theories are seldom based on observational evidence alone. Rather, theories are evaluated and compared not only in terms of the accuracy of their predictions but also with respect to their explanatory scope and logical coherence.

The model of science outlined also may foster some distorted impressions about the practice of scientific inquiry. For one thing, scientific investigations seldom proceed along a smooth path from theory to hypothesis to observation to generalization, and so on. Reports of scientific research tend to follow this format, but that is mostly the product of hindsight and the condensation of a great many activities. Rather, the course of inquiry tends to be very irregular and circuitous, with no typical scenario. For example, the scientist may begin with a theoretical deduction, test the deduction, find that it is not confirmed, mull over the inconsistent results, revise the theory, test a new theoretical deduction, and so forth. Or, the scientist may begin with a problem from everyday life, make an educated guess about a suspected relationship, investigate the relationship, find that it does not hold, revise the idea, and formulate a new hypothesis for further study.

Sociologist Walter Wallace (1971:18–19) also points out that the process of scientific inquiry may occur

(1) sometimes quickly, sometimes slowly; (2) sometimes with a very high degree of formalization and rigor, sometimes quite informally, unself-consciously, and intuitively; (3) sometimes through the interaction of several scientists in distinct roles (of say, "theorist," "research director," "interviewer," "methodologist," "sampling expert," "statistician," etc.), sometimes through the efforts of a single scientist; and (4) sometimes only in the scientist's imagination, sometimes in actual fact.

As you can see, there is nothing mechanical or programmed about scientific work. The development of theory, the formulation of empirical tests of hypotheses, and the application of methods to carry out the tests all involve a great deal of imagination and insight and also can generate tremendous excitement and frustration.

This last observation brings us to a very important aspect of the reality of scientific practice. While the image of scientists projected by the ideal view is that of detached and dispassionate observers of the world, there is a pervasive subjective element in science. Scientists are not merely passive recorders of the social world or the world of nature. Rather, they actively interpret what they see on the basis of socially shared ideas and assumptions. And far from being detached, scientists naturally develop an intense commitment to their work, which may lead them to overlook or reject evidence that is contrary to their own ideas. In fact, such commitment may affect entire scientific disciplines. It has been shown that disciplines may adhere to theories for long periods in the face of much contradictory evidence and that major theories are displaced only after prolonged "scientific revolutions" (Kuhn, 1962).

This reinforces our earlier point about objectivity. That is, as much as scientific norms and the scrutiny and skepticism of the scientific community foster objectivity, it is impossible to eliminate completely the influence of personal values and biases. Value judgments intrude scientific inquiry in several ways, affecting problem selection, decisions about research procedures, and the interpretation of results. Beginning in the mid-1970s, for example, many scholars began to point out the impact of sexism on social research. They noted that gender differences often were ignored, studies of one sex were presented as if they were applicable to both sexes, and problems were selected and findings interpreted from a male-dominant perspective that treated women as passive objects rather than as fully human subjects (Eichler, 1988). We believe that these problems are, to a large extent, correctable because the very nature of scientific inquiry enables its own critique (Sprague and Zimmerman, 1989). As long as scientists are committed to accurate reporting and to making their assumptions and biases as explicit as possible, findings can be reviewed critically by others. And by considering alternative explanations and alternative research strategies, scientists can exercise the power of self-correction.

Still, some social scientists deny the possibility of detecting and eliminating sexism and other forms of bias. Some even contend that the application of the model of science presented in this chapter can seriously bias interpretations of the social world. We may regard this as the final reality of social science—that there are social researchers who challenge the appropriateness of adopting this so-called "positivist" or "natural science" model.

One of the oldest criticisms comes from the phenomenological or interpretive school of thought. According to this school, the natural scientist and social scientist differ because they deal with inherently different objects of study. The inanimate or nonhuman objects in the natural sciences "are not expected to interpret themselves or the environment or field in which they are located and move" (Gurwitsch, 1974:129). Therefore, the natural scientist can invoke interpretations without regard to how the objects of study may interpret their own worlds. Social scientists, on the other hand, deal with human beings who give purpose and meaning to their actions. Because of this—because the objects of study themselves interpret and act on their own interpretations of the world—social scientists should aim to understand human behavior from the subject's frame of reference only. Otherwise, if one seeks to identify the external causes of phenomena, as natural scientists do, then one's interpretations of the social world are bound to be erroneous or inadequate.

We certainly agree that it is important to understand the subject's point of view in addressing many social scientific questions. In fact, the distinction between nonhuman and human actors has many methodological consequences. We can ask people questions, probing the reasons for their behavior. We can participate in their worlds in order to gain their perspective, as field researchers often do. We also must consider how people's awareness of being questioned or observed may affect what they say and do. Consistent with the interpretive position, we see certain methodological approaches as more amenable to understanding human motivation and cognition than others. However, many social scientific issues and types of analysis need not take into account the subject's view of social reality (e.g., social class differences in morbidity and mortality). And regardless of whether one does incorporate the subject's interpretation into one's analysis, it is always best to use a variety of methodological approaches.

Challenges to the scientific conception of sociology and the other social sciences are as old as the disciplines themselves. In addition to the interpretive critique, other current criticisms include:

- critical theory, which claims that science reflects an investment in the status quo and fails to promote economic and social change that could transform social relations and empower the powerless (see Agger, 1991);
- historicism, which denies the possibility of general laws insofar as observed regularities are always tied to time and place (see Gergen, 1973);
- the "discourse" school, which emphasizes the ways that language structures and limits knowledge (see Rabinow and Sullivan, 1987); and
- postmodernism, which rejects the possibility of abstract explanation, challenges systematic empiricism, and sees one description of reality as no more valid than another (Rosenau, 1992).

In the late 1980s and 1990s these and other anti-scientific critiques touched off heated debates about the virtues of a "science of the social" (see, for example, Collins, 1987; Denzin, 1987; Cole, 1994; Trachtman and Perrucci, 2000). Following Randall Collins (1989), we take the position that while these criticisms have contributed to the development of social scientific theory and method, they have not undermined the basic scientific approach. Social scientists have created many different methods. But no matter what methods they adopt, it is clear that most social scientists today are guided by the canons of scientific inquiry outlined in this chapter.

Summary

The aim of science in the broadest sense is to know and understand the world around us. In pursuing this aim, science addresses questions that can be answered by identifying the conditions under which observable events take place. Answering such questions requires concepts that describe the phenomena of interest and general laws and theories that show how events are instances of patterned relationships. Ideally, the events to be explained can be logically deduced from laws and theories, so that it is possible both to explain the past and present and to predict the future. Scientific theories also satisfy our curiosity and render a sense of understanding by positing causal relationships and processes that connect events. This understanding is considered to be fragile and incomplete, however, since the observed patterns among events are always subject to change or reinterpretation. Thus, there are no ultimate explanations in science, and it follows that scientific theories should not be judged as true or false, only *useful*. In general, the greater the range of phenomena a theory is capable of explaining and predicting, and the more accurate and precise its predictions, the more useful it is considered to be.

The production of scientific knowledge requires a constant interplay between theory and research. The process of science therefore is cyclical, with theories leading to predictions, predictions to observations (or research), and observations to generalizations that have implications for theory. Throughout this process, scientists follow the principles of logic, reasoning inductively when they infer generalizations from specific observations and reasoning deductively when they show how theories and hypotheses imply specific facts or predictions. As they conduct research, they also are guided by three canons of inquiry: empiricism, objectivity, and control.

Empiricism means that the only admissible evidence is that which we can know directly or indirectly through our senses. Objectivity, scientists agree, is not possible in the sense of bias-free observation. On the other hand, it is possible if it means intersubjective testability—that independent observers are capable of agreeing about the results of observations. Ultimately, such objectivity is a product of science's public nature, for scientific knowledge rests with the consensus of scientists, and individual claims must be scrutinized by others. While certain biases are unavoidable, scientists do try to control for bias and error as far as possible. In fact, most of the procedures discussed in the remainder of this book could be regarded as mechanisms of scientific control.

Although the above model of science guides the activities of most social researchers, it is an ideal that in some ways does not match reality. Thus, theory in social science seldom takes the form of a deductive system of propositions and rarely, if ever, matches the accuracy of the natural sciences. Research can be very haphazard, sometimes exhilarating, and sometimes frustrating, so that to do scientific work requires a deep emotional commitment. This subjective element also affects science in other ways—to the extent that some social researchers reject the very model of science that characteristically guides contemporary social research.

Key Terms

concept	deductive reasoning
explanation	inductive reasoning
empirical generalization	empiricism
hypothesis	objectivity
law	intersubjective testability
theory	control
cause/causal relationship	serendipity pattern

Review Questions and Problems

1. What is the ultimate goal of science?

2. Identify some of the untestable assumptions of science.

3. Give examples of scientific and nonscientific questions that could be asked about the following topics: (a) capital punishment, (b) abortion, (c) intelligence.

4. State the three rules about language usage in science.

5. What are the twin objectives of scientific knowledge?

6. Briefly differentiate the following terms: hypothesis, empirical generalization, law, and theory.

7. Short of direct empirical tests, what criteria are used for judging the relative superiority of competing scientific theories?

8. Why is the identification of causal processes thought to be crucial to the development of scientific knowledge?

9. Give an example of an empirical generalization that explains but cannot predict.

10. Why is all scientific knowledge considered tentative?

11. Briefly explain how Durkheim's study of suicide illustrates the cyclical nature of the scientific process.

12. Briefly distinguish between inductive and deductive reasoning.

13. At what point in the scientific process do scientists reason inductively? When do they reason deductively?

14. What are the three key principles underlying scientific inquiry?

15. What is meant by "indirect observation"?

16. Why is completely unbiased observation thought to be impossible to attain?

17. Briefly explain the scientific meaning of "objectivity"?

18. How does science's public nature contribute to its objectivity?

19. What is the purpose of control procedures in scientific inquiry?

20. In what ways do the authors suggest that the depiction of science presented in this chapter is idealized?

21. Briefly explain why some social researchers reject the positivist model of science presented in this chapter.

NOTES

1. A distinction sometimes is made between basic or pure science, concerned exclusively with the production of knowledge, and applied science, involving the application of principles to specific, limited problems (see chapter 13). The heart of science, however, is the search for understanding, not the solution of existing problems.

2. The division of philosophy that investigates the foundations of knowledge and understanding is called epistemology.

3. On the other hand, it would be possible to investigate scientifically the effects of prosecution on the incidence of pornography or the relationship between efficiency and morale.

4. Though generally true, there are exceptions to this distinction. As John Kemeny (1959:112) notes, an inductive conclusion need not be a generalized statement. From careful observations of electoral politics, a political scientist may reason that a Democrat will be elected President in the year 2008. This is a particular event, and yet it is also an inductive conclusion. "And deduction need not start with a generalization either. For example, from 'there are at least five students in the course' and from 'there are at most seven students in the course' we can deduce that 'there are either 5, or 6, or 7 students in the course.'"

I

■ ■

RESEARCH DESIGN

In outlining the goals and norms that guide scientific inquiry, we have placed social research in the context of science. Having filled in the background, we are now ready to learn about the details of social research.

Science is the process of producing generalized understanding (theory) through systematic observation (research). Research involves the planning, execution, and interpretation of scientific observation. The three chapters in this section deal with the planning phase. Focusing on the selection and formulation of the research problem, chapter 3 introduces the basic terminology of social research. Chapters 4 and 5 then address two major problems in planning a study: devising operations to measure the phenomena of research interest, and selecting cases for observation. Together these chapters specify the key elements and considerations in the overall plan, called the *research design*. The overview they provide will set the stage for the treatment, in the remainder of the book, of the execution and interpretation phases of research.

The language of social research introduced in chapter 3 represents a shift in terminology from our discussion of the nature and logical structure of scientific theory in chapter 2. As you will see, the tools of thinking on the abstract, theoretical level (concepts, propositions) differ somewhat from the tools of research on the empirical level (variables, hypotheses). The process of moving from the abstract to the concrete is itself an essential part of social research that we consider still further in chapter 4.

3

✓

Elements of Research Design

All social research focuses on a particular topic and addresses specific research questions. We begin this chapter by considering the social forces and personal motives that affect topic selection. We then consider three main concerns as the researcher narrows in on researchable questions: (1) What entities (e.g., individual people, groups, formal organizations, nations) are to be studied; (2) what aspects or characteristics of these entities are of interest; and (3) what kinds of relationships among the characteristics are anticipated. By considering these key elements of research design, we can grasp the language of social research and what it means to state the problem in researchable terms.

Origins of Research Topics

The starting point for research is the selection of a topic. Once a topic is chosen and the research question is set, we can discuss rules and guidelines for conducting research that will generate the most valid data and the most definitive answers. But there are no rules for selecting a topic. Given that anything that is "social" and "empirical" could be the subject of social research, there is a nearly endless variety of potential topics. So, *how* are specific topics likely to emerge in the social sciences? We have identified five factors that explain the origin of most topics.

1. *The structure and state of the scientific discipline.* With the scientific goal of advancing knowledge, most researchers select topics suggested by the ongoing development of theory and research in their particular fields of study. The organization of disciplines casts the framework for topic selection. Social psychologists, for example, divide their discipline with respect to various forms of social behavior, such as aggression, altruism, interpersonal attraction, and conformity, which act as organizing themes or areas of research interest. Similarly, sociologists frequently study aspects of various institutions like religion, politics, education, and the family, around which the discipline is organized. As knowledge in an area develops, inconsistencies and gaps in information are revealed that researchers attempt to resolve through research.

2. *Social problems.* The focus and development of the social sciences are intimately related to interest in basic problems of the "human condition." Historically, this has been a major source of research topics, especially in sociology. The most eminent sociologists of the nineteenth and early twentieth centuries—people like Emile Durkheim, Karl Marx, Max Weber, and Robert Park—concerned themselves

43

with problems emanating from great social upheavals of their day, such as the French and Industrial revolutions and massive foreign immigration to the United States. The problems wrought by these events—alienation, deviance, urban crowding, racism, and many others—have remained a major focus of the discipline ever since. Indeed, many people are attracted to the social sciences because of their perceived relevance to social problems.

3. *Personal values of the researcher.* To carry out a research project, with its inevitable complications, obstacles, and demands for time and money, requires considerable interest and commitment on the part of the investigator. What sustains this interest more than anything else are highly personal motivations for doing research on a particular topic. Thus, an investigator may choose a topic not only because it is considered theoretically important, novel, or researchable, but also because it stimulates the researcher's interest. According to social psychologist Zick Rubin (1976:508–9), one reason for his embarking on the study of romantic love was that he was "by temperament and avocation, a songwriter. Songwriters traditionally put love into measures." And so he set out to find a way of measuring love scientifically. In a similar fashion, it is not surprising that members of particular groups often have pioneered research on those groups; for example, women have led the way in research on women and African Americans in research on blacks (King, Keohane, and Verba, 1994:14).

4. *Social premiums.* There are also powerful social determinants of topic selection. Through the availability of supporting funds, the prestige and popularity of the research area, and pressures within the discipline and within society, social premiums are placed on different topics at different times. Typically, these premiums will reinforce one another, with the social climate affecting funding, which in turn affects prestige. This was certainly true of the space program in the 1960s. Today, in the social sciences, the aging of the population as a whole has raised interest and support for research on the elderly, just as it has caused a dramatic increase in federal expenditures on and services available to older people. Similarly, in the 1970s the Women's Movement spurred a dramatic increase in research on gender issues that has continued to this day.

5. *Practical considerations.* An overriding concern in any research project is cost. Research requires time, money, and personnel. Limitations on these resources, as well as other practical considerations such as the skill of the researcher and the availability of relevant data (see chapter 11), will shape both the nature and scope of the problem that the researcher can pursue.

The choice of any given research topic may be affected by any or all of the factors mentioned. Consider, for example, a recent study by Beckett Broh (2002), which examined the effects of participation in extracurricular activities on high school academic achievement. Using data from a national survey of high school students, Broh's study was designed to find out who benefits from participating in sports and other school activities and why. The study continued a line of inquiry on the impact of the extracurriculum of theoretical interest to sociologists of education and sport. Social scientists, school officials, and the general public have long debated whether sport, in particular, builds character and has positive educational benefits. Given the costs of extracurricular programming, especially school sports, and the public concern about boosting academic achievement, Broh's study also had important practical implications. Finally, the topic was of special personal interest to Broh. She herself was a high school athlete, and after her collegiate athletic career was cut short by an injury, she turned to coaching. For the past decade she has coached middle and high school basketball in Michigan and Ohio. These experiences naturally sparked her interest in sport and education as a PhD student in sociology. And when her mentor suggested that she look at the questions in the National Educational Longitudinal Study, she found the means of testing some of her ideas about the impact of athletes' network of relationships on their academic achievement.

Once a general topic has been chosen, it must be stated in researchable terms. This involves translating the topic into one or more clearly defined, specific questions. To get to this point, the investigator usually conducts a literature search. In the process, he or she may discover several preliminary questions that must be answered before the main problem can be pursued; or the topic may be recast to fit a particular research strategy or to fit some other need. It is not uncommon, in fact, for the researcher's interest to become permanently shifted to one of these narrower or preliminary questions. Regardless of the direction it takes, however, the formulation of a researchable problem or question boils down to deciding what *relationships* among what *variables* of what *units* are to be studied. We will now turn our attention to these important terms.

Units of Analysis

The entities (objects or events) under study are referred to in social research as **units of analysis**. Social scientists study a variety of units (sometimes called elements or cases). These include individual people; social roles, positions, and relationships; a wide range of social groupings such as families, organizations, and cities; as well as various social artifacts such as books, periodicals, documents, and even buildings. Ordinarily, the unit of analysis is easily identified. The unit is simply what or who is to be described or analyzed. For example, a researcher wanting to determine if larger organizations (in terms of the number of employees) have more bureaucratic rules and regulations than smaller ones would treat the *organization* as the relevant unit and would gather information on the size and bureaucratic complexity of different organizations. In Broh's study of the impact of extracurricular activities on academic achievement, the unit of analysis was *individuals* or, more precisely, individual high school students.

In these examples, the purpose of the study dictates what or who is to be described, analyzed, and compared, hence what is the appropriate unit of analysis. Selecting and identifying the unit of analysis is not as simple as it may seem, however. Consider the problem of investigating a theory of cultural change. David Riesman (1950) theorized that there was a trend in the twentieth century toward "other-directedness"; people's actions became less motivated by intrinsic values and more influenced by the actions of others. But how can one study long-range trends in individual motivation when it is impossible to analyze individuals from the past? One social scientific solution is to rely on various social artifacts and to assume that such artifacts reflect the individual values and behavior of direct interest. To test Riesman's theory, for example, Sanford Dornbusch and Lauren Hickman (1959) chose as their units of analysis advertisements in a mass-circulation women's magazine for the period 1890–1956, to see if the advertising had appealed increasingly over time to the standards of others (other-directedness). Indeed it had.

Aggregate Data

Another problem arises from the practice of combining information about individuals to describe the social unit to which they belong. Information about one set of units that is statistically combined to describe a larger social unit is called **aggregate data**. Each year, *U.S. News and World Report* uses aggregate data to rank America's best colleges: They gather information about individual students at each college to characterize the college as a whole. Among their indicators of academic quality, for example, is each school's graduation rate, which is calculated by dividing the number of enrollees in a given class into the number who graduate within six years of their enrollment. Other aggregate measures include average SAT or ACT test score; the proportion of enrolled freshman who graduated in the top 10 percent of their high school classes; and the acceptance rate, the ratio of the number of students admitted to the number who apply.

In *U.S. News'* rankings, the unit of analysis is colleges; that is what is being described and compared. But the use of aggregate data does not always imply a collective unit of analysis. In another recent study of adolescents' extracurricular participation, Andrew Guest and Barbara Schneider (2003) wondered whether the effect of such activities depended on the social context of the school and community. For example, sports may have a greater effect on academic achievement in lower-class communities, which value sports as paths to financial gain, than in upper-class communities, which value sports for their health and aesthetic benefits. Their unit of analysis, like Broh's study, was individual high school students; however, they created aggregate measures to study the impact of the community and school context. Their measure of the community's socioeconomic class was based largely on the average income and education of the neighborhoods where the students lived, and a school context measure consisted of the percentage of students from each student's high school who went on to four-year colleges after graduation.

Thus, when information about individuals is aggregated to describe groups or collectivities, the unit of analysis may be either the individual or the group. How can you tell? In their analyses, researchers ordinarily compare a number of instances of a particular unit—for example, a number of individuals, or a number of cities, or a number of colleges. To identify the unit of analysis, therefore, ask yourself what is being described in each instance and what sorts of units are being compared—individuals or groups. If the aggregate data are used to compare different groups, the unit of analysis is the group. If the data are used to compare individuals who belong to different groups, the unit is the individual.

One reason it is important to identify accurately the unit of analysis is that confusion over units may result in false conclusions about research findings. Generally speaking, assertions should be made only about the particular unit under study. (Actually, assertions should be even more circumscribed than this, as we will see in chapter 5.) To draw conclusions about one unit on the basis of information about another is to risk committing a logical fallacy.

Ecological Fallacy

The most common fallacy involving the mismatching of units is the **ecological fallacy** (Robinson, 1950). This occurs when relationships between properties of groups or geographic areas are used to make inferences about the individual behaviors of the people within those groups or areas. This is quite similar to what logicians call the "fallacy of division": assuming that what holds true of a group also is true of individuals within the group. Knowing that Sally attended a college whose students had relatively low average SAT scores, you would commit this fallacy if you assumed that Sally herself had low SAT scores.

Political analysts who use aggregate data from elections to study individual voting behavior are particularly susceptible to the ecological fallacy. Suppose, for example, that a researcher wanted to know whether registered Democrats or Republicans were more likely to support an Independent party candidate in a city election, but that the only information available was the percentage of votes the candidate received and the percentages of Republican and Democratic voters *in each precinct*. In short, the researcher wants to draw conclusions about *individual voters* but only has collective information about *precincts*. Knowing that the candidate received a relatively larger number of votes in precincts with greater percentages of Republicans does not permit the conclusion that Republican voters were more likely to support the candidate than were Democratic voters. In fact, it is quite plausible that Democrats in predominantly Republican precincts were more likely to support the Independent party candidate than were Democrats in other precincts. Because the unit of analysis here is the precinct and not the individual voter, we simply do not know how individual voters within each precinct voted.

Social scientists of a few decades ago frequently performed ecological analyses such as the one above. For example, criminologists analyzed crime and delinquency rates in relation to other characteristics of census tracts in order to draw conclusions about characteristics of individual criminals and delinquents. A typical erroneous conclusion might be that foreign-born persons commit more crimes than native-born persons because the crime rate is higher in areas with greater proportions of foreigners. But such a conclusion is clearly unwarranted because we do not know who actually committed the crimes—foreign or native-born persons. Similarly, Durkheim's classic study of suicide was subject to the ecological fallacy by inferring that Protestants commit more suicides than Catholics from the observation that suicide rates were higher in predominantly Protestant nations than in predominantly Catholic ones.[1]

It is not always wrong to draw conclusions about individual-level processes from aggregate or group-level data. Social scientists have identified conditions under which it is reasonable to make such inferences (e.g., Firebaugh, 1978), but it is often difficult to determine if these conditions are met. The implications of the ecological fallacy are clear: Carefully determine the units about which you wish to draw conclusions and then make sure that your data pertain to those units. If you are interested in individuals but only aggregate data are available, then draw conclusions very tentatively, recognizing the possibility of an ecological fallacy.

Variables

While the researcher observes units of analysis, it is relationships among characteristics of units that are of primary interest. Characteristics of units that vary, taking on different values, categories, or attributes for different observations, are called **variables**. Variables may vary over cases, over time, or over both cases and time. For example, among individuals, any set of characteristics that may differ for different people, such as age (range of years), gender (male and female), and marital status (single, married, divorced, widowed, etc.), is a variable. And for an individual, any characteristic that may vary from one time period to the next, such as age, level of education (first grade, second grade, etc.), and income (dollars earned per year), is a variable.

It is not unusual to see some confusion between variables and the attributes or categories of which they consist. "Gender" is a variable consisting of the categories male and female; "male" and "female" by themselves are not variables but simply categories that distinguish persons of different gender. Likewise, "divorced" and "Republican" are not variables but categories of the variables "marital status" and "political party affiliation," respectively. To keep this distinction clear, note that any term you would use to describe yourself or someone else (e.g., sophomore, sociology major) is an attribute or category of a variable (academic class, major).

You are now in a position to test your understanding of the concepts of unit of analysis and variable. Table 3.1 is designed to help you do this. The first column presents seven research questions or hypotheses; the second and third columns identify the relevant units of analysis and variables. Read the first column while covering up the second and third columns, and record the unit of analysis and variables on a separate sheet of paper. Then check your answers by examining the full table.

Types of Variables

Social scientists find it necessary to classify variables in several ways. One type of classification is necessitated by the complexity of social phenomena. For any given research problem, the researcher can observe and measure only a few of the many potentially relevant properties. Those variables that are the object of study—part of some specified relationship—are called **explanatory variables**, and all other variables are **extraneous** (Kish, 1959).

There are two types of explanatory variables: dependent and independent. The **dependent variable** is the one the researcher is interested in explaining and predicting. Variation in the dependent variable is thought to depend on or to be influenced by certain other variables. The explanatory variables that do the influencing and explaining are called **independent**. If we think in terms of cause and effect, the independent variable is the presumed cause and the dependent variable the presumed effect. Independent variables are also called *predictor variables* because

TABLE 3.1. **Sample Research Questions, Units of Analysis, and Variables**

Research question/hypothesis	Unit of analysis	Variables
[WHAT ONE WANTS TO KNOW]	[WHAT ENTITIES ARE DESCRIBED AND COMPARED]	[WITH RESPECT TO WHAT CHARACTERISTICS]
Are older people more afraid of crime than younger people?	Individuals	Age, fear of crime
The greater the growth of air passenger traffic at a city's airport, the greater the economic growth.	Cities	Growth of air traffic, economic growth
The higher the proportion of female employees, the lower the wages in nineteenth-century factories.	Factories	Proportion of employees who are female, average wage
Does economic development lower the birth rate?	Nations	Level of economic development, birth rate
The longer the engagement period, the longer the marriage.	Couples (dyads)	Length of engagement, marriage duration
Fan support in the NBA, as measured by attendance, is not related to the proportion of black players on the team.	NBA teams	Racial composition of the team, average attendance
A student's grade-point average is directly related to his or her class attendance.	Individuals	Grade-point average, attendance record

their values or categories may be used to predict the values or categories of dependent variables. For example, when Broh studied the impact of extracurricular involvement on academic achievement, her independent variable consisted of whether students participated in specific school activities such as interscholastic sports and her dependent variable was level of academic achievement. One research question was whether sport participation explained (or predicted) differences in academic achievement.

Research studies in the social sciences often involve several independent variables and sometimes more than one dependent variable. Also, a variable is not intrinsically independent or dependent. An independent variable in one study may well be a dependent variable in another, depending on what the researcher is trying to explain. Finally, it is conventional in mathematics and science for the letter X to symbolize the independent variable and for the letter Y to represent the dependent variable. This is a practice we shall follow in the remainder of the book.

Extraneous variables, which are not part of the explanatory set, may be classified in two important ways. First, in relation to specific independent and dependent variables, they may be **antecedent** or **intervening**. An antecedent variable occurs prior in time to both the independent and dependent variable; a variable is intervening if it is an effect of the independent variable and a cause of the dependent variable. Antecedent variables in Broh's study were parents' income and a student's race and gender; each of these variables may affect both extracurricular involvement

A. Antecedent Variable

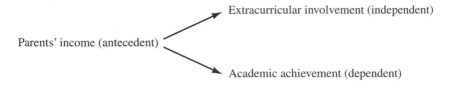

B. Intervening Variable

FIGURE 3.1. Antecedent and intervening variables.

and academic achievement. An intervening variable was students' self-esteem. Extracurricular involvement could affect self-esteem, which in turn could affect a students' academic performance. Figure 3.1 depicts these examples of antecedent and intervening variables. Each arrow in the figure represents causal direction. We discuss the concept of "cause" below, and we cover "arrow diagrams" further in chapter 15.

Extraneous variables also may be categorized as controlled or uncontrolled. Controlled or, more commonly, **control variables** are held constant, or prevented from varying, during the course of observation or analysis. This may be done to limit the focus of the research or to test hypotheses pertaining to specific subgroups—for example, all males or all males under 18 years of age. Basically, the value or category of a control variable remains the same for a given set of observations. Several techniques for holding variables constant are discussed at length in the following chapters. Some examples would be selecting only individuals of the same age and gender, observing groups of the same size, creating uniform laboratory conditions or social settings in which to observe people or groups, and statistically controlling for specific attributes.

Whenever a variable is held constant in research, that variable cannot account for (or explain) any of the variation in the explanatory variables. Suppose, for example, that you wanted to explain differences (i.e., variation) between people in their level of aggression. If you controlled for gender by studying only males, then the variable "gender" could not account for any of the observed variation in aggression. Holding variables constant thus simplifies complex social situations. It is a means of ruling out variables that are not of immediate interest but that might otherwise explain part of the phenomenon that the investigator wishes to understand. Indeed, one aim of efficient research design is to identify potentially relevant extraneous variables in order to measure and control as many as is feasible (Kish, 1959). Broh measured numerous extraneous variables, including parents' income and students' race, gender, and self-esteem. This enabled her to statistically control and test the effects of these variables on the relationship between extracurricular activities and academic achievement.

Another important distinction is made between quantitative and qualitative variables. Actually, this is a rather crude way of pointing to some significant differences in the numerical representation of variable categories. We make more precise distinctions along these lines in the next chapter, but for now appeal to the common understanding of quantitative and qualitative. A variable is **quantitative** if its values or categories consist of numbers and if differences between its categories can be expressed numerically. For example, the variable "income," measured in dollars, signifies a quantitative difference—a certain number of dollars—between people with different incomes. **Qualitative variables** have discrete categories, usually designated by words or labels, and nonnumerical differences between categories. For example, with the variable "gender," consisting of the discrete categories male and female, we can make categorical, but not numerical, distinctions between people of different gender.[2]

Relationships

Social scientists' ultimate objective is to make sense of the social world by discovering enduring relationships among phenomena. Much research is therefore aimed directly at developing and testing relationships. There are other, more immediate purposes for which research is conducted, such as exploration and description, which we discuss later in the chapter. Yet, even when the researcher's goal is discovery or description, research findings will depend to a large extent on what particular **relationships** are anticipated. Research is not like the kind of fishing trip in which you drop your line anywhere, hoping you will catch something. Investigators do not make random observations. Whatever their goals, they must decide what to observe or ignore, how to go about making their observations, and how to interpret them. Such decisions inevitably are based on the researcher's expectations about how variables are related to one another.

Anticipated relationships are implicit in the researcher's disciplinary focus. If a sociologist looks at dormitory rooms and classrooms, for example, "it is not with the eyes of an architect," but with an interest in how these rooms and their contents are related to the people using them (Miles and Huberman, 1994:17). Similarly, you cannot do any kind of research without some guiding orientation. Consider the investigator who wants to study "everything" about families, but "let the facts speak for themselves" (Batten, 1971:9–11). Without *any* expectations, how is the researcher to decide what constitutes a "family"? Should first cousins be included even if they live far away or seldom keep in touch? Should a family include all persons living in the same household, no matter how remote the blood tie (Batten, 1971)? When collecting data, should the researcher include the hat size and shoe size of each family member? Such considerations ultimately depend on the social researcher's *expectations* about salient properties and *relationships* regarding families.

Facts never speak for themselves. Not only which facts are sought but also how they are interpreted depends again on anticipated relationships—on what particular answers the researcher expects the "facts" to provide. A trenchant example is related by sociologist Herman Smith (1975:22). According to Smith, it is a fact that African Americans save less money than whites. However, if the fact that blacks earn less than whites is taken into account, it turns out that blacks save proportionately more of their incomes than whites. Thus, blacks would appear to be *more* frugal than whites. But this conclusion would not have been reached if the researcher had not entertained the notion that the relationship between race and savings might be affected by a more complex set of relationships involving how much of his or her income a person saved.

It is clear, then, that all research carries expectations about the nature of what is being investigated. As a result, an important tenet of social research, which unfortunately is not always followed, is that one's expectations—that is, anticipated relationships and guiding theoretical explanations—should always be identified as far as possible. Beckett Broh's (2002) selection of variables for her study was guided largely by three theoretical explanations of the link between sports participation and educational achievement: (1) Developmental theory—sports teaches skills, such as a strong work ethic and perseverance that help students achieve in the classroom; (2) the leading crowd hypothesis—athletes gain social status and membership in a peer group of disproportionately college-oriented high achievers, which facilitates higher academic performance; and (3) social capital theory—sports create strong social ties among students, parents, and teachers that provide educational benefits. Broh derived the social capital model in part from her experience as a basketball coach; she noticed that her players tended to spend more time with their parents and had better relationships with them than other students.

Thus far we have relied on the reader's intuitive grasp of the term "relationship." Everybody has experienced relationships at some time in their lives. One might think of relationships among kin; "serious" relationships, as between lovers; and relationships among the members of teams and work groups. We also have a sense of a relationship when one event regularly precedes or follows the occurrence of another, as, for example, when the appearance of dark clouds is regularly followed by rain. All such relationships have two features. First, they always involve two or more entities: persons, objects, or events—such as parent and child, leader and follower, or clouds and rain. Second, the pairs or combinations of things usually occur together and change together; thus, the appearance of one thing signals the appearance of the other and the absence of one implies the absence of the other. For example, by definition every parent has a child and every child has (or had) a parent; we cannot have one without the other. Also, by observation we know that certain kinds of clouds produce rain and that without clouds it cannot rain.

The kind of relationships with which social scientists are concerned, relationships among variables, have these same two features. Two or more variables are related, or form a relationship, to the extent that changes in one variable are accompanied by systematic changes in the other(s). Since the manner in which the variables change or vary together will depend on whether the variables are qualitative or quantitative, we will consider the nature of relationships separately for each of these types of variables.

Relationships among Qualitative Variables

Consider the two qualitative variables, race and political party affiliation. If two individuals have the same party affiliation, say Democrat, then the category of this variable does not change as we look from one individual to the other. If they have different affiliations, say one is a Democrat and the other is a Republican, then the category of the variable does change. Assuming similar statements about race, we would say that a relationship exists between race and political party affiliation if a comparison of a pair of individuals reveals that a change in race is accompanied by a change in party affiliation. More generally, the basic idea of a relationship, or association, between qualitative variables can be incorporated into two assertions (Leik, 1972:26): (1) If one variable changes, the other variable changes; and (2) if one variable does not change, the other does not change. If these two assertions were true for all pairs of cases, the result would be a perfect one-to-one correspondence between the categories of one variable and the categories of the other. Table 3.2A depicts a perfect relationship between race and political party affiliation among twenty individuals.

In actual research, of course, we never see such perfect associations. To the researcher, therefore, the important question is not whether a given pair of variables is perfectly associated, but how strongly they are related. That is, how closely do the data approximate a perfect association between variables? Statistical techniques to assess this are called measures of association. These techniques, as well as the concept of "strength of relationship," are best understood if assertions about concomitant changes in variables are treated as predictions. Table 3.2A suggests two predictions: (1) If a person is black, then he or she will be a Democrat, and (2) if a person is white, then he or she will be a Republican. The proportion of times such predictions are correct for all pairs of cases is an index of the strength of the relationship. A high proportion indicates that the variables are strongly related; a low proportion indicates a weak relationship. Furthermore, if the proportion is so low that knowledge of one variable is of no use in predicting the other, the variables are said to be unrelated. The rest of Table 3.2 gives a possible combination showing a

TABLE 3.2. **Varying Degrees of Association**
between Two Qualitative Variables:
Race and Political Affiliation

A. Perfect association	White	Black	Total
Democrat	0	10	10
Republican	10	0	10
Total	10	10	20
B. Moderate association	White	Black	Total
Democrat	3	7	10
Republican	7	3	10
Total	10	10	20
C. No association	White	Black	Total
Democrat	5	5	10
Republican	5	5	10
Total	10	10	20

moderate relationship between race and political party affiliation (B) and a distribution indicating no relationship (C). Statistical indices of association may be computed for each of these distributions. Ordinarily, these indices will range from 0, indicating no relationship, to 1.00, indicating a perfect relationship.

Relationships among Quantitative Variables

As we move from qualitative to quantitative variables, it becomes possible to say
whether a change in a variable represents an increase or a decrease in value. With
this additional property, we can measure not only the strength of the relationship
but also two other aspects: direction and linearity.

A relationship may be either positive or negative in direction. A **positive** or **direct relationship** between variables exists if an increase in the value of one variable is accompanied by an increase in the value of the other, or if a decrease in the
value of one variable is accompanied by a decrease in the value of the other. In
other words, the two variables consistently change in the same direction. We would
expect a positive relationship between sons' heights and fathers' heights (e.g., the
taller a father, the taller his son will tend to be) and between students' scores on the
Scholastic Aptitude Test and their college grade-point averages (e.g., as scores increase, grades tend to increase). A **negative** or **inverse relationship** between variables exists if a decrease in the value of one variable is accompanied by an increase
in the value of the other. Thus, changes in one variable are opposite in direction to
changes in the other. We would find a negative relationship between a person's age
and how long he or she is expected to live (as age increases, life expectancy decreases) and between the speed and accuracy with which people perform many
tasks (the faster one does something, the less accurately one is likely to do it).

Relationships among quantitative variables are usually depicted with graphs,
such as those in Figure 3.2. The lines in these two graphs illustrate the characteristic
of "linearity." The straight line in Figure 3.2A depicts a *linear* relationship. (Actually,
this line depicts a *positive linear* relationship. A straight line running from the upper
left corner to the lower right corner would depict a *negative linear* relationship.) Notice that one variable changes at the same rate and in the same direction (positive)
over the entire range of the other variable. The curved line in Figure 3.2B depicts a
curvilinear relationship. In this case, the rate of change in one variable is *not* consistent over all values of the other: Variable Y increases more rapidly for low values than
for high values of variable X and then reverses direction. We would expect this pattern of relationship to occur between the age and annual earnings of adult workers.
Earnings will generally increase with age up to retirement and then will decline.

Tabular and graphic representations of relationships between variables and
other statistical analyses are discussed at length in chapter 14. There as well as elsewhere in the book we focus on linear relationships, since this pattern is most often
assumed and analyzed in the social sciences. A common statistical measure of the
strength and direction of linear relationships between two quantitative variables is
called the Pearson product-moment coefficient of correlation, or **correlation coefficient** for short. Symbolized by the letter r, the correlation coefficient may vary
between -1.00 and $+1.00$. The signs, $-$ and $+$, indicate the direction of the rela-

A. Linear relationship

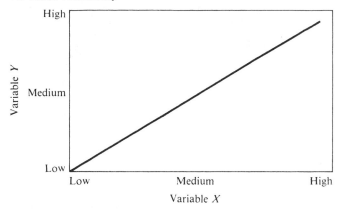

B. Curvilinear relationship

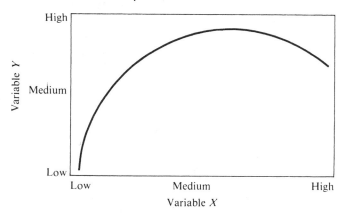

FIGURE 3.2. Linear and curvilinear relationships between two quantitative variables.

tionship, positive or negative; the magnitude of the coefficient, ignoring the sign, indicates the strength of association. Among the students in Broh's sample, there was a strong positive correlation of .74 between grades in English and grades in math, and there was a weak positive correlation of .08 between number of hours spent on homework and grades in English.

Relationships between a Qualitative and a Quantitative Variable

Another way of assessing relationships is used when both qualitative and quantitative variables are involved. Most often, in such cases, especially in experiments, the independent variable is qualitative and the dependent variable is quantitative. This is the type of relationship considered here.

It will be helpful, once again, to think in terms of predictions. A relationship is said to exist if the different categories of the independent variable predict differ-

**TABLE 3.3. Relationship between
a Quantitative Variable (Median
Income in Constant Dollars) and
Qualitative Variable (Race), 2000**

	Whites	*Blacks*
Median income	$53,256	$34,192

Source: U.S. Census Bureau, *Statistical Abstract of the United States: 2002,* (122nd edition), Washington, D.C., 2002, Table No. 710, p. 461.

ent values for the dependent variable. Thus, if each category of the independent variable is treated as a distinct group, then a relationship can be described in terms of the *differences among groups* on the dependent variable. We might compute an average value on the dependent variable for each group. No differences in these averages across groups would then indicate no relationship. And, in general, the larger the differences, the stronger the relationship.

For example, suppose a researcher were interested in examining the relationship between race and annual income. Since annual income, as measured in dollars earned, is a quantitative variable, average incomes could be computed for each racial group (i.e., for each category of the qualitative variable race), as shown in Table 3.3.[3] Note in the table that there is a difference in the averages across groups: In 2000, whites earned $53,256 on the average and blacks earned $34,192. Thus, we may conclude that a relationship exists between race and income.[4]

Statistically Significant Relationships

Social scientists do not ordinarily consider an association between two variables meaningful unless the association is **statistically significant**. Consider the moderate association between race and party affiliation in Table 3.2B. Note that there are only twenty cases in this table. Now suppose that these twenty cases represent a random sample of the U.S. population. It would not be appropriate to conclude from these data that there is an association between race and party affiliation in the general population. Why? Because in a sample this small the difference in party affiliation between blacks and whites easily could have occurred by chance (i.e., as a result of random selection) even if there is no relationship in the larger population.

Statistically significant associations are those that are *not* likely to have occurred by chance or random processes. Table 3.4 shows the relationship between race and party affiliation in a recent national sample of the adult population. The respondents in this survey were asked if they usually thought of themselves as a Democrat, Republican, or Independent. The table shows only those respondents who described themselves as either Democrats or Republicans. Blacks were far more likely than whites to identify themselves as Democrats (91.6 percent compared to 48.9 percent); given the size of the sample (1531), this difference is highly unlikely to have occurred by chance and therefore is statistically significant. When this property of relationships is reported in the research literature, it is indicated

**TABLE 3.4. Race by Political
Party Preference,*
2000 General Social Survey**

	White	Black
Democrat	48.9%	91.6%
Republican	51.1	8.4
	100.0%	100.0%
(*N*)	(1257)	(274)

*Party preference indicates respondents who described
themselves as either "strong" or "not very strong"
Democrats (Republicans).

with an italic lowercase p followed by < and a decimal; for example, $p < .05$. This means that the probability is less than 5 in 100 that the relationship could occur by chance, assuming that there is no relationship in the larger population from which the sample is drawn. With odds this low, we would conclude that the association did not occur by chance and therefore that a relationship between race and party affiliation exists in the United States. (See chapter 14 for a brief discussion of tests of statistical significance.)

So far we have examined some common ways of depicting relationships. Also, we have noted four properties of relationships: strength, directionality, linearity, and statistical significance. Statistical significance indicates whether a relationship exists or is likely to be the product of random processes. The strength of a relationship refers to the extent to which variables are associated or correlated. Directionality and linearity tell us *how* changes in one variable are related to changes in another. Do the variables change in the same or the opposite direction? Is the rate of change in one variable consistent over all values of the other? Together these two properties describe the *form* of the relationship. Knowing the strength and form of relationships as well as whether it is statistically significant will often satisfy the researcher's curiosity. However, if our interest is in explaining social phenomena, we also will need to know about the causal link between variables. And, these statistical properties are never sufficient to establish a cause-and-effect relationship.

The Nature of Causal Relationships

In chapter 2 we noted that for purposes of explanation and prediction, scientists find it helpful to think in terms of cause-and-effect relationships. But how does one identify such a relationship? What is meant by the term "causality"? At first glance, the task of defining "causality" seems simple. Since we are so accustomed to thinking causally, and causal terms are so frequently used in everyday life, the concept would appear to be widely understood. In lay terms, a cause is something that makes something happen or change. It seems obvious that a rock thrown against a window will cause the glass to shatter. And the fact that drinking too much soda causes me to get a stomachache is a causal relationship that you can comprehend even if you fortunately have not had the same experience.

In contrast to the implicit understanding of causality that seems to exist in everyday life, the meaning of the concept of cause has been hotly debated by philosophers and scientists for centuries. Much of this debate stems from the philosopher David Hume's analysis (1748). Hume argued that all that one can observe is a constant or stable association between events. From such association we infer a causal connection; however, there is no way of logically or empirically showing that a causal connection actually exists. A causal relationship exists only in the observer's mind; it is something inferred from an observed association between events. Following Hume's line of reasoning, some philosophers and some scientists (e.g., Kerlinger, 1973) have maintained that the concept of cause ought to be discarded from scientific work. Yet many people regard causal relationships as the heart of scientific understanding. Furthermore, even if such relationships cannot be "proven" empirically (just as no generalization can be proven by scientific evidence), researchers have found it helpful to *think* causally (Blalock, 1964:6) and have found working with causal hypotheses to be a very productive way of doing science.

The important point of Hume's analysis, therefore, is that we should understand the bases for making causal inferences. In other words, what kind of evidence supports the belief that a causal relationship exists? Social scientists generally require at least three kinds of evidence to establish causality. These requisites are association, direction of influence, and nonspuriousness.

Association. For one variable to be a cause of another, the variables must be statistically associated. If the pattern of changes in one variable is not related to changes in another, then the one cannot be producing, or causing, changes in the other. Thus, for instance, if intelligence is unrelated to delinquency—that is, if adolescents of high and low intelligence are equally likely to be delinquent—then intelligence cannot be a cause of delinquency.

Associations, of course, are almost never perfect; and so a perfect association between variables is not a criterion of causality. According to logicians, in fact, the very idea of causation implies imperfect associations between events. Causes can have invariable effects only in "closed systems" that exclude all other factors that might influence the relationship under investigation. Many of the laws of physics, for instance, are said to apply exactly only in a vacuum. However, vacuums are not found in nature; neither is it possible in real social situations to eliminate completely the influence of extraneous factors. Perfect associations may be expected, therefore, only under the theoretical condition that "all other things are equal," but not in the "real world" of observations.

Barring "perfect" associations, then, the application of this first criterion necessarily involves a judgment about whether an association implies a meaningful causal relationship. In the social sciences, causal relationships often are implied from comparatively "weak" associations. One reason for this is that many measurements in the social sciences are relatively imprecise. The primary reason, though, is that in explaining human action, multiple causes may independently or jointly produce the same or similar effects. A weak association may mean that only one of several causes has been identified, or it may mean that a causal relationship exists, but not under the conditions or for the particular segment of the population in which the weak association was observed. Rather than strength of association, therefore, social scientists rely on tests of statistical significance to determine whether a meaningful, interpretable association exists between variables. Although Broh found a weak correlation between time spent on homework and grades, this association was still statistically significant; therefore, it was construed as a cause (among others) of academic performance.

Direction of influence. A second criterion needed to establish causality is that a cause must precede its effect, or at least the direction of influence should be from cause to effect. In other words, changes in the causal factor, or independent variable, must influence changes in the effect, or dependent variable, but not vice versa. For many relationships in social research the direction of influence between variables can be conceived in only one way. For example, characteristics fixed at birth, such as a person's race and gender, come before characteristics developed later in life, such as a person's education or political party affiliation, and it is hard to imagine how changes in the latter could influence changes in the former.

Direction of influence is not always so easy to determine. Suppose you found a correlation between racial prejudice and interracial contact showing that the more contact a person has with members of other races, the less prejudiced he or she is apt to be. One possible interpretation is that racial contact increases familiarity and contradicts stereotypes, thereby reducing prejudice. An equally plausible interpretation is that prejudiced people will avoid contact while tolerant people will readily interact with other races, so that racial prejudice influences racial contact. Without any information about the direction of influence between these variables, there is no basis for deciding which variable is the cause and which is the effect. To take another example, a correlation between grades and class attendance may mean that greater attendance "increases the amount learned and thus causes higher grades" or it may mean that "good grades lead students who obtain them to attend class more frequently" (Neale and Liebert, 1986:89–90).

Direction of influence was an issue in the Broh study. An association between sports participation and academic performance could mean that playing sports has educational benefits, but it also could mean that higher achieving, "good" students are more likely to choose or be selected to play sports than other students. Thus, as she designed her study, it was important for Broh to rule out the possibility that superior academic performance leads to sports participation.

The requirement that causes influence effects has two major implications for research: (1) Hypothesized relationships should always specify the direction of influence among variables, and (2) whenever the direction cannot be established theoretically, it should be tested empirically. As you will see, this task is relatively easy in experiments but often difficult in other kinds of research.

Nonspuriousness (elimination of rival hypotheses). If two variables happen to be related to a common extraneous variable, then a statistical association can exist even if there is no inherent link between the variables. Therefore, to infer a causal relationship from an observed correlation, there should be good reason to believe that there are no "hidden" factors that could have created an accidental or spurious relationship between the variables. When an association or correlation between variables cannot be explained by an extraneous variable, the relationship is said to be *nonspurious*. When a correlation has been produced by an extraneous third factor, and neither of the variables involved in the correlation has influenced the other, the relationship is called a **spurious relationship**.

The idea of spuriousness is obvious when we consider two popular examples in the social sciences. The first is a reported positive correlation in northwestern Europe between the number of storks in an area and the number of births in that area (Wallis and Roberts, 1956:79). Although this correlation might explain how the legend got started, one could hardly accept the conclusion that storks bring babies. The correct interpretation is that storks like to nest in the crannies and chimneys of buildings; and so, as the population and thus the number of buildings increases, the number of places for storks to nest increases. And as the population increases, so does the number of babies. We also would expect to find a positive correlation between the number of firefighters at a fire and the amount of damage done. But this does not imply that firefighters did the damage. The reason for the correlation is the size of the fire: Bigger fires cause more firefighters to be summoned and also cause more damage.

In the above examples the original relationship is an incidental consequence of a common cause: an antecedent extraneous variable. In the first example, the size of the population accounts for *both* the number of storks and the number of births; in the second, the severity of the fire determines *both* the number of firefighters and the amount of damage. These relationships are depicted in Figure 3.3. The examples are intuitively obvious, and the third factor is fairly easy to identify. In actual research, however, spurious relationships are much less apparent, and since their detection depends on the investigator's knowledge and insight, the possibility often exists that an unknown variable may have produced an observed association.

To infer nonspuriousness, the researcher ideally must show that the relationship is maintained when all extraneous variables are held constant. Circumstances

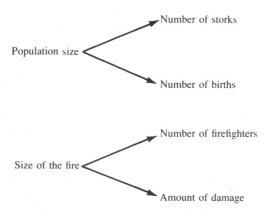

FIGURE 3.3. Examples of spurious relationships.

seldom allow a researcher to control *all* variables, however. Therefore, one attempts to control or evaluate the effects of as many variables as possible. The greater the number of variables that are controlled without altering a relationship, the greater the likelihood that the relationship is not spurious. An example involving the relationship between smoking and cancer will show how this works (Labovitz and Hagedorn, 1981).

Smokers develop lung cancer at a rate about six to seven times greater than that of nonsmokers. The belief that this indicates a causal link between smoking and cancer is strengthened by the fact that this rate remains the same when other variables are controlled. Consider, for example, the variables gender, urban–rural residence, and socioeconomic status. When the incidence of lung cancer among smokers and nonsmokers is computed separately for males and females, for urban and rural residents, and for persons of high and low socioeconomic status, we would expect in every case that smokers are approximately seven times more likely to develop lung cancer than nonsmokers. Each of these variables is a potential rival explanation to the interpretation that smoking *causes* lung cancer. An association but no causal connection between smoking and cancer could occur if males were both more likely to smoke *and* more likely (for some reason other than smoking) to get lung cancer than females. Similarly, urban–rural residence could produce a spurious association between smoking and lung cancer if urban areas have more smokers as well as sources of lung cancer (e.g., greater outdoor air pollution) than rural areas. Thus, if controlling for any one of these variables revealed no difference in the rate of lung cancer between smokers and nonsmokers, the relationship between smoking and cancer would be considered spurious. For example, the finding of no difference in the cancer rate between smoking and nonsmoking men and between smoking and nonsmoking women would suggest that the variable "gender" had produced a spurious association between smoking and cancer. (Box 3.1 provides another example of the importance of the nonspuriousness criterion. In this case, the causal interpretation that exercise reduces the risk of heart attacks was challenged by several rival explanations.)

BOX 3.1

**Problems in Causal Interpretation:
The Case of Exercise and Heart Attacks**

Of the three criteria needed to establish a causal relationship, the most difficult to assess is nonspuriousness. One can never be sure that a causal connection exists between correlated variables. Indeed, mistaken impressions of causality may remain undetected for years. An interesting example of this problem in social science research is related by psychologists Schuyler Huck and Howard Sandler (1979:151,152,227).

In recent years there has been much interest in the relative benefits of regular exercise. One controversial claim is that exercise can reduce the risk of heart attacks. An early study by Dr. J. N. Morris of London shows, however, just how difficult this is to establish. Examining drivers and conductors of London's double-decker buses, Morris found that the drivers were far more likely to suffer from heart disease and to die from coronaries than were the conductors. Since the drivers sat in their seats all day while the conductors ran up and down stairs to collect fares, he concluded that it was the differential amount of exercise inherent in the two jobs that brought about the observed differences in health. Before reading further, you might try to think of variables other than exercise that could have produced the difference in heart problems between the drivers and conductors. Morris uncovered one variable in a follow-up study, and Huck and Sandler mention two others.

Some time after the publication of the above results, Morris examined the records maintained on the uniforms issued to drivers and conductors and discovered that drivers tended to be given larger uniforms than conductors. Therefore, he concluded, differences in weight rather than exercise might be the causal factor. That is, heavier men, who were more coronary prone to begin with, may have chosen the sedentary job of driver, whereas thinner men chose the more physically active job of conductor.

Another explanation is related to the amount of tension associated with the two jobs. As Huck and Sandler (1979:227) point out,

> The conductors probably experienced very little tension as they went up and down the bus collecting fares from the passengers; the worst thing that they probably had to deal with in their jobs was a passenger who attempted to ride free by sneaking around from one seat to another. Normally, however, we suspect that the conductors actually enjoyed their interaction with other people while on the job.
>
> But on the other hand, each driver had the safety of everyone on the bus as his responsibility. And as anyone who lives in or visits a city knows, driving in rush-hour traffic is anything but restful. Having to dodge pedestrians, being cut off by other vehicles, watching for signal changes—these activities can bring about temporary outbursts of anger and chronic nervousness. Imagine how it would affect your heart to be in the driver's seat of a bus for eight hours each working day!

Finally, a third variable that could account for the different rate of heart problems is age. If mobility or seniority or some other function of age were related to job assignment, then employees assigned to the driver jobs may have been older and those assigned to the conductor jobs younger. And since we would expect more heart attacks among older persons, age rather than the nature of the job could be the causal variable.

In this example it is impossible to tell which cause—exercise, weight, job stress, or age—may have produced the observed differences in health between drivers and conductors. Since both weight and age are antecedent to job type and heart disease, either of these uncontrolled extraneous variables could have created a spurious relationship. However, if exercise or job stress were the correct interpretation, then the original relationship would not be spurious, since exercise and job stress specify intervening variables through which the job itself can make a person more or less susceptible to heart problems. The following diagram shows the difference in these two outcomes.

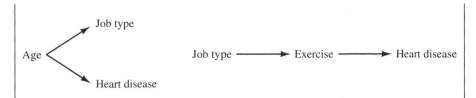

Of course, it is possible that two or more of these variables are operating jointly to produce the health differential between the two groups. The only safe conclusion is that we really do not know which interpretation is correct.

In general, correlation does not imply causation. All correlations must be interpreted; like any fact, they do not speak for themselves. To infer a causal relationship from a correlation, an investigator must detect and control for extraneous variables that are possible and plausible causes of the variable to be explained. The fatal flaw in Morris's study is that relevant extraneous variables were not controlled; without directly assessing the effects of such "hidden" causes, we cannot tell which interpretation is valid.

In one way or another, tests for spuriousness entail controlling for extraneous variables. The type of statistical control employed in our smoking–cancer example is very common in nonexperimental research. Its major drawback is that one can control statistically only for those variables that have been observed or measured as part of the research. Hence, the effects of any unknown or unmeasured variables cannot be assessed. A stronger test of nonspuriousness is provided in experiments through a process called *randomization* that makes it theoretically possible to control for all extraneous variables. Experimental controls are discussed in chapter 6, and causal analysis techniques involving statistical manipulation of nonexperimental data are discussed in chapter 15.

Causation, intervening variables, and theory. Recall that extraneous variables may be either antecedent or intervening in relation to the independent and dependent variables. An antecedent variable, which is causally prior to both the independent and dependent variable, can produce a spurious relationship. By contrast, the identification of an intervening variable or mechanism linking the independent and dependent variables strengthens the causal inference. Indeed, this is sometimes advocated as a fourth criterion—in addition to association, direction of influence, and nonspuriousness—for establishing that one variable causes another (see Hyman, 1955). For example, one may argue that the belief that smoking causes lung cancer will be enhanced considerably if and when it is established that certain chemical agents from cigarettes produce cancerous cells. Knowing the causal process through which smoking produces cancer would provide one last shred of evidence against a spurious correlation. However, once the criterion of nonspuriousness is firmly established, a causal relationship is generally inferred even if the intervening mechanisms are not known. Few scientists today doubt that smoking causes cancer. Thus, while specifying the intervening variables in a relationship may lead to a better theoretical understanding and more accurate prediction, it is "not part of the minimum requirements for demonstrating causality. Holding a match to a pile of leaves is a cause of their bursting into flame, even if one cannot describe the intervening chemical reactions" (Hirschi and Selvin, 1967:38).

Though not a necessary causal criterion, intervening variables are nonetheless an essential part of scientific inquiry. Often, in fact, this is what the development and testing of theory is all about. For example, Durkheim's theory of suicide stipulated the intervening causal mechanism—social integration—for a number of relationships. The reason that fewer suicides are found among Catholics than among Protestants and that there are fewer suicides among married than among single people, according to the theory, is that being a Catholic and being married each engenders a greater sense of social integration which, in turn, reduces the likelihood that anyone within the group will commit suicide. Broh tested the effects of several intervening variables. Having found that participation in interscholastic sports benefits students' academic performance, she found that this relationship was best explained by developmental and social capital theories. High school athletes develop a greater work ethic and sense of control over their lives than do non-athletes, and their athletic participation generates stronger ties among students, parents, and teachers, all of which have positive effects on academic performance.

Yet, theory plays a much larger role in causal analysis than specifying intervening variables. Theories not only render a more complete understanding of the causal processes that connect events, but also provide the general framework for investigating the nature of all relationships. Theories tell the researcher which relationships to observe, what extraneous variables are likely to affect the relationships, and the conditions under which a causal relationship is likely to exist. It is only in terms of some theory, in short, that the researcher can determine how to assess the meaningfulness of a "weak" association and how to test for direction of influence and nonspuriousness. Thus we see again the importance of the interplay between theory and research in science. Theory guides research, and research provides the findings that validate and suggest modifications in theory.

Stating Problems and Hypotheses

Having introduced the language of units of analysis, variables, and relationships, we are now ready to examine statements of the research problem. Scientific investigations always start with a problem or question that can be solved or answered empirically. Arriving at this starting point for research can be a long and difficult process. Experienced as well as novice researchers often begin with only a vague notion of the problem, or they may be motivated by a question so broad in scope that it provides little or no immediate direction for research. Many well-known social scientists seem to have been stimulated by just these kinds of "grand questions." For example, Stanley Schachter, well known in part for his work on affiliation, was interested initially in what motivates people to be around others (Evans, 1976:159), a question nearly as encompassing as the entire field of social psychology. In tracing the development of the ideas for his study *The Adolescent Society*, sociologist James Coleman (1964:184) says that his major interest, from the time he entered graduate school, was in "the relation of the individual to society," or, being only slightly less general, "the dilemma that confronts each society, on the one hand, to maintain social order and, on the other, not to restrict the freedom of the individuals within it." These are certainly important questions, but they are too broad to be scientifically answerable. Before Schachter and Coleman could begin to do research, they had to reformulate their problems so that they pointed to identifiable variables and relationships. After reading and speculating about "affiliative tendencies," Schachter eventually focused on the problem of how fear affects the desire to be with others. Coleman, having been influenced by a casual discussion among friends about high school experiences, decided to study various determinants and consequences of high school status systems.

To provide sufficient direction for research, the statement of a research problem should always suggest observations that offer some solution to the problem. For most research, this means that a problem statement should, first of all, express or ask a question about a relation between two or more variables (Kerlinger, 1973:17). This rules out moral, philosophical, and religious issues as well as any questions of the general form, "What causes *A*?" or "What are the effects of *B*?" Second, the variables in the problem statement should be observable or at least potentially observable. A major difficulty with the problems with which Schachter and Coleman began is that their concepts—"being around others," "social order," "freedom"—are too complex to be amenable to observation.

Beckett Broh progressively narrowed the focus of her research. Beginning with the question of whether extracurricular programming enhances academic achievement and informed by a review of the research literature, she came up with three unanswered questions about this relationship:

- Why does sports participation boost students' achievement? Does sports participation benefit students' development and social networks, and are these the mechanisms that link participation to educational outcomes?
- Are the educational benefits of sports participation unique to sports, or do nonsports extracurricular activities also promote achievement?
- Do nonsports extracurricular activities benefit students' development and social networks? (Broh, 2002:73)

The tentative answers to research questions are called hypotheses. Formally defined, a **hypothesis** is an expected but unconfirmed relationship between two or more variables. Hypotheses come from a variety of sources, including everything from theory to direct observation to guesses and intuition. Sometimes the formulation of hypotheses is the principal outcome of research. At other times, hypotheses are never made explicit, even though they implicitly guide research activities. However, whenever the research objective is clearly one of testing relationships among variables, hypotheses should be stated formally and precisely so that they carry clear implications for testing the stated relations (Kerlinger, 1973:18).

While stated in a variety of ways, all hypotheses should speculate about the nature and form of a relationship. An adequate hypothesis statement about two variables should indicate which variable predicts or causes the other and how changes in one variable are related to changes in the other. For example, if we thought that education generally increases tolerance, we might hypothesize that "an increase in education will result in a decrease in prejudice." This statement implies two features about the relationship: first, which variable causes, explains, or predicts the other (education predicts prejudice); and second, how changes in one variable are related to changes in the other (as education increases, prejudice decreases). Hypotheses that specify the form of the relationship are said to be testable because it is possible, assuming each variable has been measured adequately, to determine whether they are true or false, or at least whether they are probably true or probably false.

There are several forms of expressing testable hypotheses, such as the one relating education and prejudice:

1. *"If–then" (conditional) statements.* These statements say that if one phenomenon or condition holds, then another will also hold. An example would be, "if a person has a high level of education, then he or she will have a low level of prejudice." Alternately, one could say, "if a person has a low level of education, then he or she will have a high level of prejudice." In logic, such statements are called **conditionals**. A conditional consists of a connection between two simple statements, each pointing to a condition or category of a variable. As used in science, the connection asserted by a conditional is that the condition (or variable category) following the "if" *causes* the condition (or variable category) following the "then." Social research hypotheses seldom are specified in this form. Still, it is always possible to restate testable hypotheses as conditionals; and by using this standard logical form, some scientists contend that it is easier to ascertain the kinds of inferences that legitimately can be made from research findings to the hypothesis (McGuigan, 1993:37).

2. *Mathematical statements.* Many hypotheses may be stated in the form of the standard mathematical formula $Y = f(X)$, which reads "Y is a function of X." An example is Einstein's famous formula $E = mc^2$ (i.e., energy equals mass times the speed of light squared). Of course, though once a hypothesis, $E = mc^2$ is now called a scientific law because it has been confirmed repeatedly. Mathematical formulas represent precise formal statements of hypotheses. Because variables in social research generally are measured with less precision than in the physical sciences, many social scientists choose not to state hypotheses in this form. Nonetheless, mathematical formulas are the ideal in science, because they yield precise predictions and express complex relationships parsimoniously. The mathematical form is also equivalent to the conditional. $Y = f(X)$ merely says "If (and only if) X is this value, then Y is that value" (McGuigan, 1993:38).

Considering our education–prejudice example and assuming that each variable could be measured numerically, an equation for the relationship might be $P = 10 - \frac{1}{2}E$; that is, prejudice (P) equals 10 minus one-half times education (E). Prejudice might be scaled such that zero indicated an extremely low level of prejudice and 10 an extremely high level, with intermediate values indicating intermediate levels. Education might be quantified in terms of the number of years of schooling. Thus, a person with a college education, or sixteen years of schooling, would be hypothesized to have a prejudice level of 2, since $10 - \frac{1}{2}(16) = 2$; and a person who had only finished the fourth grade would be hypothesized to have a prejudice level of 8 $[10 - \frac{1}{2}(4) = 8]$.

3. *Continuous statements*. Hypotheses of the form "the greater the X, the greater (or lesser) the Y" indicate that increases in one variable (X) are associated with increases (or decreases) in another variable (Y). For example, as education increases, prejudice decreases; or, expressed in slightly different form, the higher the level of education, the lower the prejudice.

4. *Difference statements*. Statements in this form assert that one variable differs in terms of the categories of another variable. For example, people with high education are less prejudiced than people with low education. Whether "continuous" or "difference" statements are used to express a hypothesis will depend on whether the variables in the hypothesis are quantitative or qualitative. If both variables could be "quantified," as we assumed in the case of the formula $P = 10 - \frac{1}{2}E$, then the relationship could be stated in the continuous form. But if either variable consisted of discrete categories, such as "high" and "low" prejudice, then the relationship would need to be stated in the difference form.

Both continuous and difference statements clearly specify the *form* of the relationship. However, both types of statements are ambiguous about the causal connection between variables. Ordinarily, a statement of the form "the greater the X, the greater the Y" is meant to imply that X causes Y. But it also can mean that Y causes X or that X and Y cause one another. As you saw in our discussion of causation, it is important to know which variable is presumed to cause the other; in addition, since most hypotheses take the form of continuous or difference statements, the causal linkage can be problematic. Fortunately, in most research articles and reports, researchers make this connection clear in their discussions of the hypothesis.

Once the causal variable has been identified, it is easy to transform the hypothesis statement into the form of a conditional. Thus, for example, the statement "The higher the level of education, the lower the level of prejudice" becomes "If education is high, then prejudice will be low."

At this point we should reiterate an important tenet of scientific research. Even though all of the above forms of expression would appear to assert that the relationship is absolutely true or false, hypotheses in science can only have probabilistic, not exact, confirmation. Thus, while the statement "If X, then Y" logically can only be true or false, it is assumed that observations will show it to be "probably true" or "probably false."[5] One often sees this kind of assumption built into statements of hypotheses in the form of qualifiers such as "tends to" or "in general." For example, one might say that "increased education will *tend* to reduce prejudice." Such statements acknowledge that tests of hypotheses are always restricted by the limited accuracy of our measures and our inability to specify and control all the variables affecting events.

How a hypothesis is expressed in a given study will depend on several factors: the researcher's discretion, the present state of knowledge about the research problem, and whether qualitative or quantitative variables are involved. Regardless of how hypotheses are expressed, however, they should indicate at least the form of the relationship between variables and, ideally, should specify the causal linkage between variables; for ultimately it is causal relationships in which scientists are interested.

Research Purposes and Research Design

In the previous pages we have emphasized the role of relationships in social research. The sense that social scientists make of the social world is expressed in terms of relationships among variables. Furthermore, although they may be only vaguely defined or implicit and unbeknownst to the researcher, anticipated relationships structure the researcher's every activity, from deciding which variables to measure to deciding how observations should be made and interpreted. As mentioned earlier, however, not all research is conducted for the immediate purpose of testing relationships. Research is undertaken for three broad purposes: (1) to *explore* a phenomenon such as a group or setting in order to become familiar with it and to gain insight and understanding about it, frequently in order to formulate a more precise research problem for further study; (2) to *describe* a particular community, group, or situation as completely, precisely, and accurately as possible; and (3) to examine and formally to *test relationships* among variables. Whether a study is conducted primarily for the purpose of exploration, description, or testing of relationships is important to know, for these three functions have different implications for research design.

Exploratory studies are undertaken when relatively little is known about something, perhaps because of its "deviant" character or its newness. Falling into this category of research would be observational studies of street gangs and radical political and religious movements; clinical case histories of persons, groups, and events; and anthropological accounts of entire cultures. When attempting to explore a topic or phenomenon about which one knows very little, one necessarily begins with a general description of the phenomenon. This sounds easy but in fact is probably the most difficult kind of study for the novice researcher to undertake. There are no clearly delineated independent and dependent variables and, therefore, no preset categories of observation and analysis. The researcher may have few, if any, guidelines to help determine what is important, whom to interview, or what leads to follow up on. For these reasons, the research plan in an exploratory study is more open than in other kinds of research. Decisions are made about the kinds of instruments needed (e.g., photographic equipment, tape recorders) and the key persons with whom one will need to speak at first, but the paths down which these initial steps may lead are almost impossible to foresee. In chapter 10, on field research, we discuss some data-gathering approaches that frequently are devoted to exploration.

The objective of a **descriptive study**, as the name implies, is to describe some phenomenon. The nature of the description, however, differs considerably from exploratory research. A descriptive study is much more structured. Basically a fact-finding enterprise, it focuses on relatively few dimensions of a well-defined entity and measures these dimensions systematically and precisely, usually with detailed numerical descriptions. The information is gathered from a set of cases that are carefully selected to enable the researcher to make estimates of the precision and generalizability of the findings. Examples of descriptive studies are the various censuses conducted periodically at the local and national levels. A census may provide information about everything from the age and racial composition of a community to its employment and housing costs. Also having a descriptive purpose are the ubiquitous opinion polls that attempt to estimate the proportion of people in a specified population who hold certain opinions or views, or who behave in certain ways. For example, how many favor capital punishment? How many say they will vote for candidate A in the next election?

The third purpose for which research is conducted is to test relationships. Studies with this purpose are sometimes called **explanatory studies**, because they formally seek the answers to problems and hypotheses. Since all research involves description at some level, the primary difference between descriptive and explanatory studies lies in the scope of the description. Purely descriptive research operates at a lower level of description by merely seeking information about isolated variables, whereas explanatory research goes beyond this step to a description of relationships among variables.

Both descriptive and hypothesis-testing research are highly structured and must be carefully planned. With these kinds of research it is important, therefore, to have a complete, detailed strategy worked out before the data are collected. This preliminary strategy or outline is what we have called the **research design**. Basically, it consists of a clear statement of the research problem as well as plans for gathering, processing, and interpreting the observations intended to provide some resolution to the problem. To formulate a research design is to anticipate the entire research process, from beginning to end. To do this, one needs to have an adequate knowledge of every stage of social research. Examining these stages now will serve not only to clarify the key components of research design but also to introduce the reader to the remainder of the book.

Stages of Social Research

Figure 3.4 outlines the major steps in the research process. Although most research follows this pattern, steps may be omitted, depending on the type of research, and there may be numerous feedback loops. In short, this is an idealized model; some research is much less orderly than it implies.

Stage 1: Formulation of the Research Problem

Research begins with a question or problem. Problems initially chosen almost always require more precise formulation to be amenable to research. From a general idea, one must decide more specifically what one wants to know and for what purpose one wants to know it. The best ideas on how to refine the problem are likely to be found in the scientific literature. Indeed, a thorough review of previous research in journals and books is considered essential in science. Besides helping to

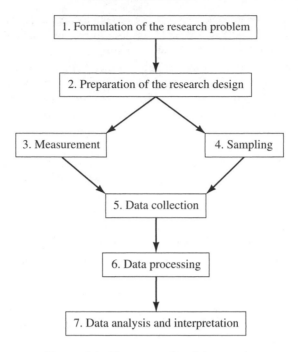

FIGURE 3.4. The stages of social research.

narrow and refine the problem, a review of the literature may reveal its broader theoretical significance. Literature reviews also may help to identify relevant control
variables and should suggest pertinent methods and procedures by indicating how
other researchers have addressed the problem.

Stage 2: Preparation of the Research Design

Once the problem has been clearly formulated, the researcher must develop an overall plan or framework for the investigation. To do this, he or she must, in effect,
anticipate all of the subsequent stages of the research project. Preliminary decisions
have to be made about what sort of observations are needed to solve the research
problem or to provide an adequate test of the hypothesis. The researcher must then
select an appropriate strategy for making the observations—experiment, survey,
field research, or use of available data. Each of these approaches has its unique
strengths and weaknesses that determine its suitability for given problems. Often
the best strategy, as we argue in chapter 12, is a combination of approaches. Within
the context of selecting an overall strategy, decisions also must be made on the unit
of analysis, on which variables to observe and control and how they should be measured, and on how best to analyze the data. Thinking through all of these problems
in advance should prevent serious mistakes and omissions in a study. Of course, not
all problems can be foreseen, especially in exploratory research, and many of the
decisions at the design stage will be arbitrary and subject to change.

Two problems—measuring variables and selecting units of analysis—warrant special attention and are ordinarily worked out in detail after the basic research design is complete. These are therefore considered separate, concurrent stages.

Stage 3: Measurement

Part of the research plan involves devising operations that will link specific concepts to empirically observable events. This process of operationalization and measurement will be taken up in chapter 4, a substantial part of which describes techniques for assessing the quality or goodness of measures.

Stage 4: Sampling

Besides deciding on the unit of analysis, the researcher must also determine how many units should be selected and how to go about choosing them. The problems and methods related to sampling are addressed in chapter 5.

Stage 5: Data Collection

Once the research design is completed, the researcher is ready to make the observations—to collect the data. Since the general approach to data collection affects decisions about both measurement and sampling, the approach to be taken is determined early in the design phase. As we have pointed out, there are four basic choices: experiment, survey, field research, and use of available data. The underlying logic of each of these approaches, as well as their distinctive problems, advantages, and disadvantages, are covered in chapters 6 through 11.

Stage 6: Data Processing

Having made the observations, the researcher is ready to analyze and interpret them. In most cases, however, the form of the data does not allow easy interpretation. The data must be transformed or processed for analysis. In this era, most data processing involves, at some point, the hardware and software of computers. Chapter 14 begins with a discussion of data processing, giving special attention to the preparation of data for computer analysis.

Stage 7: Data Analysis and Interpretation

Once the data are ready for analysis, they must be manipulated further so that their meaning and bearing on the problems and hypotheses that initiated the inquiry can be extracted. There are several types of analysis, many of which involve statistical tests, a topic that is beyond the scope of this textbook. Without any training in statistics, however, one can learn how to read and to present data properly in tables and graphs. One can also learn when it is appropriate to apply certain statistical procedures. Also, it is possible to develop a solid understanding of the logic of analyzing causal relationships. These topics are also covered in chapters 14 and 15.

Having analyzed the data, one draws conclusions about the hypotheses and theory that guided the research and, if appropriate, assesses the practical implications of the findings. Finally, one reports the results.

Summary

Our purpose in this chapter has been to introduce the basic terms in the technical language of social research as these terms relate to problem formulation and research design. There are many sources of ideas and factors affecting problem selection. A basic requirement is that a problem be amenable to scientific research—that it be resolvable with reference to observational evidence. Beyond this requirement, problem selection is affected by such factors as theoretical and practical relevance, social premiums, and the personal values and resources of the researcher.

Problems are refined in the course of working out the overall study plan, or research design, the key elements of which are units of analysis, variables, and relationships. Units of analysis are the entities about whom or which the researcher gathers information. These include individual people, groups and organizations of all kinds, communities, nations, and social artifacts. Researchers often aggregate information about individuals in order to describe the social unit that the individuals comprise. In general, conclusions should be restricted to the unit of analysis to which the data pertain. Thus, conclusions about individuals should not be drawn from group-level data; otherwise, one risks committing an ecological fallacy.

Variables are the characteristics of units that may vary in successive observations. Research focuses on explanatory variables while attempting to eliminate the influence of extraneous variables. The dependent variable is the explanatory variable that the researcher tries to explain or predict; an independent variable is a presumed cause of the dependent variable. Other variables may be either antecedent or intervening in relation to specific independent and dependent variables, and either controlled or uncontrolled during the course of the study. Quantitative variables have categories that express numerical distinctions, whereas qualitative variables involve differences in kind rather than in number.

Anticipated and predicted relationships guide all social research. Relationships occur when the changes in two or more variables form a predictable pattern. This pattern has two properties—strength and form—which are depicted differently according to whether the variables are qualitative or quantitative. In addition to statistical measures of strength of association, such as the correlation coefficient, tests of statistical significance indicate whether a relationship is likely to exist or whether it is likely to be the product of random processes. Social scientists are particularly interested in causal relationships. To establish that variable X causes variable Y, one must show that X and Y are statistically associated, that the direction of influence is from X to Y, and that the association between X and Y is nonspurious. Theories that identify intervening variables also may strengthen the inference that X causes Y.

Problem statements ideally express or ask a question about a relation between two or more variables. A hypothesis is a conjecture about a relationship between variables. In social research, a hypothesis may take the form of a conditional, a mathematical equation, a continuous statement, or a difference statement. Although much social research is undertaken to test hypotheses, it also may be done for the purposes of exploration and description.

Key Terms

unit of analysis	*correlation coefficient*
aggregate data	*statistical significance*
ecological fallacy	*causal relationship*
variable	*association*
explanatory variable	*direction of influence*
extraneous variable	*spurious relationship*
dependent variable	*nonspuriousness*
independent (predictor) variable	*hypothesis*
antecedent variable	*conditional*
intervening variable	*mathematical statement*
control variable	*continuous statement*
quantitative variable	*difference statement*
qualitative variable	*descriptive research*
relationship	*exploratory research*
positive (direct) relationship	*hypothesis testing (explanatory) research*
negative (inverse) relationship	*research design*

Review Questions and Problems

1. What are some of the factors that influence topic selection in social research?
2. Indicate the unit of analysis suggested by each of the following statements.
   a. Homicide rates are lower in European countries than in the United States.
   b. Ecks College has a lower proportion of minority students than any other college in the state.
   c. Children from one-parent families are more likely to commit delinquent acts than are the children from two-parent families.
   d. Among blacks, high self-esteem is associated with positive family and friendship relations.
   e. Wendy Griswold (see chapter 11) studied American culture and character by analyzing 130 novels written in the late nineteenth and early twentieth centuries. For each novel, she asked several questions (e.g., what is the protagonist's social class? Is adult heterosexual love important to the plot? Is money important to the novel?)
3. What is the "ecological fallacy"?
4. A researcher examining data on schools finds that the higher the average income of the parents whose children attend a school, the higher is the average achievement test score for all students in the school. What is the unit of analysis of these data? Can the researcher conclude from the data that the higher the income of a student's parents, the better the student's achievement test score will be? Why or why not?

5. Specify the type of variable (independent, dependent, extraneous, control) that applies to the underlined term in the following statements:

    a. We believe that the effect of <u>school quality</u> on <u>academic achievement</u> found in prior research is spurious, because researchers have not examined the <u>social class level</u> of the students studied.

    b. When <u>pay rate</u> was held constant, we found no influence of <u>job satisfaction</u> on <u>productivity</u>.

    c. Sherif's camp studies demonstrated that <u>conflict between groups</u> increases <u>cohesion within groups</u>.

6. Explain how anticipated relationships guide the collection and interpretation of research evidence.

7. Give one example, other than those mentioned in the text, of (a) a positive and (b) a negative relationship between two quantitative variables.

8. Distinguish between the strength and form of relationships. Which of these aspects may be applied to relationships among qualitative variables? Which may be applied to relationships among quantitative variables?

9. Beckett Broh reported that the relationship between sports participation and grades was statistically significant at $p < .001$. Carefully explain the meaning of "$p < .001$" with reference to this relationship.

10. What are the three criteria necessary to establish causality in the social sciences?

11. Explain the function of intervening variables in establishing causal relationships.

12. Explain the meaning and give an example (other than one mentioned in the text) of the statement, "Correlation does not imply causation."

13. In a sociological study, Galle, Gove, and McPherson (1972) found a positive statistical association between population density, or crowding, and several measures of social pathology (e.g., mortality rate, juvenile delinquency rate). Identify a variable that might have created a spurious relationship between crowding and social pathology. Then briefly explain how the spurious relationship could occur.

14. Suppose that you want to test the hypothesis that students who have taken a course in methods of social research will receive higher grades in subsequent sociology courses than students who have not taken such a course.

    a. Identify the independent and dependent variables in this hypothesis.

    b. List three extraneous variables. One of them must be of the kind that reasonably could be expected to produce a spurious relationship between the independent and dependent variables.

    c. Briefly explain how one of your extraneous variables could make the hypothesized relationship spurious. (You may assume that methods of social research is not a required course.)

15. Evaluate the following statements as hypotheses. That is, discuss how clearly each spells out the nature of the relationship.

    a. Social class is related to party affiliation.

    b. As the frequency of interaction with a person increases, the degree of liking for the person increases.

    c. Among adults, intellectual ability declines with age.

d. Broken homes cause delinquency.

16. Formulate three hypotheses, each relating two variables from the following list. For each hypothesis, specify the independent and dependent variables.

Gender (male/female)

Level of education (highest grade completed)

Marital status (married/widowed/divorced/separated/never married)

Party identification (Republican/Democrat/Independent/none)

Belief in life after death (yes/no)

Attitude toward capital punishment (favor/oppose)

17. Express one of the hypotheses formulated in question 16 in the form of a (a) conditional, (b) continuous statement (if possible), and (c) difference statement.

18. What are the three broad purposes for which research is undertaken?

19. Explain the difference between exploratory research, on the one hand, and descriptive and hypothesis-testing research, on the other. Now differentiate between descriptive and hypothesis-testing research.

20. Outline the stages of social research.

NOTES

1. When Frans van Poppel and Lincoln Day (1996) recently tested Durkheim's theory with individual-level data from the Netherlands at roughly the same period as Durkheim, they found that the Catholic–Protestant difference in suicide rates could be accounted for by how the causes of deaths were recorded. Catholic deaths were far more likely than Protestant deaths to be recorded as "sudden death" or "death from ill-defined or unspecified cause"; these deaths would have been categorized as suicides had they occurred among Protestants. Although Durkheim's theory may be supported by other data, this analysis shows the pitfalls of using group-level data to make inferences about individuals.

2. We caution the reader not to confuse this distinction with the distinction between quantitative and qualitative research or quantitative and qualitative measurement. Both quantitative researchers—typically survey researchers and experimenters who rely on numbers and statistical methods—and qualitative researchers—who do intensive interviews, participant observation, and depth analyses of historical materials and rely on discursive methods—use both kinds of variables in their analyses (see King, Keohane, and Verba, 1994).

3. The table reports a type of "average" called the median, which is equal to the fiftieth percentile: half of the group earn less and half earn more.

4. Determining the level of confidence in the conclusion that a relationship exists, as well as estimating the strength of the relationship, is the job of statistics and is therefore beyond the scope of this textbook. In general, confidence and strength will be greater to the extent that (a) the observed differences between groups are large, (b) the computed averages are based on a large number of people, and (c) people in the same group are quite similar to one another and different from those in other groups.

5. Determining whether a statement is probably true or probably false, like assessing the existence and strength of a relationship, is a matter of applying the laws of probability, which is the subject of statistics.

4

✓

Measurement

Measurement is the process of assigning numbers or labels to units of analysis in order to represent conceptual properties. This process should be quite familiar to the reader even if the definition is not. For example, we measure every time we "rate" something, such as a movie, restaurant, or blind date: "The movie was 'pretty good' "; "the new restaurant definitely merits a four-star rating—the decor, service, and food are excellent, and the price is right"; "on a scale of 1 to 10, I would give him a 2—not the worst date I have ever had but close to it." In a somewhat more refined manner, you may have "measured" someone's "intelligence" by his or her grade-point average; and you probably have measured your weight on a bathroom scale. Each of these examples contains the essentials of measurement: Labels or numbers ("pretty good," "four-star," a "2," a particular GPA, a pointer reading on a scale) are assigned to objects (movies, restaurants, people) to represent properties (the overall quality of a movie, restaurant, or date; intelligence; weight).

There is a difference, of course, between these everyday examples of measurement and the process of measurement in social research. In the examples, the rules for assigning labels or numbers to objects are more or less intuitive, whereas in social research these rules must be spelled out in detail. Scientific norms require that we fully describe our methods and procedures so that others can repeat our observations and judge the quality of our measurements. In this chapter we outline the measurement process, provide several examples of measurement in social research, and then discuss three criteria for evaluating the nature and quality of measurements.

The Measurement Process

The measurement process begins as the researcher formulates his or her research problem or hypothesis. Every problem or hypothesis contains terms—concepts or variables—that refer to aspects of reality in which the researcher is interested. Problem formulation involves thinking about what these terms mean in both an abstract and an empirical sense. The ultimate goal of measurement is to specify clearly observable referents of the terms contained in one's hypothesis, but to get to this point one must first consider the abstract meaning of the terms. Thus, the entire measurement process consists of moving from the abstract (concepts) to the concrete (measures of concepts).

Conceptualization

Recall Beckett Broh's study of extracurricular involvement and academic achievement, which we introduced in chapter 3. Broh theorized that extracurricular activities increase social capital which, in turn, enhances academic achievement. This theory relates three terms: "extracurricular activities," "social capital," and "academic achievement." The terms are merely labels for concepts. To understand fully what the theory means and to arrive at an appropriate set of observations for testing it, one must know the meaning of these concepts. Thus, the initial step in measurement is to clarify the concepts embedded in one's theories and hypothesis with words and examples, ultimately arriving at conceptual or theoretical definitions.

Broh considered the meaning of each of her key concepts. She relied on common understandings of extracurriculum and academic achievement. Academic achievement generally refers to "cognitive learning outcomes which are products of [school] instruction or aimed at by [such] instruction" (Helmke and Schrader, 2001:13552); the extracurriculum pertains to school activities outside the set of courses offered at a school. Social capital, according to Broh (2002:72), "is generally recognized as the ability to accrue benefits through membership in social networks."

Theoretical definitions of this sort direct the search for appropriate measures of concepts, establish a basis for judging the quality of one's measures, and enable others to evaluate the meaning of one's research findings. Such definitions, however, are not worked out anew with each research project, nor are they the arbitrary invention of each individual investigator making sure that others understand what he or she means. If this were so, there would be no basis for developing a shared body of knowledge. Rather, the process of formulating and clarifying concepts, called **conceptualization**, is linked to theory testing and construction. This ongoing process may occur prior to any particular empirical investigation, and it usually continues through research, as theories and their constituent concepts are refined and elaborated.

Broh derived her theoretical definition of social capital from analyses of this concept by, among others, sociologists James Coleman and Alejandro Portes. Coleman (1990:304) distinguished social capital, "embodied in the relations among persons," from human capital, "embodied in the skills and knowledge acquired by an individual." He also argued (Coleman, 1988) that the family is a primary site of social capital, while Portes (1998) analyzed important extrafamilial networks. Taking into account these theoretical analyses, Broh (2002:72) concluded that "participation in sports and other extracurricular activities may serve to create social capital within the family by providing opportunities for increased social interaction between the parents and the child"; these activities further create social capital outside the family "by offering opportunities for the formation and intensification of social ties among students, parents, and the school." Operating through these networks, social capital facilitates academic achievement in two ways: It exerts social control over students by encouraging them to comply with school norms and values, and it provides channels for students to acquire important educational information and resources.

The conceptualization of complex concepts such as social capital often involves making careful distinctions among similar ideas and breaking down the concept into various components or dimensions. Thus, in her conceptualization, Broh distinguished between social capital and human capital, and she identified different social ties—parent–child, parent–teacher, student–teacher, and student–student—in which social capital is grounded. With regard to the extracurriculum, she carefully noted the numerous activities in which students participate, such as sports, drama, music, and vocational clubs; and she further distinguished between types of sports activities, such as interscholastic sports, intramural sports, and cheerleading. This sort of analysis further clarifies the meaning of concepts and generates more precise statements of problems and hypotheses. Beginning with the general theoretical relationship between the extracurriculum and social capital, Broh concentrated on the less abstract relationship between participation in interscholastic athletics and social ties among parents, students, and teachers.

Two aspects of concepts are especially relevant to the measurement process. First, a concept may signify a single category, such as "male" or "'A' student," or a concept may imply several categories or values, such as "gender" or "grade in English." Measurement assumes the possibility of assigning *different* values or categories to units of analysis; hence, we measure concepts that vary, which we refer to as *variables*. Second, many social science concepts are not directly observable. For example, we cannot "see" social capital or academic performance in the same sense that we can see a table or a horse or the color red. On the other hand, while we cannot see school performance, we can observe how many questions students answer correctly on standardized tests and the grades they receive in core academic subjects such as English and math. After conceptualization, the next step is to identify such manifestations of one's concepts, and it is at this point that we move from a language of concepts to a language of variables.

Just where this shift in language occurs is difficult to pinpoint, and researchers often use the terms "concept" and "variable" interchangeably. Still, it is important to realize that these terms connote different levels of abstraction. Once the researcher begins to speak in terms of a variable, he or she generally has some observable events in mind that represent the underlying concept.

Operationalization

Once the meaning of a concept has been clarified and the concept is construed as a variable, the researcher begins the process of **operationalization**. The counterpart of a conceptual definition is an operational definition. An *operational definition* describes the research operations that will specify the value or category of a variable on each case. Broh operationalized the variables in her study by using responses to survey questions from the National Educational Longitudinal Study (NELS), which administered questionnaires to students in the 8th, 10th, and 12th grades. In both the 10th and 12th grades, for example, students were asked whether they had participated on an interscholastic sport team—that is, "your school team competes with other schools' teams." Based on these questions, Broh (2002:74) operationally defined participation in interscholastic sports as "whether a student participated in interscholastic sports during both the 10th and 12th grades (1 = participated in both years, 0 = did not participate in both years)."

To understand better the notion of operational definitions, let us consider a simple illustration from everyday life. Suppose your friend bakes you a delicious carrot cake. You ask your friend how he made it, since you would like to make one. Your friend says, "Oh, you take some carrots, flour, sugar, eggs, and so forth, add some nuts, bake it, and voilà!—you have a carrot cake." Would you be able to make an identical cake with these directions? Not likely. What you need is an operational definition of your friend's concept of "carrot cake." You would need to have the complete directions—that is, details such as all of the ingredients, the amount of each ingredient to use, the steps necessary to combine the ingredients, the oven temperature, and baking time. In short, your friend's operational definition should look like an ordinary recipe card. Using the recipe (operational definition), you should be able to produce a very similar cake.

Many operational definitions are possible; social scientists must choose or develop one that they believe corresponds reasonably well to the concept in question. To return to the carrot cake example, how could you be certain that your friend's recipe represented an "authentic" carrot cake? Are nuts really an essential ingredient? Suppose you substituted whole-wheat flour for white; would you still have a carrot cake? If you compared his recipe with others, you would no doubt find some differences. How are you to conclude which is the correct recipe? In the end you would find that there is no correct recipe, but you would still have to decide for yourself whether your friend's operational definition (recipe) "really" corresponded to your idea of what a carrot cake is. As you can see, operational definitions, so essential to social research, are somewhat arbitrary and restricted expressions of what a concept "really" means.

When creating operational definitions, a researcher may consider many different empirical representations or indicators. An **indicator** consists of a single observable measure, such as a single questionnaire item in a survey. If each indicator classified units in exactly the same way, the choice would be wholly arbitrary. However, no two indicators measure a given concept or variable in the same way, and no one indicator is likely to correspond perfectly to its underlying concept. Indicators provide imperfect representations of concepts for two reasons: (1) They often contain errors of classification and (2) they rarely capture all the meaning of a concept. Consider one indicator of social capital in Broh's study: whether students talk to their teachers outside class about their school work. Whether this promotes social capital will depend on why students speak with their teacher. Are they doing so for disciplinary reasons at the insistence of the teacher or because they seek guidance on an assignment? And, of course, there are many sources of social capital other than student–teacher relations, including students' relations with other students and with parents and parent–teacher relations.

Because of the imperfect correspondence between indicators and concepts, researchers often choose to rely on more than one indicator when operationalizing a concept. Sometimes several indicators of a given concept are analyzed separately, yielding multiple tests or cross-checks of a hypothesis. At other times, indicators are combined to form a new variable, as when answers to several questions, each a distinct indicator, are combined to create the variable "IQ score." Researchers generally use several indicators to operationalize a complex concept like social capital. With simpler concepts like participation in interscholastic sports, a single indicator will suffice. James Davis (1971:18) suggests this rule for deciding whether to use

BOX 4.1

Operationalizing the Concept of Religiosity

Sociologist Ronald Johnstone (1983:289–304) provides an excellent illustration of the processes of concept clarification and measurement with respect to the concept of "religiosity." Johnstone notes, first, that the conceptualization of religiosity should begin with a definition of religion: "Religion is a set of beliefs and practices, centered around a belief in the supernatural and an orientation toward the sacred, that are shared by members of a group" (p. 290). Having defined religion, one could say that religiosity is the concept of "being religious." This conceptual definition suggests several ways of operationalizing religiosity:

1. The group affiliation approach focuses on the religious group to which a person belongs. In this case, a person is religious if he or she professes to be a member of some religious group, such as a Protestant or Catholic, while nonmembers are nonreligious. Measures of religious affiliation focus on group differences, but fail to capture the intensity of belief or degree of religious interest, which is closer to the concept of individual religiosity.
2. Single indicators of individual religiosity typically have emphasized "ritual participation"—in particular, the frequency of attendance at formal religious services. The General Social Survey (Davis, Smith, and Marsden, 2002) includes such a measure:

   How often do you attend religious services?

   [ ] Never
   [ ] Less than once a year
   [ ] About once or twice a year
   [ ] Several times a year
   [ ] About once a month
   [ ] 2–3 times a month
   [ ] Nearly every week
   [ ] Every week
   [ ] Several times a week

   Related measures tap frequency of prayer or extent of involvement in the total organizational life of the congregation. The problems with such measures are that they (1) are subject to systematic error and (2) assume that religiosity is a one-dimensional phenomenon. Attendance may reflect, for example, family or other group pressures, habit, or the desire to socialize with friends after services, rather than religious commitment. Moreover, people who rank high on one dimension of religiosity may rank low on another, so that different conclusions about the impact of religion could be reached, depending on which measure of religiosity is used. For example, Stephen Ainlay and James Hunter (1984) found that while church attendance declined with age among persons over 50, nonchurch participation measures such as Bible reading and listening to religious radio programs increased with age.
3. A frequently cited example of the multidimensional approach is Charles Glock's (1962) identification of five dimensions of religiosity: experiential, ritualistic, ideological, intellectual, and consequential. Joseph Faulkner and

Gordon DeJong (1966) have developed sets of questions for measuring each of Glock's dimensions. For example, the experiential dimension concerns the degree of emotional attachment to the supernatural. Items developed by Faulkner and DeJong to measure this dimension include:

Would you say that one's religious commitment gives life a certain purpose which it would not otherwise have? (1) Strongly agree; (2) Agree; (3) Disagree; (4) Strongly disagree.

All religions stress that belief normally includes some experience of "union" with the Divine. Are there particular moments when you feel "close" to the Divine? (1) Frequently; (2) Occasionally; (3) Rarely; (4) Never.

4. The final two approaches identified by Johnstone conceive of religiosity in terms of (1) open-ended "ultimate concerns" and (2) intrinsic-extrinsic religious orientation. The ultimate-concern approach attempts to define religiosity in terms of basic religious feelings, without reference to traditional religious forms or institutionalized religious groups. The intrinsic–extrinsic concept distinguishes between extrinsically motivated persons for whom religion represents a self-serving instrumental conformity to social conventions and intrinsically motivated persons for whom religion provides a framework for living and understanding life. Here are two sample items from Joe Feagin's (1964) intrinsic–extrinsic religious orientation scale:

The church is most important as a place to formulate good social relationships. (1) I definitely disagree; (2) I tend to disagree; (3) I tend to agree; (4) I definitely agree.

My religious beliefs are what really lie behind my whole approach to life. (1) This is definitely not so; (2) Probably not so; (3) Probably so; (4) Definitely so.

single or multiple indicators to represent a concept: "If you have to ponder about the best way to measure a key [concept], it is worth measuring in two or more different ways. . . ." (See Box 4.1 for examples of different ways to operationally define the concept of religiosity.)

Operational Definitions in Social Research

There are two general kinds of operational definitions in social research: manipulated and measured. *Manipulation* operations are designed to change the value of a variable, whereas *measurement* operations estimate existing values of variables. Both types are nicely illustrated in a study of people's reactions in a common situation—a car failing to proceed immediately when a traffic signal turns green. Anthony Doob and Alan Gross (1968) used this setting to investigate unobtrusively the relations among status, frustration, and aggression. They hypothesized that frustration in traffic caused by a higher status person would elicit fewer aggressive responses than would frustration caused by a lower status frustrator. The independent variable, status of the frustrator, was *manipulated* by blocking traffic with two different automobiles: a new luxury automobile for the high-status condition and an older vehicle for the low-status condition. To operationalize the dependent variable, aggression, they used a *measured* definition—number and frequency of horn-honking responses by drivers blocked by the experimental vehicle. The hypothesis was confirmed: For example, 84 percent of the blocked drivers in the low-status condition honked at least once in twelve seconds, compared with only 50 percent of those blocked in the high-status condition.

The operations involved in the manipulation of frustrator's status are spelled out in detail by Doob and Gross. These include such fine detail as the models and ages of the experimental cars, the clothes worn by drivers of these cars, and the amount of time the drivers remained stopped after the signal changed to green. Similarly, precise details are given on the measured operations (observers, stopwatches, and tape recorder) used to determine horn honking. Unless investigators explicitly spell out the details of their manipulations and measurements, other researchers will not be able to replicate or judge the quality of the research.

Manipulation of an independent variable is by definition experimental, and we will have a good deal more to say about this in chapter 6. For now, let us examine some of the various approaches to operationalization of measured variables.

Verbal Reports

By far the most common form of social measurement is the **verbal** or **self-report**. Such reports consist of replies to direct questions, usually posed in interviews or on questionnaires. Self-reports provide simple and generally accurate measures of background variables such as age, gender, marital status, and education. They also are used extensively to measure subjective experiences, such as knowledge, beliefs, attitudes, feelings, and opinions.

All the variables in Beckett Broh's study were operationalized by means of self-reports. She used a single item from the first year of the NELS survey to measure parents' income: What was your total family income from all sources in 1987? (possible responses ranged from 1 = none to 15 = $200,000 or more).

Composite measures. In self-report attitude measurement, responses to several questions frequently are combined to create an **index** or **scale**. As we noted earlier, it is best to use several indicators to measure complex concepts. Scales and indexes (the terms often are used interchangeably) condense or reduce the data generated by multiple indicators into a single number or scale score. This not only simplifies the analysis but also increases precision and provides a means of assessing the quality of the measurement.

Broh created several composite measures in her study, combining from two to seven questions. For example, she added together the answers to two parts of one question to measure the amount of time students spent on homework each week:

Overall, about how much time do you spend on homework EACH WEEK in and out of school?

	In school each week	Out of school each week
None	00	00
Less than 1 hour	01	01
1–3 hours	02	02
4–6 hours	03	03
7–9 hours	04	04
10–12 hours	05	05
13–15 hours	06	06
16–20 hours	07	07
Over 20 hours	08	08

To operationalize self-esteem, Broh drew on seven items from Morris Rosenberg's widely used self-esteem scale. Respondents were asked to indicate whether they strongly agree, agree, disagree, or strongly disagree with each of the following seven statements. Values between 1 and 4 were assigned to the response categories, with a 4 representing strong agreement with a positive statement about the self (or, conversely, strong disagreement with a negative statement).

1. I feel good about myself. (Strongly agree = 4)
2. I feel I am a person of worth, the equal of other people. (Strongly agree = 4)
3. I am able to do things as well as most other people. (Strongly agree = 4)
4. On the whole, I am satisfied with myself. (Strongly agree = 4)
5. I feel useless at times. (Strongly disagree = 4)
6. At times I think I am no good at all. (Strongly disagree = 4)
7. I feel I do not have much to be proud of. (Strongly disagree = 4)

An individual's responses to these seven questions were added together to produce a single scale score that could range from 7 (low self-esteem) to 28 (high self-esteem).

As with most scale construction, the development of the Rosenberg self-esteem scale involved some rather sophisticated statistical techniques that are beyond the scope of this book. Because of the difficulty of creating scales and because literally thousands of scales and indexes now exist, we recommend that the beginning researcher use well-validated scales to measure attitudes, opinions, and other subjective experiences whenever possible. Chapter 12 contains a more advanced discussion of the underlying logic of scaling. Also, at various points below, we will note how composite measures increase the quality and precision of measurement.

Verbal reports vary widely with respect to question wording and response formats. The number of response categories ranges from two to seven for most attitude measures, but the researcher may provide many more categories or none at all.

Instead of labeling all response categories, as in the self-esteem scale, investigators may ask respondents to place a check mark along a line whose end points represent opposite ends of a continuum.

Verbal reports also are elicited with pictures and diagrams, which can simplify complex issues and are particularly useful with children. To measure attitudes toward residential integration, for example, Maria Krysan and Reynolds Farley (2002) presented respondents five cards with diagrams depicting neighborhoods containing 14 homes. Each card showed a different interracial mixture ranging from all-black to all-white with three racially mixed neighborhoods. Respondents "were asked to imagine that they had been looking for a house and found a nice one they could afford." Then they were asked to rank the cards from the most to least attractive and to indicate if there were any of the neighborhoods that they would not want to move into.

Because slight changes in phrasing can drastically alter the meaning of a question, wording is very important. We will discuss question formats and wording at length in chapter 9, which deals with interview and questionnaire construction.

Observation

Doob and Gross measured drivers' levels of aggression by direct observation of behavior: They observed how quickly and how often the drivers honked at a blocking vehicle. Lesley Joy and her colleagues (1986) developed an observational measure of children's aggression to compare a Canadian town before and after it first received television reception in 1974 with two similar "control" towns that had one or several television channels prior to this time. Trained observers recorded grade school children's physically aggressive behavior (hitting, pushing, chasing, etc.) and aggressive words (threatening, arguing, insulting, etc.) on school playgrounds during recess. Summary measures of physical and verbal aggression (average number of acts per minute of playground observation) increased for both sexes following the introduction of television.

Observation provides direct and generally unequivocal evidence of overt behavior, but it also is used to measure subjective experiences such as feelings and attitudes. For example, one could measure interpersonal attraction by observing and recording the physical distance that two people maintain between themselves, with closer distances indicative of greater liking. Similarly, Zick Rubin (1970) operationally defined romantic love by observing the length of time couples spent gazing into one another's eyes.

Besides firsthand observation, hardware such as videotapes, audiotapes, and counters are commonly used for recording purposes. To measure which television programs people watch, the Nielsen Organization attaches an electronic monitoring device to the television set of each person in their sample, which automatically records, minute by minute, the channel to which the set is tuned.

Archival Records

Archival records, which refer to existing recorded information, provide another invaluable source of measurement. The various types of archival data, discussed in chapter 11, include statistical records, public and private documents, and mass communications.

Using public data from the United States 1990 and 1980 censuses, Reynolds Farley and William Frey (1994) found modest declines in black–white residential segregation in metropolitan areas during the 1980s. Residential segregation was operationally defined by the index of dissimilarity, which indicates the percentage of whites (or blacks) who would have to change their census block of residence to produce zero segregation. In 1990 the indexes of dissimilarity ranged from 91 for Gary, Indiana (the most segregated), to 31 for Jacksonville, North Carolina (the least segregated).

Another example of an operational definition derived from archival records comes from a study testing Riesman's hypothesis that there was a trend in the twentieth century from "inner-" to "other-directedness." Sanford Dornbusch and Lauren Hickman (1959) analyzed advertisements in a popular magazine, *Ladies' Home Journal*, sampled over a sixty-seven-year period. An advertisement was operationally defined as other-directed if it used endorsements by persons or groups (e.g., "Billie Burke wears Minerva Sweaters," "Housewives like the Singer Sewing Machine") or claimed that use of a product would benefit interpersonal relations ("He'll like you better if you use Revlon"). Beginning about 1920, the authors found a dramatic shift upward in the frequency of other-directed advertising themes, thus supporting Riesman's hypothesis.

Selection of Operational Definitions

Given that you have a concept in mind, how do you decide on an appropriate operational definition? First of all, your decision will be made in the context of an overall research strategy, the choice of which depends to a degree on the specific research problem or hypothesis. As we shall see, each of the four basic approaches has its distinctive strengths and limitations, which must be taken into account in deciding how to study a given problem. Some hypotheses, for example, contain variables that may be impractical or unethical to manipulate, hence, to study experimentally. No one would propose inducing varying amounts of emotional suffering in people to study effects on physical health.

Each of the different approaches favors certain types of operational definitions. For the most part, survey research involves verbal reports; field research entails observational measurement; and the use of available data, by definition, includes archival records. Experiments, on the other hand, use a combination of measures— verbal reports and/or observation in addition to manipulation procedures. Field researchers often supplement their observations with verbal reports. And survey researchers sometimes use observational measures; for example, an interviewer may observe the type of household and neighborhood in which an interviewee resides as a measure of social class.

With an overall research strategy in mind, the most basic requirement is to select an operational definition that fits the concept well. While we have said that no operational definition can capture a concept's meaning perfectly or completely, this does not license the researcher to select just any measure. It is still desirable to get the best possible fit between concept and measure, and the best way to do this is by carefully considering the meaning of the concept, especially as it relates to the theory in which it is embedded. The National Television Violence Study, for example, developed a coding scheme for measuring television violence based on the theory that television violence is more harmful to the viewer when the depicted perpetrator is physically attractive, portrayed as a hero, and goes unpunished and when the victim exhibits no pain cues or evidence of harm (Kunkel et al., 1995).

Another example of a study in which theory guided the selection of an appropriate operational definition is Albert Pierce's test (1967) of Durkheim's (1951) hypothesis that suicide rates increase in periods of rapid economic change independently of the direction of change (boom or bust). Durkheim theorized that marked economic changes can disturb the existing goals and norms toward which people orient their lives, can thrust individuals into new social settings in which they are ill suited to manage, and hence can increase the probability of suicide. Data for white males during the peacetime years 1919 to 1940 were examined. At first, Pierce correlated the suicide rate with various *objective* measures of economic change, based on income, percentage of labor force unemployed, and housing construction, with indecisive results. Finally he struck upon the notion of using a measure—the "index of common stock prices"—that would reflect the *public definition* of the economic situation, which is more in tune with Durkheim's theory. That is, rapid fluctuations of stock-market prices may be viewed as indicators of public economic uncertainty, resulting in disruption or discontinuities in perceived goals and norms. Pierce's analysis revealed that suicide rates correlated highly with the rate of change in the public definition of economic conditions as operationally defined by the index of stock-market prices.

Beyond attending to the basic research strategy and the concept's meaning, the choice of operational definitions is largely a matter of creativity, judgment, and practicality. One's selection also should be aided by considering three characteristics that describe the quality of information provided by operational definitions: levels of measurement, reliability, and validity.

Levels of Measurement

Speaking now in terms of variables, we can define measurement as "the assignment of numbers or labels to units of analysis to represent variable categories." One characteristic of measurement emerges from the nature of the variable categories. It turns out that we tend to use different empirical rules for sorting cases into categories, and each rule results in different interpretations of the numbers that may be assigned to the various categories. Unlike the numbers derived from the measurement of length, time, mass, and so forth in the physical sciences, the numbers assigned to different categories in social research do not always have a simple and straightforward interpretation. The various meanings of these numbers, which reflect basic empirical rules for category assignment, are what is meant by **levels of measurement**. The four general levels usually identified are nominal, ordinal, interval, and ratio.

Nominal Measurement

The lowest level, **nominal measurement**, is a system in which cases are classified into two or more categories on some variable, such as gender, race, religious preference, or political party preference. Numbers (or more accurately, numerals)[1] are assigned to the categories simply as labels or codes for the researcher's convenience in collecting and analyzing data. For example, political party preference might be classified as

1. Democrat
2. Republican
3. Independent
4. Other
5. No preference

Since we are merely using numbers as labels, no mathematical relationships are possible at the nominal level. We cannot say that $1 + 2 = 3$ (Democrat plus Republican equals Independent) or that $1 < 2$ (Democrats are "lower" on political preference than Republicans). We can say, however, that all 1's share the same political preference and that 1's differ from 2's in their political preference.

With nominal measurement, the empirical rule for assigning units to categories is that cases placed in the same category must be equivalent. Also, the categories of the variable should possess two characteristics: They must be both exhaustive and mutually exclusive. To be **exhaustive** means that there must be sufficient categories so that virtually all persons, events, or objects being classified will fit into one of the categories. The following set of categories for the variable "religious preference" does not meet this criterion:

1. Protestant
2. Catholic

You can probably think of other categories needed to make this measure exhaustive, especially if you happen to have no religious preference or if you are Jewish or Muslim or a member of some other religion. Even if one expected few non-Catholic or non-Protestant respondents, one should at least add the categories "None" and "Other" to cover all the possibilities.

The criterion of **mutual exclusivity** means that the persons or things being classified must not fit into more than one category. Suppose that a researcher hastily came up with the following categories for the variable "place of residence":

1. Urban
2. Suburban
3. Rural
4. Farm

You can see that some persons would fit into both categories 3 and 4. The following set of categories would be an improvement:

1. Urban
2. Suburban
3. Rural, farm
4. Rural, nonfarm

Ordinal Measurement

In **ordinal measurement**, numbers indicate the rank order of cases on some variable. Psychologist S. S. Stevens (1951), who developed the idea of measurement level, used hardness of minerals as one example of ordinal measurement. We can determine the hardness of any two minerals by scratching one against the other: Harder stones scratch softer ones. By this means, we could number a set of stones, say five, from 1 to 5 according to their hardness. The numbers thus assigned, however, would represent nothing more than the order of the stones along a continuum of hardness: "1" is harder than "2," "2" is harder than "3," and so on. We could not infer from the numbering any absolute quantity, nor could we infer that the intervals between numbers are equal; in other words, we could not say how much harder one stone is than another.

Another example of ordinal measurement would be an individual's ranking of certain leisure activities in terms of the pleasure derived from them. Suppose you ranked three activities as follows:

1. Playing tennis
2. Watching television
3. Reading sociology

From this ordering we could not make any statements about the intervals between the numbers; it may be that you enjoy watching television almost as much as playing tennis but that reading sociology is not nearly as pleasurable as watching TV. In this sense, ordinal measurement is like a very elastic tape measure that can be stretched unevenly; the "numbers" on the tape measure are in proper order, but the distances between them are distorted.

One virtue of ordinal measurement, as Julian Simon (1978:231) notes, is "that people can often make an accurate judgment about one thing *compared to another*, even when they cannot make an accurate *absolute* judgment." Simon (1978:231) illustrates the accuracy of comparative judgments with a familiar example:

> [Y]ou can often tell whether or not a child has a fever—that is, when the child's temperature is two or three degrees above normal—by touching the child's face to yours and comparing whether her skin is warmer than yours. But you would be hard-put to say whether the temperature outside is 40° or 55°F, or whether a piece of metal is 130° or 150°F.

Similarly, in the realm of social measurement one can probably say with some certitude whether security or chance for advancement is the more important job characteristic, without being able to say just how important either characteristic is.

The ability of human observers to make such comparative judgments permits a wide range of reasonably accurate social measurements at the ordinal level—for example, measures of socioeconomic status, intelligence, political liberalism, various preference ratings, and attitude and opinion scales. On the other hand, ordinal measurement is still rather crude. At this level we cannot perform most mathematical (statistical) operations in analyzing the data. We cannot add, subtract, multiply, or divide; we can only rank things: $1 < 2$, $2 < 3$, $1 < 3$.

Interval Measurement

Interval measurement has the qualities of the nominal and ordinal levels, plus the requirement that equal distances or intervals between "numbers" represent equal distances in the variable being measured. An example is the Fahrenheit temperature scale: The difference between 20°F and 30°F is the same as the difference between 90°F and 100°F—10 degrees. We can infer not only that 100°F is hotter than 90°F but also how much hotter it is. What enables us to make this inference is the establishment of a standard measurement unit, or *metric*. For Fahrenheit temperature, the metric is degrees; similarly, time is measured in seconds, length in feet or meters, and income in dollars.

When numbers represent a metric, the measurement is "quantitative" in the ordinary sense of the word. Thus, we can perform basic mathematical operations such as addition and subtraction. However, we cannot multiply or divide at the interval level. We cannot say, for example, that 100°F is twice as hot as 50°F, or that 20°F is one-half as hot as 40°F. The reason is that interval measures do not have a true or absolute zero but an arbitrary one. That is, the zero point on the scale does not signify the absence of the property being measured. Zero degrees Fahrenheit does not mean that there is no temperature; it is simply an arbitrary point on the scale. Its arbitrariness is illustrated by comparison with another interval scale designed to measure the property of temperature: 0°F equals about -18°C (Celsius or centigrade), and 0°C equals 32°F.

While social researchers often aim to create interval measures, most of what passes for this level of measurement is only a very rough approximation. IQ score, for example, is sometimes treated as an interval level measure, even though it makes no sense to add IQ scores or to infer that equal numerical intervals have the same meaning. (Is the difference between IQ scores of 180 and 190 equal to the difference between 90 and 100?) The empirical rule defining interval measurement is to create equal intervals between numbers. Some attitude scaling techniques attempt to do this, although most scales (e.g., Rosenberg's self-esteem scale) have ordinal-level measurement.

Ratio Measurement

The fourth level, called **ratio measurement**, includes the features of the other levels plus an absolute (nonarbitrary) zero point. The presence of an absolute zero makes it possible to multiply and divide scale numbers meaningfully and thereby form ratios. The variable income, measured in dollars, has this property. Given incomes of $20,000 and $40,000, we can divide one into the other (that is, form a ratio) to signify that one is twice (or one-half) as much as the other.

Many measures in social research have a well-defined metric and a zero point that meaningfully signifies none of the property being measured. Besides income, other examples are age in years, number of siblings, and years of employment. Ratio-level measures often are obtained by simply counting—for example, number of horn honks, number of siblings, number of people in a social network. Also, aggregate variables, which characterize collectivities of people, frequently are measured at this level by counting and then dividing by a population base—for example, crude birth rate (number of births per 1000 people in the total population),

TABLE **4.1.** Information Provided by the Four Levels of Measurement

Information provided	Nominal	Ordinal	Interval	Ratio
Classification	X	X	X	X
Rank order		X	X	X
Equal intervals			X	X
Nonarbitrary zero				X

divorce rate (number of divorces per 1000 existing marriages), percentage of labor force unemployed, percentage Democrat.

Discussion

The level of measurement achieved depends upon the empirical procedures used to operationalize a concept. A field researcher, for example, may obtain an ordinal measure of *age* by using people's appearance, manner, and other observed characteristics to classify them as "children," "young adults," "middle-aged," and "seniors." Or date-of-birth information might be used to measure *age* as a ratio scale.

It is interesting to note that the four levels of measurement themselves form an ordinal scale with regard to the amount of information they provide. Each level has the features of the level(s) below it plus something else. Table 4.1 illustrates this.

In most social science research, the distinction between interval and ratio levels of measurement is not very important compared with the differences among interval, ordinal, and nominal measures. Many older statistical techniques (including Pearson's correlation coefficient) assume interval measurement and are therefore inappropriate for lower levels of measurement. Some newer techniques are well suited for drawing meaningful inferences about nominal and ordinal measures.[2]

Finally, researchers may use words rather than numbers to represent gradations in conceptual properties (Sorokin, 1937:21–22). If a historian describes the extent of political unrest in various epochs as "low," "high," and "extremely high," an ordinal scale is being used to measure political unrest. If a field researcher classifies the homeless as "mentally ill," "drug dependent," and "other," the categories represent a nominal scale. The use of words rather than numbers to represent variable categories does not imply poorer or better measurement (King, Keohane, and Verba, 1994:151–52). Whether words or numbers are used, the quality of a measure is judged in terms of reliability and validity, as explained below.

Reliability and Validity

Level of measurement provides a framework for interpreting the categories of a variable. It tells us what sort of inferences we can make about cases assigned to different categories. (Are they merely different? Can we say that one is greater or lesser than the other? And so on.) But what about the adequacy of the set of categories as a whole and of the operationalization procedure for assigning cases to categories? In other words, how does one evaluate the goodness of specific operational definitions?

We have seen that for any concept a large number of operational definitions are possible, and that creative insight, good judgment, and relevant theory aid in the development of operational definitions. Admittedly these aids are rather subjective in nature; however, once an operational definition is selected, there are more objective ways to evaluate its quality. Social scientists use the terms "reliability" and "validity" to describe issues involved in evaluating the quality of operational definitions.

Reliability is concerned with questions of stability and consistency. Is the operational definition measuring "something" consistently and dependably, whatever that "something" may be? Do repeated applications of the operational definition under similar conditions yield consistent results? If the operational definition is formed from a set of responses or items (e.g., scores on the self-esteem scale), are the component responses or items consistent with each other? An example of a highly reliable measuring instrument is a steel tape measure. With such an instrument, a piece of wood 20 inches long will be found to measure, with negligible variation, 20 inches every time a measurement is taken. A cloth tape measure would be somewhat less reliable in that it may vary with humidity and temperature, and in that we can expect some variation in measurements depending on how loosely or tightly the tape is stretched.

Measurement **validity** refers to the congruence or "goodness of fit" between an operational definition and the concept it is purported to measure. Does this operational definition truly reflect what the concept means? Are you measuring what you intend to measure with this operational definition? If so, you have a valid measure. An example of a valid measure is amniocentesis, a technique for determining various genetic characteristics of an unborn child, including sex. It is a valid measure of biological sex because it can determine with virtually perfect accuracy whether the unborn will be a boy or a girl. At one time, a number of invalid "measures" of the unborn's sex existed in the form of folk wisdoms. One belief, for example, involves tying a string to the pregnant woman's wedding band and holding the band suspended over her abdomen. If the band swings in a circle, the baby will be a girl; if, however, the band swings back and forth, the child will be a boy.

A highly unreliable measure cannot be valid—how can you measure something accurately if the results fluctuate wildly? But a very reliable measure still may not be valid; that is, you could be measuring very reliably (consistently) something other than what you intended to measure. To take a facetious example, let us suppose we decide to measure the "intelligence" of students by standing them on a bathroom scale and reading the number off the dial (Davis, 1971:14). Such an operational definition would be highly reliable, as repeated scale readings would yield consistent results. However, this obviously would not be a valid measure of an individual's intelligence.

Sources of Error

When we apply an operational definition to a set of cases, we use different labels, ranks, ratings, scores, and so forth, to represent differences or variation among the cases. There are three potential sources of variation. By examining these, we can better understand the ideas behind reliability and validity assessment. The three sources of variation in any measurement are expressed in the following equation:

$$\text{Observed value} = \text{true value} + \text{systematic error} + \text{random error}$$

The first source of variation is *true differences* in the concept the operation is intended to measure. One would hope that this would account for most of the variation in the measurements; after all, this is what validity is all about! In the ideal situation, with a perfectly valid operational definition, *all* of the measured variation would reflect differences in the concept under study. Observed differences in IQ scores obtained with an IQ test, for example, ought to reflect only true differences in intelligence and nothing else. However, since perfect measurement is unobtainable, a realistic approach is to be aware of other possible sources of variation and to try to eliminate or reduce their effects as much as possible.

Social scientists refer to sources of variation other than true differences in the variable being studied as "error." The main problem in interpreting the observed variation is to determine what part of it can be explained by true differences and what part is due to one or more sources of error. There are two basic types of measurement errors: systematic and random.

Systematic measurement error results from factors that systematically influence either the process of measurement or the concept being measured. Assuming interval-level measurement, systematic error would be reflected in ratings or scores that are consistently biased in one direction—either too high or too low. A cloth tape measure that has stretched with wear would create error in the form of constant underestimates of length. An example of systematic error in social measurement is the cultural bias of IQ tests. Most IQ tests contain problems and language that tend to favor particular groups in society. Given the same "true" intelligence level, the person familiar with the test problems and language will always score higher than the person who is unfamiliar with the test problems or who speaks a different language than the one in which the test is communicated. Thus, differences in IQ scores may reflect a systematic error introduced by the cultural bias of the test, as well as differences in intelligence.

Many of the systematic errors that contaminate social measurement arise from respondents' reactions to participating in research. When the respondent's sensitivity or responsiveness to a measure is affected by the process of observation or measurement, we refer to this as a **reactive measurement effect** (Webb et al., 1966:13). Just as people behave differently alone than in front of an audience, or with friends than with strangers, they tend to react differently when in a research setting. Awareness of the presence of a social scientist "observer," for example, can increase or decrease the incidence of some observed behaviors.

It has been shown that people are less willing to admit to holding undesirable positions and attitudes when they are aware of being "tested." This is why verbal report measures generally underestimate (a systematic error) the prevalence of socially unacceptable traits, behaviors, and attitudes such as psychiatric symptoms, deviant behaviors, and racial prejudice. A good example is John McConahay's (1986) Old-Fashioned Racism Scale. This measure asks respondents whether they agree or disagree with palpable racist statements: For example, "Blacks are generally not as smart as whites"; "If a black family with about the same income and education as I have moved next door, I would mind it a great deal." In this post-civil-rights era, however, it is no longer socially acceptable to support acts of open discrimination or to endorse blatant racist beliefs about black intelligence, ambition, and other stereotyped characteristics. "This form of racism," as McConahay (1986:93) says, "is as out of style in trendy circles as are wide ties and spats." Consequently, many white Americans, knowing the socially desirable answers, may not express their true feelings when responding to the Old-Fashioned Racism Scale or similar measures. Indeed, it is precisely for this reason that researchers have questioned evidence of a decline in racial prejudice in recent years. That is, the apparent decline may be a function of social desirability effects rather than of real changes in attitudes (Crosby, Bromley, and Saxe, 1980).

Besides this **social desirability effect**, there are other response tendencies that can introduce systematic measurement error. Respondents are more likely to agree than to disagree with statements irrespective of their content (called the acquiescence response set); also, when sequences of questions are asked in a similar format, respondents tend to give stereotyped responses, such as endorsing the right-hand or left-hand response (Webb et al., 1966). Such tendencies produce systematic error when they correspond to supposed variation in the measured property. For example, if a question measuring political liberalism is worded such that agreement indicates a liberal view, then the researcher could not be sure whether a person's agreement indicated a liberal view or simply a tendency to agree with statements regardless of their content.

Systematic errors differ from the true value of a variable by a constant amount. Therefore, they bias measurements in a particular direction, underestimating or overestimating the true value, which affects their accuracy or validity. Because of their constancy, however, systematic errors do not adversely affect reliability. Reliability is undermined by inconsistencies in measurement that arise from random errors.

Random measurement error is unrelated to true differences in the concept being measured. It is the result of temporary, chance factors, such as transitory upswings and downswings in the health and mood of subjects and respondents, temporary variations in the administration or coding of a research measure, or momentary investigator fatigue. A tired or bored respondent, for example, may give erroneous responses by not attending carefully to the questions asked. Similarly, an ambiguously worded question will produce random errors by eliciting responses that vary according to respondents' interpretations of the question's meaning.

Such error is random because its presence, extent, and direction are unpredictable from one question to the next or from one respondent to the next. Thus, random errors in a measure of the variable "age" would not be consistently high or low, but rather would fall on either side of respondents' real ages, so that the average error would be zero. Random error could be demonstrated by asking someone whose visual acuity is impaired (perhaps by drunkenness) to measure the length of an object several times. It is likely that this person's measurements will vary about the object's true length. Sometimes the errors will vary in one direction (overestimating length) and sometimes in the other (underestimating length); sometimes they will be large and sometimes small. Random errors produce imprecise and in-

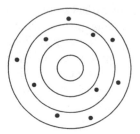 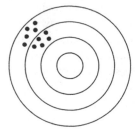 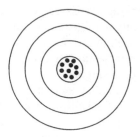

Low reliability   High reliability   High reliability
Low validity   Low validity   High validity
High random error   Low random error   Low random error
Low systematic error   High systematic error   Low systematic error

FIGURE 4.1. Analogy of target to reliability, validity, and measurement error. Adapted from Babbie (1995).

accurate measurements, affecting reliability; however, because they are unsystematic, random errors tend to cancel each other out with repeated measurements. Thus, they do not bias the measure in a particular direction.

In Figure 4.1, a target is used to illustrate the relationship between reliability, validity, and the two sources of measurement error. Measurement is an attempt to hit the bull's eye, which represents the theoretical definition of the concept. A tight pattern, irrespective of its location on the target, reflects a reliable measure, because it is consistent. Validity is a reflection, however, of how closely the shots cluster about the bull's eye. Random error affects the tightness of the pattern as well as distance from the center, hence both reliability and validity; systematic error affects only the distance of shots from the bull's eye, hence only validity.

Reliability Assessment

So far we have said that reliability indicates consistency, or the extent to which a measure does not contain random error. Because we can never know for certain the precise true value of that which we measure, measurement errors can only be examined indirectly. In fact, we infer random error from the degree of consistency observed across measurements. If a measure yields the same result time after time, then it is free of random error; furthermore, the greater the variation in repeated measurements, the greater the random error. Reliability assessment is essentially a matter of checking for such consistency—either over time (as when the same measurements are repeated) or over slightly different but equivalent measures (as when more than one indicator or more than one observer/interviewer/recorder is used).

Test–Retest Reliability

The simplest method for assessing reliability, the **test–retest** procedure, involves testing (i.e., measuring) the same persons or units on two separate occasions.[3] For example, a researcher might administer the self-esteem scale to the same group of students on consecutive days. One then calculates the statistical correlation between the sets of "scores" obtained from the two measurements, and the resulting value serves as an estimate of reliability. Such correlations range from 0 (indicating a completely unreliable measure with total random error) to 1.00 (indicating a perfectly reliable measure subject to no random error). For the test–retest procedure, the correlation tends to be high, with anything less than .80 considered dangerously low for most measurement purposes. Test–retest reliability checks of the self-esteem scale have produced correlation coefficients of .82 to .88 for one- and two-week intervals (Rosenberg, 1979; Gray-Little, Williams, and Hancock, 1997); however, test–retest reliability coefficients for this scale are much lower for longer periods of six months (.63) and one year (.50) (Gray-Little, Williams, and Hancock, 1997).

While simple in principle, the test–retest method has several problems that limit its usefulness as an estimate of reliability. First, either the persons responding to questions or the persons recording observations may remember and simply repeat the responses they gave the first time, thereby inflating the reliability estimate. Second, real change in the concept being measured may occur in the interim between the two "tests." In attitude measurement, new experiences or new information may result in a shift in attitude. For example, positive or negative experiences between administrations may raise or lower a respondent's self-esteem; the loss of a job may change one's attitude toward unemployment insurance or social welfare programs. Because such true changes are inseparable from random errors in test–retest correlations, they falsely lower the reliability estimate. Third, the first application of a measure may itself bring about conceptual changes in the persons under study. Suppose, for example, that a scale designed to measure traditional sex-role attitudes is administered on two occasions to the same group of persons. If, after the first administration, the persons began to think through some of their assumptions about women and as a consequence changed some of their beliefs, a subsequent administration of the scale would yield different scores and a lowered estimate of reliability.

To a certain extent, these problems are manageable. For example, one can try to time the second measurement optimally so that responses to the first testing will have been forgotten but little real change in the concept will have had time to occur. Also, the above difficulties may be more or less problematic depending on the type of measure under study. Using a test–retest reliability estimate for an attitude measure would be fraught with problems, because such measures tend to be highly reactive and genuine changes in attitudes are likely to take place over time. On the other hand, the test–retest procedure provides a good evaluation of the reliability of many relatively stable concepts such as characteristics of organizations or political units and individual background variables.

Split-Half and Internal Consistency Reliability

Rather than obtain a *stability* estimate based on consistency over time, as in test–retest reliability, a second set of procedures for assessing reliability estimates the agreement or *equivalence* among the constituent parts or items of a multi-item measure. If we assume that each component of a measure represents the same underlying concept, a lack of agreement among the components would indicate a high degree of random error, hence low reliability. Like the test–retest estimate, all of the statistical estimates of equivalence yield coefficients that run from 0 to 1.00.

A commonly used equivalence estimate is the **split-half method**. In this procedure, a scale or index (i.e., a measure containing several items) is applied once to a sample of cases, after which the items of the scale are divided into halves, usually by random selection; each half is then treated as a subtest with the results of the two subtests correlated to obtain an estimate of reliability. The higher the correlation, the more equivalent the halves, and the greater the reliability of the measure.

The split-half technique assumes the existence of equivalent subsets of items. From there it is a short step to the assumption that every item in a scale is equivalent to every other item. This gives rise to another technique for assessing reliability, called **internal consistency**. With this approach, the researcher examines the relationships among all the items simultaneously rather than arbitrarily splitting the items. The basic question is, To what extent are the items homogeneous—that is, to what extent do they measure the same concept? Homogeneity or internal consistency may be estimated via a number of statistical procedures that are beyond the scope of this text. One procedure involves computing the average of the correlations among the responses to all possible pairs of items; another involves computing the average of the correlations between responses to each item and the total scale score. Numerous studies have reported internal consistency reliability coefficients for the self-esteem scale, ranging from a low of .72 for a sample of men 60 years or older to a high of .88 for a group of college students (Gray-Little, Williams, and Hancock, 1997).

Intercoder Reliability

A second type of equivalence measure examines the extent to which different interviewers, observers, or coders using the same instrument or measure get equivalent results. Assuming that the different users have been properly trained, a reliable operational definition must yield comparable results from user to user. Estimates of equivalence are calculated by comparing the records of two or more researchers who independently apply the same operational definition. For example, in the aforementioned study of other-directedness (Dornbusch and Hickman, 1959), two coders were directed to judge whether magazine advertisements contained some form of other-directed appeal. A reliability check was made by comparing the number of such appeals independently analyzed by each coder in two issues of the magazine. The level of agreement, or **intercoder reliability,** was very high.

It is the norm in social research to check for intercoder reliability whenever measures are derived from systematic observation or from archival records. With regard to the other types of reliability, the split-half and internal consistency techniques are the most frequently used, even though they are limited to multi-item measures. The test–retest approach is less common, not only because of the problems mentioned above but also because of the impracticality of applying the same measure twice to the same sample of cases.

Improving Reliability

At some point in this discussion of reliability assessment you might have wondered, "What can be done if your measure turns out to have low reliability?" Should you discard it and start over with another measure? In some cases you may decide to do just that. However, there are ways to raise the reliability of an operational definition to an acceptable level.

1. Exploratory studies, preliminary interviews, or pretests of a measure with a small sample of persons similar in characteristics to the target group are ways to gain crucial information about whether the measure is clearly understood and interpreted similarly by respondents. The need for preliminary work with actual respondents before the final form of an instrument is completed cannot be overstated. Indeed, it is a topic we will consider again in relation to experiments and survey research.

2. Simply adding items of the same type to a scale will usually increase reliability. Other things being equal, a composite measure containing more items will normally be more reliable than a composite measure having fewer. There are two reasons for this. First, as we noted earlier, random errors deviate on either side of the "true" value. Thus, with repeated measurements or additional items, such errors will tend to cancel each other out, yielding a more stable and accurate measure of the true value. Second, since any given set of items represents a sample of the possible measures of a concept, adding items increases sample size. As you will see in the next chapter, a basic principle of sampling is that the larger the sample, the more reliable the estimate.

3. An item-by-item analysis will reveal which items discriminate well between units with different values on a particular variable. Those items that do not discriminate appropriately should be omitted. For instance, if both persons scoring high and persons scoring low on a test measuring knowledge of research methods are equally likely to answer a given question incorrectly, the question may be ambiguous or misleading. By keeping only those items or questions that correlate highly with the total score, reliability may be greatly improved.

4. Clues for improving reliability may be found in the instructions to respondents. Are they clear, or is there some room for misinterpretation? One should also examine the conditions under which the instrument is used or administered. Are they consistent? Finally, one might question whether the users of the instrument have been adequately and uniformly trained.

Of course, it is important to bear in mind that although a highly unreliable measure cannot be valid, it is possible to have highly reliable but invalid measures. Therefore, unless validity has been demonstrated, caution should be used in drawing conclusions about the "goodness" of even the most reliable measure.

Validity Assessment

Reliability assessment is relatively simple; the major forms outlined above use straightforward procedures that yield precise estimates of consistency and random error. These procedures are independent of the theories under investigation; that is, they can be applied and interpreted without regard to what is actually being measured. Validity assessment, by contrast, is more problematic. Systematic errors, which affect validity but not reliability, are more difficult to detect than random errors. And the issue of measurement validity generally cannot be divorced from larger theoretical concerns; sooner or later you must ask what the nature of your concept is, what it means, and whether your operational definition faithfully represents this meaning or something else.

Validity cannot be assessed directly. If it could—if we knew a case's true value on a variable independent of a given measure—then there would be no need for the measure. Or, if we had perfectly valid, established measures of concepts, assessing validity would simply be a matter of checking to see if the application of a new operational definition corresponded with the application of an existing one. If we invented a new measure of length, for example, we could easily check its validity by determining whether we get the same results with standard instruments—tape measure, yardstick, transit, and so on—for measuring length. But there are very few established operational definitions of concepts in the social sciences. Therefore, to assess validity, one must either (1) subjectively evaluate whether an operational definition measures what it is intended to or (2) compare the results of the operational definition with the results of other measures with which it should or should not be related. As you will see, the relevant kinds of subjective judgments and objective evidence depend on the purpose of measurement.

Subjective Validation

There are two methods of validity assessment based on subjective evaluation of an operational definition: face validity and content validity. **Face validity** refers simply to a personal judgment that an operational definition appears, on the face of it, to measure the concept it is intended to measure. In some cases this claim alone would seem reasonable to establish a measure's validity. Few would dispute the face validity of common indicators of variables such as age, gender, and education. Many observational measures of behavior have similar palpable validity—for example, "hitting another person" as an indicator of aggression and "offering assistance to a stranger" as an indicator of helping. As a method of validity assessment, however, face validity is generally not acceptable. Most operational definitions have it. After all, why would an instrument be offered as a measure of some concept if it did not appear to be valid? Face validity is based solely on personal judgment rather than objective evidence. Furthermore, it suggests that validity is an all-or-none matter when, in fact, measures have degrees of validity. For example, several operational definitions of age are possible. One could ask respondents directly what their age is, ask for their age at their last birthday, or ask them when they were born. While these all have face validity, they are not equally accurate.[4]

One would not know which operationalization is most accurate without resorting to a validation method other than face validity.

Content validity concerns the extent to which a measure adequately represents all facets of a concept. A more acceptable form of subjective evaluation, this type of validation is used most often in psychology and education where it is applied to measures of skill, knowledge, and achievement. An instructor testing the reader's knowledge of this chapter, for example, ought to be concerned with the test's content validity—that is, with whether it includes questions on all sections of the chapter. Such a test would not have content validity if it omitted questions on reliability and validity and only contained questions on the measurement process and levels of measurement.

Psychologists and educators speak of the performance or content "domain" in relation to content validity. To demonstrate content validity, one must be able to identify clearly the components of the total domain and then show that the test items adequately represent these components. This is not too difficult for most tests of knowledge. With respect to knowledge of the present chapter, one could list all the major topics and subtopics and then develop test items for each of these, making sure that the number of items per topic was proportionate to the breadth of coverage. However, such a process is considerably more complex when measuring the abstract concepts typical of the social sciences. The domain of concepts like social capital, alienation, and social status is not easily specified; therefore, it is difficult to determine how adequately the domain has been tapped by specific indicators.

To some extent, the problems associated with face and content validity are not unique. All forms of validation are subjective in the sense that judgments on the validity of an operational definition ultimately rest with the verdict of the scientific community. However, social scientists generally do not find content validity evidence as persuasive as the kinds of "external" evidence provided by the validation procedures examined in the next two sections. Evidence that is external to the investigator is less subject to unintentional distortion and is easier to verify.

Criterion-Related Validation

Criterion-related validity applies to measuring instruments that have been developed for some practical purpose other than testing hypotheses or advancing scientific knowledge. One may wish to devise measures that will identify children with learning disabilities, determine a person's ability to fly an airplane or drive a car, or predict success in college. Under these circumstances, the investigator is not interested in the content or apparent meaning of the measure but in its usefulness as an indicator of a specific trait or behavior. The trait or behavior is called a *criterion,* and validation is a matter of how well scores on the measure correlate with the criterion of interest. The higher the correlation, the more valid the measure with respect to that criterion. As Jum Nunnally (1970:34) notes, with this form of validation the criterion variable is the only necessary standard of comparison: "If it were found that accuracy in horseshoe pitching correlated with success in college, horseshoe pitching would be a valid measure for predicting success in college."

The selected measure may indicate either an individual's *present* or *future* standing on the criterion variable. For example, a mental health inventory designed to identify those in need of psychiatric care could be given to a sample of "well" persons and a sample of persons currently under psychiatric care. Its validity would be indicated by the degree to which the inventory distinguishes between the present two groups. Or the measure may predict a person's future standing on the criterion variable. A college entrance examination, for example, might be validated by comparing the exam scores of high school students with a criterion measure of their later success in college, such as grade-point averages or whether or not they graduate.

Since criterion-related validity rests on the correspondence between a measure and its criterion, it is only as good as the appropriateness and quality of the criterion measure. Unfortunately, this may present major difficulties. By what standards do you choose the criterion? What if no reasonable criterion exists? What if the criterion exists but practical problems prevent using it? For example, how would you demonstrate the validity of a county civil service test developed to assist in the hiring of probation officers? Logically you could suggest that the county hire high-, average-, and low-scoring persons; then at a later time you could compare some measure of their job performance, such as supervisors' ratings, with their scores on the civil service test. Most likely, however, the county will hire only the top scorers; and regardless of their performance on the job, you would not know how it might have compared with the job performance of those who scored average or low. Thus you could not assess the criterion-related validity of the measure.

Despite such problems, evidence of criterion-related validity is crucially important when a test or measure serves a specific, practical end. Thus, if a test is designed to screen and select candidates for certain jobs or to place students in ability tracks or special programs, then it is important to know how well it works for the given purpose. Except for applied areas of psychology and education, however, social science measures are not developed to help solve practical problems of this sort. Operational definitions are created to reflect the meaning of certain concepts, and there is seldom a clear and adequate criterion variable for evaluating validity.

Construct Validation

When neither a pertinent criterion of prediction nor a well-defined domain of content exists for determining validity, investigators turn to construct validation. (The term "construct" is interchangeable with the term "concept"; a concept developed for scientific purposes is sometimes called a construct.) **Construct validation** emphasizes the meaning of the responses to one's measuring instrument. How are they to be interpreted? Is the instrument measuring the intended concept (or construct), or can it be interpreted as measuring something else? While this sounds like face validity, the orientation is quite different; construct validity is based upon an accumulation of research evidence and not on mere appearances.

According to the logic of construct validation, the meaning of any scientific concept is implied by statements of its theoretical relations to other concepts. Thus, the validation process begins by examining the theory underlying the concept being measured. In light of this theory, one formulates hypotheses about variables that should be related to measures of the concept. At the same time, one considers other variables that should *not* be related to measures of the concept, but might produce systematic error. Then one gathers evidence to test these hypotheses. The more evidence that supports the hypothesized relationships, the greater one's confidence that a particular operational definition is a valid measure of the concept.[5]

An example of construct validation is Morris Rosenberg's validation (1965) of his self-esteem scale. Self-esteem refers to an individual's sense of self-respect or self-worth; those with high self-esteem have self-respect, those with low self-esteem lack it. Rosenberg reasoned that, if his "scale actually did measure self-esteem," then scores on it should "be associated with other data in a theoretically meaningful way" (p. 18). Thus, because clinical observations indicated that depression and neurosis often accompany low self-esteem, people who score low on the scale should report more depressive feelings such as unhappiness and gloom, appear more depressed to outside observers, and reveal more symptoms of neurosis. Also, given the sociological proposition that an individual's self-esteem is determined largely by what others think of him or her, students with high self-esteem scores should be chosen more often as leaders by classmates and described more often as commanding the respect of others. Evidence confirmed these and other theoretical expectations, thereby supporting the construct validity of the self-esteem scale.

Table 4.2 depicts the differences between construct validation and criterion-related validation. The test of criterion-related validity is the ability of the measure to classify, group, or distinguish persons (or other units of analysis) in terms of a single criterion. What the measure means aside from its ability to make such distinctions is of little concern. What is important is the strength of the correlation between the predictive measure and a measure of the criterion; the stronger the correlation, the higher the validity.

In construct validation, on the other hand, one is less interested in the accuracy of a prediction per se than in what a relationship reveals about the meaning of the concepts being measured. One does not necessarily expect the correlation between measures of two theoretically related concepts to be extremely high because the two

TABLE 4.2. **Comparison of Criterion-related and Construct Validity**

	Criterion-related validity	*Construct validity*
Validity a matter of:	ability to classify units with precision	ability to capture the meaning of the concept
The measure is used for:	practical application	theoretical application
Assessment a matter of comparison with:	a single, agreed-upon independent criterion	no clear, single criterion
Degree of validity a matter of:	predictive accuracy	a consistent pattern of relationships

concepts do not mean exactly the same thing. That is why it is important to examine the relation of the measure in question to several other variables rather than base the assessment of validity on a single prediction. All the tested relations contribute to the evaluation of construct validity; it is their cumulative effect that supports or disputes the validity of the measure.

Evidence of construct validity consists of any empirical data that support the claim that a given operational definition measures a certain concept. Because such evidence may be derived from a wide variety of sources, construct validation is not associated with a particular approach or type of evidence. We will now consider four of the more common types of evidence used to establish construct validity. Remember, though, that no single study or piece of evidence is sufficient; the construct validity of a concept is only as compelling as the amount and diversity of evidence supporting it.

1. *Correlations with related variables.* If a measure is valid, it should correlate with measures of other theoretically related variables. Rosenberg (1965) validated his self-esteem scale in this way by showing that scores on it were correlated with symptoms of depression and neurosis and with peer ratings.

2. *Consistency across indicators and different methods of measurement.* Different measures of the same concept should be correlated, and because each methodological approach (e.g., self-reports, observation, archival records) is subject to different sources of systematic error, measures of concepts should not be tied to a particular method. Thus, one of the most convincing evidences of construct validity is the correspondence of results when a concept is measured in different ways. This is called **convergent validity** because the results converge on the same meaning, namely that conveyed by the underlying concept.

Charles Glock and Rodney Stark (1966) provided such evidence for their Index of Anti-Semitic Beliefs. Scores on the index were determined by level of agreement with six statements about Jews (e.g., "Jews believe they are better than other people," "Jews are more likely than Christians to cheat in business"); hence, respondents were forced to agree or disagree with characteristics imputed by the investigators. To measure anti-Semitism in a different way, Glock and Stark had respondents furnish their own images of Jews by requiring them to complete the following sentences: "It's a shame that Jews . . ." and "I can't understand why Jews. . . ." When their answers were divided into those indicating negative, neutral, or positive images of Jews, it was found that 73 percent of those scoring high on the Beliefs index as opposed to 27 percent of the low scorers projected a negative image.

3. *Correlations with unrelated variables.* A valid operational definition should separate the concept being measured from other concepts from which it is intended to differ. In other words, there are some variables (representing systematic errors) with which a measure should not be highly correlated. This is called **discriminant validity**.

A good example is Zick Rubin's validation (1970) of his thirteen-item Love Scale. A valid measure of love should differentiate love from liking, as these two concepts are empirically related but conceptually distinct. Rubin therefore developed a parallel scale of liking. When both the love and liking scales were administered, he found that their scores were only moderately correlated. Also, whereas respondents liked their dating partners only slightly more than they liked their friends, they loved their dating partners much more than their friends. Additional evidence showed that the Love Scale tapped an attitude toward a specific other person rather than a general response tendency. For example, Love Scale scores were uncorrelated with scores on the Marlowe–Crowne Social Desirability Scale, designed to measure the tendency to give socially desirable responses.

4. *Differences among known groups.* When certain groups are expected to differ on the measure of a concept, one source of validating evidence would be a comparison of the groups' responses. Milton Rokeach (1960) used this approach to test the validity of his Dogmatism Scale. This scale consisted of items intended to tap the degree to which a person is closed-minded in his or her thinking and beliefs, irrespective of the content of the beliefs. Rokeach administered the scale to several groups, such as (a) friends and acquaintances whom graduate students identified as open- or closed-minded and (b) Catholics, Protestants, and nonbelievers among American college students. Consistent with expectations, Catholics and persons perceived by peers as closed-minded had higher scores than their comparison groups. (See Box 4.2 for an example of construct validation that uses a variety of evidence.)

BOX 4.2

Validation of the Attitudes toward Feminism Scale

At the height of the Women's Liberation Movement in the mid-1970s, Eliot Smith, Myra Marx Ferree, and Frederick Miller (1975) developed a twenty-item scale to measure attitudes toward feminism. Each scale item consists of a profeminist or antifeminist statement; for example, "Women have the right to compete with men in every sphere of activity," and "A woman who refuses to bear children has failed in her duty to her husband." Respondents indicate their level of agreement with each statement, numbers are assigned to the answer categories, and then scale scores are calculated by adding up responses to the twenty items. The numerical range of the answer categories is 1 to 5, with the highest number representing a profeminist response; so the scale has a possible range of 20 (extreme antifeminism) to 100 (extreme profeminism). (See Box 12.1 for a description of how the authors created this scale.)

There is unusually good evidence validating this measure, called the FEM Scale (an acronym based on the authors' first names). The creators of the FEM Scale tested its reliability as well as its construct validity with data from one hundred Harvard summer school students. Royce Singleton and John Christiansen (1977) also assessed the scale's validity with data from a larger, more heterogeneous sample of respondents. On the next page is a summary of the evidence regarding the scale's reliability and validity.

Reliability

Both of these studies obtained a reliability estimate, based on internal consistency, of
.91, which is quite acceptable for attitude measurement.

Intercorrelations and Convergent Validity

Smith, Ferree, and Miller tested the validity of the FEM Scale by correlating it with three
other variables: measures of identification with the Women's Movement, activism in the
movement, and the Rubin–Peplau Just World Scale. High scores on the latter scale reflect a belief that the world is a just place and that people generally get what they deserve. Smith, Ferree, and Miller reasoned that feminists are unlikely to view the world
in general as a just place, since they tend to perceive that women have been treated un-
justly. Consistent with expectations, the results showed that FEM Scale scores were positively correlated with the identification and activism measures (evidence of convergent
validity) and negatively correlated with scores on the Just World Scale.

     Singleton and Christiansen correlated scores on the FEM Scale with measures of
dogmatism, antiblack prejudice, and identification with the Women's Movement.
They reasoned that dogmatism, a tendency to adopt traditional views, would include
an antifeminist orientation. Also, prejudice toward blacks would reflect a general tendency toward prejudice with which antifeminist attitudes would be consistent. The
correlations of individuals' scores on the FEM Scale with their scores on these other
measures were in fact uniformly high.

Discriminant Validity

In addition to the above measures, Smith, Ferree, and Miller administered the Rotter
I–E Scale to their respondents. "I–E" stands for internal–external locus of control.
High "internals" are persons who believe that they have a great deal of personal control over their lives; high "externals" are persons who tend to believe that their lives
are controlled by forces outside themselves. Because there was reason to expect that
feminism would be mildly correlated with both of these tendencies, Smith, Ferree, and
Miller expected no correlation with the FEM Scale when internality and externality
were treated as a single scale. Once again, the results supported their prediction.

Known-Groups Validity

Singleton and Christiansen also administered the FEM Scale to members of two
groups with opposing views on women's issues: the National Organization for Women
(NOW) and Fascinating Womanhood. NOW was the largest and most prominent organization in the Women's Movement; Fascinating Womanhood was an antifeminist
organization of the early to mid-1970s that strongly advocated a traditional, dependent
role for women. FEM Scale scores of the members of these two organizations were
widely divergent as expected. Recall that the scale has a range of 20 to 100. NOW
members had an average score of 91, whereas members of Fascinating Womanhood
had an average score of 51.

While construct validation is now considered the model validation procedure for most social measurement, it is not without its problems. Obviously it is cumbersome and requires abundant evidence; more important, however, it can lead to inconsistent and equivocal outcomes. If a prediction is not supported, this may mean that the measure lacks construct validity. On the other hand, such negative evidence may mean that the underlying theory is in error or that measures of other variables in the analysis lack validity. Only if one's theoretical predictions are sound and the measures of other variables are well validated can one confidently conclude that negative evidence is due to lack of construct validity (Zeller and Carmines, 1980).

A Final Note on Reliability and Validity

The procedures for assessing validity and reliability may seem so complex and cumbersome that one may wonder if investigators ever pass beyond this stage of research.[6] Fortunately, many investigators avoid the issue by borrowing, from previous studies, measures that have established records of validity and reliability. Also, few researchers apply more than one of the simpler procedures discussed above to ascertain the reliability or validity of their new measures. What usually happens is that once a new measure of some sort is introduced (perhaps with minimal evidence of reliability or validity), the measure is widely used for awhile until invalidating features are found (such as the middle-class bias of IQ tests) and the instrument is revised or replaced. Thus, validity and reliability assessment is not confined to intrastudy or intra-investigator efforts, but is an ongoing process that extends across studies and investigators and over a considerable length of time.

It is also true that the most elaborate procedures were developed in response to the difficulties of operationalizing some concepts, such as attitudes, that are relatively unstable and pose reactivity and other measurement problems. More stable and less reactive measures are not as problematic.

In speaking about the issues validity raises, James Davis (1971:14–15) aptly observes that "[a]t the extreme [validation] constitutes a philosophical thicket which makes a dandy hiding place from which antiempirical social scientists can ambush the simple-minded folk who want to find out what the world is like rather than speculate about it." Although it is true that such difficulties can immobilize die-hard perfectionists, for most social scientists the validation problem presents challenging opportunities to exercise their creativity. No measure is perfect, but an imperfect measure is better than none at all. Or, as Davis further notes, "Weak measures are to be preferred to brilliant speculations as a source of empirical information" (p. 15).

Summary

Measurement is the process of assigning numerals or labels to units of analysis in order to represent conceptual properties. This process involves conceptualization (the development and clarification of concepts) followed by operationalization (the description of the research procedures necessary to assign units to variable categories to represent concepts). Because single indicators do not correspond perfectly to concepts, researchers often use multiple indicators, which may be combined to create an index or scale. Operational definitions may be formed either by experimentally manipulating a variable or through nonmanipulative procedures such as verbal reports, observations of behavior, and archival records. One selects operational definitions in the context of an overall research strategy with an eye toward obtaining the best possible fit with the concept being measured.

Operational definitions are described in terms of their level of measurement and are evaluated with respect to their reliability and validity. Measurement level alerts us to the various ways that we can interpret the numerals assigned to different variable categories. In nominal measurement, the numbers are simply labels that signify differences of kind. Variables measured at this level form a classification system that should be exhaustive and mutually exclusive. In ordinal measurement, different numbers indicate the rank order of cases on some variable. In interval measurement the numbers form a metric, so that different numbers imply not only rank order but also countable distances. Ratio measurement contains these features plus an absolute zero point, making it possible to form ratios of the numbers assigned to categories.

Reliability refers to the stability or consistency of an operational definition, whereas validity refers to the goodness of fit between an operational definition and the concept it is purported to measure. A valid measure is necessarily reliable, but a reliable measure may or may not be valid. One can see this in relation to the three sources of variation in all measures: true differences and systematic and random measurement errors. A completely valid measure reflects only true differences, which means that it is free of both systematic and random error. A completely reliable measure is free from random error but may reflect true differences and/or systematic error.

We assess reliability by calculating the correlation between (1) repeated applications of the measure (test–retest reliability) and (2) responses to subsets of items from the same measure (split-half reliability); by (3) examining the consistency of responses across all items (internal consistency); or by (4) observing the correspondence among different interviewers, observers, or coders applying the same measure (intercoder reliability). Of these approaches, the first is used least often. One can increase reliability by adding items to a scale, by omitting items that do not discriminate well, and by clarifying questions and instructions contained in one's operational definition.

We assess validity by subjectively evaluating an operational definition, by checking the correspondence between the operational definition and a specific criterion, or by determining whether the operational definition as a measure of a given construct correlates in expected ways with measures of several other constructs. Subjective validation involves judgments of either whether an operational definition appears to be valid (face validity) or whether it adequately represents the domain of a concept (content validity). Content validity is important in educational testing, but otherwise subjective judgment per se is unacceptable as a source of validation. Criterion-related validation applies to measures (or "tests") that are intended to indicate a person's present or future standing on a specific behavioral criterion. It is especially important to assess when a measure is a practical, decision-making tool. Construct validation is based on an accumulation of research evidence. This evidence may include differences among groups known to differ on the characteristic being measured, and correlations with related variables, with different measures of the same concept (convergent validity), and with measures from which the concept should be differentiated (discriminant validity).

Key Terms

conceptualization

operationalization

indicator

verbal (self-) report

index/scale

level of measurement

    nominal

    ordinal

    interval

    ratio

exhaustive

mutually exclusive

reliability

validity

random measurement error

systematic measurement error

reactive measurement effect

social desirability effect

test–retest reliability

split-half reliability

internal consistency reliability

intercoder reliability

subjective validation

    face validity

    content validity

criterion-related validation

construct validation

    convergent validity

    discriminant validity

Review Questions and Problems

1. What are the two steps in the measurement process?
2. Why do researchers use multiple indicators to measure a concept?
3. What is an operational definition?
4. Explain the difference between manipulated and nonmanipulated operational definitions, and give an example of each.
5. Differentiate between an indicator and a scale (or index).
6. Give an operational definition of any two of the following concepts: leadership; campus involvement; quality of life; social class; interpersonal attraction.
7. Indicate whether the source of each of your operational definitions in question 6 is a verbal report, an observation, or an archival record.
8. What do the numbers assigned to variable categories signify with nominal measurement? With ordinal measurement?
9. Indicate the level of measurement of each of the following variables.
   a. *Seriousness of criminal offense*: measured by having judges rank offenses from the most to the least severe
   b. *Political activism*: measured by the total number of politically related activities in which an individual participates

   c. *Ethnic group membership*: measured by having respondents check one
     of these categories: black, Hispanic, Oriental, Caucasian, other

   d. *Educational attainment*: measured by asking respondents to check one
     of the following categories: eighth grade or less; 9 to 11 years; high
     school graduate; some college; college graduate

   e. An item measuring an attitude or opinion that uses the following response
     format: strongly agree, agree, undecided, disagree, strongly disagree

10. Although only one level of measurement typically is associated with a given variable, it is frequently possible to measure a variable at more than one level. For example, while the variable "age" generally is measured at the ratio level, one could also measure age at the ordinal level by placing respondents in one of the following age categories: under 20 years, 20–39, 40–59, 60 and over. How might you measure the variable "income" (i.e., what categories would you establish) if you treated it as (a) a nominal variable, (b) an ordinal variable, and (c) a ratio variable?

11. Compile a list of categories for the variable "religious affiliation." Make sure that the list is *exhaustive* and *mutually exclusive*, but also keep the list fairly short (say, no more than six categories).

12. For each of the following variables, indicate whether the list of categories is exhaustive and mutually exclusive. Then indicate, where necessary, the changes or additions to the categories that would have to be made to meet these two requirements.

   a. Income: $3000–7999; $8000–11,999; $12,000–14,999; $15,000–24,999;
     $25,000 and over

   b. Employment status: working full-time; working part-time; student;
     housewife; unemployed

   c. Age: under 18 years; 18–30 years; 30 years and over

13. Carefully state the relationship between the reliability and validity of measures. Is it possible to have a reliable but invalid measure? To have an unreliable but valid measure?

14. What are the three primary sources of variation in operational definitions?

15. Suppose that members of a class in research methods were given an examination on this chapter. Assuming that the examination is designed to measure students' knowledge of the material in the chapter, describe three possible sources of measurement error (either systematic error or random error) in the set of examination scores. For each source of error, explain whether it is likely to affect measurement validity, reliability, or both.

16. Which type of measurement error—random and/or systematic—affects reliability? Which type of error affects validity?

17. What are some of the problems involved in using a test–retest procedure (or stability estimate) to estimate the reliability of a measure?

18. What is the difference between stability and equivalence estimates of reliability? Which of these estimates is preferable if a change in the variable is likely to occur over time? Explain.

19. How is the logic behind split-half and internal consistency reliability similar?

20. What is intercoder reliability?
21. Identify three ways of increasing reliability.
22. Why is face validity generally an unsatisfactory method of validation?
23. When is content validity most appropriate as a method of validation?
24. In what sense are all forms of validation "subjective"?
25. Under what conditions is it important to use criterion-related validation? What are its drawbacks?
26. Explain the difference between criterion-related validity and construct validity.
27. Identify four types of evidence used to establish construct validity.
28. Indicate the type of reliability (test–retest, split-half, internal consistency, intercoder) or validity (face, content, criterion-related, convergent construct, discriminant construct) to which each of the following assertions refers.

   a. The correlation between scores on the odd and even items of the multiple-choice exam was very high.
   b. The study indicated a moderately strong association between total score on the Graduate Record Examination and performance in graduate school, as measured by grade-point average.
   c. Zick Rubin (1970) found that scores on his Love Scale were correlated with marriage probability and the feeling of being "in love."
   d. The set of final examination questions was judged to be thoroughly representative of the material covered in the course.
   e. The scale is an improvement over previous measures of authoritarianism, in which right-wingers tended to score higher than left-wingers, because both left- and right-wing authoritarians tend to score high.
   f. The scale was administered twice to the same group. Scores obtained the second time were nearly identical to scores obtained the first time (coefficient of correlation = .98).
   g. Michael Armer and Allan Schnaiberg (1972) found that four measures of modernity (a set of attitudes and behavior that facilitates life in modern society) were no more highly correlated with one another than they were with measures of anomia and alienation.

29. Look through recent issues (1990–present: vol. 69 and up) of *Social Forces* and find an article reporting an empirical study.

   a. Give a full bibliographical citation for the article (i.e., author, "article title," *journal name*, year, volume number, pages).
   b. State the problem or hypothesis being tested (if more than one problem or hypothesis, state only one).
   c. Briefly describe how each concept or variable in the problem or hypothesis is measured.
   d. What is the level of measurement of each variable?
   e. Evaluate each measure from the standpoint of reliability. Does the author(s) cite or provide evidence of reliability?
   f. Evaluate each measure from the standpoint of face validity. Does the author(s) cite or provide evidence of construct validity?

NOTES

1. At times we will use the word "number" where technically the term "numeral" is more accurate. The difference, simply put, is that numbers are abstract concepts (such as the number 2), whereas numerals are the squiggly lines used to represent the concepts. In the nominal level of measurement, numerals do *not* represent the number concept but rather are arbitrarily assigned to categories for coding purposes.

2. Choosing an appropriate statistical technique, however, is not always easy, as an actual measure may fall between two levels of measurement. One might think of educational attainment (years of schooling), for example, as providing more information than an ordinal scale but not attaining the interval-scale level.

3. As the terminology suggests, most of the procedures for determining reliability were developed in connection with psychological testing.

4. Studies have shown that if a single question is used, it is best to ask respondents in what year they were born. However, the way to get the most accurate measure is to ask both date of birth and age at last birthday, check one against the other, and then inquire about any discrepancies (Sudman and Bradburn, 1982).

5. As you can see, this process is quite similar to general hypothesis testing. In fact, construct validation "is not simply a matter of validating a [measure]. One must try to validate the theory behind the [measure]" (Kerlinger, 1973:461).

6. The foregoing discussion of reliability and validity does not exhaust the use of these concepts in the social sciences; for in addition to judging the adequacy of operational definitions, the terms are also applied in the evaluation of other aspects of a research study. For example, the term "validity" is used in reference to the adequacy of a research design (chapters 6 and 7). The concept of reliability is used frequently in judging the quality of a sample (chapter 5).

5

✓

Sampling

Sampling, whether we are aware of it or not, is part of everyday life. For instance, after eating at one of a chain of restaurants, a person may decide that all the restaurants in the chain serve poor food and provide poor service. A student's decision to take a given course may be based upon the opinions of friends who have already taken it. Having met a few people from New York, someone may conclude that New Yorkers are pushy and aggressive. In each of these examples, inferences about a whole class of objects are made from observations of a subset of such objects. The examples implicitly contain the basic idea behind sampling:

1. We seek knowledge or information about a whole class of similar objects or events (usually called a **population**).
2. We observe some of these (called a **sample**).
3. We extend our findings to the entire class (Stephan and McCarthy, 1958:22).

While simple in principle, sampling can be fraught with difficulties in practice. Consider some possibilities. The restaurant patron may have picked a day when the head cook had quit and been replaced by the busboy, or she may have patronized the worst franchise in the chain. The student talked to friends, who are likely to have highly similar opinions that may differ markedly from the opinions of other students who have taken the course. Finally, characterizations of groups of people, like the one of New Yorkers, seldom apply to even a majority of the group. Generalizations such as the above, drawn from casual observation, are likely to err because they are based on inadequate samples of information. In this chapter we discuss some rigorous yet surprisingly simple techniques that are designed to reduce the hazards of generalizing from incomplete information.

Chapter 4 dealt with the measurement of variables. Before actual measurements are taken, researchers must select an appropriate set of units (or cases). Selecting a set of cases raises several crucial questions. The first of these was addressed in chapter 3: What is the unit of analysis—individual people, married couples, newspaper editorials, cities? The answer to this question, recall, hinges largely on the research topic, which determines what the researcher seeks to describe and compare. Thus, research on the relationship between a nation's literacy rate and its economic development would use nations as units; a study of the influence of years of schooling on prejudice would concern individuals. The decision about *what type of unit* to examine will not be considered further in the present chapter; we will assume that the appropriate type of unit has been determined. The interests here will be with *how many* such units of *what particular description* should be *chosen by what method.* But before examining each of these issues, let us take a brief look at some of the reasons that sampling in social research, as in everyday life, is a practical necessity for informed decisions.

Why Sample?

Scientists seek to establish the broadest possible generalizations, applicable to infinitely large classes of events. Yet, it is obviously impossible to observe all relevant events. In the physical sciences, the nature of the elements studied simplifies this problem. Particular physical and chemical elements are assumed to be identical or nearly identical with respect to pertinent properties. Thus, any sample of one or more cases suffices; one test tube of hydrogen, or distilled water, or nitroglycerine will be like any other. As we move from the physical to the biological and social sciences, however, this assumption of homogeneity becomes increasingly risky. Because people and other social objects vary widely on nearly every imaginable property, studying any one case simply will not suffice as a basis for generalizing. The heterogeneity of cases requires careful procedures designed to ensure that the range of variation in the population will be represented adequately in one's sample of observations.

Beyond the need to represent population variability adequately, practical considerations usually necessitate sampling. Researchers often want to know something about a specific social group or population that, for reasons of size, time, cost, or inaccessibility, cannot be studied in its entirety. Indeed, unless the researcher is willing to restrict his or her inferences to a very small set of narrowly defined cases or unless one has unlimited time and funds, there is no getting around sampling.

To interview the entire 20,000-student population at a university, a population that is relatively small by survey research standards, would require a long period of time or a large number of interviewers. However, time is often of the essence. A lengthy period of data collection would render some data, such as attitudes about current issues or voter preferences, obsolete by the time the information was completely in hand. Moreover, the responses of persons interviewed late in the investigation could not be considered comparable to those of persons interviewed early. Responses could be affected by current events, or rumors and scuttlebutt about the ongoing survey may influence the responses of persons interviewed late. A large staff of interviewers also would present problems. Not only would this add to the total costs of the study, but it would be more difficult to train and supervise interviewers adequately. To employ a large number of interviewers, one may also be forced to hire some who are not well qualified, thereby reducing the accuracy of the data.

This last point brings us to a third reason for sampling. Paradoxically, the attempt to observe all cases may actually describe a population less accurately than a carefully selected sample of observations, especially in survey studies of large populations. The reason is that the planning and logistics of observation are more manageable with a sample. Greater attention can be given to the design of interviews or questionnaires, to procedures for locating difficult-to-find respondents, and, once again, to the hiring, training, and supervision of a competent staff of interviewers, all of which will increase the quality of the data collected.

A case in point is the decennial Census, a complete enumeration of the U.S. population made every ten years. The Census is an enormous undertaking; the 2000 Census, which counted more than 280 million people, cost about $6.5 billion to collect, tabulate, and publish, and the Bureau of the Census hired more than 500,000 interviewers just to track down those who did not return their census forms in the mail (Government Accounting Office, 2001a, 2001b). Yet, despite its efforts the Census Bureau has estimated a net undercount of over 3 million people; an estimated 7.6 million people may have been missed and 4.3 million more may have been counted twice (Schmitt, 2001). As James Gleick (1990) said about the 1990 Census, there were simply "too many doors to knock on, and too many people living without doors, . . . [and too high] a rate of noncooperation." These obstacles are much easier to overcome in a sample. That is why data from some sample surveys, such as the 50,000-household Current Population Survey, are considered more accurate for many purposes than the Census. A post-enumeration sample survey is used to estimate the accuracy of the Census and to make statistical adjustments to the count. And to increase accuracy and reduce costs, many statisticians recommend that the Census be replaced with a survey of a large sample.[1]

We hasten to add that only in the case of extremely large populations would we expect a sample to yield more accurate information about a population than a survey of the whole population. But the justification for sampling need not rest on a claim of greater accuracy. More to the point, carefully selected samples are an efficient way of producing accurate information. You can see this for yourself on the next election day. Note the accuracy with which the major news networks predict certain election outcomes, long before all the votes have been tabulated. This accuracy is made possible by the careful sampling procedures of expert pollsters. (The polls have not always been so accurate, however, as revealed in Box 5.1.)

Population Definition

After determining the unit of analysis, the first task in sampling is to define the population of interest—to describe the particular collection of units that make up the population. Sociologist Kenneth Bailey (1982:86) notes that the experienced researcher always gets a clear picture of the population before selecting the sample, thus starting from the top (population) and working down (to the sample). "In contrast, novice researchers often work from the bottom up." Rather than making explicit the population they wish to study, they select a predetermined number of conveniently available cases and assume that the sample corresponds to the population of interest. Consider a sample consisting of "randomly" chosen passersby at a shopping center on a Saturday afternoon. What could this sample possibly represent? There is simply no way of knowing. It almost certainly would not be representative of people in the surrounding community. For one thing, weekend shoppers would probably overrepresent people who work during the week and underrepresent the retired and unemployed. And if the shopping area happens to be a luxurious shopping mall, the sample is likely to be heavily weighted in favor of the financially well-off. At best, this sample would represent Saturday afternoon shoppers at the

BOX 5.1

Sources of Errors in Survey Sampling:
Two Notorious Failures in Political Forecasting

In recent years, political pollsters have been able to predict election outcomes with amazing accuracy. With the use of sophisticated probability methods to select the sample, a Reuter/Zogby poll of registered voters conducted just before the 1996 presidential election estimated that Bill Clinton would receive 49 percent of the votes and Bob Dole would receive 41 percent. That is precisely what each candidate received. Although it is unusual to see this level of accuracy, most pre-election polls fall within a few percentage points of the actual vote. Political polls, however, have not always been so accurate, as two infamous examples from the annals of sample surveys reveal.

Perhaps the biggest polling debacle occurred in the presidential election of 1936, when *Literary Digest* magazine predicted that Alfred Landon would be a landslide winner, by 57 to 43 percent, over Franklin Roosevelt. At this time, the *Literary Digest* was well known for its polls on public issues and enjoyed considerable prestige, having predicted the winner in every presidential election since 1920. Its 1932 poll erred by less than two percentage points. However, in 1936 it missed calling the election by a wide margin. What went wrong? With over 2 million individuals polled, the *Digest's* sample was certainly large enough. Indeed, it was enormous by current standards. In 1996, a sample of only 2000 to 3000 people was required to predict accurately the voting behavior of over 100 million voters.

There were two major reasons for the failure of the *Literary Digest* poll. The first was the manner in which the sample was selected, which produced *coverage error* (see p. 145). The *Digest* conducted its polls by mailing ballots to millions of people. The names and addresses of these people came from a variety of sources, including phone books, automobile registration lists, and the *Digest's* own subscription list. Because such sources tended to exclude the poor, who could not afford telephones or automobiles, the sample did not provide a representative cross section of American voters. With rich and poor voting similarly before 1936, this bias against the poor apparently had little effect on the predictions. But in 1936, the rich tended to vote for Landon, the poor voted overwhelmingly for Roosevelt, and the bias inherent in the *Digest's* initial sample contributed to the error.

A second problem with the *Digest* poll has to do with what is called *nonresponse bias* (see p. 145). With any survey, there will be a certain percentage of the selected sample who do not respond or who cannot be contacted. Studies have shown that these nonrespondents tend to differ in important ways from respondents. For example, both lower-class and upper-class people are less likely to respond to questionnaires or personal interviews than middle-class people. Respondents are also likely to have a stronger interest in the survey topic than nonrespondents. Although the *Digest* mailed 10 million sample ballots to prospective voters, it based its predictions on 2.4 million responses. Peverill Squire (1988) has shown that this low response rate combined with a nonresponse bias produced a substantial error in the 1936 poll. Feeling more strongly about the election than did the pro-Roosevelt majority, the anti-Roosevelt minority was more likely to respond to the *Digest* poll.

Another notorious polling failure occurred in 1948, known as "the year the polls elected Thomas E. Dewey President." All three major polls—Gallup, Crossley, and Roper—that covered the 1948 campaign projected that Dewey would be the winner with 50 percent or more of the popular vote, but he ended up with just over 45 percent. Several factors combined to produce this failure. For one thing, those who were undecided about their election choice when the polls were taken went predominantly for Truman. Critics of the 1948 polls, however, agree that the way the samples were selected also contributed to the prediction error.

By this time the pollsters were using a procedure called quota sampling (see text discussion). With quota sampling the population is divided into subgroups (e.g., men and women, blacks and whites), and interviewers are assigned a fixed quota of persons to interview in each of the subgroups. For example, an interviewer might be required to interview three men under 40 years of age and four over 40, as well as four women under 40 and four over 40. Quotas are determined so as to guarantee that the sample will be representative of the voting population with respect to important characteristics thought to affect voting behavior. One shortcoming of this method is that the quotas are theoretical; they are an indirect means of creating a representative sample of the voting population *before the election*. However, demographic characteristics of the voting population cannot be known with certainty until after the election is held. Another problem is that the interviewers, who are free to choose anybody they like within the assigned quota, may be subject to selection bias. In fact, Gallup and Crossley poll results from 1936 to 1948, based on quota sampling, revealed that interviewers consistently preferred Republicans (Katz, 1949). With Democratic candidate Roosevelt possessing a large lead in 1936, 1940, and 1944, Gallup and Crossley were able to predict the winner in spite of the Republican bias of their polls. But this was too much to overcome in an election as close as that of 1948.

shopping center in question on the day the data were collected, which is a strange definition of the population and surely not the one in which the researcher would be interested.

Defining the population is a two-step process. First, one must clearly identify the **target population**, that is, the population to which the researcher would like to generalize his or her results. To define the target population, the researcher must specify the criteria for determining which cases are included in the population and which cases are excluded. The relevant criteria depend on the type of unit and the research topic. With individual people, some combination of locale, age, and selected demographic variables such as gender, race, marital status, and education is ordinarily used (Sudman, 1976:12). For example, in his study of the Boston antibusing movement, Bert Useem (1980) defined the target population as "white Boston residents between the ages of 25 and 53 who were United States citizens."

For the National Education Longitudinal Study (NELS), which Beckett Broh (2002) used to analyze the relationship between extracurricular activities and academic achievement, the target population for the base year, 1988, consisted of students enrolled in "all public and private schools containing eighth grades in the fifty states and District of Columbia" (Spencer et al., 1990:6). This definition was clarified further by taking into account several pragmatic considerations, as the researchers note:

> Excluded . . . are Bureau of Indian Affairs (BIA) schools, special education schools for the handicapped, area vocational schools that do not enroll students directly, and schools for dependents of U.S. personnel overseas. The student population excludes students with severe mental handicaps, students whose command of the English language was not sufficient for understanding the survey materials (especially the cognitive tests), and students with physical or emotional problems that would make it unduly difficult for them to participate in the survey. (p. 6)

If the unit is groups or organizations, then organizational type and size as measured by number of members or employees are often specified. For instance, one study of organizations limited the population to social service agencies with staffs of ten or more in a large midwestern city (Lincoln and Zeitz, 1980). Studies of families also invoke unique definitional criteria: for example, presence or absence of children, number of generations, and intact or single parent. Which set of criteria is used depends on the researcher's purposes.

Two defining characteristics that always implicitly or explicitly define the target population are its geographic and time referents. Notice that each of the above examples of target populations has a clear geographic boundary (city of Boston; United States; midwestern city); and although it was not made explicit in Useem's study, each has a distinctive time frame (mid-1970s; 1987–88 academic year).

The researcher next must find a way of making the target population operational. This involves the second phase of population definition: constructing the sampling frame. The **sampling frame** denotes the set of all cases from which the sample is actually selected. Since the term can be misleading, please note that the sampling frame is *not a sample*; rather, it is the *operational definition of the population* that provides the basis for sampling.

There are two ways of constructing a sampling frame, which correspond to the two ways to define a set (or subset) in logic: (1) listing all cases and (2) providing a rule defining membership. For example, in a city telephone survey, the sampling frame could consist of the city phone book (a listing) or the set of all telephone numbers with certain telephone exchanges (a rule). In survey research, establishing a sampling frame often amounts to obtaining an adequate listing—either of the population as a whole or of subgroups of the population. But listing is not always possible or preferable. As long as cases can be identified, a rule procedure can usually be devised for finding and selecting cases. Suppose that you wanted to observe the behavior of inmates in a mental institution. Listing all acts before they occur is obviously impossible. However, if we consider that all acts within the institution occur at specified places, days, and times, then this would provide the basis for a three-dimensional rule (site, time, and day) for identifying and selecting cases. Similarly, if you wanted to interview people attending a rock concert, the fact that everyone must arrive at the concert at a particular time allows you to establish a rule based on time of arrival.

It is the researcher's hope that the sampling frame and the target population will be identical. Unfortunately, this usually occurs only for very small, geographically concentrated populations. Because it is often impossible or impractical to create an accurate list of the target population, one must rely on existing lists; and such lists are inevitably incomplete. For Useem's antibusing study, the sampling frame consisted of the 1977 City of Boston "Annual Listing of Residents," which provided names, addresses, birth dates, and citizenship information. However, not only was it likely that many names were inadvertently omitted from this list, but through deaths and migration in and out of Boston, the target population was bound to have changed somewhat by the time the interviews were actually conducted. Thus, the sampling frame could not have matched precisely Useem's population of interest.

Strictly speaking, inferences should be made only about the population represented by the sampling frame. Yet, it is the target population to which we wish to generalize. Therefore, one should always evaluate the extent to which cases in the target population have been omitted from the sampling frame. How many omissions are there? How are they likely to differ from cases included in the sampling frame? Because they frequently differ in a systematic way from those included in the frame, excluded cases can seriously bias findings. Telephone directories, for example, exclude the poor who cannot afford telephones and the more wealthy who tend to have unlisted numbers. Whenever such biases are known to exist, the researcher should decide whether to use the list or to find an alternative sampling frame. Regardless of the frame that is used, however, the nature of possible excluded cases should be acknowledged and carefully taken into account when making inferences about the target population.

Obviously, the problem of omitted cases is solved best by finding a good list to begin with. At the local level, many organizations (e.g., unions, schools, churches, professional associations) have membership directories, which constitute excellent sampling frames when appropriate. For most medium-size cities in the range of about 50,000 to 800,000, population and household directories are available (Sudman, 1976:58). Street address directories of households can provide particularly good sampling frames when the unit of analysis is the individual, such as head of household, or the family. At the national level few lists exist. An explicit list of all eighth-grade students in the United States, for example, is simply not available. To sample national populations, researchers generally break the target population down into natural groupings for which lists are available or can be constructed at low cost. For the National Education Longitudinal Study, the researchers obtained a list of public and private schools in the United States, a sampling frame that comprised an implicit list of all eighth-grade students. We discuss this sampling strategy further below.

Equally problematic is finding or constructing sampling frames for studies of rare or special target populations, such as Vietnam War veterans, people with a particular illness or disability, or people with incomes above or below a given amount. If a list of the general population is available, it may be possible to screen the rare population from the larger sampling frame. In a study of the elderly, for example, if the sampling frame for the general population contained information on age, the frame could be culled to include only people over 65 years of age. Alternatively, members of the special target population, such as people over age 65, could be identified at the data collection stage.

Finally, some populations defy identification and listing. Imagine trying to identify for sampling purposes members of a terrorist group or other radical political groups, such as Aryan Nations, or deviant populations such as drug abusers, criminals, or delinquents. For obvious reasons, political radicals and deviants tend to resist identification by anyone outside their own group. In studying such populations, therefore, the process of population definition breaks down because an adequate sampling frame is unobtainable.

Sampling Designs

Ideally in sampling we would like to obtain a sample that will be representative of the target population. To be "representative" means to provide a close approximation of certain characteristics of the target group. If the population consists of the students at Alpha College, then a perfectly representative sample would be like Alpha College students in all respects. The sample would contain the same proportion of first-, second-, third-, and fourth-year students, the same proportion of commuter students, the same proportion of sociology majors, and so forth, as is contained in the student body as a whole.

While intuitively appealing, however, the concept of representativeness has nearly disappeared from the technical vocabulary of sampling (Kish, 1965). Not only is it extremely unlikely that one will be able to draw a *perfectly* representative sample, it is rarely possible to evaluate a specific sample in terms of its overall representativeness. Because the populations we study are not known in all respects (which is, of course, the reason we study them), there is no way of knowing just how representative a given sample is. Therefore, we use the term "representative" in reference to specific, known population characteristics but not in reference to the overall quality of the sample.

The quality of a sample must be judged in terms of the procedure that produced it, that is, in terms of its sampling design. **Sampling design** refers to that part of the research plan that indicates how cases are to be selected for observation. Sampling designs are generally divided into two broad classes: probability and nonprobability. **Probability sampling** is scientifically more acceptable, although it is not always feasible or economical. Its essential characteristics are that all cases in the population are randomly selected and have a known probability of being included in the sample. In **nonprobability sampling**, the chances of selecting any case are not known because cases are nonrandomly selected.

Probability sampling designs offer two major advantages over nonprobability sampling designs. The first advantage is that they remove the possibility that investigator biases will affect the selection of cases. The second advantage is that by virtue of random selection, the laws of mathematical probability may be applied to estimate the accuracy of the sample. With probability sampling, one knows to which population the sample may be generalized as well as the limits of generalizability, but with nonprobability sampling, the population itself is undefined and the laws of probability do not apply.

Probability Sampling

Random Selection

Probability sampling always involves the process of **random selection** at some stage. In popular usage, "random" describes something that occurs or is done without plan or choice; random events or choices are haphazard or nondeliberate. As used in sampling, however, "random" has a more specific, technical meaning. It refers to a process that gives each element in a set, such as each case in a population, an equal chance of being selected. If for any reason the selection process favors certain cases, or if the selection of one case increases or decreases the likelihood that another case will be selected, then the selection is biased. By this definition, your circle of friends would clearly be biased as a sample of the student population at your college. So also would a variety of other, more or less haphazardly chosen samples, such as the students enrolled in introductory sociology classes, or students who happen to be in the library on a weekday night, or those students who pass in front of the campus center at a given time. In each of these samples, it is a good bet that certain types of students are more likely to appear than others; therefore, they are not random samples of the student body.

To satisfy the condition of randomness, the investigator cannot simply pick cases haphazardly or in any hit-or-miss fashion; subtle and often unconscious biases will invariably enter into the selection process. Rather, mechanical or electronic aids should be used to ensure that chance alone dictates selection. One popular "mechanical" procedure is the lottery method. All cases are numbered; the numbers are written on equal-size objects, such as balls or disks; the objects are thoroughly mixed in a container; and then the requisite number of "cases" are selected one by one. This method is cumbersome and impractical, however, when applied to populations of social scientific interest.[2] In actual practice, social researchers usually draw random samples by using a computer program that generates random numbers or selects cases randomly from a computerized list of the population.

Simple Random Sampling

The basic probability sampling design that is incorporated in all the more elaborate probability sampling designs discussed below is called a **simple random sample**. The defining property of a simple random sample is that every possible *combination* of cases has an equal chance of being included in the sample. For example, in a population of four cases, numbered 1, 2, 3, 4, there are six possible samples of size two: (1, 2), (1, 3), (1, 4), (2, 3), (2, 4), and (3, 4). In a simple random sample, each of these pairs of cases would have the same chance of selection. To guarantee this property, two requirements are necessary: (1) a complete list of the population and (2) the random selection of cases to be included in the sample.

With the concepts of random selection and simple random sampling now in mind, we are in a position to examine the principles of probability sampling theory.

Although a complete understanding of the theory would require advanced training in statistics, the reader can gain a good intuitive grasp of the essential concepts through the following small-scale hypothetical example.[3]

Suppose that you are interested in conducting a study of alcohol consumption on your campus. Your interest perhaps stems from recent reports that problem drinking is increasing among college-age youth. Very limited time and resources prevent you from studying the student population as a whole, and so you focus instead on all the students who live in your off-campus condominium. There are eight residents in all, which makes it easy to create a list of the target population. You realize, of course, that you would not need to draw a sample of such an incredibly small population. But to understand how samples vary, let us look at some characteristics of samples drawn from this imaginary population. Your dependent variable is alcohol consumption, which you measure by administering a questionnaire in which you ask each resident how many drinks he or she consumes on a typical weekend night. (You also tell your respondents to consider one drink as a bottle or glass of beer, a glass of wine, a wine cooler, a shot glass of liquor, or a mixed drink.)

The following tabulation contains hypothetical data for the population of eight students:

Student	Ann A	Bea B	Cora C	Dee D	Ed E	Fred F	Greg G	Hal H
Gender	F	F	F	F	M	M	M	M
Class standing	U	G	U	G	U	G	U	G
Glasses of beer	3	1	0	2	3	4	6	5

Notice that, in addition to alcohol consumption, information is given on gender and undergraduate versus graduate student status. There are four females (F) and four males (M); four undergraduates (U) and four graduate students (G). These two variables will be considered later.

Characteristics of a population are called **parameters**. For our population of eight students, we are interested in the average (or mean) number of drinks consumed. We determine this parameter by adding up all of the reported drinks (24) and dividing by the number of cases (8), which equals 3.0. Of course, in the real research situation, the parameter would not be known, and our task would be to obtain an estimate from a sample of observations. Sample estimates of population parameters are called **statistics**. Just as we calculated the mean number of drinks consumed in the population, we can estimate the population mean by calculating the mean number of drinks consumed in a sample. To get an idea of how such sample estimates will vary, let us examine all possible simple random samples of two students and of four students that could be drawn from the population. By seeing how the sample statistics vary in relation to the population parameter, we also can see the kinds of generalizations about a population that are possible from a single sample.

There are twenty-eight possible combinations of two cases each that can be drawn randomly from eight cases; thus, there are twenty-eight simple random samples of size two. You can check this for yourself by systematically arranging the possibilities in the following manner: AB, AC, . . . , AH, BC, BD, . . . , GH. In fact, we have done this for you in Table 5.1, which also gives the mean number of drinks for each combination.

Similarly, there are seventy simple random samples of size four. To see how the estimates of alcohol consumption will vary from sample to sample, let us calculate the mean number of drinks consumed for each possible sample of size two and size four. Calculating a statistic, such as the mean, for all possible samples of a given size results in a **sampling distribution**. The sampling distribution of the mean for samples of size two and size four are presented in Figure 5.1 and in columns two and four of Table 5.2. Note first the sample of two cases: Only one combination (BC) yields a sample mean of 0.5 (Bea has 1 drink and Cora has 0, for an average of 0.5); only one combination (CD) has a sample mean of 1.0; three combinations (AC, BD, CE) have sample means of 1.5; and so on. Now examining samples of four cases: Two combinations (ABCD and BCDE) yield sample means of 1.5, two combinations (ABCE and BCDF) yield sample means of 1.75, and so on.

From the sampling distributions one can calculate the probability that any given sample will be selected. (Probabilities, which range from 0 to 1, correspond to percentages. Thus, an event with a probability of .40 is likely to occur 40 percent of the time.) Recall that with simple random sampling, each possible combination of cases is equally likely to be selected. This means that the likelihood, or probability, of selecting any particular combination of two cases (e.g., BC) from the above population will be equal to one divided by the total number of combinations (or 1/28 =

TABLE 5.1. List of All Possible Samples of Size Two

Combination of cases	Mean number of beers	Combination of cases	Mean number of beers
AB (Ann, Bea)	2.0	CE (Cora, Ed)	1.5
AC (Ann, Cora)	1.5	CF (Cora, Fred)	2.0
AD (Ann, Dee)	2.5	CG (Cora, Greg)	3.0
AE (Ann, Ed)	3.0	CH (Cora, Hal)	2.5
AF (Ann, Fred)	3.5	DE (Dee, Ed)	2.5
AG (Ann, Greg)	4.5	DF (Dee, Fred)	3.0
AH (Ann, Hal)	4.0	DG (Dee, Greg)	4.0
BC (Bea, Cora)	0.5	DH (Dee, Hal)	3.5
BD (Bea, Dee)	1.5	EF (Ed, Fred)	3.5
BE (Bea, Ed)	2.0	EG (Ed, Greg)	4.5
BF (Bea, Fred)	2.5	EH (Ed, Hal)	4.0
BG (Bea, Greg)	3.5	FG (Fred, Greg)	5.0
BH (Bea, Hal)	3.0	FH (Fred, Hal)	4.5
CD (Cora, Dee)	1.0	GH (Greg, Hal)	5.5

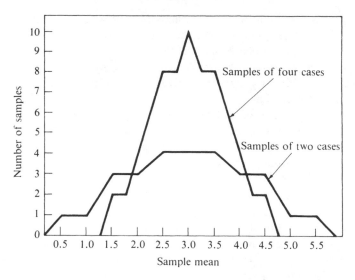

FIGURE 5.1. Frequency distributions of sample means for simple random samples of two cases and four cases drawn from a hypothetical population of eight cases with a mean of 3.0.

.036).[4] This is also the probability of drawing a sample with a mean of 0.5 or of drawing a sample with a mean of 1.0, since each of these means is the result of one and only one combination of two cases. To get the probability of selecting a sample with a mean of 1.5, we simply add the probabilities of each combination that yields a mean of 1.5 (1/28 + 1/28 + 1/28 = .107), which, as you can see, equals the number of such combinations (3) over the total (28). The remaining probabilities are given in columns three and five of Table 5.2. From the table, notice that the probability of obtaining a particular sample mean increases as the estimate approaches the actual population mean of 3.0 drinks. By the same token, the more a sample mean deviates from the population mean, the lower its probability of selection.

It is also possible to calculate the probability of obtaining sample estimates within a given range of the population mean. For example, there are eighteen samples (count them) of two cases with means between 2.0 and 4.0; thus, the probability of obtaining a sample mean within this range is 18/28 = .64. Similarly, with samples of four cases, the probability of getting a sample mean within the range of 2.0 to 4.0 is 62/70 = .89; and with samples of six cases (not shown), the probability is 1.0 (i.e., all samples have means between 2.0 and 4.0). This illustrates a very important principle in sampling theory: The larger the sample, the closer its mean is likely to be to the population mean.

The amount that a given sample statistic deviates from the population parameter it estimates is known as **sampling error**. For example, in our hypothetical population, a sample mean of 0.5 has a sampling error of 2.5 because this is how much it differs from the known population mean of 3.0. Similarly, a sample mean of 1.5 has a sampling error of 1.5 (3.0 − 1.5 = 1.5). The statistical measure of the "average" of such errors for an entire sampling distribution is called the **standard error**.

TABLE 5.2. Means and Probabilities of Simple Random Samples of Two Cases and Four Cases Drawn from a Hypothetical Population of Eight Cases with a Mean of 3.0

SAMPLE MEANS	Sample of two cases		Sample of four cases	
	NUMBER OF SAMPLES	PROBABILITY	NUMBER OF SAMPLES	PROBABILITY
0.50	1	.04		
0.75				
1.00	1	.04		
1.25				
1.50	3	.11	2	.03
1.75			2	.03
2.00	3	.11	4	.06
2.25			6	.09
2.50	4	.14	8	.11
2.75			8	.11
3.00	4	.14 } .64	10	.14 } .89
3.25			8	.11
3.50	4	.14	8	.11
3.75			6	.09
4.00	3	.11	4	.06
4.25			2	.03
4.50	3	.11	2	.03
4.75				
5.00	1	.04		
5.25				
5.50	1	.04		
Total number of samples	28		70	
Mean of sample means	3.0		3.0	

Using this concept, then, another way of stating the principle about sample size is, the larger the sample, the smaller the standard error.

So far, we have demonstrated that a knowledge of the sampling distribution of the mean enables one to make the following kinds of statements regarding the accuracy of a sample mean: The probability is .89 that the mean of a randomly selected sample of four cases will deviate from the population mean by 1 or less (i.e., will fall within the range of 2.0 to 4.0). Of course, in the above example, the sampling distributions were constructed by calculating means for all possible random samples from a *known* population. In actual research, we select only one sample in order to estimate an *unknown* population characteristic. The key to being able to make the same kind of statement about sample accuracy in the actual research situation is provided by the mathematical theory behind probability sampling. According to this theory, the sampling distributions of various statistics (such as the mean) form stable, predictable patterns. Consequently, even though the population parameter is not known, the theory indicates *how* sample estimates will be distributed (by specifying the sampling distribution) and provides a statistical formula for calculating the standard error, a measure of *how much* the sample estimates will tend to vary.

More rigorous accounts of sampling theory and sample estimation procedures can be found in the inferential statistics section of most statistics textbooks. In actual research, sample inferences about a population parameter are arrived at in the following manner. From a single sample, drawn randomly:

1. The sample statistic (e.g., the sample mean) is considered the best single estimate of the population parameter (e.g., the population mean).
2. The extent to which the sample statistic tends to deviate from the population parameter, indicated by the standard error, is calculated on the basis of variation within the sample.
3. Theoretical knowledge about the sampling distribution is utilized to attach a probability, or level of confidence, to a calculated range within which the population characteristic should fall.

This range, called a **confidence interval**, is established around the sample statistic. From this procedure we end up with statements such as the following: "We are 95 percent confident that the population mean is between 2.0 and 4.0." With the mean as the midpoint of this interval, the margin of random sampling error—the amount by which a sample mean is likely to deviate from the population mean—is plus or minus 1. In presenting the results of opinion polls, newspapers and magazines usually give the margin of error for an unstated 95 percent level of confidence; for example, when reporting the percentage of respondents who gave a particular opinion, they may note that the "margin of error is plus or minus 4 percentage points, based on a sample of 750 adults."

A major advantage of probability sampling is that the size of the confidence interval (i.e., sample precision), or the amount by which the sample statistic is likely to differ from the population parameter, can be estimated *before* a study is carried out. Recall that the possible error in sample statistics is a function of sample size: The larger the sample, the smaller the standard error. Therefore, one can get a more precise sample estimate by selecting a larger sample. Sample precision also may be increased by using a more complex sampling design known as stratified random sampling.

Stratified Random Sampling

In **stratified random sampling**, the population is first subdivided into two or more mutually exclusive segments, called **strata**, based on categories of one or a combination of relevant variables. Simple random samples then are drawn from each stratum, and these subsamples are joined to form the complete, stratified sample.

To illustrate, let us return to our hypothetical data. Note that the population of eight cases can be broken down into two strata—male and female—according to categories of the variable "gender," or into two strata—undergraduate and graduate—according to categories of the variable "student status." A stratified random sample of four cases could be drawn by randomly selecting an equal proportion of males and females. In other words, one could draw independent random samples of two cases from each stratum, male and female, and then combine these into a single sample. This would not produce a simple random sample since there are several combinations of cases that are not possible—for example, the combinations of all females (ABCD) or all males (EFGH). There are thirty-six possible stratified random samples of four cases with equal proportions of males and females. By computing the mean number of drinks consumed for each of these possible samples, we again obtain a sampling distribution of the mean. This distribution can be compared with the sampling distribution based on simple random sampling to demonstrate the effect of stratifying on sample precision.

Table 5.3 presents the sampling distributions for samples of four cases based on simple random sampling, stratified random sampling with gender as the stratification variable, and stratified random sampling with student status as the stratifica-

TABLE 5.3. **Means of Samples of Four Cases Drawn by Simple Random Sampling and Stratified Random Sampling with Gender and Student Status as Stratifying Variables**

Sample means	Simple random samples	Samples stratified by gender	Samples stratified by student status
1.50	2		2
1.75	2		
2.00	4	1	2
2.25	6	2	6
2.50	8	5	2
2.75	8	6	2
3.00	10	8	8
3.25	8	6	2
3.50	8	5	2
3.75	6	2	6
4.00	4	1	2
4.25	2		
4.50	2		2
Total number of samples	70	36	36
Mean of sample means	3.0	3.0	3.0
Percentage of sample means between 2.5 and 3.5	60	83	44
Percentage of sample means between 2.0 and 4.0	89	100	89

tion variable. Notice by examining the last two rows of the table that, compared with simple random sampling, sampling with gender stratification yields a distribution of sample means that cluster more tightly about the population mean. Thus, it is possible for a stratified sample to give a better estimate than a simple random sample. On the other hand, stratifying by student status offers no such improvement; indeed, the percentage of sample means between 2.5 and 3.5 (i.e., that deviate from the population mean by as little as .5) is lower—44 percent—than in simple random sampling—60 percent.

Clearly, as these comparisons reveal, stratifying can contribute to sampling efficiency. Whether it does depends on whether the stratifying variable is related to the dependent variable under study. In our hypothetical population, gender is related to alcohol consumption but student status is not; that is, men tend to drink more than women, whereas undergraduate and graduate students drink about the same amount. Consequently, stratifying by gender increases sample precision but stratifying by student status does not.

Technically speaking, stratifying by variables correlated with the dependent variable increases the precision of estimates because it systematically controls relevant sources of variability (or heterogeneity) in the population. The effect of this is to eliminate a source of sampling error—for example, the error that could occur if our sample of students contained all men or all women. Thus, when there are differences across strata, stratified sampling ensures that these differences are accounted for and are not free to vary within the sample. In fact, in the extreme instance, when all the variation in the dependent variable is across strata and each stratum is completely homogeneous, the researcher needs to sample only one case per stratum for a perfectly accurate estimate. In our hypothetical population, this would occur if, say, each woman had one drink and each man drank five drinks. The population mean would be 3.0, and a sample of one woman and one man would yield a mean estimate of 3.0 [(5 + 1)/2 = 3.0)].

With simple random sampling, only an increase in sample size can reduce the variation across strata that contributes to sampling error. A stratified random sample, therefore, will be comparable in precision to a *larger* simple random sample, and hence more efficient, provided that the stratifying variable is related to the variable under study. Since we also can increase sample precision by increasing sample size, the greater efficiency of stratifying also depends on whether the cost of stratifying is low relative to the cost of sampling more cases. Obtaining a stratified sample necessitates classifying cases according to categories of the stratifying variable; for example, if you want to stratify by gender, you need to know *prior to drawing the sample* whether each person in the population is a male or a female. Otherwise, you cannot draw separate samples from each stratum. Often, however, the information needed to stratify is not available and is either impossible or too costly to obtain, which limits the use of stratified random sampling.

In addition to increasing efficiency, stratified random sampling may be used to guarantee that variable categories with small proportions of cases in the population are adequately represented in the sample. Suppose, for example, that we wanted to examine ethnic attitudes among various ethnic groups on a campus where 90 percent of the students are white, 5 percent are black, and 5 percent are Asian. A simple random sample of one hundred would yield, on the average, ninety whites, five blacks, and five Asians. However, the number of cases in the latter two sampled groups is so small that statistical estimates derived from them would be very unreliable. To get around this problem, we could obtain a stratified random sample in which we select a greater proportion of blacks and Asians for our sample than are found in the population. We might select forty whites, thirty blacks, and thirty Asians. This is called **disproportionate stratified random sampling**, because the proportion of cases in each stratum of the sample does not reflect the proportion in the population.

When strata are sampled proportionate to the population composition, each case has an equal probability of being selected and one can generalize directly from sample to population. But with disproportionate sampling, the probability of selection varies from stratum to stratum and one must make a statistical adjustment before estimating population parameters.[5] Disproportionate stratified random sampling still constitutes a probability sample because the probability of case selection is *known*. Furthermore, probability sampling theory applies, since the subsamples drawn from each stratum are simple random samples.

Cluster Sampling

Both simple random sampling and stratified random sampling assume that a complete list of the population is available. What do you do, however, when your target population is so large that it is either impossible or impractical to list all its members? The only lists of the U.S. population—income tax forms and census forms filed every ten years—are confidential and not available to the public. Lists of most city and all state populations simply do not exist, and it would be prohibitively expensive to compile lists of these and other very large populations. In such instances, the researcher often is able to obtain a sample in stages, using a method called **cluster sampling**.

In cluster sampling, the population is broken down into groups of cases, called clusters. The clusters generally consist of natural groupings, such as colleges and churches, or geographic areas, such as states, counties, cities, and blocks. Unlike stratified sampling, which draws cases from each stratum, cluster sampling draws cases only from sampled clusters. To draw a cluster sample, one first selects at random a sample of clusters. Then one obtains a list of all cases within each selected cluster. If all the cases in each sampled cluster are included in the sample, the design is called a *single-stage cluster sample* in that sampling occurs once—at the cluster level. More frequently, cluster sampling involves sampling at two or more steps or stages, hence the term **multistage cluster sampling**. An example of a two-stage cluster sample would be a random selection of four-year colleges (first stage), followed by a random selection of students within each sampled college (second stage). The sampling units in the first stage of a multistage sample are termed **primary sampling units** (or PSUs); units in the second stage are termed secondary sampling units, and so on.

While stratified random sampling is used either to increase sample precision or to provide a sufficient number of cases in small strata, the principal reason for cluster sampling is to reduce the costs of data collection. In face-to-face interview stud-

BOX 5.2

Sampling Design for a Nationwide Survey

Survey organizations such as the Survey Research Center (SRC) at the University of Michigan use multistage cluster sampling to conduct nationwide surveys. The steps

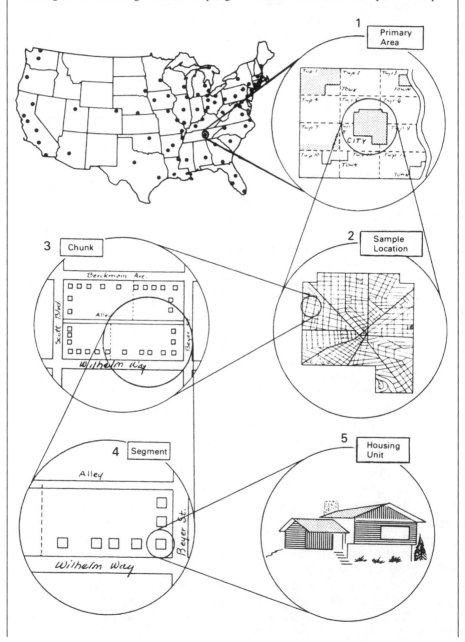

involved in selecting the SRC's national sample in the 1970s are roughly diagrammed in the accompanying figure. The steps are numbered and labeled according to the type of unit selected.

Step 1. The United States is divided into *primary areas* consisting of counties, groups of counties, or metropolitan areas. These areas are stratified by region, and a proportionate stratified sample of seventy-four areas is selected.

Step 2. The seventy-four areas are divided into *locations* such as towns, cities, and residual areas. After these have been identified and stratified by population size, a proportionate stratified sample of locations is drawn within each area.

Step 3. All sample locations are divided into *chunks*. A chunk is a geographic area with identifiable boundaries such as city streets, roads, streams, and county lines. After division into chunks, a random sample of chunks is drawn.

Step 4. Interviewers scout each sample chunk and record addresses and estimates of the number of housing units at each address. They then divide the chunks into smaller units called *segments*, and a random sample of segments is selected.

Step 5. Within each sample segment, either all or a sample of the housing units, usually about four, are chosen for a given study. Finally, for every housing unit in the sample, interviewers randomly choose one respondent from among those eligible, which ordinarily consists of all U.S. citizens 18 years of age or older.

Source: Page 36 of Survey Research Center, *Interviewer's Manual,* revised edition (Institute for Social Research, The University of Michigan, 1976). Used by permission.

---

ies of large, widely scattered populations, two major costs are interviewer travel and the listing of population elements. Simple random and stratified random methods produce isolated interviews at dispersed localities, which can create substantial travel costs to reach respondents. However, clustering concentrates interviews within fewer and smaller geographic areas, thereby spreading the travel costs over several cases and reducing the costs of any one interview.

Since the listing of population elements is a prerequisite for simple random or stratified random methods, clustering also can reduce costs by limiting the compilation of lists of cases to selected clusters rather than compiling a list of the entire population. Moreover, multistage cluster sampling may be the only viable method of drawing a probability sample when an exhaustive list of population elements is unavailable or impractical to create. Often, however, it is possible to obtain lists of subpopulations (clusters) into which the population is naturally grouped or can be subdivided (Babbie, 1995:213). For example, although a single list of U.S. high school students does not exist and would be difficult and extremely costly to compile, lists of school districts within each state could be obtained fairly easily. To arrive at a nationwide sample of high school students, one could initially sample school districts, then obtain a list of high schools within selected districts and sample high schools, then list and sample students within each school. (Box 5.2 provides an example of a multistage sampling design for a national survey of the adult population.)

Multistage sample designs may involve either simple random sampling or stratified random sampling at each stage of the design. In other words, one can stratify clusters just as one stratifies individual cases. The National Education Longitudinal Study (NELS), for example, used a two-stage stratified, cluster sample design. The first stage consisted of schools, and the second stage consisted of eighth-grade students within the selected schools. At the first or cluster stage, schools were divided into several strata according to four variables: school type (public, Catholic private, other private), region of the country, urbanicity (whether the school's location was urban, suburban, or rural), and percent minority. A number of schools were selected within each stratum, and then an equal number of students (24) were selected within each school in the sample.

One problem with cluster sampling is that natural clusters often vary considerably in the numbers of cases they contain. This, in fact, was true of the schools in the NELS. There are two ways of handling this problem in order to reduce potential error. First, you can stratify clusters by population size. In this way, a relatively few clusters with extremely large populations can be sampled from a separate stratum to guarantee that they are represented in the sample. Otherwise, with simple random sampling one runs the risk of not selecting clusters that account for a major proportion of the population. Imagine, for example, drawing a cluster sample, with counties as the primary sampling units, of the population of Nevada, in which over 80 percent of the people reside in two of the state's sixteen counties. Any sample that excludes these two counties would be a biased sample of Nevada residents. Yet the chances are fairly high that neither of the state's two largest counties would be included in a simple random sample of counties (e.g., the probability that neither would be selected is 55 percent in a sample of four counties and 23 percent in a sample of eight counties). The best procedure, therefore, would be to stratify by county size, placing the two most populous counties in the topmost stratum, and then sample 100 percent from this stratum (i.e., select both counties).

When clusters vary in size, another common solution is to make the selection of clusters or cases within clusters proportionate to the size of the cluster. This method, called **probability proportionate to size** sampling, was applied to the selection of schools in the NELS. One way it works is to assign each cluster a probability of selection proportionate to the number of cases in the cluster. Thus, a school with 1000 students would be twice as likely to be selected as a school with 500 students. If an equal number of students is selected from each school, then each student in the population has an equal probability of being selected.[6]

While cluster samples are more cost efficient, they are less precise, size for size, than either simple random or stratified random samples. The latter designs have a single source of sampling error; however, there are sampling errors associated with each stage of a multistage cluster sample. For example, in a two-stage cluster sample of college students at four-year colleges, the sample of four-year colleges would represent the population of colleges within a range of error, and the sample of students within a selected college represents all students in the college within a range of error. The sampling error in the total sample is thus compounded and can be quite large relative to the error produced by one simple random selection.

In stratified sampling, efficiency increases to the extent that strata are internally homogeneous; for example, the drinking behavior of women is similar and the drinking behavior of men is similar. By contrast, the ideal in cluster sampling is for clusters to be internally *heterogeneous* compared with the differences between clusters. In general, however, there is much less variability (hence sampling error) within than across natural clusters. For example, residents in a single block are likely to be fairly homogeneous with respect to income, but quite different in terms of average income from the residents in another block. For this reason, one way of increasing efficiency is to select more clusters and fewer elements within the clusters. By increasing the number of clusters, sampling error is reduced at the stage that is subject to the greatest error.[7]

Although increasing the number of clusters generally decreases sampling error, it also increases the cost of cluster sampling. A greater number of clusters means more widely scattered interviews, hence more time and expense invested in travel, and more time and expense required for listing elements within the selected clusters. Reducing costs, of course, is the reason for cluster sampling. Consequently, researchers are likely to resolve this dilemma by simply selecting as many clusters as they can afford (Babbie, 1995:215).

Systematic Sampling

Before the computer age—before random number programs and computerized lists became available—social scientists often used a technique called systematic sampling to closely approximate simple random sampling. Simple random sampling requires not only a complete sampling frame, such as a list, but also the numbering of population elements. (In effect, one selects random numbers that correspond to case numbers.) A list in a computer file meets both of these requirements. But if you only have an unnumbered hard-copy list of the population, and the list is quite long, such as a university student directory, it is much easier to draw a systematic sample than a simple random sample.

Systematic sampling consists of selecting every Kth (e.g., fifteenth or twentieth) case from a complete list or file of the population, starting with a randomly chosen case from the first K cases on the list. Such a procedure has two requirements: a sampling interval (K) and a random start (Sudman, 1976). The **sampling interval** is merely the ratio of the number of cases in the population to the desired sample size. A *random start* refers to the process of randomly selecting the initial case between 1 and K. For example, suppose you wanted to draw a sample of 100 students from the 2500 students listed in the campus directory. Dividing 2500 by 100, you obtain a sampling interval of 25. You would then select at random a number between 1 and 25, and starting with that number, select every twenty-fifth student thereafter. Suppose the random number turns out to be 19. Your sample then would consist of cases numbered 19, 44, 69, 94, 119, . . . , 2494.

Although each case in a systematic sample has an equal chance of being selected, each *combination* of cases does not. (There are only 25 possible combinations in the above example.) Technically speaking, therefore, a systematic sample is not the equivalent of a simple random sample. It is a random sample, however, and in practice researchers regard it as a close approximation of a simple random sample.

The only potential problem with systematic sampling arises from the fact that most available lists are not random, but rather are ordered in some fashion, such as alphabetical, or by rank, age, or size of unit. The danger is that the available population listing may have a periodic or cyclical pattern that corresponds to the sampling interval. A classic example is a World War II study in which a 1/10 systematic sample of soldiers was drawn. The list from which the sample was drawn, however, was ordered by squads of ten soldiers, with each squad ordered by rank (sergeants, corporals, privates). When the sample was drawn, the interval of 10 corresponded to all the sergeants on the list.

Fortunately, the danger of periodicity in a systematic sample is actually quite small. Still, to counteract this possibility, the researcher should carefully examine the list from which a systematic sample will be drawn. If the list has a cyclical pattern, steps should be taken (e.g., randomizing the start before selection on each page of the student directory) to eliminate the possibility of bias.

Nonprobability Sampling

Nonprobability sampling refers to processes of case selection other than random selection. Without random selection, nonprobability samples have two basic weaknesses: (1) They do not control for investigator bias in the selection of units, and (2) their pattern of variability cannot be predicted from probability sampling theory, thereby making it impossible to calculate sampling error or to estimate sample precision. However, while one should be ever mindful of these weaknesses, it would be a mistake to rule out nonprobability sampling. In many instances, this form of sampling either is more appropriate and practical than probability sampling or is the only viable means of case selection.

1. Consider the situation in which very few cases can be included in the sample. For an investigator doing an intensive study in which the unit of analysis is the city, corporation, or university, the expense of studying more than one or a few cases would be prohibitive. As we have seen, probability sampling is less reliable the smaller the sample. With extremely small samples of one or few cases, generalization from sample to population essentially becomes a matter of judgment. The selection of cases is therefore better left to expert judgment (in other words, nonrandom selection) than to the whims of chance (Wallis and Roberts, 1956:117–18).

2. When studying past events, the archaeologist or historian often finds only a fraction of relevant materials available or accessible. Similarly in contemporary societies, certain individuals or institutions may refuse to cooperate in an inquiry. Under these circumstances, the researcher must either accept a nonprobability method of case selection or abandon the study altogether.

3. In the early stages of investigating a problem, when the objective is to become more informed about the problem itself, probability sampling simply may be

unnecessary. It will suffice to select a range of cases nonrandomly without concern for precise statistical generalization.

4. If the population itself contains few cases or if an adequate sampling frame cannot be obtained or constructed, there is no point in considering probability sampling. With small populations (say, fewer than 100), each case should be studied in its own right in comparison with all others. If the population is unknown or not readily identifiable, as in many sociological studies of deviance, sampling generally will consist of studying any and all identifiable and cooperative units.

Because nonprobability sampling is a residual category pertaining to any method of *non*random case selection, the various types of nonprobability samples are far ranging and less precisely defined than the probability sampling designs examined in the previous section. With this in mind, let us now examine three primary types of nonprobability samples: convenience, purposive, and quota.

Convenience Sampling

In this form of sampling (also called haphazard, fortuitous, and accidental sampling), the researcher simply selects a requisite number from cases that are conveniently available. In terms of the study of campus alcohol consumption, you might decide to (1) ask a professor for permission to administer a questionnaire to all the students in his or her classes, (2) interview whoever comes down the dormitory hall when you happen to be there, or (3) find a convenient spot in the campus pub from which to observe behavior. Television stations and newspapers wanting to tap public opinion on specific issues may interview conveniently available commuters, shoppers, store clerks, and others (Chein, 1981). Such methods of case selection are easy, quick, and inexpensive. If the research is at an early stage and generalizability is not an issue, then they may be perfectly appropriate. However, convenience sampling is a matter of catch-as-catch-can. There is no way of determining to whom, other than the sample itself, the results apply. Thus, in attempting to make inferences from such a sample, "one can only hope that one is not being too grossly misled" (Chein, 1981:424).

Purposive Sampling

In this form of sampling, the investigator relies on his or her expert judgment to select units that are "representative" or "typical" of the population. The general strategy is to identify important sources of variation in the population and then to select a sample that reflects this variation. One might select a single unit or subpopulation that is thought to be typical of the population in important respects or select a few units that correspond to key population differences. For example, in his study of "community ideology"—the values and beliefs associated with different kinds of communities—David Hummon (1990) selected residents of four distinct communities in northern California: a central city, an upper-class suburb, a working-class suburb, and a rural small town. Because the type of community in which people lived was likely to affect their community ideology, this was a crucial variable in Hummon's study. He therefore wanted to be sure that it was represented adequately in his sample. Furthermore, in selecting the specific communities, Hummon carefully examined census data to identify typical areas or towns and to avoid populations that contained relatively large proportions of aged, minority, or institutionalized persons. Such purposive sampling fit the aims of the study extremely well, because Hummon's interest was not in estimating the distribution of various beliefs about communities within a particular population, but in identifying the key elements in various community ideologies.

Another purposive sampling technique, applied to election forecasting, is the selection of "barometer" states or precincts that have served as reliable predictors of overall election returns in previous years. Still another is the selection of deviant or extreme cases in order to discover why they deviate from the norm. Finally, one may select both typical and extreme instances within the same study. For example, if one were testing an innovation in the schools, it would be wise to investigate at least one instance of the "typical school" in a particular city (or state or nation) and at least one instance of the best and worst problem schools (Cook and Campbell, 1979:76). If comparable results were found in all three instances, one would have a reasonably firm basis for inferring that the effect applies to the full range of schools.

As with any nonprobability method of case selection, purposive sampling for heterogeneity and/or typicality is an unacceptable substitute for probability sampling when precise and accurate generalizations are required. However, with studies of more limited scope or in situations that preclude random selection, purposive sampling is an acceptable alternative. It generally offers much stronger, less tenuous inferences than convenience sampling, although such inferences are very much dependent on the researcher's expert judgment. The major weakness of purposive sampling is that making an informed selection of cases requires considerable knowledge of the population before the sample is drawn.

Quota Sampling

Quota sampling is a form of purposive sampling that bears a superficial resemblance to proportionate stratified random sampling. Like the latter, quota sampling begins by dividing the population into relevant strata such as age, gender, race, and geographic region. The fraction of the population in each stratum is then estimated or determined via external data such as the census, and the total sample is allocated among the strata in direct proportion to their estimated or actual size in the population. Finally, to obtain the correct proportions in the sample, interviewers are asked to speak to a fixed quota of respondents in each stratum: so many men and so many women, so many of a given age or income, and so on. To fill the quotas, interviewers are free to choose anyone who meets the quota requirements. For example, in the study of campus alcohol consumption, one might decide to obtain a quota sample, with a quota-control for gender, in light of the known effects of this variable on consumption. Suppose the campus population was 55 percent male and 45 percent female. Then a sample of 200 would require quotas of 110 men and 90 women. How these respondents were chosen would be up to the investigator.

The difference between quota sampling and stratified random sampling lies precisely in how cases are selected once quotas have been set. In stratified random sampling, the requisite number of cases within each stratum must be drawn by simple random sampling. But in quota sampling, the quota of cases within a stratum may be filled in whatever way the investigator chooses. Each stratum in a quota sample thus constitutes a convenience sample of the corresponding stratum of the population (Chein, 1981:426); moreover, the total sample is also a convenience sample, albeit one that resembles the population with respect to some key characteristics.

The quota method assumes that a sample that agrees with the population in important characteristics should be like the population in other ways as well. Experience has shown, however, that this is an unsafe assumption. Interviewers allowed to self-select respondents are subject to several kinds of bias. If left to their own devices, they will interview their friends in excessive proportions; they also have been known to fill quotas by concentrating on areas where there are large numbers of potential respondents, such as transportation or entertainment centers, college campuses, and business districts (Chein, 1981:426). When quotas are filled by home visits, interviewers tend to select houses that are perceived as more attractive or as housing persons with relatively high income (Carter, Troldahl, and Schuneman, 1963). The potential biases in such procedures are obvious: Friends are likely to resemble closely the interviewers themselves; people who gravitate to population centers may differ sharply from those who do not; and a preference for nicer neighborhoods and homes will almost certainly create a strong socioeconomic bias. Thus, representative quotas on some characteristics do not ensure representation on others.

For some years before the election forecast failure in 1948 (see Box 5.1), quota sampling was the predominant sampling design in opinion surveys. Probability sampling designs are now preferred. Yet, in spite of its weaknesses, quota sampling continues to be used by some market research and opinion survey organizations, because of two main advantages (Kalton, 1983). First, unlike probability sampling, there is no need to construct a sampling frame for selecting respondents. Second, whereas probability sampling requires that interviewers make several call-backs, if necessary, to contact predesignated respondents who are not at home, call-backs are unnecessary in a quota sample. The interviewer must simply find any eligible person according to the relevant quota criteria. For these two reasons, interviewing can be completed more quickly, more easily, and at much lower cost in quota sampling studies. To reduce the hazards of the quota technique, investigators have introduced tight geographic controls, specifying the section of the city, block, and even household where respondents may be selected. This will not eliminate sample biases entirely, but it does refine quota sampling to the point that it "is clearly superior to loose judgment or convenience samples" (Sudman, 1976:200).

Other Sampling Designs

In addition to the foregoing "pure" forms, investigators have developed a variety of other sampling techniques and designs. Each of these methods addresses a recurring problem in social research: what to do when research purposes require the rig-

orous, systematic selection of cases, but available resources or other practical problems preclude the use of conventional probability sampling designs.

Consider, for example, the Chicago Homeless Study (Rossi et al., 1987;
Rossi, 1989), which attempted to estimate the composition and size of Chicago's
homeless population. Because of the difficulties in conducting empirical research
on the homeless, estimates of the extent of homelessness vary widely and knowledge of the conditions that produce it is minimal. Conventional probability sampling in surveys assumes "that persons can be enumerated and sampled within
their customary dwelling unit"; however, this assumption fails by any definition
of the homeless. For the Chicago study, therefore, the investigators devised a
strategy that sampled persons from nondwelling units at times of maximum separation between the homeless and those with homes. The sampling design consisted of two complementary probability samples: (1) a systematic sample of persons spending the night in over twenty shelters provided for homeless persons and
(2) a one-stage, stratified cluster sample of the 19,409 census blocks within the
Chicago city limits. Blocks were stratified by the expected number of homeless
to be found on each, according to police estimates. Within each selected block,
between the hours of 1 AM and 6 AM, interviewers conducted thorough searches
of every conceivable place, including alleys, hallways, roofs and basements, and
parked cars. All persons encountered were first given a short screening interview
to determine if they were homeless. If so, the person was given a fifteen- to
twenty-minute interview.[8]

John Watters and Patrick Biernacki (1989) devised a very different strategy for
sampling another "hidden" population—injecting drug users. This is a group at high
risk for the transmission of the HIV virus that causes AIDS. Due to the clandestine
nature of illicit drug use, members of this target population are very difficult to locate. One option rejected by Watters and Biernacki was use of a convenience sample of injecting drug users enrolled in methadone maintenance treatment programs.
While this option would have provided easy access to some of the target population, there was reason to believe that persons in methadone clinics were a biased
sample of drug users who differed in many ways from those outside the clinics.[9]
The sampling strategy they decided on, which they called "targeted sampling," contained several steps: (1) Through observation and the use of several sources of information, they determined which neighborhoods had the highest concentrations of
drug users and drug-related activity; (2) on the basis of intensive observation and
interaction with people in these areas, they identified potential respondents; and (3)
they established field sites in each area and developed specific plans for recruitment. During the course of the study, Watters and Biernacki were careful to select
adequate numbers of particular groups of respondents and were sensitive to the effects of time and field site location on recruitment.

Combined Probability and Nonprobability Sampling

To reduce the costs associated with probability sampling, probability and nonprobability sampling may be combined in one design. This is possible whenever
sampling is carried out in stages (Chein, 1981:438–39). Cases can be selected ac-

cording to nonprobability procedures at one stage and by probability procedures at another. Two combinations are common in social research. The first involves multistage probability sampling of clusters, with a quota sampling of individual respondents at the final stage. Thus, one might "select a probability sample of counties in a state; within each of these counties, a probability sample of neighborhoods; and within each of the selected neighborhoods, a quota sample controlled for, say, age and sex" (Chein, 1981:438). While sometimes called "probability sampling with quotas," such a design produces, strictly speaking, a *non*probability (quota) sample—with geographic restrictions that sharply reduce interviewer selection bias.

The second combination reverses the first strategy by drawing a probability sample of cases within a nonprobability (purposive) sample of areas. For example, in a study of crime and deterrence, Charles Tittle (1980) surveyed the population aged 15 and older in New Jersey, Iowa, and Oregon. Within each state he drew a probability sample of respondents; however, the states themselves formed a purposive national sample, carefully selected to represent various degrees of urbanization and industrialization and to avoid unusual age, gender, and racial distributions. With this design, mathematical sampling theory applies to inferences from each probability sample to its respective state population, while more risky investigator judgment must be used in making generalizations to the total population.

Referral Sampling

Another set of techniques has been developed for sampling target populations that comprise small subgroups of the larger population (see Sudman and Kalton, 1986; Sudman, Sirken, and Cowan, 1988): for example, users of a particular service or product, members of a minority ethnic group that is widely dispersed in a larger population, laid-off workers, or persons with AIDS. If resources are plentiful and members of the target population are readily identifiable, probability sampling can be carried out simply by choosing a large enough fraction of the larger population and screening for members of the target population. However, extensive screening is very costly and time-consuming, and it is also possible to miss persons because they are incorrectly identified.

Often the sampling technique devised to handle these problems utilizes some form of referral, wherein respondents who are initially contacted are asked to supply the names and addresses of members of the target population. In **network sampling**, respondents initially contacted in screening a probability sample of the larger population are asked to identify members of the target population who are socially linked to the respondent (e.g., relative, neighbor, co-worker, friend). In a study of male Vietnam veterans, for instance, George Rothbart, Michelle Fine, and Seymour Sudman (1982) first selected respondents by screening the larger population for eligible persons. Each respondent to a screening call was then asked if he or she had a son, brother, or nephew who was a veteran. The sample of 1011 consisted of 535 veterans who were directly contacted and 476 veteran kin who were nominated in the initial screening process. Since veterans living within initially contacted households comprised only 6.2 percent of the larger population, a sample of 1011 would have required 16,439 interviews without network sampling. With network sampling, however, the number of screening interviews was slightly more than half this total—8698. Thus, the major advantage of this technique is a reduction in screening costs. On the other hand, the final probability sample creates unequal selection probabilities that increase sampling error and that must be taken into account in the analysis, and failures by informants to identify members of the target population may result in bias.

Another referral technique, called **snowball sampling**, uses a process of chain referral: When members of the target population are located, they are asked to provide names and addresses of other members of the target population, who are then contacted and asked to name others, and so on. A basic assumption of snowball sampling is that members of the target population often know each other. This technique has been used to create sampling frames (Sudman and Kalton, 1986) and is sometimes associated with probability sampling (Goodman, 1961), but most applications involve nonprobability methods of selection. Patrick Biernacki and Dan Waldorf (1981:144) note that snowball sampling is particularly applicable to studies of deviant behavior, where "moral, legal, or social sensitivities surrounding the behavior in question . . . pose some serious problems for locating and contacting potential respondents." In these studies, members of the target population are often socially invisible by virtue of their illicit, clandestine activities. Their characteristics, therefore, are unknown, and drawing a probability sample is virtually impossible. Often the best that one can do is to use all available means to find eligible respondents and start referral chains. The quality of the sample ultimately depends on the researcher's ability to develop initial contacts and referral chains that represent a range of characteristics in the target population.

Factors Affecting Choice of Sampling Design

Now that we have examined the basic sampling designs, let us look more closely at some of the factors that enter into the researcher's selection of an appropriate design. Which sampling design is adopted depends on several preliminary considerations:

1. What is the stage of research?
2. How will the data be used?
3. What are the available resources for drawing the sample?
4. How will the data be collected?

As you will see, these considerations are interrelated and vary in their relative importance in affecting the choice of a sampling design.

Stage of Research and Data Use

The first two considerations—stage of research and data use—dictate how accurate the sample must be as a description of the population (Sudman, 1976). Accuracy is least important in the exploratory phases of research, when the goal is to discover interesting patterns and generate hypotheses for later study. In fact, under these circumstances, generalizing to a specified population and estimating sample precision are usually unimportant or irrelevant. The researcher often must rely on his or her judgment in drawing a sample and may end up selecting cases for such reasons as availability or willingness to participate in the research; therefore, convenience or purposive sampling is appropriate.

Accuracy would appear to be most important in large-scale fact-finding studies that provide input for major policy decisions. Perhaps the best example of this is the aforementioned Current Population Survey (CPS). The CPS is the only up-to-date source of information on a number of important characteristics of the total population—providing, for example, monthly estimates of unemployment and employment. As Seymour Sudman (1976:3) notes, "major government economic and welfare programs are influenced by changes of a few tenths of a percent in CPS data from month to month." Consequently, a very large (approximately 50,000) and carefully controlled probability sample is necessary to guarantee a high degree of precision.

Obviously, the desired level of precision in most studies lies somewhere between exploratory data gathering and the CPS. The important point here is that the researcher must have some sense of how good the sample must be to meet the objectives of the research. For example, if you need to assess opinions about student government among students at your school for the purpose of documenting support for government reforms, a haphazard, poor-quality sample would be inappropriate. You would need to make sure that the sample is adequate for the task of making reasonably accurate generalizations about the student population. On the other hand, if you merely wanted to get some sense of the variability in opinions about student government for a class project, a small-scale convenience sample would suffice.

Available Resources

If sample accuracy were the sole criterion, selecting an appropriate sampling design would be a simple matter of using the procedure that yields the smallest margin of error. However, accuracy ultimately must be balanced against cost. Available resources such as time, money, materials, and personnel place limitations on how cases can be selected. The primary reason for multistage cluster sampling, as we have seen, is that it reduces time and expense due to interviewer travel and the compilation of necessary case listings. Therefore, some form of this design is recommended for all large-scale surveys. Because it requires less time, systematic sampling sometimes is used in lieu of simple random sampling. And the popularity of quota sampling similarly rests on critical savings in time and expense in comparison with probability sampling.

For the student doing unfunded research, such comparisons probably seem irrelevant. The underlying message, however, is that one should make efficient use of available resources in designing one's sample. The sampling design should be appropriate for available resources, but lack of funds should not be used as an excuse for drawing a haphazard, low-quality sample. As a general rule, one should define the target population to fit the scope of the study; if the study is small enough, a well-designed and executed sample is possible with very limited resources.

Method of Data Collection

A common impression of sampling is that it is only a tool of survey researchers. Social scientists who employ the other major forms of data collection (experimentation, field research, and documentary research) have been seen as having a peripheral interest in sampling. The truth is, however, that all researchers must deal with case selection. The four data collection strategies simply handle the issue of sampling in different ways. As you will see in subsequent chapters, convenience sampling is the rule in experiments, which tend to use small samples drawn from readily available populations. Some form of probability sampling is found in most surveys, purposive or judgmental sampling typifies field research, and—to the extent that the population is definable—probability sampling often is used in the analysis of available data.

Factors Determining Sample Size

Having carefully defined the target population, obtained a good sampling frame, and come up with an appropriate sampling design, the researcher finally must decide on an adequate sample size. As with the choice of a sampling design, several interrelated factors affect the decision about sample size: (1) heterogeneity of the population, (2) desired precision, (3) type of sampling design, (4) available resources, and (5) number of breakdowns planned in data analysis. The most sophisticated research applications enter these factors into mathematical equations for determining sample size. Such technical matters are, of course, largely beyond the scope of this book. Still, we think that understanding some of the statistical sampling theory underlying sample size considerations is important. The few mathematical principles that we introduce in the following discussion apply directly to simple random sampling. However, they also apply, in a more complex fashion than we discuss, to other forms of probability sampling, and, in both a logical and intuitive sense, to nonprobability sampling designs.

Population Heterogeneity

Heterogeneity refers to the degree of dissimilarity (and conversely, homogeneity to the degree of similarity) among cases with respect to a particular characteristic. In general, the more heterogeneous the population with respect to the characteristic being studied, the more cases required to yield a reliable sample estimate. The logic of this principle can be seen by considering the extremes: If all cases were exactly alike, a sample of one case would suffice; and if no two cases were alike on a given characteristic, only a complete census could satisfactorily represent the population.

The populations studied by social scientists are rarely uniform on any characteristic; indeed, it is their natural heterogeneity that compels us to sample in the first place. The degree of heterogeneity or variability depends on the specific population and variable in question. In a study of a college student population, political attitudes should be more heterogeneous, and therefore require a larger sample, than attitudes toward higher education. On the other hand, both of these sets of attitudes (or variables) should be more heterogeneous, and therefore require an even larger sample, in an urban population than in a college population.

The best statistical measure of population heterogeneity for a quantitative variable is the **standard deviation**, conventionally symbolized by the Greek letter sigma (σ). There is a direct link between this measure and the concept of standard error, introduced earlier in our discussion of probability sampling theory. The standard error, recall, indicates the degree of error in a sample estimate (the "average" amount by which a sample estimate deviates from the population value it estimates). The formula used to calculate the standard error is $\sigma/\sqrt{N}$, that is, the standard deviation divided by the square root of the sample size N. From this formula one can see that the standard error is directly related to the heterogeneity of the population as measured by σ and is inversely related to sample size. Also, the formula itself is a statement of the first principle regarding sample size: The greater the heterogeneity of the population, the larger the sample necessary to achieve a given level of precision.

Desired Precision

Technically speaking, precision refers to the degree of variability or error in a sample estimate, hence to the standard error. Intuitively, however, the concept of precision is perhaps best conveyed by relating it to the size of the confidence interval used to estimate a population value. Thus it is more precise to say that the average number of beers consumed is likely to fall between 2.0 and 4.0 than to say that the average is likely to fall between 1.0 and 5.0. For a given confidence level (say, 95 percent), the size of the confidence interval is directly related to the standard error; that is, the smaller the standard error, the smaller the confidence interval and the *more* precise the sample estimate. Of course, the larger the sample, the smaller the standard error. Therefore, it follows that the larger the sample, the greater the precision of the sample estimate.

Two facts about this relationship are especially noteworthy because they defy intuition to a certain extent. First, ordinarily it is the absolute size of the sample rather than the proportion of the population sampled that determines precision. As long as the population is relatively large, the proportion of the population sampled has a negligible effect on precision. For example, in 2000 the population of Vermont was a little over 600,000 and the population of Massachusetts was over 6 million. Now, if one were to take a simple random sample of 2000 in each of these states, the sample proportion of the total population would be about 1 of every 300 persons in Vermont and about 1 of every 3000 persons in Massachusetts. Yet, based on these samples, an estimate (say, of average income) would be just as precise for Massachusetts as for Vermont.

We can get a mathematical understanding of this relationship by reexamining the formula for the standard error. Although the formula given above shows that the standard error is determined only by the standard deviation and sample size, this formula actually applies to populations of theoretically infinite size. For finite populations, the formula should be multiplied by a correction factor equal to $\sqrt{1 - f}$, where f is the **sampling fraction**, or proportion of the population included in the sample (Kish, 1965:43–44). Notice, however, that if the sampling fraction is very near zero, then the correction factor becomes $\sqrt{1}$, or 1, which has no effect on the standard error. In most practical examples, the population is so much larger than the sample that f is extremely small—near zero—and the correction factor can be ignored. Only with small populations would we expect f to be much larger than zero; however, for a small population a small f implies a small sample size, and it is the latter that has the greater impact on the standard error.

Although precision is governed primarily by the absolute numerical size of the sample rather than by the proportion of the population sampled, the sample need not be enormous in size to yield very precise results. This is the second crucial fact about precision and sample size. The sampling error tends to be quite small for a sample of size 2000 to 3000, and increasing the sample size beyond this number decreases the error by so little that it usually is not worth the additional cost.

The mathematical explanation for this once again can be found in the standard error formula. Notice that the standard error goes down as the *square root* of the sample size goes up. Because of the square root function, each time we wish to decrease the standard error by one-half we must increase the sample size fourfold. At this rate, the precision gained with increased sample size reaches a point of minute, diminishing returns after a few thousand cases. Consider, for example, how sample size affects the standard error of a percentage, such as the estimated percentage of the vote a candidate will receive in an election. With two candidates and an evenly split vote, the standard error will be 5.0 percent for a sample size of 100. This error decreases to 2.5 percent when the sample reaches 400, and to 1.0 percent when

TABLE 5.4. **Standard Error of a Percentage of 50 Percent, Broken Down by Sample Size***

Sample size	Standard error (percent)
100	5.0
400	2.5
2,500	1.0
10,000	0.5

*Standard errors are smaller for percentages greater than or less than 50 percent.

the sample reaches 2500, as Table 5.4 shows. To get the error down to 0.5 percent would require a sample size of 10,000.

The reader should now begin to understand how election forecasters can make accurate predictions using samples of a few thousand out of millions of voters. The huge size of the population has no effect on the precision of sample estimates. And a sample size of 2000 to 3000 is large enough to predict accurately all but the closest elections.

We hasten to add that 2000 to 3000 should not be regarded as *the* standard size for reliable sample results. Not only does sample size depend on factors other than precision, but necessary levels of precision also vary widely from one study to the next. At one extreme, the CPS requires a sample of some 50,000 housing units, a sample "large enough so that the sampling errors of the total estimates of unemployment are only about 0.1%" (Sudman, 1976:3). At the other extreme, thirty cases generally is regarded as minimally adequate for statistical data analysis, although most social researchers would probably recommend at least one hundred.

Sampling Design

The type of sampling design also affects decisions about sample size. Recall that one way of increasing precision other than selecting a larger sample is to use stratified rather than simple random sampling. In other words, for the same level of precision, a stratified random sample requires fewer cases than a simple random sample. A cluster sample, on the other hand, requires a somewhat larger number of cases for precision equal to that of a simple random sample. A nonmathematical explanation for these comparisons rests on the concept of heterogeneity.

Remember that stratified random sampling provides greater sampling efficiency (or precision) when the stratifying variable is related to the variable one is estimating. If it is related, much of the variation or heterogeneity in the estimated variable resides in differences between the strata, and each stratum tends to be relatively homogeneous. With respect to alcohol consumption, for example, there is much less variability among men or among women than between men and women. By sampling every stratum, the effect of stratified random sampling is to eliminate this *between* source of heterogeneity, leaving only the variation within the strata. And because of their homogeneity, each stratum requires a relatively small sample.

Although cluster sampling has the advantage of low cost, it lacks efficiency in precision. In two-stage cluster sampling, for example, there is variability both between and within the clusters. By taking a sample of clusters, the "between source" of heterogeneity that was eliminated in stratified sampling is still present. If the variability between clusters tends to be large compared with the variability within the clusters, then the sampling error could be considerable, depending on how many clusters are selected. (For this reason, we want clusters to be heterogeneous compared with differences between the clusters—just the opposite of the strategy in stratified sampling.) Furthermore, each stage in a multistage cluster design contributes a source of variability or error to the total sample; consequently, the more stages, the larger the total sampling error tends to be, and the larger the sample required for a given level of precision.

Available Resources

Each individual case requires an expenditure of available resources. Consequently, at some point, cost must enter into the equation for determining sample size. When a fixed amount of money and/or time has been allocated for a project, Sudman (1976:88–89) offers the following rule of thumb for survey research: Allocate one-half of both money and time to data collection (and the other half to data analysis). Once the data collection procedure is specified, the sample size can be determined on a time- and cost-per-case basis. That is, the number of cases will be equal to the total time for data collection divided by the time per case, or the total funds for data collection divided by the cost per case.

Number of Breakdowns Planned

The number of variables and variable categories into which the data are to be grouped and analyzed also must be taken into account in determining sample size. In general, the more breakdowns planned in the analysis—the more complex the relationships under investigation or the more distinct subcategories of separate interest—the larger the sample must be. Consider, for example, what happens when a sample of 1000 is divided into males/females, then into blacks/whites, then into people over/under 18 years of age, then into urban/rural residence. If we were interested in describing rural black young men, we might find that a breakdown of the 1000 cases looks something like this:

Sample	1000
Males	489
Black males	60
Young black males	20
Rural young black males	4

With just four cases available, the sample clearly would be too small for a reliable analysis of this particular subgroup. To avoid this kind of problem, it is important to estimate the number of breakdowns to be made during data analysis and to make sure that the total sample size will provide enough cases in each subcategory. If the requisite sample size turns out to be rather large, it might be more efficient to sample the relevant subcategories separately, as in stratified and quota sampling.

Final Notes on Sampling Errors and Generalizability

In sections on probability sampling and sample size considerations, we spoke repeatedly of sampling error—the deviation of a sample estimate from the true population value. The sampling error referred to in our discussions is random error, produced by the random selection of elements. Though unavoidable in sampling, this error can be estimated and reduced by increasing the size or efficiency of one's sample. There is, however, another type of sampling error, called **sample bias**,[10] which is nonrandom, difficult to detect, and often much more damaging to sample accuracy.

In probability sampling designs, the two most common sources of sample bias are **coverage error** due to incomplete sampling frames and **nonresponse bias** due to incomplete data collection. As an example of coverage error, we mentioned earlier that telephone directories provide inadequate sampling frames to the extent that they exclude the poor who cannot afford telephones and the more wealthy who tend to have unlisted numbers. The problem of nonresponse bias arises when, through refusals to cooperate, unreturned questionnaires, missing records, or some other means, the sample turns out to be a fraction of the number of cases originally selected for observation. The crux of this problem is that nonobservations tend to differ in systematic ways from observations. Thus in surveys, mail surveys in particular, highly educated respondents are more likely to cooperate than poorly educated ones. Also, those who feel most strongly about the topics or issues of a study are more likely to respond than those in the middle (see Box 5.1).

Obviously, the researcher should do everything possible to avoid these biases. With respect to nonresponse bias, this may entail several call-backs to not-at-home respondents, three or four mailings of questionnaires, or interview follow-ups of respondents not returning questionnaires. Despite such efforts, however, in virtually all surveys some respondents designated for the sample ultimately will not be included. With probability sampling, the greater the proportion of this nonresponse, the greater the likelihood of bias. Therefore, it is very important to pay attention to response rates. For interview surveys, a response rate of 85 percent or more is quite good; 70 percent is minimally adequate; below 70 percent there is a serious chance of bias. In questionnaire surveys, response rates tend to be about 20 percent lower than in comparable interview surveys. (For a further discussion of response rates, see chapter 8.)

This chapter has dealt exclusively with the issue of generalizing from samples to populations. As we have seen, the manner of selecting cases determines to whom and with what level of precision research results may be applied. Sample generalizability is the primary generalization issue addressed in social science research, especially survey studies, which are often called "sample surveys" because the sampling of units is such an integral part of the research design. Survey researchers are also largely responsible for the development of many of the sampling techniques discussed in this chapter. So it is no wonder that most of our examples came from survey studies and involved people as units.

However, the issue of generalizability is not limited to units of analysis, nor is the sampling of units solely the province of survey research. Generalizability pertains to all features of research, including the time of the study, the research setting, and the operational definitions. We might ask, for example, whether the same results would be obtained if a different set of questions were asked or if the study were conducted in a different place or at a different time of day or year. The social scientific ideal is to establish theoretical propositions that hold under all conditions—that do not pertain to any particular population, time, or setting. With this goal in mind, social researchers have no particular target population as the focus of their research. To establish the broadest possible generalizations, researchers use a variety of techniques in addition to random sampling, which we discuss in later chapters. These include replication (chapter 6), theoretical sampling (chapter 10), and triangulation (chapter 12).

Summary

Sampling is the process of selecting a subset of cases in order to draw conclusions about the entire set. Sampling is unavoidable given the scientific goal of generalization, and it requires special attention in social research given the inherent variability of social units of analysis. Sometimes sampling can yield more accurate information than "complete" enumerations of the population. Yet, even if this were never true, we would still sample because it is usually impossible for practical reasons to examine all cases, and observing a sample of cases is simply more efficient anyway: It saves time and money and can be as accurate as research purposes demand.

Prior to sampling, one must select the unit of analysis. Sampling then begins with a description of the target population, the collection of units about which one wishes to generalize. For sampling to be feasible, the target population should be defined by objective criteria that clearly indicate its limits of inclusion. Even then, there is often an imperfect fit between the target population and the sampling frame, which consists of either (a) a list of cases from which the sample is actually selected or (b) a rule defining membership that provides a basis for case selection.

The procedure for selecting a sample is called the sampling design. The major distinction among designs is between probability and nonprobability sampling. Probability sampling is based on a process of random selection, which gives each case in the population an equal chance of being included in the sample. This process, which is absent from nonprobability sampling, eliminates investigator bias in selecting cases and permits the application of mathematical probability theory for estimating sample accuracy.

Probability sampling designs include simple random sampling, stratified random sampling, cluster sampling, and systematic sampling. In simple random sampling, random selection from the entire population makes it equally possible to draw any combination of cases. The distribution of a statistical property for all possible combinations of random samples of a fixed size is called the sampling distribution. A given sample statistic differs from the estimated population value by an amount known as the sampling error; an index of the size of such errors in a given sampling distribution is called the standard error. In general, the larger the sample, the smaller the standard error. To take into account random sampling error, researchers use interval estimates, called confidence intervals, in making inferences from a sample statistic to its population parameter.

In stratified random sampling, the population is divided into strata and independent random samples are drawn from each stratum. The number of cases in each stratum of the sample may be either proportionate or disproportionate to the number of cases in the population. Stratifying improves sampling efficiency, provided that the stratifying variable is related to the variable under study and that the cost of stratifying is low compared with the cost of increasing sample size. It also may be used to increase the number of cases in certain variable categories that would prove too small if a simple random sample were drawn.

In cluster sampling, the population is divided into natural groupings or areas, called clusters, and a random sample of clusters is drawn. When this is done in stages, as it usually is, moving from larger to smaller clusters, it is referred to as multistage sampling. Clustering reduces the costs of interviewer travel and sampling frame construction, but it does so at a loss of sample precision. Systematic sampling, which often provides a reasonable approximation to simple random sampling, consists of selecting cases from an available list at a fixed interval after a random start.

Nonprobability sampling designs include convenience, purposive, and quota samples. Convenience sampling is a rubric for various nonrandom and unsystematic processes of case selection that offer no basis for generalizing. Purposive sampling involves the careful selection of typical cases or of cases that represent relevant dimensions of the population. Quota sampling allocates quotas of cases for various strata and then allows for the nonrandom selection of cases to fill the quotas. While this procedure has been abused in the past, it can be used effectively in combination with probability sampling and with tight controls on respondent selection.

Other sampling strategies have been devised when research goals require rigorous, systematic methods of case selection but conventional probability sampling methods are not feasible. If selection can be done in stages, using probability sampling at one stage and nonprobability sampling at another can reduce costs. For rare target populations, sampling may entail a process of referral. Network sampling asks respondents to identify members of the target population who are socially linked to the respondent in a specified way. Snowball sampling uses a chain of referrals, with initial contacts asked to name other members of the target population with particular characteristics, who are asked in turn to name others, and so on.

Factors affecting the choice of a sampling design include (1) the stage of research and data use, with research in later stages intended to provide accurate population description requiring the most sophisticated probability sampling designs; (2) available resources such as time, money, and personnel; and (3) the method of data collection. In general, the more heterogeneous the population, the greater the desired precision and available resources, and the larger the number of breakdowns planned during the data analysis, the larger the sample should be. Holding sample size constant, one will generally get the greatest precision with a stratified sample, followed by a simple random sample, and then a cluster sample. Finally, the quality of a sample ultimately depends not only on sample variability due to random selection but also on sample bias in the form of coverage error and nonresponse error.

Key Terms

population
sample
target population
sampling frame
sampling design
probability sampling
    simple random sampling
    stratified random sampling
    cluster sampling
    systematic sampling
random selection
    parameter
    statistic
    sampling distribution
    sampling error
    standard error
confidence interval
stratum

disproportionate stratified sampling
multistage sampling
primary sampling unit
probability proportionate to size sampling
sampling interval
nonprobability sampling
    convenience sampling
    purposive sampling
    quota sampling
network sampling
snowball sampling
heterogeneity
standard deviation
sampling fraction
sample bias
coverage error
nonresponse bias

Review Questions and Problems

1. Give three reasons for sampling.

2. Why is a sample sometimes more accurate than a census of the population?

3. What were the principal reasons for the failures of the *Literary Digest* presidential poll of 1936 and the Gallup presidential poll of 1948?

4. Describe the two-step process involved in population definition.

5. How does one go about constructing a sampling frame?

6. In judging sample quality, why do social researchers prefer to assess the quality of the sampling design rather than sample representativeness?

7. Briefly distinguish between probability and nonprobability sampling.

8. When is case selection biased? How do researchers meet the requirement of random selection?

9. What is the defining property of a simple random sample?

10. How can one increase the probable accuracy of a simple random sample?

11. When is stratified random sampling more efficient than simple random sampling?

12. When is it advantageous, or even necessary, to employ *dis*proportionate stratified random sampling?

13. Explain the difference between a single-stage cluster sample and a stratified random sample.

14. What are the primary reasons for using cluster sampling?

15. Assuming relatively homogeneous clusters, how can one reduce sampling error in a cluster sampling design?

16. Explain how sampling based on probability proportionate to size solves the problem of clusters that vary widely in size.

17. Describe the principal advantage of systematic sampling. What is the potential problem with this method?

18. When is nonprobability sampling justified?

19. What is the difference between convenience and purposive sampling?

20. What is the difference between quota sampling and stratified random sampling?

21. What are some of the potential biases in quota sampling?

22. How can one combine probability and nonprobability sampling within the same sampling design? Why would the researcher choose to do this?

23. What sampling strategies are used to sample "rare" populations—subpopulations that comprise very small proportions of the larger population?

24. List four considerations affecting the selection of a sampling design and briefly indicate *how* each affects design selection.

25. Identify the five factors to consider in determining sample size. How does each factor affect the decision about sample size?

26. Because of your developing expertise about social research, someone asks you, "What proportion of the population should I sample to give me adequate precision?" How would you respond to this question?

27. What are the two most common sources of sample bias?

28. Indicate the type of sample you think is most appropriate for each of the following research objectives, and state the rationale for your choice.

    a. A study of the career plans of sociology majors at your college or university

    b. An in-depth study of the gay community in Boston to determine their social and psychological characteristics

    c. A national survey of Democrats' favored candidates for the next presidential election

29. This exercise will help familiarize you with some types of probability sampling. First, using the A section of the latest issue of your campus telephone directory as a starting point, draw up a sampling frame composed of the first fifty names listed.

    a. *Simple random sample.* Select a random sample of ten names using the Research Randomizer (http://www.randomizer.org/). List all the random numbers you select and then list the ten names in your sample. Repeat this procedure in drawing a random sample of five names.

    b. *Stratified systematic sample.* Divide the names in your sampling frame into strata on the basis of gender. Begin with a random start, and indicate the random number in each stratum with which you began. Then select a 1/5 systematic sample within each stratum. List the names that you obtain.

30. Suppose you would like to do a survey of students on your campus to find out how much time on the average they spend studying per week. You obtain from the registrar a list of all students currently enrolled and draw your sample from this list.

    a. What is your sampling frame?

b. What is your target population?

c. Explain how you would draw a simple random sample for this study.

d. Assume that the registrar's list also contains information about each student's major. One then could select a stratified random sample, stratifying on major. What main benefit can result from using a stratified random sample instead of a simple random sample? Would you expect this benefit to be obtained by stratifying on major? Explain.

e. How might you obtain a cluster sample? When should you consider using this type of sampling design?

f. Which type of sampling design is most appropriate for this research problem? Explain.

31. Now you want to find out the same information (as in question 30) for all college students in the state of Massachusetts. To do so you obtain a list of all four-year and community colleges in the state. As a first step you draw a random sample of colleges. Then you get a list of students enrolled in each of the colleges you selected in the first step. Finally, you draw a random sample of students from these lists.

a. What type of sample is this?

b. A significant proportion of students in four-year colleges go to a few large schools in the state (e.g., University of Massachusetts, Boston University, Northeastern University). If you were to give each school in your first stage of sampling an equal chance of being selected, you might not obtain any of the larger schools (because there are more smaller than larger schools). This could create problems in obtaining an accurate estimate of the time students spend studying, since larger schools may require more (or less?) work. How would you resolve this problem while still drawing a probability sample?

32. Following the 1994 Senatorial race in California, an article in the *Los Angeles Times* pointed out that the polls are not as reliable as media portrayals would suggest. The author gave several examples of seemingly contradictory poll results in pre-election surveys; for example, one poll had Senator Diane Feinstein ahead of Representative Mike Huffington by 10 points and another had her trailing by 2. Suppose someone asks you to explain how this could occur. Assuming that all the polls were telephone surveys that used probability sampling, identify and briefly describe three possible sources of sampling error in the polls.

33. Refer to the article from *Social Forces* that you used in question 29 of chapter 4.

a. Describe the sampling procedures employed in the study reported in this article. Did the authors use one of the sampling designs reported in this chapter? If so, which one?

b. What is the target population? What is the sampling frame? Does the sampling frame provide a good fit with the target population?

c. What particular sampling problems (e.g., incomplete lists, missing cases, nonresponses), if any, did the authors encounter? How were these problems dealt with?

NOTES

1. The U.S. Constitution mandates a complete enumeration of the population every ten years. It therefore would require a constitutional amendment to replace the Census with a survey of the U.S. population. The primary purpose of the Census is to reapportion seats in the U.S. House of Representatives. Therefore, it would require a very large sample to provide detailed information on small geographic areas, as the Census does.

2. The lottery method also has proven inadequate on occasion due to insufficient mixing. Two dramatic examples of this problem are the military draft lotteries of 1940 and 1970. Statistical analyses convincingly have shown that both lotteries were biased, apparently due to the failure of physical mixing to achieve randomness (Fienberg, 1971). The 1970 lottery, based on birthdays, was set up in the following way: 366 cylindrical capsules with rounded ends were used; slips of paper with the January dates were inserted in thirty-one capsules and placed in a large, square wooden box; the February dates were inserted and then placed in the box and mixed with the January dates, and this procedure was repeated for each of the remaining months, in turn; the box then was shut and shaken several times; finally, the 366 capsules were poured from the box into a large bowl, from whence they were drawn. When the lottery drawing sequence was analyzed, it was shown that the sequence was not random, but rather a reflection of "the order in which capsules were placed in the wooden box during the initial mixing procedure" (Fienberg, 1971:260). As a result, those with birthdays in the later months of the year had lower lottery numbers, hence were more likely to be drafted, than those with birthdays in the early months of the year.

3. This example is modeled after presentations by Morris James Slonim (1957, 1960) and Isidor Chein (1981).

4. If each one of a set of events is equally likely to occur, then the probability of any one event occurring is defined as 1 divided by the number of events. Assuming a perfect coin, for example, we have two events—a head and a tail—with the probability of one event (say, a head) in a single flip equal to 1/2.

5. Basically, this is accomplished by a weighting procedure that compensates for over-sampling in some strata. The necessary mathematical formulas can be found in Leslie Kish (1965).

6. The following example illustrates how the probabilities are equal. Suppose that the total number of students in the population is 500,000 and that 100 schools are selected. The probability of selecting a school A, with 1000 students, is $100 \times 1000/500,000$, or .20. The probability of selecting a school B, with 500 students, is $100 \times 500/500,000$, or .10. If fifty students are selected from each school, the probability of selecting a student from school A is .20 x 50/1000, or .01, which is the same as the probability of selecting a student from school B ($.10 \times 50/500 = .01$).

7. Another problem with cluster sampling is that, except for rare cases in which clusters are equal in size, the probabilities of case selection may vary widely from cluster to cluster. Consequently, estimates of population characteristics require some rather complex statistical solutions, which are beyond the scope of this book.

8. Richard Appelbaum (1990), who contends that counting the homeless is an intractable problem and that "every effort is likely to produce an undercount," criticized the Rossi street survey on two counts. First, since the homeless were self-identified, there is the strong possibility of response bias—either through avoidance of interviewers, refusals to be interviewed, or unwillingness to admit to being homeless. Second, the survey reached only the visible homeless, which excludes the sizeable number of peo-

ple in rooming houses, jails, and halfway houses, as well as people riding trains and buses.

9. In spite of the potential bias, studies of noninstitutional hidden populations are rare. Indeed, "classic studies of deviance have depended largely or wholly on populations captured in the nets of institutions of social control" (Watters and Biernacki, 1989:417).

10. These two types of error—random sampling error and sample bias—are analogous to random and systematic measurement error.

II

■ ■

METHODS OF
DATA COLLECTION

The chapters in this section cover the four most distinctive and widely used approaches to social research: experiments, surveys, field research, and research using available data. Several factors influence an investigator's selection of an approach: the nature of the research problem, research goals, available resources, and disciplinary and personal preferences. All too often the choice is bound to a particular theoretical perspective, which makes the researcher unduly committed to one means of making observations. Indeed, each approach has developed largely independently of the others and, as a consequence, tends to have its own distinctive terminology for describing various features of the method. This is reflected, for example, in the terms applied to units of analysis, which are labeled variously as "subjects" (experiments), "respondents" (surveys), "informants" (field research), and "items" (available data research).

Once a given approach is selected, it has an overriding effect on nearly every other facet of the research, from measurement and sampling to data analysis. Thus, even though we already have dealt broadly with elements of research design, in the following chapters we will return again and again to design issues. In fact, we devote whole chapters to technical design features of experiments (chapter 7) and surveys (chapter 9). Otherwise, our principal aim in the four main chapters (6, 8, 10, and 11) is to describe each approach's unique process of executing a study. Then, in chapter 12, we present some strategies for using a combination of methods and approaches. Throughout most of this section we assume the goal of basic social research—to understand the social world. In the final chapter (13), we examine a form of applied social research called evaluation research, whose aim is to assess social programs and policies.

6

✔

Experimentation

People readily associate the term *experiment* with scientific research. Typically they have read about or conducted experiments in elementary and high school science courses. Many have learned that experimentation is the hallmark of "the scientific method." In fact, we have found that some students refer to any scientific study as an experiment. This usage of the term, however, is technically incorrect and can be misleading. Much of social research is nonexperimental; the word "experiment" denotes studies with several distinctive features.

The key features of the experimental approach are manipulation and control. To test hypotheses, the experimenter deliberately introduces changes into the environment of subjects and observes or measures the effects of the changes. Because greater control is exercised over the conditions of observation than in any other research strategy, experiments more effectively eliminate the possibility of extraneous variables offering alternative interpretations of research findings. For this reason, experimental studies long have been regarded as the optimal way to test causal hypotheses. Even when a "true" experiment is impractical or impossible and some other approach must be used, the logic of experimentation serves as a standard by which other research strategies are judged.

In this chapter we introduce the essential features and causal logic of experiments as found in social research. We outline the process of "staging" an experiment and then discuss the social nature of experiments, including ways to prevent this from adversely affecting their scientific value. Finally, we discuss some variants of the experimental approach: experiments conducted in natural settings, the application of experimental design to social surveys, and the use of units of analysis other than individuals.

The Logic of Experimentation

The main reason for doing an experiment is to test a hypothesis that one variable affects another variable. Thus all experiments possess certain basic requirements that permit strong inferences about cause and effect. Research designs that fill these requirements are called true experimental designs; those that do not, which are discussed in chapter 7, are called pre-experimental or quasi-experimental designs. In this section we focus on the logic of experimentation by first identifying those essential features that make true experiments a model for testing causal relationships, and then we relate these features to the criteria for inferring causality.

Testing Causal Relations

The basic features of an experimental design are nicely illustrated by a simplified version of Ellis Page's study (1958) of teacher comments and subsequent student performance. Page wanted to determine whether teacher comments written on test papers would motivate students to improve their scores on the next test. (This seems like a relevant question to study in view of the hours teachers spend writing comments on students' papers!) To conduct the experiment, teacher "Smith" gave one of her classes a scheduled objective test and scored the tests in her usual way, assigning grades A through F. Then she assigned the test papers, by tossing a coin, to one of two piles. One pile of papers received the experimental treatment, a specified comment that depended on the letter grade, as follows (Page, 1958:174):

A: Excellent! Keep it up.

B: Good work. Keep at it.

C: Perhaps try to do still better?

D: Let's bring this up.

F: Let's raise this grade!

Papers assigned to the second pile received no comment, providing a control group. The effect of the comments on student performance was judged by comparing the scores of students in the two groups on a subsequent test given and scored in the usual way. Results showed that the group that had received the written comments scored higher on the second test than the group that had received no comments.

What basic features of an experimental design are illustrated in the foregoing experiment? A *manipulated* independent variable (whether or not the teacher wrote comments on the first test) is *followed by* a measured dependent variable (student performance on the second test). There are two groups: One receives the experimental **treatment**, and another, the control, does not receive the treatment. Except for this experimental manipulation, the treatment and control groups are treated *exactly alike* to avoid introducing extraneous variables and their effects. Finally, subjects (or in this case their first test papers) are assigned to one or the other group *randomly*.

How do these features meet the requirements of causal inference? Although we can never prove beyond all doubt that two variables (say, X and Y) are causally related, recall that certain types of empirical evidence are regarded as essential for causal statements: (1) association (i.e., evidence that X and Y vary together in a way predicted by the hypothesis); (2) direction of influence (evidence that X affected Y rather than Y affected X); and (3) the elimination of plausible rival explanations (evidence that variables other than X did not cause the observed change in Y). The first two kinds of evidence show that X could have affected Y; the third kind shows that the relation between X and Y is nonspurious—that other variables are not responsible for the observed effects. Let us refer back to our simplification of Page's experiment to see how these types of evidence were provided.

1. *Association.* It was found that the independent variable, teacher comments, was associated with the dependent variable, scores on the subsequent test, in the manner hypothesized. That is, the treatment group, which received comments, scored higher on the test than the control group, which received no comments.

2. *Direction of influence.* Evidence that the independent variable (X) influenced the dependent variable (Y), and not the other way around, is based on time order in experiments: Y cannot be the cause of X if it occurred after X. In the above experiment, we know that the subsequent test scores (Y) could not have caused or affected the teacher comments (X), because the experimenter made sure that the comments occurred first.

3. *Elimination of rival explanations.* What might be plausible reasons why one group of students would score higher than another group on a test? Personal qualities such as intelligence and motivation might have an effect; experiences such as having a cold on the test day, missing breakfast, or being in love also might affect individual scores. These extraneous variables are controlled by random assignment of persons to the treatment and control groups. **Random assignment** means that the procedure by which subjects are assigned (in this case, by tossing a coin) ensures that each subject has an equal chance of being in either group. By virtue of random assignment, individual characteristics or experiences that might confound the results will be about evenly distributed between the two groups. Thus, the number of students who are bright or dull, motivated or unmotivated, fully nourished or hungry, in love or not in love, and so forth, should be about the same in each group.

In addition to controlling pre-experimental differences through random assignment, the researcher makes every attempt to ensure that both groups are treated exactly alike during the experiment except for the experimental treatment that one group receives. In the Page experiment, the tests given, time of testing, and intervening classroom experiences were the same for both groups. Examples of violations of this principle would have been if the treatment and control groups had not had the same teacher or if students had been told that they were in an experimental or control group.

In an airtight experimental design, there is only one rival explanation: The results could have occurred by chance. This would mean that the process of randomly assigning persons to the experimental and control groups resulted, by chance, in an unequal distribution between the groups of variables related to test performance, such as intelligence, interest in school, and health. The lower test scores of the control group in the Page experiment, for example, could have resulted from the chance assignment of fewer of the brighter students to this group than to the treatment group.

To assess the likelihood that the results of an experiment could have occurred by chance, experimenters use a **test of statistical significance**. Recall from chapter 3 that significance tests indicate the likelihood or probability that an association is due to random processes. Such tests express this probability in decimal form. So, when we read that the results of an experiment were found to be significant at the .05 level, this means that only about 5 percent of the time, or 5 times in 100, would differences this large between the experimental and control groups occur by chance when the experimental variable actually has no effect. With such a low probability it would be reasonable to rule out prior differences uncontrolled by the randomization process as a plausible rival explanation of the experimental results. On the other hand, if the results were not found to be statistically significant, it would not be reasonable to rule out differences due to chance assignment and we could not have much confidence that the experimental treatment caused the effects. In short, a statistical test of significance assesses the likelihood that the observed difference between the groups is real (significant) and not of a magnitude that would occur frequently by chance.[1]

Matching and Random Assignment

Some researchers attempt to eliminate prior differences between groups by **matching** subjects on characteristics that logically seem to be related to the experimental outcome. If, for example, an experimenter wanted to learn which of two methods of teaching Russian is most effective, potential students for the two language methods groups might be matched on variables such as grade-point average and verbal aptitude test scores. For each student with, say, above-average verbal aptitude and average grades, a second student who scored very nearly the same on the two variables would have to be found. Then, each matched pair would be split so that one of the pair would be in each group, thus ensuring that the composition of the groups would be highly similar on the matching variables.

The reader should note carefully that matching should be used in conjunction with and *not* as a substitute for randomization. Matching is a powerful technique whose object is similar to that of stratification in random sampling: to increase the efficiency of the experimental design by creating treatment groups that are similar with respect to characteristics related to the dependent variable. However, matching on some characteristics does not guarantee an equal distribution on other possibly relevant extraneous variables. For example, in the study of language teaching methods, another variable that might affect the learning of a foreign language is auditory discrimination, the ability to discriminate similar sounds. Only with randomization can one be sure of the approximate equivalence on *all* extraneous variables, including those unknown to the researcher.

One problem with matching is that researchers do not always know what variables to match or control for. Another problem is that, unless the pool from which the subjects are drawn is extremely large, it may be difficult to find enough pairs of subjects who scored alike on the relevant variables to make up similar matched groups. In other words, it may be difficult to form treatment groups large enough to produce reliable results. This is especially the case when more than one or two matching variables are involved.

There are several ways to assign subjects randomly to experimental and control groups. The method previously mentioned was tossing a coin for each subject; "heads" meant one group and "tails" meant the other. For experiments with more than two groups we recommend using a computer program or table of random numbers. The important point is that "random" does not mean haphazard; it is a technical term which means that every case has an equal and independent chance of being assigned to any experimental condition. If matching procedures are used, one should first match subjects on relevant variables and then randomly assign the members of each matched pair to different groups.

A final word of caution relates to the difference between the random *assignment* of subjects in experiments and the random *selection* of cases in probability sampling. Although both processes invoke randomness, they occur at different points in the research process and serve different purposes. Sampling occurs first, for example, when a pool of subjects is selected for an experiment; although random sampling facilitates inferences from sample to population, it is seldom used in experiments. Random assignment occurs after the sample has been selected, when subjects are assigned to different experimental groups; its function is to make groups approximately equal on all uncontrolled extraneous variables, and it is an essential aspect of true experiments.

Internal and External Validity

The Page study possessed all the basic requirements of a true experiment:

- Random assignment
- Manipulation of the independent variable
- Measurement of the dependent variable
- At least one comparison or control group (i.e., at least two groups, experimental and comparison)
- (Excluding experimental manipulations) the constancy of conditions across groups

Experiments with these minimum characteristics, which provide relatively sound evidence of a causal relationship, will be generally high in **internal validity**. We will have more to say about this in chapter 7; suffice it to say here that an experiment is internally valid to the extent that it rules out the possibility that extraneous variables, rather than the manipulated independent variable, are responsible for the observed outcome of the study. As we saw in the Page study, experiments eliminate rival explanations associated with extraneous variables in two ways. First, effects of prior differences between subjects, such as personal qualities and experiences, are "neutralized" by randomly assigning subjects to treatment and control groups, thus initially ensuring approximate equivalence of the groups. Second, aside from the introduction of the experimental variable, treatment and control groups are treated exactly alike, thus ensuring equivalence of the groups during the experiment.

A related concern is that experiments have **external validity**. This is basically a question of generalizability, or what the experimental results mean outside of the particular context of the experiment. For example, regarding Page's study of teacher comments and student performance, we might question whether the same results would be obtained with different classes, teacher comments, subject matter, or age groups. At this point we will describe the Page study (1958) more completely, as it also provides an excellent example of an experiment high in external validity.

For his experiment, Page selected seventy-four teachers at random from twelve secondary schools (grades 7–12) in three school districts. These teachers were given

detailed instructions in how to carry out the experiment, including the random selection of one of her or his classes for the experiment. This procedure ensured that
the experiment would include a great variety of subject matter as well as students
at every grade level. Over 1200 students participated, unaware that they were experimental subjects.

In addition to the "no comments" group (the control group) and the "specified
comments" group that received the comments listed in our earlier discussion, a third
group, called the "free comments" group, received whatever comments the teachers felt were appropriate in the circumstances. Random assignment of the initial set
of test papers to one of the three groups was actually carried out by means of a specially marked die. The "specified comments" group scored significantly higher than
the "no comments" group on the subsequent set of tests, with the "free comments"
group scoring highest of all. Analysis of the data showed consistent results regardless of the particular class, school, or grade level (grades 7–12). Because of the consistency of the experimental results in different settings, with different teachers and
students, we can say the experiment was high in external validity.

Sampling in Experiments

The relatively high external validity of the Page study is rare in experiments. External validity is usually very limited, especially with regard to generalizing from
sample to population. Because experimental manipulation often involves a laboratory setting and/or elaborate staging, it is usually impractical either to sample subjects over wide areas or to utilize a large number of subjects. As a consequence, experimenters tend to use small samples drawn from readily available populations. In
fact, because most experimentation is done in universities, very frequently the subjects are either college students (over 70 percent of published studies in some
areas; Higbee, Millard, and Folkman, 1982; Sears, 1986), volunteers, or—worse
yet—college students who have volunteered. Differences between college students
and people in general would include socioeconomic level, age, occupational goals,
education, and interests. Differences between volunteers and nonvolunteers are also
considerable (see Rosenthal and Rosnow, 1969).

With such circumscribed samples, generalizations from any one experiment are
severely limited. Experimenters, however, have tended to rationalize this limitation.
Some contend that human nature is universal; therefore, demographic characteristics should have little or no effect on subjects' reactions in the experimental situation. Men will react the same as women, old people will react the same as young
people, someone from New England will react the same as someone from the south-
west, and so forth. Others argue that the generalizability of experimental outcomes
depends primarily on the meaning subjects impart to the experimental stimulation
and the responses they make (Berkowitz and Donnerstein, 1982). As long as their
interpretation of events is the same, subjects' laboratory reactions will parallel their
behavior in other settings. Some investigators (e.g., Festinger, 1959; Oakes, 1972;
Mook, 1983) also maintain that sampling considerations are of minor importance
as long as the goal is to test causal relationships, which is the main task of experiments. In an experimental study of altruism, for example, the primary concern

should be designing a valid test of a hypothesis, such as the positive effect of a good mood on helping behavior. The researcher would, of course, like to be able to generalize to a variety of persons, settings, and helping behaviors, but this is deemed less important than simply demonstrating the existence of the effect of a good mood on helping. Once this causal relationship is established for a given sample of subjects, the researcher can address, through subsequent research, the issue of whether the relationship extends to other, unsampled populations and to other settings and measures of helping.

Thus, experimenters often skirt the issue of population generality. They choose cases for convenience because this enables them to gain the necessary control over subjects required for experimentation, and they either overgeneralize or deemphasize the importance of generalizing across subject populations. Yet, despite the trade-off for experimental control and other justifications for convenience sampling, this is a major weakness of experimentation. Time and again, research has shown that the nature of the sample can have a direct impact on the results of a study. If, therefore, an all-male or all-female sample is used, a relatively common practice in experiments, it should not be assumed that the findings will generalize to the population as a whole. Indeed, gender differences have been found repeatedly in some areas of research (cf. Carlson, 1971; Hall, 1984; Eagly, 1987).

With regard to social psychology's overreliance on college student subjects, David Sears (1986:515) has gone so far as to say that "this narrow data base may have unwittingly led us to a portrait of human nature that describes rather accurately the behavior of American college students in an academic context but distorts human social behavior more generally." Sears recommends conducting more experiments with adult samples, but we would go even further. If the experimenter has specified a target population of persons or settings, then probability sampling should be used if at all feasible. And even if the experimenter has no specific target group in mind, it is still desirable to utilize probability sampling or purposive sampling for heterogeneity. According to inductive logic, the broader the range of cases included in the sample, the more generalizable the findings. Thus, the inferences that could be drawn from a study with a homogeneous sample of college sophomores enrolled in introductory psychology are far more restricted than the inferences possible from a probability sample of people from the town where the college is located. One might therefore draw the latter sample, not because it is meaningful to generalize to all residents of the town, but because the greater heterogeneity among town residents permits stronger inferences about generalizability.

Convenience samples of American college students also constitute a very narrow cultural base from which to generalize about human social behavior (Fish, 2000). Recent research in social psychology has shown that robust findings from research in American and Western cultures may not apply to non-Western cultures (see, for example, Choi, Nisbett, and Norenzayan, 1999). Therefore, to further increase external validity, more experimental research needs to be carried out in non-Western cultures.

Finally, the issue of external validity applies not only to samples of subjects but also to experimental settings, observers, and experimenters and to the time of the study. Because all of these aspects limit the external validity of individual experiments, the usual strategy for increasing the generalizability of experimental findings is **replication**. That is, the experiment is repeated—by the same or another investigator who conducts the research at a different time, in a different setting or with slightly different procedures, or with a different sample of subjects. Indeed, the strongest argument for generality is that widely varying experimental tests have produced similar results. (A technique called meta-analysis, discussed in chapter 12, enables researchers to synthesize and summarize the results of numerous studies addressing the same research question, thereby providing systematic evidence of external validity.)

Staging Experiments

Experiments are most frequently conducted in laboratory settings to which the experimenter brings subjects to have them participate in some individual or social activities. Planning and carrying out a laboratory experiment is much like producing a play. There are "scripts" to write and rewrite; a sequence of "scenes," each contributing something vital to the production; a "cast" of experimental assistants to recruit and train; "props" and "special effects"; and "rehearsals." And once the stage is set, the experimenter must publicize the experiment and sell potential subjects on participation, for without an audience there can be no play.

In writing a play the playwright must consider how each scene will contribute to the success of the play; likewise a researcher designing an experiment must consider how each part of the experiment will contribute to the entire production. Figure 6.1 shows the key points in planning and conducting an experiment. The main parts are (1) introduction to the experiment, (2) manipulation of the independent variable, (3) measurement of the dependent variable, and (4) concluding activities, which usually include a debriefing and sometimes a postexperimental interview. To illustrate these parts, we first summarize an experiment and then refer back to it as we describe each part.

An Example: Who Will Intervene?

Why do bystanders sometimes fail to aid people immediately in crisis situations? This was the question that social psychologists John Darley and Bibb Latané asked after the tragic murder of a woman named Kitty Genovese in New York City in 1964. Trying to understand how 38 of her neighbors failed to come to her aid in time to thwart her attacker, Darley and Latané (1968) hypothesized that the more bystanders who witness an emergency, the less likely it is that any one bystander will come to the victim's assistance and the greater the amount of time that will elapse before intervention.[2] The setting was a simulated group discussion where the experimental subject witnessed (over an intercom system) and believed others to be witnessing an apparent epileptic seizure of one of the discussants.

Subjects were men and women enrolled in introductory psychology courses at New York University. The subjects participated to fulfill part of a class requirement, but were not told the nature of the experiment before reporting to the labo-

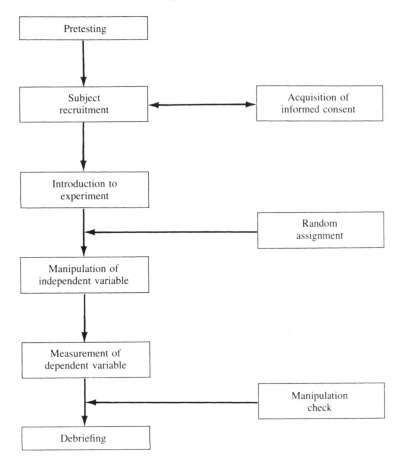

FIGURE 6.1. Key points in planning and conducting an experiment.

ratory. On arrival they were met by an assistant to the experimenter who led them down a corridor to a small room, seated them, and had them fill out a background information form. Each subject was then given headphones with a microphone attached and was instructed to listen for further directions. Over the intercom system the experimenter stated that the research involved the personal problems of college students and that, because of the personal nature of the discussion in which he or she would be participating, measures had been taken to minimize embarrassment for the students and to protect their privacy. First, anonymity would be preserved by their physical separation. (In reality, the separation permitted tape-recorded simulation of other subjects' participation and of the emergency.) Second, the experimenter would not be listening to the discussion but would obtain their reactions afterward. (This explanation permitted the experimenter's absence from the scene of the emergency.)

The experimenter went on to say that some organization of the discussion was necessary and that each person in turn would present his problems to the group.

Next, each person in turn would respond to the others' remarks, with further discussion at the end. Each person's microphone would be on for two minutes and then would automatically shut off, allowing only one person to be heard at one time. (These instructions ensured that the subjects would realize two things at the time of the "emergency": Only the "victim's" microphone was on, and they had no way to determine what the other discussants were doing.)

The simulated discussion then began. The "victim" spoke first and, among other problems, mentioned a proneness to seizures. Then the other "participants" and the subject spoke. In the second round of the discussion, the "victim" made several comments and then, after about seventy seconds, began in a distressed and somewhat incoherent voice to ask for help, because he was having a seizure. After 125 seconds the "victim's" speech was cut off. The length of time it took the subject to report the emergency was measured from the start of the apparent epileptic fit.

The number of other people the subject believed to be in the group discussion was the major independent variable. The discussion groups (three treatment conditions) consisted of two persons (the subject and the "victim"), three persons, or six persons. The major dependent variable was the length of time from the onset of the seizure until the subject left the room. If the subject did not leave the room in six minutes, the experiment was ended.

Subjects who left the room before six minutes had elapsed found the experimental assistant seated in the hall. As soon as the emergency was reported, or at the end of six minutes, debriefing began. The real purpose of the experiment was then explained and the subject's emotional reactions discussed. Then, the subject was asked to complete a questionnaire and several personality trait scales.

Briefly, results showed that the number of discussants believed to be participating strongly affected subjects' reporting of the incident. All subjects in the two-person groups reported the emergency, with approximately 80 percent of those in the three-person groups and 62 percent of those in the six-person groups reporting. In regard to speed of response, subjects in the three-person groups reported about as quickly as those in the two-person groups; the small difference obtained was not statistically significant. However, subjects in the six-person groups took significantly longer to report.

The Darley and Latané experiment provides an excellent example of the work and planning involved in staging an experiment. The subject is brought into the setting where the production will take place. Appropriate "props" have been prepared and are in place: desk, chair, headphones, microphone, background information form, prerecorded tapes, chair in hallway, and additional scales and a questionnaire. There is a cast of characters. In addition to the experimenter and persons clearly perceived by subjects to be assistants to the experimenter, frequently there are also "confederates," or persons who appear to be subjects participating in the experiment but who are actually persons trained by the experimenter to play the subject role in order to affect the real subject in some way. The Darley and Latané experiment had a cast consisting of the experimenter's assistant, the experimenter, and confederates posing as subjects. (In this experiment the subject's only contact with the experimenter and confederates was through the tapes.) The cast carefully follows a script memorized in advance; only the subject is free to vary his or her behavior, some measure of which is the dependent variable. Every effort is made to ensure that the same "play" is presented to each subject in order to preserve internal validity. (For a further description of Darley and Latané's program of research on bystander intervention, see Box 6.1.)

BOX 6.1

External Validity and the Social Inhibition of Helping

The epileptic seizure experiment was part of a program of research carried out by social psychologists Bibb Latané and John Darley (1970) on bystander intervention in emergencies. The program consisted of a series of experiments, each designed to examine the kinds of factors that influence a person's decision to help or not to help another. A description of additional experiments by Latané and Darley will show how successive experimentation can increase external validity as it extends our knowledge of a social phenomenon.

Latané and Darley believed that a key factor in determining whether a bystander will intervene in an emergency is the presence of other bystanders. They hypothesized that as the number of bystanders increases, any one bystander will be less likely to *notice* an emergency incident, less likely to *interpret* it as an emergency, and less likely to *intervene* or take action. In ambiguous situations, which most emergencies are, people tend to look to others to gauge their reactions. Thus, others' apparent lack of concern and inaction will inhibit helping. When others are present, one also runs the risk of embarrassment by misinterpreting the situation. Moreover, the costs for not helping are reduced because one feels less personally responsible for taking action.

In their initial test of this explanation, Latané and Darley had subjects fill out questionnaires in a waiting room either alone or in the presence of two strangers. As the subjects worked, smoke was piped into the room through a wall vent. The experimenters, observing subjects' reactions through a one-way mirror, found that the majority of subjects who were alone noticed the smoke in less than five seconds and reported it to the experimenter in less than two minutes; subjects in the presence of others took an average of twenty seconds to notice, and most failed to report before the six-minute experimental period had ended. In a postexperimental interview, the researchers also found that many of the latter subjects had interpreted the smoke as a nondangerous event—that is, as something other than fire. The "smoke" was explained variously as "steam or air-conditioning vapors," "smog, purposely introduced to simulate an urban environment," and "truth gas."

A second experiment, involving a woman in distress, was similar in design to the smoke-filled-room study. After setting subjects to work on a questionnaire, a female researcher exited the waiting room through a curtained doorway to work next door in her office. Four minutes later she could be heard climbing up on a chair (to reach a book) and then crashing to the floor and screaming as the chair fell over. She then cried, "Oh, my God, my foot . . . I . . . I . . . can't move . . . it. Oh, my ankle, I . . . can't . . . can't . . . get . . . this thing off . . . me." This was followed by moaning and struggling for about two minutes until she limped out of her office door. The main dependent variable was whether subjects intervened to help the victim: 70 percent of the alone subjects did, but in only 40 percent of the pairs of strangers did either person offer help to the injured woman.

Besides these two studies and the epileptic seizure study, Latané and Darley conducted several other experiments on the social inhibition of helping, each producing similar findings. These experiments utilized a wide range of emergency situations. The situations varied in their seriousness. Some, such as the smoke-filled room, involved danger to the subject, while others, such as the fall and the seizure, involved danger to the victim. The experiments also utilized a range of subject populations. In addition to the above experiments in which male and female college students participated, other studies included men and women from the general public. Finally, Latané and Darley performed field experiments as well as the laboratory experiments reported here. Thus, the external validity of the basic finding, which would be low in any one experiment, was made impressively high by a succession of studies that varied in their settings, procedures, measures, and samples.

In the decade following the publication of Latané and Darley's research, more than fifty studies were performed on bystander intervention in emergencies. About 90 percent of these showed that the presence of others inhibits helping (Latané and Nida, 1981). This research not only further documented an important social phenomenon; it also extended our knowledge by refining our theoretical understanding and by identifying some conditions under which the effect is reduced or eliminated. It is now clear, for example, that the presence of others is much less inhibiting when the emergency nature of the situation is made less ambiguous.

Subject Recruitment and Acquisition of Informed Consent

Before the start of the "production," subjects must be recruited and the investigator must obtain the subjects' informed consent to participate. As is typical of experiments, Darley and Latané's subjects were a convenience sample of college students who participated to fulfill a course requirement. Frequently, also, subjects volunteer or are paid for their participation. Informed consent, which we discuss in chapter 16, is an ethical guideline requiring that subjects learn about foreseeable risks and discomforts before agreeing to participate in an experiment. Nowadays, to ensure subjects' freedom of choice to participate, subjects are given an informed consent form that (a) explains the experimental procedures and potential risks and benefits to the participants or to others and (b) informs them that their participation is voluntary and that they have the right to leave the experiment at any time without penalty.

Introduction to the Experiment

The first "scene" of an experiment consists of some sort of introduction to the study. Basically, this involves an explanation of the purpose or nature of the research, together with instructions to the subject. In the bystander intervention study, subjects were told that the research involved the personal problems of college students, and that to avoid embarrassment they would carry on a discussion with other students who were physically separated from them. Then they were told how the discussion would proceed.

It is essential that the first scene have enough impact on the subject to arouse interest. Obviously, if the subject is not paying attention to the directions or to the events being staged, experimental "findings" will be worthless. The explanation of the research purpose also must make sense to the subject; that is, it must be understandable and believable. This is especially important because the explanation often is intended to deceive the subject, through a **cover story**, as to the real nature of the research. Although this practice raises ethical questions, many investigators believe it is necessary because subjects will often try to guess the hypothesis and sometimes even try to "help" the experimenter by behaving in ways consistent with the guessed hypothesis. A cover story may prevent this preoccupation with the true purpose of the study. Also, without deception some topics probably could not be explored at all. Think, for example, how the behavior of the subjects in the Darley and Latané study would have differed had they known that the experimenter was really interested in their willingness to intervene in an emergency. Still, deception should be used only if it is essential to the study and justified by its importance, and only then if it does not conceal possible risks or discomforts that would affect subjects' willingness to participate. (See chapter 16 for a further discussion of deception in social research.)

The Experimental Manipulation

The manipulation of the independent variable may be thought of as the second scene of the experiment. This is the point at which some set of stimuli is introduced that serves as an operational definition of the researcher's independent variable and to which the subject is expected to respond. The major independent variable in the foregoing study was the size of the simulated discussion group. There were three levels of the independent variable or three conditions to which subjects were assigned randomly: the two-person condition, the three-person condition, and the six-person condition. (Random assignment may occur at any time before the experimental manipulation.) The group size was manipulated by means of an assistant's comments pertaining to the size of the group and by the number of voices heard over the earphones.

A major concern in experiments is the possible meanings that subjects may attribute to the experimental manipulation. Essentially a matter of measurement validity, this has been referred to as the problem of "multiple meanings" (Aronson and Carlsmith, 1968). For example, a manipulation meant to arouse embarrassment in the subject is invalid if it produces disgust or anger instead. In general, the more complex the set of stimuli presented to the subject, the less sure the researcher may be that a manipulation appropriately measures the independent variable. When interpreting the results of any experiment, therefore, one must be sensitive to possible alternative explanations for any effects found. Evidence that the manipulation had the intended effect is gained by conducting a series of experiments in which the same theoretical concept is operationally defined differently, and by performing manipulation checks.

Manipulation Checks

An immediate way to obtain evidence that the manipulation of the independent variable was experienced or interpreted by the subject in the way the experimenter intended is to incorporate some sort of **manipulation check** into the experiment. This might involve asking subjects, either directly or by means of a written instrument, what they felt or thought during or immediately after the experimental manipulation. A manipulation check may also be used to determine whether subjects understood or recalled essential directions or facts related to the manipulation.

In the Darley and Latané study, subjects were given a fifteen-item checklist of thoughts that might have occurred to them during the seizure. In addition, subjects were asked whether at the time of the seizure they had been aware of other persons who might be witnessing it—an awareness crucial to the meaning of the independent variable. (Data from two subjects who found the seizure unconvincing were not included in the statistical analysis.)

Different viewpoints exist regarding the best place in an experiment to administer a manipulation check. Frequently, a manipulation check is taken after the independent variable is manipulated but before the dependent variable is measured. The advantage here is that the manipulation is still fresh and the subject's memory of it has not been distorted by later events. However, it may not be feasible at this point, as in the Darley and Latané study, where the check was made part of the post-experimental interview. (Certainly it was more appropriate for the subjects to respond at once to the "emergency" than to a checklist!) An additional problem with having a check administered between the experimental manipulation and the dependent variable is that of reactivity; that is, the manipulation check may alter subjects' subsequent behavior (the dependent variable) by calling attention to or emphasizing the manipulation.

One solution to this dilemma may be found through pretesting, in which the experiment is tried out on a number of subjects. The pretest subjects might be run in the usual manner through the manipulation of the independent variable and then interviewed as to how it affected them (Aronson and Carlsmith, 1968). In this way a manipulation check is carried out without affecting the data of the actual experiment. This procedure makes good sense also in view of the fact that there would still be time to make changes in the experiment before it is conducted with actual subjects whose data would be collected and analyzed.

Measurement of the Dependent Variable

The dependent variable, which always follows the introduction of the independent variable, is measured in experiments with either self-reports or observations of behavior. Darley and Latané used behavioral observation, with the dependent variable consisting of the length of time from the onset of the seizure until the subject left the room to report the emergency. A behavioral measure of the dependent variable—grades on a second test—also was used in the Page study of the effect of teacher comments on student performance.

The use of verbal versus observational measures of the dependent variable is a controversial point among experimenters. Our examples notwithstanding, verbal reports are more common, even though they often contain serious weaknesses. Verbal measures have the advantage of being easy to devise, allowing for more numerous and varied assessments of the dependent variable. They also tend to be high in face validity. Using a verbal measure, for example, the experimenter interested in willingness to help could simply ask: "To what extent are you willing to help?" There are two major problems with such self-reports, however. First, subjects may censor their responses, especially when they construe the "truth" to reflect negatively on themselves; second, research consistently has shown differences between what people do and what they think and say they will do (Deutscher, Pestello, and Pestello, 1993).

With observations of behavior, on the other hand, subjects tend to be less aware or even unaware of the measure. Behavioral measures also can be more precise; recall that Darley and Latané recorded the length of time to respond to the emergency in seconds. Finally, when a specific behavior (e.g., helping) is of interest, it is better to get a direct measure of that behavior than an indirect measure of how subjects *say* they will behave.

Debriefing

The closing scene of the experiment is a **debriefing** session in which the experimenter discusses with the subject what has taken place. When subjects have been deceived, it is ethically imperative that they be told at this point about the nature of and reasons for the deception and that their feelings about being deceived be explored fully (see chapter 16). The experimenter also may try to learn what the subject experienced throughout the experiment: Did the subject understand the directions? If a cover story was used, did the subject believe it? Why did the subject respond as he or she did to the experimental manipulation? Did the subject experience psychological stress or discomfort? How does the subject feel about the experiment as a whole?

The experimenter should be aware that the manner in which the debriefing session is conducted may make a great deal of difference in the feelings of the subject about being deceived (if the subject has been deceived), about this research and researcher, and about social science research in general. Thus the experimenter should explain the real purpose of the research and why it is of importance. If deception has been used, the subject must be gently informed of this and the reasons why it was necessary. If the manipulation aroused the subject's emotions, this, too, should be justified and every effort made to relieve any remaining discomfort. Any negative feelings of the subject toward the study should be brought into the open and discussed. The subject should be encouraged to ask questions about the study.

Because many subjects in their experiment experienced stress and conflict, Darley and Latané took great care in explaining the necessity of the deception and seeing that subjects left the experiment feeling positive about their participation. While they did not gather systematic information about subjects' reactions to the experimental experience, Shalom Schwartz and Avi Gottlieb (1981) administered an "ethics questionnaire" to measure subjects' feelings about their participation in three different experiments on bystander intervention, including a close replication of the Darley and Latané study. Very few subjects felt any negative affect such as being upset, embarrassed, or nervous, or feeling angry at the experimenter and self, and subjects generally evaluated their experience quite favorably. The vast majority found their participation enjoyable, believed that the research was ethically justified, and were not resentful about having been deceived. The relative absence of negative reactions, Schwartz and Gottlieb contend, was most probably due to the thorough debriefing provided in all three experiments.

Finally, subjects must be convinced not to talk to others about the experiment. This is a serious problem in that frequently potential subjects are acquainted with one another. Certainly, experiments requiring deception will not yield valid results if subjects coming to the experiment have been informed of its true purpose. Even experiments not requiring deception will usually suffer if subjects previously have been told the hypothesis or what the experimental manipulation is. If the debriefing process has been an open, satisfying experience for the subject up to this point, he or she is very likely to respect the researcher's wishes in regard to secrecy.

Pretesting

Pretesting an experiment may be compared to rehearsals of a play in that the pretests provide an opportunity for the director of the research to (1) train the "cast," (2) test the "props," instructions, and cover story, (3) check whether the manipulation has the intended effect, (4) revise and practice the "script," and so forth. Pretests are carried out on a few preliminary subjects to see how the experimental procedures affect them. Feedback provided by pretest subjects may be used to modify the manipulation of the independent variable (e.g., by increasing the level of a stimulus such as praise, or by changing the behavior of confederates in some way), to change the dependent measure, or to improve some other part of the experiment such as the instructions, setting, or cover story. The time it takes for the actual performance of a play is usually a fraction of the time required to write the play and prepare for its performance. Similarly, the amount of time spent by a researcher in planning and pretesting an experiment will typically be many times greater than the time spent running subjects through the experiment.

Experimental and Mundane Realism

One thing the experimenter may learn from pretesting is the extent to which pretest subjects become involved in the experiment—that is, whether they are compelled to attend to it and take it seriously or, on the other hand, remain detached. When an experiment is found to have impact on subjects and to seem real to them, it is said to have **experimental realism** (Aronson and Carlsmith, 1968). The bystander intervention study achieved a very high degree of experimental realism for subjects. As Darley and Latané (1968:381) report,

> Subjects, whether or not they intervened, believed the fit to be genuine and serious. "My God, he's having a fit," many subjects said to themselves (and were overheard via their microphones) at the onset of the fit. Others gasped or simply said "Oh." Several of the male subjects swore. One subject said to herself, "It's just my

kind of luck, something has to happen to me!" Several subjects spoke aloud of the confusion about what course of action to take, "Oh God, what should I do?"

This type of experiment is sometimes called an *impact experiment* (Aronson, Brewer, and Carlsmith, 1985) because the event in question—witnessing an emergency by hearing an apparent epileptic seizure—happened to the subjects themselves. Impact experiments tend to be high in experimental realism, although the stimuli presented are often complex, increasing the likelihood of "multiple meanings" from subject to subject. By contrast, *judgment experiments,* in which subjects make judgments about stimulus materials presented by the experimenter, have little direct impact on subjects. For example, subjects might be asked to indicate how much they like a stimulus person about whom they read a description or whom they see on film. This type of experiment allows a great deal of control over the events or stimuli presented, but the gain in control may undermine subject involvement and thereby lower experimental realism. In general, there often is a tension between the goal of experimental realism and the goal of control over the experimental situation. Ways to increase experimental realism include using a "live" experimenter rather than tape-recorded or written instructions, making the cover story more interesting, selecting a confederate with substantial acting ability, and developing elaborate apparatus or other props.

A second type of "realism" that experiments may have to different degrees is called **mundane realism** (Aronson and Carlsmith, 1968). This type of realism refers to the similarity of experimental events to everyday experiences. The Page experiment on teacher comments, which took place in a natural setting, was clearly high in mundane realism. Receiving general comments on exams is something that has happened to every student. The Darley and Latané experiment, however, was low in mundane realism. Carrying on a highly regulated discussion with unseen peers over an intercom is not likely to be a common experience.

Experiments may be high in both experimental and mundane realism, high in one type of realism but low in the other, or low in both. Of the two types, mundane realism is considered less important in that an experiment is by nature a contrived situation (Aronson and Carlsmith, 1968). Therefore, mundane realism is of less concern in planning and pretesting. To control many variables and isolate others for study, some degree of mundane realism must be sacrificed. However, as long as an experiment is properly designed, so that the relationship between variables is interpretable, its findings will be important even if it is artificial in a mundane sense.

The Experiment as a Social Occasion

Unlike an audience for a stage play who assume a passive role, subjects in a laboratory experiment are both audience and active participants. As participants, they bring to the experimental setting their own personal qualities, needs, and expectations. And as they interact with the experimenter (or the experimental assistants), the event takes on social as well as scientific aspects.

Scientifically, an experiment is an occasion to measure subjects' responses to certain intentionally and systematically varied stimuli. However, other stimuli related to the social aspects of the occasion may have unintended effects, which account for subjects' responses as much or more than the intended experimental manipulation. A good example of this was the famous Hawthorne experiments, mentioned in chapter 2 (see Box 2.1). Measuring the production rate of workers in response to a series of changes in working conditions (e.g., working hours, temperature, method of payment), the investigators found to their surprise that every change introduced resulted in an increase in productivity. This heightened productivity was not a response to the specific changes, however, but to the special attention given the group of workers as participants in an important experiment.

In chapter 4, we referred to the responses that are due to subjects' awareness of being studied as **reactive measurement effects**. An example was the self-censoring that occurs with verbal report measures. While such effects are present in varying degrees in survey and field research, they are most problematic in laboratory experiments. Subjects in a laboratory experiment are acutely aware that they are participants in an experiment. Usually, their participation has brought them to a place they have never been before to interact with people whom they have never met before. They realize that they may be asked to do some strange things in the name of scientific inquiry, and they are likely to suspect that the true nature of the experiment is being concealed from them. They are aware that they are being observed and that certain behaviors are expected of them. Let us take a look now at how such thoughts and expectations might affect subjects' behavior.

Demand Characteristics

In any situation, from classroom to athletic field to experimental laboratory, there are norms and role expectations that govern behavior. Subjects entering an experiment, for example, implicitly agree to place themselves under the control of the experimenter and to perform a wide range of tasks without questioning their purpose or duration (Orne, 1962). These expectations were strikingly demonstrated by psychologist Martin Orne (1962) in the course of his research on hypnosis. To study the difference between the degree of control inherent in the hypnotic relationship and in a waking relationship, Orne tried to develop boring, meaningless, or unpleasant tasks that waking subjects would refuse to do or would stop doing after a short period of time. However, Orne found instead that subjects would persist hour after hour in apparently meaningless tasks. In one of these, subjects were instructed to perform additions of adjacent numbers on a sheet filled with hundreds of random numbers, to tear up the sheet in a prescribed manner, and then to go on to the next sheet and do the same thing, continuing in this manner until told to stop. Despite many efforts, Orne could find no task that would be refused or quickly discontinued by subjects once they agreed to participate in an experiment.

To Orne, these results revealed that a previously unimagined degree of control exists in the experimental setting. As a consequence of "being in an experiment," subjects feel justified in carrying out all sorts of tedious, noxious, even dangerous tasks. In one experiment, Orne and Evans (1965) found that subjects fearlessly complied with a request to reach into a cage containing a poisonous snake, only to be prevented from doing so by an invisible pane of glass. The reason why subjects will perform such tasks is that the "demands" placed upon them in an experiment go beyond the experimenter's verbal instructions. Because of the knowledge that one is in an experiment, endlessly boring tasks are viewed as endurance tests and seemingly dangerous acts are seen as really safe.

The particular cues in an experimental situation that communicate to subjects what is expected and what the experimenter hopes to find are called **demand characteristics** (Orne, 1962, 1969). These cues, which frequently are very subtle, range broadly. They can be communicated through campus scuttlebutt about the experiment, information provided during the recruiting of subjects, experimenter qualities such as appearance, the laboratory setting, experimental procedures, and communications during the experiment. According to Orne (1962), what makes subjects especially susceptible to such cues is their determination to play the role of "good subject." The good subject believes in the value of social science research and hopes by his or her participation to make a contribution toward the advancement of science. Whatever the purpose of the experiment, he or she assumes it to be worthwhile. Such subjects will gladly comply with virtually any request of the experimenter. And in order to "help" the experimenter, they are sensitive, consciously or unconsciously, to cues that indicate how to behave so as to validate the experimental hypothesis. Support for this viewpoint is provided by the fact that subjects often express concern about their behavior at the close of an experiment, saying something like, "I hope I didn't ruin the experiment."

The crux of the problem is that, in some experiments, unintended demand characteristics may influence subjects' responses more than the intended experimental manipulation. Consider, for example, laboratory studies of the effect of persuasive messages on attitude change. When presented with a message or argument, followed by attitude or opinion measures, most subjects realize that their acquiescence to the message is being studied. If they are motivated to conform to the experimenter's expectations, then compliance to demand characteristics rather than the persuasiveness of the message accounts for their responses. One study in which this was demonstrated (Silverman, 1968) presented subjects with a 250-word report advocating the use of closed-circuit television tapes to present lectures in large classes. It was found that subjects showed more agreement with the message when they were told that they were in an experiment than when this was not explicitly conveyed to them.

Evaluation Apprehension

Besides their concern about being helpful and cooperative, subjects in experiments often experience anxiety about being evaluated. Viewing the experimenter, typically a psychologist, as having special skills to determine their true character or personality, subjects come to experiments expecting the possibility that they will be evaluated. When this suspicion is confirmed, they are likely to experience **evaluation apprehension**. According to Milton Rosenberg (1965:29), who coined the term, subjects whose evaluation apprehension is aroused are concerned that they "win the positive evaluation of the experimenter, or at least that [they] provide no grounds for a negative one." This may cause the subject to be overly sensitive to cues regarding what constitutes a good, healthy, able, or "normal" performance of the task, and thus not to respond spontaneously to the independent variable.

Evidence that subjects may behave in a way that is thought to project a favorable image comes from an experiment by Rosenberg (1969). Subjects who believed they were participating in a social perception study were asked "to judge how much they liked or disliked various pictured persons." Before carrying out this task, however, one group of subjects was told that past research indicated that psychologically mature and healthy people show greater liking for strangers than do immature people, while a second group was told the opposite. For both groups, subjects' "liking" judgments reflected their beliefs about how psychologically mature individuals would respond.

For many subjects in the Rosenberg experiment, "looking good" may have seemed consistent with "being a good subject" and complying with demand characteristics. What happens, however, when there is a conflict between projecting a favorable image and confirming the experimenter's hypothesis? The evidence suggests that subjects will choose to look good. In one experiment (Sigall, Aronson, and Van Hoose, 1970), for example, subjects who knew the experimenter's hypothesis responded so as to disconfirm it when they thought that cooperating would reveal an unfavorable personality type.

Other Motives of Experimental Subjects

Motives of experimental subjects are not limited to those of the good subject who carefully attends to demand characteristics in order to "help" the experimenter or to the anxious subject intent on putting his or her best foot forward. When 110 experienced subjects were questioned regarding what they liked about the last experiment in which they participated (Straits and Wuebben, 1973), responses referred to the nature of the experimental task or the experimenter, the challenge of a new experience or of being successful in the experiment, the opportunity to learn something, and figuring out the experiment's purpose. Other common motivators are course credit or pay.

Another possible subject role is that of the negative or "bad" subject who tries to sabotage the research by deliberately providing useless or invalid responses. Chris Argyris (1968:188) wrote, for example, that

> [i]n one major university, a formal evaluation was made of the basic psychology course by nearly 600 undergraduates [and] the students were very critical, mistrustful, and hostile to the requirement [that they had to participate in experiments]. In many cases they identified how they expressed their pent-up feelings by "beating the researcher" in such a way that he never found out.

Why would subjects feel this way? Argyris, borrowing from organizational theory, has argued that experiments "tend to place subjects in situations that are similar to those organizations create for the lower level employees" (p. 193). Unaccustomed to being subordinates in a highly authoritarian system, research subjects may react by adopting employee ploys such as covert withdrawal or opposition.

Despite Argyris's claim, the negativistic subject seems to be less prevalent than the apprehensive or good subject (Weber and Cook, 1972). On the other hand, studies on the motivation of experimental subjects, taken together, seem to suggest that human subjects are too complex and diverse to describe by simple models presuming good, bad, or anxious subjects. For example, subjects may hold both hostile and favorable feelings toward experimentation and the social sciences. Certain features of experiments, such as required participation or unpleasant tasks, may evoke bad subject motives and behavior; other features, such as an impressive or attractive experimenter, may stimulate good subject motives. Clearly, one cannot assume that the subject will be a passive responder to the experimental manipulation. Furthermore, there is always the strong possibility of subject bias whenever experimental procedures make the hypothesis transparent.

Experimenter Effects

Another source of bias due to the social nature of experiments is the experimenter. Experimenters can affect the results of their research in many ways that are not unique to experimentation, for example, by making recording errors, computational errors, and errors of interpretation, or by intentionally falsifying their data (recall from chapter 2, Box 2.2, the case of Cyril Burt). However, the most problematic experimenter effects are influences on subjects' behavior. Robert Rosenthal (1966, 1967, 1969), who investigated such effects extensively, showed that numerous experimenter traits, including gender, race, status, anxiety, and warmth, affect the behavior of subjects. Just what effects these traits have depend on the particular experiment and on characteristics of the subject. Also, to a certain extent, such effects can be limited through training and appropriate controls.

More unsettling and operating at a more subtle level are effects due to the **experimenter's expectations** about how the experiment will turn out. Several studies by Rosenthal and others have shown that experimenters may unintentionally communicate to subjects their expectations about how the subjects "should" respond so as to confirm their hypotheses. One study involved a "person-perception" task (Rosenthal and Fode, 1963). Graduate student experimenters, who believed they were replicating a previous study, were told to present a set of photographs of individuals and ask subjects to rate each photograph as to how successful the individual appeared to be. The pictures had been selected on the basis of pretests to include only individuals who appeared neither especially successful nor unsuccessful. However, half the experimenters were informed that subjects would generally perceive the persons photographed as experiencing success (high ratings); the other half were led to expect that subjects would perceive the individuals as unsuccessful (low ratings). Even though the experimenters read identical instructions to their subjects, those experimenters expecting high success ratings tended to get higher ratings from their subjects than those expecting low ratings.

The means by which experimenters communicate their expectancies to subjects is not well understood, although there have been a number of studies on this question. Some studies have demonstrated the importance of auditory cues—voice quality or tone of voice. For example, Edward Zoble and Richard Lehman (1969) showed that if subjects performing the person-perception task described above were denied visual contact with the experimenter, about one-half of the expectancy effect remained. This study, as well as others (Rosenthal, 1969:253–54), also provides indirect evidence that visual cues such as facial expressions and gestures may mediate expectancy effects.

Fortunately, although there is little question of the existence of experimenter expectancy effects, it is doubtful that such effects are either very strong or widespread. Those studies designed to demonstrate an expectancy effect, such as the study involving person perception, differ from most other experiments in two regards: (1) The stimulus was highly ambiguous, which may have caused the subject to pay unusual attention to any possible cues from the experimenter, and (2) the experimenters for the most part ran subjects in one experimental condition only. Elliot Aronson and J. Merrill Carlsmith (1968:67) have pointed out that an experimenter would be less likely to bias subject behavior when running subjects in more than one condition, because he or she would probably notice any systematic differences in his or her behavior toward subjects. Still, the general problem of experimenter bias is one that researchers can ill afford to ignore.

Minimizing Bias Due to the Social Nature of Experimentation

While experiments provide an ideal model for testing causal relations, the success of that model depends on the experimenter's ability to eliminate or minimize potential biases emanating from an experiment's social nature. Several strategies have been developed for handling the problems raised by demand characteristics and experimenter bias.

The most straightforward way of detecting demand characteristics is simply to ask subjects about their perception of the experimental situation (Orne, 1969). Did the subjects entertain any hypotheses? Did it appear to them that the experimenter expected them to behave in a certain way? How do they think others might have reacted in the situation? This sort of probing could take place in a pretesting phase, in which subjects are asked for their impressions at different points in the experiment, or during the debriefing.

The most widely used means of controlling for demand characteristics is a cover story that provides the subject with a false hypothesis about the purpose of the study. If a cover story satisfies subjects' suspicions about the purpose of the experiment, the subjects will not be busily trying to figure out the true hypothesis; therefore, they will be less likely to act deliberately in ways consistent or inconsistent with it. Similarly, experiments high in experimental realism (partly achieved with a good cover story) have such an impact on subjects that there is little chance for them to be distracted by evaluation apprehension or other suspicions.

A second approach to circumventing the problem of demand characteristics is to measure the dependent variable in a setting different from the one in which the independent variable is manipulated. By separating these processes physically, the experimenter hopes the subjects will dissociate the events psychologically. For example, Milton Rosenberg (1965) arranged for subjects to participate in two apparently unrelated studies conducted by different experimenters. In the first study, conducted in the education department, subjects were paid to write essays counter to their own views on a particular issue, with the size of the payment being the independent variable. Then, in a subsequent opinion survey, conducted in the psychology department, subjects' attitudes on the same issue were measured. A less elaborate separation of these parts of the experiment occurred in three studies testing the hypothesis that guilt increases compliance (Freedman, Wallington, and Bless, 1967). The investigators first manipulated subjects' feelings of guilt. Then, when the experiment appeared to be over and the subject was about to leave the laboratory, they measured compliance by asking subjects if they would be willing to take part in another study, without pay, being conducted by another person in the department.

A third technique for controlling demand characteristics is to keep subjects unaware that they are actually participating in an experiment. In this way, subjects should behave naturally without wondering about the "true" nature of the situation. The best place to conduct such "disguised experiments" is in a natural rather than a laboratory setting (Campbell, 1969a). A good example is the Page experiment on teacher comments.

Finally, there is some evidence that the effects of demand characteristics can be minimized by asking subjects to adopt the role of the "faithful subject." Faithful subjects believe that they should follow instructions scrupulously, regardless of their suspicions about the true purpose of the experiment (Weber and Cook, 1972). Getting subjects to adopt this role, however, might be difficult if the experiment is likely to evoke a high level of evaluation apprehension.

A number of approaches also have been developed to eliminate or reduce bias introduced by the experimenter. One possibility, the **double-blind technique**, prevents the experimenter from knowing which condition a subject is in. This would be akin to studies of new drugs in which neither the subject nor the research assistant interviewing the subject knows whether the subject received the drug or a placebo (inert substance). With this method, a coding system enables the research supervisor to keep track of which subjects received which treatment.

In most studies it is not possible to keep the experimenter blind to the subjects' condition, because differences in the treatment conditions are obvious to the experimenter. In these cases, a partial solution may be to utilize two or more experimenters, with each "blind" to some part of the experiment. For example, when the manipulation of the independent variable is separated from the measurement of the dependent variable, as in the guilt-compliance study mentioned earlier, these two processes could be carried out easily by different experimenters.

Another effective means of controlling the effects of experimenter bias is to have a single experimental session that includes all subjects. The experimenter might read general instructions to all subjects, but manipulate the independent variable by varying additional written instructions. If the latter instructions were randomly assigned, the experimenter could not systematically influence the subjects in any one group.

Finally, one could reduce the amount of contact between the experimenter and subjects by using taped recordings or written instructions. This averts the possibility of an experimenter unknowingly introducing differences in the intended manipulation through slight variations in voice quality, inflections, and volume; by smiling more at some subjects than at others; and so forth. On the other hand, this approach also would reduce experimental realism, as subjects are likely to be more attentive to a live experimenter.

Experimentation Outside the Laboratory

In the last two sections we have focused on experiments carried out in a laboratory. By far the most common setting for the experimental approach, the laboratory permits a great deal of control—control over subject assignment and of the events to which subjects are exposed. Control is obtained, however, at some cost: The sample of subjects is usually small and from a highly restricted population; the setting is often unrealistic in the mundane sense; and the subjects are aware that the experimenter has created the situation to test some hypothesis about their behavior.

Some experimental designs avoid these particular problems by moving outside the laboratory into a more natural social setting. When experiments take place "in the field," mundane realism tends to be high and demand characteristics are minimized because subjects often are unaware that they are participating in a study. Experimental designs also may be incorporated into nonexperimental research approaches, such as social surveys. Finally, as further evidence of the versatility of the experimental approach, the "subjects" randomly assigned to experimental conditions may consist of social units such as families, classrooms, clinics, and organizations, as well as individuals.

Field Experiments

Field experiments refer to studies that meet all the requirements of a "true" experiment but are conducted in a natural setting. As in a laboratory experiment, there is a staging of events in a field experiment. But this staging occurs in an environment that is familiar to the subject and is rendered in such a way that it appears to be a "natural" (albeit slightly out of the ordinary) part of that environment. Recall, for example, Alice Isen and Paula Levin's (1972) experiment on the effects of mood on helping, described in chapter 1. To manipulate mood, these investigators stocked a telephone in a phone booth with a dime; to measure helping, they staged an accident—someone dropping a folder of papers—and then recorded whether the subject stopped to help. The experiment took place as subjects were going about a common activity, and the manipulations and observations were so subtle and unobtrusive that subjects' normal behavior was not disrupted.

Social researchers increasingly have gone outside the research laboratory to conduct experiments in a wide variety of settings. In the study of helping behavior alone, field experiments have been performed in department stores and municipal parking lots (Bryan and Test, 1967; Shotland and Stebbins, 1983), in a suburban shopping mall (Taylor, 1998), in a college library (Isen and Levin, 1972), in elevators (Latané and Dabbs, 1975), on a highway (Bryan and Test, 1967), on city sidewalks (Levine et al., 1994), and in the New York City subway (Piliavin and Piliavin, 1972). Conducting experiments in such settings offers several advantages. Without being aware that a study is in progress, subjects should not respond self-consciously to demand characteristics. External validity generally increases, not only because the setting and measures are more realistic but also because it is possible to observe the behavior of a more heterogeneous sample of subjects. Field experimentation also lends itself well to applied research—that is, research intended to provide input into problem solving. Some of the field experiments on helping behavior, for example, have been directed at factors affecting blood donating (Piliavin, Callero, and Evans, 1982) and contributions to charitable organizations (Cialdini and Schroeder, 1976). We will now examine one of these studies to illustrate the utility and nature of experiments carried out in a real-life setting.

Research has shown that heightening concern about one's self-image may predispose one to help others as a means of maintaining or restoring a favorable image. Robert Cialdini and David Schroeder (1976) demonstrated this in a field experiment performed in a door-to-door fund-raising context. With the permission of the American Cancer Society, they asked pairs of college students to solicit contributions for the society in a middle-class suburban area. Solicitors requested contributions in one of two ways. In the first method, they made a standard request: "I'm collecting money for the American Cancer Society. Would you be willing to help by giving a donation?" In the second strategy, solicitors added the sentence, "Even a penny will help." Cialdini and Schroeder predicted that helping would be greater when the latter statement was added, because it legitimizes trivial requests and makes the solicitation more difficult to turn down without damaging one's self-image. Supporting their hypothesis, 29 percent of the subjects in the standard request condition contributed, averaging $1.44 each, as opposed to 50 percent of the subjects in the even-a-penny condition, who averaged $1.54 each. (See Box 6.2 for the story behind the origins of this study.)

With the advantages cited above, one may wonder why the field has not supplanted the laboratory as the primary setting for experimental research. Alas, there are disadvantages, the major drawback being the lower degree of control present in field experiments. Often researchers can only approximate a true experimental design in the field. It may not be possible to assign subjects (or other units of analysis) randomly to the various treatment conditions. Sometimes it is not possible to have a true control group because of ethical considerations or subject preferences. Furthermore, field experimenters often relinquish some control over the experiment by their dependence on other persons such as administrators or teachers to carry out parts of the study (a potential problem in the Cialdini and Schroeder study). Consequently, it is much more difficult outside the laboratory to ensure that there are no systematic differences in the experiences of subjects other than those resulting from the manipulation of the independent variable.

A related problem with field experimentation is that the manipulation of the independent variable may be less controllable and more open to interpretation. This is apparent in studies that attempted to evaluate the educational impact on American preschoolers of the television series "Sesame Street" (Ball and Bogatz, 1970; Cook and Conner, 1976; Liebert, 1976). Ideally, to investigate the effects of viewing, it would be desirable to have a treatment group that viewed the series and a

BOX 6.2

On the Origins of Research Ideas

In chapter 3 we outlined some of the sources of ideas for social research. As we noted, many studies derive from existing theory. This is especially true of the hypothesis-testing research that characterizes experiments. Occasionally, however, investigators get their research ideas from everyday observations and experiences. This was, in fact, the origin of two of the experiments described in this chapter.

According to John Darley, his and Bibb Latané's research on bystander intervention stemmed from a widely publicized incident in New York City. A young woman named Kitty Genovese was brutally murdered while thirty-eight of her neighbors watched from their windows without so much as calling the police until her assailant had departed. Shocked by this incident, Darley and Latané

> met over dinner and began to analyze the bystanders' reactions. Because we were social psychologists, we thought not about how people are different nor about the personality flaws of the "apathetic" individuals who failed to act that night, but rather about how people are the same and how anyone in that situation might react as did these people. By the time we finished our dinner, we formulated several factors that together could lead to the surprising result: no one helping. Then we set about conducting experiments that isolated each factor and demonstrated its importance in an emergency situation. (Reported in Myers, 1983:394)

Robert Cialdini (1980:27–28), whose research involves social influence processes, tells how a personal experience led him to investigate a highly effective fundraising tactic.

> I answered the door early one evening to find a young woman who was canvassing my neighborhood for the United Way. She identified herself and asked if I would give a monetary donation. It so happened that my home university has an active United Way organization and I had given in-house a few days earlier. It was also the end of the month and my finances were low. Besides, if I gave to all the solicitors for charity who came to my door, I would quickly require such service for myself. As she spoke, I had already decided against a donation and was preparing my reply to incorporate the above reasons. Then it happened. After asking for a contribution, she added five magic words. I know they were *the* magic words because my negative reply to the donation request itself literally caught in my throat when I heard them. "Even a penny will help," she said. And with that, she demolished my anticipated response. All the excuses I had prepared for failing to comply were based on financial considerations. They stated that I could not afford to give to her now or to her, too. But she said, "Even a penny will help" and rendered each of them impotent. How could I claim an inability to help when she claimed that "even a penny" was a legitimate form of aid? I had been neatly finessed into compliance. And there was another interesting feature of our exchange as well. When I stopped coughing (I really had choked on my attempted rejection), I gave her *not* the penny she mentioned but the amount I usually allot to charity solicitors. At that, she thanked me, smiled innocently, and moved on.

Together with his then-graduate student Dave Schroeder, Cialdini analyzed the situation and concluded that two sources of social influence had been activated by the addendum, "Even a penny will help." First, it removed any excuses for not offering at least some aid. Second, it made it more difficult to maintain one's altruistic self-image without contributing. Cialdini and Schroeder then set out to find a naturalistic fund-raising context for testing their ideas.

control group that did not. However, because there was no practical way to prevent the control group children from viewing the series in their homes, it was decided that the experimental treatment would be "encouragement to view." This treatment included weekly visits by trained staff who encouraged parents and children to watch the programs and who brought along literature, toys, and games designed to stimulate viewing. The control group children received no "encouragement" and could view or not. Both groups of children were given a battery of tests before the first viewing season and at its end, and the results showed that the group encouraged to view made greater gains on the posttests. Unfortunately, this did not establish that viewing the programs caused the gains, as there were systematic differences in the experiences of the two groups aside from the viewing experience; that is, the effects of viewing were confounded with the effects of "encouragement." It is possible that the social and intellectual stimulation provided by the "encouragement" alone was sufficient to cause the gains.[3]

Finally, field experiments often raise ethical and legal issues. Is it ethical or legal, for example, to expose passersby to someone who collapses or feigns a heart attack, as has been done in bystander intervention research? In laboratory experiments, subjects' rights are protected by obtaining their prior consent to participate and by debriefing. But these safeguards may be impossible to incorporate in a field experiment. Obtaining "informed consent," for instance, in many cases would destroy the cover for the experiment. Thus, there is a greater demand on field experimenters to demonstrate that their research presents no more than minimal risk of harm to subjects.

Experimental Designs in Survey Research

The versatility of the experimental approach is evidenced not only by extensions into the field but also by the use of experimental design in survey research. For example, several surveys have investigated the effects of slight changes in the wording of a question during an interview. Generally, as part of a larger survey, a mini-experiment is conducted by directing a question with one wording to a randomly selected subsample of respondents and directing a differently worded question to the remaining respondents. (See Box 9.1 for a specific example.)

Another common way of incorporating an experimental design into surveys is through the use of vignettes. Vignettes are short, detailed, and concrete descriptions of situations that contain references to factors that are thought to be important in decision making. Some survey researchers believe that vignettes produce more valid responses than the briefer but more general or abstract questions normally used in opinion surveys (see Alexander and Becker, 1978). To test experimentally which factors in a given situation significantly affect respondents' decision making, a number of versions of the vignettes are developed by systematically varying the details of the situation. The different versions are then randomly assigned to respondents. For example, to study college women's fertility plans, Bruce Straits (1985) used six vignettes, each of which described a married woman facing a decision directly or indirectly bearing on her childbearing plans. The information that was varied in each vignette concerned the direct costs of children due to changes in earning power and living standards, the indirect costs of children due to the loss of other opportunities for self-fulfillment (forgoing further schooling or occupational advancement, for example), and the perceived cultural support for parenthood. Contrary to some journalistic accounts, Straits found that the college women in his sample had a strong commitment to motherhood that took precedence over a career and other direct and indirect costs of childbearing.

It is also possible to perform an experiment via a sample survey by constructing different sets of questionnaires. Consider, for example, a study by Robert Navazio (1977) on the so-called bandwagon effect. This is the idea that voters are influenced by public opinion poll results to the extent that they tend to "get on the bandwagon" and support what they believe to be the majority opinion on an issue. To study this phenomenon, Navazio mailed experimental and control questionnaires to two samples of respondents. The questionnaires contained four opinion questions evaluating President Nixon's performance. On the experimental questionnaire, each question followed a statement of recent national poll results that showed that a majority of people had responded negatively to the question. On the basis of "bandwagon psychology," one would predict that the experimental group, having access to the critical responses of others, would respond more negatively than the control group. However, the results did not support this hypothesis.

Units of Analysis Other than Individuals

Experimental designs do not always use individuals as the unit of analysis. Numerous laboratory experiments have been performed over the years treating pairs of subjects or small groups as units. Although less common, experimental units of analysis also have consisted of larger groupings such as organizations or neighborhoods.

One illustrative field experiment on patrol staffing in San Diego, California, used police "beats" as the units, assigning them to either a one-officer or a two-officer condition. The object of this study was to evaluate whether staffing police patrol cars with two officers as opposed to one officer resulted in increased quality of service, efficiency, and safety, making the practice cost effective (Boydstun, Sherry, and Moelter, 1978). It had been determined that the difference in cost between fielding a two-officer patrol unit and a one-officer patrol unit was over $100 per unit for an eight-hour period. Pairs of beats were matched on various characteristics and then randomly assigned to the one-officer or two-officer staffing condition, with forty-four patrol units involved. The findings revealed that quality of performance and efficiency were as high with the one-officer units as with the two-officer units and that the two-officer units were more often associated with suspects resisting arrest or assaulting officers. The study concluded, therefore, that the staffing ought to be primarily one-officer units.

Another study, a massive field experiment carried out on the island of Taiwan in the city of Taichung, used neighborhoods as units of analysis (Berelson and Freedman, 1964). This study sought to determine the extent to which "family planning" would be implemented with information and service programs that required different levels of effort and cost. Each of Taichung's 2389 *lin's* (neighborhoods of twenty to thirty families) was randomly assigned to one of four experimental treatments. The treatments varied in terms of the cost of providing family planning information: In the lowest-cost treatment, educational posters were distributed and neighborhood meetings were held; in the highest-cost treatment, a nurse-midwife visited the home of every married couple. The researchers found that the proportion who accepted contraceptives was highest in the highest-cost condition, as expected. But there was also a marked indirect effect by word-of-mouth communication from the high-cost home visit *lin's* to *lin's* receiving lower cost treatments. The researchers therefore concluded that contraception use can be spread economically by a mixture of low- and high-cost programs.

Summary

Experimental research is intended for the purpose of testing hypothesized causal relationships. Controlling extraneous variables is the key to doing this effectively. First, random assignment of subjects to treatment and control groups ensures that pre-experimental differences will be "neutralized" or distributed approximately evenly among the groups. Then, treatment and control group subjects must experience the same events during the experiment except for the manipulation of the independent variable. Only in this way can we confidently infer that the experimental manipulation produced differences in measures of the dependent variable.

Because experiments permit relatively strong inferences about cause and effect, providing clear evidence of direction of influence and controlling effectively for extraneous variables, they are high in internal validity. On the other hand, experiments, especially those performed in research laboratories, tend to be limited in generalizability—that is, tend to be low in external validity. This is most apparent with respect to the sample of subjects, who typically are college students. Whereas external validity is sometimes increased by using more heterogeneous samples, more often it is achieved through replications that test the same hypothesis but in a different setting, with different variable manipulations and measures and with subjects drawn from different populations.

The staging of an experiment has four main parts: (1) an introduction, which provides subjects with instructions and a rationale for the experimental procedures; (2) manipulation of the independent variable, ideally followed by a manipulation check that examines subjects' interpretations of the manipulation; (3) measurement of the dependent variable, either by verbal reports or, preferably, by behavioral observation; and (4) a debriefing session, which is intended to explain the purpose of the experiment, to explore subjects' reactions, and to assuage subjects' anxieties about their "performance" or participation.

Before experiments are carried out, they should be pretested on a few preliminary subjects to check the efficacy of the procedures. At this time one can determine the study's experimental realism, or the extent to which the experiment engages and has an impact on subjects. Also important, though generally of lesser concern, is the study's mundane realism, which refers to the similarity of experimental procedures to "real-world" events.

Perhaps the most problematic aspects of the laboratory experiment stem from its social nature. Subjects react not only to experimental manipulations but to the social meaning of the situation. Thus their responses may be determined by their sensitivity to cues, called demand characteristics, which communicate the hypothesis being tested; by their apprehensiveness about the evaluation of their performance; or by their resentment about being "coerced" into taking part in an experiment. In addition, experimenters may nonverbally communicate their own expectations to subjects.

To a large extent, these potentially biasing factors can be controlled. Subject biases might be detected by pre-experimental and postexperimental interviews. Methods of controlling such biases include using a good cover story that inhibits subjects' suspicions, placing the manipulation of the independent variable and the measurement of the dependent variable in different contexts, conducting a disguised experiment, or asking subjects to adopt the role of the "faithful subject." Experimenter biases are controlled most effectively by keeping experimenters blind to the subjects' conditions. One also may use two experimenters, each blind to a part of the experiment, or carry out the experiment in a single session. Also effective, though less desirable, is the automation of the experiment through the use of audiotapes or videotapes.

One other means of controlling for biases is to perform an experiment in a natural setting where subjects are unaware that a scientific investigation is taking place. Such field experiments also increase external validity and are an effective tool for applied research. However, in moving from the laboratory to the field, one generally sacrifices control over extraneous variables and over the manipulation of the independent variable, and one may find it more difficult to protect subjects' rights and safety.

Evidence of the versatility of experimentation comes from the incorporation of experimental design methodology into sample surveys and from the use of units of analysis other than individuals. Because of its greater degree of control, experimentation is the preferred approach for testing causal hypotheses. However, there are frequently problems in applying true experimental designs to social research that may result in a less-than-ideal execution of the experiment or in a compromise in the design itself. In the next chapter we will consider a variety of research designs, some of which are extensions and some of which are approximations to the model of the true experiment presented in this chapter.

Key Terms

treatment

random assignment

test of statistical significance

matching

internal validity

external validity

replication

cover story

manipulation check

debriefing

pretesting

experimental realism

mundane realism

reactive measurement effects

demand characteristics

evaluation apprehension

experimenter expectancy effect

double-blind technique

field experiment

Review Questions and Problems

1. Briefly explain *how* experiments provide the types of evidence required to establish causality: association, direction of influence, and elimination of rival hypotheses.

2. What purpose does a test of statistical significance serve in an experiment?

3. Should matching be substituted for random assignment in an experiment? Explain.

4. Differentiate random assignment from random sampling.

5. Briefly distinguish between internal and external validity.

6. Describe the typical sample of subjects in an experiment.

7. How do experimenters rationalize the convenience samples typical of experiments?

8. How can one increase the external validity of an experiment?

9. What are the four main parts of an experiment?

10. What is the purpose of a cover story?

11. Explain the problem of multiple meanings in experimental manipulation.

12. What is the purpose of manipulation checks?

13. Why are behavioral measures generally preferred over self-report measures of the dependent variable in experiments?

14. What purposes does debriefing serve?

15. When is an experiment high in experimental realism? When is it high in mundane realism?

16. What is the difference between an "impact experiment" and a "judgment experiment"? Which is higher in experimental realism?

17. Why is it important to consider the social nature of an experiment?

18. Describe the role expectations of the typical experimental subject.

19. Briefly describe Orne's model of the "good subject." How is this model related to the problem of demand characteristics?

20. Explain the motives of the "anxious subject" and the "bad subject" in experiments.

21. Describe various ways in which the experimenter can affect the outcome of an experiment.

22. How are experimenter expectancies communicated to subjects?

23. How do experiments demonstrating experimenter expectancy effects differ from most other experiments?

24. Identify two methods for minimizing demand characteristics and two methods for reducing experimenter effects.

25. What are the advantages and disadvantages of using a "live" experimenter rather than a taped recording to provide instructions to subjects?

26. Compare the advantages and disadvantages of field experiments versus laboratory experiments.

27. How can the experimental approach be incorporated into survey research?

28. Do the units of analysis in experiments always consist of individuals? Explain.

29. Find an article in *Social Psychology Quarterly* or the *Journal of Personality and Social Psychology* that reports the results of a laboratory experiment.

    a. State the hypothesis under investigation.

    b. What is the principal independent variable? How was it manipulated?

    c. What is the dependent variable? How was it measured?

    d. Identify any control variables present in the study.

    e. Do the results of the study support the hypothesis? Explain.

    f. Evaluate this experiment in terms of its experimental and mundane realism.

30. Looking through the same journals, find an article that reports a field experiment.

    a. What is the hypothesis being tested in this study?

    b. What is the independent variable? How is it manipulated?

    c. What is the dependent variable? How is it measured?

    d. Which of the four main parts of an experiment is missing?

    e. Comparing the experiments in questions 29 and 30, which is higher in mundane realism? Which is higher in experimental realism? Explain.

NOTES

1. Note that in this sense the word "significance" does not refer to the importance or triviality of the research findings.

2. This hypothesis is explained partly by the theory that the presence of others at an emergency is likely to create a "diffusion of responsibility" for helping. That is, with others present, we feel less personally responsible for taking action and are more likely to rationalize that "someone else is doing something."

3. This study is a good example of how a group of subjects who receive "no treatment" is not always an appropriate comparison group. Ideally the experience of the treatment and control groups should be similar in every way except for the variable the researcher intends to manipulate. A better comparison group for the Sesame Street study would be one in which families also received weekly visits with toys and games but in which the content of the materials was not designed to encourage viewing Sesame Street.

7

✔

Experimental Designs

By now you should have some pretty clear ideas about the experimental approach—its key features, strengths and weaknesses, and the steps in carrying out an experiment. This chapter will provide additional knowledge necessary to become an informed consumer of research. Understanding the language and logic of experimental designs should be especially valuable to you as a citizen, as experimental designs increasingly are applied to the study of social policy issues. Reading this chapter is, in fact, a prerequisite to reading chapter 13, on the nature of policy assessment research.

Although the topic of experimental design may sound formidable, and some experiments with their statistical baggage do appear rather complex, the basic principle of good design is simply the idea of "doing only one thing at a time." For the results of an experiment to be as unequivocal as possible, the only plausible explanation of changes in the dependent variable must be the manipulated independent variable. Therefore, a good design is one that rules out explanations of the results other than the effect of the independent variable. We learned in chapter 6 that this is best accomplished by randomly assigning subjects to experimental conditions (thereby controlling for pre-existing subject differences) and by making sure that the events occurring within each experimental condition are exactly the same except for the manipulated independent variable (thus controlling for extraneous factors and experiences during the experiment). The principle, then, is to allow only one factor, the independent variable, to vary while controlling the rest.

In this chapter, the first three designs we consider are inadequate; they do not follow the principle of good design. Before we examine the flaws in these "pre-experimental" designs, we identify the kinds of uncontrolled variables, or threats to internal validity, that provide plausible rival explanations of study results. Next we consider three basic, true experimental designs, which stand up better against threats to validity and thereby yield less ambiguous results. Then we examine designs for testing the joint effects of two or more independent variables. The need for these more complex "factorial" designs exists because in the "real world," unlike in the typical laboratory experiment, many variables may be at work simultaneously. Finally, we examine some "quasi-experimental" designs, used when it is not practical or possible to meet all the conditions of true experiments.

Threats to Internal Validity[1]

In chapter 6 we introduced the notion of internal validity. Recall that an experiment has internal validity when one can make strong inferences about cause and effect, inferring with confidence that the independent variable rather than an extraneous variable has produced the observed differences in the dependent variable. When we cannot separate the effects of the independent variable from possible effects of extraneous variables, we say that the effects are *confounded*. Imagine, for example, that a businesswoman wants to determine whether taking two aspirin tablets after work will get rid of the headaches she suffers in the evenings.[2] To test this hypothesis, she decides to take the aspirin on some evenings but not on others, so that she can compare the effects of the treatment (aspirin) with a control condition (no aspirin). However, she always washes the aspirin down with a glass of milk, which she eliminates along with the aspirin on control days. Her test would not be internally valid because the possible effects of the aspirin are confounded with the possible effects of the milk. Because she has not isolated the aspirin "treatment," she cannot be confident that this, and not the glass of milk, accounts for any observed differences between her treatment and control conditions.

The ideal research design effectively controls extraneous variables that threaten the internal validity of a study. We say "threaten" because uncontrolled extraneous variables pose explanations of study results that rival the hypothesized effects of the independent variable. To facilitate the evaluation of research designs, investigators have classified several common **threats to internal validity**, which we will now consider. Each of these threats signifies a distinctive class of extraneous variables.

One threat to internal validity is **history**. This consists of events in the subjects' environment, other than the manipulated independent variable, that occur during the course of the experiment and that may affect the outcome. In this sense a "historical event" may be a major event of social or political importance, such as an assassination of a public figure or a prolonged strike, or it may be a minor event that occurs within the experimental setting and has no significance outside it, such as a hostile remark by a subject. For example, suppose that you are studying the impact of a series of written persuasive communications on attitudes toward U.S. immigration policies. During the course of your experiment, many of your subjects happen to view at home a feature television program on the plight of illegal immigrant workers. Should the results of your study show that subjects' attitudes toward U.S. immigration policies have changed, it would be impossible for you to tell whether this change was caused by your independent variable (written communications) or by the television program. The confounded effects of the experimental manipulation and history preclude a clear causal interpretation of the results.

Another frequent rival explanation for research findings is **maturation**. By this we mean any psychological or physical changes taking place within subjects that occur with the passing of time regardless of the experimental manipulation. Even during a one- or two-hour experiment, subjects may become hungry or tired. Over a long-term experiment, subjects may grow physically or intellectually, become more rigid or more tolerant, or develop health problems or improved health. The effects of such maturational factors may be confounded with treatment effects. For example, in a study of the effectiveness of a new physical therapy program for stroke victims, any progress that the stroke victims would make naturally over time without therapeutic intervention (a phenomenon known as spontaneous remission) might incorrectly be attributed to the therapy.

Testing effects represent a third possible source of internal invalidity. Similar to reactive effects discussed in chapters 4 and 6, testing effects refer to changes in what is being measured that are brought about by reactions to the process of measurement. Typically, people will score better or give more socially desirable or psychologically healthier responses the second time a test or scale is administered to them. This is true even when a different but similar measure is used. There are a number of reasons why this occurs. On some measures, such as intelligence tests, the tasks simply become easier after practice. Attitude scales, on the other hand, may alert subjects to the purpose of the scale, causing them to give socially desirable responses or perhaps to reexamine their own attitudes. Such effects are potentially confounded with the effects of the independent variable whenever subjects are measured twice in the same study and the initial measurement arouses their awareness of being studied.

A fourth threat to internal validity, **instrumentation**, refers to unwanted changes in characteristics of the measuring instrument or in the measurement procedure. This threat is most likely to occur in experiments when the "instrument" is a human observer, who may become more skilled, more bored, or more or less observant during the course of the study. Instrumentation effects also may occur when different observers are used to obtain measurements in different conditions or parts of an experiment. Such an effect would be analogous to a shift in an instructor's grading standards while grading a set of essays, or to inconsistent standards on the part of two instructors grading subsets of the same essays.

The fifth threat to internal validity is **statistical regression**, the tendency for extreme scorers on a test to move (regress) closer to the mean or average score on a second administration of the test. Also known as *regression toward the mean*, this phenomenon is likely to affect experimental results when subjects are selected for an experimental condition because of their extreme scores. Consider, for example, an experiment to assess the effectiveness of an assertiveness training program in helping shy, introverted persons become more socially outgoing. Subjects are given a previously validated scale of extroversion, and the most introverted subjects— those who score in the bottom quartile—are assigned to the experimental condition, where they undergo an eight-week assertiveness training program. The remaining subjects serve as a control group, receiving no such training. At the end of eight weeks, both groups are retested. Assuming that subjects in the experimental group showed more significant gains in extroversion, on average, than the control group, we cannot confidently attribute this difference to the assertiveness training program. The students chosen for assertiveness training were those scoring in the bottom 25 percent on a measure of extroversion. Because of this, the observed increase in extroversion scores may have been due to statistical regression rather than the training program.

Statistical regression can explain many events in everyday life. An example should clarify how its effects occur. Suppose that Instructor Young gives his class two exams. In each case the average grade is B. Table 7.1 compares the performance of individuals on the two tests. Young is disappointed to see, from the first row of Table 7.1, that of the fifteen persons who received A's on Exam I, only ten

TABLE 7.1. Grade on Exam II by Grade on Exam I (Hypothetical Data)

	Exam II grade			
Exam I Grade	A	B	C	Total
A	10	4	1	15
B	3	22	5	30
C	2	4	9	15
Total	15	30	15	60

received A's on Exam II, with four receiving B's and one receiving a C. He concludes that five of the students became overconfident after the first exam and slacked off. Then he looks at the C scorers and is delighted to see that of the fifteen who scored C initially, two raised their scores to A and four to B. He feels some satisfaction that at least these students hit the books to bring their grades up. Such conclusions could be correct, but it is more likely that the results are due to regression toward the mean.

Because measurement error is always present, there is never a perfect correlation between scores from separate administrations of the same test or measure. A relatively large amount of measurement error will be reflected in a low correlation of scores and will result in more regression toward the mean. Another way to think of it is that the extreme scorers, as a subgroup, are affected more by chance factors we might call luck. On the first exam, some of the high scorers are particularly lucky whereas some of the low scorers are particularly unlucky. But it would be rare for extremely lucky students on the first exam to repeat their good fortune on the second exam (or for unlucky students to repeat their misfortune), which results in subgroup scores closer to the mean. Initially average scorers, on the other hand, are likely to include about as many lucky as unlucky individuals, so that changes in luck will tend to cancel out and not influence results on the second test.

A sixth threat to internal validity, **selection**, is present whenever there are systematic differences in the composition of the control and experimental groups. Such selection bias is especially likely when naturally existing groups are studied. Suppose, for example, a study compared one-year recidivism rates of apparently recovered alcoholics who received help through Alcoholics Anonymous with the recidivism rates of those who received in-hospital treatment. One possible systematic difference in the two groups that might affect abstinence is economic standing. If economic well-being aids recovery and if those choosing in-hospital treatment were in fact more affluent, then the hospital treatment group might have a better record of recovery because of their economic status, apart from any benefits of the treatment. Or, another possibility, also a matter of selection, is that the people entering the two treatment programs differed in the severity of their alcohol abuse, with more severe cases, who were also less likely to be "cured," receiving in-hospital treatment.

An additional example where selection would be a confounding factor is a study comparing the academic progress of pupils in an alternative school with that of pupils in a conventional school. Even if attempts were made to match the alternative school with a conventional school on such relevant characteristics as class size and socioeconomic status of pupils, there still might be confounding differences between the two groups. For example, the parents of the alternative-school children might be more permissive or differ in other unknown ways from the parents of the conventional-school pupils. Whenever the groups are not equivalent at the beginning of the experiment, it is difficult to interpret differences on the dependent variable.

Another rival explanation for experimental results involves the loss of subjects from the experimental groups. The reasons for subjects dropping out range from illness or moving out of the area to disenchantment with the experience of being a subject. The loss of subjects in an experiment is called **attrition**.[3] Attrition poses the greatest threat to internal validity when there is **differential attrition**—that is, when the conditions of an experiment have different dropout rates. Invariably, those subjects who drop out differ in important ways from the ones who remain, so that the experimental conditions are no longer equivalent in composition; thus differential attrition undermines the effects of random assignment. In an experiment to test the effectiveness of certain behavior modification techniques on fingernail biting, for example, nail biters might be randomly assigned either to the experimental treatment or to the control group. But what if nail biters who are making the least progress drop out of the experimental group? The measure of nail biting at the end of the treatment will tend to reflect greater success than if all subjects had remained in the experimental group. Thus the effect of differential attrition will be confounded with the treatment.

Finally, experimental findings may be confounded by an *interaction* between two or more of the threats to internal validity we have discussed. This simply means that two of these threats, say selection and maturation, act together to affect the outcome on the dependent measure. You will recall the example we used to illustrate the possible confounding effects of maturational processes, a hypothetical study of the effectiveness of a new physical therapy program for stroke victims. It was pointed out that some degree of spontaneous remission might be confounded with the therapy effects. Now suppose that patients were allowed to select either the new therapy program, where treatment took place at a hospital, or the usual program, which involved visits by a physical therapist to the patient's home. We can conjecture how this process of selection might interact with effects of the normal recovery process (maturation). Those patients who volunteered for the new treatment program would differ from those who did not in one obvious way: They would have to have transportation to the hospital. For most patients, this would mean a family member or some other person available and willing to take them and wait for them while they had the therapy. Perhaps stroke victims who have someone around who is willing to make such an effort are also receiving more social and emotional support (and perhaps other benefits) than are those patients who do not have such a person available. Such benefits could possibly facilitate spontaneous remission for patients in this therapy group. Thus the interaction effects of selection (differences between patients choosing and not choosing the new program) and maturation (spontaneous remission) would be confounded in this study with the effects of the therapy program.

We now examine three research designs in which threats to internal validity pose rival explanations for the results, thus preventing meaningful interpretation. Because these designs lack one or more features of true experimental designs, they are termed pre-experimental.

Pre-experimental Designs

Design 1: The One-Shot Case Study

X   O

In the simplest possible design, dubbed the **one-shot case study,** some treatment is administered to a group, after which the group is observed or tested to determine the treatment effects. The above diagram illustrates this design; X stands for the treatment condition of the independent variable and O stands for the observation or measurement of the dependent variable. Time moves from left to right.

To illustrate this design, imagine a teacher who is having a problem with her fourth-grade pupils frequently talking out of turn. She decides to conduct the following "experiment" one day. Every time a child speaks out of turn, the teacher says, "You are talking out of turn," and then immediately turns her attention to the pupil who was interrupted or to another who is modeling desirable behavior. (This is the treatment, symbolized by the letter X in the diagram.) Toward the end of the day a teacher's aide carefully records the number of incidents for each child and finds that few children are talking out of turn and that the number of incidents is low. (This is the measurement of the dependent variable, symbolized by the letter O.) The teacher concludes that her treatment is effective and recommends it to other teachers.

Unfortunately for the teacher's efforts, such a conclusion is clearly unwarranted; several other explanations may account for the apparent change in behavior. Maybe one of the more recalcitrant talkers left after lunch for a date with the dentist; this would result in an attrition effect. Maturational variables also might threaten the study's internal validity if, for example, some of the children were particularly tired that day. Finally, history could offer an alternative explanation for the results; perhaps early in the day the class had a music lesson in which they let off steam by doing a lot of energetic singing and so felt less inclined to interrupt during class discussions. Attrition, maturation, and history represent threats to the internal validity of any study based on the one-shot case study design.

The critical flaw in this design is that it provides no adequate basis for comparing the findings with other observations; and some process of comparison is essential to scientific inference. We cannot tell in our example what the incidence of talking out of turn would have been with a different intervention, with no intervention, with a different group of students, or on a different day. All we know is that the teacher intuitively sensed that talking out of turn decreased.

Many of our day-to-day assumptions about causality are based on "experiments" similar to one-shot case studies. Suppose a jogger buys a new brand of running shoes and afterward finds that she is running faster than before. Concluding that the shoes have "helped" her, she recommends them to you. Can you think of other explanations for her increase in speed?

Design 2: The One-Group Pretest–Posttest Design

$$O_1 \quad X \quad O_2$$

A second pre-experimental design, the **one-group pretest–posttest design,** involves observing or measuring a group of subjects (the pretest), introducing a treatment (the independent variable), and observing the subjects again (the posttest). The pretreatment observations are represented by O_1, the independent variable by X, and the posttreatment observations by O_2. For example, the performance of a group of joggers might be timed before (O_1) and after (O_2) they received a new brand of running shoes (X). Design 2 is commonly found in educational, organizational, and clinical research. It is an improvement over design 1 because it provides a basis of comparison, but it is still subject to major sources of invalidity.

We may illustrate this design by changing our design 1 example slightly. Suppose the teacher's aide counted talking-out-of-turn incidents on the day before as well as the day of the experiment. How would this change in design affect the study's internal validity? First, the attrition threat is controlled effectively in design 2 studies, because only the data from those subjects observed both before and after the treatment would be used in analyzing the effects of the independent variable. In addition, the pretreatment observation makes it possible to determine whether those who dropped out before the second observation differed initially from those who remained.

Two other threats found in the one-shot design, maturation and history, also are found in one-group pretest–posttest designs. In fact, the longer the period between pretest and posttest, the greater the likelihood that either of these threats will confound the results. If in our example a weekend or holiday intervened between pretest and posttest, the children might be "talked out" or worn out on the posttest day.

Additional threats to internal validity—testing, instrumentation, and sometimes statistical regression—may present rival explanations to the hypothesis in design 2 studies. To continue with our example, it is possible that recording talking-out-of-turn incidents could inhibit children who notice their behavior is being observed and recorded; this would be a testing effect. Instrumentation would threaten internal validity if the teacher's aide was not consistent in measuring the problem behavior. For instance, he might record every incident zealously during the pretest but become bored during the posttest and fail to count some incidents. On the other hand, he might be more accurate on the second day of observation due to practice. Finally, statistical regression can be a problem in design 2 studies if a group representing an extreme position on the dependent variable is used. This was not the case in our classroom example, since the whole class served as subjects.[4]

Design 3: The Static-Group Comparison

$$X \quad O_1$$

$$O_2$$

A third pre-experimental design, the **static-group comparison,** like design 2 is an improvement over the one-shot case study in that it provides a set of data with which to compare the posttreatment scores. Whereas design 2 provided pretreatment scores on the same group, design 3 provides the scores of a control group. As symbolized above, the rows represent separate groups. X stands for the experimental treatment, the blank space under X stands for the no-treatment control, and O represents the dependent-variable measure. Notice that each group is measured just once.

Our classroom example again may be altered slightly to fit this design. Let us suppose that, because of rapid growth in the area, the school is on double sessions, so that the teacher has one class in the morning and a different one in the afternoon. On the treatment day she tries out her new approach on the morning class only, but records talking-out-of-turn incidents for the pupils in both groups.

Although the static-group comparison does a better job of controlling threats to internal validity than do the other two pre-experimental designs, some threats remain. The threat of history confounding the findings is controlled, for the most part, as the two groups should experience the same major environmental events. Since there is no pretest, the threats of testing and statistical regression are absent. And as long as measurements are equally reliable and valid for the two groups, instrumentation is not a problem. On the other hand, selection is a serious threat to internal validity; for without the random assignment of subjects to the experimental and control groups, there is no control of possible pretreatment differences. Attrition also is uncontrolled and there are no pretest data by which one may learn whether subjects who drop out of a group are similar or dissimilar to those who remain. Groups that were similar in all important aspects at the beginning of a study may become dissimilar through differential attrition. Finally, maturation also may be a threat if maturational factors are operating differently in the two groups. Indeed, it seems plausible that the afternoon class will be less lively and less likely to talk out of turn than the morning class, simply because it is later in the day.

We turn now to a discussion of true experimental designs, in which threats to internal validity are better controlled.

True Experimental Designs

The designs described in this section differ from the preexperimental designs in that there are always two or more groups, and subjects are assigned to them randomly to ensure approximate equivalence of the groups.

Design 4: The Pretest–Posttest Control Group Design

$$O_1 \quad X \quad O_2$$
$$R$$
$$O_3 \qquad O_4$$

The **pretest–posttest control group design** involves measuring the experimental group before and after the experimental treatment. A control group is measured at the same time but does not receive the experimental treatment. As symbolized before, the rows represent separate groups, and time moves from left to right. The R to the left indicates that subjects are randomly assigned to the groups; each O stands for an observation; the X symbolizes the treatment condition of the independent variable; and the blank space under the X indicates the no-treatment control condition.

Our earlier example of the study of assertiveness-training effectiveness may be altered to illustrate this design. In the original example, which was not a true experiment, subjects who scored in the bottom 25 percent on an extroversion scale were assigned to the experimental treatment, with the remaining 75 percent serving as controls. To fit design 4, the entire pool of available subjects would be randomly assigned to the treatment and control groups. Both groups then would be given the extroversion scale (O_1 and O_3 pretest measurements). Only the experimental treatment group would receive the assertiveness training; at the conclusion of the training, both groups would again be given the extroversion scale (O_2 and O_4 posttests).

How does this design deal effectively with the common threats to internal validity? To consider history first, any event in the general environment that would produce a difference between the pretest and posttest in the experimental group (O_1–O_2) would produce about the same difference in the control group (O_3–O_4).[5] Similarly, changes due to maturation, testing, or instrumentation would be felt equally in both groups. Therefore, these factors cannot account for differences between the posttests, O_2 and O_4. Random assignment also eliminates the factors of selection and regression, within the limits of chance error. Comparison of O_1 and O_3 provides a check on the randomization procedure with regard to initial differences on the dependent variable. And even if the subject pool consisted only of extreme scorers—for example, all introverts—random assignment of these subjects to experimental and control groups should ensure initially equivalent groups that regress about the same amount on the posttest. Finally, this design permits the assessment of possible attrition effects; one can compare both the number of subjects and the pretest scores of those who drop out of each group.

Since true experimental designs adequately control threats to internal validity (without which we cannot tell whether the independent variable was responsible for the results), it is appropriate to examine these designs for possible threats to external validity. You will recall that external validity refers to the extent to which a study's findings have meaning outside the particular circumstances of the experiment—that is, the extent to which the results may be generalized.

The pretest–posttest control group design suffers from the external-validity threat of testing interacting with the independent variable, called *testing–X interac-*

tion or *testing–treatment interaction*. This simply means that the effect of the independent variable may be different when a pretest is present than when it is not. Sometimes an independent-variable effect can be produced only with subjects who have been sensitized to the experimental treatment by pretesting. To continue with our example, it may be that the assertiveness training is effective in helping people become more socially outgoing only when they have been made particularly conscious of their introversion (or extroversion) by responding to the pretest extroversion scale. If that were true, results of the study could be generalized only to other similarly pretested groups.

The extent to which one need be concerned about an interaction between testing and treatment depends on the experimental situation. In educational settings, where test taking is the norm, the effects of a testing–treatment interaction would probably be negligible; and the learning situations to which one would be generalizing are likely to involve testing. The classroom experiment described in chapter 6 on the effects of teacher comments on student achievement (Page, 1958) is an example of the usefulness of the pretest–posttest control group design. Since regular classroom tests and procedures were used in this study, there is no reason to believe the pretests interacted with the treatment to any significant extent. On the other hand, in studies of attitude change or persuasion, a pretest may very well alert subjects to the treatment to follow in such a way as to make them more receptive (or resistant) to it. In such cases, the findings would have little external validity, and it would be better to use the following design.

Design 5: The Posttest-Only Control Group Design

$$R \quad \begin{matrix} X & O_1 \\ \\ & O_2 \end{matrix}$$

The simplest of the true experimental designs, the **posttest-only control group design** incorporates just the basic elements of experimental design: random assignment of subjects to treatment and control groups, introduction of the independent variable to the treatment group, and a posttreatment measure of the dependent variable for both groups. Notice that, except for one crucial difference—subject randomization—design 5 resembles the pre-experimental static-group comparison design. Unlike this design, however, design 5 controls for the common threats to internal validity adequately.

Some researchers seem to feel more confident that groups are equivalent before the experimental manipulation when they can check pretest scores. Yet in reality the random assignment of subjects is sufficient to ensure approximate equivalence. Therefore, under most circumstances, design 5 is preferable to design 4, the pretest–posttest control group design. By eliminating the pretesting step, design 5 has two major advantages. First, it is more economical. Second, and more important, it eliminates the possibility of an interaction between the pretest and the experimental manipulation. Still, there are special situations requiring a pretest and other situations in which a pretest would be useful. Imagine, for example, a long-term experiment in which you expect a higher than usual number of subjects to drop out. In such a situation, pretest scores on each group would help in determining if there was an interaction between attrition and the experimental manipulation.

Design 6: The Solomon Four-Group Design

$$O_1 \quad X \quad O_2$$

$$O_3 \quad \quad O_4$$

$$R$$

$$X \quad O_5$$

$$O_6$$

A third true experimental design, the **Solomon four-group design,** is really a combination of designs 4 and 5, as may be seen in the above symbolic representation. Here we have an experimental group and a control group that are pretested, along with an experimental and a control group that are not pretested.

The Solomon four-group design has the advantages of both of the two previously discussed experimental designs; information is available regarding the effect of the independent variable (O_2 and O_5 compared with O_4 and O_6), the effect of pretesting alone (O_4 versus O_6), the possible interaction of pretesting and treatment (O_2 versus O_5), and the effectiveness of the randomization procedure (O_1 versus O_3). While this design provides more information than either of the other two experimental designs, the requirement of two extra groups makes it much more expensive to use.

Within-Subjects Designs

Each of the three true experimental designs requires the random assignment of subjects to conditions. Randomization is, of course, intended to create groups that are equivalent on uncontrolled extraneous variables. Another solution to the problem of equivalence is to have the same subjects participate in both the treatment and control conditions of the experiment. In other words, an experimenter might expose subjects to a treatment (X_1), apply the measure of the dependent variable (O_1), expose the same subjects to a control (or comparison treatment) condition (X_2), and then measure the effect a second time (O_2), as diagrammed below:

$$X_1 \quad O_1 \quad X_2 \quad O_2$$

This type of study is called a **within-subjects design,** because each subject acts as his or her own control—that is, O_1 is compared with O_2 for each subject. By contrast, designs 4–6 are called **between-subjects designs** because different groups of subjects are compared with one another.

Within-subjects designs have a long history in the natural sciences and are used in some areas of psychological research such as sensation and perception. They have two principal advantages. First they require fewer subjects; a within-subjects design with a treatment and a control condition, for example, would require half as many subjects as design 5. Second, by having each individual experience and react to every condition of the experiment, they reduce the error associated with how different people react to these conditions. But alas, within-subjects designs also create threats to internal validity that often make them inappropriate for social research. A study by R. Brent Gallupe and associates (1992) illustrates these threats and the general strategy for estimating their effects.

Gallupe and colleagues sought to compare the effectiveness of traditional brainstorming with electronic brainstorming. From the time it was introduced in the 1950s, brainstorming has been a popular method for enhancing group creativity. To stimulate ideas through group discussion, members of brainstorming groups are asked to express as many ideas as they possibly can while withholding comments and criticisms. Despite its widespread use, however, research has shown that brainstorming groups do not outperform noninteracting individuals. Group researchers attribute this to various inhibitors, such as evaluation apprehension, present in interacting groups. To reduce these inhibitors, they recently have introduced a new technique called electronic brainstorming in which group members simultaneously type ideas into a computer that then distributes the ideas to all members of the group.

To compare the productivity of traditional verbal brainstorming with electronic brainstorming in a within-subjects design, one simply could have the same groups first generate ideas verbally and then electronically. This is, in part, what Gallupe and colleagues did, and they used the number of nonredundant ideas each group produced as their primary measure of the dependent variable. Suppose more ideas were produced following electronic brainstorming than verbal brainstorming. Besides the different form of communication, what might account for this effect? One possibility is a testing effect; with practice, groups became better at generating ideas. (Alternatively, if they produced fewer ideas over time, this might be due to fatigue.) Another possibility is that subjects may become aware of the experimenter's hypothesis; if subjects realized after the first, traditional brainstorming session that their idea-generation was being compared under two conditions, they might behave differently in the second session, perhaps viewing electronic communication as a novel and more interesting challenge.

More generally, in any within-subjects design, there is always the possibility that observed changes are due to the sequencing or order of the treatment and control conditions rather than to the treatment. The principal method of controlling for order effects is **counterbalancing**. This consists of reversing the sequence of the treatment and control conditions, so that different groups of subjects experience either sequence. Gallupe and colleagues' experiment was counterbalanced; half the subjects brainstormed verbally first and the other half brainstormed electronically first, with the order determined randomly. With random assignment, the within-subjects design becomes a true experiment, effectively controlling for threats to internal validity. Testing effects should be manifested equally in both sequences, and the effects of the order of the treatment and control condition can be estimated by comparing differences in the measures of the dependent variable in one sequence with differences in the other. But even though testing is manifested equally and order effects can be tested, the randomized within-subjects design does not eliminate these effects. Consequently, if it is likely that participating in one condition of an experiment will influence how subjects respond to another, as often occurs in social psychological experiments, this design should not be used.

Gallupe and colleagues actually carried out two experiments comparing verbal with electronic brainstorming. Besides counterbalancing the different forms of communication, both experiments manipulated group size or the number of group members and both used two different idea-generation problems to reduce the testing effect. The researchers found that neither the type of problem nor the order of the brainstorming techniques had an effect, which simplified the interpretation of the findings. Except in two-member groups, electronic brainstorming produced more ideas than verbal brainstorming.

Overview of True Experimental Designs

Many simple variations of experimental designs are possible. Although designs 4 and 5 were presented as having just two groups (an experimental group and a control group), the logic of either design may be extended easily to three or more groups: One might, for example, want to compare several clinical approaches for treating depression or a number of methods of teaching reading. Similarly, groups may be added to vary the intensity of the independent variable; for example, we might induce a high level of frustration in one group, a moderate level in another, and a low level in a third group.

Sometimes ethical considerations preclude withholding treatment from a control group. This is frequently the case in the fields of correction, clinical psychology, medicine, and education. Also, a true no-treatment control group, one that is exactly identical to the treatment group except for the treatment manipulation, is impossible to implement in many situations. The hypothetical study discussed earlier, in which a new approach to physical therapy for stroke victims was compared with a standard approach, illustrates the common variation of experimental design in which there is no true control group; rather, two or more treatments are compared for their relative effectiveness.

We have pointed out the importance of random assignment of subjects as a means of controlling for pre-existing differences (known and unknown) in subjects. However, randomization introduces one other threat to internal validity: The observed results might have occurred by chance rather than being caused by the experimental variable. Recall that tests of statistical significance are used to determine the likelihood of this occurring, thereby screening out trivial results that could have occurred easily by chance. Having noted this, we stress again that the random assignment of subjects is an integral part of any true experimental design.

The matter of external validity warrants further comment. As noted earlier, external invalidity results from an interaction of the treatment, or independent-variable manipulation, with some other variable. The presence of such interaction means that treatment effects apply only under certain conditions inherent in the experiment. Earlier, for example, we discussed the threat of a testing–treatment interaction as a particular concern in the pretest–posttest control group design. This interaction limits the generalizability of results to situations in which subjects have been pretested. External validity similarly may be threatened by interactions of the treatment with characteristics of the subject population, time, or some other feature of the experimental setting. We now elaborate on a few of these sources of external invalidity.

Sample selection often restricts external validity. Because the sample of subjects participating in an experiment typically consists of homogeneous groups such as college students, the possibility of sample selection interacting with the independent variable may be present in any of the experimental designs. Thus, extreme caution must be used in generalizing any effect of the independent variable to dissimilar groups. A cigarette-smoking cessation treatment, for example, might succeed with volunteer subjects (who are highly motivated) but be ineffective with the general population of smokers who wish to quit.

Maturation also may interact with the independent variable; that is, the effect of the treatment may occur only with subjects in a certain physical or mental state. For example, the findings of an experiment conducted at four o'clock on a hot summer day may be generalizable only to hot, tired subjects. Solutions to this problem include (1) deliberately varying the conditions that would seem to affect maturational states as part of the experimental design and (2) replicating the basic experiment under varying conditions.

Finally, the effect of the treatment might be peculiar to the historical circumstances surrounding the experiment. For example, a study of the effects of certain experiences on Christians' attitudes toward Jews might produce significant results only because the experiment took place at the time of a highly rated television series on the Holocaust. In viewing it, subjects became more receptive to the treatment. Replicating experiments under different historical circumstances is an effective way of ruling out the threat of such treatment-history interactions.

Factorial Experimental Designs

Social events often are caused or influenced by a number of variables. Therefore, it frequently makes sense to study several possible causes, or independent variables, at the same time. When two or more independent variables are studied in a single experiment, they are referred to as *factors*, and the designs that enable us to explore their effects jointly are called **factorial designs**. Although more than one variable is manipulated, it is possible to assess the effect of any manipulated variable while controlling for the impact of other variables. Hence, the basic principle of good design, "doing only one thing at a time," still applies.

An interesting example of a factorial design is Jody Gottlieb and Charles Carver's (1980) experiment on "the anticipation of future interaction and the bystander effect." As you may recall, Darley and Latané (1968) demonstrated the bystander effect—the larger the number of bystanders who witness an emergency, the less likely that any one person will help—in an experiment described in chapter 6. Gottlieb and Carver's study was quite similar to Darley and Latané's. Subjects (college students) were asked to engage in a discussion of the problems of college living with other subjects over an intercom system; the other discussants were tape recorded; the number of discussants varied, either one or five others; and the dependent measure consisted of the length of time that subjects took to respond to a staged emergency (one of the supposed fellow discussants, who apparently had been eating, began choking and struggling for breath, and cried out for help). So, one independent variable or factor was the number of discussants or "bystanders." Gottlieb and Carver reasoned, however, that the bystander effect may occur because of the anonymity of the subjects; that is, they never saw nor did they expect ever to meet their co-subjects face-to-face. If subjects expected to interact with other by-standers face-to-face in the future, they might be more willing to help to avoid being blamed by others for their inaction. Thus, Gottlieb and Carver manipulated a second factor, anticipated interaction, by telling some subjects that they would be meeting afterward face-to-face and telling the others that they would not meet the co-subjects at all.

The Gottlieb and Carver experiment represents the simplest case of a factorial design. Two variables (number of bystanders and anticipated interaction) are manipulated, with each variable having two levels or categories. This design requires four experimental conditions, one for each combination of variable categories: one discussant (the emergency victim)/anticipated interaction; one discussant/no anticipated interaction; five discussants/anticipated interaction; and five discussants/no anticipated interaction. When a design has two independent variables, each having two levels, we call it a 2×2 (two by two) factorial design. A design that had three levels of one factor and four levels of another would be a 3×4 factorial design having twelve conditions. In every case the number of conditions of a factorial design may be determined by multiplying the number of levels of the first factor by the number of levels of the second factor and, if there are additional factors, by the number of levels of each in turn. Theoretically, a factorial design may utilize any number of factors, although there are practical limits.

As you can see, factorial designs are simple extensions of the basic experimental designs. In fact, we already have introduced one design, the Solomon four-group design, which may be viewed as a factorial design. We depicted this design as follows, with each row representing a separate group.

$$O_1 \quad X \quad O_2 \quad \text{first group}$$

$$O_3 \quad \quad O_4 \quad \text{second group}$$

$$R$$

$$ \quad X \quad O_5 \quad \text{third group}$$

$$ \quad \quad O_6 \quad \text{fourth group}$$

Table 7.2 presents the Solomon four-group design in factorial form. Note that this design has two factors: the treatment and the pretest. Also, like the Gottlieb and Carver experiment, both levels (categories) of one factor are combined with both levels of the second, forming the four experimental groups in the cells of the table. So, this is another example of a 2×2 factorial design.

Ideally, each cell will have the same number of subjects. When this is not possible (because of subject attrition or other reasons), the dependent-variable data in the various cells can be analyzed after statistical adjustment has been made to com-

TABLE 7.2. **Solomon Four-Group Design Represented as a**
2 × 2 Factorial Design

Treatment condition (factor A)	Pretest condition (factor B)	
	PRETEST	NO PRETEST
Treatment	First group, O_2	Third group, O_5
No treatment	Second group, O_4	Fourth group, O_6

pensate for the uneven number of subjects. As always with true experimental designs, subjects are assigned to the various conditions (cells) by a random device to control for pre-experimental differences.

You may be wondering how the effects of the various factors are determined in a factorial design. To answer this question, let us consider a hypothetical study of the effect of a sympathetic movie portrayal of the gay community (the treatment) on attitudes toward gay rights (the dependent variable). The results from the Solomon four-group experiment are shown in Table 7.3. Each cell contains the average (mean) posttest attitude score for that experimental group. A higher score indicates a more positive attitude toward gay rights.

First, factorial designs provide information about the **main effect** of each factor—that is, the overall effect of the factor by itself. We have labeled the treatment variable "factor A" and the pretest variable "factor B." The main effect of factor A is determined by comparing the overall mean score of subjects who received the experimental treatment (which in this case is 25) with the overall mean score of subjects who did not receive the experimental treatment (in this case 15).[6] Clearly, subjects who saw the movie were more supportive of gay rights than those not exposed to the movie. Whether this treatment effect is "significant" would have to be determined by an appropriate statistical test. Let us assume that all effects are statistically significant.

Likewise, the main effect of factor B is determined by comparing the overall mean score of pretested subjects (30) with the overall mean of subjects not pretested (10). Thus, exposure to the pretest also enhanced posttest attitudes toward gay rights. While this result is not unexpected, it is nonetheless discouraging, since ideally treatment effects (the movie) should be much more powerful than measurement artifacts (pretesting effects).

Interaction Effects

Notice that we determined the main effects of each factor by averaging over all levels of the other. Assessing main effects in this way actually can be very misleading, as it may conceal how the two factors, acting together, produce the outcome. A major advantage of factorial designs is that they also provide information about the *joint effects* of the factors. If there is an interaction between two factors, the effect of one factor on the dependent variable varies according to the value or level of the other. In other words, the effects of the factors together differ from the ef-

**TABLE 7.3. Hypothetical Results of a Study
Using a 2 × 2 Factorial Design**

Treatment condition (factor A)	Pretest condition (factor B)		
	PRETEST	NO PRETEST	OVERALL MEANS OF A
Treatment	40	10	25
No treatment	20	10	15
Overall means of B	30	10	

fects of either alone. Because of this possibility, it is always best to check first for an interaction; otherwise, conclusions based on main effects may be incorrect.

The presence of the pretesting effect in our example should lead us to question the generalizability of the movie effect. Specifically, there may be an interaction between the pretest and the movie, with the pretest sensitizing subjects to the topic and thereby enhancing the movie's impact. Inspection of the cell means in Table 7.3, graphed in Figure 7.1, does indeed reveal a testing–treatment interaction: The movie has an impact only on pretested subjects. Consequently, its value outside the laboratory as an attitudinal change agent appears to be very limited.

Interaction effects do not always look like the idealized results in Figure 7.1. Some other possible outcomes are graphed in Figure 7.2. The movie treatment may affect all subjects but more so for those pretested (Figure 7.2A), may have no effect on pretested subjects (Figure 7.2B), or may even have a reverse effect on pretested subjects (Figure 7.2C). Finally, when there is no interaction, the lines connecting the mean scores for pretested and not-pretested subjects will be parallel, as shown in Figure 7.2D. (Box 7.1 describes a factorial experiment that produced an interaction effect.)

Besides providing information on interaction effects, factorial designs are cost efficient. A factorial design can increase the amount of information provided by a

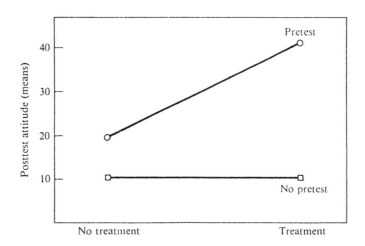

FIGURE 7.1. Graph of cell means from Table 7.3.

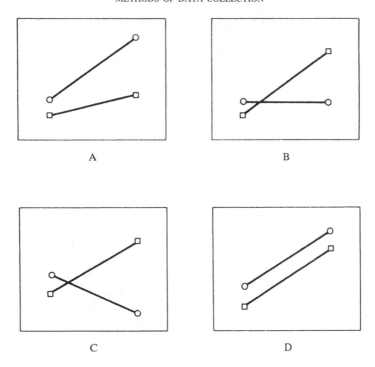

FIGURE 7.2. Illustrative outcomes for 2 × 2 factorial designs. Symbols are the same as in
Figure 7.1.

study with little increase in cost over a nonfactorial experimental design. Consider
the Gottlieb and Carver experiment, for example. By adapting the procedures of the
Darley and Latané experiment and manipulating the number of discussants, this
study replicated the bystander effect. In effect, it addressed the following question:
Does the number of bystanders affect helping in emergencies with a different sample of subjects? But by including another relevant independent variable, anticipated
interaction, the factorial design addressed two additional questions: (1) Does anticipated face-to-face interaction affect helping? (2) Will anticipated interaction diminish the impact of the bystander effect—that is, will expected future encounters
with bystanders reduce the difference between helping in the absence and presence
of bystanders? As it turned out, Gottlieb and Carver did not find an interaction effect, as expected. Rather, there were main effects for both factors: Anticipated interaction reduced the time to respond to the emergency, irrespective of the presence
of bystanders, and response time was longer in the bystander than in the non-
bystander condition.

A factorial design also may enhance external validity by permitting determination of the effects of a key variable under several conditions. When the effects
are consistent under diverse conditions, we are more confident that the findings
generalize to additional situations. For example, we may want to study the effects
of counseling on troubled marriages, with our dependent measure being the percentage of participant couples still together one year after completion of counsel-

BOX 7.1

An Example of a Factorial Design: Beautiful but Dangerous

In an interesting study employing a 2 × 3 factorial design, Harold Sigall and Nancy Ostrove (1975) investigated the effects of type of criminal offense (swindle or burglary) and physical attractiveness of the offender (attractive, unattractive, or no information) on the severity of the sentence received. Subjects in each of the six conditions were presented with a case account describing the offender and the crime. Then they were asked to circle a number between 1 and 15 to complete the statement, "I sentence the defendant, Barbara Helm, to _____ years of imprisonment" (p. 412).

For the factor "type of criminal offense," the researchers chose a swindle and a burglary. Swindles appeared to be attractiveness related, in that the offender could use his or her attractiveness to commit the crime. The crime of burglary, however, appeared to be unrelated to attractiveness. In the swindle account, the defendant Barbara Helm had become friendly with a middle-aged bachelor and persuaded him to invest $2200 in a nonexistent corporation. In the burglary account, the defendant had illegally entered a neighbor's apartment and stolen $2200 in cash and goods. To manipulate the attractiveness factor, the researchers attached a photograph of a physically attractive woman to one-third of the case accounts, a photograph of a physically unattractive woman to one-third of the accounts, and no photograph to the remainder.

Sigall and Ostrove predicted an interaction: When the crime was unrelated to attractiveness (the burglary), subjects would sentence the attractive defendant to a shorter prison term than the unattractive defendant. But when the offense was attractiveness related (the swindle), the attractive defendant would receive a more severe sentence. The first prediction follows from evidence that attractive people are better liked and that liking for a defendant increases leniency. In the case of the second prediction, the authors reasoned that a beautiful criminal would be regarded as more dangerous and as having taken advantage of a "God-given gift" if her attractiveness helped her to commit the crime. As shown below, the data supported the hypothesis, with a statistically significant interaction of attractiveness and offense.

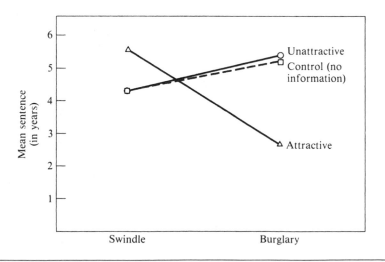

ing. A $2 \times 3 \times 2$ factorial design might utilize two counseling approaches, let us say "behavior modification" and "eclectic"; three counselor conditions, such as "male–female counselor team," "male counselor only," and "female counselor only"; and two cost-of-counseling conditions, perhaps "fixed fee" and "free." Since this design explores the effects of marriage counseling under twelve conditions, the study should be high in external validity.

Quasi-experimental Designs

Legal, ethical, or practical considerations make it impossible to employ a true experimental design in some research situations. Frequently, random assignment of persons (or other units) is not possible. At other times, control or comparison groups cannot be incorporated into the design. Sometimes, random assignment to treatment and control groups can be carried out but the researcher cannot exercise the tight control over subjects' experiences required for a true experiment. To deal with these problems, researchers have developed a number of **quasi-experimental designs**, so named because they take an experimental approach without having full experimental control.

In terms of complexity and effectiveness in controlling extraneous threats to validity, these designs generally lie between pre-experimental and true experimental designs. Some of them resemble pre-experimental designs but with added features. Others are similar to true experimental designs but with something lacking, such as a control group or the process of randomization.

An example of the first type is the **separate-sample pretest–posttest design** (Campbell and Stanley, 1963), diagrammed as follows:

$$\begin{array}{ccc} & O_1 & X \\ R & & \\ & X & O_2 \end{array}$$

R in this design signifies random assignment to the time of measurement. The top line represents the group randomly selected for pretreatment measurement. This group receives the treatment but is not measured afterward. The second group is randomly selected for posttreatment measurement. Since the treatment effect is estimated by comparing pretest (first-group) scores with posttest (second-group) scores, this design resembles the pre-experimental one-group pretest–posttest design (O_1 X O_2). However, some of the threats to validity found in the latter (e.g., testing and testing–X interaction) are eliminated by using separate samples. The most serious challenge to the internal validity of the design is history.

The separate-sample pretest–posttest design may be useful in those circumstances in which the entire population of interest, such as residents of a city, employees of a large firm, students in a university, or soldiers in a military unit, receives the same treatment. Although one cannot randomly assign subjects to different treatments, the design may be applied if one can determine the timing of the measurement of the dependent variable and randomly select those who are measured before and after the treatment. For example, measurement might take the form of an attitude survey conducted prior to and following alcohol education week (the treatment) at a certain college.

Nonequivalent control group designs exemplify those quasi-experimental designs that are similar to but lack a crucial feature of true experiments. These designs often are used when the experimental treatment is administered to intact groups, such as school classes, making random assignment of individual subjects impossible. In one such design, symbolized below, pretests and posttests are administered both to the experimental group and to a nonequivalent but similar control group.

$$O_1 \quad X \quad O_2$$

$$O_3 \quad\quad O_4$$

Except for the missing R representing randomization, this design looks exactly like the pretest-posttest control group design. Randomization, of course, should be used if at all possible. But if it is not possible, then this quasi-experimental design is often worth using. The inclusion of a control group, especially one highly similar to the experimental group in known respects, makes it superior to the one-group pretest–posttest design. For if the groups are similar in recruitment and history, then the design controls for history, maturation, testing, and regression.

Another important type of quasi-experimental design involves time-series data, which consist of multiple observations of the same or similar units over time. The **interrupted time-series design** resembles the one-group pretest–posttest design except that instead of a single observation before and after the treatment, there are multiple observations before and afterward, as shown below. (*Note*: There are no limitations, other than practical ones, on the number of observations in the series.)

$$O_1 \quad O_2 \quad O_3 \quad O_4 \quad X \quad O_5 \quad O_6 \quad O_7 \quad O_8$$

The treatment may be systematically introduced into the series by the researcher or it may consist of some naturally occurring intervention. Social researchers often use this design when periodic measurements of an effect of interest are available, such as regularly administered school achievement tests, business records of absenteeism and productivity, or myriad institutional records on events such as automobile accidents, divorces, and crimes. For example, to assess the deterrent effect of a gun control law mandating one-year minimum sentences for anyone convicted of carrying a firearm without an appropriate license, one could examine homicide rates several years before and several years after the law went into effect (see Deutsch and Alt, 1977). If the law had an impact, one would expect an "interruption" or discontinuity in the time series—the homicide rates—at the point where the law was introduced.

The use of several observations makes the interrupted time-series design superior to the one-group pretest–posttest design. Any change from pretest to posttest in the latter design may reflect a long-term trend or a temporary upswing or downswing in a fluctuating pattern. But these effects can be distinguished from treatment effects in a time-series design by comparing the overall pattern with any change at the point of intervention. The biggest threat to internal validity with the interrupted time-series design is history, since it is possible that some more or less simultaneous event other than X may have produced the change. Also, if the time-series is taken from official records, an instrumentation effect should be ruled out by checking carefully to see if there has been a change in record-keeping procedures.

The best way to control for history in a time-series analysis is to examine two or more time series, one of which was exposed to the treatment and the others of which were not. This extension of the interrupted time-series design, diagrammed below, is known as the **multiple time-series design**.

$$O_1 \quad O_2 \quad O_3 \quad O_4 \quad X \quad O_5 \quad O_6 \quad O_7 \quad O_8$$

$$O_1 \quad O_2 \quad O_3 \quad O_4 \qquad O_5 \quad O_6 \quad O_7 \quad O_8$$

The subscripts here represent points in time. Now, if a change from O_4 to O_5 occurs in the first group but does not occur in the second group, the change is not likely to be due to a treatment-correlated historical event. This quasi-experimental design is particularly effective in controlling for sources of invalidity. But like the nonequivalent control group design, which is contained within it, the strength of inferences in a multiple-time-series design depends on how comparable the control group is to the interrupted group.

Since the design possibilities are so numerous, we limit further discussion of quasi-experimental designs to some general ideas and a detailed description of two quasi-experimental studies that used one or more of the designs outlined above.[7] The objective of such studies, as with true experiments, is to determine treatment effects by eliminating plausible rival explanations of experimental results. Lacking subject randomization or other features of true experiments, however, quasi-experimental studies use a variety of approaches to establish internal validity. Threats to internal validity are ruled out individually in several ways (Cook, Cook, and Mark, 1977): (1) including special design features, (2) examining additional data that bear on each threat, and/or (3) reasoning, on the basis of theory or common sense, that a particular threat is an unlikely alternative explanation.

An example of a design feature that strengthens causal inferences in a quasi-experiment is the use of a pretest. This is a nonessential feature in most true experiments because randomization creates initially equivalent groups. But in a quasi-experimental study, a pretest permits a vital check on the initial difference between nonequivalent groups (Cook, Cook, and Mark, 1977). An example of the second approach—examining additional data—comes from a study of a smoking-cessation treatment (Berglund et al., 1974). The researchers obtained a measure of motivation from pretreatment interviews with participants. By showing that motivation scores were unrelated to subjects' success in withdrawing from smoking, they eliminated one selection threat as a possible rival explanation. Finally, an example of the third approach would be ruling out testing as a serious threat in an educational setting where the measures are similar to typical classroom testing procedures.

Let us further examine how these approaches are applied in two carefully conducted quasi-experimental studies.

Example 1: Interracial Attitudes and Behavior at a Summer Camp

Can contact between "opposite-race" children under favorable circumstances improve interracial attitudes and behavior? To test this idea, social psychologist Gerald Clore and his colleagues (1978) set up a summer camp for underprivileged black and white children that was designed to provide a positive interracial experience. Previous research suggested that prolonged, intimate contact between racial groups of equal size and similar socioeconomic background could significantly reduce prejudice. Therefore, the camp was structured so that blacks and whites of similar status were equally represented among the campers, counselors, and staff. For example, children were assigned to tents that accommodated three black and three white campers of the same sex and age group (8–10 or 11–12), as well as one black and one white counselor. In all, 196 children were randomly assigned to attend one of five one-week camp sessions.

The experimenters used three dependent measures to assess whether the camping experience affected racial attitudes and behavior. First, they administered an attitude measure, based on four questions regarding feelings toward children of the "opposite" race. The procedure approximated the separate-sample pretest–posttest design, with half the children administered the measure on the first day of camp and the other half near the end (fifth or sixth day). Results showed the camp to be effective for girls but not for boys. While the girls had somewhat more negative cross-race attitudes at the beginning and shifted toward neutrality, the boys were relatively neutral at the beginning and showed no change.

A second measure, obtained for three of the five weeklong sessions, involved making inexpensive loaded cameras available to the children and allowing them to photograph whatever and whomever they wished. Within age, sex, and race categories, children were randomly assigned to either a pretest group that took pictures on the second day or a posttest group that took pictures on the fifth or sixth day. The dependent variable was the proportion of persons in the resultant photographs who were not of the photographer's race. Thus, this measure, like the first, was based on the separate-sample pretest–posttest design. But unlike the first measure, the photo taking was unobtrusive and behavioral. Analysis of the photos revealed a slight but nonsignificant overall treatment effect: For only one of the three weeks measured did photos taken at the end of the week reveal a significantly higher proportion of cross-race persons than photos taken at the beginning.

A third set of measures, also behavioral, consisted of interpersonal choices the children made in three games played on the first day of camp and again on the fifth or sixth day. Counselors recorded the choices, with the dependent variable being the proportion of choices that were interracial. The design for this measure, referred to by the researchers as a multiple-group pretest–posttest design, resembled the preexperimental one-group pretest–posttest design but was an improvement over it in that it was replicated over five camp sessions ("multiple groups"). Results showed a slight shift toward more cross-race choices from the beginning to the end of the sessions. As with the attitude measure, the change was evident for girls only. While showing no significant change from pretest to posttest, the boys made a higher proportion of cross-race choices overall than did the girls.

Thus, the dependent measures, taken together, indicated that the camp experience was effective in changing the interracial attitudes and behavior of the girls but not of the boys, who evidenced more positive attitudes and behavior from the beginning. The authors of the study described how they were able to rule out rival explanations to the hypothesis that the camp experience itself caused the observed changes. To do so, they invoked special design features, additional data, and reasoning based on common sense.

Some crucial design features incorporated in the study enabled Clore and co-workers to eliminate several validity threats. These included the use of two different quasi-experimental designs, three very different dependent measures (attitude questions, photographs, and interpersonal choices), and replications. Using more than one quasi-experimental design strengthens a study, because different designs ordinarily will not share the same weaknesses. For example, testing effects cannot be ruled out in the multiple-group pretest–posttest design (which produced the shift in cross-race choices), since pretests and posttests are administered to the same persons. However, testing is not a threat in the separate-sample pretest–posttest design (which produced the change in attitudes), since individuals receive either the pretest or the posttest but not both.

The use of dissimilar measures also strengthens inferences by controlling for systematic error in any one measure. Moreover, the measurement processes were replicated three to five times (weekly camp sessions), controlling for the most part the threats of instrumentation and history. Instrumentation could be ruled out because with pretests and posttests repeated over several weeks, it was unlikely that scorers' expertness, effort, or enthusiasm would differ systematically from pretest to posttest across all sessions. And since the measurements were replicated at different times and produced consistent results for both the attitude and choices measures, the rival explanation of history was ruled out for these two measures. On the other hand, one could not rule out entirely the possibility that historical conditions were responsible for the change in the photo measure, implausible as this explanation seems, since this measure showed significant effects for only one week.

Two possible rival explanations for certain of the findings were ruled out through the examination of additional data. First, it was conjectured that the changes in the interpersonal-choices data might be attributable to children making their choices from among their acquaintances. That is, if children were acquainted with more same-race children than cross-race children at the beginning of camp, they might choose more same-race children on the pretests and move toward a higher proportion of cross-race posttest choices as they became acquainted with the cross-race children. Since the names of initial acquaintances of each child were available (the children had been asked in one game to circle the names of all the other children whom they knew), it was possible to test this argument. Data for two camp sessions were reanalyzed, discarding choices of children known to the subject before camp. The results of the reanalysis were consistent with the original findings, ruling out this rival explanation.

A second possible explanation for the choices data, that choices in the posttest games might reflect allegiance to the child's living unit, was also evaluated. The choices data were reanalyzed using the proportion of cross-unit choices as the dependent variable. No significant effects were found, thereby ruling out this second possibility.

Finally, Clore and colleagues were able to rule out some other threats through reasoning based on common sense. For example, maturation was an unlikely explanation for the changes because the camp sessions lasted only one week each. The threat of regression was implausible, because subjects were not selected on the basis of extreme attitudes or behavior.

Example 2: The Connecticut Crackdown on Speeding

In late December 1955, Governor Abraham Ribicoff of Connecticut instituted a crackdown on speeding in the hope of reducing the number of deaths from automobile accidents, which had risen to a high point of 324 in 1955. New, stiffer penalties for speeding involved automatic suspension of the offender's driver's license: thirty days for the first offense; sixty days for the second offense; and indefinitely for the third offense, with a hearing after ninety days. Although opposed by many, the crackdown was carried out and suspensions for speeding increased dramatically. When the number of traffic fatalities declined to 284 in 1956, Governor Ribicoff was quoted as saying, "With the saving of 40 lives . . . we can say the program is definitely worthwhile" (Campbell and Ross, 1968).

But did the program actually cause the reduction in traffic deaths? Donald Campbell and H. Lawrence Ross (1968) addressed this question while demonstrating the utility of quasi-experimental time-series designs. First, they noted that the data Ribicoff cited, although impressive, covered only two years—the year before and the year after the crackdown. If these data alone were used in determining whether the crackdown (the treatment) caused the decrease in deaths (the dependent variable), the design would be the one-group pretest–posttest design, which fails to control for most of the common threats to validity.

Because of the weakness of the one-group pretest–posttest design, Campbell and Ross did an analysis based on an interrupted time-series design. Data for this design are graphed in Figure 7.3, which shows the number of traffic fatalities from 1951 through 1959. The decrease in traffic fatalities in 1956 now appears much less impressive in view of the comparable decreases shown in 1952 and 1954 and the unusually high number of fatalities in 1955.

Campbell and Ross then extended their evaluation by using a multiple time-series design. The researchers obtained traffic fatality statistics for the years 1951 through 1959 for four states adjacent to Connecticut, which were assumed to be similar in weather and driving patterns. Figure 7.4 shows the time-series data for the five states. Note that for the year 1955, four of the five states showed an increase in fatalities over the previous year, with Connecticut showing the greatest increase. All five states showed a decrease for 1956. These facts, as well as the fact that the 1956 decrease in Rhode Island closely resembled that in Connecticut, might argue against the hypothesis that the decrease in Connecticut was caused by the crackdown. However, Connecticut was the only one of the five states to show consistent year-to-year decreases following the crackdown; Rhode Island, by contrast, showed consistent increases after 1956.

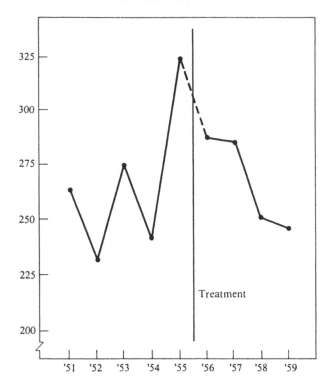

FIGURE 7.3. Connecticut traffic fatalities, 1951–59. *Source:* Page 42 of Campbell and Ross (1968). Reprinted by permission of the Law and Society Association and Blackwell Publishing Ltd.

Let us now examine how the major threats to validity were dealt with in this study.

History is a possible threat in that some event of 1956 other than the crackdown may have caused the reduction in fatalities. Possible rival explanations included better weather conditions in 1956 than in 1955 and improved safety features on 1956-model automobiles (Campbell and Ross, 1968). While the researchers reasoned on the basis of available data that neither of these explanations appeared plausible, the threat of history cannot be ruled out altogether, especially in view of the fatality rate decreases for 1956 in all of the four control states. Some event common to all five states still may have caused the decrease in fatalities. However, history is not a plausible rival explanation for the post-1956 decreases in Connecticut, since the adjacent states failed to show the same pattern.

Maturation is normally associated with human physical and psychological processes. In the Connecticut study, maturation would be a threat if, for example, the driving population as a whole were becoming more skilled drivers. Although this is rather implausible, Campbell and Ross extend the idea of maturation to processes external to subjects. Thus, they defined as a maturation threat the possibility of a long-term trend toward a reduction in death rates due to such factors as improved medical services and improved highways. But since no such trend appears in the time-series or multiple time-series data, this threat may be ruled out.

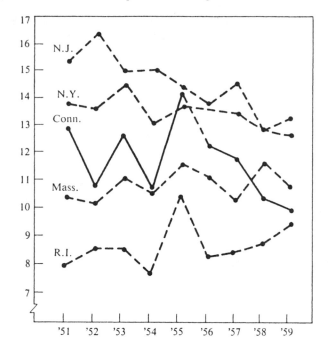

FIGURE 7.4. Traffic fatalities (per 100,000 persons) for Connecticut, New York, New Jersey, Rhode Island, and Massachusetts. *Source:* Page 45 of Campbell and Ross (1968). Reprinted by permission of the Law and Society Association and Blackwell Publishing Ltd.

The threat of *testing* must also be evaluated: Could the pretest by itself have caused the change? In this case, the pretest consists of the 1955 traffic fatalities statistic. It seems unlikely that mere keeping of records would have much impact on the next year's statistic, but the widespread publicizing of the high 1955 figure conceivably could have increased driver caution, thus lowering the subsequent year's statistic. This threat cannot be ruled out with certainty for 1956; however, it seems implausible that publication of the 1955 figure would result in the continued year-to-year decreases that were observed in Connecticut.

Instrumentation would be a threat if there had been a post-crackdown change in record keeping. Campbell and Ross reported that they found no evidence of this.

Regression is a threat whenever a treatment is administered on the basis of a high pretest score. It may be argued that this was the case with the Connecticut crackdown on speeding, which was instituted following an extreme year. On the basis of data from 1951 through 1956, regression or simple instability of the data would indeed offer a plausible rival explanation. However, since the rate of traffic deaths continued to decrease in the years following the crackdown, these factors do not explain the findings adequately. The Campbell and Ross study is an example of rigorous quasi-experimental research. While the absence of a true experimental design made it impossible to exert optimal control over the threats to validity, the researchers gained valuable knowledge by making use of better quasi-experimental designs, relevant available data, and common sense. By these means they were able to conclude with a large degree of confidence that the Connecticut crackdown on speeding had some effect.

Summary

The basic principle of good experimental design is "doing only one thing at a time"—that is, allowing only one independent variable to vary while controlling all other variables. In this chapter we examined pre-experimental designs, true experimental designs, and quasi-experimental designs in the light of this basic principle. We found that the pre-experimental designs violate this principle by permitting a number of variables to go uncontrolled, presenting serious threats to the internal validity of the study. Features of the true experimental designs, on the other hand, permit researchers to rule out these threats as rival explanations to the hypothesis. Although quasi-experimental designs control extraneous variables imperfectly, rival explanations frequently may be ruled out through the intelligent use of design features, additional data, and common sense.

Experimental designs are evaluated in terms of how well they control for extraneous variables that threaten a study's internal and external validity. Thus, we began by identifying several common threats to internal validity: history (specific events other than intended experimental manipulations that occur during the course of an experiment), maturation (psychological and physiological changes in subjects), testing (the effects of being measured once on being measured a second time), instrumentation (unwanted changes in the measuring instrument or procedure), statistical regression (the tendency for extreme scorers on one measurement to move closer to the mean score on a later measurement), selection (differences in the composition of experimental and control groups), attrition (the loss of subjects during the course of an experiment), and interactions with selection (differences between treatment groups due to the combined effect of initial differences and history, maturation, or testing). These threats, or classes of extraneous variables, are sources of invalidity insofar as they can account for study results.

Pre-experimental designs lack one or more features of true experiments, such as a comparison group or random assignment. Therefore, they are subject to several validity threats and their findings cannot be interpreted meaningfully. Three pre-experimental designs are the one-shot case study, the one-group pretest-posttest design, and the static-group comparison.

All the basic true experimental designs control adequately for the major sources of internal invalidity. However, the external validity of the pretest–posttest control group design suffers from the possibility of a testing–treatment interaction, in which experimental effects occur only for pretested subjects. This threat is eliminated in the more economical posttest-only control group design, albeit at the loss of pretest information. The Solomon four-group design offers the advantages of both of these designs by combining them in a single experiment. Randomized within-subject designs offer the advantage of comparing the same individuals in both experimental and control conditions, but are seldom used in social research because responses in one condition are likely to affect responses in a subsequent condition. While strong in internal validity, studies incorporating true experimental designs may still be weak in external validity. Besides testing–treatment interaction, external validity may be threatened by the interactions of the treatment with sample characteristics, history, and maturation.

External validity is generally better in factorial designs. These are simple extensions of basic experimental designs in which two or more independent variables are manipulated. Other advantages of factorial designs include their ability to demonstrate both main effects and joint effects and cost efficiency. Each manipulated variable in a factorial design is called a factor. Main effects refer to the effects of a single factor by itself. Joint or interaction effects refer to outcomes in which the effect of one independent variable depends on the level or value of another.

Quasi-experimental designs, like pre-experimental designs, lack some feature (usually randomization) of true experiments. Examples are the separate-sample pretest–posttest design, in which both groups receive the treatment, but one is tested before the treatment and the other afterward; nonequivalent control group designs, which incorporate control groups but without random assignment; the interrupted time-series design, which involves a series of observations before and after the treatment; and the multiple time-series design, which extends the latter design by adding a series of observations on a nonequivalent control group. By virtue of special design features and supplementary data that test specific validity threats, and by rendering threats implausible through reasoning, quasi-experiments often permit relatively strong inferences about cause and effect. As a result, they often are used to assess the effects of social policies and social programs, a subject we will address at length in chapter 13.

Key Terms

threats to internal validity
  history
  instrumentation
  statistical regression
  selection
  attrition
  differential attrition
  maturation
  testing effects
pre-experimental designs
  one-shot case study
  one-group pretest–posttest design
  static-group comparison
true experimental designs

pretest–posttest control group design
posttest-only control group design
Solomon four-group design
within-subjects designs
between-subjects designs
counterbalancing
factorial experimental designs
  main effect
  interaction effect
quasi-experimental designs
  separate-sample pretest–posttest design
  nonequivalent control group design
  interrupted time-series design
  multiple time-series design

Review Questions and Problems

1. What is the basic principle of good design?

2. What is meant by "threats to validity" in a research design?

3. Complete this statement: If "history" or some other threat to internal validity is present in an experimental design, then the possible effects of an extraneous variable are *confounded* with the _____.

4. Explain the difference between history and maturation effects; between testing and instrumentation effects.

5. Under what circumstance is regression toward the mean likely to be a threat to internal validity?

6. The authors give an example of an experiment in which the *interaction* effect of selection and maturation is a threat to internal validity. Imagine the following hypothetical experiment. To study the effects of new writing-intensive courses at a college, a researcher examines two groups of students during a single semester. One group consists of first-year students enrolled in writing-intensive courses, and the other group consists of mostly upperclass students who are not enrolled in such courses. Tests given at the beginning and end of the semester reveal a much greater improvement in writing skills for the group enrolled in writing-intensive courses than for the group not enrolled. How could a selection-maturation effect account for this outcome?

7. Which threats to internal validity are likely to be present in the (a) one-shot case study, (b) one-group pretest–posttest design, and (c) static-group comparison?

8. Explain how the pretest–posttest control group design adequately controls for each of the major threats to internal validity.

9. Explain why random assignment to experimental conditions can or cannot be used to rule out the following threats to internal validity: (a) maturation, (b) history, (c) instrumentation, (d) selection, (e) statistical regression.

10. What is the principal threat to *external* validity in a pretest–posttest control group design?

11. Why is the posttest-only control group design generally preferred over the pretest–posttest control group design?

12. The interaction of the independent variable with some other variable (e.g., a variable represented by history or maturation) poses a threat to external validity in experiments. What are some solutions to problems of (a) sample selection–X interaction, (b) maturation–X interaction, and (c) history–X interaction? (Recall that X is an independent variable.)

13. What are the advantages and disadvantages of within-subjects designs? Why are they seldom used in social research?

14. The Solomon four-group design may be viewed as a 2×2 factorial design. What are the factors and the levels of each factor in this design?

15. What kind of effect—main or interaction—was found in the Sigall and Ostrove experiment (Box 7.1)? Suppose they had found that the defendant's attractiveness had no effect on sentencing, irrespective of type of crime, but that sentences were significantly longer for the burglary than the swindle. What kind of effect is this?

16. What are the principal advantages of factorial over nonfactorial (i.e., single-factor) experimental designs?

17. How do quasi-experiments differ from true experiments?

18. Give examples of two quasi-experimental designs, and explain how each design controls for the major threats to internal validity.

19. What are the three ways that rival explanations are ruled out in quasi-experimental designs? Describe one application of each of these techniques in (a) the Clore and co-workers camp study and (b) the Campbell and Ross study of the Connecticut speeding crackdown.

20. Over 50 years ago, social psychologists Morton Deutsch and Mary Evans Collins (1951) conducted a study on the impact of an interracial residency pattern on racial attitudes. To assess this impact, they interviewed tenants of two *integrated* interracial housing projects in New York (families were assigned to apartments without consideration of race) and tenants of two *segregated* biracial housing projects in Newark (black and white families were assigned to different buildings or different parts of the project). In general, they found less prejudice among tenants in the integrated housing projects.

    a. Which pre-experimental design does this study design resemble?

    b. Identify three threats to internal validity in this study. Briefly explain how each threat (or extraneous variable) could account for the observed difference in prejudice between the two projects.

21. The following example is taken from F. J. McGuigan (1993:75):

> The problem of whether children should be taught to read by the word method or by the phonics method has been a point of controversy for many years. Briefly, the word method teaches the child to perceive the word as a whole unit, whereas the phonics method requires that he break the word into parts. To attempt to decide this issue an experimenter plans to teach reading to two groups, one by each method. The local school system teaches only the word method. "This is fine for one group," the experimenter says. "Now I must find a school system that uses the phonics method." Accordingly, a visit is made to another town that uses the phonics method. . . . [where] a sample of third-grade children is tested to see how well they can read. After administering an extensive battery of reading tests, it is found that the children who used the phonics method are reliably superior to the children who learned the word method. It is then concluded that the phonics method is superior to the word method.

    a. What is wrong with this study design?

    b. Briefly explain how you would redesign this study to provide an adequate test of the researcher's hypothesis.

NOTES

1. This section and the next three sections draw heavily on Donald Campbell and Julian Stanley's classic treatment of these subjects (1963).

2. This example is adapted from John Neale and Robert Liebert (1986:100).

3. Campbell and Stanley (1963) originally used the term "mortality" to describe this source of invalidity. However, attrition, which is now commonly used, seems better to capture the intended meaning.

4. However, if the teacher initiated the experiment one day because of a sharp increase in talking out of turn, the incidence of this behavior may regress toward a more typical classroom level on the posttest.

5. However, this design does not by itself control for effects of unintended events that might occur *within* a treatment group. For a discussion of this problem and suggestions for dealing with it, see Campbell and Stanley (1963:13–14).

6. Notice how the principle of "doing only one thing at a time" applies in interpreting factorial results. The only difference between the first-row and the second-row groups is the factor-A manipulation. The two groups are equivalent on factor B (each row has an equal number of pretested and nonpretested subjects) and should be approximately equivalent on extraneous variables as a result of subject randomization.

7. For a more complete discussion, see Campbell (1969b) and Cook and Campbell (1976, 1979).

8

✔

Survey Research

Survey research in its many forms has become a very common activity in today's world, and most of us have had some experience with it in one form or another. Perhaps you have been stopped on the street by a radio news reporter and asked your opinion on some issue of local or national importance. You may have responded to a reader survey found in a popular magazine. Or perhaps you have filled out and returned a brief questionnaire that came with a small appliance or other product you purchased. You or someone else in your household very likely responded to the last U.S. Census, which attempted to enumerate and gather confidential information about every person living in the United States. You have been a consumer of survey research if you have read in the newspaper the results of Gallup or Roper public-opinion surveys. You have done a little "survey research" of your own if you moved to a new community and asked a number of residents about local restaurants or where to obtain various services.

General Features of Survey Research

The survey examples above differ in their degree of formality and in the extent to which they conform to these typical features of professional survey research:

1. A large number of respondents are chosen through probability sampling procedures to represent the population of interest.
2. Systematic questionnaire or interview procedures are used to ask prescribed questions of respondents and record their answers.
3. Answers are numerically coded and analyzed.

As we now elaborate on these three features through reference to actual studies, we will also describe exceptions to the general rule for each feature.

Large-Scale Probability Sampling

Professional surveys make use of large samples chosen through scientific sampling procedures to ensure precise estimates of population characteristics. National opinion polls typically number around 1000 respondents, but surveys of national samples can be much larger. In the National Educational Longitudinal Study (NELS), for example, the probability sample interviewed in 1988 consisted of 24,599 eighth-graders from 1052 public and private schools. Participating students were asked about a wide range of school, family, and home experiences, and these data were supplemented by information obtained from parents and teachers as well as achievement test scores and school characteristics such as teacher and student composition. Beckett Broh (2002) analyzed the NELS data in her study of the impact of extracurricular involvement on academic achievement. Using data from follow-up surveys of NELS respondents, Thomas Deleire and Ariel Kalil (2002) examined the effect of family structure on four developmental outcomes among teenagers: whether they graduate from high school, attend college, smoke or drink, and initiate sexual activity. As previous researchers had found, youths from nonmarried families did not fare as well as youths from married families on all four outcomes. A major exception to this pattern, however, was youths from single-parent multigenerational families, who did just as well as youths from married families.

The NELS was conducted by the National Opinion Research Center on behalf of the National Center for Educational Statistics of the U.S. Department of Education. Such national studies require considerable resources—time, money, and personnel—that are beyond the capacity of independent researchers or small research teams. Many surveys, therefore, involve somewhat smaller samples drawn from state or local populations. The 1979 Detroit Area Study, for example, entailed interviews with 640 respondents from randomly selected households in a stratified cluster sample of the city of Detroit (Young, 1991). The survey focused on attitudes toward crime and the criminal justice system. Among the findings was a difference between blacks and whites in the factors that influenced support for the death penalty. Whites, who are far more likely than blacks to support capital punishment, tended to base their support on perceptions of the causes of criminals' actions; blacks' support, however, depended on their degree of trust in the police.

Many useful surveys also are conducted with still smaller samples as well as with nonprobability sampling methods. In 1990 the Worcester Area Project on Aging interviewed 229 people aged 65 or older who were randomly selected from the annual city census of Worcester, Massachusetts (Ainlay, Singleton, and Swigert, 1992). Many other surveys of the elderly, in particular, are conducted with nonprobability samples. Gay Young and Winifred Dowling (1987), for example, surveyed 123 members of five El Paso, Texas, chapters of the American Association of Retired Persons (AARP), who returned questionnaires distributed at chapter luncheons.

Thus, while large-scale probability samples are the ideal, surveys vary considerably in sample size and sampling design. There are legitimate reasons for doing a small-scale survey, particularly if you have a low budget or some specialized or applied research purpose. Indeed, students can often conduct their own low-budget research if they have a research problem that can be studied appropriately with a brief questionnaire survey of the home campus or a telephone survey of the local dialing area.

At the other end of the spectrum from surveys of local populations are surveys that draw samples from more than one nation. In **comparative** or **cross-national surveys**, equivalent surveys are conducted in different countries. For example, based on interviews with over 25,000 men and women from 22 different nations, Haya Stier and Noah Lewis-Epstein (2003) analyzed preferences for the amount of time spent at work. There is considerable cross-national variation in weekly working hours and trends in working hours; for example, during the 1980s and early 1990s working hours increased in the United States and the United Kingdom but declined in Japan and Germany. Stier and Epsten-Lewis found that preferences for working hours were affected by both individual-level and country-level characteristics. At the individual level, people with higher education and income and the elderly preferred to work fewer hours, whereas the opposite was true for those with lower education and income. At the societal level, a highly developed economy and low economic inequality were associated with a preference to reduce the time spent at paid work.

Units of analysis. While in most surveys the units of analysis are individuals, this is not always the case. An example of a survey treating cities as units involved community decisions about whether to fluoridate water supplies to reduce tooth decay. A controversial issue in many communities in the 1950s, the proposal to fluoridate provided social scientists with an excellent opportunity to study the political decision-making process in cities. To learn how cities had dealt with the issue of fluoridation, Robert Crain, Elihu Katz, and Donald Rosenthal (1969) sent questionnaires to three informants in each of 1181 cities: the public health officer, the publisher of the largest city newspaper, and the city clerk. The units of analysis were, again, the cities. One finding was that when the issue was decided by referendum, the odds against fluoridation were five to one.

Systematic Procedures: Interviews and Questionnaires

Surveys obtain information through interviews and/or self-administered questionnaires. The Detroit Area Study illustrates the use of interviews; the U.S. Census uses a combination of interviews and self-administered questionnaires; the 1969 study by Crain, Katz, and Rosenthal of political decision making in cities made use of questionnaires only.

An additional example of the use of questionnaires is Henry Wechsler and associates' (1994) widely cited survey of American college students' drinking habits. The survey's 20-page questionnaire, completed by 17,592 students at 140 colleges, asked numerous questions about drinking behavior and other health issues. The most controversial findings concerned binge drinking. Operationally defining binge drinking as the consumption of five or more drinks in a row for men and four or more drinks in a row for women during the two weeks prior to the survey, the researchers found that 44 percent of the students responding to the survey were binge drinkers. Binge drinkers, especially those who frequently binged, were far more likely than nonbinge drinkers to experience a variety of alcohol-related and other health problems, such as engaging in unprotected and unplanned sex, getting in trouble with campus police, damaging property, and getting hurt or injured.

Unstructured versus structured interviewing. Regardless of whether the survey researcher makes use of interviews only, questionnaires only, or some combination of the two, the procedures tend to be standardized for all respondents in order to enhance the reliability of the data. This epitomizes a **structured interview**: The objectives are very specific, all questions are written beforehand and asked in the same order for all respondents, and the interviewer is highly restricted in such matters as the use of introductory and closing remarks, transitions or "bridges" from topic to topic, and supplementary questions to gain a more complete response (called "probes"). There are exceptions to this rule, however, as informative and scientifically useful interviewing is sometimes carried out in a less formal or structured manner.

In an **unstructured interview**, the objectives may be very general, the discussion may be wide ranging, and individual questions will be developed spontaneously in the course of the interview. The interviewer is free to adapt the interview to capitalize on the special knowledge, experience, or insights of respondents. An everyday example of an unstructured interview might be a journalist's interviewing a celebrity to learn more about his or her personal background, interests, and lifestyle. Between the two extremes, the **semistructured interview** would have specific objectives, but the interviewer would be permitted some freedom in meeting them. The scope of the interview would be limited to certain subtopics, and key questions probably would be developed in advance.

The choice of a highly structured, semistructured, or unstructured approach depends on the researcher's objectives. For example, in their study of undocumented migration among rural Mexicans, Douglas Massey and associates (1987) wanted to gather quantitatively rigorous data, but ruled out a highly structured approach because of the sensitive nature of the study and the respondents' limited background (many were poorly educated or illiterate). Their semistructured interview form listed subtopics or data to collect for each household member. The interviewers were given considerable discretion as to question wording and timing to ensure that the interview was informal and not threatening to the respondents. To make sure that the flexible, semistructured interviews produced comparable or standardized information from each respondent, the interviewers were given extensive training and field supervision. This approach, when combined with probability sampling of households in four carefully chosen communities, yielded precise quantitative information on Mexican migration to the United States.

When the research purpose is not to derive facts or precise quantitative descriptions, but to understand the meaning of respondents' experiences (see Warren, 2002), unstructured interviews often are adopted. This approach allows maximum flexibility in the development of hypotheses and theory; however, it seldom is associated with survey research because it invariably involves small nonprobability samples and qualitative analysis. An example is Kristin Luker's (1975) study of the relationship between contraception and abortion. By using a relatively unstructured approach in interviewing a sample of fifty abortion-seeking women who had experience with effective methods of contraception but who had taken risks during their last menstrual cycle, Luker was able to develop a theory of contraceptive risk taking. She found that a woman's decision not to contracept was not a symptom of psychological problems, as often has been assumed by health care professionals, but rather a rational decision based on the perceived costs and benefits to the woman of contracepting and the perceived risks, costs, and benefits of pregnancy. Costs associated with contraception included medical side effects, inconvenience, lack of spontaneity, male resistance, and so forth. To most of the women interviewed, the risk of pregnancy seemed slight, and all were aware of the possibility of obtaining an abortion. Benefits to getting pregnant included testing fertility (many were of the impression that they had some physical problem that decreased their chances of getting pregnant) and testing the partner's commitment.

For some research purposes, a social scientist might utilize two or three sets of interviews, beginning with very loosely structured interviews and progressing to a final set of highly structured interviews. A freer interviewing style in the preliminary stages would yield rich and varied information. This would assist the researcher in formulating or refining hypotheses, clarifying objectives, and specifying subtopics for subsequent semistructured interviews. Findings from a second set of interviews might be applied to the development of a highly structured questionnaire.

Quantitative Data Analysis

Data analysis techniques depend on whether the survey's purpose is descriptive, explanatory, or a combination of the two. Surveys that are primarily **descriptive** seek to describe the distribution within a population of certain characteristics, attitudes, or experiences and make use of simpler forms of analysis. **Explanatory surveys**, on the other hand, investigate relationships between two or more variables and attempt to explain these in cause-and-effect terms. Sorting out the relationships between the variables in an explanatory survey requires the use of more sophisticated data analysis techniques. (Data analysis will be dealt with further in chapters 14 and 15.)

An illustration of a primarily descriptive study is the National Health and Social Life Survey (NHSLS) in which a national probability sample of adults between the ages of 18 and 59 were interviewed about their sexual attitudes and practices (Laumann et al., 1994). Originally prompted by the lack of national statistics on the prevalence of various sexual behaviors relevant to the AIDS epidemic, NHSLS was transformed by actions of federal agencies and hostile politicians into a study with a somewhat broader focus, a much smaller than planned sample (3432 people were interviewed rather than 20,000), and a sponsorship by private rather than by public funding.

Among the interesting NHSLS findings are estimates of same-gender sexual activity and forced sexual behavior. Only 1.4 percent of the women and 2.8 percent of the men during the interview identified themselves as "homosexual" or "bisexual." Yet in a short self-administered questionnaire that the respondent placed in a sealed envelope, 4.3 percent of the women and 9.1 percent of the men reported having engaged in a sexual act with someone of the same gender since puberty. These and other NHSLS estimates of homosexuality are substantially lower than reported in the Kinsey report and other studies that did not use probability sampling (Laumann et al., 1994:286–90). Perceptions of unwanted sexual activity varied by gender. Although only 2.8 percent of the men reported ever having forced a woman to do something sexual that she did not want to do, 21.6 percent of the women reported forced sex by a man.

The aforementioned NELS represents explanatory survey research. The study began with a baseline survey of students' school and school-related experiences in the eighth grade and continued with follow-up surveys two, four, six, and twelve years later. The general purpose of the NELS was to relate the eighth-grade experiences to high school performance and, in turn, to later achievements in life. The wealth of data enables investigators to examine the impact of numerous factors— for example, students' school experiences and activities, their relationships with peers, parents, and teachers, and characteristics of their schools—on students' academic achievement, persistence in school, participation in postsecondary education, and career choices.

Secondary Analysis of Surveys

In most of the examples presented thus far, each survey had a central topic, and the investigators were responsible for all phases of the research project, from the formulation of ideas and research design to the collection, analysis, and presentation of the data. Although this was once the dominant approach, researchers today are more apt to analyze survey data collected by some other person or agency than to conduct an original survey themselves (Presser, 1984). The analysis of survey data by analysts other than the primary investigator who collected the data is called **secondary analysis**. Analyses of the NELS data by Beckett Broh and others represent this form of research.

One of the many advantages of this research strategy is that sample size can be increased greatly by combining data from several surveys. For example, in their study of the long-term effects of education, Herbert Hyman, Charles Wright, and John Shelton Reed (1975) drew together fifty-four surveys conducted between 1949 and 1971, involving 76,671 respondents, from three sources: the Gallup poll, the National Opinion Research Center (NORC) of the University of Chicago, and the Survey Research Center at the University of Michigan. Not surprisingly, a very strong positive relationship was found between amount of education and correct answers to knowledge questions. However, this was true not only for "academic"-type questions taken from the arts and sciences, but for questions relating to current affairs and popular culture as well. Furthermore, the relationship persisted over time, suggesting that one of the lasting effects of education is a lifelong openness to learning or tendency to seek information.

The earliest application of secondary analysis was to census data and then, beginning in the 1950s, to opinion-poll data. These data, however, were collected primarily for administrative and journalistic purposes. The major impetus for secondary analysis came in the 1970s with the advent of surveys designed expressly for the purpose of making high-quality data available to the social science research community (Glenn, 1978). The first large-scale survey of this type, called the General Social Survey (GSS), began in 1972 and was conducted annually (except for 1979, 1981, and 1992) until 1994. Each GSS involved personal interviews with about 1500 respondents, drawn from a probability sample of the adult population of the United States. Starting in 1994 the GSS shifted to biennial surveys with twice the normal sample size.

In contrast to most surveys, which have a central topic, the GSS is eclectic, with questions pertaining to a broad range of attitudes and behavior. A small portion of each GSS includes a common core of questions that are replicated from year to year to facilitate research on social trends. The remainder of each survey is devoted largely to topical and cross-national modules, which comprise blocks of questions relating to special topics. The cross-national modules, which are sponsored by the International Social Survey Program (ISSP), are included in national surveys in over 30 collaborating countries. The Stier and Lewis–Epstein comparative study of work time preferences used the 1997 ISSP module on Work Orientation.

The 2002 GSS contained topical modules on computers and the Internet, racial and ethnic prejudice, child mental-health stigma, participation in the arts, trust in doctors, quality of working life, non-wage compensation for workers, altruism, transition to adulthood, and sexual behavior, as well as two ISSP modules, one on family, gender, and work and the other on social networks and support, for comparative studies. The altruism module included questions on empathy, blood donation, charitable contributions, voluntarism, and spontaneous helping. The ISSP family, gender, and work module, which replicated some questions from 1988 and 1994, contained items on sex-role attitudes, work history before and after marriage and children, household division of labor, marital decision-making, and family and work stress.

Data from the GSS are often used in the teaching of sociology and other social science courses, especially statistics (see Babbie, Halley, and Zaino, 2003; Fox, 2003). Moreover, analyses of GSS data can be found in over 7000 books, articles, chapters, and dissertations (T. W. Smith, personal communication, 2003). We make extensive use of GSS data in chapters 14 and 15. In this chapter and the next, we will report some of the survey methods and materials used in producing these data so that the reader may become more familiar with this important data base.

The Uses and Limitations of Surveys

Now that we have examined a wide range of surveys, we are in a position to consider the uses as well as the strengths and weaknesses of this approach. With the exception of the NELS, conducted by a federal government agency, all of the studies cited above were carried out by social scientists for social scientific purposes. In fact, "surveys are the most widely used method of collecting data in the social sciences, especially in sociology and political science" (Bradburn and Sudman, 1988:61). Yet the use of surveys as a scientific tool outside the scientific community is even more extensive. The ubiquitous opinion polls, oft reported in the news media and eyed warily by politicians, monitor public reactions to people, events, and policies. Marketing research by businesses, advertising agencies, and other organizations tests consumer reactions to new products and services, assesses customer satisfaction, and compiles audience profiles for various media. And the single largest user of surveys, the federal government, conducts or commissions scores of surveys every year to help in planning, decision making, and policy assessment. Given the importance of surveys in shaping major decisions by politicians, businesspeople, and government officials, we all need to know something about surveys (Bradburn and Sudman, 1988:2). What can they tell us better than other methods of social research? And what are their major limitations?

Whereas experiments are used almost exclusively for explanatory, hypothesis-testing research, surveys are used extensively for both descriptive and explanatory purposes. Among all approaches to social research, in fact, surveys offer the most effective means of social description; they can provide extraordinarily detailed and precise information about large heterogeneous populations. By using probability sampling, one can be certain, within known limits of error, whether the responses to a sample survey accurately describe the larger target population. Furthermore, the topics covered and the questions that may be included in surveys are wide ranging. Topics of the studies cited above ranged from academic achievement to alcohol consumption and from sexual activity to attitudes toward capital punishment. The scope of possible survey questions is suggested by the following classification (Schuman and Kalton, 1985):

1. Social background information (e.g., What is your religious preference? What is your date of birth?)
2. Reports of past behavior (e.g., Did you vote in the last presidential election? Have you ever been the victim of a crime? On an average day, about how many hours do you personally watch television?)
3. Attitudes, beliefs, and values (e.g., Do you believe that there is a life after death? Do you think there should be laws against marriages between blacks and whites?)
4. Behavior intentions (e.g., If the presidential election were held today, whom would you vote for? Would you yourself have an abortion if there is a strong chance of serious defect in the baby?)
5. Sensitive questions (e.g., Have you ever been arrested for a crime? Have you used cocaine in the past month?)

For categories 1, 2, and 5, which pertain to behavior and personal characteristics, the information may be verifiable from records or observer reports, but it is often impractical, unethical, or even illegal to obtain it from sources other than the individuals themselves (Bradburn and Sudman, 1988). For subjective phenomena such as categories 3 and 4, the information can be directly known, if at all, only by asking the individuals themselves (Turner and Martin, 1984).

As this listing suggests, surveys can address a much broader range of research topics than experiments can. Ethical considerations preclude studying some topics experimentally—for example, the effect of emotional traumas on mental health—while practical considerations rule out many others; for instance, one normally cannot experimentally manipulate organizations or nations. Besides this flexibility, surveys can be a very efficient data-gathering technique. While an experiment usually will address only one research hypothesis, numerous research questions can be jammed into a single large-scale survey. Furthermore, the wealth of data typically contained in a completed survey may yield unanticipated findings or lead to new hypotheses.

The secondary analysis of surveys also affords many unique advantages. The cost of obtaining the data for analysis is usually a small fraction of the cost of collecting and coding the data. Survey data made available for secondary analysis tend to come from professional polling and research centers with the resources to obtain high-quality information from large, national samples. In addition, secondary analysis may enable one to (a) assess social trends by examining questions repeated over time and (b) increase sample size by combining data from several surveys.

The major disadvantage of surveys relates to their use in explanatory research. Beyond association between variables, the criteria for inferring cause-and-effect relationships cannot be established as easily in surveys as in experiments. For example, the criterion of directionality—that a cause must influence its effect—is predetermined in experiments by first manipulating the independent (or causal) variable and then observing variation in the dependent (or effect) variable. But in most surveys this is often a matter of interpretation, since variables are measured at a single point in time. Consider also the criterion of eliminating plausible rival explanations. Experiments do this effectively through randomization and other direct control procedures that hold extraneous variables constant. In contrast, surveys must first anticipate and measure relevant extraneous variables in the interviews or questionnaires, and then exercise statistical control over these variables in the data analysis. Thus, the causal inferences from survey research generally are made with less confidence than inferences from experimental research.

Although surveys are quite flexible with respect to the topics and purposes of research, they also tend to be highly standardized. This makes them less adaptable than experiments and other approaches in the sense that it is difficult to change the course of research after the study has begun. That is, once the survey instrument is in the field, it is too late to make changes. The experimenter, in contrast, can modify the research design after running a few subjects with the loss of only those subjects.

A more serious weakness of surveys is one they share with laboratory experiments: They are susceptible to reactivity, which introduces systematic measurement error. A good example of this, noted in chapter 4, is the tendency of respondents to give socially desirable answers to sensitive questions. Another inherent weakness is that surveys rely almost exclusively on reports of behavior rather than observations of behavior. As a consequence, measurement error may be produced by respondents' lack of truthfulness, misunderstanding of questions, and inability to recall past events accurately and by the instability of their opinions and attitudes. Finally, a brief encounter for the purpose of administering a survey does not provide a very good understanding of the context within which behavior may be interpreted over an extended period of time. For this kind of understanding, the best approach is field research, discussed in chapter 10.

Survey Research Designs

Research design generally refers to the overall structure or plan of a study. The crucial design features of experiments, with their focus on hypothesis testing, reveal how a given study will test a specific hypothesis. Surveys place much less emphasis, however, on this aspect of research design. The basic idea of a survey is to measure variables by asking people questions and then to examine the relationships

among the measures. The major design option is to ask the questions once or to repeat the questions over time.

Cross-Sectional Designs

The most commonly used survey design by far is the **cross-sectional design**, in which
data on a sample or "cross section" of respondents chosen to represent a particular
target population are gathered at essentially one point in time. By "one point in time"
we do not mean that respondents are interviewed or that self-administered questionnaires are collected simultaneously (although questionnaires might be in some studies). Rather, the data are collected in as short a time as is feasible. For the 2002 GSS,
it took over three months—February to May—for about 190 interviewers to complete
interviews with nearly 3000 respondents (T. W. Smith, personal communication,
2003). Most of the studies cited earlier are cross-sectional designs.

Two variations on the cross-sectional survey design have been developed out
of sociological interest in studying the influence of social contexts and interpersonal
relations on individual behavior (Glock, 1967). Cross-sectional surveys are limited
by the amount and accuracy of the information that individual respondents can ca-
pably report about the groups and milieus to which they belong. Contextual designs
and social network designs address this problem by studying individuals and relationships found within the same social context.

Contextual designs sample enough cases within particular groups or contexts
to describe accurately certain characteristics of those contexts. Doris Entwisle, Karl
Alexander, and Linda Olson (1994) employed this design to study if the gender gap
in math achievement favoring boys over girls might be explained by the contextual
resources of their schools and their neighborhoods. The investigators first sampled
twenty Baltimore elementary schools and then sampled children from each first-
grade classroom in the selected schools. Student improvement in math skills during
the first two years of school was predicted from individual-level variables (including initial math reasoning score, race, sex, parent's education, family economic
standing) and contextual-level variables (average number of years of schooling for
parents of sampled children in each of the twenty schools, racial composition of
each school, and median neighborhood household income). The analysis revealed
that the boys' gains in math skills were more affected by resources outside the home
(school and neighborhood contexts) than were the girls'.

Social network designs focus on the relationships or connections among social actors (people, organizations, countries, etc.) and the transaction flows (processes) occurring along the connecting links.[1] Network adherents reject analytical
approaches that isolate actors from their social environment (network linkages) and
that interpret behavior solely in terms of actor attributes (characteristics). For example, social psychologists may hypothesize that the likelihood of two people becoming friends increases (a) if they share common interests and values (the traditional attribute approach) or (b) if they share a friend in common (the network
approach).

Social network designs typically require the interviewing of every person in the
group under study. This makes it possible to delineate networks of personal rela-

tionships by asking respondents to provide such information as who their best friends are, whom they most like to work with on a certain project, or to whom they would go for advice. In a social network study of a male-dominated advertising firm, Herminia Ibarra (1992) found that women had to form costly, differentiated interactional networks by choosing (a) other women as friends and sources of support and (b) men mostly as instrumental (work-related) resources. The men, in contrast, chose other men for both expressive and instrumental purposes.

Longitudinal Designs

Because cross-sectional designs call for collection of data at one point in time, they do not always show clearly the direction of causal relationships and they are not well suited to the study of process and change. Of course, investigators can make inferences about the logical relations among variables, and respondents can be asked about both past and present events. But both of these sources of evidence are highly fallible. To provide stronger inferences about causal direction and more accurate studies of patterns of change, survey researchers have developed **longitudinal designs**, in which the same questions are asked at two or more points in time. The questions may be asked repeatedly either of independently selected samples of the same general population or of the same individuals. This results in two main types of longitudinal designs: trend studies and panel studies.

A **trend study** consists of a repeated cross-sectional design in which each survey collects data on the same items or variables with a new, independent sample of the same target population. This allows for the study of trends or changes in the population as a whole. Trend studies may be illustrated by the monthly government surveys used to estimate unemployment in the United States (target population), as well as by repeated public-opinion polls of candidate preferences among registered voters (target population) as an election approaches. Ideally, all trend information would be obtained through measures repeated frequently at regular intervals. However, much of our trend survey data come from infrequent replications of studies. For example, a classic study by Samuel Stouffer (1966) surveyed opinions regarding the threat of communism and attitudes toward civil liberties among a cross section of the American population and a separate sample of community leaders. One finding was that, while a solid majority of community leaders expressed support for the rights of dissidents to freedom of expression, a minority of the sample from the general population did so. Stouffer predicted a future trend toward increased tolerance. A careful replication of this study did indeed find an increase in the proportions of civic leaders and of the general public expressing tolerance, but as a group the civic leaders remained somewhat more tolerant than the population in general (Nunn, Crockett, and Williams, 1978). The replication also revealed that the relationships found in the Stouffer study between support of civil liberties and such variables as gender, section of country, and education still held.

Danching Ruan and associates (1997) in 1993 replicated a 1986 social network survey in urban China to see if structural changes in Chinese society would be reflected in changes in personal relationships. Both surveys asked respondents to name others with whom they have discussed important matters over the last six months. The discussion partners named in 1986 were primarily co-workers (44 percent) and relatives (39 percent). The 1993 replication revealed a dramatic shift in personal connections: More friends and associates and fewer co-workers and relatives were named as discussants. The 1986–93 changes in people's discussion networks were consistent with concurrent large-scale social changes, including a diminished role of the traditional work place in people's lives and the new opportunities provided by an emerging market economy.

Most trend studies measure changes in the general population over time. To study the developmental effects of aging as well as chronological changes, it is also possible to focus on a specific cohort of persons. A *cohort* consists of persons (or other units such as organizations and neighborhoods) who experience the same significant life event within a specified period of time (Glenn, 1977). Most often the life event that defines a cohort is birth, but it also might be marriage, completion of high school, entry into medical school, and so forth. Demographers long have analyzed birth cohorts from census data to predict population trends. In the past forty-five years, social researchers also have begun to do **cohort studies** of various attitudes and behaviors by tracing changes across cohorts in repeated cross-sectional surveys. Cohorts are identified (or tracked) by their birth date; for example, the 1962 cohort would be 18 years old in a 1980 survey, 28 years old in a 1990 survey, and 38 years old in a 2000 survey.

Cohort trend studies enable one to study three different influences associated with the passage of time. To get a sense of these influences and of the difficulty of studying them at a single point in time, consider a cross-sectional survey containing measures of age and attitudes toward premarital sex. The GSS, for example, includes the following question: "There's been a lot of discussion about the way morals and attitudes about sex are changing in this country. If a man and woman have sex relations before marriage, do you think it is always wrong, almost always wrong, wrong only sometimes, or not wrong at all?" If we found that responses to this question became more conservative (premarital sex is always or almost always wrong) with age or time, this could be due to one of three kinds of influences: *life course* (as people grow older, they become more conservative), *cohort* (older generations are more conservative than younger generations), or *historical period* (the prevailing culture has become more conservative over time, making it less socially acceptable to hold liberal views toward premarital sex).

The problem with cross-sectional data is that one cannot begin to disentangle these various effects. Longitudinal data in general and cohort analyses in particular are generally superior for this purpose, although the reader should be aware that these techniques seldom provide clear causal inferences (Glenn, 1977). An example of a cohort study is David Harding and Christopher Jencks' (2003) analysis of age, cohort, and period effects on changing attitudes toward premarital sex. Using GSS data from 1972 to 1998, data from a 1965 NORC survey, and Gallup surveys in 1962, 1969, and 1973, Harding and Jencks broke the samples down into ten-year age cohorts according to the decade when respondents turned 18 years of age, from the 1920s to the 1990s. In general, they found a sharp increase in liberal attitudes toward premarital sex since 1962, with much of the change occurring in the early 1970s, which they attributed to a period effect. Within each cohort, they also found an increase in conservatism after people turned age 30, which they attributed to an aging effect.

Whereas trend studies identify which *variables* are changing over time, **panel studies** can reveal which *individuals* are changing over time because the same respondents are surveyed again and again. Paul Lazarsfeld, Bernard Berelson, and Hazel Gaudet's 1948 classic study of voter behavior, *The People's Choice*, exemplifies the panel method. Before the 1940 presidential election, 600 persons were interviewed repeatedly between May and November. The analysis revealed that persons who expressed a clear preference for candidates Roosevelt or Wilkie at the first interview were unlikely at the second interview one month later to remember having seen or heard any campaign propaganda from the party of the opposing candidate. Because of this phenomenon of selective attention, few voters changed their preferences over the course of the study.

The time interval between data collection in panel surveys may vary from weekly, as in some market research, to monthly, as in the 1940 study of electoral behavior, to annually or longer. Some of the best-known panel studies have analyzed data from small highly selective samples over long periods of time. Glen Elder's (1999) 30-year follow-up study of the impact of the Great Depression on the life course analyzed data from a panel study that began in 1932 with the selection of 167 fifth-grade children from five elementary schools in Oakland, California. These individuals were observed, tested, and questioned more than a hundred times before they graduated from high school in 1939. They then completed a short questionnaire in 1941, were interviewed extensively in 1953–54 and 1957–58, and completed a final follow-up mailed questionnaire in 1964. In a study of attitude change among Bennington College students, women who were surveyed initially in the late 1930s either were interviewed or completed a mailed questionnaire in 1960 and then again in 1984 (Alwin, Cohen, and Newcomb, 1991). A major finding of this study was the persistence of political attitudes over the adult years, as the Bennington women, who were liberalized in the college years, remained politically liberal in later life.

The 30- and 45-year survey periods in the latter two studies are highly unusual. Indeed, panel studies of any duration were a rarity in the social sciences until the late 1960s, when the federal government began conducting large-scale longitudinal studies for secondary data analysis. In addition to the NELS, which surveyed a sample of eighth graders in 1988 and then did follow-up surveys of these same respondents in 1990, 1992, 1994, and 2000, other examples include the Panel Study of Income Dynamics (PSID) and the National Longitudinal Survey of Youth (NLSY). The PSID has collected data on a sample of U.S. households annually from 1968 to 1997 and biennially beginning in 1999; by the end of 2003, over 65,000 individuals had been surveyed. Starting in 1979 with interviews of over 12,000 individuals 14–22 years of age, the NLSY reinterviewed this sample annually through 1994 and biennially since then.

One drawback to studies of this magnitude is that they are very expensive. Another is that they take time. In addition, panel surveys have two problems not found in cross-sectional designs: respondent attrition and reactivity stemming from repeated measurement (Duncan, 2001). Panel attrition occurs when respondents interviewed in the initial wave do not respond in later waves. The more respondents who drop out, the less likely that follow-up samples will be representative of the original population from which the initial sample was drawn. Therefore, researchers typically make great efforts and devote sizeable resources, including incentive payments, to retain a high percentage of the initial sample in follow-up surveys. The NLSY, for example, offered respondents $10 for their time. In the early years, over 95 percent of the initial respondents were reinterviewed; by 1992, 13 years after the initial, 1979 interview, the NLSY was still able to interview 90 percent of the original sample (Brandon, Gritz, and Pergamit, 1995). No matter what the rate of follow-up response, however, a panel survey is like the experimental pretest–posttest design in its ability to assess and control for the effects of attrition. That is, initial information on respondents who fail to participate in later waves can be used to assess nonresponse bias and to make necessary statistical adjustments.

Interviewing respondents repeatedly also may affect how individuals respond to the survey. Known as "time-in-sample bias" or "panel conditioning," one manifestation of this effect is simply a change in reporting behavior. For example, panel participation may become routinized to the point that respondents merely repeat what they have said before, rather than carefully consider their current feelings and actions. Or realizing from previous interviews that a "yes" response leads to follow-up questions, respondents may avoid answering the extra questions by answering "no" (Kalton and Citro, 1993). Panel conditioning also may stimulate real attitude or behavioral changes, so that respondents' attitudes and behavior are no longer representative of the larger population. In national election studies, for example, Michael Traugott and John Katosh (1979) found that voter registration and turnout increased with the number of times participants were interviewed. On the other hand, G. J. Duncan (2001:11011) argues that "pervasive behavioral effects" are unlikely in panel surveys, "especially when changes in the behavior under investigation require more effort than making a trip to the polls." He also contends that data from subsequent waves may be less biased as respondents understand better the purpose of the study and become more motivated to give accurate answers.

Steps in Survey Research: Planning

The activities in doing surveys fall into three broad categories: (1) planning, (2) field administration, and (3) data processing and analysis. The remainder of this chapter is devoted to planning and field administration. Chapters 14 and 15 deal with data processing and analysis.

In planning a survey, a few activities may be thought of as key decision points. These are represented in the flowchart shown in Figure 8.1. Under each major activity we have indicated the chapters that deal with it.[2]

The initial stages in planning a survey are essentially the same as in other forms of research. The first step is to select a topic and formulate a problem in researchable terms. One then reviews relevant journal articles, books, and other published materials to determine what is known about the topic and what work remains to be done. During the course of this review, the researcher inevitably will refine and further specify his or her objectives; also he or she may become aware of existing mea-

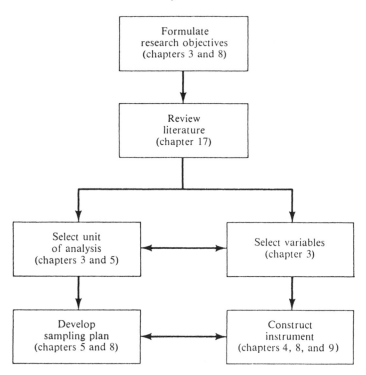

FIGURE 8.1. Key decision points in planning a survey.

sures or scales that may be incorporated into the prospective study. The selection of units of analysis and variables occurs in light of research objectives. In survey research, the units of analysis are either individuals or groups of individuals (including families, organizations, cities); the particular variables selected depend on which characteristics should be studied to meet research objectives.

A very effective planning device when thinking about variables is to work backward mentally from the final steps in the study to the earlier steps in the planning phase. Serious mistakes can be avoided by anticipating the data analysis. To do this, one works out the actual data analysis along with the steps likely to be taken in the event of various outcomes. One might ask questions such as these: If the data support my hypothesis, what will I do next? If the data are the opposite of my hypothesis, what will I do next? (I might decide that I need to control additional variables to test the hypothesis properly.) Have I included all the variables I might want to use? By anticipating the data analysis in this way, the survey content can be planned better. (But, then again, this is not as easy as it sounds, as James Davis reveals in his report of a social survey that we recount in Box 8.1.)

Having selected the unit of analysis and identified key variables, the survey researcher turns his or her attention to the development of the sampling plan and survey instrument. As the flowchart in Figure 8.1 shows, these plans are made concurrently, as each affects the other and both depend on the objectives and resources

BOX 8.1

An Informal Account of a Large-Scale Survey

Researchers do not, as a rule, report the false starts, unsolvable roadblocks, embarrassing problems, and mistakes that are a normal part of the process of doing surveys. James Davis (1964b), however, has provided a humor-filled account of a national survey, the Great Books study, from its inception to the publication of a book. Davis describes the events as an illustration of how survey research is carried out in a large research organization.

The parties involved in the Great Books study included the National Opinion Research Center (NORC), with James Davis as study director; the Fund for Adult Education, as client; and the object of the study, the Great Books Foundation. The Fund for Adult Education, a subsidiary of the Ford Foundation, had been supporting, through grants, various educational activities and programs, including Great Books. The Fund hoped by commissioning an evaluation study to gain concrete evidence of the value of the Great Books program and to determine whether the continuation or expansion of support was merited. The Great Books Foundation, a nonprofit corporation, believed in its program, according to Davis, but seriously doubted the usefulness of a survey in evaluating it. The parties in the study agreed at the outset that the study would be concerned with the effects on participants of participation in Great Books.

The Great Books program in 1957–58 involved approximately 1960 discussion groups throughout the United States, with additional groups in Canada and elsewhere, which met every two weeks from September to June. At each meeting, the members discussed a book that they had been assigned to read. Book selections were organized into blocks of one year. The size of the groups varied, with the sample average eleven. The groups were sponsored chiefly by public libraries, but also by churches, businesses, and individuals. One or two persons served as leaders of each group. No tuition was charged, and no certificates of completion were given. Readings could be bought from the Foundation inexpensively if desired.

The design of the study fell naturally into two parts: sampling and questionnaire construction. In regard to sampling, the "ideal" design would have been a field experiment in which a large probability sample of persons were randomly assigned to a control group or to a Great Books discussion group. After a specified period, both groups would be measured on the dependent variables. However, such a design clearly was not feasible. Among other problems the effects were expected to take a long time to appear, and a report had to be delivered in about a year. The compromise design would use beginning participants as a control group and compare them with advanced-year members on a number of variables. The sample was stratified to overrepresent the advanced-year groups where the effects might be expected to show. Groups were asked to distribute and complete self-administered questionnaires at a regular meeting. Thus, although it would have been ideal to have had a sample of randomly assigned *individuals* in and out of the Great Books program, practical considerations resulted in a stratified sample of Great Books discussion *groups*.

Constructing the questionnaire presented more difficulties than devising the sampling plan. The Fund for Adult Education, the Great Books Foundation, and the study director Davis had different ideas about the program's effects. The Fund, interested in community participation, argued that participants would become more involved in community affairs as a result of their exposure to great literature. Davis and the Great Books Foundation doubted that this was the case. The Great Books Foundation insisted that its program did not have any specific purposes that could be evaluated by a survey. Under pressure from Davis, the Foundation was able to make some very general statements regarding the program's objectives: Participants should become more open-minded, develop more critical thinking skills, become more intellectually sophisticated, and so forth, effects that would be difficult to measure. Davis was interested in members' philosophies, ideologies, and tastes. He also wanted to include some social network questions to see how a person's acceptance or nonacceptance by the group affected his or her reactions to the program. However, the Great Books Foundation ruled out the social network questions as possibly offensive to participants. Instead, questions were asked about roles played by the respondent and others in the group. The final questionnaire contained items reflecting the Fund's interest in community participation; a few items related to aesthetics, open-mindedness, and critical thinking; measures of tastes, ideologies, and philosophies; and the role questions.

Over 90 percent of the sampled groups returned the questionnaires. Analysis of the survey results showed marked differences in knowledge between beginners and advanced-year members, slight differences in tolerance and open-mindedness, and few behavioral differences.

A report for the sponsor was completed on time in August 1958. The project, however, was not finished. Davis immediately conceived the idea of doing a follow-up study to find out which respondents had dropped out of the groups during the year, so that data from these individuals could be subtracted. The remaining data would be reanalyzed to see whether omission of the dropouts affected the findings. The Fund agreed to sponsor the follow-up study. It turned out that controlling for dropouts had little effect.

A new study then was conceived to analyze, with the budget money remaining, the factors associated with dropping out. The idea was not only to learn why Great Books members drop out, but to view the data more broadly as "why some small-scale social systems lose the commitment of their members" (p. 228). Davis admitted he hoped by this study to impress his colleagues that he was capable of theory-building research, as opposed to purely empirical work. The study was to lead to the publication of *Great Books and Small Groups*.

The study showed that retention of participants was greatest where a large percentage of members played active roles. Theories that the content of the roles is important were not supported, nor was Davis's hunch that retention was related to a balance of power in the group.

At the end of Davis's account (1964b:233–34) of the Great Books study, he gives a beautiful description of the satisfactions of doing research:

> There is a lot of misery in surveys, most of the time and money going into monotonous clerical and statistical routines, with interruptions only for squabbles with the client, budget crises, petty machinations for a place in the academic sun, and social case work with neurotic graduate students. And nobody ever reads the final report. Those few moments, however, when a new set of tables comes up from the machine room and questions begin to be answered; when relationships actually hold under controls; when the pile of tables on the desk suddenly meshes to yield a coherent chapter; when in a flash you see a neat test for an interpretation; when you realize you have found out something important that nobody ever knew before—these are the moments that justify research.

of the researcher. Constructing the survey instrument or questionnaire requires a great deal of time and thought and the making of many decisions. We devote the entire next chapter to this aspect of survey design.

A critical aspect of survey instrumentation is deciding on the mode of asking questions—face-to-face interviews, telephone interviews, self-administered questionnaires (usually delivered and returned by mail but increasingly completed electronically), or some combination of these modes. This choice depends partly on other planning decisions such as the research objectives, units of analysis, and sampling plan. For example, in the Wechsler et al. (1994) study of binge drinking, the sampling plan required contact with a very large number of respondents at 140 geographically dispersed colleges and universities. These requirements ruled out both face-to-face and telephone interviews as too expensive, time-consuming, and impractical, and questionnaires were used. In the study of contraceptive risk taking by Kristin Luker (1975), personal interviews were necessitated by the sensitivity and complexity of the topic and by the researcher's need for an approach flexible enough to permit the development of hypotheses.

The choice of survey mode, in addition to the overriding factor of cost, will determine the optimum sampling design. The most expensive and time-consuming mode of survey research is face-to-face interviewing, the major costs of which are incurred from direct interviewing time and travel to reach respondents. If respondents are widely dispersed geographically, this method also will require an efficient sampling procedure for locating respondents. Under these circumstances, the most cost-efficient procedure is multistage cluster sampling. Almost all large-scale surveys are multistage, with stratification at one or more stages.

If respondents are reached by mail or phone, there is no reason for use of clustering. Simple random or systematic sampling may be implemented easily, with or without stratification, provided that an adequate sampling frame can be obtained. Unfortunately, for phone surveys telephone directory listings often provide inadequate sampling frames because they exclude new and unlisted numbers, which constitute as many as 50 percent of the phones in the largest cities (Lavrakas, 1993). This coverage error problem has been circumvented in recent years by a procedure called random digit dialing, which is described later.

As you can see, survey planning is not a linear series of decisions. Rather, it requires the simultaneous consideration of the likely costs and benefits of a number of choices. Also, as planning progresses, revisions in previous decisions and plans frequently are needed. Survey costs and benefits are best viewed from Robert Groves' (1989) "total error perspective," which identifies four types of errors that threaten the accuracy of survey results. We discussed each of these error sources in the chapters on sampling and measurement:

1. *Coverage error*: Differences between the target population and the sampling frame; this is produced when the sampling frame does not include all members of the population, as when a telephone survey omits people without telephones.
2. *Sampling error*: The difference between a population value and a sample estimate of the value that occurs because a sample rather than a complete census of the population is surveyed.

3. *Nonresponse error*: Differences in the characteristics of those who choose to respond to a survey and those who do not.
4. *Measurement error*: Inaccurate responses associated with the respondent, the interviewer, the survey instrument, and the postsurvey data processing.

Ideally, the survey planner effectively allocates available funds and resources to minimize the impact of these potential errors. This is difficult because the errors may be interrelated (reducing one may increase another), certain types of error may be too costly to reduce appreciably, and information on the extent of the errors may be limited or lacking. The choice of a stratified random sampling plan, for exam-ple, might reduce sampling error but increase coverage error compared with a sim-ple random sampling design. Reducing nonresponse error by efforts to convert re-luctant respondents may inadvertently increase measurement error (Lavrakas, 1993:78). Survey error can never be totally eliminated. When it is too expensive to reduce a source of error, it may be possible to estimate the magnitude and direction of the error and make suitable adjustments in the data analysis.

We now consider various survey modes. Although we focus primarily on the traditional distinction between face-to-face and telephone interviews and mailed questionnaires, recent developments in computer-assisted interviewing and telecom-munications have rapidly expanded the options and encouraged the use of multiple modes. Therefore, we also discuss some of these options to traditional methods. Each mode, as you will see, has its distinctive advantages and disadvantages, espe-cially with respect to error reduction. Because sampling error is primarily a func-tion of sampling design, sample size, and population heterogeneity, and not a func-tion of the data collection mode, our concern here is with the other three sources of error, especially coverage error and nonresponse error.

Face-to-Face and Telephone Interviewing

Both the face-to-face interview and the telephone interview require trained inter-viewers proficient in the use of the survey's **interview schedule**. The interview schedule consists of instructions to the interviewer together with the questions to be asked and, if they are used, response options. Interviewers and an interview sched-ule permit a great deal more flexibility than is possible with a self-administered questionnaire. For example, when research objectives necessitate the use of *open-ended questions*, which require respondents to answer in their own words, in con-trast to *closed-ended questions*, for which specific response options are provided, an interviewer usually will be able to elicit a fuller, more complete response than will a questionnaire requiring respondents to write out answers. This is particularly true with respondents whose writing skills are weak or who are less motivated to make the effort to respond fully. In addition, interviewers can easily utilize ques-tion formats in which certain questions are skipped when they do not apply to a par-ticular respondent, while such a format may be confusing for respondents complet-ing a questionnaire. Furthermore, in cases where it is important that questions be considered in a certain order, the self-administered questionnaire presents problems because the respondent may look over the entire form before beginning to answer.

Other advantages of interviewing include the ability of an interviewer to clarify or restate questions that the respondent does not at first understand. An interviewer may also help respondents clarify their answers by using *probes*, such as
"I'm not sure exactly what you mean," or "Can you tell me more about that?" Interviewers help to ensure that every relevant item is answered; tedious or sensitive
items cannot be passed over easily as in self-administered questionnaires. Even
when a respondent initially balks at answering an item, a tactful explanation by
the interviewer of the item's meaning or purpose frequently results in an adequate
response.

In addition to these characteristics that both modes of interviewing share, each
has its own set of advantages and disadvantages.

Face-to-Face Interviewing

The oldest and most highly regarded method of survey research, **face-to-face** or **in-
person interviewing** has a number of advantages in addition to the ones already
mentioned. The **response rate**, the proportion of people in the sample from whom
completed interviews (or questionnaires) are obtained, is typically high—approximately 80 percent except in large cities, where the rate declines for surveys of the
general public (Dillman, 1978). The GSS response rates from 1972 to 1990, for example, typically ranged from 85 percent in rural counties to 67 percent for large
central cities (Davis and Smith, 1992:58). The overall response rates for the 2000
and 2002 GSS were 70 percent. A high response rate means less nonresponse error
or bias. Reasons for the high response rate probably include the intrinsic attractiveness of being interviewed (having someone's attention, being asked to talk
about oneself, the novelty of the experience); the difficulty of saying "no" to someone asking for something in person; and possibly the fact that the importance and
credibility of the research are conveyed best by a face-to-face interviewer who can
show identification and credentials.

This survey mode is appropriate when long interviews are necessary. Face-to-
face interviews of one hour's length are common, but they sometimes go much
longer. (GSS interviews take about ninety minutes for completion of some 400
questions.) When face to face, one can use visual aids such as photographs and
drawings in presenting the questions, as well as cards that show response options.
The cards may be useful when response options are difficult to remember or when
it is face-saving for respondents to select the option or category on the card rather
than to say the answer aloud. Finally, face-to-face interviewing permits unobtrusive
observations that may be of interest to the researcher. For example, the interviewer
may note the ethnic composition of the neighborhood and the quality of housing.

There are some disadvantages to this method, the greatest of which is cost. The
budget for a face-to-face survey must provide for recruiting, training, and supervising personnel and for interviewer wages and travel expenses, plus lodging and
meals in some cases. In one experiment by Herschel Shosteck and William Fairweather (1979) in which comparable surveys of physicians were conducted by mailed
questionnaires and by personal interviews, the field cost per initial respondent—that
is, the data-gathering expenses divided by the number in the sample—amounted to

approximately $63 for personal interviews and $24 for the mailed questionnaire. These figures excluded the costs of initial planning and data coding, processing, and analysis. The full cost of the 2002 General Social Survey, from sampling through release of the data to the public, was about $750 per respondent (T. W. Smith, personal communication, 2003).

The difficulty of locating respondents not at home when the interviewer first calls is another disadvantage of this survey mode. In more and more households, no adult is at home during the day. This necessitates call-backs in the evening or, as in the GSS, generally restricting contacts to weekdays after 4 PM and on weekends. Even then, many persons in large cities will not open their doors to strangers in the evening, and many interviewers refuse to go into certain areas of cities at night. Fear of strangers and the desire for privacy may be the causes of another disadvantage: The response rate for heterogeneous samples in metropolitan areas has been declining for several years. However, this is not true for rural areas or among specialized target groups.

Staff supervision presents special difficulties. Frequently, interviewers, data coders, and the researcher are geographically dispersed. If an interviewer has not recorded responses adequately, effective coding is impossible. Furthermore, many interviews may be completed by an interviewer before feedback gets back to the individual. This is less of a problem when interviewer supervisors go over each interview schedule soon after it is completed. Some of the problems associated with interviewer mistakes may be minimized with **computer-assisted personal interviewing** (CAPI). A computer program, usually on a portable laptop computer, prompts the interviewer with instructions and question wording in the proper order, skips questions not relevant to particular respondents, ensures that the interviewer enters appropriate response codes for each question, and may even identify when respondents are giving inconsistent responses to related questions. CAPI has become the standard for large-scale survey research in the United States; the GSS switched to CAPI in 2002 and most U.S. government in-person surveys now use CAPI (Couper and Hansen, 2002).

Finally, with the personal-interview method, interviewers may introduce bias into the data in a number of ways. For example, they may fail to follow the interview schedule in the prescribed manner or may suggest answers to respondents. Bias also may be introduced through a respondent's reaction to the interviewer's gender, race, manner of dress, or personality. In chapter 6 we spoke of the experiment as a social occasion and the related possibilities of bias. A face-to-face interview is no less a "social occasion" than an experiment; consequently, interviewers must be carefully trained to be sensitive to the ways in which they may wittingly or unwittingly affect their interviewees' responses.

Telephone Interviewing

Like face-to-face interviewing, **telephone interviewing** has its advantages and disadvantages. Substantial savings in time and money are two of the reasons why survey researchers choose to use this method. Large survey research organizations that have a permanent staff can complete a telephone survey very rapidly, and even those researchers who must hire and train interviewers can complete a telephone survey faster than one requiring face-to-face interviews or mailed questionnaires. The costs for sampling and data collection in telephone surveys have been estimated to be 45 to 64 percent of those for face-to-face interview surveys (Groves and Kahn, 1979). However, telephone survey costs will exceed those for mailed questionnaires, even with several follow-up mailings included.

Another major advantage of telephone interviewing is the opportunity for centralized quality control over all aspects of data collection (Lavrakas, 1993), including question development and pretesting, interviewer training and supervision, sampling and call-backs, and data coding and entry. Administration and staff supervision for a telephone survey are much simpler than for a personal interview survey. No field staff is necessary; in fact, it is possible to have the researcher, interviewers, and coders working in the same office. This arrangement permits supervisors to monitor ongoing interviews, allowing immediate feedback on performance and helping to minimize interviewer error or bias. Coders may be eliminated and the interviewers can enter numbers corresponding to respondent answers directly into a computer terminal. If they are used, coders may provide immediate feedback to interviewers and their supervisors.

Response rates for this survey mode approach those for face-to-face interview studies and may exceed them. Robert Groves and Robert Kahn (1979) report response rates about 5 percent below what may be attained with face-to-face surveys. For metropolitan areas, telephone surveys usually will attain higher response rates than will face-to-face interview studies. In addition, required call-backs may be made more easily and economically with telephone surveys than with face-to-face surveys. Contrary to the fear that the proliferation of answering machines might lower response rates by screening out phone surveys, there is some evidence that households using answering machines at the first call attempt are eventually more accessible and more likely to complete an interview than households initially producing a no answer or a busy response (Tuckel and Feinberg, 1991; Xu, Bates, and Schweitzer, 1993).

In terms of sampling quality, the telephone survey mode falls between the face-to-face interview and the mailed questionnaire. In the past, lists of telephone subscribers were used in the sampling process, creating a problem of coverage error. Two groups went unsampled: (1) that part of the population that did not have telephones and (2) those who had unlisted telephone numbers. The problem of bias resulting from the omission of nonsubscribers has diminished because an increasingly larger percentage of U.S. households, at least 95 percent, have telephones (Lavrakas, 1993). However, certain groups are still underrepresented, such as rural people and the poor. The second problem, missing those with unlisted numbers, may be resolved through **random-digit dialing** (RDD) procedures in which telephone numbers are chosen randomly. For example, telephone prefixes (exchanges) within the target geographic area are sampled, and then the last four digits of the telephone number are randomly selected.

Besides random digit dialing, which was introduced in the 1960s and improved and further developed in the 1970s, the introduction of **computer-assisted telephone interviewing** (CATI) in the 1970s greatly enhanced the efficacy of this survey mode (Nathan, 2001). CATI refers to a set of computerized tools that aid interviewers and supervisors by automating various data collection tasks. The uses of CATI include sampling and dialing phone numbers, scheduling call-backs, screening and selecting the person to be interviewed at each sampled phone number, prompting the interviewer with appropriate introductions and questions in the proper sequence, skipping irrelevant questions, identifying when responses are inconsistent with replies to earlier questions, ensuring that the interviewer enters legitimate response codes for each question, recording the responses into a computer data file, and producing immediate sampling and interviewing updates for supervisors (Lavrakas, 1993).

Still, telephone surveys have their limitations. For one thing, the complexity of the questions asked is an issue. While the interviewer may repeat a question, it is desirable to develop questions simple enough to be understood and retained by respondents while they formulate an answer. A related issue is the adequacy of data attained by open questions. Groves and Kahn (1979), as well as others, have found that open-ended questions yield shorter, less complete answers in telephone interviews than in face-to-face interviews. Furthermore, closed questions may present difficulties in that the interviewer cannot present the options on cards but must read and, if necessary, repeat them to respondents at the risk of boring them. For these reasons, the telephone survey mode lacks the advantages of the face-to-face mode in regard to the types of questions that are used.

Another disadvantage of the telephone interview is that it is more difficult for interviewers to establish trust and rapport with respondents than it is in face-to-face interviews; this may lead to higher rates of nonresponse for some questions and underreporting of sensitive or socially undesirable behavior. Robert Groves (1979) compared the results of two identical telephone surveys based on separate samples with the results of a face-to-face survey asking the same questions. At the end of the questionnaire were items about respondents' reactions to the interview. Among other questions, respondents were asked if they felt uncomfortable talking about certain topics, such as income, their income tax refund, political opinions, or racial attitudes. For each of the sensitive topics, more telephone respondents felt uncomfortable, with the largest differences for the income and income tax questions. Not surprisingly, the telephone surveys showed lower response rates to the income questions. Other studies confirm that respondents are less likely to divulge illegal or socially undesirable behavior to an interviewer by telephone than face to face (Aquilino, 1994: 211,214).

Despite these disadvantages, telephone surveys became the most popular survey method in the United States and Western Europe in the last quarter of the twentieth century. Reduced time and cost are major advantages. Furthermore, closer supervision, developments in random digit dialing and CATI, and the high percentage of households with telephones make the quality of telephone surveys only slightly inferior to face-to-face interviewing. The biggest challenges to the continued widespread use of telephone interviewing stem from recent developments in telecommunications technology and the increased prevalence of telephone marketing (see Nathan, 2001). The rapid proliferation of mobile telephones, now increasingly adopted as an alternative to a fixed-line telephone, poses major coverage problems, as it becomes more difficult to apply RDD sampling and to interview individuals who may be anywhere. While answering machines, as we noted earlier, seem to have had a beneficial effect on survey response, the effects of "call forwarding" and caller identification may increase the likelihood of nonresponse. Finally, perhaps the biggest threat to telephone surveys is the pervasive calling by telemarketers. Some survey researchers see this factor not only as the primary cause of declining response rates in telephone surveys, but as a threat to the survival of this survey mode (Kalton, 2000). In light of all these mounting obstacles to telephone surveys, others foresee an increasing reliance on self-administered questionnaires (Dillman, 2000).

Self-Administered Mailed Questionnaires

Occasionally, the site of a **self-administered questionnaire** is a school or organization, where the questionnaire may be hand delivered and filled out in a group or individually. Most often, however, the setting of either an interview or a questionnaire survey is the home (Schuman and Kalton, 1985). To get to this setting, almost all self-administered questionnaires are mailed to respondents. Therefore, we will discuss the pros and cons of this method as a *mail survey*.

This is the least expensive of the three survey modes, even though the budget for printing and postage must be sufficiently high to permit follow-up mailings. No interviewers or interviewer supervisors are needed, there are no travel or telephone expenses, and very little office space is required. In some surveys, the staff may consist of just one or two persons in addition to the researcher.

The time required to complete the data-collection phase of the survey is greater than that for telephone surveys but usually less than that for face-to-face surveys. The sample size may be very large, and geographic dispersion is not a problem. Furthermore, there is greater accessibility to respondents with this method, since those who cannot be reached by telephone or who are infrequently at home usually receive mail.

Compared with interviews, self-administered questionnaires offer several advantages to motivated respondents (Mangione, 1995). Respondents are free to select a convenient time to respond, and to spend sufficient time to think about each answer. The absence of an interviewer also assures privacy, which may explain why respondents are less willing to reveal illegal or socially undesirable behaviors or attitudes to an interviewer than in a self-administered questionnaire (Tourangeau and Smith, 1996:277–79).

On the other hand, coverage and nonresponse error may be magnified with this survey mode. The researcher must sample from a mailing list, which may have some incorrect or out-of-date addresses and which may omit some eligible respondents. Also, the response rate with mailed questionnaires tends to be much lower than with other survey modes. However, even though rates of 50 percent or lower are fairly common, it is possible to obtain high response rates. Donald Dillman (1978) reported response rates from 60 to 75 percent in lengthy surveys of the general public that used his Total Design Method.

The most important factors in generating high return rates are reducing the costs for the respondent and increasing the perceived importance of the survey (Heberlein and Baumgartner, 1978; Yammarino, Skinner, and Childers, 1991). Costs are reduced by including postpaid return envelopes, enclosing small cash prepayments (rather than monetary incentives conditional upon survey completion), and making the questionnaire shorter and easier to complete (Dillman, Sinclair, and Clark, 1993; Warringer et al., 1996). The importance of the survey is impressed on respondents by using stamped rather than metered mail, by making special appeals within the cover letter, by personalizing correspondence (e.g., with real signatures and salutations with respondents' first names), and by making repeated contacts in the form of preliminary notification and follow-ups emphasizing different appeals (Dillman, 2000; Mangione, 1995).

In addition to a generally lower overall response rate, self-administered questionnaires may introduce nonresponse bias due to response selectivity. Certain groups of persons, such as those with little writing ability and those not interested in the topic, would be less likely to respond to a mailed questionnaire than to a personal interview request. Also, more questions are left unanswered with self-administered questionnaires than with interview methods. The problem of item nonresponse may be alleviated to some extent by instructions explaining the need for every item to be answered, by assurances of confidentiality, and by making items easy to understand.

While interviewer bias is eliminated, so are the advantages of an interviewer. There is no opportunity to clarify questions, probe for more adequate answers, or control the conditions under which the questionnaire is completed or even who completes it. A mailed questionnaire usually yields the most reliable information when closed questions are used, when the order in which questions are answered is unimportant, and when the questions and format are simple and straightforward.

The questionnaire may serve the research purposes well under the following conditions: with specialized target groups who are likely to have high response rates,[3] when very large samples are desired, when costs must be kept low, when ease of administration is necessary, and when moderate response rates are considered satisfactory.

Self-Administered Electronic Surveys

The advent of computers and the Internet have spawned several new data-collection technologies. We have already mentioned computer-assisted personal and telephone interviewing (CAPI and CATI). By automating many tasks and simplifying others, these methods reduce interviewer errors and facilitate the interview process. However, they do not displace the interviewer; they simply make his or her job easier. More recently, researchers have developed a variety of computer-mediated surveys that are self-administered. These include electronic surveys via e-mail, the World Wide Web, Interactive Voice Response (IVR), and computerized self-administered questionnaires.

E-mail and Web surveys are conducted over the Internet. Both involve computer-to-computer transmission of a questionnaire; in e-mail surveys the questions are sent as the text of an e-mail message or in an attached file, whereas in Web surveys the questionnaire is on specially designed Web pages. IVR surveys are conducted by telephone, as respondents listen to pre-recorded, voice-read questions, and then use Touch-Tone data entry or give verbal answers, which are tape-recorded. In **computer-assisted self-administered interviewing** (CASI), the questionnaire is transmitted on a program that may be on a computer disk mailed to respondents or on a laptop provided by the researcher. Of these innovations, Web surveys have had the broadest application. IVR surveys, which may not be suitable for long or complex questionnaires, have been used extensively in consumer marketing research but have had limited application in general social surveys. CASI often has been used in conjunction with interview-administered surveys. We focus here on the advantages and disadvantages of Web surveys.

One of the greatest advantages of Web surveys is reduced cost. Compared to self-administered questionnaires, the cheapest of the traditional modes, Web surveys eliminate the costs of paper, postage, assembly of the mailout package, and data entry (Dillman, 2000). The principal costs, assuming the requisite computer equipment is available, are Internet service provider fees and telephone costs. But phone calls for Internet use are already free in many places; free Internet access is increasingly available; and for research on populations with institutional access to the Internet, such as colleges and universities, the cost is zero (Mann and Stewart, 2002). A related advantage is time savings. Web surveys require much less time to implement than other survey modes; compared to mail surveys, which may take weeks or months for questionnaires to be delivered and returned, Web surveys may be completed in only a few days (Kwak and Radler, 2002). Finally, Web surveys can substantially reduce the cost of increasing sample size, because once the electronic questionnaire has been developed, the cost of surveying each additional person is far less than in an interview or mail survey (Dillman, 2000).

Another advantage of Web surveys, one they share with other computer-mediated methods, is flexibility in the questionnaire design. As Don Dillman (2000:354) points out, the questionnaire can be designed "to provide a more dynamic interaction between respondent and questionnaire" than is possible in a paper survey. Web questionnaires can incorporate extensive and difficult skip patterns, pop-up instructions for individual questions, and drop-down boxes with lists of answer choices. They can use a great variety of shapes and colors and can add pictures, animation, video-clips, and sound.

At this point, the great practical advantages and enormous design potential of Web surveys for social research are offset by some major weaknesses. Perhaps the greatest of these is coverage error. This error derives from two related problems: the proportion of the general population who are Internet users and the difference between users and non-users. By year 2000, only a third of the U.S. population used the Internet at home or elsewhere (Couper, 2000). Given the rapid growth rate of the Internet, this percentage should increase significantly over the next several years. Yet it remains to be seen whether the Web will approach the 95 percent penetration level of the telephone. Even if it does, the population of Internet users may differ from the general U.S. population in several respects. Presently, the "digital divide" is large, for example, college graduates are 16 times more likely than others to have Internet access, and black and Hispanic households are only about 40 percent as likely as white households to have home Internet access (Couper, 2000:471). At the least, Internet users must be able to read, which makes literacy a limitation for Web surveys in the same way that it is for mail surveys (Couper, 2000).

Nonresponse error poses another problem for Web surveys. Early studies comparing response rates for mail surveys and electronic, mostly e-mail surveys generally found lower response rates for electronic surveys (Couper, 2000). Although some recent studies produced opposite results (see McCabe et al., 2002), response rates were still low (63 percent and lower) in comparison with in-person interviews. On the other hand, studies also have shown that Web respondents are less likely than mail respondents to leave specific questions unanswered and tend to write longer answers to open-ended questions (Kwak and Radler, 2002).

Despite these problems, Web surveys have developed so rapidly in recent years that some have argued that they eventually will replace traditional survey modes. Solutions to some of the problems are being addressed. For example, the coverage problem can be handled by limiting Web surveys to studies of populations with near-universal Web access, such as college students, or by making access available to those included in the sample (Couper, 2000). Special design features have been applied to improve data quality and reduce nonreponse error (Couper, Traugott, and Lamias, 2001). Still, consumers should be wary of Web polls and surveys for the foreseeable future. Such surveys will vary widely in format or design, and most are likely to entail self-selected samples that merely reflect the views of those who choose to respond.

Mixed Mode Surveys

Choosing a data-collection mode is difficult when none of the primary modes (face-to-face interviews, telephone interviews, or self-administered mail questionnaires) seems optimum for the intended research. An alternative solution is to design a **mixed mode survey,** which uses more than one mode to sample and/or collect the data (Lavrakas, 1993). In this way the weaknesses of one mode may be offset by the strengths of another mode. For example, relatively inexpensive phone surveys may be used to locate specialized populations, such as people with a rare disease, for a study requiring expensive, face-to-face interviews. Another example would be increasing the response rate of the sampled population by conducting telephone or face-to-face interviews with those who did not respond to an initial mail questionnaire.

Mixed mode surveys also may be designed to make effective use of the new computer-mediated methods. One solution to the coverage problem in Web surveys, for example, is a mixed-mode approach whereby those without Web access are surveyed in-person or by mail (Dillman, 2000). Audio-CASI, in which respondents listen to questions on headphones plugged into a computer, is now widely used in surveys of sensitive topics (Couper and Hansen, 2002; Tourangeau and Smith, 1996). Typically, an interviewer administers the largest part of the interview, but then provides the respondent with the equipment to complete the self-administered portion that requests the most sensitive information. In this way, respondents are less susceptible to social desirability biases, which are more likely when questions are administered by an interviewer. An early application of this strategy occurred in the 1992 National Health Interview Survey of Youth Risk Behavior (NHIS-YRBS), which used an audio questionnaire to collect sensitive information about drug use, sexual intercourse, cigarette smoking, and other unhealthy behaviors from adolescents (Willard and Schoenborn, 1995). Teens listened to the questions on a Walkman-type portable audio headset and recorded their answers on an answer sheet that did not contain any information by which parents or other household members would know the questions being answered. Besides providing privacy to the young respondents, this data collection mode was more effective than a written questionnaire with younger teens and those with poor reading skills. In addition, the prerecorded questions provided greater standardization (wording, tone of voice, etc.) than when questions are asked by interviewers.

Field Administration

Once the planning is completed, fieldwork can begin. This phase of the research begins with the recruitment and training of interviewers, continues with the field interviews, and concludes when follow-up efforts have been completed on initially unresponsive persons in the sample. Figure 8.2 is a flowchart that summarizes the various aspects of a survey's fieldwork phase.[4]

Interviewer Selection

Although there are no universally agreed-on criteria for the selection of interviewers, experience and common sense suggest that certain qualities are desirable. These would include articulateness; a pleasant personality that inspires cooperation and trust; a neat, businesslike appearance; freedom from prejudices or stereotypes toward the population being interviewed; interest in the survey topic; a legible handwriting; and the ability to listen, use neutral probes when needed, and record responses accurately. We suspect that the presence of these qualities is evaluated to some degree during the selection and training processes. This should create reasonably well-qualified interview staffs and would explain why research has found no consistent correlates between interviewer characteristics and the quality of interviewing (Fowler, 1991).

Unless the survey is being done by a large research organization that has a permanent staff, the researcher must recruit all the interviewers for a given survey. The process of recruiting interviewers is basically the same as hiring for any job (Weinberg, 1983). That is, positions are advertised; applicants are screened and selected. Beyond minimum reading and writing skills, availability and readiness to meet job requirements are the principal selection criteria. Other interviewer attributes are largely dependent on market forces. The majority of interviewers, according to data from a sample of interviewers at U.S. government statistical agencies, do not regard their job as a primary source of income or career, perhaps because of the intermittent

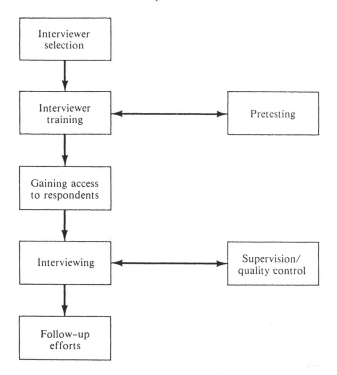

FIGURE 8.2. Flowchart illustrating a survey's fieldwork phase.

nature of the work (Groves and Couper, 1998:198). This work feature as well as job requisites also may account for the composition of the interviewer workforce, which is predominantly female, young to middle-aged, with above-average education. Since such attributes are largely beyond the control of the researcher, it is fortunate that they appear to be much less important in determining the quality of a survey than the interviewer's ability achieved through careful training and experience.

Interviewer Training

Interviewers receive training in general interviewing skills and techniques as well as in specific procedures required for a particular survey project. In practice, these two aspects of training often are combined, with survey-specific materials (e.g., questionnaire or sampling procedures) used for practical application (Weinberg, 1983). More specifically, the training process must accomplish several goals:

1. Provide interviewers with information regarding the study's general purpose, sponsor, sampling plan, and uses or publication plans.
2. Teach basic interviewing techniques and rules, such as how to gain respondents' cooperation, establish rapport without becoming overly friendly, ask questions and probe in a manner that will not bias the response, deal with interruptions and digressions, and so forth.

3. Acquaint interviewers with the interview schedule and special instructions for
   its use, such as how to introduce a topic or record responses.
4. Provide demonstrations and supervised practice with the interview schedule.
5. Weed out those trainees who do not possess the motivation and ability to do an
   acceptable job.

The typical training program combines home study with a series of classroom
sessions. The first session might begin with a general introduction to the study, followed by a presentation and instruction in basic interviewing skills and responsibilities. In the second session, the researcher would thoroughly familiarize interviewers with the survey questionnaire, going over the entire instrument item by
item, explaining the importance of each item, and giving instructions for recording
responses and examples of problematic responses and ways to deal with them. Next,
the researcher would conduct a demonstration interview and then divide interviewers into pairs for supervised practice interviewing. Third and subsequent sessions
would involve further practice, possibly including field experience, and further
evaluation. Experienced interviewers generally receive survey-specific training
through home study of the project's special interviewing procedures and survey instrument followed by discussions or mock interviews with a field manager.

Pretesting

A pretest consists of trying out the survey instrument on a small sample of persons
having characteristics similar to those of the target group of respondents. The basic
reason for conducting a pretest is to determine whether the instrument serves the
purposes for which it was designed or whether further revision is needed. **Pretesting** may be carried out before, at the same time as, or after the interviewers are
trained. An advantage to completing the pretest before interviewer training is that
the final instrument may be used during training. An advantage to delaying pretesting is that the interviewers can assist with this step, either during the field practice
part of interviewer training or after the formal training is completed. A disadvantage to delaying pretesting is that there may be a time gap between the completion
of training and the start of the "real" interviews while the instrument is being revised. The subject of pretesting is discussed in more depth in chapter 9.

Gaining Access

Gaining access to respondents involves three steps: getting "official" permission or
endorsement when needed or useful, mailing a cover letter introducing the study to
persons or households in the sample, and securing the cooperation of the respondent.

When doing a community interview survey, it is usually a good idea to write
a letter to the local sheriff or chief of police describing the general purpose of the
study, its importance, the organization sponsoring it, the uses to which the data will
be put, the time frame, and so forth. A follow-up visit to the sheriff or chief of police may be made. In addition, endorsement letters from relevant local organizations
may be sought, such as the county medical society if doctors will be interviewed,

or the chamber of commerce if businesses are being sampled. Press releases to local newspapers and television stations also may help to open doors.

Respondent cooperation also will be enhanced by a good **cover letter**. In interview surveys, the cover letter is usually mailed a few days before the interviewer is to call on the respondent. In surveys using mailed questionnaires, the cover letter is sent with the questionnaire either as a separate sheet or attached to the questionnaire. Occasionally, cover letters are mailed out in advance of phone surveys when mailing addresses are known. The objective of the cover letter, to persuade the respondent to cooperate with the survey, may be met by (1) identifying the researcher and survey sponsor and the phone number of a contact person, (2) communicating the general purpose and importance of the study, (3) showing how the findings may benefit the individual or others (e.g., the results will be used to improve health care or to increase understanding of marriage relationships), (4) explaining how the sample was drawn and the importance of each respondent's cooperation to the study, (5) assuring individuals that they will not be identified and that their responses will be kept confidential and will be combined with those of others for data analysis purposes, (6) explaining that the questionnaire will take only a few minutes to fill out or that the interview will be enjoyable and will be held at the respondent's convenience, and (7) promising to send respondents a summary of the study's findings. (See Box 8.2 for an example of a cover letter.) Also, response rates may be increased by including a token incentive, such as $1 or an inexpensive gift, with the cover letter (Willimack et al., 1995:79).

A third step in interview surveys is gaining the cooperation of the respondent. Interviewers must contact or reach the sample person and then persuade him or her to cooperate by completing the survey. Making contact with designated households is primarily a matter of persistence and overcoming barriers. Interviewers vary the time of attempted contacts and may make repeated callbacks, typically at least 6 for face-to-face surveys and 10 or more for telephone surveys (Fowler, 1993). We discuss follow-up efforts further below as a final phase of fieldwork.

Avoiding refusals is a more difficult problem that requires special interviewer skills. According to Robert Groves and Mick Couper's (1996, 1998) theory of survey participation, which applies mainly to in-person interviews, in the initial moments of the survey encounter, the sample person is actively trying to comprehend the purpose of the interviewer's visit. He or she uses cues from the words, behavior, and physical appearance of the interviewer to arrive at an explanation (or identify a "script") and then evaluates the costs of continuing the conversation. Whether the person eventually agrees or refuses to participate depends on the interviewer's ability to quickly and accurately judge the particular script reflected in the householder's initial response and to react accordingly.

The theory is consistent with analyses of interviewer-householder interactions. For example, Robert Groves, Robert Cialdini, and Mick Couper (1992) found that experienced interviewers use two related strategies to convince respondents to participate. First, they tailor their approach to the sample unit, adjusting their dress, mannerisms, language, and arguments according to their observations of the neighborhood, housing unit, and immediate reactions of the householder. Second, they maintain interaction, which maximizes the possibility of identifying relevant cues

BOX 8.2

Sample Cover Letter for Household Survey, with
Key Features Identified in Left-Hand Margin

Official letterhead	**WASHINGTON STATE UNIVERSITY** PULLMAN, WASHINGTON 99163 DEPARTMENT OF RURAL SOCIOLOGY Room 23, Wilson Hall
Date mailed	April 19, 1971
Inside address in matching type	Oliver Jones 2190 Fontana Road Spokane, Washington 99467
What study is about; its social usefulness	Bills have been introduced in Congress and our State Legislature to encourage the growth of rural and small town areas and slow down that of large cities. These bills could greatly affect the quality of life provided in both rural and urban places. However, no one really knows in what kinds of communities people like yourself want to live or what is thought about these proposed programs.
Why recipient is important (and, if needed, who should complete the questionnaire)	Your household is one of a small number in which people are being asked to give their opinion on these matters. It was drawn in a random sample of the entire state. In order that the results will truly represent the thinking of the people of Washington, it is important that each questionnaire be completed and returned. It is also important that we have about the same number of men and women participating in this study. Thus, we would like the questionnaire for your household to be completed by an <u>adult female</u>. If none is present, then it should be completed by <u>an adult male</u>.
Promise of confidentiality; explanation of identification number	You may be assured of complete confidentiality. The questionnaire has an identification number for mailing purposes only. This is so that we may check your name off of the mailing list when your questionnaire is returned. Your name will never be placed on the questionnaire.
Usefulness of study "Token" reward for participation	The results of this research will be made available to officials and representatives in our state's government, members of Congress, and all interested citizens. You may receive a summary of results by writing "copy of results requested" on the back of the return envelope, and printing your name and address below it. Please <u>do not</u> put this information on the questionnaire itself.
What to do if questions arise	I would be most happy to answer any questions you might have. Please write or call. The telephone number is (509) 335-8623.
Appreciation	Thank you for your assistance.
Pressed blue ball point signature Title	Sincerely, *[signature]* Don A. Dillman Project Director

Source: Page 169 of Dillman (1978). Copyright 1978 by John Wiley and Sons, Inc. Used by permission.

for tailoring the conversation to present the most effective arguments. In a subsequent analysis, Groves and Couper (1996) concluded that the most effective interviewer adaptations were those that addressed the real concerns of the householder. Moreover, experimental tests of a training program to help interviewers anticipate and address such concerns were shown to increase cooperation (Groves and McGonagle, 2001).

Interviewing

Although we noted earlier that interviews may be more or less structured, nearly all surveys, especially large-scale surveys, use structured or "standardized" interviewing. The goal of standardization is to expose each respondent to the same interview experience, so that any differences in recorded answers are due to differences among respondents "rather than differences in the process that produced the answer" (Fowler and Mangione, 1990:14). To standardize the measurement process, survey instruments consist almost entirely of closed-ended questions that are presented in the same order for all respondents, and interviewers are instructed to carefully follow prescribed procedures. Ideally, interviewers should be perfectly consistent, neutral intermediaries of the survey researcher. In short, "the goal [of standardized interviewing] is nothing less than the elimination of the interviewer as a source of measurement error" (Groves, 1989:358).

Specific practices vary somewhat from one survey organization to another, but the following four rules of standardized interviewing, according to Floyd Fowler (1991:264; also see Fowler and Mangione, 1990), are given almost universally to interviewers:

1. Read the questions exactly as written.
2. If a respondent does not answer a question fully, use nondirective follow-up probes to elicit a better answer. Standard probes include repeating the question, asking "Anything else?," "Tell me more," and "How do you mean that?"
3. Record answers to questions without interpretation or editing. When a question is open-ended, this means recording the answer verbatim.
4. Maintain a professional, neutral relationship with the respondent. Do not give personal information, express opinions about the subject matter of the interview, or give feedback that implies a judgment about the content of an answer.

(Further, more detailed, interviewer guidelines from a community survey are provided in Box 8.3.)

Considerable empirical evidence and sound theoretical arguments justify standardization principles (Fowler, 1991; Fowler and Mangione, 1990). For example, if questions are not asked as worded, one cannot know what question was posed; and numerous experiments have shown that small changes in the wording of questions can alter the distribution of answers (Schuman and Presser, 1981). Also, experiments have demonstrated that suggestive questioning (presenting only a subset of answer alternatives that are presumed to be relevant) and suggestive probing can affect response distributions and relationships with other variables (Smit, Dijkstra, and van der Zouwen, 1997).

BOX 8.3

Guidelines for Survey Interviewers

Organizations sponsoring surveys, such as the National Opinion Research Center, which oversees the GSS, usually produce an interviewers' manual that explains rules and procedures to follow to minimize the effects of error. The rules and guidelines outlined below have been adapted from an interviewers' manual used in a community survey conducted in a medium-sized city; however, they apply to any well-conducted personal interview survey.

Rules

Three basic rules are suggested.

1. *Courtesy, tact, and acceptance.* It is of utmost importance that your manner be at all times courteous, tactful, and nonjudgmental. Under no circumstances are you to argue or debate anything that is said. The primary function of the interviewer is to learn what the respondent believes about the items on the schedule without judging or influencing that response in any way. No matter what the respondent says, the interviewer should accept it without showing surprise, approval, or disapproval. Respondents will be less likely to share confidential data about their personal lives, for example, with an interviewer who appears to disapprove of them.

2. *Dress.* Three things should be kept in mind in selecting clothing for interviewing: the expectations that surround the role of the interviewer, the persons being interviewed and their probable response to one's dress, and comfort. Within the limits of good taste, the individual interviewer should make adjustments for the neighborhood in which he or she is working.

3. *Confidentiality.* Under no circumstances is the interviewer to give out to anyone except the supervisor any information gathered in the course of interviews. Incidents that occur or any information gained while interviewing are strictly confidential and should not be discussed with anyone who is not part of the project. Project workers should never discuss interview data, even among themselves, in a public place where the conversation could be overheard.

Procedures in Conducting an Interview

The following procedures have been found to be helpful in conducting interviews and obtaining accurate, honest responses. In many cases, deviating from these procedures will influence the respondent and introduce bias.

1. *Initiate the interview.* When the respondent comes to the door, introduce yourself by name. Show identification. Explain briefly what the study is about and whom it is you wish to interview. Be prepared to answer briefly questions regarding who is

sponsoring the study and how or why the respondent was chosen. Letters of endorsement and newspaper clippings may be presented.

Proper groundwork by the researcher and a positive approach on the part of the interviewer will help to minimize the problem of refusals. In addition, the interviewer can frequently overcome an initial refusal by listening to the respondent's concerns and then addressing those concerns. For example, is the respondent "too busy"? Stress the brief and enjoyable nature of the interview, or, when necessary, make an appointment to call back. Does the respondent appear suspicious about the uses to which the data will be put? If so, explain again the study's purpose, provide an assurance of confidentiality, and explain that the data will be combined so that no individual's responses can be identified or linked to that person. Of course, firm refusals must be respected.

2. *Put the respondent at ease.* This is a major part of successful interviewing. A conversational, convivial attitude may help put the respondent at ease. Try to be relaxed and "natural."

3. *Be businesslike.* While it should be relaxed, an interview should not be long-winded. Remember that you and the respondent are busy people. If the respondent strays far afield from the point of a question, politely pull him or her back on the track.

4. *Keep the interview situation as private as possible.* If you are in a room with other people, do not let your attention wander to other parts of the room. Direct your questions to the respondent, and maintain eye contact. This will help both you and the respondent focus on the task.

5. *Avoid stereotyping.* Do not try to "peg" the respondent, as your preconceptions may interfere with your objectivity and may influence the respondent. You can also help to prevent the respondent from stereotyping you by not identifying yourself with any particular group or ideology.

6. *Be thoroughly familiar with the survey instrument.* Know the instrument so well that you can look at the respondent while asking questions.

7. *Ask every question in its proper sequence and exactly as written.* The interview schedule should have been carefully constructed. Questions are in the order presented because it is easier for interviewers to ask them in this order, because there is a logical flow of the topics, because the order helps respondents think through or recall material, or for similar reasons. Remember that very slight changes in the wording of items have been shown to affect the results.

8. *Do not assume the answer to any question.* A respondent may imply the answer to a question in answering a previous question but may respond differently when asked the question formally.

9. *Speak slowly in a clearly understood, well-modulated voice.* If respondents are to give reliable answers, they must understand the questions.

10. *Do not put answers in the respondent's mouth.* This is one of the most common mistakes of interviewers. If a respondent seems unsure of an answer, pause and then repeat the question exactly as worded. Do not suggest an answer or a series of answers. Not all interviewers would suggest the same responses, and, therefore, respondents would not be choosing from the same suggestions. This would result in biased data.

11. *Use an appropriate, neutral probe when needed.* Probing is used when the initial response is incomplete, ambiguous, or irrelevant. A variety of probes are possible, but they must be neutral; that is, they must stimulate a more valid response without suggesting an answer. Sometimes, as suggested above, pausing or repeating the

question may be sufficient to motivate the respondent to add to or clarify the response. At other times, a neutral question such as one of the following may be needed: Is there anything else? Can you tell me more? In what ways? The survey instrument designer may include on the interview schedule certain probes to use with particular items when needed.

12. *Record responses on the interview schedule as you go along.* Do not try to re-create the interview later. Before leaving the residence, skim the instrument to be sure all questions have been answered. Later, check to be sure responses will be understandable to the coders. Add notes in parentheses if necessary.

While there is little doubt that standardization reduces the interviewer's contribution to measurement error, a more serious, longstanding concern is that presenting a standard stimulus in and of itself can produce measurement error. According to this view, standardized interviewing stifles interviewer–respondent communication in two ways: (1) It inhibits the ability to establish rapport, which motivates respondents to cooperate and give complete and accurate answers; and (2) it ignores the detection and correction of communication problems (Beatty, 1995).

Regarding motivation, some respondents feel irritated by the unilateral nature of a structured survey; they cannot converse with the researcher or interviewer, they cannot qualify or expand answers, and they may be forced to choose among alternative answers that they find unsatisfactory. Fowler (1995:99–102) believes that respondents' resistance to standardized survey interviewing can be overcome by initially orienting or training them to play the role of a respondent. Since interviewer–respondent interaction in a highly structured survey is quite different from everyday conversation, respondents should be given an explanation of the rationale and the rules of standardized surveys to prepare and motivate them for the interview task.

Standardization also may reduce validity if respondents' misinterpretations of questions are ignored or uncorrected. In a widely cited article, Lucy Suchman and Brigitte Jordan (1990) argued that standardization suppresses elements of ordinary conversation that are crucial for establishing the relevance and meaning of questions. Interviewers who are trained to read questions as written and to discourage elaboration are not prepared to listen carefully for misunderstandings and correct them. From videotapes of standardized interviews, Suchman and Jordan gave several examples of miscommunication, such as an interviewer failing to correct a respondent who interprets "alcoholic beverages" to include hard liquor but exclude wine, which led to invalid responses. Such problems could be resolved, they claimed, if interviewers were granted the freedom and responsibility to negotiate the intended meaning of questions through ordinary conversational conventions.

While acknowledging the communication problems identified by Suchman and Jordan, advocates of standardized interviewing tend to disagree with them about causes and remedies. Some advocates contend that problems arise chiefly because of poorly worded questions, and whether respondents interpret questions consistently and accurately depends on adequate question pretesting (Kovar and Royston, 1990). Detractors of standardization maintain that efforts to improve question wording are rarely, if ever, sufficient. Researchers need interviewers to help ensure consistent interpretations, but this is unlikely unless interviewers are given a freer hand in communicating with respondents than standardization allows.

Paul Beatty (1995) notes that advocates on both sides of this debate tend to take extreme positions that seem incompatible. He argues, following Nora Cate Schaeffer (1991), that while the problems of standardization should not be overlooked, it also is foolish to ignore its merits. The real issue for him is, "How can researchers solve communication problems while harnessing the full benefits of standardization?" One means is the development of better questions; another may involve adapting the role of the interviewer.

The standardization controversy aside, a serious weakness of surveys, alluded to earlier, is their reactivity. This is especially problematic in interviews, where biases may be produced not only by the wording, order, and format of the questions, but also by the interaction between interviewer and respondent. Like the subject in an experiment, the respondent's chief concern often is with gaining the interviewer's social approval, or at least with avoiding his or her disapproval (Phillips, 1971). And even though the interviewer's main goal is to obtain valid responses, interviewers may unknowingly affect responses in myriad ways. In survey research, the general term for such effects, or measurement errors, is **response effects.** More precisely, a response effect is "the amount of the error in response to a question that is associated with a particular factor" (Sudman and Bradburn, 1974). Chapter 9, on survey instrument design, suggests ways in which to minimize response effects related to the interview schedule (or questionnaire), such as question wording or position. Here we focus on effects due to the interaction of interviewer and respondent.

One source of response effects is the interviewer's physical characteristics. For example, the race of the interviewer has been shown to have a considerable impact on certain types of responses. In general, blacks express fewer antiwhite sentiments to white than to black interviewers, and whites give fewer antiblack answers to black than to white interviewers (Schuman and Kalton, 1985). A 1989 pre-election survey also found a significant race-of-interviewer effect on expressed voter preferences for a black versus white gubernatorial candidate (Finkel, Guterbock, and Borg, 1991). Respondents in the state of Virginia were more likely to support the black candidate L. Douglas Wilder (subsequently elected as the nation's first black governor) when the interviewer was black and were more likely to favor the white candidate J. Marshall Coleman when the interviewer was white.

Less is known about whether other demographic variables such as age, gender, and class have the same effect as race, although this seems likely when a specific interviewer trait is particularly relevant. For instance, Emily Kane and Laura Macaulay (1993) found gender-of-interviewer effects on several items measuring gender-role attitudes, with both male and female respondents tending to give more egalitarian responses to female than to male interviewers.

In a fashion similar to experimenter effects, interviewers also may inadvertently communicate their expectations to respondents about how they should respond. To illustrate, if an interviewer believes a respondent to be of limited intelligence and inarticulate, he or she may expect shorter, less articulate responses and may communicate this indirectly by short pauses. Since the respondent is looking to the interviewer for clues to the appropriateness of his or her behavior, he or she will likely provide short responses, thus fulfilling the interviewer's expectations.

On the other side, the respondent's reports to an interviewer may easily be distorted by such things as poor memory, desire to impress the interviewer, dislike for the interviewer, or embarrassment. Similarly, a respondent's feelings about the topic of the study or toward the organization sponsoring it may also affect the quality of data obtained. Finally, settings for interviews may present problems. A housewife who is being interviewed while supervising children may not be able to focus on the tasks of the interview sufficiently to provide as full and accurate responses as she might in another situation. In the British Household Survey, the presence of a spouse during an interview led to greater agreement between husbands and wives on several attitudinal and behavior items (Zipp and Toth, 2002). A study by Anne Zanes and Euthemia Matsoukas (1979) showed that eleventh graders were more likely to report incidents of drug use when questioned at school than when questioned at home.

Supervision and Quality Control

Once the interviewing phase of the survey begins, the researcher or an interviewer supervisor oversees all aspects of the data collection. The supervisor's role involves three interrelated sets of activities: managing the work of the interviewers, monitoring their performance, and administering quality control procedures. In their management role, supervisors provide materials, collect completed questionnaires, pay for work done, make themselves available to answer questions and provide help, identify and resolve problems, hold regular meetings with interviewers, and review and give feedback on the interviewers' work.

To detect problems and review interviewers' progress, supervisors monitor their performance. In virtually all surveys, part of performance monitoring involves careful record keeping and evaluation of completed interviews. Records kept on the number of hours worked, amount paid, number of eligible contacts, and number of refusals provide critical information on interviewer productivity, survey costs (e.g., time and dollars per interview), and survey quality (response and refusal rates). By reviewing completed questionnaires, supervisors also can clarify uncodable responses and check to see if interviewers are following instructions and recording answers appropriately. To tell if interviewers ask questions exactly as written, use neutral probes, and record answers correctly, many survey organizations also monitor or observe the interview process. In face-to-face interview surveys, supervisors may observe interviewers by either accompanying them on interviews or having them make tape recordings of all or a sample of their interviews. In telephone interview surveys, special monitoring phones allow supervisors to listen to ongoing interviews without being heard by either the interviewer or the respondent.

Reviewing completed questionnaires and observing interviews are two mechanisms of controlling the quality of interviewers' work and thereby determining the quality of the data. Two other processes are retrieving missing data and validating interviews (Weinberg, 1983). When data are missing, particularly for factual items that are critical to the survey, respondents may be recontacted to retrieve the information. Also, it is standard in all well-conducted surveys to verify that the interview actually took place and that the interviewer did not fabricate some responses or deviate from prescribed procedures. Validation usually is done by reinterviewing a sample of respondents for each interviewer. Respondents may be asked a subset of items and, in the case of in-person surveys, the reinterviews often are carried out by telephone.

Finally, another important aspect of the supervisory role is sustaining interviewers' motivation and enthusiasm and preventing feelings of isolation. It is easy to assume that interviewers will do better work as they gain experience; however, studies have shown that the opposite may be the case. For example, validity studies of reports of hospitalizations and physician visits found that the more interviews an interviewer had done, the greater the problem of underreporting (Cannell, Marquis, and Laurent, 1977). Thus, supervisors should meet with interviewers regularly throughout the interviewing period not only to provide continuing feedback and reinforcement of skills but also to communicate the importance of good interviewing. GSS interviewers report, mostly via e-mail, to their field supervisors at least weekly, but usually more often, to go over the status of their assignments (T. W. Smith, personal communication, 2003).

Follow-Up Efforts

The final phase of fieldwork consists of following up on nonrespondents in an attempt to gain their cooperation. If no contact is made initially, then GSS interviewers are instructed "to try several follow-up procedures, such as (a) calling back at different times and days of the week, (b) asking neighbors when people are usually at home or how they might be contacted, (c) leaving notes, and (d) using a reverse directory to get a telephone number for the household" (Davis and Smith, 1992:51). Follow-up efforts help to ensure that an adequate response rate is obtained and therefore are an important component of all kinds of surveys.

The question of what constitutes an adequate response rate has no definitive answer, but in surveys of the general public, response rates of approximately 75 percent for face-to-face interviews, 70 percent for telephone interviews, and 60 percent for mailed questionnaires are frequently considered acceptable. With concerted effort from the planning stage through follow-up, and with specialized groups, higher rates can be obtained (Dillman, 2000). Besides follow-up efforts, response rates may be improved (1) by appropriate efforts to gain access, discussed earlier; (2) in interview surveys, by proper interviewer training and supervision; and (3) for mailed questionnaires, by inclusion of a stamped return envelope and a token prepayment, as well as by attention to the length, difficulty, and appearance of the questionnaire (see chapter 9).

The particular follow-up activities depend on the survey mode. For telephone and face-to-face surveys, the major problem is dealing with refusals. In many surveys, more experienced interviewers or supervisors are used to try to gain the respondent's cooperation on the second try. The National Health and Social Life Survey (NHSLS) dealt with some initial refusals by employing follow-up interviewers who specialize in converting reluctant respondents and by sending out "conversion letters" that answered special concerns that potential respondents were raising (Laumann et al., 1994). In response to a clear refusal, however, one follow-up call or visit should be the limit to avoid respondent feelings of harassment.

Because the NHSLS investigators were worried about reaching their target response rate (75 percent), they started offering incentive completion fees to reluctant respondents on a selective basis in low-response areas (Laumann et al., 1994:56–57). Although incentive fees ranging from $10 to $100 were offered for interviews, the fees were viewed as cost efficient given the high cost of interviewer wages and travel costs (the cost of completed interviews averaged $450). The fees and other techniques for converting reluctant respondents eventually paid off with a final 79-percent response rate.

Since response rates are typically lower for mailed questionnaires, follow-up efforts are especially important with this mode. Typically, three follow-up mailings are used. For example, in Henry Wechsler and associates' (1994) college alcohol survey, respondents received four separate mailings, approximately 10 days apart: the initial mailing of the questionnaire, a postcard thanking those who had completed the questionnaire and urging those who had not to do so, a mailing with a another copy of the questionnaire again appealing for its return, and a second reminder postcard. Given that this survey was truly anonymous, all persons in the sample had to be sent the subsequent mailings. If questionnaires have been coded so that the researcher knows who has responded, there can be a savings in postage and paper, as only nonrespondents need receive the follow-up mailings.[5]

In the Tailored Design Method, Don Dillman (2000) recommends three more widely spaced follow-ups, each of which entails new and more persuasive appeals. The first follow-up, sent out about two weeks after the original mailing, consists of a postcard thank you/reminder as in the Wechsler et al. alcohol survey. The second follow-up, mailed two weeks later, is sent only to nonrespondents and contains a replacement questionnaire; the cover letter for this mailing communicates that the respondent is receiving individual attention, emphasizes their importance for the success of the survey, and notes that others have responded as a means of encouraging response. The third follow-up, mailed four weeks later, invokes special procedures, such as special mail or contact by telephone, to emphasize the importance of the respondent's cooperation. When Dillman (2000:185) used certified mail for this final request in five statewide surveys of the general public, he raised the response rates from an average of 59 to 72 percent. These follow-up efforts should yield adequate response rates, but pushing rates higher is very expensive and difficult; therefore, additional follow-mailings are seldom used.

Summary

Social surveys have three common features: a relatively large number of respondents generally chosen by some form of probability sampling, formal observation procedures involving interviews and/or questionnaires, and computerized statistical analysis of data. The units of analysis in sample surveys are typically individuals selected from a single community or nation; however, surveys of social units other than individuals are also done and samples from different countries are sometimes combined, as in comparative studies. While standardization is the norm, data-collection procedures vary along a continuum from highly formal and structured to less formal and structured, the choice of which depends on the researcher's objectives.

Surveys are used extensively for both scientific and nonscientific purposes, largely because of their ability to describe large populations in terms of a broad range of characteristics, attitudes, and behavior. Relative to other research strategies, surveys generally are more flexible in that they can be used with equal facility for both descriptive and explanatory research and can address a wider range of research topics. On the other hand, surveys present greater problems for inferring causal relationships, are less easily altered once the study has begun, are limited to reports of behavior rather than observations of behavior, and, like laboratory experiments, are subject to reactive effects.

Survey research designs are divided into two broad categories: (1) cross-sectional studies, in which data are gathered from a sample of a community or larger grouping at essentially one point in time; and (2) longitudinal studies, in which data are gathered at two or more points in time from either the same sample of respondents (panel study) or independently selected samples of the same population (trend studies). Two variants of the cross-sectional design have been developed to study social structural influences: (1) contextual studies, in which different groups are sampled to examine the effects of the group or context on individuals, and (2) social network studies, in which every individual in a group is studied to delineate networks of personal relationships. Cohort studies, a special instance of trend studies, trace changes across cohorts to separate the effects of age, cohort or generation, and historical period.

Of the three steps in conducting a survey, planning and field administration were considered in this chapter. Data processing and analysis are covered in chapter 14. The initial stages in planning a survey depart from other research strategies primarily in the construction of the survey instrument (interview schedule or questionnaire), which we discuss at length in the next chapter, and the development of the sampling plan. Survey data may be conducted through personal face-to-face interviews, telephone interviews, self-administered questionnaires, or a combination of these modes (mixed mode survey).

Interviews, in comparison with questionnaires, offer greater flexibility in the type and format of questions, provide the opportunity to clarify questions and elicit fuller responses, and tend to have higher response rates. Face-to-face interviews also permit lengthy interviews with complex questions, although they may introduce greater bias through interviewer–respondent interaction, and they tend to be very expensive. By comparison, telephone interviews offer a substantial savings in time and money and are easier to administer, although they require simpler questions and may elicit less complete responses. Mailed self-administered questionnaires are the least expensive survey mode, but they tend to have lower response rates, result in more nonresponse to individual questions, and must contain simpler questions for reliable responses. New electronic self-administered methods, which are rapidly gaining acceptance, may reduce time and cost and allow for more varied and user-friendly questionnaire design; however, Internet surveys, in particular, suffer from coverage error, and their most productive use in the short run may be as a complement to interviews in mixed mode surveys.

Field administration in survey research begins with interviewer selection and training and instrument pretesting, continues with interviews and staff supervision, and ends with follow-up efforts to reach initial nonrespondents. Interviewers must be able simultaneously to put the interviewee at ease, to ask questions and guide the interview to its completion, and to record responses. To accomplish this requires careful interviewer selection and training. Before data are gathered from respondents, the survey instrument should be pretested and access to respondents should be gained by contacting appropriate community officials and mailing a cover letter. During the course of interviewing, interviewers must (1) be wary of introducing bias; (2) be courteous and tactful, dress appropriately, and guard the confidentiality of respondents' replies; (3) be relaxed but businesslike; and (4) be thoroughly familiar with the instrument so as to maintain rapport, use probes when necessary, and record answers as they go along. Supervision of interviewees—keeping a record of each interviewer, checking completed interview schedules, and so forth—is essential for quality control, while follow-up efforts to contact initial nonrespondents are essential to obtain an adequate response rate, especially in mail surveys.

Key Terms

cross-national surveys
structured interview
semistructured interview
unstructured interview
descriptive and explanatory surveys
secondary analysis
survey research designs
   cross-sectional design
     contextual design
     social network design
   longitudinal design
     trend study
     panel study
     cohort study

interview schedule
response rate
face-to-face interview
computer-assisted personal interviewing
telephone interview
computer-assisted telephone interviewing
random-digit dialing
self-administered questionnaire
computer-assisted self-interviewing
mixed mode survey
pretesting
cover letter
response effect

Review Questions and Problems

1. What are the three principal features of professional survey research?
2. Give an example of a survey study in which the unit of analysis is not the individual.

3. Contrast the objectives of unstructured, structured, and semistructured interviews.

4. What is the General Social Survey (GSS)?

5. Describe the kinds of questions that can be included in a survey.

6. Discuss the advantages and disadvantages of surveys in relation to experiments.

7. What inherent weakness does the survey share with the laboratory experiment?

8. What limitation of cross-sectional surveys is addressed by contextual designs and social network designs?

9. What is the difference between a trend study and a panel study? Which of these study designs permits the assessment of individual change?

10. What are the three kinds of influences examined in cohort analysis?

11. Outline the major decision points in planning a survey.

12. What are the relative advantages and disadvantages of structured versus unstructured survey procedures?

13. Which sampling design is likely to be used with face-to-face interviews? Why?

14. Explain how interviews provide greater flexibility than self-administered questionnaires.

15. What particular problems are associated with face-to-face interviewing?

16. Relative to face-to-face interviewing, what advantages does telephone interviewing offer?

17. In what ways can computer-assisted personal and telephone interviewing (CAPI and CATI) assist the interviewer?

18. Compare face-to-face interviews, telephone interviews, and self-administered questionnaires with respect to (a) response rates and sampling quality, (b) time and cost, and (c) type—complexity and sensitivity—of questions asked.

19. Under what conditions is a mail questionnaire survey recommended?

20. What are the strengths and weaknesses of Internet surveys?

21. Give an example of a mixed mode survey.

22. Outline the key steps in the field administration phase of survey research.

23. What qualities are desirable in an interviewer?

24. Describe the steps involved in interviewer training.

25. Explain the purpose of pretesting.

26. What should a cover letter communicate to the respondent?

27. What are the principal arguments pro and con regarding the use of standardized interviewing procedures?

28. Describe some sources of measurement error in surveys attributable to the (a) interviewer and (b) respondent.

29. What activities does the supervision of interviewers involve?

30. Why is it suggested that supervision and contact with interviewers be maintained throughout the interviewing period?

31. Why are follow-up efforts necessary? At what point should they be abandoned in interview surveys? How many follow-up mailings typically are used in mail surveys?

NOTES

1. Social network analysis is an interdisciplinary paradigm that developed primarily from earlier work in American sociology and social psychology (sociometry) and British anthropology (Wasserman and Faust, 1994).

2. Whereas the flowchart in Figure 8.1 shows the top-to-bottom and sideways influences, in reality later decisions may result in modifications of earlier decisions. For example, sampling-plan cost considerations may bring about a change in the research objectives.

3. See Shosteck and Fairweather (1979) for a study comparing physician response rates to mailed and personal interview surveys.

4. Fieldwork is not always carried out exactly in this order. Pretesting, for example, may occur before, during, or after the training of interviewers. Efforts to gain access to respondents may well begin earlier than depicted.

5. Another strategy is to enclose a postage-paid postcard that identifies the respondent (name or identification number) in the first mailing (Mangione, 1995). Respondents are asked to mail the postcard separately from the anonymous questionnaire, and they are told that the postcard indicates that the questionnaire has been returned and they will receive no reminder notices.

9

✔

Survey Instrumentation

The two most critical features for successful survey research are the sample and the survey instrument. Accurate generalizations about populations of interest depend on the quality of the sample. But no matter how carefully the sample is selected, a sample survey is only as good as the design of the questionnaire or interview schedule.

Survey instrument design is a creative process, partly art and partly science (Payne, 1951). Like an artist, the survey designer selects "raw materials" and combines them creatively within certain principles of design. For the artist, raw materials may consist of paper or canvas; pencil, charcoal, chalks, watercolors, acrylics, or oils; brushes; and so forth. The survey designer's raw materials are such things as free response and fixed-choice questions, direct and indirect questions, question-and-response formats, overall physical layout, and instructions.

However, the survey designer is unlike the artist in at least one important way. An artist is mainly concerned with expressing his or her own personal ideas, emotions, or other subjective experience, whereas the designer of a survey instrument must be concerned ultimately with getting reliable and valid reports about other people. This concern is what makes the survey designer a scientist rather than an artist. The reports may be of subjective experiences such as values, opinions, fears, and beliefs, or they may be of overt experiences such as job history, salary, political behavior, place of residence, consumer behavior, or leisure activities. The verbal reports obtained in surveys are, of course, answers to questions; survey instrumentation is thus the science of asking questions.

In this chapter we focus on standardized instruments, in which the wording and order of questions is the same for all respondents. Yet many of the principles discussed here apply to less structured interview approaches. Also, we generally do not treat separately the primary modes of asking questions (self-administered mail questionnaire, face-to-face interview, and telephone interview), although these sometimes require different questions and formats. The survey designer generally has fewer options with self-administered than with interviewer-administered questionnaires. Questions, response formats, and instructions must be simpler in mail surveys, and certain questions—for example, questions of knowledge in which the consulting of other sources would be undesirable—are inappropriate.

We begin by discussing cognitive and communication theories of how people answer survey questions. Then we consider "materials" available to the survey designer—types of questions and response formats. Next we examine the overall design or "sketch" of the survey instrument. Then we look at practical guides for "filling in the sketch"—writing items to arrive at a first draft. Finally, we discuss the pretesting operations that are necessary to transform a draft instrument into a finished product.

The Survey as a Social Occasion

Until recently, the science of asking questions was based largely on two sources of information: the experience of professional survey researchers and empirical evidence from experiments on question wording. For example, experience has shown that it is best for question crafters to use simple, plain-spoken language (Converse and Presser, 1986); research has shown that respondents are more likely to give a "no opinion" response if it is explicitly offered as a response alternative (Schuman and Presser, 1981). Such wisdom has resulted in some important guidelines for questionnaire design, but these guidelines are ad hoc and often not clearly understood. What has been needed is a solid theoretical understanding of how people go about answering survey questions. Fortunately, over the past two decades survey methodologists have drawn heavily on work in cognitive and social psychology (for detailed discussions, see Schwarz, 1996; Sudman, Bradburn, and Schwarz, 1996; Sirken et al., 1999; Tourangeau, Rips, and Rasinski, 2000) to develop theoretical models of the response process.

Scientifically, the survey interview is an occasion to obtain valid responses to a series of questions; however, it also is a social occasion subject to the influences of the social world. Being interviewed is an uncommon, sometimes anxiety-provoking experience for many respondents. Unfamiliar with the canons of structured interviewing, they turn to the social and linguistic rules governing everyday conversation for guidance on how they should behave as respondents. In answering each question, they also attend to a sequence of cognitive tasks with certain levels of ability and motivation. What can each of these perspectives tell us about designing a survey instrument?

From the perspective of cognitive processing, answering survey questions requires that respondents (1) comprehend the question, (2) retrieve the information requested from memory, (3) formulate a response in accord with the question and the information retrieved, and (4) communicate a response deemed appropriate (Sudman, Bradburn, and Schwarz, 1996:58–75; see also Tourangeau, Rips, and Rasinski, 2000). Each of these steps involves mental tasks that can give rise to response errors. For example, to comprehend a question according to what the researcher had in mind, the respondent must understand both its literal and intended meaning. Therefore, the question–answer task breaks down not only when the question wording is vague but also when the purpose of the question is misunderstood. Consider the question, "What have you done today?" While the literal meaning of the words may be clear, this may not be sufficient to answer the question, because the respondent still needs to know what sort of activities are of interest to the researcher. Would this include, for example, mundane activities such as brushing one's teeth and taking a shower (Schwarz, Groves, and Schuman, 1998)? Analyses of the other cognitive steps in the response process indicate that response errors are likely to occur when there is insufficient time to access relevant information from memory, when the accessed information does not fit the response options provided in the question, and when the respondent modifies the information to project a favorable image to the interviewer. We discuss ways to minimize these problems later in this chapter.

Another perspective, conversational analysis, suggests that respondents make sense out of structured interviews and self-administered questionnaires by relying upon tacit assumptions underlying ordinary conversations. This perspective draws on the work of philosopher of language Paul Grice (1989). According to Grice, conversations generally run smoothly because speakers and listeners follow four maxims:

1. Speakers should not say things that they believe to be false. [Truthfulness]
2. Speakers should make comments that are relevant to the purposes of the conversation. [Relevance]
3. Speakers should make their contributions as informative as possible and not repeat themselves. [Nonredundancy]
4. Speakers should express themselves as clearly as possible. [Clarity]

As respondents follow these conversational maxims to infer the intended meaning of questions, they may be unintentionally influenced by subtle aspects of the survey instrument and administration, such as prior questions, response formats, and other cues irrelevant to the intended purpose of the current question. The principle of relevance, for example, implies that respondents will see everything about the survey as relevant to a given question, including seemingly irrelevant design features such as the numeric values on a rating scale. Norbert Schwarz and associates (1991) demonstrated this by asking respondents to answer the question, "How successful would you say you have been in life?" on an 11-point scale with endpoints labeled "not at all successful" and "extremely successful." The answers, as it turned out, depended on the numeric values assigned to these endpoints. When the endpoints ranged from 0 (not at all successful) to 10 (extremely successful), 34 percent endorsed a value from 0 to 5, whereas when the endpoints ranged from −5 (not at all successful) to +5 (extremely successful), only 13 percent endorsed a formally equivalent value of −5 to 0. Follow-up questions revealed that the numeric values affected how respondents interpreted the endpoints. When accompanied by a value of 0, they interpreted "not at all successful" to mean the absence of success, but when accompanied by a value of −5, they interpreted this to mean explicit failure.

Another study shows how the methodological strategy of exploring complex topics by asking a series of related questions runs counter to the conversational principle of nonredundancy. Fritz Strack, Norbert Schwarz, and Michaela Wänke (1991) asked German students to answer two questions about their lives: One question asked them to rate their happiness, and another asked them to rate their satisfaction with life as a whole. Both questions had 11-point rating scales with similar endpoints (11 = very happy and 11 = very satisfied). Happiness and life satisfaction are nearly identical concepts. Not surprisingly, when both questions were asked in ostensibly unrelated questionnaires, the two measures were highly correlated; however, when the questions were introduced in the same questionnaire with the sentence "Now, we have two questions about your life" and then were asked one after the other, the correlation was much lower. Apparently, asking both questions in the same conversational context implied that they were intended to convey a different meaning; after all, asking the same question twice would not make sense.

Finally, a third theoretical perspective, rational choice theory, focuses on how respondents' *motivation* to provide acceptable answers to survey questions can affect their responses (Krosnick, 1991, 1999). Answering survey questions requires a great deal of mental effort. At the least respondents must go through the four cognitive steps outlined above. Of course, some questions, such as those that require memory recall or thoughtful opinions on controversial issues, require more work than others; and lengthy interviews require more effort than shorter ones. When respondents exert the maximum effort to generate a complete and unbiased answer, they are said to be "optimizing"; when they do not expend the necessary effort but take shortcuts, such as not searching their memories thoroughly, they are said to be "satisficing." Satisficing may explain why some respondents tend to give "no opinion" or "don't know" responses; it requires less effort to express no opinion than to think through one's position. On attitude questions that ask respondents whether they agree or disagree with a series of statements, satisficing also may account for the tendency to agree more often than disagree, because it is easier to politely agree with reasonable assertions than to generate reasons why they may not be true.

Theoretically, the likelihood of satisficing behavior increases with question difficulty and decreases with the respondent's motivation and ability to answer the question. One recent study (Holbrook, Green, and Krosnick, 2003) compared evidence of satisficing responses in telephone versus personal interview surveys. As evidence of their lesser motivation to provide optimal answers, telephone respondents were judged to be less cooperative and engaged in the interview and expressed more dissatisfaction with the length of the interview. Consistent with the theory, they also evidenced more satisficing behavior. For example, they were more likely to give "no opinion" answers on several attitudinal items and were more likely to express agreement on yes/no and agree/disagree questions.

Although these theories are in an early stage of development, their methodological implications are clear. To identify likely problems when designing survey instruments, researchers need to understand the conversational, cognitive, and motivational processes that underlie question asking and answering (Sudman, Bradburn, and Schwarz, 1996:258). As we examine the options available to the question designer, we will consider these perspectives on the response task. Given the complexity of this task, however, decisions about questionnaire design are best worked out in a thorough process of pretesting. Indeed, one of the most important products of this theoretical movement is the development of rigorous diagnostic procedures for pretesting survey instruments, which we discuss at the end of the chapter.

Materials Available to the Survey Designer

Like the artist, the survey designer has a number of choices about raw materials. We now offer some guides regarding choices among certain types of questions and response formats and regarding the use of visual aids and questions from previous research.

Open-Ended and Closed-Ended Questions

A major choice among "materials" concerns open-ended and closed-ended questions. The **open-ended** (also called the **free-response**) **question** requires respondents to answer in their own words (in written form on a questionnaire or aloud to an interviewer). The **closed-ended** (or **fixed-choice**) **question** requires the respondent to choose a response from those provided. Here are examples of two questions written in both open and closed forms.

1. How would you rate the President's performance in office so far? (OPEN)
1. How would you rate the President's performance in office so far? (CLOSED)
   ( ) Poor
   ( ) Below average
   ( ) Average
   ( ) Above average
   ( ) Excellent
2. What do you think is the number one domestic issue the President should be concerned with? (OPEN)
2. Which one of the domestic issues listed below should the President be most concerned with? (CLOSED)
   ( ) Unemployment
   ( ) Inflation
   ( ) Reform of the welfare system
   ( ) Balancing the budget
   ( ) The energy crisis
   ( ) Other

The choice between open- and closed-ended questions is a complex one, because each has a number of advantages and disadvantages. The greatest advantage of the open question is the freedom the respondent has in answering. The resulting material may be a veritable gold mine of information, revealing respondents' logic or thought processes, the amount of information they possess, and the strength of their opinions or feelings. Frequently the researcher's understanding of the topic is clarified and even completely changed by unexpected responses to open questions. But, alas, this very quality of open questions, the wealth of information, has a drawback: the "coding" problem of summarizing and analyzing rich and varied (and often irrelevant and vague) responses. Coding such material is a time-consuming and costly process that invariably results in some degree of error (Sudman and Bradburn, 1982). (See chapter 14 for a further discussion of coding.)

Open questions also require interviewers skilled in "recognizing ambiguities of response and in probing and drawing respondents out . . . to make sure they give codable answers" (Sudman and Bradburn, 1982:151). The following interviewer–respondent exchange illustrates the importance of probing to give respondents encouragement and time to think and to clarify their responses (Sudman and Bradburn, 1982:150):

Interviewer:	What are the most important problems facing the nation today?
Respondent:	I don't know, there are so many.
Interviewer:	That's right, I'd just like to know what you think are the most important problems.

Respondent:	Well, there's certainly inflation, and then government spending.
Interviewer:	Government spending . . . how do you mean? Could you explain that a little? What do you have in mind when you say "government spending"?
Respondent:	There's no end to it. We have to cut down federal spending somehow.
Interviewer:	Any others?
Respondent:	No. I think those are the most important ones.

Other problems with the open question include (1) the varying length of responses (some people are unbelievably verbose; others, exceedingly reticent), (2) the difficulty with inarticulate or semiliterate respondents, (3) the difficulty interviewers have in getting it all down accurately, and (4) the reluctance of many persons to reveal detailed information or socially unacceptable opinions or behavior. Open-ended questions also entail more work, not only for the researcher but also for the respondent. Indeed, open questions should be used sparingly, if at all, in self-administered questionnaires, where respondents must write rather than speak.

Closed-ended questions are easier on the respondent because they require less effort and less facility with words. The presence of response options also enhances standardization by creating the same frame of reference for all respondents. When used in an interview, closed questions require less work and training to administer, and the interview may be shortened considerably.

On the other hand, good closed questions are difficult to develop. It is easy to omit important responses, leading respondents to choose among alternatives that do not correspond to their true feelings or attitudes. Research shows that respondents tend to confine themselves to the alternatives offered, even if they are explicitly given a choice such as "Other _____ (please explain)" (Schuman and Presser, 1981). This would be consistent with Grice's relevance principle, because respondents are likely to view the list of response options as indicative of the researcher's interests. To provide a list of response options that are meaningful to the respondent, the recommended procedure is to use open questions in preliminary interviews or pretests to determine what members of the study population say spontaneously; this information then may be used to construct meaningful closed alternatives for the final instrument. Unfortunately, this procedure is not always followed; time and financial limitations may prevent pretesting of sufficient scope to yield adequate information on the population's responses.

Even when the range of possible responses is known, they may be too numerous to list in a closed question. It is better, obviously, to ask the open question, "In what state or foreign country were you born?" than to list all states and foreign countries. Similarly, questions about occupations, medical conditions, favorite television shows, and the like, are best asked open-ended (Fowler, 1995).

Given these advantages and disadvantages, when should one choose open or closed questions? Robert Kahn and Charles Cannell (1957) suggest these five considerations: (1) the objectives of the survey, (2) the level of information possessed by respondents in regard to the topic, (3) how well respondents' opinions are thought out or structured, (4) motivation of respondents to communicate, and (5) the extent of the researcher's knowledge of respondents' characteristics.

1. Consider first the study's objectives. If you simply want to classify respondents with respect to some well-understood attitude or behavior, the closed question would probably be appropriate and most efficient. However, the open question is usually preferable when the survey objectives are broader and you are seeking such information as the basis on which opinions are founded, the depth of respondent knowledge, or the intensity with which respondents hold opinions.

2. A second consideration is the amount of information that respondents already have on the topics of interest. If you believe that the vast majority will have sufficient information regarding the survey's topics, the closed question may be acceptable. On the other hand, if you are uncertain as to the level of information of the respondents or if you anticipate a wide range in the amount of knowledge, the open question is more appropriate. With closed questions, uninformed respondents may conceal their ignorance by making arbitrary choices, yielding invalid reports. And even adding the response option "don't know" may not resolve the problem, since this option is unlikely to be popular with respondents who are sensitive about appearing ill-informed.[1] It is easier, for example, to respond "approve" or "disapprove" of the Supreme Court decision *Roe v. Wade* than to admit not knowing what it is.

3. A related consideration is the structuring of respondent thought or opinion. Are respondents likely to have thought about the issue before? Can they take a position or express a definite attitude? If respondents are likely to have given previous thought to the matter *and* the range of typical responses is known to the researcher, the closed question may be satisfactory. This might be the case, for example, with a survey designed to measure the attitudes of registered voters toward the performance of the President. However, if respondents' ideas are less likely to be structured, open questions may be preferable. Suppose you wanted to ascertain why college students chose XYZ University or why couples desired a certain number of children; for such questions, the reasons may be numerous and not always immediately accessible to respondents. A series of open questions would allow respondents time to recall, think through, and talk about various aspects of their decisions, rather than hastily selecting a possibly incomplete or inappropriate response provided by a closed question.

4. Motivation of respondents to communicate their experiences and thoughts is a further consideration. In general, the open question will be successful only when the respondent is highly motivated, because this question type is more demanding in terms of effort, time, and self-disclosure. Therefore, with less motivated respondents, closed questions may lead to better quality data. On the other hand, closed questions sometimes dampen respondent motivation, in that some people prefer to express their views in their own words and find being forced to choose among limited fixed-choice responses very irritating.

5. A fifth important consideration in choosing between open and closed questions is the extent of the researcher's previous knowledge of respondent characteristics. That is, how well does the researcher understand the vocabulary and amount

of information possessed by the respondents, the degree of structure of respondents' views, and their level of motivation? Unless the researcher has done similar studies previously or has done extensive preliminary interviewing, the most likely answer is "not very well." If this is the case, open questions should yield more valid (albeit more difficult to summarize and analyze) data.[2]

One approach is to use the different types of questions at different stages of research, first utilizing open questions in preliminary interviewing and using the information provided by these early interviews to develop closed questions or a combination of open and closed questions on the final instrument. Or, you may decide from the start upon some combination of open and closed questions appropriate to your purposes. (For a further comparison of open and closed questions, see Box 9.1.)

Direct and Indirect Questions

Another choice of "materials" concerns the use of direct and indirect questions. A **direct question** is one in which there is a direct, clear relationship between the question that is asked and what the researcher wants to know. The bulk of questions used in survey research are direct. "What is your total family income?" and "What do you think is the ideal number of children for your family?" are examples of direct questions.

With **indirect questions**, the link between the researcher's objectives and the question asked is less obvious. An investigator interested in studying the sex-role attitudes of male factory workers, for example, might ask the indirect question, "Do you believe your co-workers would mind having a woman as supervisor?," instead of the direct question, "Would you mind having a woman as supervisor?" Although the investigator really wants to determine the respondents' own sex-role attitudes, he or she may suspect that they will be unwilling to admit personal sexist sentiments to an interviewer. Knowing, however, that individuals' attitudes and beliefs shape the way they perceive the world about them, the researcher assumes that respondents will impute their own attitudes to their co-workers.

Indirect questions may be appropriate when the researcher is interested in characteristics or experiences that the respondent is unwilling or unable to reveal in direct terms. Respondents may be unwilling because the behavior in question is considered socially undesirable or unacceptable; they may be unable because the characteristics— motives, needs, fears—are below their level of conscious awareness.

Most indirect measurement is based on the notion of projection: that individuals tend to attribute their own inner needs, feelings, opinions, and values to the outer world. Thus, an individual presented with ambiguous stimuli will tend to interpret the material in ways that reflect his or her own needs and values. Some of the more common projective techniques are word association, sentence completion, and storytelling. In word association, respondents say the first thing that comes to mind in response to each of a list of words read by an interviewer. Sentence completion requires respondents to finish incomplete sentences, such as "When I think of cities, I think of _____." Storytelling involves asking respondents to interpret such ambiguous stimuli as inkblots and pictures.[3]

BOX 9.1

An Experimental Comparison of Open and Closed Questions

Discussions of the advantages and disadvantages of open and closed questions are based largely on common sense and the unsystematic experiences of survey researchers. One of the few exceptions is Howard Schuman and associates' (Schuman and Presser, 1981; Schuman, Ludwig, and Krosnick, 1986; Schuman and Scott, 1987) use of an experimental design within large-scale sample surveys to compare systematically responses elicited by parallel open and closed questions. The table shows the outcome of one of these experiments (Schuman and Scott, 1987), in which half of the respondents in a national telephone survey were randomly assigned to an open version and half were assigned to a closed version of the same question about the most important problem facing the country.

The open question has been used repeatedly in national surveys. This particular closed version listed four problems, each of which had been mentioned rarely in recent uses of the open question. As expected, only 2.4 percent of the sample mentioned any of these four problems in response to the open question. The categories most frequently mentioned were unemployment and general economic problems. In response to the closed question, however, 60 percent of the respondents chose among the alternatives offered to them, in spite of the fact that the question explicitly instructed them to consider other alternatives. Furthermore, unemployment, mentioned by 17 percent of respondents on the open version, was named by only 6.2 percent of respondents on the closed version. As Schuman and Scott (1987:957) point out, "the issues mentioned on the open question give the better overall picture of American concerns and . . . the findings on the closed question are distorted by the constraint or inertia produced by listing the four problems as part of the question."

Open question		*Closed question*
What do you think is the most important problem facing this country today?		Which of the following do you think is the most important problem facing this country today—the energy shortage, the quality of public schools, legalized abortion, or pollution—or if you prefer, you may name a different problem as most important?
1. The energy shortage	0.0%	5.6%
2. The quality of public schools	1.2	32.0
3. Legalized abortion	0.0	8.4
4. Pollution	1.2	14.0
Subtotal	2.4	60.0
5. All other responses	93.0	39.3
6. Don't know	4.7	0.6
	100.0%	100.0%
Number of respondents	(171)	(178)

Source: Reprinted with permission. Copyright 1987 American Association for the Advancement of Science.

This experiment clearly demonstrates how differences in the form of a question can produce quite different results. Although these data suggest the superiority of the open version, other evidence indicates that open and closed questions will ordinarily lead to the same conclusion, so long as the closed form includes as alternatives the most frequently mentioned issues in response to the open form (Schuman and Presser, 1981). When in doubt about response alternatives, investigators should be careful not to impose their own frames of reference on respondents, but should begin with open questions and then use the "free" responses to construct a set of "fixed" alternatives. In addition, open questions may be necessary as "why" follow-ups to closed questions; when alternatives are too complex or too many to present easily in a closed version; and when rapidly changing events undermine the adequacy of closed alternatives (Schuman and Presser, 1981).

Most indirect measures were developed for clinical use and designed to aid in the diagnosis of emotional disorders by revealing an individual's personality and needs. This remains their principal use, although they also have been used in attitude and motivation research, especially in marketing. To illustrate the indirect approach, let us examine a classic study from marketing research, conducted in 1950. (For a more complete discussion of the use of indirect questions and approaches, see Kidder and Campbell, 1970.)

Mason Haire (1950) was interested in attitudes toward instant coffee, one of the early instant-food preparations. Using direct questioning, Haire found that when women who reported not using instant coffee were asked, "What do you dislike about it?," most of them said that they did not like the flavor. Suspecting, however, that this was a stereotypic response that concealed other motives, Haire developed an indirect approach to measure consumers' attitudes. He prepared two grocery shopping lists that were identical, except that one contained "Nescafé instant coffee" while the other contained "1 lb Maxwell House coffee (drip ground)." He then asked subjects to read one or the other shopping list and to describe the personality and character of the woman who made it out. As it turned out, Nescafé and Maxwell House coffee users were perceived quite differently. For example, nearly half of the subjects described the Nescafé user as lazy and failing to plan household purchases, whereas the Maxwell House purchaser was rarely described in these terms. The evidence from the indirect approach thus suggested that the decision to buy instant coffee was influenced as much by prevailing attitudes about what constitutes good housekeeping as by the flavor of instant coffee. Although a 1968 replication of this study produced essentially the same results (Webster and von Pechmann, 1970), it would be interesting to see if the findings would be repeated today, given the apparent changes in attitudes toward gender roles and housework in the past three decades.

While one should be aware of the possibility of indirect questioning, it is used relatively infrequently in survey research today. One likely reason is that its use often requires intensive training in the administration, scoring, and interpretation of responses. Some researchers also question the validity of such measures. On the infrequent occasions that tests of validity and reliability have been done, the results have not been encouraging (Kidder and Campbell, 1970). Furthermore, there are some serious ethical concerns with the use of indirect questions. To what extent are respondents giving their "informed consent" (see chapter 16)? To what extent is deception being used, and is its use justifiable?

Response Formats

In addition to making decisions about the broad categories of open and closed questions and direct and indirect questions, the creative survey designer will consider the possibilities offered by various **response formats** for closed-ended questions. The simplest response option is a simple "yes" or "no." This would be appropriate for such questions as "Do you belong to a labor union?" and "Have you ever been threatened with a gun?" However, even though many types of information form natural dichotomies, this kind of question appears less frequently than you might think. With many apparently dichotomous items, respondents may prefer to answer "don't know," "uncertain," or "both." About 10 percent of GSS national samples, for instance, respond "don't know" to the question "Do you believe in life after death?" (Davis, Smith, and Marsden, 2002).

The decision to encourage or discourage "don't know" or "no opinion" responses is a complex one (Fowler, 1995:164–65). When respondents are truly uninformed or lack firsthand experiences with the subject of the question, the researcher needs to learn this by explicitly providing a "don't know" option and, in some circumstances, including a statement that sanctions a know-nothing response. Otherwise, respondents may haphazardly pick a response to conform to normative expectations that they should answer the question (Grice's relevance principle). When measuring feelings or subjective states, on the other hand, respondents who are ambivalent, indifferent, or even lazy are likely to choose an explicit "don't know" option rather than attempt to express their feelings (satisficing strategy). In such situations, it may be more appropriate to omit "don't know" response categories, thus limiting no opinions to volunteered responses.

Ordinal response scales are commonly used to measure the strength or intensity of respondents' feelings. One of the most popular formats, the **Likert response** scale used in Likert scaling (see chapter 12), consists of a series of responses ranging from "strongly agree" to "strongly disagree." This is a common way of measuring attitudes. The respondent is presented with a statement and asked to indicate the extent of his or her agreement. For example,

Men have greater sexual needs than women.

( ) Strongly agree
( ) Agree
( ) Uncertain
( ) Disagree
( ) Strongly disagree

Besides degrees of agreement, a variety of other rating scales exist for assessing attitudes and opinions. To evaluate objects ranging from consumer products to personal attributes to government policies, respondents could be given the categories "excellent," "very good," "good," "fair," and "poor," as in the following question.

> Compared with the jobs that your friends have, would you say that your job is excellent, very good, good, fair, or poor?
>
> ( ) Excellent
> ( ) Very good
> ( ) Good
> ( ) Fair
> ( ) Poor

One can also create scales by asking respondents "how" they feel and then using a series of adverbs to modify the intensity of opinion. The following item from the GSS measures job satisfaction in this way.

> On the whole, how satisfied are you with the work you do—would you say you are very satisfied, moderately satisfied, a little dissatisfied, or very dissatisfied?
>
> ( ) Very satisfied
> ( ) Moderately satisfied
> ( ) A little dissatisfied
> ( ) Very dissatisfied

It is also common to use numerical rating scales, with verbal ratings provided for the numerical endpoints, as in the GSS item below (Davis, Smith, and Marsden, 2002).

> I am going to name some institutions in this country. Some people have complete confidence in the *people running* these institutions. Suppose these people are at one end of the scale at point number 1. Other people have no confidence at all in the *people running* these institutions. Suppose these people are at the other end, at point 7. And, of course, other people have opinions somewhere in between at point 2, 3, 4, 5, or 6. Where would you place yourself on this scale for banks and financial institutions?

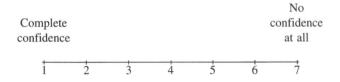

Another popular rating approach measures people's reactions to stimulus words or statements on a 7-point scale with end points anchored by opposing adjectives (such as "good" and "bad," or "fast" and "slow").[4] Respondents are asked to rate the stimulus word or statement as it relates to each pair of adjectives. For example,

President Bush

Fun	:		:		:	x	:		:		:		:		:		:	Boring
Real	:		:		:		:		:	x	:		:		:		:	Fake
Strong	:	x	:		:		:		:		:		:		:		:	Weak
Cold	:		:		:		:	x	:		:		:		:		:	Warm

Here a hypothetical respondent evaluated President Bush to be slightly fun and fake, and extremely strong, and was neutral or undecided on the cold-warm dimension.

A particular advantage with this format is that it is easily adapted for people from different backgrounds by using words appropriate to their vocabulary. Robert Gordon and colleagues (1963) adopted this format to test predictions from several delinquency theories regarding the values of gang, nongang lower-class, and nongang middle-class boys. With use of such adjective pairs as "clean—dirty," "good—bad," "brave—cowardly," and "smart—sucker," the boys studied were asked to rate various stimulus descriptions (e.g., "someone who works for good grades at school," "someone who shares his money with his friends," "someone who knows where to sell what he steals," "someone who stays cool and keeps to himself"). The gang boys were found to endorse middle-class norms to a much greater extent than predicted.

In creating a rating scale, two important considerations are the number of categories to use and whether the scale should be defined primarily by numerical or adjectival labeling (Fowler, 1995:52–55). Should the response format comprise two categories (e.g., "yes," "no"), five categories (e.g., Likert), seven categories (e.g., the preceding two examples), or even more? Unless respondents' views are limited to a few categories, seven to eleven categories seem best for measuring the full range of their attitudes, beliefs, or feelings. In studies comparing different length rating scales, including a contrast between seven- and eleven-category scales, Duane Alwin (1992, 1997) found that scales with more response categories were generally more reliable and valid than shorter scales. An exception to the principle of using longer scales to obtain more precise information is the telephone survey, in which respondents may not retain all of the scaling instructions because, unlike other survey modes, they cannot be handed a visual aid or questionnaire portraying the scale. When scales are administered by telephone, it is best to keep them short and provide a description that is easy to remember.

Adjectival labeling of each response category conveys less ambiguity to the reader than numerical values alone, or numerical values with verbal labeling of endpoints (Fowler, 1995). Suppose that respondents are asked to rate the honesty of a particular politician, either on scale A from 0 ("Not at all honest") to 6 ("Extremely honest") or on scale B from −3 ("Not at all honest") to +3 ("Extremely honest"). Although both scales have seven categories and the same endpoint labels, as we discussed earlier, respondents will actively use the numerical information in determining an appropriate answer (Schwarz et al., 1991). Thus, they are likely to interpret scale B as bipolar, with categories ranging from degrees of dishonesty (negative values) to degrees of honesty (positive values). In contrast, scale A may be construed as unipolar categories representing degrees of honesty ranging from its absence (0) to its highest presence (6). Also, the "0" category of version B better conveys a middle or neutral position than the somewhat ambiguous "3" of version A. If the intended scale was conceptualized as bipolar, the following adjectival labeling format might be used instead of numerical values:

Extremely dishonest	Moderately dishonest	Slightly dishonest	Neither dishonest nor honest	Slightly honest	Moderately honest	Extremely honest

Ranking questions present another possibility to the survey designer, as in this example.

> A number of factors influence people's career choices. Rank the factors listed below from 1 to 5, according to their importance to you in choosing a career:
>
> _____Making a lot of money
> _____Being creative
> _____Being free from supervision
> _____Having opportunities for advancement
> _____Avoiding a high pressure job

Although ranking questions frequently are handy and appropriate to use, we have chosen this example to illustrate several potential problems. First, unless pretesting with an open-ended question has been done, who can say these five factors are the most salient to the respondents? You can probably think of other important factors, especially if you are interested in working with people and helping others. (This, of course, is a general problem with closed questions.) Even if these factors have been shown to be the most important ones, further questions of validity may be raised. Do people really *know* why they choose certain careers? If so, will they tell you? How many respondents would freely admit that, to them, "making a lot of money" is the most important factor? Would "being creative" tend to get a spuriously high ranking? (For several additional examples of ranking questions, see Sudman and Bradburn, 1982:158–65.)

Visual Aids

An effective survey instrument also may include miscellaneous aids such as illustrations, photographs, films, and cards that contain written material. The use of illustrations in a self-administered questionnaire may improve clarity and appeal, increasing respondent motivation and perhaps improving the completion rate. In interviewing, photographs and films sometimes are used to acquire data not obtainable through questioning alone. In a study of early socialization practices, for example, photographs of mothers with their young babies might be taken to stimulate the mothers to discuss their child-rearing attitudes and behavior, especially if the mothers have difficulty answering highly abstract questions.

Other aids used with an interview may speed up the interview or make it easier for the respondent to answer accurately. The latter purpose may be served by presenting respondents a card containing the responses to a fixed-choice question, so that the respondent can view the choices while answering the question. As a rule, cards are used whenever the response categories are lengthy or more than five or six in number. For example, GSS interviewers hand respondents a card similar to the one shown below when they ask, "Which of the categories on this card come closest to the type of place you were living in when you were 16 years old?" (Davis, Smith, and Marsden, 2002).

```
1. In open country but not on a farm
2. On a farm
3. In a small city or town (under 50,000)
4. In a medium-size city (50,000–250,000)
5. In a suburb near a large city
6. In a large city (over 250,000)
```

Existing Questions

Of all the raw materials available to the survey researcher, perhaps the most important are questions that have been used in previous research. Most survey instruments contain existing questions, at least in adapted form, and it is easy to understand why. The use of existing questions shortcuts the measurement and testing processes. It also enables researchers to compare results across studies, to estimate trends, and, under certain conditions, to estimate response reliability (Sudman and Bradburn, 1982:14). Lest one be concerned about the ethics of using another person's questions, Seymour Sudman and Norman Bradburn (1982:14) note that "the mores of social science in general and survey research in particular not only permit but encourage the repetition of questions." Unless questionnaire items have been copyrighted, no permission is required.

Many sources of questions are available on most topics. Literature reviews on the research topic should uncover references with pertinent questions. One may also consult more general sources of questions, such as the CBS–*New York Times* poll, as indexed in the *The New York Times Index*, and the polls section of *Public Opinion Quarterly*, or data archives, such as the Roper Center and National Opinion Research Center. Finally, every survey contains some demographic questions on age, gender, marital status, and so forth. An excellent critical discussion of alternative ways to word these basic questions about respondent characteristics may be found in Floyd Fowler (1995:166–76).

"Sketches" or Preliminaries

Having considered likely raw materials, the survey designer, like the artist, will go on to make a "sketch." The sketch for the survey designer essentially is an outline of the question topics to be covered in the interview or questionnaire.

The most general principle to follow is to formulate your research objectives clearly before you begin. We could not agree more with Sudman and Bradburn's recommendation (1982:41), especially for beginning researchers, "that—before you write any questions—you put down on paper the aims of the study, hypotheses, table formats, and proposed analyses." This material then "should not become a straightjacket for you," but should guide you in writing items, clarifying their meaning to respondents, and organizing them into a meaningful sequence.

Beyond a formal statement of objectives, certain practices in survey design have been shown to enhance the effectiveness of the research instrument. For instance, when a topic is somewhat abstract, using a number of items or questions results in better quality data. In general, the more abstract the topic, the more items are required; however, this principle must be balanced by the need to keep the instrument reasonably short. The principle may be illustrated by a hypothetical interview schedule investigating job satisfaction. Topics to be included might be wages, hours or shift worked, opportunities for learning and advancement, whether the work is interesting, supervisor–worker relations, and other working conditions. The topic concerning hours or shift worked might well be covered by a couple of questions, whereas "supervisor–worker relations" is a bit more abstract, and several distinct questions probably would be needed to get an accurate picture of the worker's satisfaction or dissatisfaction in this area.

Finally, the instrument design should reflect the perspectives of the target population as well as the survey designer. The job satisfaction survey outlined above, for example, could be ineffective if it excludes topics important to workers. **Focus group** discussions, which are unstructured discussions among a small group of participants led by a skilled interviewer, are often used to learn how people think about a survey topic (Fowler, 1995:105–10; Krueger and Casey, 2000). In planning a survey of sexual practices among teenagers, for example, teen focus groups could provide insight into how teens cognitively organize, label (vocabulary), and retrieve sexual information.

The Opening

At this point, one should decide what the opening topic will be and draft the opening questions. It is best to have an interesting and nonthreatening topic at the beginning that will get respondents involved and motivate them to cooperate in completing the interview or questionnaire. The first question should be congruent with respondents' expectations: It should be a question they might reasonably expect to be asked, on the basis of what they have been told by the interviewer about the study. This sometimes involves using a question that has no research purpose other than motivating respondents by conforming to their preconceptions about what should occur in a competent survey. The first question also should be relatively easy to answer, thus preventing respondents from becoming discouraged or feeling inadequate to fulfill their role as respondents.

If both open-ended and closed-ended questions are used, the beginning is a good place to have an open-ended question.[5] Most people like to express their views and have someone listen and take them seriously. An interesting opening question is a good way to meet this need of respondents and also get them to open up and warm to the respondent role. Here are two examples:

> As far as you're concerned, what are the advantages of living in this neighborhood? What do you like about living here?

> Let's talk first about medical care. What would you say are the main differences between the services provided by doctors and hospitals nowadays compared with what they were like when you were a child?

The Placement of Sensitive and Routine Questions

It would be prudent to avoid both boring, routine questions and sensitive, personal questions in the beginning; build up interest, trust, and rapport before risking these. Uninteresting routine questions such as background information (e.g., age, gender, marital status) are often placed toward the end of the survey instrument. Asking personal questions (e.g., racial prejudices, income, sexual activity, alcohol or drug use, religious beliefs) prematurely may embarrass or otherwise upset respondents and possibly cause them to terminate the interview or question the researcher's motives.

Some researchers place sensitive or personal topics at the end of an interview, arguing that, if the respondent fails to cooperate at this point, not much information will be lost. However, this may leave respondents with a bad taste in their mouths and may promote negative feelings toward survey research. Probably it is best to introduce such questions after the interview is well under way, because the respondent will have invested time and effort by then and possibly will have developed trust toward the research and/or interviewer. In addition, sensitive questions should fit into the question sequence logically; they should be preceded when possible by related but less sensitive questions or topics, so that the relationship of the personal questions to the topic and to the research is clear to the respondent. It also may be helpful to precede the most sensitive questions with a direct explanation of their importance to the research and to repeat an assurance of confidentiality.

Order, Flow, and Transition

After decisions have been made regarding the first topic and questions and you have a general idea of how you plan to introduce both sensitive and routine questions, the next task is to put the remaining topics in some reasonable order. What additional considerations go into the organization of topics?

The respondent's point of view must be considered as the researcher attempts to order the topics. The order must seem logical to respondents if their thinking about the questions is to be facilitated and motivation enhanced. Early topics should be easy to answer and of interest to the respondent; subsequent topics should seem to flow naturally from the early ones. It may even be that the survey instrument will begin with topics of little or no interest to the researcher but that will facilitate the introduction at a later point of topics more pertinent to the research objectives. An excellent example of topic flow is provided by the University of Michigan Surveys of Consumer Finances. According to Robert Kahn and Charles Cannell (1957:161–62),

> the objectives of these annual surveys [was] to ascertain the respondent's income, his savings patterns and the amount he has in various forms of savings, his buying intentions and major items purchased over the past year, his indebtedness, and his feeling about his own financial situation, both present and anticipated. The questionnaire starts with broad attitudinal questions on how the respondent feels about economic conditions generally, and moves to questions on his feelings about his own financial position and his expectations for the next few years. The interview then considers the respondent's assets, beginning with home ownership. How much is the house worth? When did he buy it? Does he have a mortgage? How much does he still owe on the mortgage? Similarly, ownership of automobiles is discussed. Then other major purchases are discussed. Next comes the topic of plans to purchase goods in the near future, which leads logically to the problem of sources of funds for such purchases. Will the money come from savings, from current income, or where? This introduces the topics of how much income is available and how much savings the person has. Last, to round out the picture, the amount of money already committed (debts) is discussed.

If there are to be questions that demand hard work on the part of the respondent, these should not be at the beginning but included sometime later, when commitment and momentum have been developed but before the respondent could become tired.

The researcher also must be sensitive to the problem of question-order effects. A topic or question appearing early in an interview may start the respondent thinking in a way that will affect later responses by activating or changing the information readily accessible in memory. Since respondents tend to truncate memory searches as soon as they have enough information for an acceptable answer, the most accessible information is likely to be that used recently to answer previous questions (Sudman, Bradburn, and Schwarz, 1996). For example, questioning cigarette smokers early in an interview about their beliefs in a link between cancer and smoking could influence their responses to later questions about perceived benefits and drawbacks of continued smoking. Even questions appearing later in self-administered questionnaires can influence responses to earlier questions since respondents may skip ahead and then return to the earlier questions (Sudman, Bradburn, and Schwarz, 1996:82).

Research indicates that questions vary in their susceptibility to order effects (McFarland, 1981; Schuman and Presser, 1981). In particular, general questions are more susceptible than questions with more specific content. When, for example, a general question about abortion followed a specific question (abortion in the case of a defect in the unborn child), respondents were less likely to support abortion than when the general question preceded the specific (Schuman and Presser, 1981:37). Responses to the specific question, however, were unaffected by its placement. This pattern of findings is consistent with Grice's nonredundancy principle. After responding to the specific question, respondents interpreted the subsequent general question as excluding birth defects in order to avoid reiterating information already provided.

On the other hand, respondents sometimes include, rather than exclude, information previously given to specific questions in responding to a general question (Sudman, Bradburn, and Schwarz, 1996). That is, they assimilate the old information, which is readily accessible in memory from answering previous questions, into their response to the general question. For example, in an experiment with college students, the correlation between a specific question on dating frequency and a general question on life satisfaction dramatically increased when the specific question preceded the general question (Strack, Martin, and Schwarz, 1988). When respondents perceive specific and general questions as belonging together, however, they may exclude the information already given to specific questions from the general question to avoid being redundant (Schwarz, Strack, and Mai, 1991). Thus, whether responses from previous questions are included or excluded from subsequent general questions is difficult to predict in advance. Careful instrument pretesting may clarify how respondents are being influenced by question ordering.

A number of strategies mitigate unintended influences of earlier questions on later questions: Eliminate the earlier questions, reword the later questions to make them more specific and less ambiguous, increase the separation between the earlier and later questions by adding intervening "buffer" questions, use separate boxes or pages to visually separate them in a questionnaire, and provide explicit instructions to include or exclude certain information in answering the later questions (Sudman, Bradburn, and Schwarz, 1996).

After the researcher has made an outline of the topics, considered the location of routine and sensitive questions and the problem of question-order effects, and written the opening questions (and perhaps a few others), transitions between major topics should be considered. Transitions indicate that one topic is completed and another topic is to be discussed; the main objective is to focus the respondent's attention on the new topic. Transitions also may be used to explain briefly why the new topic will be discussed or how it relates to the research purposes. Although they are not needed between every change in topic, transitions can improve the flow of an interview or questionnaire as well as respondent understanding and motivation. The following are examples of topic transitions:

> "Now I would like to ask some questions about your family. As you were growing up, let's say when you were around 16, how much influence do you remember having . . . ?"

> "Okay, now I'd like to change the subject slightly to one part of campus life that we're particularly interested in. As you may know, ..."

> "I would like to shift the subject slightly and get some of your opinions about . . . ."

> "Fine. Now we have just a few background questions."

The sketch of the instrument will be completed by drafting an introduction. The introduction should explain briefly the general purpose of the study, assure the respondent of confidentiality, and provide basic instructions for responding to the interview or questionnaire. Of course, the researcher never divulges specific hypotheses or relationships of interest during the introduction, for to do so would be an invitation to respondents to give the desired or expected responses.

Filling in the Sketch: Writing the Items

Drawing on the raw materials outlined earlier, the survey designer is now ready to "fill in the sketch" by writing the individual items. An artist has elements such as line, perspective, light effects, and color to aid in filling in a sketch. Are there principles or "elements of design" by which the survey designer likewise may be guided? We now consider useful principles for wording questions, for grouping questions to achieve greater effectiveness, and for avoiding common problems.

Using Language Effectively

In writing question items, using language effectively presents a real challenge. Even slight altering of the wording of a question can greatly affect responses, whether the question is open-ended or closed-ended. For example, a question might be written, "What is your annual income?" or "What is your total annual income from all sources?" A person answering the first item might neglect to consider income from such sources as interest on stocks or savings, sale of stocks, and rental income.

In general, research findings on question wording indicate that it is potentially very important but difficult to predict whether a wording change will have an effect (Converse and Presser, 1986). For this reason, it is essential to pretest new questions adequately. Furthermore, it is generally a good idea not to base conclusions on results from a single item. Approaches to the problem of wording effects include asking multiple questions on a topic; using two forms of the question, each with a different, randomly selected subset of respondents; and using open-ended questions as follow-ups to closed-ended questions to probe for the respondent's meaning (Converse and Presser, 1986). Edward Laumann and associates (1994:292–301), for example, used six different sets of questions in the NHSLS to examine components of homosexuality (self-identification, homoerotic fantasies, and actual practice).

Additional guidelines for using language to obtain better data have been developed on the basis of survey researchers' experiences and of validity and reliability testing. While some of these guidelines seem to be self-evident or common-sense suggestions, the plethora of poorly worded items continually being produced would seem to indicate a need for more attention to the language of items. The following questions provide a framework for examining the language of the items.

1. Are the items unambiguous, easily read, and sufficiently brief? Clarity and precision are essential qualities of well-worded items. At times, an item that appears perfectly clear to the designer may be very confusing or carry a different meaning to someone with a different background and point of view. The point is easily illustrated by the question, "How many years have you been living here?" To one respondent, "here" may mean the present house or apartment, to another, the city, and to another, the United States.

Especially troublesome are indefinite words such as "usually," "seldom," "many," "few," "here," "there"; these will have different meanings to different respondents. Following are two alternative items illustrating the problem; the second is an improvement over the first because the responses are specific and thereby have the same precise meaning for both researcher and respondent.

1. How often do you attend religious services?

( ) Seldom or never
( ) Often
( ) Very often
( ) Every day

2. How often do you attend religious services?

( ) Never
( ) Less than once a year
( ) About once or twice a year
( ) Several times a year
( ) About once a month
( ) Two or three times a month
( ) Nearly every week
( ) Every week
( ) Several times a week

Items also should be easy to read or hear accurately. Succinct wording of items will enhance the accuracy of responses, as will avoiding the use of negative words such as "not." Some respondents will skip over or tune out the negative word in an item and respond the opposite of the way the question is actually intended. If negative words must be used, it is wise to print them in all capitals, underline them, or verbally emphasize them.

If key terms are subject to multiple meanings, definitions should be provided before they are used in a question. In a self-administered section of the NHSLS, for example, the respondents were asked about sexual partners after the following definition of "sex" was provided:

> People mean different things by sex or sexual activity, but in answering these questions, we need everyone to use the same definition. Here, by "sex" or "sexual activity," we mean any mutually voluntary activity with another person that involves genital contact and sexual excitement or arousal. That is, feeling really turned on, even if intercourse or orgasm did not occur.
>
> . . . please include all persons or times . . . where you had direct physical contact with the genitals (the sex organs) of someone else and sexual excitement or arousal occurred. Certain activities such as close dancing or kissing without genital contact should NOT be included. (Laumann et al., 1994:622)

If a key term is defined within a question, the definition should precede the actual question. Otherwise, respondents may skip or tune out the definition after hearing the question (Fowler, 1995). In the following question, for example, female respondents might report only pregnancies that resulted in live births *if* the definition of "pregnancy" had followed the actual question:

> Now I would like to ask you about *any* pregnancies you might have had. I'm interested in all your pregnancies, whether they resulted in a live birth, stillbirth, abortion, or miscarriage, even those which ended very early. How many pregnancies have you ever had, NOT including a current pregnancy? (Laumann et al., 1994:619)

2. Is the instrument's vocabulary appropriate for the respondents you intend to interview? If the intended study population is highly heterogeneous, the vocabulary must be kept extremely simple, and the survey designer should be aware of regional and other group differences in the meanings of words. To exemplify the problem of translating social science concepts into language understandable by nearly everyone, let us assume for a moment that you are studying "socialization" among a random sample of American parents. You decide to start the interview with a broad, open question. While any of the three examples that follow could be used, the third would doubtless be most effective.

> What do you consider to be the most important factors in the socialization of children?
>
> What child-rearing practices do you think are most important?
>
> What things do you think are most important for parents to do if they want to bring up their children right?

On the other hand, with some surveys, "talking down" may be a potential problem. When sampling a more homogeneous or specialized group (say, city managers, doctors, or nuclear engineers), use vocabulary that is appropriately sophisticated and technical for that group.

In choosing an appropriate vocabulary to characterize sexual practices, Laumann and associates (1994) steered a middle course between language that would be too technical (e.g., "fellatio") or too colloquial or slangy (e.g., "blow job") to be widely understood in a national survey. Their solution was to use simple, standard English (e.g., "oral sex") and to provide definitions when terms were first introduced.

3. Do the questions contain a single idea, or are any of them addressing two or more issues at once? A **double-barreled question** is one in which two separate ideas are presented together as a unit. An example (perhaps from the "socialization" study) might be: "What factors contributed to your decision to marry and have children?" The researcher seems to assume that marrying and having children is a single act or decision, whereas in fact there are two questions being asked here. It is a good idea for the survey designer to examine all questions with the words "and" or "or" in them to be sure that they are not double-barreled.

Consider the following question that was included in a "questionnaire" distributed by a political interest group:

Do you believe that for every dollar of tax increase there should be two dollars in spending cuts with the savings earmarked for deficit and debt reduction?

( ) Yes
( ) No

About four ideas are hidden within this "quadruple-barreled" question. Should taxes be increased? Should every tax increase dollar be matched by two dollars in spending cuts? Should spending cut savings be applied to deficit reduction? Should savings be applied to debt reduction?

The single-idea principle may also be violated in response formats as illustrated by asking workers to describe their boss using such fixed-choice categories as "Very professional and friendly," "Generally professional and friendly," "Somewhat unprofessional and unfriendly," and "Very unprofessional and unfriendly." Even the popular Likert response categories combine two ideas as in the following example.

A preschool child is likely to suffer if his or her mother works outside the home.

( ) Strongly agree
( ) Agree
( ) Disagree
( ) Strongly disagree

The respondent is given response choices that combine two different dimensions: agreement and strength of feelings (Fowler, 1995). The first response might be selected because the respondent is in complete agreement *or* has a very strong emotional conviction about how to raise young children. Floyd Fowler (1995) suggests an alternative wording to avoid such double-barreled response categories:

( ) Completely agree
( ) Generally agree
( ) Generally disagree
( ) Completely disagree

4. Are the items free of emotionally loaded words and other sources of bias? Emotionally loaded words and phrases, such as "communists," "racial preferences," "pro-life," "cops," or even "the President's statement," may evoke cognitive responses that have little to do with the real attitudes or opinion of the respondent regarding the issue the researcher is attempting to study.[6] In general, try to word questions in a neutral way, and avoid identifying a statement or position with any controversial or prestigious person or group. Notice the loaded words ("union czars," "forcing," "knuckle under") in the following question (Sudman and Bradburn, 1982:2):

Are you in favor of allowing construction union czars the power to shut down an entire construction site because of a dispute with a single contractor, thus forcing even more workers to knuckle under to union agencies?

This question was part of a questionnaire distributed by a political lobbying group for fund-raising purposes, a practice that social scientists consider deceptive and unethical.

Another source of bias is **leading questions**. Leading questions suggest a possible answer or make some responses seem more acceptable than others. The question, "How often do you smoke marijuana?," may seem to imply that everyone indulges at least occasionally.[7] A question that begins, "Do you agree . . . ?," may suggest to some persons that they ought to agree. The generally accepted practice is to balance attitudinal questions by using such phrases as "agree or disagree," "favor or oppose," and "satisfied or dissatisfied" (Sudman and Bradburn, 1982).[8]

An incomplete listing of alternatives either in the question or in the response options given is another common error. An example of the former would be the question, "When you discipline your children, do you spank them, take away privileges, or what?" It would be better to either give a complete listing of alternatives or give none. The problem of making sure the responses to a closed question are exhaustive was discussed earlier in the chapter; it is also important that the responses be balanced. For example, if the responses represent attitudes toward the United Nations, it would be judicious to have an equal number of positive and negative statements, as well as a neutral statement. Furthermore, you would want to represent both extreme and moderate attitudes in each direction. Otherwise, respondents interpret an unbalanced set of response options as relevant to question intent and indicative of the range of typical or normal responses.

Consider the following question, which was used in a mail questionnaire to gauge University of California employee satisfaction with their health maintenance organizations (HMOs).

Based on the experience of everyone in your family, how satisfied was your family with your HMO plan in 1995?

1. Very satisfied   3. Neither satisfied nor dissatisfied   5. Very dissatisfied
2. Satisfied   4. Dissatisfied   6. Don't know or doesn't apply

Both the question and the formatting of the response categories skew the responses in the direction of satisfaction. A more neutral wording, such as "How would you rate your HMO?," is likely to produce more critical responses than asking "How satisfied . . . ?" Note also that the two "satisfied" categories (1 and 2) are spatially grouped together in such a way as to be seen next after reading the end of the question. The scale endpoint printed first tends to draw more responses than if the categories are reversed and it is printed last (Sudman, Bradburn, and Schwarz, 1996:157). It is not surprising, then, that some HMOs received 80 percent or higher satisfaction ratings (combining "very satisfied" and "satisfied" responses) on this leading question.

5. On personal and sensitive questions, is the wording as tactful, diplomatic, and face-saving as possible? The topic of sensitive questions was discussed earlier in reference to their placement in the instrument. It was pointed out that motivation could be enhanced not only by logical placement of the item but also by showing the relevance of the question to the research purpose, reassuring the respondent of

confidentiality, and including a wide range of response options. In addition to these efforts, careful diplomatic wording of the items may boost motivation and facilitate more candid responses. A housewife may feel irritated or defensive if asked, "Do you work?" but perhaps not if asked, "Do you work outside the home?"

A sensitive question might also be preceded by a statement that in effect sanctions the less socially desirable response, such as, "Some people feel that smoking marijuana is pleasant and harmless, while others feel that it is harmful. What do you think?" or "Many people have taken an item from a store without paying for some reason. Have you ever done this?"

Finally, to make the best use of language, the survey designer will usually need to make, test, and revise several successive drafts of the questions. Early drafts should be subjected to careful scrutiny by both the researcher and colleagues with the aforementioned wording issues in mind. Then, cognitive interviewing techniques, discussed later in this chapter, should be used to identify further problems by probing the thought processes employed to answer the questions. Finally, a semifinal draft should be field pretested under realistic conditions with a population similar to the one for which the survey instrument is designed.

The "Frame of Reference" Problem

Often the questions we ask people seem clear in meaning to us but can be answered from several perspectives or frames of reference. For example, suppose a survey of second-semester college students asked, "Generally speaking, how satisfied are you with your decision to attend State University?" Students giving the same response, such as relatively satisfied, could have very different reasons for doing so. One may feel relatively satisfied because she has a generous scholarship and feels the school is as good as most others from an academic standpoint. Another may be thinking of the social life, and a third of intramural sports activities. Yet, from their answers, the researcher would not know what the respondents' reasons were for their satisfaction or dissatisfaction.

There are a number of ways to determine or to control the respondent's frame of reference. A straightforward way to determine the frame of reference is to follow the question with a probe such as, "Can you tell me why you feel that way?" "What things specifically do you feel are satisfactory (or unsatisfactory) about State University?" Another simple means of controlling the frame of reference for individual questions is to specify the frame of reference within the question, such as, "Compared with other universities in the state system, how do you feel about the intellectual life at Caufield State?"

By particular arrangements of questions, the researcher also can direct the respondent to the investigator's frame of reference. A **funnel sequence** (Kahn and Cannell, 1957:158–60) moves from a very general question to progressively more specific questions. Suppose one wanted to study the impact of inflation on people's attitudes about the performance of the President. Research on question-order effects, reported earlier, suggests that asking specific questions about inflation first might impose this frame of reference on respondents, so that later, general questions about the President's performance are judged with reference to the President's inflation efforts. Instead, a funnel sequence could start out with general questions about achievements ("What do you think about the President's performance in office?" "Why do you feel this way?"), which will likely disclose the respondents' frame of reference. These questions then could be followed by questions on inflation ("Do you think we have a serious inflation problem?" "Has it had much effect on you?") and, finally, specific questions about the President's activity in this area ("Do you believe the President is doing a good job of fighting inflation?").

The previous example illustrates the effectiveness of a funnel sequence in avoiding the possibility that asking more specific questions first will influence responses to more general questions. This sequence also offers the advantage of beginning with the respondent's ideas and perspectives, which may increase interest and motivation. Funnel sequences may consist entirely of open-ended questions or of an open-ended question (or questions) followed by closed-ended questions.

A common frame of reference also may be established through an **inverted-funnel sequence** of related questions (Kahn and Cannell, 1957:160). Here one begins with the most specific questions and ends with the most general. While this approach lacks the advantages of the funnel sequence, it is useful in some situations. First, it may be used to ensure that all respondents are considering the same points or circumstances before expressing their general opinions. For example, if we wanted to make sure that respondents were judging the President's performance in office on similar bases, an inverted-funnel sequence would enable us to bring up and question performance in specific areas (inflation, unemployment, foreign policy) before asking for a general evaluation. A second advantage of the inverted-funnel sequence is that, whether or not respondents have previously formed an opinion regarding the final question in the sequence, all will have time to think through certain aspects of a complex issue before giving their opinion. Instead of asking respondents to express immediately their attitude toward liberalizing laws on abortions, for example, one might ask about approval of abortion in various specific circumstances (if there is a strong chance of a birth deformity, if the woman became pregnant as a result of rape, if the woman's own health is seriously endangered, if the woman is married and does not want the child, if the family cannot afford any more children), at the end of which the respondents' general opinion would be sought. (See Box 9.2 for additional examples of a funnel sequence and inverted-funnel sequence.)

Will an inverted-funnel sequence be susceptible to order effects, since respondents may avoid being redundant by excluding previously given information from the final general question? There is limited evidence (Schwarz, Strack, and Mai, 1991) that another conversational norm, a request for a summary judgment, may operate when a general question follows a block of specific questions as in the second example of Box 9.2.

Reason Analysis

The funnel sequence illustrates the benefits of using a sequence of questions to explore complex issues. Similarly, a well-devised series of questions is invariably

BOX 9.2

Examples of Funnel and Inverted-funnel Sequences of Questions

Here is a sample funnel sequence from a study of union printers (Lipset, Trow, and Coleman, 1956:493–49).

7. (a) All things considered, how do you like printing as an occupation?
     Do you dislike it?
     Are you indifferent?
     Do you like it fairly well?
     Do you like it very much?
   (b) Why do you feel this way?
8. (a) Is there any occupation you would like to have other than the one you now have—either in or outside the printing trade?
     (If so) Which one?
9. Let's look at it another way: If you were starting all over again, what occupation would you want to get into?
10. (a) How would you rate printing as an occupation? For example:
      (1) Would you rate the *pay* as excellent, good, fair, or poor?
      (2) How about *job security* in the printing trade? Would you rate it as excellent, good, fair, or poor?
      (3) How about the *prestige* printing receives from people outside the trade?

A brief inverted-funnel sequence used to measure perceptions of well-being (Andrews and Withey, 1976:376) is reproduced here.

13. Here are some faces expressing various feelings. Below each is a letter.

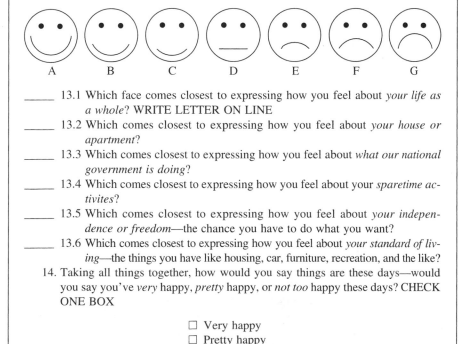

_____ 13.1 Which face comes closest to expressing how you feel about *your life as a whole*? WRITE LETTER ON LINE
_____ 13.2 Which comes closest to expressing how you feel about *your house or apartment*?
_____ 13.3 Which comes closest to expressing how you feel about *what our national government is doing*?
_____ 13.4 Which comes closest to expressing how you feel about your *sparetime activites*?
_____ 13.5 Which comes closest to expressing how you feel about *your independence or freedom*—the chance you have to do what you want?
_____ 13.6 Which comes closest to expressing how you feel about *your standard of living*—the things you have like housing, car, furniture, recreation, and the like?
14. Taking all things together, how would you say things are these days—would you say you've *very* happy, *pretty* happy, or *not too* happy these days? CHECK ONE BOX

☐ Very happy
☐ Pretty happy
☐ Not too happy

more effective than the simple question "Why?" in finding out the reasons for people's behavior.[9] Suppose we ask undergraduates why they decided to attend UCLA, and we receive the following responses: Mary—"My parents convinced me"; Sam—"Because I live in LA"; Pascual—"for a scholarship"; Irma—"To be with my boyfriend"; Reuben—"It's a fun school and I wasn't accepted at the other schools I applied to." Not only are these reasons brief and quite diverse, they seem incomplete; surely these students selected UCLA for more than one reason (only Reuben mentioned two reasons). Perhaps Mary and Sam also were influenced by scholarships; maybe Irma was not alone in having a close friend at UCLA, or Reuben was not the only one turned down by other schools. Also, other determinants of the respondents' choice of UCLA may have been overlooked, such as the recommendations of high school teachers, the academic reputation of UCLA, and the climate of southern California.

The simple "why? question implies that a simple, prompt answer is desired. Consequently, respondents may expend minimum effort (satisficing) to generate quickly a plausible answer that is easy to verbalize. How, then, can we go about discovering the main factors that influenced our respondents to attend UCLA? Fortunately, Hans Zeisel (1968) systematized the process of asking "Why?" The key idea in Zeisel's **reason analysis** is the development of an "accounting scheme" outlining the general categories of reasons, or dimensions of the decision, which, in turn, provides a model or structure for formulating a comprehensive series of questions.

The accounting scheme is based on the research objectives (not all reasons may be of interest), on the researcher's creativity, and usually on informal exploratory interviewing or focus group discussions with members of the group under study. Unless one is reasonably well informed about the various categories of reasons for an action (perhaps from previous research or experience), these are sought through exploratory interviewing. The information from these preliminary interviews is culled for reasons not pertinent to the research objectives,[10] and the remaining responses are creatively grouped into an integrated model of relevant categories to form the accounting scheme.

Often an accounting scheme is structured in terms of the typical stages in a decision process. To return to our example, for many students the decision to attend UCLA involved (1) a decision to attend college, (2) the selection of schools to apply to for admission, and (3) the final choice of UCLA. At each of these stages the respondent's behavior may be influenced by sources of information (knowledge, gossip, rumors learned from the media, friends, and strangers), advice from significant others (recommendations of friends, parents, teachers), constraints or limitations (financial needs, health requirements, need to live with or near a friend or relative), the respondent's particular needs (academic interests, vocational objectives, social and recreational interests), perceived characteristics of the schools considered (reputation or image, strengths and weaknesses, location and climate, housing availability, costs), and responses by the schools (offers of aid or scholarships, athletic awards, special recruitment efforts, rejection of admission application).

After a systematic outline of the accounting scheme just sketched out is made, the final step in our reason analysis would be to write a series of questions to assist the respondents in reviewing the stages of their decisions to attend UCLA:

"When did you first seriously consider going to college?" "How did you reach this decision?" "Did you apply to any other colleges or universities? Which ones?" "What were the characteristics of UCLA that you particularly liked?" "Did your parents, friends, teachers or any other persons help you come to your decision? Who?" "How much influence did this have on you?" Although the process of reason analysis in this situation obviously calls for intense mental labor, we would end up knowing immensely more about the college decisions of Mary, Sam, Pascual, Irma, and Reuben than had we simply asked, "Why UCLA?"

The sequence of stages of a decision process is not the only basis for accounting schemes. Zeisel (1968) discusses in detail several common schemes. In studies of why people move from place A to place B (or shift jobs, or, in general, change preferences from A to B), the reason analysis focuses particularly on the negative aspects of A and the positive aspects of B. This is called the push–pull scheme in migration studies, since the decision to move may be precipitated by factors that push one out of the old location (e.g., an increase in rent, a change in neighborhood character, the loss of a job) and/or that pull or attract one to a new habitat (e.g., the anticipation of employment, a better wage, a better environment). Another common accounting scheme used in studies of consumer behavior has three major dimensions: the perceived attributes of the consumer product (its effects, price, etc.), the motives or needs of the respondent to be satisfied by the product, and the influences that affect the purchase decision (advertising, recommendations of friends, etc.).[11]

Reason analysis thus is a very useful and general technique for guiding questionnaire construction and for avoiding superficial and incomplete answers to important questions. The researcher basically is asking many specific "whys?" rather than a general "why?" question. Compared with a general question, a comprehensive series of specific questions better conveys to the respondent the information sought by the researcher, as well as facilitating information retrieval by triggering different memory associations.

Memory Problems

There are two kinds of memory problems. First, respondents may be unable to recall information the researcher is seeking about life events. According to Cannell and Kahn (1968), the ease with which material may be recalled depends on three factors: how long ago the event occurred, how significant the event was when it occurred, and how relevant the event is to the respondent's life currently. Generally, respondents will have a longer memory for significant rare and costly events in their lives, such as getting married or having major surgery, than for more trivial habitual occurrences, such as losing a small amount at gambling or the content of the previous evening's television programs. Furthermore, they will remember more effectively events of continuing importance in their lives. The presence of an unsightly scar, for example, is a reminder of the accident that produced it.

A second difficulty arises from memory distortion. People do not uniformly recall events objectively; rather, memories seem to be distorted either in the process of organizing one's past and making it consistent or in an unconscious effort to maintain a positive self-image. One common type of memory distortion in responses to survey questions is called "telescoping" (Sudman and Bradburn, 1974). This occurs when a respondent erroneously recalls the timing of an event as having occurred more recently than it did. When respondents are asked about events that occurred within a specific reference period, such as visits to doctors in the past six months, telescoping leads to overreporting, because some events that happened before the reference period (e.g., a doctor visit seven months ago) are remembered as occurring during the reference period.

What can be done to stimulate accurate recall? Here are some suggestions (see Cannell and Kahn, 1968; Converse and Presser, 1986; Sudman, Bradburn, and Schwarz, 1996):

1. Shorten the reference period. As a rule, the shorter the recall period, the more accurate the report. Sudman and Bradburn (1982) emphasize the appropriateness of the time period—with memory of a year or more for high-salience events (e.g., major accidents or illnesses) and a few weeks to a month for low-salience events. For example, the NHSLS (Laumann et al., 1994) asked about sexual partners during the last twelve months, whereas the NHIS-YRBS (Willard and Schoenborn, 1995) used a shorter reference period of thirty days to ask youth about episodes of heavy drinking. Jean Converse and Stanley Presser (1986) recommend that, for certain events, the time period be narrowed to the immediate past, such as yesterday or last week. For example, to obtain an estimate of the amount of time students spend studying, it would be better to ask, "How much time did you spend studying on weekdays during the past week?" than to ask "How much time per day do you spend studying?"

2. Give respondents more time to search their memories for a response. This may be accomplished by increasing the length of the question, by instructing the respondents that the question may take some time to answer, and by training interviewers to allow adequate time for a response (Sudman, Bradburn, and Schwarz, 1996:225).

3. Provide a helpful context and question sequence as in "reason analysis." Rather than asking a respondent, for example, "At what addresses have you resided in the last ten years?" begin with the present, asking, "How long have you lived in Atlanta?" A second question might ask if the respondent had lived at other addresses in Atlanta, and a later question might ask about residences before moving to Atlanta. Or one might ask the respondent to recall an important past event, such as completing school or leaving the parental home, and then guide the respondent to recall subsequent events (marriage, first job, etc.) in a forward time sequence.

4. Some questions demanding accurate memory may be best asked by means of closed questions utilizing lists. Doctors sometimes present new patients with a list of illnesses and ask them which they have had. Social researchers likewise may present lists for aiding recall of such things as magazines read, television programs watched, and organizational memberships.

5. Conduct a household inventory with the respondent. Studies of consumer behavior have revealed that even the current day's grocery purchases (type, brand, size) are best documented by examining with respondents their refrigerator and pantry provisions.

6. Where appropriate, ask respondents to check their records (birth and marriage certificates, school records, financial information, scrapbooks, photographs, etc.).

The first suggestion as well as suggestions 3 through 5, which involve the use of "aided-recall" procedures, deal directly with the problem of forgetting but also may contribute to some memory distortion. A shorter reference period, for example, decreases omission errors but increases dating errors (telescoping). The use of records deals most effectively with both kinds of memory problems, although this information is often difficult to acquire.

Response Bias Problems

Other instrumentation problems arise from the social situation surrounding the administration of interviews and questionnaires. Just as experimenters must be concerned about how the laboratory setting may produce disingenuous subject behavior, the survey researcher must be alert to how the social situation in surveys may produce responses irrelevant to the object of measurement. We discussed this problem briefly in chapter 8 in relation to response effects introduced by the interaction between interviewers and respondents, and extensively in this chapter from the perspective of cognitive, conversational, and motivational theories. Here we focus on biases produced by respondent tendencies to answer in certain ways as a function of the content or form of survey questions.

One frequent response tendency is to answer in the direction of **social desirability** (see DeMaio, 1984). We all have our private self-image to maintain; in addition, many respondents will want to make a good impression on the researcher by appearing sensible, healthy, happy, mentally sound, free of racial prejudice, and the like. Some individuals and groups demonstrate this tendency more than others. Indeed, Derek Phillips (1971:87–88) suggests that the consistent finding of greater happiness, better mental health, and lower racial prejudice among middle-class compared with lower-class respondents may not reflect true class differences in these variables but instead a greater concern among the middle class to give socially desirable responses. Some common techniques for minimizing social desirability bias have been mentioned previously: use of indirect questions, careful placement and wording of sensitive questions, assurances of anonymity and scientific importance, statements sanctioning less socially desirable responses, building of rapport between interviewer and respondent, and collection of sensitive information within face-to-face interviews with self-administered forms or other modes that provide privacy to the interviewees.

A second response bias is the **acquiescence response set**. This is the tendency for respondents to be very agreeable: Presented with a question having such an option as "yes/no" or "agree/disagree," they are more apt to agree or say yes than to disagree or say no. This tendency also extends to such formats as the Likert scale where there are gradations of agreeing or disagreeing. One way of circumventing the problem is to give specific content to the response options. For example, one may construct the second item below to avoid a possible acquiescence effect in response to the first item.

1. Rent control is necessary in order for many of the people of River City to obtain adequate housing.

( ) Completely agree
( ) Generally agree
( ) Uncertain
( ) Generally disagree
( ) Completely disagree

2. From the following statements, select the one that most closely represents your opinion about the need for rent control in River City.

    a. Rent control is necessary in order for many of the people of River City to obtain adequate housing.
    b. Rent control is necessary in order for some of the people of River City to obtain adequate housing.
    c. I am uncertain whether rent control is necessary or not.
    d. Very few people are really helped by rent control.
    e. Rent control is unnecessary.

One problem with this approach, however, is that it requires much greater effort on the part of the survey designer.

Another way to control as well as check for an acquiescence response set when the researcher wishes to retain a yes/no or an agree/disagree format is to include within the instrument two items measuring the same concept that are roughly opposite in meaning. Obviously, the items should be located at different points in the instrument. The following item pair from the F scale, a measure of authoritarianism, illustrates this approach (Bass, 1955:619):

1. Human nature being what it is, there will always be war and conflict.
2. Human nature being what it is, universal peace will come about eventually.

Responses to the two conflicting statements may be compared to see whether a significant number of persons answered both statements affirmatively. The major problem with this approach is the difficulty of constructing truly contradictory items. It would not necessarily be inconsistent, for example, to reject both of the above statements.

Ordinal or position biases represent a third response tendency. Some respondents mark options located in a certain position, such as the first choice in a multiple-choice format or a particular position in a horizontal rating scale. This is a potential problem whenever questions are asked in a very similar format. Hence, one way of addressing this type of response set, as well as the tendency to acquiesce, is to vary the arrangement of questions and the manner in which they are asked. A second approach is to give response options more specific content, as in the rent control question above.

Format Considerations

Finally, the format or physical organization of the survey instrument must be planned. Obviously there are many possibilities, but a few main points should be considered.

Probably most important, the physical form of the instrument should be appealing to respondents and interviewers. In addition, the design should facilitate the tasks of reading, completing, and coding. Numbering items consecutively throughout, using clear type, and allowing sufficient space between items and between response options can help greatly. With interview schedules, different type styles (or capitalization and underlining) should be used to differentiate instructions to the interviewer from material to be read aloud to interviewees.

While planning the physical organization, it would be appropriate to consider whether using "filter" (screening) and "contingency questions" would improve the instrument. **Contingency questions** are intended for only a part of the sample of respondents. By addressing only those persons for whom the questions are clearly relevant, contingency questions avoid the waste of time and possible decline in respondent motivation that may occur when the same questions are asked of all respondents. Responses to a **filter question** determine who is to answer which of subsequent contingency question(s). One format is illustrated below from a hypothetical survey of adolescent sexual attitudes and practices.

19. Have you ever had sexual intercourse?   (FILTER QUESTION)

    (   ) Yes (Please answer questions 20–29.) (CONTINGENCY QUESTIONS)
    (   ) No (Go to question 30. Please skip questions 20–29.)

(Box 9.3 presents a series of filter and contingency questions from a GSS interview schedule.)

Pretesting

Throughout the chapter, we repeatedly have emphasized the importance of pretesting—of evaluating survey questions to determine if respondents clearly understand and are able to answer them. Failure to conduct adequate pretesting can result in a meaningless study. Once the study has been conducted, it is too late to benefit from the information, for example, that in one item, 99 percent of the respondents chose the same option, or that a large number of respondents misunderstood the meaning of a question. Experience has shown that the amount of effort expended on study planning and pretesting is related directly to the ease with which data may be analyzed and to the quality of results.

Pretesting should begin as soon as the survey instrument, or portions of it, have been drafted. Traditionally, pretesting has been done solely "in the field," that is, in the homes of respondents drawn from the target population. However, sparked by the recent interest in cognitive aspects of surveys, researchers have begun to test questions in the laboratory. We first review new procedures developed in the laboratory, which have proven to be very effective in identifying potential wording, ordering, and formatting problems. The information gained through these procedures gives direction to further revision efforts. Often several pretests and revisions of a questionnaire may be necessary to arrive at a good semifinal draft. Once the ques-

BOX 9.3

Examples of Filter and Contingency Questions

The following is one page from an interview schedule for the General Social Survey. The physical layout is designed to facilitate interviewing and computer processing.

29. Last week were you working full time, part time, going to school, keeping house, or what?

CIRCLE ONE CODE ONLY. IF MORE THAN ONE RESPONSE, GIVE PREFERENCE TO SMALLEST CODE NUMBER THAT APPLIES.

HAND CARD C	Working full time .... (ASK A) .... .01 09–10/ Working part time .... (ASK A) .... .02 With a job, but not at work because of temporary illness, vacation, strike .... (ASK B) .... .03 Unemployed, laid off, looking for work .... (GO TO Q.30) ..... .04 Retired .... (ASK C) .... .05 In school .... (ASK C) .... .06 Keeping house .... (ASK C) .... .07 OTHER (SPECIFY AND ASK C) _____08

A. **IF WORKING, FULL OR PART TIME:** How many hours did you work last week, at all jobs?

Hours: ☐☐   11–12/

NOW GO TO Q.30

B. **IF WITH A JOB, BUT NOT AT WORK:** How many hours a week do you usually work, at all jobs?

Hours: ☐☐   13–14/

NOW GO TO Q.30

C. **IF RETIRED, IN SCHOOL, KEEPING HOUSE, OR OTHER:** Did you ever work for as long as one year?

Yes ..... (ASK Q.30) 1   15/
No ..... (SKIP TO INSTRUCTIONS BEFORE Q.33) 2

tionnaire is in this form, it is routinely tested in the field; therefore, we also discuss various techniques used in field pretesting.

Cognitive Laboratory Interviews

The goal of **cognitive interviewing** is to understand the thought processes involved in answering survey questions. Verbal reports from respondents, collected during or after their response to pretest questions, are used to identify problems and revise questions. The cognitive laboratories established at the Census Bureau and other federal statistical agencies typically use paid subjects who are recruited for intensive sessions lasting one to two hours; however, cognitive interviewing also may take place outside a laboratory facility (e.g., in subjects' homes) and involve only a tape or a video recorder (Fowler, 1995; DeMaio and Rothgeb, 1996). In either case, the primary methods are "thinkaloud" interviews, probing questions, and paraphrasing follow-ups (for a more complete review, see Forsyth and Lessler, 1991).

"Thinkaloud" interviews. The respondents are asked to think out loud, reporting everything that comes to mind, while arriving at answers to the questions. They verbalize their thought processes either concurrently as they work out an answer to each question or retrospectively after they answer each question or complete the survey. Here is an example of an improved question resulting from cognitive interviewing:

> One question asked, "How many times during the past twelve months have you stopped smoking for one day or longer?" The intent of this question was to measure attempts to quit smoking. However, the question was not always interpreted this way. Several respondents included instances when they had not smoked for at least one day because of illness, excessive drinking the previous day, or other extraneous circumstances. The revised version makes the intent clearer, asking specifically, "How many times during the past twelve months have you stopped smoking for one day or longer because you were trying to quit smoking?" (DeMaio and Rothgeb, 1996:182–83).

Probing questions. A weakness of the thinkaloud technique is that some respondents have great difficulty verbally describing their thought processes. Instead, an interviewer can focus on particular aspects of the cognitive processes by special probes, such as, "What did you think I meant by 'stopping smoking'?" Probes may directly follow each question (when the information used to answer the question is freshest in memory) or may come at the end of the survey (to avoid reactivity associated with the probing). Here is an example of probes used to pretest a question intended for elderly people (Jobe, Keller, and Smith, 1996:201):

> By yourself and without using special equipment, how much difficulty do you have bathing or showering: some, a lot, or are you unable to do it?
>
> Probes: "I said without using special equipment. What sort of things do you think would be special equipment?" "Do you use anything to help you bathe or shower?"

Paraphrasing follow-ups. Another technique is to ask respondents to summarize or repeat the question in their own words. Not only is this a good test of whether respondents understand the literal and intended meaning of the question, but it may also reveal better ways to word the question.

Cognitive diagnostic procedures are only a partial solution to good instrument development. First, they are better at diagnosing problems than providing solutions. Second, since they are usually based on small, unrepresentative samples of paid subjects, they may not detect problems that will occur in subgroups of larger, more diverse populations. Third, different problems may occur in the "field" under more realistic interviewing conditions. We now examine techniques to field test survey instruments.

Field Pretesting

Field pretesting a survey instrument consists of trying it out on a small sample (usually 25–50) of persons having characteristics similar to those of the target group of respondents. The pretest group is normally not a probability sample, since you are not planning to publish your pretest findings. However, it should be as heterogeneous as the target population. For example, if your target group is a national sample of college and university students, the pretest group should include college students at all levels (first-year through graduate students) and from different types of institutions (large, small, religious, secular, liberal arts, technical, etc.).

Field pretesting should provide answers to questions such as these:

> Does the level of language match the sophistication of the target population? Are instructions to respondents and to interviewers clear? Are transitions smooth and informative?
> Are the questions and question format varied enough to retain respondents' interest and attention?
> Are responses to open questions so diverse as to be impossible to analyze?
> Are the choice options to closed questions clear and exhaustive?
> Are interviewing aids such as cards or photographs effective and practical?
> Are there questions that respondents resist answering?
> How long, generally, does the interview take to complete?
> What is the completion rate?

For some time, field pretesting to identify such problems has consisted of having either experienced interviewers or interviewers in training both administer the draft questionnaire and observe the process. The interviewers might take notes during the interviews or file reports afterwards, but their observations generally are conveyed in a group oral debriefing (Converse and Presser, 1986). However, this process has several limitations (Fowler, 1995; Fowler and Cannell, 1996). Playing the role of interviewer may interfere with the task of observing the process; each interviewer's observations are based on a small number of interviews, which may not be adequate for reliably assessing question problems; the standards for evaluation may not be well articulated or may be applied inconsistently, resulting in a lack of agreement about problem questions; and the recognition of question comprehension problems is limited to items in which respondents ask for clarification or give inappropriate answers. Some of these problems may be addressed by cognitive laboratory interviewing. Recently, however, several strategies have been applied to make field pretesting more systematic and reliable. These include behavior coding, respondent debriefings, interviewing ratings, split-panel tests, and response analysis.

Behavioral coding. Systematically coding live or taped interviewer–respondent interactions is an effective technique for identifying instrument problems under realistic field conditions. Coding consists of categorizing responses and counting the number in each category (see chapter 14). In **behavioral coding** of pretest interviews, interactions with respect to each question are coded to identify the frequency of problematic respondent and interviewer behaviors, such as interviewers incorrectly reading or skipping questions, respondents interrupting interviewers before the question is completely read, respondents requesting that the question be repeated or clarified, and interviewers probing to follow up on inadequate answers (Fowler, 1995:116–21). For example, behavioral coding revealed that a question commonly used in governmental health studies, "When was the last time you had a general physical examination or checkup?" elicited a high proportion (87 percent) of inadequate answers because respondents did not understand the meaning of "general physical examination or checkup" and if the "when" requested a date, elapsed time, or their age (Fowler and Cannell, 1996). Behavioral coding is designed to identify potential problems. The next two pretest techniques, which involve the active participation of respondents and interviewers, are better at identifying the nature of the problem.

Respondent debriefings. In chapter 6 we discussed how debriefing sessions following experiments provide valuable insights into subjects' understanding and motivation during the experiment. Similarly, **respondent debriefings**, which are structured follow-up questions at the end of pretest interviews, may reveal question-and-answer problems as well as the sources of the problems (for procedural details, see DeMaio and Rothgeb, 1996:188–94). Since the results of cognitive interviews tend to be limited in generalizability due to very small, unrepresentative samples, respondent debriefing provides a way to assess the external validity of cognitive testing results.

Interviewer debriefings. Another perspective on question-and-answer problems may be sought from the pretest interviewers. Although interviewer debriefings customarily entail informal group discussions with the interviewers, Fowler (1995:121–24) recommends that more systematic information be collected by having the interviewers fill out standardized ratings of each question prior to the debriefing session.

Split-panel tests. Experimental manipulations of question ordering, wording, and formats, which survey designers commonly call split-panel or split-ballot tests, are a costly but effective way to check out suspected problems or weaknesses under field conditions (see discussion of survey experimental designs in chapter 6 and Box 9.1). Split-panel tests require random assignment of adequate-sized samples of pretest respondents to the versions being tested. For example, the results of cognitive interviewing might suggest a serious problem of question-order effects. This suspicion could be experimentally tested by randomly assigning pretest respondents to two forms of the instrument in which the order of related questions differs, and then comparing the responses on the two forms.

Response analysis. The responses of the pretest respondents also can be tabulated and examined for such problems as a low response rate to sensitive questions, the incidence of "don't know" responses, items where nearly everyone makes the same response, the adequacy of responses to open-ended questions, or confusion as to the meaning of questions. The generalizability of a **response analysis** is dependent on the pretest sample size and the degree to which the pretest respondents resemble the target population.

Each of these pretesting techniques offers a slightly different window on the question-and-answer process: Behavior coding allows the researcher to see interviewer–respondent interaction under actual field conditions, respondent debriefings and other cognitive interviewing methods reveal problems from the respondent's perspective, interviewer debriefings expose problems from the interviewer's perspective, response analysis reveals problems from the researcher's perspective, and split-panel tests show differences among instrument versions. This suggests that some pretest methods are better than others at identifying particular types of question problems.

To test this idea, Stanley Presser and Johnny Blair (1994) systematically compared four pretest methods: conventional field pretesting with oral group debriefings, behavior coding of live pretest interviews, cognitive interviewing combining follow-up probes with concurrent and retrospective thinkalouds, and panels of experts. Each method was applied to a single questionnaire in repeated trials. Results indicated that behavior coding was the most reliable and conventional pretesting least reliable; expert panels identified the largest number of problems and were the least costly; experts and cognitive interviewing were the only methods likely to spot problems affecting the data analysis; and conventional pretesting and behavior coding were the only effective methods for spotting problems involving the interviewer.

Noting that the expert panel was the most cost effective, Presser and Blair argued that questionnaire drafts should be routinely subjected to a peer review process. Their results also imply that questionnaires should be subjected to more than one form of pretesting. After reviewing an evaluation of the U.S. Current Population Survey, James Esposito and Jennifer Rothgeb (1997) concluded that the use of multiple techniques is critical to any comprehensive program of pretesting, because it capitalizes on the strengths of individual techniques while compensating for the unique weaknesses associated with each.

Summary

Survey design is indeed an art as well as an evolving science that draws upon communication, cognitive, and behavioral theories. The design of the instrument must (1) ensure effective two-way communication between the respondents and the researcher; (2) assist the respondents in recalling and clarifying their experiences, attitudes, and thoughts; and (3) keep the respondents interested and motivated. The principles and procedures discussed in this chapter are intended to facilitate these tasks.

In gathering "raw materials," the survey designer chooses among open and closed questions, direct and indirect questions, and a wide variety of response formats. The researcher may also select visual aids and will almost certainly draw upon questions developed in previous research. Open questions are most appropriate in face-to-face interviews when the researcher is unsure of response categories or is dealing with complex issues that require an in-depth understanding. They often are used effectively in preliminary interviewing to determine appropriate closed questions and response alternatives. However, the use of open questions in the final survey instrument is somewhat limited because responses are difficult for researchers to code and require more time and effort on the part of respondents. Closed questions are best used when both researcher and respondent have ample information on the topic. While easier for researchers to analyze and for respondents to complete, closed questions are more difficult to develop, may bias results by structuring responses, and may dampen respondents' interest in the survey. Most questions in surveys are linked apparently or directly to what the researcher wants to know. However, when examining characteristics that respondents are unable or unwilling to report directly, researchers may use indirect questions that disguise the researcher's intent.

After considering raw materials, the survey designer makes a "sketch" of the instrument—an outline of topics to be included. Focus group discussions may be used to learn how people think and talk about a survey topic. The researcher decides at this point on opening questions, on the placement of sensitive and routine questions, and on the order of topics. Opening questions are critical for motivating respondents to complete the survey; therefore, they should be interesting, relatively easy to answer, and consistent with respondents' expectations. Sensitive questions are best placed somewhere between the middle and end of the instrument; routine background items are usually placed at the end. But all questions should be ordered in a way that seems natural and logical to the respondent and that does not produce unintended order effects. Transitions may improve the flow from topic to topic.

As one begins to fill in the sketch—to write the items—one should keep the objectives of the study in mind. Properly worded items are clear and precise, are written in a vocabulary appropriate for the respondents, contain a single idea, are free of emotionally loaded words and phrases, and are tactfully worded. To control the respondent's frame of reference in investigating complex topics, one can arrange questions in a funnel sequence, moving from general to progressively more specific questions, or in an inverted-funnel sequence, moving from the most specific to the most general questions. Complex issues also can be examined through reason analysis. This involves the development of an accounting scheme, based on preliminary interviewing, that identifies the key dimensions of reasons for an action and integrates them into a model of the action.

Besides the error and bias introduced by improper question wording, the survey designer must be alert to problems of forgetting and memory distortion and to various response bias tendencies. Response accuracy may be improved by shortening the recall period, by giving respondents more time to respond, by aided-recall procedures (e.g., providing a helpful context or list), or by encouraging the use of records. Among the ways to minimize the social desirability bias are careful placement and wording of questions as well as assurances of anonymity. Response set problems are best handled by varying the type of questions and response format. It is also important for the format of the instrument to be neat and appealing. To save time and prevent adverse reactions, the format might include filter questions that direct respondents to appropriate contingency questions.

The pretest-and-revision process begins early with first drafts of questions and continues until the survey is successfully field pretested on a group of respondents similar to those in the target population. Initially, cognitive interviewing techniques ("thinkaloud" interviews, probing questions, and paraphrasing follow-ups) are used to diagnose question wording, ordering, and formatting problems. Field pretesting techniques, including behavior coding, respondent debriefings, interviewer debriefings, response analysis, and split-panel tests, are then used to evaluate the survey instrument under realistic field conditions.

Key Terms

open-ended (free-response) question
closed-ended (fixed-choice) question
direct question
indirect question
response format
Likert response scale
focus group
double-barreled question
leading question
funnel sequence
inverted-funnel sequence
reason analysis

response bias tendency
   social desirability bias
   acquiescence response set
   position response set
contingency question
filter question
cognitive interviewing
field pretesting
   behavioral coding
   respondent debriefings
   interviewer debriefings
   split-panel tests
   response analysis

Review Questions and Problems

1. What cognitive steps are necessary to answer a survey question?

2. Explain how the conversational principles of "relevance" and "clarity" could affect a respondent's answer to a survey question.

3. When are respondents likely to adopt a "satisficing" strategy in answering questions? When are they likely to adopt an optimizing strategy?

4. Compare the advantages and disadvantages of open versus closed questions. When is it advisable to use open rather than closed questions? Why should open questions be used sparingly in self-administered questionnaires?

5. For each of the following research conditions, indicate whether an open or closed question is most appropriate.

    a. The survey seeks broad, in-depth information.

    b. Respondents have a high level of information about the topic of interest.

    c. Respondents are not likely to have given much thought to relevant issues.

    d. Respondents are not highly motivated.

    e. The researcher has little prior knowledge of respondents.

6. Schuman and Scott's (1987) experiment (Box 9.1) showed that people responded differently to open and closed versions of a question regarding the most important problem facing the country. Which version gives the best overall picture of American concerns? Why?

7. Why do researchers resort to indirect questions? What special problems do they present to the researcher?

8. Is it considered unethical to borrow questions from previous research? Explain.

9. Describe some characteristics of a good opening question in an interview or questionnaire.

10. Suppose you are constructing a questionnaire for the purpose of conducting a survey of sex-role attitudes. What would be the best placement (beginning, middle, end) of the following questions?

    a. How many sisters do you have?

    b. Does your mother work outside the home?

    c. Mothers should put their children before themselves.

        ( ) Strongly agree

        ( ) Agree

        ( ) Disagree

        ( ) Strongly disagree

    d. Would you say that women nowadays are more likely to work outside the home than they were when you were growing up?

11. Which of the following questions (from the GSS) is more susceptible to an order effect: (a) Do you think it should be possible for a pregnant woman to obtain a *legal* abortion if there is a strong chance of serious defect in the baby? (b) Do you think it should be possible for a pregnant woman to obtain a *legal* abortion if the woman wants it for any reason? Explain.

12. Give an example, other than one cited in the text, of a "transition." What purpose do transitions serve?

13. As a general guide to writing items and organizing the entire survey instrument, what should you do before you begin to write individual questions?

14. The text identifies five common wording problems in constructing survey questions: (1) lack of clarity or precision, (2) inappropriate vocabulary, (3) double-barreled question, (4) loaded word or leading question, and (5) insensitive wording. Identify the wording problem(s) in each of the following questions and then rewrite the questions to make them more satisfactory.

    a. How many siblings do you have? ( ) 0–2 ( ) 3–7 ( ) 8 or more.

   b. Do you think the man should initiate and pay for the first date?
   c. In divorce or separation cases, the man has just as much right as the woman to have custody of the children.
      ( ) Strongly agree
      ( ) Agree
      ( ) Disagree
      ( ) Strongly disagree
   d. Because women are less aggressive than men, a woman's place is in the home.
      ( ) Strongly agree
      ( ) Agree
      ( ) Disagree
      ( ) Strongly disagree
   e. Do you hold traditional sex-role attitudes?
   f. Does your mother work?
   g. Is the leadership in your family matriarchal, patriarchal, or egalitarian?

15. How can a funnel sequence or inverted-funnel sequence solve the survey researcher's frame-of-reference problem?

16. Suppose you want to know why students choose a specific major (e.g., sociology). Applying reason analysis, construct a series of questions to find out the reasons for students' choice of major.

17. What are the two types of memory problems with which survey researchers must deal? Identify three ways of increasing the accuracy of respondents' recall.

18. How can one minimize the tendency to give socially desirable responses?

19. Identify two methods of avoiding acquiescence and positional response sets.

20. What is the relation between a filter question and a contingency question?

21. What does it mean to pretest a survey instrument? What purposes does pretesting serve?

22. What is the difference between cognitive interviewing techniques and field pretesting? When is each technique used? What purposes and information does each technique provide?

23. Describe three primary methods of cognitive interviewing.

24. Describe five primary methods of field pretesting.

NOTES

1. For experimental investigations of the effects of including "don't know" options in opinion questions, see Howard Schuman and Stanley Presser (1981).

2. Even when the researcher has had relevant personal experiences, this should not take the place of pretesting.

3. Indirect questioning should not be confused with proxy reporting, which involves asking respondents information about others in their households or social environments (spouses, relatives, co-workers, neighbors, etc.). Proxy reporting reduces interviewing costs because information about several persons (for example, all household members) may be col-

lected during a single interview. In the November 1984 Current Population Survey (CPS), for example, about 40 percent of the reported presidential election participation (voting turnout) figures were based on proxy reports (U.S. Bureau of the Census, 1986: table 18). The rationale underlying indirect questioning, that respondents will perceive others to be like themselves, is a potential source of error in proxy reporting.

4. This response format is used in, but not limited to, the semantic-differential scaling technique. For details see Charles Osgood, George Suci, and Percy Tannenbaum (1957).

5. This rule applies to interviews only. As indicated earlier, open-ended questions are usually inappropriate in mail surveys and, if placed at the beginning of a self-administered questionnaire, may discourage respondents from completing the survey.

6. A test of question wording shows how the word "communist" can alter the tone of the question. Schuman and Presser (1981:284–86) compared the responses to two questions regarding support for American military intervention: "If a situation like Vietnam were to develop in another part of the world, do you think the United States should or should not send troops?" and "If a situation like Vietnam were to develop in another part of the world, do you think the United States should or should not send troops to stop a communist takeover?" When these questions were asked in separate but comparable national sample surveys in 1974, 1976, and 1978, an average of 15 percent more people favored sending troops when the communist-takeover phrase was added.

7. For certain underreported behavior, this type of question may be necessary (Sudman and Bradburn, 1982). Although the marijuana question appears to assume that the respondent smokes, a "never" answer is still possible.

8. Research supports this practice. A famous study by Donald Rugg (1941), replicated by Schuman and Presser (1981:276–78), compared responses to two freedom-of-speech questions, one using the word "forbid" and the other the antonym "allow": "Do you think the United States should allow public speeches against democracy?" and "Do you think the United States should forbid public speeches against democracy?" When these questions were asked in three separate but comparable national sample surveys in the 1970s, over 22 percent fewer people, on average, were willing to "forbid" than to "not allow" such speeches.

9. This section is adapted, in part, from the discussion in Zeisel (1968).

10. If the UCLA administration had hired us to study the impact of financial aid programs on the quality of undergraduate admissions, for example, our accounting scheme would definitely incorporate financial considerations; and the sample under study also should include UCLA applicants who are accepted but choose to go elsewhere to school. If, instead, our client were the UCLA student government, which wanted to improve programs serving the needs of first-year students, our accounting scheme would focus on these needs and would likely omit information about other schools considered.

11. Sometimes an accounting scheme guides the entire research design, not just the wording of a few questions. Nine years after the first major announcement in 1953 of a possible link between cigarette smoking and lung cancer, Bruce Straits (1967) conducted a survey to study why the health reports were apparently having only slight effects on cigarette smokers. His study was designed around the accounting scheme that this anxiety-arousing information was having negligible impact on smokers because they (a) were unaware of the reports, (b) disbelieved them, (c) were not motivated to give up smoking, or (d) were unable to translate their motivation into action.

10

✓

Field Research

When we introduced experiments and surveys, we appealed to the reader's casual familiarity with these approaches—either from having read about or participated in actual studies. In this chapter, however, we appeal to a different sense of familiarity. The field research approach resembles the natural inquisitiveness that is part of everyday life. At one time or another you have joined a group or organization or entered an unfamiliar setting (e.g., your first time in a bar, your first rock concert, the first day in your research methods class), where you have watched and listened closely to others to learn what is going on and how you should act. You also have reflected occasionally on the actions, thoughts, and feelings of others in situations you encounter every day—at work, in class, at meals, in the library. Each of these examples captures the essence of field research: to render our daily lives socially intelligible and meaningful by keenly observing others as well as reflecting on our own experience.

This is not to say that everyone is a field researcher or that common sense is all there is to it. The major point of similarity between field research and other forms of common sense inquiry is "the observation of naturally occurring everyday events" (Johnson, 1975:21). The ultimate goal of field research, however, is not personal but rather scientific—to build a general, abstract understanding of social phenomena. Moreover, field researchers have developed special skills and techniques for observing, describing, and understanding everyday life.

Although we have chosen the label **field research**, several other terms often are applied to the methodological approach examined in this chapter. Some call it "qualitative" (as opposed to "quantitative") research (see Filstead, 1970; Schwartz and Jacobs, 1979; Taylor and Bogdan, 1984) because observations typically are reported in ordinary language, much as in the daily newspaper. But this is somewhat misleading, as it implies that there is no place for counting or assigning numbers to observations. Field research may, in fact, generate data on the frequency of certain behaviors and events, and it may include accounting schemes for recording behavior. Qualitative research also usually includes in-depth or unstructured interviews (sometimes called qualitative interviews). However, this method overlaps with survey research, and we will treat it here as an adjunct to field observation rather than as a separate approach.

Others have referred to field research as "observational" research or, more commonly, "participant observation" (see Bruyn, 1966; McCall and Simmons, 1969). But these labels also are misleading. Not only is observation basic to all scientific inquiry, but the picture of detached observation that science sometimes conjures up is contrary to the kind of understanding that field research seeks. Field researchers often aim to see the world from the subject's own frame of reference. To do this requires more than a backstage view of reality; indeed, field researchers may actively participate in the lives of the people and situations that they are studying. Yet, to call this approach simply participant observation is too limiting. Although observation yields the fundamental data, field research may or may not involve direct interaction with the people observed, and is not limited to observational data. Any evidence that provides firsthand information and enables the researcher to get close to the subjects being studied—from direct experience to documents to unstructured interviewing—may supplement field observation. What brings these activities together, aside from the desire to describe the social world as subjects see it, is that they always take place *in the field*—in a natural social setting familiar to the subject (see Shaffir, Stebbins, and Turowetz, 1980; Emerson, 1983).

Two other terms are also associated with this approach. Because much of field research examines a single social phenomenon or unit of analysis—for example, a particular community, organization, or small informal group—it becomes a *case study* (see Feagin, Orum, and Sjoberg, 1991). However, although many case studies involve field research, not all field research is restricted to the holistic analysis of a single setting or unit of analysis. Similarly, many field studies are called "ethnographies," a label derived from cultural anthropology. Ethnography refers to the description of a culture. In anthropology, it is assumed that this description is based on an extended stay in the field, where the investigator's aim is "to understand another way of life from the native point of view" (Spradley, 1980). While this clearly falls within the purview of field research, ethnography is a less inclusive category.

Outside anthropology, field research has tended to focus substantively on community or ethnic groups, deviance and powerlessness, occupations and professions, and, more recently, aspects of everyday life. Some field studies of elites have been done (e.g., Ostrander, 1993; Morrill, 1995), but field research generally has entailed "studying down"—focusing on the poor, the powerless, and the marginal members of society.[1] Perhaps it is more difficult to gain access to the rich and powerful than it is to gain access to the "common person." Similarly, everyday aspects of social life are easier to locate than sporadic and uncommon events.

As you might imagine, there are an extraordinarily large number of "fields" in which to do field research. Consider, for example, some of the topics of studies that have been conducted in this tradition: becoming a doctor (Becker et al., 1961), "cooling out" men in singles bars and nightclubs (Snow, Robinson, and McCall, 1991), selling used cars (Browne, 1976b), doing undercover police work (Marx, 1988), dealing with chronic back pain (Kotarba, 1977), playing Little League baseball (Fine, 1987), driving a cab (Davis, 1959), drug dealing and smuggling (Adler, 1985), acquiring privacy in public places (Henderson, 1975), having a baby (Danziger, 1979), managing a corporation (Kanter, 1977), living in a new community (Gans, 1967), and experiencing a religious conversion (Bromley and Shupe, 1979).

We begin our examination of field research by considering the kinds of problems best suited to this approach, as well as some of its strengths and limitations compared with experiments and surveys. Then we describe key aspects of sampling, field observation, and field interviewing. Finally, we turn our attention to the various stages of field research.

The Potentials and Limitations of Field Research

For a long time there has been tension between so-called quantitative researchers, on the one hand, and field researchers, on the other, with each denying the validity of the data of the other approach. For their part, many field researchers contend that by structuring one's observations—choosing what to observe and describe on the basis of preconceived notions of scientific interest—social scientists create an artificial, distorted understanding of the social world. To really know what people think and how they act, to understand what they understand, and to get behind the misinformation, lies, and evasions that survey and experimental studies often produce, one must eschew the usual mechanisms of control, disregard the possibility of generalization, and learn to see the world as the actors themselves see it (see, for example, Douglas, 1976; Schwartz and Jacobs, 1979; Taylor and Bogdan, 1984; Lincoln and Guba, 1985). While we neither dispute the kernel of truth in these criticisms nor deny the differences in method and perspective, we see no necessary conflict between field research and other approaches. Field research may complement other approaches both by providing suggestive leads for explanatory research and by adding depth and meaning to survey and experimental results. It also is simply more appropriate for certain research purposes and goals.

A major reason for doing field research is to get an insider's view of reality. For example, one of the fundamental goals of Meredith McGuire's field study (1982:19) of pentecostal Catholics was to obtain "an understanding of believers' actions from their point of view." This, she tells us, "means trying to take the role of the other, seeing things as believers see them and using their categories of thought in the organization of experience." She refers to this position as **methodological empathy**, which "differs from sympathy in that it is not necessary to agree with a perspective in order to understand it." The religious beliefs and practices that McGuire observed were understood by her as they were understood by those in the movement. But to say this is not to say that she adhered to them as did the believers, only that she empathized. Methodological empathy is a hallmark of field research. By capturing a given actor's frame of reference and definition of the situation, researchers can understand the substance, coherence, and maintenance of views that may seem implausible to outsiders. Indeed, insofar as field research is descriptive, it may have little more than this as its goal.

Because of its flexibility, the field approach lends itself well to studies of dynamic or rapidly changing situations. Suppose you are interested in how people cope with the aftermath of a natural disaster. (Recall from chapter 1 Louis Zurcher's 1968 study of a volunteer work crew formed after a tornado struck Topeka, Kansas.) People's responses are likely to depend on the severity of the disaster and the length of time since the disaster occurred. To determine the immediate impact of a calamitous event, you would have to act quickly to get to the site and observe; otherwise, the opportunity to understand certain reactions may be lost. Drafting a questionnaire or designing a probability sample of households would result in the loss of valuable time and information.

Besides fleeting situations, certain kinds of substantive problems may require a field approach. This approach is recommended (1) when it is essential to preserve "whole" events in all their detail and immediacy (Weick, 1968); (2) when a situation is complex, involving interrelated phenomena that must be studied simultaneously and as a whole—for example, the study of a prison as an institution (Weiss, 1966); and (3) when the focus is on the relationship between the person *and* the setting, so that it is important not to separate one from the other (Weick, 1968). The methodological principle that facilitates these objectives as well as the goal of getting an insider's view of reality is preserving the natural order of things, which reduces the problem of reactivity prevalent in experiments and surveys. Similarly, field research may be used when methodological problems preclude other research strategies—for example, when subjects are unable (young children) or unwilling (deviants) to participate in a formal survey.

The decision to adopt a field approach also may depend on one's resources. Research can be costly. All research strategies require time, space, money, and personnel. Conducting interviews with a large sample of individuals can be expensive in terms of sampling, interviewer training, data collection, and so forth. Similarly, experiments, while generally on a smaller scale than surveys, can be complex and expensive to conduct. Field research, if it is to be conducted at some nearby location, can be the least expensive approach. It does not require elaborate tools or equipment and, since it is typically conducted entirely by a single investigator, requires no additional personnel or training period beyond the preparation of the investigator. On the other hand, field research can be very labor intensive. Investigators have been known to spend years in the field. Bettylou Valentine (1978), for example, lived in an inner-city community for five years in conducting her study of ghetto lifestyles. Thus, the most important resource to field researchers is field researchers themselves.

In addition to cost, ethical constraints may preclude the use of other research approaches. The control and manipulation necessary for experiments are not always possible for ethical reasons. For example, it would be too dangerous to stage many kinds of events (e.g., a riot) in order to study their consequences experimentally. Nor could one ethically use potentially harmful manipulations (e.g., randomly label some children as "dumb") or, needless to say, create certain medical conditions (e.g., physical disabilities such as blindness or paraplegia) in order to study them sociologically. In such cases, field research is often a viable option. This is not a unique feature of field research, of course, because other strategies also may be ethically sound in certain circumstances. The point is simply that a field approach can avoid some ethical problems presented by experiments and surveys. (Field research does raise other ethical issues that we address in chapter 16.)

Finally, one may turn fruitfully to field research when one knows relatively little about the subject under investigation. The less you know about the subject, the less you can afford to limit data collection. The less you know, the more you must be open to all possibilities. Experiments and surveys generally require a great deal of prior knowledge about the topic being investigated. Such knowledge is essential

for deciding what to manipulate and control, or what to ask about and what to ignore. In field research, however, you must resist carrying preconceived notions into
the field, since these notions may bear little resemblance to the experience of the
people being studied.

Field research thus lends itself best to investigating dynamic situations, settings in
which it is important to preserve the natural order of things, and settings in which the
researcher's minimal understanding makes it crucial to understand the subjects' interpretation of reality. Field research takes time, however, and may not be a very efficient
way of gathering certain kinds of information. For enumerating the distribution of certain demographic characteristics (e.g., age, gender, occupation) or beliefs and attitudes
within a certain population, surveys are much quicker and more reliable. For testing
causal hypotheses, experiments are far superior because of their greater control.

Because field research typically is carried out by a single observer who interacts with a limited number of people in a limited number of settings, it is highly
dependent on the observational and interpretive skills of the researcher, is difficult
to replicate and compare, and may lack generalizability. The usual outcome is a
richly detailed description of a segment of the social world; however, the segment
is not only necessarily small but also often selected on an ad hoc basis, for reasons
of availability and convenience. This pattern tends to undermine the ability of field
studies to contribute to a body of knowledge addressing theoretically formulated
problems (Manning, 1987:22–23). Still, the products of field research are entirely
consistent with a *science* of social life, as we show in Box 10.1.

BOX 10.1

The Products of Field Research: A Field Study of Pentecostal Catholics

Rarely does a scientific study lead immediately to a great discovery; rarely are new
laws formulated; rarely are theories supported without reservation. More typically, scientific studies lead to the gradual uncovering of empirical regularities, to the eventual
realization of general principles. Yet the end product of science *is* theoretical understanding, however rarely this may occur. And because science is cumulative, the exploratory and descriptive studies are as important to the final product as are the key
hypothesis-testing investigations.

Field studies often have an exploratory/descriptive focus and are more likely to
contribute to the discovery and development of theory than to theory testing. The field
researcher typically enters the field without a well-developed picture of the research
problem. An existing literature may help guide and inform the research, but the researcher can never be certain of just how a study of natural events in a natural setting
will fit into that literature. Let us consider an example.

Suppose that you were interested in the process of religious conversion. A thorough reading of the literature would suggest that people make changes in their religious picture of the world on the basis of social pressures, psychological predisposi-
tions, and the content of the belief system to which they are in the process of converting.

Thus, an adequate theory of conversion would have to include social, psychological, and ideational variables. How, then, might you study the process of religious conversion with this information as backdrop?

To begin, you would not want to be closed to the possibility that other factors—say, the personal charisma of a religious leader or perhaps the lack of commitment to one's former religion—might affect religious conversion. Beyond this is the problem of exactly what or whom to study. Does a traditional Catholic who becomes a pentecostal Catholic experience conversion in the same way as does someone who converts from conservative Judaism to the Unification Church of Reverend Moon? Does someone who modifies or consolidates his or her beliefs experience something similar to the person who undergoes a more radical transformation? More to the point of the methodological issue, does studying a specific group, say a group of Catholic pentecostals in New Jersey, enable you to say anything about religious conversion in general or even Catholic pentecostals in general? When you observe a prayer group and afterward interact with and interview people present in the group, are you learning anything that describes the entirety of this group? What sort of generalizable information have you learned in doing a field study of some people in some group(s) within a particular movement that may be part of a larger cultural phenomenon that crosses denominational lines?

Meredith McGuire (1982), who conducted a field study of nine groups of pentecostal Catholics, generalized beyond her sample to suggest answers to questions relevant not only to the Catholic pentecostal movement, but also to other religious movements and to the broad issue of religion and social change. She noted, for example, the consistent claim of members of the movement that they were countering the secularity of modern society. Catholic pentecostals typically bemoaned the lack of religion in the work world, education, and the family; they saw a lack of Christian norms in guiding behavior, as evidenced by parental permissiveness, "gay" liberation, widespread pornography, drugs and rock music, and restriction of prayer in the public schools. She further pointed out that in spite of the uniqueness of the Catholic pentecostal form of religion, and the specific historical processes that have given rise to the movement, her analysis of the movement corresponded to broader sociological theories of religion and social change. Thus, Catholic pentecostals' concern over "secularization" is one expression of the lack of integration in modern society. The Catholic pentecostal movement is an attempt to restore religion's role in premodern times, when religion provided a system of beliefs that unified all aspects of people's lives.

McGuire's conclusions are reasonable insofar as we recognize that all social science knowledge is tentative knowledge. She is fully conscious of the limitations of her fieldwork. She provides us not with axioms of fundamental truth but with a descriptive interpretation of one religious movement, not with social laws of religious ways of being but with an exploration of one of the ways in which people can be religious, not with predictions of how people will behave but with the beginnings of a theory of conversion.

The products of McGuire's research—her descriptions and theoretical formulations—will be useful to other researchers seeking to understand pentecostal Catholics, to those working on other questions in the sociology of religion, and even to other social scientists who might gain insights for their own work on broader questions (e.g., interpersonal communication). What Meredith McGuire has done in her own limited study of nine groups is to help accumulate information that she and other social scientists can use in their struggles to understand social life. What she has written may not describe any other new religion, may not describe even any other pentecostal Catholic group, but it does suggest what might be. In this way it contributes to the cumulative work of science.

Research Design and Sampling

Unlike experiments and surveys, in which the elements of research design—hypothesis formation, measurement, sampling—are specified before data collection, design elements in field research usually are worked out during the course of the study.[2] Typically, field researchers begin with (1) broad substantive and theoretical questions and (2) a methodological approach based on observation in natural settings—that is, settings of activity that occur without the contrivance of the investigator. Neither of these desiderata permits a rigid research design. Because preconceived images may be very misleading, the researcher avoids preset hypotheses and instead lets his or her observations in the field guide the formulation of hypotheses, the asking of questions, and sampling. And because the observed setting is not under the researcher's control and its resident activities typically are not known to the researcher before he or she enters the field, research design is necessarily emergent rather than predetermined. Let us examine sampling in field research to see the special design problems that this approach presents.

Sampling in Field Research

Initially, field research almost always involves the nonrandom selection of a small number of settings and subjects. The nature of field research generally focuses attention on interactive social units such as encounters, social relationships, organizations, and communities. These units are much less amenable to probability sampling techniques than the discrete individuals typically sampled in experiments and surveys. Smaller interactive units seldom can be enumerated before their occurrence; and studies of larger units—for example, a community, an area of the city, an organization—usually are restricted to the one case under investigation. The delicate operation of entering the field—of locating suitable observation sites and making fruitful contacts—also necessitates nonrandom selection. Convenience, accessibility, and happenstance by and large determine where researchers can begin to make observations, whom they will meet there, and whom they will find most informative. Finally, the time required to conduct field observations tends to restrict the possible sample size to a very small number of cases.

Though rarely possible before a researcher enters the field, rigorous sampling can occur in the field. Murray Melbin's research (1969) on behavioral disturbances in mental hospitals provides an example of the use of probability sampling techniques in a field study. Melbin found that among patients in a small private mental hospital, far more unusual disturbances (e.g., walking around naked, making animal-like noises, lying stiffly in front of a doorway) occurred on weekdays than on evenings and weekends, but that this pattern did not appear in a large state institution nearby. In making his observations, Melbin chose times and places according to a probability sampling design. First he listed all sites in each hospital where patients could be found, and he apportioned the waking hours of the day into two-hour units. Then he randomly selected combinations of site, time, and day of the week for observation. Melbin concluded that patients tended to behave crazily when they could get the attention of professional treatment personnel—psychiatrists, social workers, and psychologists. The private hospital had an ample professional staff, which was present on weekdays and Saturday mornings, whereas the state hospital had far fewer professionals available at any time.

Melbin's study notwithstanding, probability sampling is seldom used in the field. Melbin had the luxury of three other trained observers to help record observations. And even though he did not use pre-established observational categories, his observations were much more restricted—specifically to the conduct of aides and patients—than in most field studies. The determination of a sampling frame, a necessary ingredient of probability sampling, presupposes a detailed knowledge of the field setting that researchers seldom have before entering the field. Furthermore, the usual purposes of field research—to get an insider's view, to describe a particular social setting holistically, and to develop working hypotheses—do not require considerations of statistical generalization that underlie probability sampling. Sampling in field research, therefore, ordinarily is designed to enhance the informational value of one's observations by maximizing variation (Lincoln and Guba, 1985).

Maximizing variation may sound similar to purposive sampling for heterogeneity, described in chapter 5, but there are some crucial differences. In purposive sampling for heterogeneity, which occurs before data collection, units of analysis are carefully selected on the basis of a priori assumptions and knowledge about the population in order to enhance generalizability. In field research, however, sampling plans emerge during the course of research, for the purpose of extending the information already obtained. One way this is accomplished is by "serial selection of sample units" (Lincoln and Guba, 1985). Each unit (e.g., a person or setting) is selected and analyzed one at a time. Other units are then selected to extend, fill in gaps, or test the information obtained so far. This might be accomplished by asking initial contacts to identify others, as in snowball sampling. Since the purpose is to maximize information, sampling ceases when no new information is forthcoming.

Another way to maximize variability is to identify and sample relevant dimensions of units. Typical dimensions include time and space; variations in either can serve to protect against bias as well as increase the scope of the observations. For example, in a study of altruism in which you observe altruistic acts at the scenes of accidents, you may note that the nature of the acts differs according to the time of the day, the day of the week, or the particular place where the accident occurs. Sampling times and places will provide information about variation in acts across these dimensions. Research questions that emerge in the field can help to focus data collection and identify relevant dimensions for sampling. In a study of police work, for example, one might ask, "How do police officers interpret laws when arresting and booking suspects?" (Miles and Huberman, 1994:30). This research question suggests the dimensions of setting (e.g., precinct station, squad car, crime scene), actors (police officers and suspects with different characteristics), events (e.g., arrests and bookings), and processes (e.g., making the arrest, relating to suspects, interpreting laws) (Miles and Huberman, 1994).

A related strategy, called **theoretical sampling** (Glaser and Strauss, 1967), is to sample broad analytical categories that will facilitate the development of theoretical insights. In other words, sampling is directed toward gathering information relevant to a specific working hypothesis or theory. For example, in a field study of altruism, you may decide that the time required to perform an altruistic act and the amount of physical risk or suffering incurred are important factors in your developing theory of altruism. To incorporate such variability in your study, you might investigate acts that involve different time commitments (e.g., cash contributions versus volunteer work) and acts that cause different levels of hardship (e.g., donating blood versus donating a kidney).

The sampling methods and philosophy of field research are in some ways similar to experimental research. The primary objective of experiments is to achieve a rigorous test of a hypothesis. This focuses attention on the internal validity of the research design; generalizability, a secondary issue, is achieved by varying the operationalizations and experimental context in subsequent studies. Field research similarly emphasizes the internal validity of the study, albeit with a different objective, to understand naturally occurring social events and processes; generalizability to other populations and settings is secondary to clarifying one's theoretical understanding by means of dimensional and theoretical sampling.

Field Observation

The primary method of data collection in field research is observation. Field researchers nearly always begin with field observations; even when they turn to other data sources such as interviewing "informants" or analyzing personal documents, these data generally serve as supplemental evidence or cross-checks on their observations.

The kind of observation conducted by field researchers differs from both casual, everyday observation and generic "scientific observation." George McCall (1984) noted that "while nearly everyone who goes to a zoo *sees* the animals there, and many even *watch* some of those animals, very few can be said to *observe* their behavior." In contrast to casual watching, field observation is planned, methodically carried out, and intended to extract meaningful interpretations of the social world.

Field observation differs from other forms of scientific observation in two important ways. First, while the latter can be both direct and indirect, field observation involves direct observation, usually with the naked eye, rather than the sort of indirect observation that characterizes respondents' reports in questionnaires or interviews. Second, field observation takes place in a natural setting, not a laboratory or other contrived situation. Observations made in the field also tend to be less structured than those made in the laboratory, although this is not an essential difference. Field research varies in structure, but it differs primarily in terms of the extent to which the researcher actively participates in the social setting being observed. At one extreme is the passive and intentionally unobtrusive, nonparticipant observer; at the other is the active and intentionally involved, participant observer.

Nonparticipant Observation

The nonparticipant observer is, in effect, an eavesdropper, someone who attempts to observe people without interacting with them and, typically, without their knowing that they are being observed. This form of observation often is used in conjunction with participant observation, especially in the early stages of research when one is reconnoitering a social setting as preparation for more intensive study (Gold, 1958). As a separate, inclusive method, however, nonparticipant observation is comparatively little used, in spite of its amenability to studies of social phenomena. It has been applied most routinely in the field by psychologists studying children and animals.

Direct scientific observation involves the selection, recording, and encoding of behavior and events. Selection refers to the fact that scientific observers make intentional and unintentional choices about what to observe and record (Weick, 1968). Recording consists of making records of events (e.g., by taking field notes), and encoding involves the simplification of records (e.g., by categorizing or counting the frequency of different behaviors) (Weick, 1968). All of these processes may be more or less structured. Observation is **structured** when it uses explicit and preset plans for selection, recording, and encoding of data; it is **unstructured** to the extent that these processes are implicit and emergent (McCall, 1984).

The early phase of most field research involves relatively unstructured observation. As the researcher gains a greater understanding of the setting, his or her observations may become more selective and structured. For example, the investigator may become increasingly specific about when and where to observe; what specific aspects of the setting or behavior to observe; and how to make and record the observations. As the research is delimited in this way, even more structure may be introduced in the form of area and time sampling of observation sites and checklists or other more elaborate schemes for categorizing behavior.

A good example of unstructured, nonparticipant observation is Lyn Lofland's study (1971, 1973) of how people in cities—strangers in public places—relate to one another in terms of appearance and spatial location. Although Lofland drew upon other materials, her study was based largely on hundreds of hours of observations. She made the observations in and around Ann Arbor and Detroit, Michigan, in bus depots, airports, libraries, stores, restaurants, bars, theaters, and parks; aboard buses; and on the streets. In most of these settings, she was able to "blend into the scenery," even for periods of several hours. Imagining herself viewing others through a one-way mirror, Lofland attempted to record everything within her line of vision. She did not systematically sample observation sites or resort to checklists for recording behavior. As the study progressed, she concentrated at times on certain kinds of behavior—for example, seating patterns and entrance behavior—but in general she simply recorded as much as she could.

One of Lofland's observation sites was a glass-walled hallway, called the Fishbowl, between two buildings on the University of Michigan campus. Here she became sensitized to the "grooming" actions people go through as they are about to enter a public setting. Lofland (1971:303) describes how she made this discovery:

> One wall of the Fishbowl, the one which contains the doors, is solid glass, so that whenever I happened to be observing from a bench close to the doors, I could not fail to be struck by the preparation behavior that occurred over and over again as student after student neared the door, stopped, groomed himself [or herself], and

then entered. There were many instances of this behavior recorded in my notes before I ever "recognized" it as a pattern, but once I did, I was led to look for similar activities in other settings and eventually to "see" the full entrance sequence.

Lofland maintains that some of her discoveries were made possible by her prolonged periods of observation in only a few sites. This provided sufficient familiarity with the settings to enable her to recognize faces and to make important distinctions among the different inhabitants, such as residents, patrons, customers, and newcomers. If her observations had been more structured, it seems unlikely that she would have discovered many of the patterns she reports. On the other hand, more structured observation could have provided other important kinds of sociological information, such as the duration and frequency of occurrence of the behavior patterns Lofland observed.

The advantage of structured observation lies in its greater control of sampling and measurement error, which permits stronger generalizations and checks on reliability and validity. We can see how this is possible in one of the relatively few sociological studies of this type, an investigation of crime and law enforcement by Albert Reiss (1967).

Among other things, Reiss observed police–citizen transactions in eight high-crime areas of three large cities. To do so, he assigned twelve observers and a supervisor to each city. Because he wished to generalize about transactions with citizens, Reiss (1968:358) sampled a number of units: "days of the week, watches of the day, and the officer based unit of the beat within precincts." He also used standardized procedures for recording observations. Following each eight-hour period of observation, observers completed booklets for each encounter of two minutes or more duration. Each booklet contained a sequence of questions about the transaction. By systematically recording observations and using multiple observers, Reiss was able to show that the race of the observer was related to differences in reporting of officer deviance: White observers were less likely than black observers to report the undue use of force among black officers. Thus, he was able to uncover a source of error that in all likelihood would have gone undetected in a solo unstructured observation study.

With highly structured observation, it is assumed that the categories of observation established by the researcher reflect the meaning of events to those who are studied. Because field researchers tend to challenge this assumption, most fieldwork develops "relevant categories and analytical distinctions over the course of the study" and does not use pre-established, standardized schedules for recording observations (Emerson, 1981:352).[3] In the remainder of the chapter, therefore, we will concentrate on field research that is less structured than the Reiss study.

Participant Observation

Historically, field research has been associated most closely with **participant observation**. In ideal descriptions of this method, the observer is said to participate actively, for an extended period of time, in the daily lives of the people and situations under study (see Becker and Geer, 1957; McCall and Simmons, 1969). This may require that the observer live or work in an area; it clearly assumes that the observer will become an accepted member of the group or community, able to speak informally with the people—to "joke with them, empathize with them, and share their concerns and experiences" (Bogdan and Taylor, 1975:5).

Despite the tidiness of this description, however, there is a rather fine line between nonparticipant and participant observation. As with the dimension of structure in observational studies, participation is a matter of degree. Some would argue that even a relatively unobtrusive observer sitting at a table in a restaurant taking notes influences the situation by virtue of his or her mere presence; thus, however unwittingly, such an observer is also a participant. It is more accurate, therefore, to think of the two types of field observation as poles of a continuum. At one extreme is the participant observer who becomes completely absorbed in the group under observation; at the other is the nonparticipant observer who tries to remain aloof from it. "Usually," as Jacqueline Wiseman and Marcia Aron (1970:49) note, "a researcher participates to a degree somewhere between these two extremes by either *posing* as a member or announcing himself as a scientific investigator and hoping to be accepted by the group in that role."

Because field research is rarely either detached observation on the one hand or embroiled participation on the other, participation often becomes a question of "how much"? To fully immerse oneself in the situation is to risk altering the events one observes and perhaps even losing sight of one's role as researcher. But field researchers argue that these risks are small compared with the benefits to be gained from being a participant. A stranger to a situation may easily take a word, a sigh or other gesture, or a relationship for something wholly different from what it means to a participant.

Consider, for example, the use of the Spanish phrase *de colores* in the contemporary religious movement known as Cursillo. Although the literal translation of this phrase from Spanish to English is "of colors," it means much more to those who have experienced the spiritual renewal of the Cursillo. Marcene Marcoux (1982:222), who studied the movement by participant observation, says this about the term:

> As a motto, de colores reminds members of the rainbow; the various colors merge into one phenomenon, representing the very brotherhood and sisterhood of the movement. Moreover, it conjures up the excitement and elan of initiation where this phrase was first heard . . . the spirit of the movement in terms of caring, action, piety, and community . . . that is made evident in the concrete exchange of these particular words.

It is difficult to imagine how one could see this simple phrase in all its symbolic power without actually exchanging greetings with other participants in the Cursillo.

In addition to this "language barrier," there are many other potential problems of interpretation for the outsider, or nonparticipant. Just imagine that you are one of the subjects of someone else's field research. Assume for a moment that your place of work, a club you belong to, the church you attend, a class you are taking, or a favorite tavern you visit is the setting for the researcher's observations. Now think of all the things that the researcher would have to learn in order to make appropriate judgments about the activities of the group. What do you know so well that you take for granted about the job (e.g., how the places where people take their coffee breaks serve to reinforce territorial influence and status in the work place), the conduct of the club's business (e.g., how the president influences the opinions of certain members), the symbols of your church (e.g., how the theology of your religion makes these symbols meaningful), the daily affairs of the class (e.g., what seating patterns mean in terms of social cliques), or about the differences among customers at the tavern (e.g., differences among regulars and casual visitors in terms of where they sit and how they are served)?

Even if this same researcher used you as an informant to help him or her understand the situation, there will be features that you are likely to forget, not convey accurately and completely, or omit because their understanding is assumed. In short, it is difficult to imagine full comprehension without a heavy dose of participation. Everything that you know about these various settings you learned because of your activity as a participant.

On the other hand, field research carries with it some risks. It can be an emotionally stressful experience for the researcher (see Lofland and Lofland, 1995). William Shaffir, Robert Stebbins, and Allan Turowetz (1980) describe fieldwork as "usually inconvenient, to say the least, sometimes physically uncomfortable, frequently embarrassing, and, to a degree, always tense." In the early days in the field, before learning the ropes, researchers are likely to experience awkward and embarrassing encounters; after a while they may become sensitive to hostile and suspicious challenges to their intentions and "observer" role. Eventually, researchers may come to loathe the people under observation and wish to withdraw, or may identify so strongly with the group that they cease their research. Finally, after being in the field for so long and developing deep attachments, the researcher often finds it difficult to leave.

A problem that has received much attention among field researchers is balancing the requirements of both participating and observing. Participant observation creates a difficult marginal existence; one usually participates in an alien setting, with a desire to be accepted but also a constant sense of separation from those observed that is part and parcel of the observer role. As researchers become more familiar with the setting, however, and are drawn into it more as participants, they may lose sight of their reason for being in the field. In fact, field researchers even have a label for this phenomenon: The researcher who ceases to be conscious of the observer role is said to be **going native**.

As an illustration of going native, Albert Reiss (1968:362–63) described an observer who had the role of plainclothes detective thrust on him by the police officer he was observing:

> The officer arrested two citizens, and one began to flee. The officer in this case turned to the observer, handed him his nightstick, and said: "Hold him." He then chased the fleeing man. The observer obeyed and, what is more, as he held the man against the patrol car, the man resisted and attempted to flee. And then . . . the observer threatened the citizen with the nightstick.

The problem here is judging where to draw the line between participation and observation. Reiss contends that his assistant in this case clearly went too far, that he should have responded as Reiss himself had in a similar situation—by refusing the nightstick and reminding the officer that he was an observer. On the other hand, subjects usually come to treat participant observers as at least "quasi"-members of the team or group and expect them to participate, such as by assisting a police officer in holding a suspect. Refusal to participate may jeopardize the observer's relations with subjects and his or her continued presence in the field.

To make the issue even more complicated, there may be sins of omission involved in maintaining observer distance. Sociologist Don Zimmerman (personal communication, 1986) once found himself in a situation where a social worker he was observing discovered a very young child abandoned by her caretaker. Leaving the child alone, the worker returned to the office to report the situation. Her supervisor responded by immediately calling the police and reprimanding the worker. For not assuming custody of the child, she and Zimmerman could have been held criminally culpable. Zimmerman was uncomfortable about leaving the child, but his research plan called for strict nonintervention in the work activities of the social workers. Thus, he faced a difficult dilemma in which his research plan conflicted with his personal values and civic duty. It also could be said, by the way, that Reiss's assistant performed a civic duty by assisting the officer in holding the suspect. As these examples show, the issues in balancing participant and observer roles are seldom as easy or clear-cut as they seem.

Field Interviewing

Besides observing and nearly always participating in the social words they study, field researchers also converse with the people in those worlds. Sometimes these conversations involve mere chitchat, part of being a participant, but often they are conversations with a purpose. Referred to as **field interviewing**, this aspect of the research process may serve many purposes. It is impossible to observe everything in a setting or scene; many relevant events will occur in the researcher's absence, and there may be other revealing information to which the researcher is not privy. Therefore, field researchers typically rely on the careful questioning of other participants, called **informants**, to gain information. Another important purpose of field interviewing is to question members or participants about their feelings, motives, and interpretations of events. These reactions are not only likely to be of direct interest to the researcher, but often serve as critical validity checks on the researcher's inferences.

There are two basic forms of field interviewing. Most field interviewing occurs informally, in ordinary conversations and as a natural extension of participant observation. Initially, such casual interviewing may entail orientational questions, as researchers get acclimated in a setting. For example, "Where can I find this?" "Who is she?" "What does she do?" Eventually, the questions are aimed at expanding information about specific actions and events and probing their deeper meaning. John

Lofland and Lyn Lofland (1995:70) note that field researchers devote much of their time to asking questions such as these:

What do you think she meant by that?
What are they supposed to do?
Why did she do that?
Why is that done?
What happens after _____?
What would happen if _____?
What do you think about _____?
Who is responsible if _____?

After researchers have been in the field for awhile and have begun to develop an understanding of the setting, they may conduct formal interviews with informants to secure more detailed information on individuals, to get different perspectives on events, and to round out and check information already obtained. These formal, **in-depth** or **intensive interviews** are scheduled in advance, are much less structured than those in surveys, and also take much longer, often requiring several sessions. Indeed, in-depth interviews with one or more subjects can become a major source of data in the field. For studying phenomena that lack a geographical base or transcend particular settings, intensive interviewing may be the best way to proceed (Kleinman, Stenross, and McMahon, 1994; Lofland and Lofland, 1995). This method, sometimes with limited field observation, has been applied effectively, for example, in studies of chronic illness (Charmaz, 1991), divorce (Kohler Riessman, 1990), teaching children about sex (Fox et al., 1988), and the differences in residing in small towns, cities, and suburbs (Hummon, 1990).

Although intensive interviews often are described as unstructured, they do not proceed without a great deal of preparation and they always are guided by specific topics and themes that the researcher wants to pursue. Rather than create the sort of standardized interview schedule found in surveys, however, field interviewers develop what is known as an **interview guide** (Lofland and Lofland, 1995; Kvale, 1996). Interview guides stem from the general topic of investigation and from ideas and hypotheses that emerge in the field. They may consist merely of an outline of topics in some logical order, or they may contain many specific questions, arranged thematically. In either case, the interview generally progresses from questions about concrete situations to more abstract and interpretive questions that probe an informant's experience and interpretation of events. Furthermore, the order of the questions and their exact wording will depend on the background of the informant and the general course of the conversation. Rather than ask a series of questions worked out in advance, regardless of the answers to each question, "researchers listen to each answer and determine the next question based on what is said," as in a normal conversation (Rubin and Rubin, 1995:7).

Calvin Morrill's (1995) field study of conflict management among corporate executives offers a good example of field interviewing. Morrill spent two years doing intensive fieldwork that included individual and group observation as well as informal and formal interviews. The informal interviews with executives and their staff were carried out during their daily routines. Many of these interviews consisted of "nothing more than a few conversational turns," while others stretched for an hour or more as Morrill and his informant "shot the breeze" (p. 243). Usually Morrill asked direct questions to elicit information, but he also used a procedure called "interviewing by comment" (see Snow, Zurcher, and Sjoberg, 1982). For example, to prompt the informant to say more, he repeated an informant's statement or acted puzzled by making comments such as "I don't quite follow you" or "I don't understand." In the same manner, he also got informants' views by trying out hypotheses about particular situations.

Morrill conducted the formal interviews, lasting from 30 minutes to nearly six hours, in various locales—"in executives' privated offices, favorite eating and drinking establishments, and homes" (p. 241). For these interviews, he developed an interview guide, based on his first 30 interviews, that contained clusters of questions. Initial questions asked about the nature of the informants' position and the organizational context. For example, "How many employees does _____ have?" "How many executives are at the executive levels?" "What are your responsibilities here at _____?" (p. 245). As the executives described their work, Morrill focused the questions on communications, and then he turned to issues that someone studying managers would be expected to want to know. For example, "What characteristics do you believe make an executive effective?" "How is performance measured at the executive level?" (p. 246). These questions led to more personal questions about the informants themselves, for example, about their educational background, work history, and the strengths they brought to their present position. Finally, later in single interviews or in follow-up interviews, Morrill asked questions designed to produce information on trouble cases within the corporation. Once he identified these cases, he probed further to learn "the basis of the conflict, its management, and its participants and their relationships and backgrounds" (p. 244).

To maintain as much consistency as possible, Morrill attempted to ask this repertoire of questions of every executive. But typical of field interviewing, the questions served mainly as a skeletal outline, as he varied their wording and order as the situation required. For example, whenever he detected information on organizational conflicts, he immediately plied the informant for more details. Some informants were reluctant and uneasy about answering questions; others were quickly drawn into the conversation and gave detailed information about their corporations that in effect anticipated the questions on Morrill's interview guide. Morrill also noted that he always "attempted to maintain an even emotional balance—not too excited, but interested" (p. 244). As his time in the field progressed, he became adept at reading verbal and nonverbal cues that communicated reluctance or rapport. Finally, if an executive appeared anxious toward the end of the interview, especially after disclosing conflicts, Morrill ended with wrap-up, noncontroversial questions to put the informant at ease; for example, "What are the company's goals at present?" "What do you look forward to in your job in the near and long term?" (p. 248).

Stages of Field Research

As we have noted before, scientific investigations rarely proceed smoothly in a neat sequence of steps. This is especially true of field research. Nevertheless, we can identify a series of essential problems faced by all field researchers, even if these

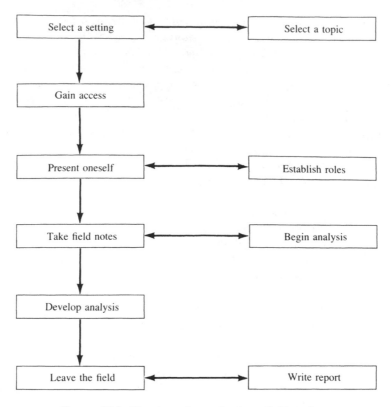

FIGURE 10.1. The stages in conducting a field study.

do not always occur in a prescribed sequence. Figure 10.1 shows the overlapping stages in conducting a field study. The major problems, considered below, are (1) selecting a research setting, (2) gaining access to the setting, (3) presenting oneself, (4) gathering information in the field, and (5) analyzing the information and developing a theoretical scheme for interpretation. To provide an overview, we first summarize a field study.

A Field Study of the Homeless

Beginning in the mid-1970s, evidence of increasing homelessness in America generated much public interest and debate. Correspondingly, social researchers began conducting studies of homelessness in communities throughout the country. The vast majority of these studies shared two characteristics: (1) They were based on questionnaire surveys, and (2) they were concerned primarily with describing personal characteristics and disabilities of the homeless, such as mental illness and alcoholism (Snow and Anderson, 1991:150). Peter Rossi's 1989 study, the sampling design for which was discussed in chapter 5, typifies this approach. Rossi used fifteen- to twenty-minute interviews with randomly selected homeless individuals to estimate the number and characteristics of the homeless population of Chicago.

For nearly a year and a half in the mid-1980s, David Snow and Leon Anderson (1987, 1991) conducted a field study of homeless individuals living in or passing through Austin, Texas.[4] In contrast to most other studies of homelessness, they were interested in understanding the "nature and texture of street life" from the perspective of the homeless themselves. In particular, they wanted to examine how the homeless managed their daily existence—the routines and strategies they used to subsist and survive and the factors that shaped these routines and strategies.

Field observations of the homeless were made over a period of one year, from September 1, 1984, to August 31, 1985, with Anderson as the principal ethnographer. His strategy was to "hang out" with as many homeless "individuals as possible on a daily basis, spending time with them in varied settings (e.g., meal and shelter lines, under bridges, in parks, at day-labor pickup sites), over the course of the twelve-month period" (1987:1342). In the end, he spent over 400 hours in twenty-four different settings with 168 homeless individuals. In addition, Snow spent another 200 hours negotiating access to records and interviewing police officers, local political officials, and personnel of agencies serving the homeless.

The principal data were based on direct observation of and interaction with the homeless, especially listening to their conversations. While Anderson asked questions and probed from time to time, mostly he engaged in relatively unobtrusive listening that took two basic forms: (1) eavesdropping (e.g., listening to others while waiting in meal lines) and (2) ordinary conversational listening when interacting with two or more homeless individuals. Some of these persons were apprised of Anderson's researcher status and some were not. Yet the nature of the encounters maintained the naturalness of the setting and of people's reactions. Even when the homeless knew Anderson's true status, they typically lost sight of it "as he continued to spend time on the street with them, dressed in old clothes, and more or less walked in their shoes" (1987:1343).

Data from observations and conversations were recorded in two steps. First, while in the field, Anderson took mental notes and jotted down key phrases and words to aid his recall of particular events. Second, as soon as possible after leaving the field, he elaborated this information into a detailed narrative account. As an aid to this process, Anderson routinely met with Snow to review his field experiences, discuss their methodological and theoretical implications, and make plans for subsequent observations.

As the study unfolded, Snow and Anderson attempted to identify the range of relevant social settings and types of homeless persons who existed on the streets of Austin. This informed their sampling strategy of maximizing variation, which involved spending "time with as many homeless as possible in the range of settings most relevant to their daily lives" (1991:155).

Initially they organized their daily recordings into three major coding categories: single focal settings (e.g., the Salvation Army, plasma centers, parks, bars), cultural domains (e.g., drinking and alcohol, sleeping and shelter, work, social relationships), and homeless individuals. Each bit of information was assigned to one or more of these categories. They soon discovered, however, that some "settings and domains were more central than others to the lives and daily routines of the homeless" (1987:1345). One of these, which was unanticipated, was the identity and self-concept domain. Snow and Anderson were surprised by the amount of talk among the people that attempted to generate personal identities that provided them with a measure of self-worth and dignity.

Different patterns of "identity talk" were identified. One of these was called "associational distancing," such as disassociating oneself from homeless persons as a social category. For example, one individual who had been on the streets for less than two weeks said, "I'm not like the other guys who hang out down at the 'Sally' [Salvation Army]. If you want to know about street people, I can tell you about them; but you can't really learn about street people from studying me, because I'm different" (1987:1349). Another pattern was labeled "fictive storytelling." This involves stories about one's experiences and accomplishments that are clearly embellished to some degree, such as (a) exaggerated claims regarding past or current wages and (b) fantasies about the future. For example, some homeless persons fantasized about becoming rich. As one said, "You might laugh and think I'm crazy, but I'm going to be rich. I know it. I just have this feeling. I can't explain it, but I am" (1987:1361).

There were many other important findings as well, but a consideration of these would go well beyond the purpose of this example: to convey the process of conducting a field study. In the remainder of the chapter we will make reference to and elaborate on other features of Snow and Anderson's research.

Selecting a Research Setting

Obviously you must begin somewhere, and for the field researcher, the first problem is deciding *where* to begin. How do you select an appropriate site in which to conduct your study? Speaking of participant observation, Steven Taylor and Robert Bogdan (1984) described the ideal setting as one that is directly related to the researcher's interests, is easily accessible, and allows for the development of immediate rapport with informants. This ideal is seldom realized, however. The homeless study satisfied the first two criteria. The site of the study—Austin, Texas—was also the location of the University of Texas, where Snow and Anderson were, respectively, a professor and a graduate student. Austin served their purposes well not only because of its proximity but also because of the relatively large and rapidly increasing number of homeless individuals living there in the mid-1980s. Immediate rapport, however, is difficult in any setting where the researcher enters as a stranger. Furthermore, broad research questions that guide field research rarely point to a particular setting. It is not uncommon, in fact, for investigators to end up in settings that are ill-suited to their interests (Geer, 1964). Consequently, the setting itself may dictate research interests, because it is only after entering the field and beginning to make observations that the researcher comes to know exactly what theoretical issues may be explored.

Regardless of the extent of the researcher's participation, the setting should permit clear observation. To the nonparticipant, it is also important not to alter the naturalness of the setting by making participants aware that they are being observed. The counterpart of this rule for the participant observer is to select a setting where he or she can participate naturally and easily become an accepted and familiar part of the surroundings. Finally, given the time required for this type of research, the setting should be as accessible as possible.

Together, these criteria suggest that novice field researchers might do well to select a setting close at hand where they can readily fit in. This does not necessarily mean a setting with which they are intimately familiar. In familiar settings, especially where they have a direct personal or professional stake, researchers often experience problems in overcoming their own particular views of reality and of holding their feelings in abeyance (Taylor and Bogdan, 1984). It is extremely difficult to be able to treat the familiar as new and to observe more as a researcher in a familiar setting than you observe as a natural participant. On the other hand, Lofland and Lofland (1995) suggest that the best starting place for field research may be "where you are." Noting that a good deal of field research is born out of accidents of the "current biography" and "personal history" of the researcher, they say: "A job; a physical mishap; the development, loss or maintenance of an intimate relationship; an illness; an enjoyed activity; a living arrangement—all these and many other possible circumstances may provide you with a topic you can care about enough to study" (p. 11). Thus, for Lofland and Lofland, "starting where you are" is a matter of interest as well as access to a social setting.

This approach has a long history dating to the 1920s and 1930s at the University of Chicago, where students were encouraged to build on their experience and to use the city as their "lab" (see Box 10.2). A recent example of this tradition is Mitchell Duneier's (1992) description of the men who frequented *Slim's Table* at a cafeteria where he ate meals as a graduate student at Chicago. Other examples of starting where you are (see also Lofland and Lofland, 1995:12) include Julius Roth's study (1963) of the passage of time in a hospital, based on his experience as a tuberculosis patient; Fred Davis's study (1959) of the cab driver, developed from his work as a cab driver while in graduate school; and a study called *Synagogue Life* by Samuel Heilman (1976), who as an Orthodox Jew had joined the synagogue before the conception of his study. In each of these cases, the researcher "naturally" belonged in the setting but was new to it, so his degree of familiarity did not encumber his observations.

Starting where you are also is likely to facilitate the researcher's efforts in other ways. Field research is not easy work. The good field researcher must be able to feel comfortable in the presence of informants who are almost always, at least at the outset, strangers, and must be able to make these informants feel comfortable as well. The ability to develop rapport is not a skill that each of us possesses to the same degree. An optimal site, therefore, may be one that encourages ease in the researcher.

Gaining Access

How do you go about getting into a group that you wish to study? The answer to this question depends first of all on the nature of the group or setting. If the setting is a formal organization, one should seek permission from those in charge, referred to as **gatekeepers** by field researchers (Taylor and Bogdan, 1984). Obtaining permission may be facilitated by having a friend vouch for the researcher or by get-

BOX 10.2

Origins of Field Research

Modern field research traces its origins to two related traditions, one in anthropology and one in sociology.* Ethnographic fieldwork, the study of native cultures by learning the native language and observing and taking part in native life, originated with the founders of modern anthropology: the German-trained Franz Boas (1858–1942) and the Polish-born British social anthropologist Bronislaw Malinowski (1884–1942). Before the work of these two men, anthropology was largely an armchair discipline relying on the testimonies of explorers, missionaries, and colonial officials for its data.

Boas, who did research on Native Americans, was particularly concerned about how the biases of Western culture affected understanding of native life. He believed that only by living among native peoples and learning the language of native thought could one come to see the world as natives saw it. Malinowski, whose major field studies took him to the Pacific islands, was the first anthropologist to provide a detailed account of how he carried out his fieldwork. These two field researchers reoriented the whole field of cultural anthropology. They and their students (e.g., Margaret Mead, Ruth Benedict, Alfred Kroeber) made it possible by their methodology to get an insider's view of the culture. This goal of understanding the subject's point of view remains a central feature of field research.

Another major source of modern field research is the social reform tradition of sociology. This tradition is as old as sociology itself. However, it became more empirically oriented toward the end of the nineteenth century, as social reformers and sociologists turned first to social surveys and then to a more varied methodology based primarily on field observation. In the United States, the latter approach became identified with the so-called Chicago School of Sociology. One of the key figures was W. I. Thomas (1863–1947), who, with his collaborator Florian Znaniecki, published a monumental study, *The Polish Peasant in Europe and America* (1918). This work contributed to the field approach by its use of a variety of techniques, including the examination of letters and life histories. Thomas also advocated the importance of understanding the individual's own "definition of the situation" as part of a more self-conscious theoretical analysis.

More than Thomas, however, it was Robert Park (1864–1944) who established the place of field research in modern sociology. Educated in Germany and trained as a journalist, Park was for many years the chairman of the sociology department at the University of Chicago. Park and his associates at Chicago inspired a generation of researchers who used the city as their social laboratory. There they investigated pickpockets, police, juvenile gangs, the Jewish ghetto, hobos, taxi-hall dancers, and other assorted groups and areas of the city. They were guided by the desire to ameliorate the problems of city living, which they saw as the natural outcome of urban crowding. One might say that Park's participant observers contributed to our understanding of different urban subcultures in much the same way that Boas- and Malinowski-inspired ethnographers promoted our understanding of different cultures.

*Although it was not until the late nineteenth and early twentieth century that this became a self-conscious method of social research, some aspects of field research are as old as recorded history. [See Hughes (1960) and Wax (1971) for historical sketches of "fieldwork."]

ting one's foot in the door, as by first visiting or volunteering to serve the organization in some way.

If the setting is public (e.g., park, street corner, public restroom), you may not need to negotiate access as an observer, although we recommend informing the police or other proper authority about what you are doing. In the homeless study, Snow negotiated and legitimated access to a number of settings for his partner Anderson. If the setting is semipublic (e.g., bar, theater, store), it is generally a good idea to speak to the manager or owner before you begin your research. It is almost impossible to spend long periods in public places without having to give a proper account of oneself. Observers can be arrested for loitering and may be suspected of shoplifting when hanging around a store. Anderson was arrested and jailed for violation of an open-container ordinance with two homeless men one evening. He was bailed out the same night, and as a result of prior negotiations with the local police, "his arrest record was subsequently expunged from the police file and the arresting officer was reprimanded" (Snow, Benford, and Anderson, 1986:395). The best practice, therefore, is to seek the cooperation of those who are likely to question what you are doing.

As a participant, you also will have to figure out ways of interacting with people and, if necessary, of becoming an accepted member of the group (Taylor and Bogdan, 1984). The usual recommendation here is simply to station yourself at an active spot and try to engage people in casual conversation. Anderson began by hanging out at the Salvation Army facility, Austin's only public shelter for the homeless, where he simply struck up conversations with strangers. Yet, there can be problems with this seemingly innocuous approach. Since people are wary of strangers, researchers must be careful that their intentions are not misconstrued. Consider the case of a highly regarded early field study conducted by William Foote Whyte (1981) in an Italian neighborhood in Boston. Having been advised that he could learn a great deal by visiting a tavern, striking up a conversation with a woman, and buying her a drink, Whyte decided to try this approach. As he recounts,

> With some trepidation I climbed the stairs to the bar and entertainment area and looked around. . . . There were women present all right, but none of them was alone. Some were there in couples, and there were two or three pairs of women together. I pondered this situation briefly. I had little confidence in my skill at picking up one female, and it seemed inadvisable to tackle two at the same time. Still, I was determined not to admit defeat without a struggle. I looked around me again and now noticed a threesome: one man and two women. It occurred to me that here was a maldistribution of females which I might be able to rectify. I approached the group and opened with something like this: Pardon me. Would you mind if I joined you? There was a moment of silence while the man stared at me. He then offered to throw me downstairs. (1981:289)

Later on, Whyte had the good fortune to be introduced by a social worker to someone, referred to as "Doc," who would be instrumental in his gaining entry into "Cornerville." Doc became Whyte's closest friend, sponsor, and major source of information. The key to opening doors in the community, such persons are called **key informants** by field researchers. Not only was Doc able to introduce Whyte to a number of people from the neighborhood, but Doc himself was well regarded in the community. Being introduced as Doc's friend thus gained Whyte immediate acceptance by people who were willing to accept any friend of Doc. Still, just as Whyte was able to bask in Doc's light, so too would he have been cast into Doc's shadow if Doc had been held in low regard by the community.

One of the problems with relying on contacts in a strange group is that one cannot always be certain how well regarded the contact may be. Martin Weinberg and Colin Williams (1972) note that frequently it is easier to meet those more peripheral to the group than it is to meet those more central. At the outset of field research, most investigators will feel ill at ease and quite alone in a new setting. Marginal members of the group may have similar feelings and thus be easier to contact. They tell the story of the first day in the field doing a study of nudists (p. 172): "The first day . . . the researcher ended up spending too much time with an unmarried male who, it was later learned, was held in disrepute. The motive imputed to this nudist as well as to other single nudists was of being there to look at other members' wives." Such situations present a dilemma for field researchers. One must be careful about whom to accept as a friend. At the same time, as an outsider one cannot afford to offend others by rejecting their friendship.

Finding out how informants stand vis-à-vis the setting or community they "inform" is also critical because of its impact on research findings. William Labov (1973) discusses this issue in terms of what he calls the "linguistic consequences of being a lame." In his study of the linguistic habits of a group of young black men, Labov found that the men most accessible and willing to serve as informants were those men who were marginal to their groups, in a word, "lames." Thus, inferences concerning linguistic patterns among blacks might reflect the habits of informants on the periphery and thereby be limited in generalizability.

Many of the settings and situations into which Whyte ventured in the community were private: homes, social clubs, political campaign meetings, and places of illegal business operations. His means of gaining entry to these settings can be traced to his contact with the social worker, who introduced him to Doc, who in turn introduced him to other "street corner boys," politicians, and racketeers, who introduced him to still others. Thus, snowball sampling is the basic approach to obtaining access to private settings. The key to its implementation is knowing where to start. Some successful strategies include checking with friends to see if they can arrange personal introductions; involving oneself in the community by using local stores and facilities and attending public meetings; going to agencies that serve the community such as churches, day-care centers, and neighborhood centers (where Whyte began); and advertising one's research interests in the local newspaper (Taylor and Bogdan, 1984:24–25).

Presenting Oneself

Related to the problem of gaining entry is deciding how to present oneself to those in the field. Certain aspects of this problem must be resolved before the researcher attempts to gain access to a setting, while other aspects cannot be anticipated fully and must be worked out during the course of the study.

As you consider how to gain access to a research setting, you must determine how to present yourself in the context of the research and how to relate to others in the setting. This issue basically boils down to deciding what role or roles to play. Roles are strategic because they greatly affect what the researcher is able to learn. The role you assume will determine where you can go, what you can do, with whom you can interact, and what you can inquire about and be told (McCall and Simmons, 1969).

The observer/participant roles. The four "master roles" from which other role relationships develop stem from the positions of scientific observer and participant (Gold, 1958; Junker, 1960). At one extreme is the *complete observer*, represented by our earlier description of nonparticipant observation. At the other is the *complete participant*, who conceals the observer role while becoming a fully accepted member of the in-group. In both of these cases, the researcher hides his or her true identity from those observed. This avoids the problem of reactivity and also has other advantages: For the complete observer, it is easier to play one role than try to balance two; for the complete participant, access may be gained to information that would escape or be withheld from an observer. But such concealment has major disadvantages: The complete observer may wish to clarify points by questioning those observed, and, most important, such covert research invariably raises ethical questions.

Covert research generally does not present serious ethical problems when the setting is public and open, where anyone has a right to be present (Lofland and Lofland, 1995). In this situation, no harm can come to the people observed, the researcher is likely to be a passive observer, and concealing one's status as a researcher is considered a mild form of deception. Many social scientists believe, however, that concealment can become a serious problem when the researcher enters a private or closed setting, especially when his or her identity is purposely misrepresented in order to gain entry (see Erikson, 1967). We consider some of the ethical questions raised by covert research in chapter 16. For now, we note that other social scientists defend covert research by maintaining that the scientific knowledge and social benefits of research may justify deceptive practices. Some research questions probably could not be investigated without complete cover for one's actions. In fact, some important, albeit controversial, studies have been conducted using a covert approach.

A well-known example is Laud Humphreys's study (1975) of impersonal sex in public places entitled *Tearoom Trade*. In this study the author, posing as a voyeur and lookout, loitered around public restrooms waiting for opportunities to study brief sexual encounters among anonymous men. While engaging in this action, Humphreys made note of participants' license plate numbers and had them traced. A year later he conducted interviews at these men's homes to find out more about them than he could learn during the covert observation of their homosexual behaviors. Humphreys's research created a heated controversy. Some applauded him for his courage in undertaking such pioneering research, for his scrupulous care in protecting the identity of the people he observed, and for contributing to the understanding of a sensitive and private aspect of social life. Others denigrated him for his vivid descriptions of homosexual activities and, more importantly, for the blatant deception involved and the dangers posed, especially during the follow-up phase of his research (Glazer, 1972).

The other two master roles that the field researcher can play combine observation and participation. The *participant as observer* role emphasizes participation. The researcher's "observer activities are *not* wholly concealed, but are 'kept under wraps' as it were, or subordinated to activities as a participant" (Junker, 1960:36). Thus, others in the field generally relate to the researcher in his or her informal participant role, and the researcher is likely to spend more time participating than observing. This master role probably occurs most frequently in community studies, where relationships with informants develop over an extended period (Gold, 1958).

Finally, the field researcher can assume the role of *observer as participant*. In this role, observer activities are overriding, as the researcher intentionally draws attention to his or her status as an observer and may even be publicly sponsored by people in the situation studied (Junker, 1960:37). Relationships with informants are thus more formal. This master role is likely to be invoked in brief encounters that do not allow relationships with informants to develop to the point of personal friendship.

Being able to relate to the people studied as a participant is likely to help one gain access to information hidden from an observer and a better understanding of the "native" point of view. Using one's professional observer/researcher identity, on the other hand, often is necessary to legitimate one's presence in the field to public officials. It also may be useful to call on this status to gather information—for example, to schedule formal interviews and secure access to institutional and agency records. Most participant observation, therefore, involves both of these two master roles, albeit at different times and in relation to different informants. Almost always the roles are assumed by the same researcher, in what is called the "lone ranger" approach. However, because the roles are often difficult to balance, some researchers (e.g., Douglas, 1976; Snow, Benford, and Anderson, 1986) recommend a team approach, with different members of the team assuming different, complementary roles. This is what occurred in the homeless study. Snow acted primarily in the role of researcher and outside observer, while Anderson was a participant observer who interacted daily with homeless persons and witnessed, if not totally shared, their experiences.

Membership roles. Given some degree of participation, the field researcher faces crucial choices about what **membership role** to adopt and how to relate to others in the setting. One "may become involved in either *peripheral, active,* or *complete* membership roles" (Adler and Adler, 1987:33). Each role affects the level of trust and rapport that can be developed with others, the extent and type of information that can be gathered, and the personal consequences of the fieldwork experience.

Peripheral members are only marginally part of the settings they observe; they limit their involvement in the group's activities, do not strive for full member status, or may be blocked from more central membership because of their personal characteristics. In her study of a Chicano youth gang, for example, Ruth Horowitz (1986) did not participate in the group's illegal activities, and she was distinguished from the gang members by her different appearance, social background, gender, and age. Gang members at first identified her as a "lady" and eventually as a "lady reporter." This identity gained her acceptance and enabled her to develop trust and respect, so that she could ask questions about fights, school, and work as well as participate in some ongoing activities. Her reporter identity also inhibited others from treating her as a sexual object, suppressing sexual teasing and advances. However, it did not allow her to gather personal information about family, girlfriends, hopes, and aspirations.

Another common type of peripheral membership is that of the "buddy-researcher," a "blending of the roles of researcher and friend" (Snow, Benford, and Anderson, 1986). Anderson assumed this dual role in the homeless study. In so doing, he

made daily institutional rounds with homeless individuals and small groups, provided individuals with minor necessities, small loans (which weren't expected to be repaid), clothes, rides, and a sympathetic ear for their hopes, troubles, and fears. (Snow, Benford, and Anderson, 1986:384)

As a buddy, Anderson received as well as gave (e.g., accepting offers of beer and marijuana), and he avoided being too distinctive in dress and speech. This generated trust and good will, while his being forthright about his researcher status lent credibility to his inquiries into personal matters.

Active membership means that researchers assume a functional role in the setting, but retain sight of its temporary nature and do not fully commit themselves to the organization or group. In his study of a college basketball team, for example, Peter Adler (Adler and Adler, 1987:50) became an assistant coach, "serving as the team's interpersonal counselor, career counselor, and academic advisor." This made him an integral cog in the program, which allowed him to relate to others in a businesslike as well as personal way. Peripheral and active members may be either covert or overt about their researcher status. In Humphreys's study of homosexual encounters in public bathrooms, mentioned above, he performed the active membership role of "lookout" who watches for police or other unfriendly strangers.

Complete membership means becoming fully immersed in the setting and attaining full-member status. In his two-year study of the peace movement, for example, Robert Benford became an "ardent activist," an active, loyal, and enthusiastic participant who "unquestioningly embraced the movement's ideology, goals, and rhetoric" (Snow, Benford, and Anderson, 1986:383). Complete membership gains researchers the greatest acceptance by other members, which affords the opportunity to gather data on the most personal and intimate matters. In addition, researchers are "able to supplement the data they gather with the greatest degree of their own subjective insight" (Adler and Adler, 1987:81). On the other hand, complete membership is like going native; it is intense and time-consuming, may have profound personal consequences, and often creates a conflict between the member and researcher roles.

Once researchers assume a particular membership role, they still must decide how to present themselves in that role. Suppose, for example, that you are considering doing a study of medical technicians. You apply for a position as a laboratory assistant so that you will be able to observe the interactions of people in a medical research setting. How, then, will you present yourself? Will you allow people to teach you to do tasks that you might already know how to do? Will you pretend to be more naive than you are so that you can see how people will explain things to a know-nothing? Or will you flaunt your expertise so that you might become a valued member of the staff? Perhaps you think that people will tell you more if they have confidence in your abilities.

These are difficult choices, each with its particular consequences. Some field researchers recommend presenting oneself as naive or as an "acceptable incompetent" (Lofland and Lofland, 1995; Taylor and Bogdan, 1984). This can be an effective way of gaining information, because it gives the impression of someone who is ignorant, needs to be taught, and therefore is expected to ask questions. On the other hand, there are some settings—for example, in studies of higher status people and "deviants"—in which it is clearly better to show competence (see Gorden, 1975:227–28). Informants are likely to judge researchers on their knowledge as well as interest in areas in which the informant is expert. Asking people about their occupation from a starting point of total ignorance usually just irritates them. Moreover, criminals may con you unless you make it clear that you are in the know.

Ultimately, the best guideline for deciding what to do is to consider how one's behavior will affect the naturalness of the setting and how it will affect the development of trust and rapport with people in the setting. This appears to be the strategy that Joseph Kotarba (1980) followed in his study of acupuncture. His goal was to cultivate the trust of the physicians and staff people with whom he was in regular contact. Using what he calls the "good boy" approach, Kotarba was able to charm his way into everyone's good graces. And by being helpful and friendly to everyone, even people he personally disliked, Kotarba learned a great deal about the practice of acupuncture.

Finally, assuming that the observer's identity as a social researcher is revealed, how much should others be told about the research? It is generally not a good idea—in fact, rarely necessary—to reveal the details of a study. One reason is that this may make people more self-conscious of the researcher's presence (Taylor and Bogdan, 1984). It is also unnecessary to volunteer information. Perhaps the best rule to follow is Joseph Howell's (1973:381) advice to field researchers to "be honest about who you are and what you are doing. You need not tell more than is asked," he suggests, "but if you are caught lying, you are finished."

Gathering Information

Gathering information in the field presents several complex problems. To get some insight into the nature of these problems, let us imagine a hypothetical field study.

Suppose that you are going to do some field research. You have solved the problem of site selection by deciding to study the class you are currently taking in research methods; therefore, the classroom in which it meets and the surrounding campus constitute the site. Choosing this setting also simplifies the problem of self-presentation; after all, you are a *student* in the class. Given what you already know about the class and its participants, you also know that you want to do a participant observation study. You are ready, as Robert Park is reported to have encouraged his students at the University of Chicago, to "go get the seat of your pants dirty in *real* research" (McKinney, 1966). Or are you ready?

Before you begin your study, you should consider the nature of your participant–observer role in the class and the limitations that this places on what you can find out. As a student, it is extremely likely that your behavior and your perceptions of the instructor's behavior will be affected by your ego involvement in the class. You will, after all, be graded; you might even be graded on your class participation. Professional ethics will prevent the instructor from giving an honest account of his or her opinions about class members and the quality and significance of their participation. Thus you are probably in the best position to study the way a student culture develops in a class, as long as you do not play too central a role in it.[5]

With this objective in mind, how do you proceed? Immediately you face the dilemma of every other participant observer: How do you perform your student (participant) role, such as listening and taking class notes, at the same time that you observe all the other activities in the classroom? Initially you will be most keenly aware of your observer role. In fact, you will probably find so much going on that you will have to forego note taking and borrow someone else's notes! How will you observe and remember the following: where people sit; who asks questions; how people address one another and interact with one another; who speaks to whom before, after, and during class; who attends regularly; who is absent or late; what people say about assignments, exams, the instructor, and so forth? If you just think about everything that goes on in a class, you will see the enormity of the problem. The vast amount of information afloat in any social setting seems especially overwhelming at the beginning of a study when you are uncertain about what is relevant or important and what is not.

There are two crucial issues here:

1. How, when, and where will you record your observations?
2. What do you observe and record?

Recording observations. While observing in the field, you have three basic choices for managing and recording data: an audiotape or videotape recorder, a notebook and pencil, and your memory. Consider some of the implications of each of these choices. A tape recorder has the advantage of allowing you to record everything that is said. But there may be nonverbal behavior to observe, so you cannot rely solely on audiotaping. Both audiotape and videotape recorders also have the distinct disadvantage of being highly obtrusive. Taping a conversation with someone is the surest way to get that person to be very careful about his or her choice of words, at least at the outset.

The advantage of *getting* everything on tape also carries with it the problem of getting *everything* off the tape. Tape-recording formal interviews is often recommended (Lofland and Lofland, 1995). This allows the researcher to take sparse notes while attending to the interviewee and the flow of the conversation. It may prove useful as a backup to the written record. And in cases where talk in the set-ting is the major focus of observation, a verbatim record furnishes a primary source of data to which the researcher (and others) might return again and again. But for many purposes, taped recordings of group interactions produce useless overload. Since it takes about six to eight hours to transcribe one hour of a taped dialogue, you can quickly find yourself overwhelmed with transcriptions. The tendency to be swamped with data in field research is great anyway; so most people shun the use of tape recorders except for dictating notes in the field.

What about the second strategy of note-taking at the scene? Although gener-ally less obtrusive than mechanical devices, extensive note-taking can be a distrac-tion to subjects and researchers alike. This technique probably would prove very easy for recording classroom observations. In interviews outside the class, however, many people would find it annoying to be talking to someone who constantly looks away to take notes. Writing things down also is very conspicuous in many settings and is inconsistent with many participant roles, and it is likely to interrupt the nor-mal flow of activities. Imagine taking notes in a bar or church or while interacting with drug dealers.

The third choice for "recording" observations is to rely on your memory. Given the caveats about taped recordings and note-taking, it is easy to understand why it is important for field researchers to develop their ability to remember. Nonetheless, practitioners of field research warn against relying heavily on one's memory: "memory is a very poor recording device" (Bernard, 1994:181); "the human mind tends to forget much that has occurred and to do so rather quickly" (Lofland and Lofland, 1995:89). So what do you do?

First, nearly all field researchers take **field jottings**—"little phrases, quotes, key words, and the like that you put down during the observation" (Lofland and Lofland, 1995:90). The general rule of thumb is to make the jottings as inconspic-uous as possible. Also, the field researcher needs to be alert to the opportunities nat-urally afforded for jotting. In her study of behavior in bars, Sherri Cavan (1966) went to the bathroom, an easily accountable act, to jot down notes. In the homeless study, Anderson often jotted down key phrases and longer quotes immediately af-ter the end of a conversation. If such opportunities do not present themselves, the researcher must rely on mental notes and quick jottings to help trigger the later re-call of important details.

Second, to guard against forgetting, the field researcher should write up **field notes** at the end of each day, or as soon after the observations as possible, just as Anderson did in the homeless study. Based on field jottings and memory, field notes provide an extensive, detailed record of events. They are the crucial data of field research, analogous to the survey researcher's completed interviews or ques-tionnaires. Field researchers, therefore, must be extremely disciplined and rigorous about recording notes. Indeed, the actual writing of notes may take as much time as the observation.

Determining what to observe and record. In field research, the "primary sources of data are the *words and actions* of the people you are interviewing or observing" (Lofland and Lofland, 1995:70). The complete observer will have to rely on listening and observing, while the participant has access to the broadest range of data. But in either case, field notes should provide as detailed and complete a *description* of events as possible. Lofland and Lofland (1995:93) point out that

> each new physical setting and person encountered merits a description. You should also record changes in the physical setting or persons. Since you are likely to encounter the same settings and people again and again, you need not repeat such descriptions, but only augment them as changes occur.

> Observers often draw maps into their fieldnotes, indicating approximate layouts and the physical placement of people in scenes, as well as their gross movements through a period of observation. Since the notes will be chronologically arranged, you should also keep records of the approximate times at which various events occur.

When recording field notes, the first rule is be concrete; take note of specific behavioral details; and avoid attaching your own abstract labels to things. As Joy Browne (1976a:77) advises, "it is crucial . . . to collect only data, not analysis. Don't interpolate or integrate—just remember. What is important or trivial is usually not evident until much later. So don't sift, just collect." In other words, force yourself to see first and conceptualize later. Earlier we alluded to Lyn Lofland's study, in which she observed the "grooming behavior" of people about to enter public places. "Grooming" was the conceptual category Lofland arrived at on the basis of more specific, concrete observations. Here are two examples of her observations of people preparing to enter a building:

> A young man approaches the door. He carries a briefcase in one hand; the other hangs free. As he nears the door he uses his free hand to brush the hair back from his forehead, then opens the door with that hand and enters.

> Two girls come toward the entrance. About three yards from the door, each begins to pass her hand over her hair, as though brushing it. They continue this until they reach the door. Apparently finished, they stop for a few seconds in front of the door while continuing the process. (Lofland, 1973:141)

As the research progresses, you might want to intersperse your record of what actually happens with your own feelings and ideas. For example, you might observe in the classroom that two students are looking intently and steadily out the window during the instructor's lecture; at the same time you feel bored and sense that others are also. You should not, however, confuse or confound your impression of "boredom" with your factual observation of students "gazing" out the window. Both kinds of observations are important, but should be kept separate (Browne, 1976a). One way to separate different kinds of notes is to assign codes (e.g., "O" for observation, "P" for personal reaction, "A" for analytical idea, "M" for methodological aside).[6]

Besides firsthand observation, the field researcher's primary source of data, you will undoubtedly obtain much information by questioning the professor and other students in the class. In the homeless study, Anderson frequently elicited information in casual field encounters by making intentional comments such as "I don't get it," "I don't understand," or "I didn't think you were a regular Sally [Salvation Army] user" (Snow and Anderson, 1987:1343). Snow and Anderson (1987:1344) also supplemented their field observations with in-depth interviews of "six homeless individuals who had been on the streets for various lengths of time, ranging from two months to 14 years."

Finally, field researchers frequently supplement observations and conversations with other sources of information, such as official records (e.g., agency records, census data, court transcriptions) and personal documents (e.g., diaries, letters, scrapbooks). Documentary data may prove especially useful in the early stages of field research, as a means of learning about the history and the physical and social characteristics of a setting. For example, Snow and Anderson examined pamphlets, records, and reports of various agencies serving homeless people. This was helpful in orienting their study, for example, providing information on the growth of homelessness in Austin and indicating how agencies (e.g., the police) dealt with the homeless. Documentary data also can serve the same purposes as interviewing—that is, to gather and cross-check factual information.

Institutional data also were collected in the homeless study to complement fieldwork findings. After several months in the field, Snow and Anderson decided to track a random sample of homeless people through selected institutions (see Snow et al., 1986; Snow, Baker, and Anderson, 1989). Because the Salvation Army operated Austin's only public shelter and was also the only facility in the city that provided free breakfast and dinner, nearly all of the Austin homeless had utilized the Salvation Army services at least once. In addition, all first-time users were required to fill out a brief questionnaire that asked for name and social security number as well as other background information. After receiving permission to use this identifying information, Snow and Anderson drew a random sample of 800 names. They then negotiated access to the records of six other local and state agencies (e.g., the city police department, the state department of mental health and mental retardation), and they tracked their sample through these institutions. An important finding related to the mental health of homeless persons: Only 10 percent of their sample had been institutionalized one or more times, and the greatest proportion of these was for substance abuse rather than purely psychiatric problems. This and related findings contradicted many estimates and claims regarding the prevalence of profound psychiatric illness among the homeless.

One of the features of field research that makes describing it difficult is that it "is not a single method gathering a single kind of information" (Zelditch, 1962:567), but a blend of methods and techniques. The ways of collecting data outlined above constitute a very short list of the means for understanding the social world used by field researchers. For example, in her study of behavior in public places, Lyn Lofland drew on a broad range of materials, including not only field observations but personal experiences, anecdotes, interviews, and historical and anthropological studies. Anything that promotes understanding is grist for the field researcher's mill.

Analyzing the Data

This brings us to the data analysis phase of field research. Unlike in other research approaches, data analysis occurs throughout the period of data collection. The act of recording field notes itself is the beginning of analyzing and making sense of field data.

A major goal of field research, as we have often noted, is to get an insider's view of reality. The data collected by the field researcher should render, therefore, a richly detailed picture of social life that describes the people on their own terms, graphically capturing their language and letting them speak for themselves. Descriptions in field research thus often involve the presentation of selected anecdotes and quotes from informants. They also provide concrete details about the setting and the actions and incidents that occur there.

Like any other form of data, however, such descriptions cannot speak for themselves. Rather, they must be integrated with concepts and ideas that help to order and explain the insider's view of reality. Description alone, in other words, is not enough. Investigators also must formulate a theoretical understanding that lends coherence to their data. This does not mean that field researchers enter the field with preset hypotheses and theoretical formulations. Many field researchers believe, in fact, that fieldwork should be directed toward the development or "discovery" of theory. Barney Glaser and Anselm Strauss (1967) refer to theory that is generated from the data as **grounded theory**, as distinguished from theory logically derived from a priori assumptions. The "grounded" approach advocates loosely structured research designs that allow theoretical ideas to "emerge from the field in the course of the study" (Miles and Huberman, 1994:17). Some field researchers contend that field studies can be used both to develop and to verify theory (see Emerson, 1983). Others point out that field researchers invariably bring *some* orienting ideas and general research questions to fieldwork that direct their data-gathering efforts (Miles and Huberman, 1994). But irrespective of these positions, the field approach to data analysis generally entails some attempt to summarize and order the data by identifying themes, concepts, propositions, and theories. How, then, does one go about doing this?

In the broadest sense, data analysis consists of "the search for patterns in data and for ideas that help explain the existence of those patterns" (Bernard, 1994:360). This process can be broken down into three interrelated tasks: (1) organizing information and identifying patterns, (2) developing ideas, and (3) drawing and verifying conclusions.

Organizing information. The raw data of the field researcher—field notes—present several problems for the data analyst. Words are harder to process than numbers; field notes can contain a massive amount of words; and there is usually little inherent structure in field notes other than a sequential and narrative account of one's observations and experiences. In the homeless study, Snow and Anderson ended up with over 600 double-spaced typed pages of field notes. Their initial task was to reduce this bulk of information into meaningful and analyzable units. To do this, they used the field researcher's most common method of organizing field notes—coding.

Coding, which is a common aspect of all social research (see chapter 14), consists of assigning symbols or numbers to categories. In survey research, numerical codes are assigned to response categories to facilitate data processing and analysis. The codes can be and usually are established before data collection, when the survey instrument is complete. In field research, codes are applied to transcribed field notes to categorize words or "chunks" of words, such as a sentence or paragraph, into units of meaning (Miles and Huberman, 1994). Because one is often working toward theory rather than from theory, the codes are usually developed from field observations. In fact, from the grounded theory standpoint, it is inappropriate to approach the field with preconceived notions or *pre*coded protocols detailing how the world is to be understood. Instead, codes (*post*codes if you will) are developed as part of making sense of the world.

To organize their field notes, Snow and Anderson used a two-step process: (1) They extracted from their field notes "data entries" that varied from a single sentence to several pages in length, and (2) they assigned these entries to one or more of three broad categories that emerged over time: focal settings, cultural domains, and homeless individuals. The twenty-four focal settings consisted of institutions and sites relevant to the daily lives of the homeless. The thirty cultural domains pertained "to categories of meaning, events, and problems that constitute the social world and life-style of the homeless (e.g., drinking and alcohol, drugs, food and eating, sleeping and shelter, social relationships, and work)" (Snow and Anderson, 1987:1345). Through this coding scheme, Snow and Anderson discovered the importance of self and identity issues in the lives of the homeless, as indicated by the number of data entries in this domain.

Developing ideas. Beyond coding, there are few guidelines and procedures for analyzing field data. In part this is because it is hard to catalogue the sources of creative insight. When an insight does occur, during coding or the proces of going over field notes and reviewing the day's observations, it is important to get it down immediately in writing. To do this, field researchers recommend writing memos. **Memos** are small pieces of analysis, usually a paragraph or two, that capture emergent ideas that help make sense of the reality one is encountering (Lofland and Lofland, 1995).

One way to focus your thinking in the field is to continually ask questions about the data. Lofland and Lofland (1995:123–48) identified several questions that can help orient field researcher's thinking. Below is a paraphrasing of some of these questions:

> What type of unit (e.g., encounter, relationship, group, organization) is this?
> What is the unit's structure and characteristics?
> What are its causes?
> What are its consequences?
> How frequently does this action or event occur?
> What social processes are occurring in this setting?
> What is the situation people face and what strategies do they use to deal with it?

In the homeless study, recall, Snow and Anderson (1991) were interested in how homeless people adapted to their environment and the factors that shaped this adaptation. This research question led them to identify three main types of adaptation and orientation among the homeless and five distinct types of organizational response. The types of organizational response ranged from the "accommodative," as exemplified by the sustenance-oriented caretaking of the Salvation Army, to "containment," as represented by the harassment of the city police.

Another, often overlooked, strategy for analyzing field data is counting. Matthew Miles and A. Michael Huberman (1994:253) note that "there is a lot of counting going on when judgments of qualities are being made. When we identify a theme or pattern, we're isolating something that (a) happens a number of times and (b) consistently happens in a specific way. The 'number of times' and 'consistency' judgments are based on counting." Counts and comparisons are also implied, they point out, whenever we make generalizations or use words such as "important" and "recurring." Resorting to counts can serve not only to verify specific hypotheses and protect against bias but also to help see the data more clearly.

One working hypothesis that emerged in the homeless study was that types of identity talk among the homeless varied according to how long the individual had been on the streets. For example, Snow and Anderson (1987) identified three types of "distancing" statements: (1) categoric distancing, which involved dissociation from the general street role identity; (2) specific or situational distancing, which included dissociation from specific groupings of homeless individuals, such as "novices" and the institutionally dependent; and (3) institutional distancing, indicated by expressions of disdain for street institutions, such as the Salvation Army and soup kitchens. Categoric distancing was thought to be more prevalent among those who had spent the least amount of time on the streets, whereas the other forms of distancing would be more likely to be used by those more entrenched in street life. To examine this relationship, Snow and Anderson divided homeless people into groups with varying amounts of time on the street and then counted the number of categoric, specific, and institutional distancing statements made by individuals in each group. Table 10.1 presents these data. Notice that categoric distancing statements were made by 80 percent of the individuals who had been on the streets less than six months, compared with 15.4 percent or less of those who had been on the streets for six months or more.

TABLE 10.1. **Types of Distancing by Time on the Streets**

	Type of distancing			
Time on the streets	CATEGORIC	SPECIFIC	INSTITUTIONAL	TOTAL (N)
Less than 6 months	80.0%	6.7	13.3	100.0% (15)
6 months to 2 years	10.0%	60.0	30.0	100.0% (10)
2 years to 4 years	4.3%	56.5	39.1	99.9% (23)
More than 4 years	15.4%	23.1	61.5	100.0% (13)

Source: Snow and Anderson (1987), p. 1353. Used by permission of the authors and University of Chicago Press.

Drawing and verifying conclusions. In the end, field researchers generally seek to identify the larger meaning of their findings, especially as these relate to existing theoretical frameworks. In Snow and Anderson's research, this meant explaining the patterned identity talk that they had identified. Why did it occur? How were the patterns they observed related to existing role-identity theory? One of their conclusions pertained to the importance of distancing behavior and other identity talk among the homeless. They questioned the assumption that the need for self-esteem is secondary to the satisfaction of physiological survival needs. Maintaining a sense of meaning and self-worth, they contend, may be especially critical for the survival of homeless and other marginal members because it enables them to "retain a sense of self and thus their humanity" (Snow and Anderson, 1987:1365).

To check the validity of such interpretations it is always a good idea to entertain alternative explanations. Explanations should be generated early and often and checked repeatedly against observations. One might seek out alternative explanations from others, for example, colleagues. A time-honored tradition in field research is to get feedback from respondents. Finally, as a further validity check on conclusions, the researcher could look for negative evidence, that is, data that oppose or are inconsistent with a particular conclusion (Miles and Huberman, 1994).

Because of the relatively unstructured nature of field research, it is critically important to consider ways of avoiding bias and enhancing validity. For the participant observer, this process begins early, when he or she attempts to establish rapport and trust with those in the field setting, in order to reduce the problem of reactivity. It continues throughout fieldwork in other ways. Researchers should constantly seek corroborating feedback for their observations from others in the setting. They should check for inconsistencies between informants and find out why they disagree (Bernard, 1994). And when possible, they should check informants' reports against other sources of data, such as institutional records. The general rule of thumb, which we discuss further in chapter 12, is to seek out a variety of evidence to support one's conclusions, for the greater the variety and the more abundant the evidence, the stronger the conclusions.

Summary

Field research implies an attempt to develop an understanding of human behavior as it is defined by the subjects themselves and/or as it is related to the situation in which the behavior occurs. To gain such understanding requires, first of all, the observation of persons in natural settings. Such observations may be augmented by the analysis of documents and virtually anything else that enables the researcher to get an insider's view of reality.

Traditionally, field research has tended to focus on the downtrodden and, more recently, on aspects of everyday life. It is most advisable to adopt this approach under the following conditions: (1) when one wishes to study a fleeting or dynamic situation, (2) when it is essential to preserve the interrelatedness of the person and situation, (3) when methodological problems, resources, or ethics preclude the adoption of other research strategies, and (4) when very little is known about the topic under investigation. However, field research is an inferior way of testing specific causal hypotheses, a very time-consuming and sometimes inefficient method of gathering data, necessarily limited to a few settings, and highly dependent on the observational skills of the researcher.

Field researchers are flexible about research design, working out the specifics of their approach during the course of the study. In sampling, for example, a flexible approach is necessitated by the nature of the social units studied and by the delicate problems of entering the field and establishing field relations. Small nonrandom samples typify the selection of subjects and settings. In the field, the general approach to sampling is to enhance the informational value of evidence by maximizing variation. Specific strategies include the serial selection of units and sampling analytical dimensions relevant to the study.

The foundational method of data collection in field research is firsthand observation. Field observation varies in terms of structure, with less structured observation characterizing the early phases of research. Highly structured observation entails formalized rules for extracting information specifying when and where observations will take place, who will make the observations, and what will be observed. Field observation also varies according to the researcher's degree of participation in the setting being investigated. At one extreme is the intentionally unobtrusive, nonparticipant observer; at the other is the engaged participant observer. Participant observation is far more common than nonparticipant observation as an inclusive method, perhaps because being a participant is seen as crucial to gaining an insider's view of the world. However, the marginal position of the participant observer makes this a difficult and often stressful role to play.

Field interviewing supplements field observations by eliciting information about unobserved events, different perspectives on events, and informants' thoughts and feelings. This may occur through casual questioning that flows from ordinary participation in a setting or by means of interviews formally arranged with informants. Interview guides consisting of question topics and questions direct formal interviews, although the order and precise wording of questions depends on what is said, as in any normal conversation.

Selecting an appropriate setting constitutes the first stage of fieldwork. For reasons of accessibility and interest, some researchers recommend "starting where you are," which has a strong tradition in field research. Gaining access to a setting is the second stage. In a formal organization this is usually a matter of getting the permission of those in charge. Public settings are more readily accessible, but require ingenuity in interacting with people and finding informants. In private settings, the principal means of gaining entry is the development of relations with key informants followed by snowball sampling.

The third stage of field research, which begins with the task of gaining entry, is presenting oneself to those in the setting. Researchers must decide, first, on the extent to which they will reveal themselves as scientific observers and the extent to which they will participate in the setting. Although not uncommon, covert field research presents ethical problems and is frowned on by some investigators. More commonly, field researchers combine undisguised observation and participation, while varying the enactment of these two roles during the course of a single study.

Second, participant or membership roles must be developed by the researcher, who may become a peripheral, active, or complete member in the field setting. Finally, in presenting oneself, it is important to consider how one's behavior will affect the development of trust and rapport with those in the setting.

The final two stages of field research, gathering and analyzing information, are concurrent. To collect data, field researchers rely on field jottings and mental notes to record detailed field notes as soon after their observations as possible. Besides firsthand observation, they also may question participants and consult records and personal documents. From this information, the researcher develops a rich description of events that conveys the experience of someone who "was there." Furthermore, throughout the process of gathering information, the researcher develops concepts and tentative hypotheses in order to make sense of the data. Aids to identifying patterns and gaining insights include coding field notes, writing memos, asking questions, and counting. It is also important to entertain alternative explanations and perform various validity checks, for example, by seeking corroborative evidence.

Key Terms

field research	*gatekeepers*
methodological empathy	*key informants*
theoretical sampling	*covert research*
structured observation	*membership role*
unstructured observation	*peripheral membership*
nonparticipant observation	*active membership*
participant observation	*complete membership*
going native	*field jottings*
field interviewing	*field notes*
informant	*grounded theory*
in-depth (intensive) interviewing	*coding*
interview guide	*memos*

Review Questions and Problems

1. Why is it misleading to use the labels "qualitative" and "observational" to characterize field research?

2. What is (a) a case study and (b) ethnography? How is each related to field research?

3. What is methodological empathy? How does it differ from sympathy?

4. When is it advisable to adopt the field research method of inquiry?

5. Identify the strengths and weaknesses of field research compared with experiments and surveys.

6. How does the field researcher's approach to research design differ from that of the experimenter and survey researcher?

7. Why do field researchers generally use nonrandom selection of settings and subjects?

8. Contrast the general sampling strategy of field research with that of survey research. How do they differ with respect to purposes and specific techniques?

9. How does field observation differ from casual, everyday observation? How does it differ from general scientific observation?

10. Distinguish between nonparticipant and participant observation. Which is more common in field research?

11. Describe how field observations can vary in structure. What are the advantages of structured field observation?

12. Why is it advantageous for a researcher to become a participant in the setting under observation?

13. How can participant observation be an emotionally stressful experience?

14. What is meant by "going native"?

15. How can field interviewing complement field observation?

16. Distinguish among structured interviewing, casual interviewing, and in-depth interviewing.

17. What are the principal stages of field research?

18. Why do Lofland and Lofland recommend "starting where you are" as a way of selecting a research setting?

19. Describe the basic approaches to gaining access to (a) formal organizations, (b) public settings, and (c) private settings.

20. Explain the functions of gatekeepers and key informants in relation to gaining access.

21. What are the four master roles for presenting oneself in the field? Which roles are most common in participant observation? Why is this the case?

22. When is covert research likely to pose ethical problems for the field researcher?

23. Describe the range of membership roles that the participant observer may perform. How do these differ in terms of (a) ability to develop trust and rapport, (b) access to various kinds of information, and (c) personal consequences for the researcher?

24. What guidelines should field researchers follow in deciding what to reveal about their research to those observed?

25. Discuss the disadvantages of a tape recorder, on-the-spot note-taking, and memory as means of recording information in the field.

26. How and when do field researchers record their field observations? What do they record?

27. What is meant by grounded theory? How does this term apply to field research?

28. What is coding and how does it contribute to data analysis in field research?

29. Describe three field research techniques for facilitating the development of theoretical ideas.

30. In what ways can field researchers enhance the validity of their findings and conclusions?

NOTES

1. Robert Park (see Box 10.2) was instrumental in establishing this focus. Trained as a journalist, Park was the press agent for the famous black educator Booker T. Washington when they co-authored a book entitled *The Man Farthest Down*. This book attracted the attention of sociologist W. I. Thomas, who invited Park to leave the Tuskegee Institute in Alabama, where he had worked with Washington, to come to the University of Chicago. Park did so in 1913, ultimately becoming chair of the sociology department and establishing the intellectual tradition of studying "those farthest down."

2. The one exception to this is structured observation, which relies on a well-developed scheme for coding behavior. The researcher observing children at play, for example, may record specific features of the play that are designed to test clearly stated hypotheses. Perhaps the hypothesis is that boys' games are more complex than girls' games. This would require pre-established observational categories based on such characteristics as the size of the play group, the rules of the games, the nature of the different task roles performed by players, and so forth (see Lever, 1978).

3. Robert Emerson (1981) likens structured observation studies to surveys insofar as each employs designs with prespecified procedures for when, where, and what to observe and sample. The only difference is the mode of data collection: asking questions versus direct observation.

4. This account of the Austin Homeless Study was drawn from several articles cited throughout the following discussion, and it was written before the publication of Snow and Anderson's 1993 book reporting their research.

5. By contrast, a student making the same kind of observations in a course in a different college, after getting the instructor's permission to observe, would face a different set of constraints. This setting probably would provide more access to the instructor's opinions, but less access to the student network outside the class. It also presents the problem of whether the student researcher should conceal his or her status in the class from other students.

6. H. Russell Bernard (1994:183–84) recommends keeping a separate personal diary to help one "deal with loneliness, fear, and other emotions that make fieldwork difficult" and provides "an outlet for writing things that you don't want to become part of a public record."

11

✔

Research Using Available Data

As different as experiments, surveys, and field studies may seem, they do have one common feature that distinguishes them from the methodological approach described in this chapter: Each involves the firsthand collection of data. Doing any of these three kinds of research entails gathering information, either by questioning or direct observation, from the people and groups who are the objects of study. Thus the data originate with the research; they are not there before the research is undertaken.

By contrast, the fourth general strategy for doing social research is to make use of available data. Sometimes the researcher uses data that were produced by another investigator for a completely different research purpose. At other times, one may use available data that were not produced for any research purpose at all. The variety of such data is tremendous; it is limited only by the researcher's imagination. As you will see in this chapter, that imagination has found sources of data in letters and diaries, government and court records, newspapers, and magazines. Even tombstones and graffiti have been used as the raw material for social research.

We begin this chapter by considering several studies that suggest the sources of and possibilities for using available data. With reference to these studies, we discuss major advantages, limitations, and methodological issues related to this approach. While we identify common issues, this discussion glosses over some important variations in the use and analysis of secondhand data. The diverse data sources give rise to very different forms of analysis, with distinctive research purposes. Therefore, we also take a brief but closer look at two of these approaches to available-data research: historical analysis and content analysis.

Sources of Available Data

The sources of available data may be placed in five broad categories: (1) public documents and official records, including the extensive archives of the Census Bureau; (2) private documents; (3) mass media; (4) physical, nonverbal materials; and (5) social science data archives. These categories provide a useful summary of data sources, although they do not constitute a mutually exclusive typology. Any data source may be placed in one or more of these categories. Also, analysts may draw on more than one data source in any given study.

Public Documents and Official Records

Exemplifying the available-data approach is the historian who searches for traces of events and processes from the past. More than any other source of evidence, the historian relies on the written record. Writing is regarded as a mark of civilization. The ubiquity of the written record is easily demonstrated. Just attempt to compile a list of all the different written materials that you encounter on a given day. This book is one example; so is the bookstore receipt that you received with its purchase, or the checkout slip filed in order to remove a copy from the library. The advertising brochure that first brought this book to the attention of your instructor is part of the written record; so is your grade for the course in which the book is being used. Each of these could find its way into the hands of a researcher using available data. The researcher could be studying anything from the reading level of textbooks to the costs of higher education; from the marketing strategies of textbook publishers to the achievement of students in different types of schools.

A great deal of the written record is public. Documents created to ensure the normal functioning of offices and departments are maintained at every level of government (not to mention by virtually every private business and organization) in every society throughout the world. These include the proceedings of government bodies, court records, state laws, and city ordinances. Many government agencies, most notably the Bureau of the Census, also maintain numerous volumes of official statistics. Add to this birth and death certificates, directories, almanacs, and publication indexes such as the *New York Times Index* and *Reader's Guide to Periodical Literature*, and one can imagine the massive information available from public records.

An especially rich data source is **vital statistics**: data on births, deaths, marriages, divorces, and the like. By state law, all births must be recorded, and death records must be filed before burial permits can be obtained. Birth records provide information not only on the child born but also on the parents, including father's full name, address, age, and usual occupation. These data make possible research ranging from a study of social class and fertility to a study of maternal age and the incidence of twin births. Similarly, death records contain, in addition to the usual biographical information, data on cause of death; length of illness (where applicable); whether injuries were accidental, homicidal, or self-inflicted; and the time and place of death. With such data, all sorts of demographic and epidemiological studies (studies dealing with the incidence or prevalence of disease in an area) are possible. Indeed, much of what we know about death has come from the analysis of death records. Ordinarily, the researcher obtains these records from an agency such as the National Center for Health Statistics in Washington, D.C., which compiles data for the nation as a whole, or from international organizations such as the United Nations, which compile such statistics for the world.[1]

One of the earliest sociological studies to make use of official records—in this case, death records—was Emile Durkheim's classic study *Suicide* (1951), which we discussed at length in chapter 2. In the late eighteenth century, many European nations began to compile data from death certificates, including cause of death as well as personal characteristics of the deceased such as sex, age, and marital status. Several scholars before Durkheim focused on suicide as a specific cause and further compiled and published data relating suicide rates to such variables as religion, season of the year, gender, and marital status. Using these data, Durkheim rejected several hypotheses popular at the time, such as that suicide was the result of mental illness, and ultimately arrived at his influential theory that a lack of social integration contributes to suicides. Supporting his theory were data showing that suicide rates were lowest when social ties were strong (as among persons who are married and members of religions that emphasize social cohesion) and highest when social ties were weak (as among the divorced and members of religions that emphasize individualism).

Another early example of the use of public data sources is Sanford Winston's study (1932) of the sex ratio at birth (the ratio of males born alive to females born alive) among upper-class families in the 1920s. Winston hypothesized that upper-class families, because of social factors and their knowledge of methods of birth control, would show a strong preference for male children that would be evident in the sex ratio. He obtained data on 5466 families from genealogical records published in the *Abridged Compendium of American Genealogy*. First he identified the sex of each child in each birth order (first child, second child, etc.). Then he computed sex ratios (the number of males divided by the number of females multiplied by 100) for three groups: (1) for last-born children in families estimated to be complete (e.g., where the mother was 45 years old or had been childless for at least nine years), (2) "for all children of incomplete families," and (3) "for all children of completed families, omitting the last child" (p. 228). In comparison with the latter two groups, the sex ratio of last-born children in completed families was higher (117.6 versus 108.8 and 109.3), indicating a preference for males and a concomitant decision to practice birth control when that preference was realized. Interestingly, when family size was controlled, the ratio of males to females among last-born children was highest in completed two-child families (sex ratio = 133.1).

Kai Erikson (1966) used several public documents to study deviance in Puritan New England. As a way of examining how the community defined deviance and, in so doing, defined its moral boundaries, Erikson examined three "crime waves" among the Puritans over a sixty-year period. The first wave, called the antinomian controversy of 1636–38, developed over a conflict concerning who was qualified to preach the Gospel in Boston and culminated in a civil trial for sedition and the banishing of two prominent citizens from the colony. The second wave involved violent, court-ordered persecutions of the Quakers from the 1650s to the 1660s, and the third wave consisted of the famous witchcraft hysteria centered in Salem in 1692. To analyze these events, Erikson relied on the extensive records of the Essex County Court and on the writings of some principals in these conflicts, such as Anne Hutchinson and the Puritan ministers John Winthrop and Cotton Mather. He concluded, in support of his hypothesis, that these historical events were in effect created by the community in order to establish its moral boundaries.

Stephen Sales (1973) made use of multiple sources of available data, including official statistics, in his study of threat and authoritarianism. Authoritarianism is a personality pattern characterized by a tendency to be unduly respectful of those in positions of authority. Authoritarians tend to admire power and toughness; to be superstitious, cynical, and opposed to introspection; and to believe in harsh treatment of those who violate group norms. Sales tested the hypothesis that these tendencies would be especially likely to occur in response to a threatening environment, such as exists in a period of economic depression. He compared existing data from the 1920s, a period of low economic threat in the United States, with data from the 1930s, the time of the Great Depression. For example, given that authoritarians wish to condemn and punish violators of in-group values, Sales expected an increase in support for police forces during the 1930s. He therefore examined the city budgets of two cities, New York and Pittsburgh, which were readily available to him. When he calculated the proportions of the budget devoted to the police force and the fire department (which he used as a control), he found that appropriations were higher for the police and lower for the fire department in the 1930s than in the 1920s. Moreover, this increase in budgeting for the police did not result from an increase in crime, because when Sales consulted the *Uniform Crime Reports for the United States*, he found a decline in crime from the 1920s to the 1930s.

Sales also found a variety of other data from public records consistent with the hypothesis that authoritarianism increased in the 1930s. For example, as indicated by the *United States Catalog*, *Cumulative Book Index*, and *Reader's Guide to Periodical Literature*, there were more books and articles published on astrology (authoritarians are superstitious) and fewer books and articles on psychoanalysis and psychotherapy (authoritarians are opposed to introspection).

Perhaps the most widely used public storehouse of data is that collected and maintained by the U.S. Bureau of the Census. The bureau gathers an enormous amount of information. According to the Constitution, every person in the nation must be counted at least once every ten years. Data from these decennial censuses, which began in 1790, are made available in two different forms: aggregate and individual. Aggregate data are released within months of their collection and describe various characteristics of the population of the states, counties, metropolitan areas, cities and towns, neighborhood tracts, and blocks. The censuses of population and housing gather detailed information on the composition of every household in the country, including data on the age, gender, race, and marital status of each person, and numerous household characteristics, such as value of home or monthly rent, number of rooms, and presence of telephone.[2] Social scientists have used these data to study everything from the ecology of cities to residential mobility to racial inequality and segregation.

Using the 1980 Census of Population and other census reports, Reynolds Farley and Walter Allen (1987) examined the difference that race makes in the lives of Americans. How does racial identity influence opportunities and outcomes for blacks and whites? Overall, their data showed "that for the *majority* of black Americans life continues to be experienced as 'separate and unequal' " (1987:410). While there has been undeniable progress for blacks since mid-century, with the gap between blacks and whites narrowing on many indicators, there are still substantial racial differences. They found, for example, that (1) whites live on average six years longer than blacks; (2) black–white residential segregation remains very high, which perpetuates segregation in the schools; (3) the unemployment rate for black men remains twice the level for white men; and (4) black men in 1980 earned 38 percent less than white men overall and 14 percent less when controlling for educational attainment, years of work experience, and region of residence.

Farley and Frey (1994) also used 1990 and 1980 census data to trace trends in racial segregation in 232 metropolitan areas with substantial black populations. Although blacks continued to be highly racially segregated, there were small declines in segregation in the 1980s. Young, southern and western areas were the least segregated and also showed the largest decreases in segregation in the 1980s.[3]

By aggregating data before release, the Census Bureau protects the privacy of individual persons, which the bureau is sworn to do. However, after a period of seventy-two years, individual census records—known as the **manuscript census**—are released to the general public. (See Box 11.1 for an example of research using the manuscript census.) Beginning with the 1960 census, the bureau also has made available individual-level data (actual census responses) on a sample of the population, called the **Public Use Microdata Sample** (PUMS). To ensure confidentiality, the bureau removes names, addresses, and all other personal identifying information from these sample files. In addition, the bureau conducts a monthly survey of some 50,000 households sampled in 754 sample areas throughout the fifty states. Known as the *Current Population Survey* (CPS), this provides, among other demographic information, the monthly unemployment figures published by the government. (Farley and Allen drew on both the PUMS and the CPS in their analyses.) Finally, there are regular censuses of business, manufacturers, agriculture, and other institutions.[4]

BOX 11.1

Using the Manuscript Census in Social Research:
Nineteenth-Century Shaker Demographics

Social scientists have been interested for many years in a religious group that has almost disappeared. The Shakers developed in England as a branch of the Quakers around the middle of the eighteenth century. In 1774 the group's prophetess Ann Lee came to America with eight others to start one of the most interesting chapters in the history of American religion. The Shakers lived a rigidly communitarian life, requiring that new members give up all personal property. They also did not believe in marriage, cohabitation, sex, or procreation. Men and women lived in different houses, and members of the opposite sex were prohibited from talking to one another in the halls or crossing one another's paths.

As celibates, the Shakers' principal means of gathering new members was voluntary joining. Yet, in spite of their austere living conditions, the sect survived for over 200 years and even thrived for a time, growing from the nine members who immigrated to America to a population that standard reference works estimate at 17,000 at the height of the movement. Some believe that this is an underestimate; indeed, the director of the Shaker Museum and Library at Sabbathday Lake, Maine, estimates that

"total membership ran to about sixty-four thousand" (Kephart, 1982:208). Other estimates are more modest; Mark Holloway (1966:70) claims that in 1830, 5000 members were scattered among eighteen different Shaker communities. What was the actual popular success of the Shaker experiment? How many Shakers were there? The
fragmentary and scattered nature of the data make all of the foregoing estimates very
rough guesses. However, William Sims Bainbridge (1982) put the original enumeration schedules of the U.S. census to good use in estimating the Shaker population in
the latter half of the nineteenth century. In so doing, he also provides insights into the
nature of recruitment, defection, and the gradual decline of this sect.

Seventy-two years after each census, the original schedules on which census enumerators recorded their data are released to the general public. These data are available on microfilm in twelve regional archives around the country. The organization of
the data files facilitates the location of individuals by persons interested in learning
more about their ancestors. In fact, the 1900 census files have a "soundex" system that
allows the genealogist to trace the location of heads of households by identifying their
names phonetically. The social scientist faces several problems in using these data.
For the first six censuses, 1790–1840, relatively little information was collected on individuals, because only heads of households were identified by name. For later censuses the sheer volume of data presents a barrier to many researchers. Recently, methods have been developed for sampling census records (see Johnson, 1978). But the
small population of Shakers made sampling inappropriate.

From historical accounts, Bainbridge first identified twenty-two colonies of
Shakers in the period 1840–1900. These colonies were located in eight states (five in
Massachusetts, four each in New York and Ohio, three in Maine, two each in New
Hampshire and Kentucky, and one each in Connecticut and Florida). Since Bainbridge
could not know in advance the last names of Shakers, he was forced to search through
some 150 rolls of microfilm reporting data for these eight states. And because the
manuscript schedules for 1890 do not exist, having been destroyed in a fire, he decided to examine the data for every other census in the period 1840–1900. Describing
the difficulties in researching the census of 1840, Bainbridge (1982:354) says that

> when one is scanning through a town which is supposed to contain a Shaker
> colony, and finds a household with 215 members, one may guess the Shakers
> have been located. But this presumption is not good enough. For one thing,
> Shaker colonies were divided into "families," sometimes as many as six of these
> subunits composing a colony, and some of the smaller families could be mis-
> taken for other kinds of groups, and vice versa. Some families in 1840 were la-
> beled "Shakers," but most were not. Many could be identified because the "head
> of household" whose name was recorded was a prominent Shaker mentioned in
> published histories.

Through painstaking cross-checking (e.g., using the 1850 census to identify some
names listed in 1840), Bainbridge estimated the Shaker population at 3489 in 1840
and 855 in 1900. By analyzing the age and sex distributions of Shakers, he also
showed that the proportion of females always was greater than in the general population and increased substantially over time, from 58 percent in 1840 to 72 percent at
the turn of the century. Contributing to this transformation to a female society was
"the defection of males, recruitment of destitute young mothers with children, and intentional differential acceptance of female children" (p. 363).

An interesting application of census data is suggested by Marcus Felson (1983), who recommends using diverse available data sets, including the Census of Manufacturers, to measure social and cultural change. The *1977 Census of Manufacturers*, for example, shows that during the 1970s increases in sales of electronic musical instruments did not result in reduced sales of traditional acoustical instruments; the shipment of neckties sharply declined while shipments of baseballs, softballs, and baseball mitts increased; and shipments of girdles declined while shipments of women's and girl's athletic shoes increased.

Private Documents

A less accessible but no less important data source is private documents: information produced by individuals or organizations about their own activities that is not intended for public consumption. Diaries and letters long have been a favorite data source for the historian; other examples would be businesses' personnel and sales records, inventories, and tax reports; hospital patient records; and college transcripts.

Perhaps the best-known research using letters is W. I. Thomas and Florian Znaniecki's classic 1918 study, *The Polish Peasant in Europe and America*. The study dealt broadly with problems of immigration and assimilation into American society. The authors drew on several sources of information, including newspaper accounts, autobiographies, and the records of social agencies such as the Legal Aid Society. But by far their largest single data source was a collection of over 750 personal letters exchanged between Polish immigrants in America and their relatives and friends in Poland. Thomas and Znaniecki's analysis of these materials was mainly descriptive. It consisted largely of introductions to sets of letters, commentaries on individual letters, and the letters themselves, nearly all of which were published as part of their study.

A second example of research using personal documents is Jerry Jacobs's analysis of suicide notes (1967). To understand how individuals justify their actions to themselves and others, Jacobs analyzed 112 notes left by persons who committed suicide in the Los Angeles area. He was able to place nearly all of the notes in six general categories: "first form notes," "sorry illness notes," "not sorry illness notes," "direct accusation notes," "will and testament notes," and "notes of instruction." The largest category, "first form notes," pertains to accounts in which the person faced an intolerable problem for which death was seen as the only possible resolution.

Victoria Swigert and Ronald Farrell's study (1977) of the effects of a criminal stereotype on the adjudication of homicide defendants combined the use of both public and private documents. Swigert and Farrell's data came from two sources in the jurisdiction of a large northeastern city: publicly accessible indictment files of the office of the clerk of courts and confidential diagnostic records from a clinic attached to the court. All persons arrested for murder were seen in the clinic; and so Swigert and Farrell were able to relate the clinical diagnoses and background characteristics of defendants to legal data on prior convictions, access to legal resources such as a private counsel, and conviction severity. They found that the use of a diagnostic category of the violent offender had important consequences for the course and the outcome of the judicial process. Defendants labeled "normal primitives" by the clinic were more likely than other defendants to be denied bail and access to trial by jury and, as a result, were likely to receive more severe sentences.

Mass Media

Also constituting part of the written record (as well as an oral and nonverbal record) are the mass media—newspapers, magazines, television, radio, films. By analyzing the content of these sources, social researchers have addressed a variety of issues.

In the aforementioned study of threat and authoritarianism, Sales (1973) also did a very simple analysis of comic strips. Because authoritarians tend to admire power and strength, Sales expected that popular fictional protagonists would become stronger and more powerful in the threatening 1930s than they had been in the relatively nonthreatening 1920s. Searching through Stephen Becker's *Comic Art in America*, Sales identified twenty comic strips that first appeared in the 1920s and twenty-one comic strips introduced in the 1930s. He and two other coders then judged whether the main character in each strip was either (1) "physically powerful or controlled great power or (2) not particularly powerful." Supporting his hypothesis, Sales found that only two of the strips started in the 1920s emphasized the power of the main character ("Buck Rogers" and "Tarzan"), whereas twelve of the strips started in the 1930s were about powerful men (e.g., "Joe Palooka," "Dick Tracy," and "Superman").

While most research on the media has analyzed verbal content, one can also analyze visual content. Erving Goffman (1979) looked at hundreds of pictures from advertisements in newspapers and magazines to see what these pictures revealed about the meaning of gender in American society. One image he identified was that of women as subordinate and dependent. This was evidenced by pictures consistently showing women bowing or otherwise on a lower plane than men, in a recumbent or reclining position, displaying a "bashful knee bend," canting (lowering) the head or upper part of the body, being victimized by men in playful games of "mocked assault," and in childlike, playful, or unserious poses.

Goffman provided a provocative description of "gender displays," but he neither chose nor analyzed his photographs in a systematic fashion. By contrast, Dane Archer and colleagues (1983) used more rigorous techniques to study one aspect of the stylistic representations of men and women in the media. They hypothesized that men and women differ in "facial prominence": The face and head—symbolizing intellect, character, wit, and other dimensions of mental life—are more prominent in depictions of men, and the body—symbolizing nonintellectual qualities like weight, physique, attractiveness, and emotion—are more prominent in depictions of women. Thus facial prominence may both reflect and influence societal images of men and women with regard to intellectual qualities. To measure facial prominence, Archer and his associates created an index consisting of the ratio of two linear measurements: the distance from the top of the head to the lowest point of the chin divided by the distance from the top of the head to the lowest visible part of the subject's body. They then calculated this index for men and women depicted in 1750 photographs from five American periodicals (e.g., *Time* and *Newsweek*), in 3500 pictures from thirteen periodicals in eleven other nations, and in 920 portrait and self-portrait paintings spread across six centuries. Except for the fifteenth and six-teenth centuries, every comparison showed a significantly higher facial prominence score for men than for women.

Finally, we mention research using newspapers and television as data sources. Contrary to popular opinion, research does not support the conclusion that capital punishment deters homicides. William Bailey examined this issue in two separate studies (Bailey and Peterson, 1989; Bailey, 1990). Both studies used monthly homi-cide figures issued by the U.S. Department of Health, Bureau of Vital Statistics. In the first study, Bailey and Peterson measured the effects of execution publicity, as found in newspapers, on the homicide rate between 1940 and 1986. Executions were classified as high in publicity if they appeared in *Facts on File* (a national in-dex of major news stories) and the *New York Times*; as moderate in publicity if they appeared in the *Times* but not in *Facts on File*; and as low in publicity if they did not receive coverage in either of these sources. In the second study, Bailey exam-ined the effects of televised execution publicity on homicide rates from 1976 to 1987. In this case, both the extent of television coverage and the type of publicity (e.g., artist drawings, witness accounts) were measured after viewing ABC, CBS, and NBC evening news programs located in the Vanderbilt Television News Archives. The findings of both studies supported the same conclusion: "Capital punishment does not provide an effective deterrent to murder."

Physical, Nonverbal Evidence

Although seldom used in the social sciences, nonverbal materials such as works of art, clothing, household items, and various artifacts constitute a rich source of evidence. Cave paintings, tools, and other artifacts are important data to archaeologists studying past civilizations, and historians find invaluable evidence in sculpture and other works of art. Furthermore, as seen in the work of Archer and colleagues (1983), social sci-entists also make use of paintings. A study of tombstones provides a further example.

Between 1690 and 1765 the Puritans, in the words of historian Richard Bush-man (1967), became Yankees. This historic transformation is evident in changes in attitudes toward death, available for all to see in the tombstones of New England's colonial cemeteries. Observing engravings on gravestones, David Stannard (1977) found that throughout the late seventeenth and early eighteenth centuries, stones in-variably bore some version of the "death's-head" carving of a winged skull, repre-senting the Puritans' rather grim vision of death. This visage dominated until the 1730s, when the death's-head motif and accompanying epitaphs steadily gave way to more romantic and optimistic designs of cherubs and angels. As this shift oc-curred, Stannard notes (1977:157), "the cemeteries in which those gravestones were placed began to become overcrowded while simultaneously falling into neglect and disarray. The Puritan community was becoming a relic of history. . . ."

Social Science Data Archives

Over the last thirty-five years, the social sciences have seen a tremendous prolifer-ation of **data archives**, repositories of data collected by various agencies and researchers that are accessible to the public. Most of these archives contain survey data, but archives also exist for collections of ethnographies, in which the whole society is the unit of analysis. Thus the use of data archives is an extension of both survey research and field research. As such, each archival data source has advantages and disadvantages associated with two different approaches to social research.

We already discussed and provided examples of the analysis of available survey data, called secondary analysis, in chapter 8. A noteworthy example, you may recall, is the General Social Survey (GSS), whose data are deposited in two main archives: the ICPSR (Inter-University Consortium for Political and Social Research) and the Roper Center for Public Opinion Research. Social scientists also analyze data derived from studies of whole societies. One valuable archive of such data, called the Human Relations Area Files (HRAF), contains information recorded on microfiche and electronically on over 400 societies. These files, fully indexed and available on the World Wide Web, are in "raw data" form, with pages from ethnographic reports organized by topic. Analysts have indexed every paragraph in the collection with subject codes denoting aspects of cultural belief and practice. Two other sources of cross-cultural data available in "coded" form, with numeric codes on several variables for each society, are the *Ethnographic Atlas* (Murdock, 1967) and the Standard Cross-Cultural Sample (SCCS) (Murdock and White, 1969). The *Atlas* contain codes on approximately forty variables for over 1100 societies; the SCCS contains more extensive data on a smaller sample of 186 societies. The following study used all three of these sources.

Obtaining data from a sample of forty-eight tribal societies, Willie Pearson and Lewellyn Hendrix (1979) tested the hypothesis that divorce increases as the status of women increases. This follows from the reasoning that as women gain economic resources they become more autonomous and less dependent on their husbands. Pearson and Hendrix's findings showed that divorce rates were moderately correlated with female status even when theoretically relevant variables such as community size, marital residence, and descent rules were controlled.

Advantages of Research Using Available Data

The foregoing studies suggest several advantages as well as some problems with research using available data. Here we discuss the principal advantages, and in the following section we address some general methodological problems. The first two advantages listed pertain to sources other than survey data archives. The remaining five benefits originally were outlined by Herbert Hyman (1972) with reference to the secondary analysis of survey data, but also apply to most other available-data research.

Nonreactive Measurement

As we saw in our previous discussion of research strategies, a major problem in much social research is reactive measurement: changes in behavior that occur because of subjects' awareness that they are being studied or observed. Research with available data also encounters this problem to the extent that the data sources are surveys or documents like autobiographies in which the author is clearly aware that what is said will be in the public domain. Still, many available-data sources are **nonreactive**. With physical evidence and many other available-data sources, there is simply no reasonable connection between a researcher's use of the material and the producer's knowledge of such use. By analyzing genealogical records, Winston's study of the preference for male children is completely nonreactive. Imagine, however, the kind of self-censorship that might have occurred if he had interviewed prospective mothers in their homes or expectant fathers in waiting rooms (Webb et al., 1981). Needless to say, we would be much less confident in this kind of evidence.

The risk of reactivity is so high in some areas of study that available data may provide the only credible evidence. Consider, for example, studies of illegal activities such as consumption of illegal drugs. Survey evidence is likely to be contaminated by concealment and underreporting; police records such as number of arrests for controlled substances may be distorted by differential efforts at law enforcement. An ingenious use of available data, however, can provide nonreactive evidence on drug use. Noting that the federal government imposes a tax and keeps a record of taxes collected on cigarette papers and tubes, Marcus Felson (1983) observed that federal taxes collected on these items changed little during the 1950s and 1960s but jumped about 70 percent over 1960s levels in 1972. Meanwhile, loose tobacco sales declined during this same period. The conclusion Felson reached is that a new market had been created for cigarette papers in the production of marijuana "joints." That market, it would appear, opened up in 1972.

Analyzing Social Structure

Despite the avowed focus of the social sciences on properties and changes in social structure, much of social research focuses on individual attitudes and behavior. Surveys are of individuals, and very few surveys utilize contextual or social network designs, which provide direct measures of social relations; experiments rarely study the group as the unit of analysis; and field studies are based on the observation of individual behavior. Available data, however, often enable the researcher to analyze larger social units. In many of the studies reviewed above, the unit of analysis was not the individual nor was the focus on individual behavior. For Durkheim and Pearson and Hendrix, the unit was the whole society; for Erikson, the community; for Farley and Frey, the metropolitan area; and for Winston, the family. Even the studies by Sales and Bailey on individual propensities toward authoritarianism and homicidal behavior, respectively, investigated these phenomena with societal-level data in terms of large-scale social processes.

Studying and Understanding the Past

Available data provide the social researcher with the best and often the only opportunity to study the past. To study some aspect of American society fifty or more years ago, it might be possible to conduct a survey of people who were alive at the time. But to do so presents several methodological problems, from the inaccuracy of respondents' memories to survivor bias in the sample. To study periods before the twentieth century necessitates the search for available data. Documentary records and other archival evidence have therefore been a favorite source of data for historians, as we saw in Erikson's and Stannard's studies of the Puritans. More recent events also can be investigated with the aid of survey data archives. In fact, many social scientists see surveys from the past as a primary data source for historians of the future (see Hyman, 1972). But studies of the past are not limited merely to understanding the past. They also can be done to test general propositions about social life, as we saw in Erikson's study, Bailey's research on the deterrent effect of capital punishment, and Sales's research on threat and authoritarianism.

Understanding Social Change

Because of the commitment and cost involved, social scientists rarely conduct longitudinal surveys or do field research over long spans of time. The analysis of available data, however, is well suited to studies of social and cultural change. Trend studies, such as Farley and Allen's analysis of black–white inequalities and Farley and Frey's study of racial segregation, have a long tradition among social demographers who rely on the census and other demographic data. Stannard's analysis of the carvings on gravestones provides an example of another source of evidence on social change. Moreover, the establishment of data archives has resulted in a marked increase in the number of studies that trace relatively recent changes in various attitudes, opinions, and behaviors (see Glenn and Frisbie, 1977). The General Social Survey was designed partly to measure trends in social conditions. And as we noted, Felson has suggested a similar use for other available data sources such as the Census of Manufacturers.

Studying Problems Cross-Culturally

In 1984, the International Social Survey Program was formed to provide cross-national survey data similar to that from the General Social Survey (Smith, 1990). By 2003, thirty-eight collaborating nations were supplementing regular national surveys with a common core of questions, with these data pooled and made available to the social science community. This is an important development, because until recently there have been few cross-cultural surveys. In fact, Hyman (1972:17) estimated "about ten documented examples of comparable large-scale multination surveys of the general population [existed] as of 1970." In spite of this development, however, other sources of available data—for example, national censuses and vital statistics as well as ethnographies—will continue to provide the primary data for cross-national studies. Pearson and Hendrix's investigation of the relationship between divorce and the status of women is but one of numerous examples.

Improving Knowledge through Replication and Increased Sample Size

Experiments and field studies use samples of very limited size, and most surveys of local populations are relatively small. Similarly, historical document analysis often focuses on a small number of cases. The use of available data, however, may afford the opportunity to generate unusually large samples. Winston obtained data on 5466 families; Archer and colleagues measured facial prominence in over 5000 photographs in eighteen diverse periodicals from twelve nations. Sample size is important for two reasons. First, large samples generally enhance our confidence in study results; with random sampling, increases in sample size increase the reliability of findings, as we saw in chapter 5. Second, by increasing sample size we may gain access to specialized problems and smaller populations that otherwise could not be studied. One reason for using census data, including sample-based data, is that the huge samples provide reliable estimates for small segments of the population. Farley and Allen based their study of black–white differences on a large sample, 450,000, which was necessary to provide a reliable comparative analysis.

Increasing sample size in effect replicates observations. Although replications are relatively rare in the social sciences, they often may be carried out easily with available data. A good example is Sales's research on threat and authoritarianism. Sales used diverse sources. We mentioned his use of municipal budgets, listings of books on astrology and psychotherapy, and comic strips. But he used several other sources that we did not mention and also analyzed changes in similar indicators for two later periods in the United States: 1959–64 and 1967–70. And that is not all. Two other researchers (Padgett and Jorgenson, 1982) replicated part of Sales's analyses for Germany in the 1920s and 1930s, using, for example, the German equivalent of the *Reader's Guide* to chart the number of articles that appeared on astrology, mysticism, and cults. The data consistently supported the thesis that threat increases authoritarianism.

Savings on Research Costs

Insofar as research using available data bypasses the stage of data collection, it can economize greatly on cost, time, and personnel. Whereas this is especially true of the secondary analysis of surveys, other sources of available data also tend to be less costly than experiments, surveys, and field studies. These costs vary depending on the nature of the data source and the time, money, and personnel required to obtain and to analyze the data. The tasks of the researcher using available data, such as searching for and coding relevant information, often are tedious and time consuming. Imagine, for example, the efforts of Archer and co-workers in obtaining periodicals, identifying eligible pictures, and measuring facial dominance and gender for some 5000 pictures, or the job faced by Swigert and Farrell in sampling and coding the information contained in court and clinic records for 444 cases of persons charged with murder. Yet, the cost per case in such studies is generally quite small compared with the cost of interviewing a respondent or running a single subject through an experiment.

General Methodological Issues in Available-Data Research

The four basic approaches to social research differ according to the stages that require the greatest labor and creativity on the part of the researcher. In experimentation, experimental design (e.g., number of conditions, measurement of key variables, instructions to subjects) is crucial; therefore, much of the effort goes into perfecting the design and preparing for its implementation (pretesting), and the data analysis is simple and straightforward. When the design is not experimental, the data analysis requires great effort and skill. And when the data were collected for another purpose, and investigators cannot directly oversee the procedures producing the data, a search for appropriate measures and the evaluation of data quality are extremely important research phases.

Searching for and Procuring Available Data

As the aforementioned studies reveal, the use of available data is a flexible and powerful approach to social research. Still, a major problem with this approach is finding and procuring relevant information. While the material to study a given topic may exist, how do you know what to look for? And how do you find it, acquire it, and/or gain permission to use it?

Perhaps the best advice is to let the research problem or hypothesis serve as a guide to appropriate sources. In one sense, this is obvious. For example, researchers like Swigert and Farrell who are interested in the adjudication of criminals will readily entertain the possibility of using judicial records. But this advice holds true in another way. Aimlessly searching through records or dredging up data from survey archives is unlikely to yield anything of value. Even though the data pre-exist, that does not mean the researcher should reverse the research process by analyzing the data and then developing some post hoc rationale for the analysis. More than likely, the outcome of such an approach will be a trivial and flawed study. It is far better to let your research problem dictate your methodology than to let your method override the substantive and theoretical focus of your research.

A second guide to locating pertinent data is to search the literature for studies by previous investigators. No doubt Erikson's study of deviance in Puritan New England was aided by the mounds of data already uncovered by earlier historians who investigated this era. It also helps to know where to go for tips on locating available data. You can learn about the location of many data sources by consulting a librarian. Robert Shafer (1980) provides a long list of bibliographic aids and sources of documentary data for historical research. In addition, there are various listings of social science data archives and other publicly available data sets (e.g., *The Federal Database Finder, American Public Opinion Index*), although nowadays the most up-to-date lists and raw data files can be found on the Internet.

Access to public sources varies among the archives and agencies holding the data. Many of these data, such as those compiled by the Census Bureau and other government agencies, are mandated for public use without restrictions. The greatest access problems pertain to private documents and confidential records. Obtaining such data may require a little ingenuity, such as Thomas and Znaniecki used in their study of letters written to and from Polish immigrants. They acquired the letters through advertisements in a Polish-language newspaper that offered to pay 10 to 20 cents per letter. Gaining access also may depend on the permission and cooperation of others. Jacobs, for example, collected his suicide notes with the aid of an acquaintance who was a deputy coroner in the Los Angeles County Coroner's Office.

Measurement of Key Concepts

Using available data is a bit like wearing someone else's shoes. They may fit perfectly well. But more likely they will either be too small, pinching your toes, or too large, causing you to stumble. Seldom will available data be ideally suited to the purposes the researcher has in mind. At best, the data may require the creative construction of measures that provide indirect evidence of a given variable. At worst, the data may be inadequate to address the research question.

In much available-data research, the investigator must develop creative measures that approximate variables of interest. Taxes collected on cigarette paper and tubes cannot be considered a direct measure of marijuana consumption. But taken in the context of loose-tobacco sales, they do provide a useful surrogate or proxy indicator, especially given the reactivity of other measures. Many of the measures in Sales's research on authoritarianism are similarly indirect. Unable to question individuals directly about their attraction to powerful people, Sales relied on the popularity of comic strip characters as an indicator of such attraction. And when no reference work covering new comic strips was available for the later periods he investigated, he speculated that individuals "attracted to strength and power in times of stress . . . might be more inclined to purchase strong and powerful dogs" (1973:52). Sure enough, an examination of American Kennel Club (AKC) registrations of some 116 breeds showed that 9.8 percent of all dogs registered by the AKC in the low-threat period (1959–64) were in the attack-dog classes (German shepherds, Doberman pinschers, Great Danes), whereas these dogs accounted for 13.5 percent of the registrations in the relatively threatening period (1967–70).

Sales's measurement of threat also is somewhat indirect, since it depends on the tenor of the times rather than on the measurable feelings of individuals. More direct measures of threat can be found in experiments where individuals have been "threatened" by being told that they have failed tests of intelligence (see Sales and Friend, 1973) or by being led to anticipate receiving electrical shocks. Sales, on the other hand, identified contiguous historical periods that appeared to pose contrasting environmental threats for the population as a whole. He ended up comparing periods marked primarily by differences in economic prosperity: the 1920s versus the 1930s, and 1959–64 versus 1967–70. These contrasts do not unambiguously represent low-versus high-threat conditions. For example, as Sales (1973:51) himself noted, the presumed "low-threat" period of 1959–64 "included the abortive Bay of Pigs invasion, the Cuban missile crisis, and the assassination of J. F. Kennedy." But the facts that he used two sets of contrasting historical periods and that the relationship between threat and authoritarianism was so consistently demonstrated lend considerable credibility to his measurement of "threat." Indeed, Sales's historical measure would appear to provide a much more powerful test of his hypothesis than weak and short-lived, albeit direct, experimental manipulations of threat.

As we argue in the next chapter, the use of several different measures of a given variable is always a good practice in social research. This is even more imperative in available-data research that uses indirect and approximate indicators. The use of multiple indicators, however, is not a panacea for inappropriate measures. One problem with available data is that their mere availability may lead researchers to use measures that are inadequate for research purposes. This is especially apparent in secondary analyses of survey data. For example, a question first asked in 1973 and now repeated each year in the GSS is, "Is there an area right around here—that is, within a mile—where you would be afraid to walk alone at night?" This has been identified in many studies as a measure of fear of crime. Yet the item makes no reference to crime or any other object of the fear, and it is entirely hypothetical, which may overestimate the individual's actual experience of fear in day-to-day situations (Ferraro and LaGrange, 1987). The point is that available data, like any tool, should be appropriate for the task at hand.

Evaluation of Data Quality

Perhaps the most important general rule that applies to the use of available data, irrespective of the source, is that the researcher must reconstruct the process by which the data were originally assembled (Riley, 1963:252). If you gather the data yourself, you generally are aware of their limitations, possible errors, and biases and you can adapt your analyses accordingly. But such adaptations also may be required of available data. Therefore, it is crucial to try to determine, so far as possible, how, when, where, and by whom the data were collected. Only then can you begin to assess the validity of the data.

Researchers using historical documents must be especially concerned about their authenticity. Authentication is a highly technical matter that requires a thorough knowledge of the historical period from which the documents are purported to originate. Besides checking the logical consistency of the content, one must examine handwriting, writing style, and even the chemical composition of ink and paper. Historian Louis Gottschalk (1969) notes that doubts about authenticity arise frequently, and if they seem not to, it is only because a skilled historian has already authenticated the sources. For this reason, social researchers like Kai Erikson usually are spared the task of authentication. Assuming authenticity, however, one must still ask how the data were collected. Is the available evidence accurate, complete, and reliable? A series of studies of colonial Boston illustrate how easy it is to be misled if you do not have a thorough knowledge of the conditions of data collection.

According to historian G. B. Warden (1976), the traditionally accepted view of colonial Boston was that of a basically egalitarian community with a town-meeting democracy and a relatively equitable distribution of wealth. These egalitarian conditions, moreover, are believed to have made the city a center of radical political agitation before the Revolution. In the 1960s a group of scholars [see, for example, Henretta (1965)] challenged this position, claiming that Boston experienced dramatic increases in social and economic inequality in the eighteenth century. Indeed, these scholars alleged that it was the resulting socioeconomic tensions that contributed to radical political agitation. The rather extensive arguments supporting the latter view are based largely on evidence from tax assessments in 1687 and 1771 (unfortunately, tax records for the intervening years are not available).

For example, one of the propositions put forth was that Boston experienced extraordinarily rapid economic growth in the eighteenth century, which increased stratification and the maldistribution of wealth. Evidence of this came from an observed increase in the total assessed wealth of Boston from 16,591 pounds in 1687 to 460,493 pounds in 1771, which translates into an annual growth rate of 33 percent per year. As Warden points out, however, these figures do not take into account how property was estimated for tax purposes. In 1687 all property was estimated for tax purposes at about one-twentieth of its true market value, whereas in 1771 real property (land and house) was estimated at about one-twelfth of its market value, and personal property (e.g., stock in trade) was estimated at close to its actual value. If appropriate adjustments are made, the estimated "simple annual growth rate is only about 2.3 percent, which is relatively low compared with other colonial communities" (Warden, 1976:589).

Warden shows how similar problems exist with other interpretations of these data. Another proposition was that the richest Bostonians possessed an increasingly disproportionate share of the wealth. But once again, the data purported to support this proposition are flawed by inconsistencies. The different assessments of real and personal property in 1771, for example, magnify the difference between the actual taxable wealth of property holders in the bottom and top halves of the distribution. As a consequence,

> there appears to be a heavy concentration of wealth in the upper half of the group; the apparent concentration occurred, however, not because the retailers and merchants were all that much richer than those in the bottom half but because the wealth of those in the top was estimated at a much higher rate than the wealth of those in the bottom half. (Warden, 1976:604)

Even for more recent data sources, the same general rule of carefully assessing the accuracy and consistency of the data applies. Consider, for example, the unwary user of crime statistics. There are two major sources of crime data: (1) self-report data from the National Crime Survey, in which people are asked to indicate crimes in which they have been personally victimized, and (2) data from official reports of crimes known to the police, which are compiled in the *Uniform Crime Reports* by the Federal Bureau of Investigation. These two sources clearly offer very different operational definitions of crime; one focuses on the victim and the other on the offense. And as it turns out, there is no simple relationship between the two measures. A single offense (e.g., a robbery of several persons in an establishment) may have more than one victim. Some offenses (murder) have no victims who can be interviewed, and other offenses (e.g., prostitution and gambling) have no victims in that the "victims" are also the offenders. Each of these measures also suffers from other methodological problems. Victimizations are limited to persons over the age of 12. Not all crimes are brought to the attention of the police (e.g., burglaries of uninsured items); also, the police themselves may fail to record incidents.

Such problems do not render crime statistics useless or totally invalid. They do, however, force the researcher to focus on a particular definition of crime—either offenses or victimizations—and to consider the implications of using data with a relatively large measurement error (Jacob, 1984). More generally, the flawed nature of these data points to the need for every researcher using available data to become acquainted with the process by which the information was gathered. How did the data collectors define categories (e.g., "crime" and "tax assessments")? If the data were collected repeatedly over time, have there been changes in record-keeping or data-collection procedures? In the case of the media and first-person documents, how might the writer's ideological position have affected his or her interpretation of events? Without recourse to the usual checks on validity, knowing how the data were collected is often the only way to determine the authenticity and accuracy of available data.

Another procedure that is especially useful for evaluating reliability is the use of several different sources of evidence. As a rule, historians do not accept an account of an event as reliable unless it is confirmed by two or more independent sources. Demographers, who analyze population statistics, often use several data sources and different estimation procedures. To estimate the annual net number of undocumented ("illegal") Mexican immigrants to the United States, David Heer (1979) used several reports of the CPS and came up with seven different estimates, each based on different assumptions about the data. Heer's estimates for the period from 1970 to 1975 ranged from 82,300 to 232,400, figures that are well below estimates of the gross flow of illegal aliens.[5]

Once the data have been evaluated, it may become necessary to refine measures. If measurement errors or changes in definitions are detected, the researcher must make the necessary adjustments to allow for proper interpretation. The historian Warden's reanalysis of tax assessments in Boston offers one example of this.

Assessment of Data Completeness

In addition to evaluating the quality of existing measures, it is essential to assess the adequacy of the existing sample of information. Consider, for example, the U.S. census. Despite the effort and cost of conducting the U.S. census, there has been much discussion in recent years of census undercount. Analyses indicate that the overall undercount is quite low—only about 1.4 percent in 2000—but that it varies by race and gender. That is, blacks are more likely than whites and males more likely than females to be omitted. Kirsten West and David Fein (1990) claim that the effects of such undercount are rarely considered by census data users. One possible effect, for example, is that the number of female-headed households among blacks is overestimated as a result of the census undercount of black males. On the other hand, Farley and Allen's analysis of the potential effects of differential undercounts indicated that this did not seriously distort their conclusions about racial differences.

In contrast to the generally high quality of census and survey archival data, cross-cultural data banks constitute nothing more than availability samples; they do not contain data on modern industrialized societies or even a representative sample of nonindustrial societies. This limits generalizations as well as the types of research that can be undertaken. Cross-cultural researchers using these data cannot make predictions or estimate worldwide societal characteristics. But they can provide limited tests of hypotheses (Lee, 1984). In their study of divorce and the status of women, Pearson and Hendrix were forced to use only those societies—forty-eight in all—for which they could obtain adequate measures on key variables. Their rationale for this data set was that it included societies from all continents except Australia and contained sufficient variation in the key variables.

The representativeness of the data is even more problematic for researchers studying the more remote past who must rely on whatever traces of information they can find. These data are certain to be incomplete and are probably biased. This is especially true of physical evidence, which invariably is subject to selective survival and selective deposit. **Selective survival** refers to the fact that some objects survive longer than others. The fact that pottery and bone survive the elements better than wood and paper has long been a problem for the archaeologist. A graver problem for users of the written record is **selective deposit**—systematic biases in the content of the evidence that is available. Records may be selectively destroyed; other information may be edited.

Eugene Webb and associates (1981) note that members of Congress are allowed to edit proofs of the *Congressional Record*, a transcript of the speeches and activities of the U.S. Congress, which means that this document hardly serves as a spontaneous account of events. As another example, these authors cite a study of the longevity of the ancient Romans based on evidence from tombstones. Wives who died after their husbands may have been underrepresented insofar as they were less likely to get a tombstone than wives who died before their husbands. Also, middle-class and upper-class Romans were probably more likely to have tombstones than the lower classes of Roman society. And the fact that mortality rates are likely to have varied across classes could bias estimates of longevity.

Similar problems may exist in studies of the written record. Only about 10 to 20 percent of those who commit suicide leave notes. The question that must be asked of the Jacobs' study, therefore, is whether the rational and coherent character of the notes he observed describes the mental condition of suicide victims *not* leaving notes. In other words, are persons who leave notes representative of the entire population of persons who commit suicide? More generally, Kenneth Bailey (1982:305–6) observes that documents may be biased by educational level. Not only are poorly educated people much less likely to write documents, but the mass media are likely to be aimed at and to be more representative of well-educated people.

For many sources of available data, there is no choice in the selection of information. Researchers simply use all the data they can obtain, and then they attempt to account for sample selection bias. On the other hand, for studies of the more recent past, probability sampling of time and space are not only feasible but often necessary because of the massiveness of the information. For example, a major data source for Farley and Allen's study was the 1980 Public Use Microdata Sample File A, a 5-percent sample of the nation's households. Budgetary constraints, however, prevented them "from tabulating and analyzing data for the entire 5-percent sample—approximately 11.5 million people—contained on 26 reels of computer tape." They therefore "selected a smaller sample [of 450,000] which could be analyzed more economically" (Farley and Allen, 1987:431). Other data sources also lend themselves to probability sampling: Actuarial, political, and judicial records usually may be sampled over time; voting records may be sampled across precincts (Webb et al., 1981); and documents and the mass media may be sampled in various ways (see discussion of content analysis below).

Historical Analysis

The analysis of available data takes as many forms as the data themselves. In part, the type of analysis is a function of research purposes and research design. Descriptive accounts of a single event or historical period differ from tests of general hypotheses, which differ from trend studies. The analysis also depends on data sources. Researchers use very different techniques for analyzing population statistics, mass media communications, and historical documents. In this section and the next, we briefly discuss aspects of two sharply different approaches to the analysis of available data: historical analysis and content analysis.

Descriptive and Analytical History

The word "history" has several meanings. It refers, for example, to (1) actual events or happenings of the past, from the recent past, such as the 2000 presidential election, to the remote past, such as the assassination of President Lincoln; (2) a record or account of what has or might have happened; and (3) a discipline or field of study (Shafer, 1980:2). One type of historical analysis refers to the set of methods that historians [represented by (3)] apply when they gather and evaluate evidence in order to describe specific moments of the past. This form of analysis stresses the accuracy and completeness of the *description* of unique, complex events. Outside the discipline of history, however, historical analysis moves beyond description to the use of historical events and evidence [represented by (1) and (2)] to develop a generalized understanding of the social world. Although this characterizes much of the field of historical sociology, we prefer the generic term **analytical history** to denote this type of historical analysis.

Surprisingly, analytical history is a relatively recent redevelopment. Despite the historical orientation of such founding fathers of modern-day social science as Karl Marx, Emile Durkheim, and Max Weber, much of social research during the past half century has lacked a historical focus. Only in the past thirty years has there been a revived interest in the historical perspective. Erikson's study of deviance in Puritan New England is representative of this work.

Erikson was careful to reconstruct events with documents of the time, much as a historian might do. But the reconstruction was not an end in itself. Rather, he attempted to use a particular historical case as a way of demonstrating and elaborating Durkheim's general theory of deviant behavior—that deviance provides a mechanism for defining community boundaries and demonstrating shared values and norms. This sort of analysis, Theda Skocpol (1984:365) points out, is valuable "because it prompts the theorist to specify and operationalize . . . abstract concepts and theoretical propositions." Thus,

Erikson must pin down historically such ideas as "community boundaries" and "group norms" and he must show us how, in terms of the symbols and social practices of the Massachusetts Puritans, deviant persons and their acts supplied "needed services to society by marking the outer limits of group experience and providing a point of contrast which gives . . . [social norms] some scope and dimension."

Erikson started with a general theory and used the specific case to explicate the theory. Another strategy for integrating social theory and history is to start with a particular historical event or pattern and then develop and test one or more explanations to account for it. For example, John Sutton (1991) attempted to explain the rapid growth of asylums in the United States between 1880 and 1920. To many observers of this period, Sutton notes, "asylum expansion was a sign that America was undergoing an epidemic of madness," which they attributed to a range of evils, including rapid urbanization and uncontrolled immigration. Using quantitative data from the states (e.g., the number of persons living in urban areas, the number of persons over age 65, the number of asylum and almshouse inmates), Sutton tested several explanations of asylum expansion: (1) As reformers succeeded in shutting down almshouses, asylums were forced to absorb the aged poor who were expelled; (2) urbanization enhanced the development of specialized and formally organized means of treatment, such as asylums; (3) asylum expansion depended on the revenues of state governments; (4) the need for asylum placements was inversely related to the distribution of direct benefits (e.g., pensions) to dependent groups; and (5) patronage politics may have supported expansion insofar as asylums were sources of jobs, contracts, and services that parties could use to reward supporters. Sutton's findings showed that all these factors, among others, contributed to asylum expansion.

Still another strategy is to search for general causal explanations of well-defined historical outcomes or patterns (Skocpol, 1984). In this case, the investigator does not focus on a particular historical event but rather on two or more similar events or cases, which are then compared systematically to identify causal regularities. For example, sociologist Theda Skocpol (1979) analyzed the causes of social revolutions by comparing the revolutions of France in 1789, Russia in 1917, and China from 1911 to 1949. Given the broad scope of her study, she did not consult original documents; instead, she drew upon the work of historians of each period and place to identify patterns of political conflict and development. Among the common factors that Skocpol identified as precipitating revolution were that each society (1) had strong peasant communities and (2) faced foreign pressures and entanglements that made it difficult to meet the needs of economic development.

Finally, historical analysts may also treat history itself as an independent variable in their analyses. That is, they may examine sequences of past events as a way of understanding the present. Used in this way, history represents the temporal dimension of social life rather than a particular outcome to be explained (as in Sutton's research) or a manifestation of large-scale social change (as in Skocpol's work).[6]

Representative of this type of analytical history is economist Paul David's analysis of the establishment of the "QWERTY" keyboard layout as a standard of the typewriter industry (1985). David showed that the influence of temporally remote events accounts for the persistence of this awkward layout on current typewriters and computer keyboards. The QWERTY format first appeared in 1873, as a result of an early effort to find an arrangement that would reduce the frequency of type-bar jamming. The format was then modified into a sales gimmick. That is, E. Remington and Sons "assembled into one row all the letters that their salesmen would need" to rapidly type the brand name TYPE WRITER without lifting their fingers from the keyboard. The future of QWERTY was not protected by technological necessities, as competitive designs introduced in the 1880s eliminated the jamming problem and a keyboard arrangement patented by Dvorak and Dealey in 1932 was demonstrably more efficient. Rather, a key event occurred late in the 1880s that locked in the QWERTY standard. The advent of "touch" typing was adapted to Remington's keyboard, so that typists began learning this design rather than others. Employers then found it less expensive to buy machines with the QWERTY arrangement than to retrain typists. Finally, non-QWERTY typewriter manufacturers adapted their machines to the QWERTY-trained typists.

Historical analysis thus consists of (1) reconstructions of past events, which emphasize the accurate description of *what* happened; (2) applications of a general theory to a particular historical case(s), which focus on *how* the theory applies; (3) tests of explanations of historical events, which examine *why* a specific event occurred; (4) the development of causal explanations of historical patterns, which also analyzes *why* events occurred but seeks a more general understanding of social phenomena; and (5) the use of history to understand the present, or explain *how* and *why* particular phenomena came to be. Each of these genres of historical research represents a slightly different level of abstraction and analysis. Descriptive historians (1) are interested in presenting sequences of specific, concrete events, whereas analytical historians (2), especially those applying abstract theories, may apply highly general concepts and propositions. Quantitatively oriented analysts engaged in testing hypotheses of a particular historical instance (3) tend to follow the traditional scientific model of investigation, and are more explicit about operationalizing concepts. Comparative historians (4), on the other hand, typically take an inductive approach similar to field researchers.[7] Finally, those who examine long-term temporal sequences and connections among events (5) may combine the historians' narrative approach with the quantitative analyses of the sociologist. Regardless of these differences, however, all historical research involves, first, the use of written residues of the past to describe the past and, second, an interpretation of past events.

Handling Documentary Evidence

Although historical researchers may use any source of available data, they tend to rely mostly on documents. Historian Vernon Dibble (1963) classifies documents into two main categories: **testimony** and **social bookkeeping**. Historians traditionally have been especially fond of direct testimony by major actors as contained in autobiographies, depositions, private letters, and the like (Tilly, 1981). Through the testimony of witnesses, historians attempt to reconstruct where, when, and what happened. Testimony, however, tends to focus the analysis on the activities and motivations of individuals, especially "major actors."

Social bookkeeping refers to documents containing recorded information produced by groups or organizations, such as bankbooks, court records, transcripts of congressional debates, vital statistics, and the list of graduates of Yale University. As the product of social systems, social bookkeeping is more likely than testimony to be used to draw inferences about social structural variables. Charles Tilly (1981:32) also points out that the numbers and abstractions that social scientists glean from such evidence have facilitated

> the bringing of ordinary people back into the historical record. . . . Ordinary people leave few diaries, letters, and novels, but their experiences leave documentary evidence nonetheless. The documentary evidence shows up in birth certificates, marriage contracts, notarized transactions, conscription registers, tax rolls, rent books, censuses, catechetical records, and other routine sources.

When drawing inferences from documents to events of the past, the historian is primarily concerned with the authenticity and credibility of the evidence. Judgments of authenticity, as we mentioned earlier, involve highly technical techniques that are best left to the professional historian or archivist. Once the evidence is authenticated, the researcher must evaluate how credible the evidence is. The best checks on the credibility of testimony are corroboration and the absence of contradiction. Consistent independent sources of testimony enhance the probability that a particular account is accurate. However, because corroboration is often impossible, historians use a variety of other checks to assess credibility. Robert Shafer's (1980:166–67) checklist includes the following suggestions:

1. Is the real meaning of the statement different from its literal meaning? Are words used in senses not employed today?
2. How well could the author *observe* the thing he [or she] reports? Were his [or her] senses equal to the observation? Was his [or her] physical location suitable to sight, hearing, touch? Did he [or she] have the proper social ability to observe: did he [or she] understand the language . . . ?
3. . . . Regarding the author's *ability* to report, was he [or she] biased? Did he [or she] have proper time for reporting? Proper place for reporting? Adequate recording instrumentation? . . . When did he [or she] report in relation to [the] observation? Sooner? Much later? [Reports written soon after an event are more likely to be accurate than reports recorded long afterward; disinterested, incidental, or casual testimony is more likely to be accurate than testimony that is ideologically relevant or intended for a particular audience.]
4. Are there inner contradictions in the document?

With their emphasis on credible testimony and the accurate description of past events, historians put much stock in the use of primary as opposed to secondary sources. **Primary sources** are eyewitness accounts of the events described, whereas **secondary sources** consist of indirect evidence obtained from primary sources. Kai Erikson used both types of evidence in his study of deviance in Puritan New England: (a) court records and the journals of those witnessing the events of the time (primary) and (b) the writings of numerous historians (secondary). Theda Skocpol relied on secondary sources for her study of revolutions. "As a general rule," Louis Gottschalk (1969:116) claims, the careful historian will be suspicious of secondary works in history, even the best ones." Gottschalk therefore recommends that these should be used for very limited purposes, such as to get general information about the setting of the historical period under investigation, to obtain bibliographic leads, and to derive tentative interpretations and hypotheses. However, it is difficult to imagine how broad-based historical analyses such as Skocpol's could ever be undertaken if she first reconstructed past events with primary sources.

Social bookkeeping requires a different kind of evaluation than does testimony. Because the documents are produced by groups or organizations, they must be read in the light of the social systems that produced them (Dibble, 1963:207). One might ask and try to discern, for example: What processes intervened between the observing and recording? Was the record subject to editing (recall our example of selective deposit in the *Congressional Record*)? For whom was the record intended? For whom might it have been valuable and who might have been hurt by it?

In general, then, when the evidence is secondhand and the subject matter remote, the investigator must be all the more thoughtful about the evidence and skeptical of his or her relationship to it (Erikson, 1970:335). Even when the researcher is confident of the authenticity and credibility of the documents, he or she must also wonder how they came to be preserved. With regard to the rich and varied documents available for the study of seventeenth-century Massachusetts, Erikson (1970:335) points out that

> one cannot spend more than a few hours in their company without wondering whose history they speak of. Not only were they originally composed by men with a vested interest in the events they were reporting, they have been passed along to us by a succession of other men, each of whom has taken a turn sifting, rearranging, and even rewriting those materials. The surviving records, then, register not only what impressed John Winthrop in the early years of settlement, but what Cotton Mather regarded as worth remembering in the second half of the seventeenth century, what Thomas Hutchinson considered "historic" in the eighteenth century, and what whole generations of chroniclers and antiquarians decided to place on the shelves in the nineteenth century.

Beyond providing more or less direct evidence of historic events, documents are an important source of indicators or measures of large-scale social structural variables and processes. In his study of asylum expansion, for example, Sutton (1991) measured urbanization, the aging of the population, and changes in the number of inmates of asylums and almshouses with data from various U.S. census publications; he used reports to the U.S. Congress by the Commissioner of Pensions to determine the number of pensioners in each state; and from gubernatorial voting data published in the *Congressional Quarterly's Guide to U.S. Elections*, he measured party patronage by the closeness of the votes for Republican and Democratic gubernatorial candidates. The quality of such indicators depends not only on the credibility of the bookkeeping sources, but also on the reliability and validity of the data as measures of particular variables. Since multiple indicators and independent sources of validation are rarely available in historical research, validity assessment is largely a matter of face validation. This was not a problem for most variables in Sutton's study because of the directness of the measures; for example, data on the number of persons over age 65 has palpable validity as a measure of the age of the population. However, for less direct measures, such as the difference in votes for party gubernatorial candidates as an indicator of patronage, face validity is less than satisfactory, albeit often the only means of validation.

Historical Interpretation

The historical analyst is interested in understanding the past. For the descriptive historian, this implies establishing what happened in a factual way. During the Salem witchcraft hysteria, for example, who was accused by whom? Who was executed? But analysis never stops here. To arrive at some *understanding* of what happened, even if the goal is merely to describe a sequence of events as accurately as possible, the researcher must order the facts according to some interpretation of the materials. As we repeatedly have noted, a tenet of social research is that facts do not speak for themselves. The search for evidence itself, however haphazard or rigorous, is always guided by a broad theory or interpretation relevant to the researcher's interest. Tilly (1981:10), for example, notes that "the American historian who examines the treatment of slaves by undertaking a detailed study of slaveholders' diaries, while neglecting the records of slave auctions, makes an implicit choice favoring a theory in which slaveholders' attitudes are significant determinants of slave experience." To examine the role of historical interpretation of particular past events, and the importance of entertaining alternative explanations, we discuss different studies of the Salem witchcraft episode, including Kai Erikson's aforementioned study of deviance in Puritan New England.

One of the three crises that Erikson analyzed was the Salem witchcraft hysteria. The events of this well-known episode have been fairly well established through court depositions and writings of that period, and the reader may be familiar with them through popular accounts such as Arthur Miller's play, *The Crucible*. In 1692 two daughters of the local minister Samuel Parris became ill, or at least they began to exhibit rather bizarre behavior. They would scream unaccountably and go into convulsions, their bodies would become contorted, and they would crawl around on all fours and bark like dogs. Possibly the girls suffered from hysteria, although nobody knew then or knows now precisely what afflicted them. Whatever it was spread quickly to other girls in the community, who began to manifest similar symptoms. In the wake of this panic, unable to bring this strange behavior under control, someone offered a diagnosis of witchcraft. And when the girls were pressed into identifying who was tormenting them, they implicated three women. One of the women was Parris's slave Tituba, who was from the West Indies and known for her practice of voodoo magic. She confessed and conveniently identified, among others, the two other women named by the girls as agents of the devil. Other confessions and accusations followed, supposed witches were arrested and put on trial, and before it was over, nineteen people were hanged and one was pressed to death.

Why did this unfortunate episode occur? Erikson, you will recall, saw this as one of three "crime" waves in the seventeenth century that served to reinforce the moral boundaries of the community. The need to reaffirm moral boundaries and community solidarity arises, according to Erikson, when the sense of community control and consensus is threatened. The threat to Salem Village, however, was not posed by the alleged witches; they were conveniently chosen deviants. Rather, it was the uncertain political status of the community. In the 1670s, Erikson points out, the colony was beset by strife between clergy and magistrates, whose alliance "had been the very cornerstone of the New England Way," and by a costly war with a confederacy of Indian tribes. Then, in the 1680s King Charles II of England imposed the establishment of an Anglican church in Boston and revoked the charter that had legally protected the colony for over half a century. At the onset of the witchcraft hysteria, colonial agents were visiting England in an attempt to restore the charter. Finally, there were many land disputes and feuds at the time, which undermined the harmony on which the community had depended. All of this, according to Erikson's interpretation, evoked a need to reaffirm the Puritan way of life.

Although Erikson's analysis of these events is thorough and persuasive, it has been challenged by other sociologists and by subsequent historical research. William Chambliss (1976) contrasts Erikson's "functionalist" explanation with "conflict" theory, siding firmly with the latter. He sees the witchcraft hysteria, in addition to the other two crime waves, as "indeed created for the consequences it had. But the consequences were not 'to establish moral boundaries'; rather, they aided those in power to maintain their position" (p. 15). Chambliss points out in support of this interpretation that the actions of court assistants were followed and criminal sanctions imposed so long as members of the ruling elite were not accused. However, when the witch finders began to overstep this bound, the witchcraft trials came to an end.

Historians Paul Boyer and Stephen Nissenbaum (1974) offer still another interpretation of these events. Using many of the same references as Erikson as well as some previously neglected sources of data (e.g., community votes, tax assessments, petitions), they noticed a split between accusers and accused that coincided with whether people supported or opposed Samuel Parris, the minister in whose home the girls first experienced their afflictions. As it turned out, this split between pro-Parris and anti-Parris factions existed before the witchcraft outbreak and went well beyond support for the local minister. Compared with supporters, for example, opponents of Parris tended to be wealthier and to live and own land close to the adjacent commercial town of Salem and were less likely to be members of the Salem Village church. Thus, in part, Boyer and Nissenbaum contend "that the accusations of 1692 represented a direct and conscious continuation of factional conflict" (p. 186).

All of this points to a major difficulty and an important caveat regarding historical analysis. Historical events invariably are subject to a variety of interpretations. It is possible for more than one interpretation to be valid, especially if the interpretations represent different levels (e.g., psychological versus sociological) or focus on different aspects of an event. For example, in explaining the witchcraft mania, one may account for not only why it took place at this point in time in the Massachusetts colony (which is what Erikson was attempting to explain), but also why it was focused in the community of Salem Village (which Boyer and Nissenbaum explained), why it began among these particular girls, why the citizens of the community actually could believe that there were witches in their midst [which historian Chadwick Hansen (1969) has attempted to explain], and so forth.

On the other hand, if the researcher assumes that some explanations may be valid and others are not, it becomes important to entertain plausible rival interpretations and to evaluate these critically in light of the evidence. How well does a given interpretation account for the evidence? What does the interpretation assume and what consequences follow from it? Chambliss assumes a singularly valid explanation in raising such questions about Erikson's hypothesis: If Erikson is right, then it follows that the witchcraft mania (as well as the other crime waves) should have increased community solidarity. Did this occur? If each crime wave increased solidarity, why did the community experience three major crime waves in a period of sixty years? These are precisely the kinds of critical issues that must be raised about *any* historical interpretation. Better yet, the historical analyst should entertain and critically evaluate multiple interpretations and hypotheses and compare the relative plausibility of each. Only then can we reach an understanding of events in the scientific sense.

Content Analysis

William Chambliss and Kai Erikson have rather divergent perspectives on the functions of crime in society. So it is not surprising that they would arrive at different interpretations of the events in Salem Village. This difference points to one of the problems with the mere *reading* of written documents—the lack of agreement or reliability. One way to overcome this problem is to be explicit about how one should read the text. In fact, it is possible to develop systematic and objective criteria for transforming written text into highly reliable quantitative data. That is the goal of content analysis.

More than just a single technique, **content analysis** is really a set of methods for analyzing the symbolic content of any communication. The basic idea is to reduce the total content of a communication (e.g., all of the words or all of the visual imagery) to a set of categories that represent some characteristic of research interest. Thus, content analysis may involve the systematic description of either verbal or nonverbal materials.

Sales's analysis (1973) of comic strips and Archer and associates' measurement of facial prominence (1983) are examples of content analysis. However, Goffman's study (1979) of the meaning of gender roles as represented in magazine advertisements is not; he neither specified his content categories before the analysis nor systematically selected and described advertisements in terms of these categories. On the other hand, Goffman's study does suggest a set of gestures and body position cues that might be used to do a content analysis. Rather than casually look for evidence of such gestures, we would need to (1) identify the categories into which the ads are to be coded (e.g., male versus female; body position—standing, sitting, recumbent); (2) define the categories according to objective criteria that can be applied by anyone; (3) systematically select and then code the advertisements in terms of these objective criteria; and (4) report the frequency of the categories into which the ads have been coded.

The process just described is exactly the same as that found in systematic observation studies. It is also the same process that one would use in analyzing responses to open-ended questions (see Box 14.1). Sociologists have used content analysis to analyze unstructured interviews, and psychologists have applied it to verbal responses that are designed to assess the psychological states of persons. So as you can see, its application is not limited to the analysis of existing data. Still, its most common application is to the available printed or spoken word. Content analysis has been applied to written documents with varied and complex content, including newspaper editorials (Namenwirth, 1969), political party platforms (Weber, 1990), novels (Griswold, 1981), and recorded speeches (Seider, 1974). Let us take a closer look at the steps in carrying out such an analysis: selecting and defining content categories, defining the unit of analysis, deciding on a system of enumeration, and carrying out the analysis (Holsti, 1969).

Selecting and Defining Content Categories

To the extent that human coders are used, selecting and defining the categories for content analysis is analogous to deciding on a set of closed-ended questions in survey research. Instead of giving the questions to respondents who provide the answers, the content analyst applies them to a document and codes the appropriate category. The "questions" applied to the document should be adequate for the research purpose, and the categories should be clearly defined, exhaustive, and mutually exclusive.

Recall that Sales asked one question of the comic strips he analyzed: Is the central character strong and powerful? Wendy Griswold (1981), who analyzed a random sample of 130 novels published in the late nineteenth and early twentieth centuries, was interested in how the American novel might reflect unique properties of American character and experience. Accordingly, she asked several questions pertaining to characteristics of the protagonist (e.g., gender? age? social class at the beginning of the novel, social class at the end?) and to the plot (e.g., What is the setting of the main action? What is the time period? Is adult heterosexual love important to the plot? Is money important in the novel?).

Both Sales and Griswold used human coders to record category "answers." In fact, Griswold's study is unusual because of her large sample of novels, which required ten readers/coders. J. Zvi Namenwirth (1969), on the other hand, used a computer program to describe the editorial orientation of British elite and mass newspapers. First, he typed the text of 144 newspaper editorials into the computer. Then he provided the computer with a "dictionary" similar in structure to a thesaurus. The dictionary contained several hundred frequently used words from the editorials to be analyzed, which were entered into one or more of ninety-nine categories. For example, words referring to buildings and building parts were placed in the category "social place"; words such as job, ability, engineer, hunter, and print were included in the category "technological."

Regardless of whether one uses a human coder or a computer, the reliability and overall value of the content analysis depends on the clear formulation of content categories and of definitions or rules for assigning units to categories.

Defining the Unit of Analysis

Content analysts refer to their units of analysis as **recording units**. The recording unit is that element of the text that is described by the content categories. It could be the single word or symbol; the sentence, paragraph, or other grammatical unit; the whole text; or some other aspect of the text such as the character or plot. Namenwirth's recording unit was the word, whereas Griswold used three different units—character, plot, and whole novel. Sales's unit, on the other hand, was the character.

In general, smaller units may be coded more reliably than larger units because they contain less information (Weber, 1990). On the other hand, smaller units such as words may not be sufficient to extract the meaning of the message, and there may be too many such units for the researcher to manage. Imagine, for example, using the word as the recording unit in Griswold's analysis of 130 novels! These limitations apply to the use of computers in content analysis because, at this time, the only units programmable for computer analysis are words, word senses, and phrases such as idioms and proper nouns.

Because it may not be possible to place the recording unit in a particular category without considering the context in which it appears, content analysts also distinguish **context units** (Holsti, 1969). One of Namenwirth's findings was that British elite newspapers were more concerned about relations with Europe and less concerned about the Cold War than mass newspapers. Concern with Cold War issues was indicated by a large number of references to the word categories "Soviet," "American," and "Atlantic." From a simple analysis of words, however, one cannot infer the extent to which editorial positions on the Cold War generally were pro- or anti-American. To make this inference, the coder would need to consider the larger context unit—the sentence, paragraph, or whole editorial—in which the words are embedded. Similarly, Sales's coders would need to be familiar with the comic strip to make judgments about the power of the main character; thus his recording unit is the character, and his context unit is the comic strip.

Deciding on a System of Enumeration

There are many ways of quantifying the data in content analysis. The most basic systems of quantification are listed here.

1. *Time/space measures.* Early content analysts of newspapers often measured the space devoted to certain topics. Using column inches as their measure, for example, Janet Lever and Stan Wheeler (1984) found that sports coverage in *The Chicago Tribune* increased from 9 percent of the newsprint in 1900 to 17 percent in 1975. Analogously, television content has been measured in time (e.g., the number of hours of televised violence). Another example is Archer and associates' measurement of facial prominence (distance from top of head to chin divided by length of whole body).

2. *Appearance.* Sometimes it is sufficient simply to record whether a given category appears in a recording unit. Sales's measurement consisted of classifying the

central character in a given comic strip as powerful or not. Many of Griswold's categories were measured in this way: Is the main character a male? Is religion important to the plot?

3. *Frequency*. The most common method of measuring content is in terms of the frequency with which a given category appears in the contextual unit. Namenwirth counted the number of times categories appeared in each newspaper editorial. In an analysis of the Democratic and Republican party platforms, Robert Philip Weber (1990) calculated the proportion of words in the category "wealth" (e.g., capital, inflation, unemployment).[8]

4. *Intensity*. When attitudes and values are the objects of the research, the content analyst may resort to measures of intensity. For example, rather than ask whether money is important to the novel's plot, one might ask *how* important it is. Devising mechanisms for making judgments of intensity is essentially the same as in the construction of indexes and scales, which we discuss in chapter 12.

How the researcher decides to enumerate the data depends on the requirements of the problem under investigation. However, the choice of a system of enumeration carries with it certain assumptions regarding the nature of the data and the inferences that one can draw from the data (Holsti, 1969). Space–time measures may appropriately describe certain gross characteristics of the mass media, but they are too imprecise to serve as indicators of most verbal content. Appearance measures also tend to be rather imprecise, although they are more flexible and can be applied to a larger range of content than space–time measures. Frequency measures are better still, but involve two crucial assumptions that should be examined: First, they assume that the frequency of a word or category is a valid indicator of its importance, value, or intensity; second, they assume that each individual count is of *equal* importance, value, or intensity. It may be that some categories or some recording units should be weighted more heavily than others. It has been suggested, for example, that front-page articles might be more important and therefore weighted more than articles appearing elsewhere in a newspaper (Holsti, 1969). (Box 11.2 also discusses the problem of making inferences from frequencies of the "manifest" content of materials.)

BOX 11.2

Perspectives on Gender Differences in Graffiti

The grist for the content analyst—recorded language and visual representations—is essentially messages in a communication process. The object of content analysis is to uncover the *meanings* of the message. Among the many possible meanings, at least one will be manifestly understood by the source as well as the receiver of the message, but a great many more meanings may be latent to one or both parties. Thus the message may reveal something about the characteristics or unconscious intent of the source or about the beliefs and values of a group or culture. But how one comes to understand these meanings depends on the theoretical orientation that informs the analysis. Nowhere is this better illustrated than in research on restroom graffiti.

Thirty years of research on restroom graffiti shows that the inscriptions written by men differ from those written by women. Edward Bruner and Jane Paige Kelso (1980) divide this research into two types. One type establishes categories of manifest observations (e.g., sexual humor, racial insults, romantic, political) and then assigns each graffito to one of these categories. These studies show where gender differences lie (e.g., men use more insults, women are more romantic) but leave unclear the meanings of these differences. In this research, according to Bruner and Kelso, "there is an implicit theory of text which assumes that the meaning is the message, and that significance will be revealed by counting the frequency with which items of manifest content appear. The graffiti mean what the graffiti say, without any attempt to interpret the text" (p. 240).

The second type of research goes beyond the manifest meaning to a deeper level of interpretation. These studies interpret graffiti in terms of such Freudian imagery as unconscious impulses, infantile sexuality, and primitive thoughts. As Bruner and Kelso point out, however, the "connection between the data and the Freudian meaning is not readily apparent," and this approach suffers from "an over-attribution of meaning compared to the under-attribution" characteristic of the first approach.

By contrast, Bruner and Kelso offer a "semiotic perspective." Noting that graffiti are never found where others will not be able to see them, they argue that restroom graffiti constitute communication among anonymous partners. "The writing of graffiti," they say, "is an essentially social act that cannot be understood in terms of the expressive functions performed for an isolated individual. To write graffiti is to communicate; one never finds graffiti where they cannot be seen by others" (p. 241). Moreover, given the segregation of restrooms in American culture, restroom graffiti must be understood as same-sex communication—men writing for other men, and women writing for other women.

Approaching the data from this perspective, Bruner and Kelso find that on the surface, women's graffiti are more interpersonal and interactive than those written by men. Men tend to write egocentric and competitive inscriptions about sexual conquests and sexual prowess and derogatory inscriptions that attack, insult, or put down; women tend to raise serious questions about love, sexual relations, and commitment, often soliciting or giving advice regarding women's relationships with men. Going beyond this surface text, Bruner and Kelso conclude that "the underlying message in both male and female graffiti is fundamentally political." "Graffiti reflect the power positions of men and women in the social structure" (p. 250). Accordingly, "men write graffiti to tell themselves and other men that they have maintained their superior position and are still in control," while women write graffiti that "express the cooperation of the dominated and reflect the strategy of mutual help employed by those in a subordinate status" (pp. 249–50).

Carrying Out the Analysis

To carry out the analysis, one first obtains a sample of material. As in survey sampling, the researcher should always be mindful of the population to which inferences are to made. Three populations are relevant to content analysis: communication sources (e.g., types of newspapers, novels, speeches), documents (e.g., specific newspaper issues), and text within documents (e.g., pages). Often a sample of documents is drawn from a single source; for example, Griswold took a random sample of all novels published in the United States between 1876 and 1910. Namenwirth first sampled communication sources, purposefully choosing three British prestige newspapers and three mass papers. Then he randomly selected twenty-four documents—newspaper editorials—from each of the papers. Although researchers also have sampled text, Weber (1990:43) recommends that the entire text be analyzed when possible because this preserves its semantic coherence. If it is necessary to sample text, then meanings are best preserved by sampling paragraphs rather than sentences.

Having selected the sample, one proceeds to code the material according to the coding categories and system of enumeration. This gives the analyst a description of the communication content. Finally, the content analyst truly engages in *analysis* by relating content categories to one another or by relating the characteristics of the content to some other variable. Griswold compared the content of novels written by American and foreign authors, finding many similarities but also some interesting differences. For instance, American authors were likely to place protagonists in the middle class; foreign authors favored the upper class. American authors also were more likely to set their novels in small towns and less likely to set the action in the home.

Weber's content analysis of party platforms (1990) showed how Democrats and Republicans have varied over time in their concerns. Figure 11.1 shows the pattern of change with respect to the percentage of each platform devoted to economic matters. The vertical axis is based on the percentage of words in the platform that fall into the category "wealth."

Weber points out several features of the figure: (1) The general rise between 1844 and about 1952 in the level of concern about economic matters, perhaps reflecting the increasing importance of the federal government in the management of economic affairs; (2) the relatively constant level of concern from 1952 to 1984; and (3) the change over time in the relationship between the two parties' concern with economic matters, as the parties manifested similar levels of concern between 1896 and 1952 and moved opposite to one another before and after this period.

Summary

In contrast to research strategies that rely on data collected firsthand, the available-data researcher mines secondhand information. The sources of such information include the written public record, ranging from court proceedings, vital statistics, and publication indexes to the voluminous data files of the Census Bureau; private doc-

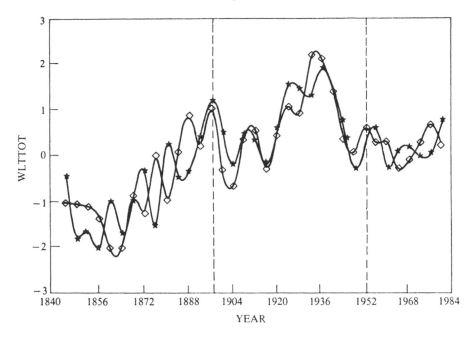

FIGURE 11.1. Democratic and Republican concern with wealth, 1844–1980. Diamonds, Republican platforms; stars, Democratic platforms. *Source:* Page 139 of R. P. Weber, "Computer-Aided Content Analysis: A Short Primer," *Qualitative Sociology,* vol. 7, 1984. Used by permission of Human Sciences Press.

uments such as diaries, letters, business records, and tax reports; the mass media; nonverbal physical evidence such as works of art, clothing, and other artifacts; and social science data archives generated from surveys and ethnographies.

Available-data research, including the secondary analysis of existing survey data, is currently the most popular method of social research. Compared with other research strategies, it is better suited to the analysis of social structural variables, to cross-cultural research, and to studies of the past and of social change. In addition, it often provides nonreactive measures of concepts, can afford the researcher the means to increase sample size and to replicate research, and generally costs less to the individual researcher.

When one uses data collected for another purpose, the search for appropriate data and the evaluation and refinement of the data become extremely important research phases. In general, the research problem should guide the search for sources of available data. The research literature also may provide useful leads for locating sources, which may be augmented by consulting a librarian or various listings of publicly accessible data sets.

Some sources of information may require the creative construction of substitute or indirect measures of key variables, or the use of multiple indicators. It is important, however, to be wary of less than satisfactory measures that may be adopted merely because of the data's availability. It is also essential to assess the validity of the data—to determine their authenticity, whether definitions used in compiling records have changed over time, whether the meaning of words and phrases in written documents has changed, and so forth. Following such evaluation, it is often necessary to refine or make adjustments to allow for proper interpretation.

Finally, one should consider the adequacy of the data as a sample of information. Much of the data from the census and various survey archives are based on unusually good, though not error-free, samples. Written records from the more remote past, however, invariably suffer from selective deposit, and physical materials are subject to selective survival. For voluminous data sets, probability sampling based on time and/or space is often possible and necessary.

The analysis of available-data research depends on research purposes and the nature of the source of information. Historical analysis may involve attempts to reconstruct past events (descriptive history) as well as the use of historical evidence to generate and test social theories (analytical history). In either case, the basic evidence consists of documents—testimony and social bookkeeping. Historical researchers judge testimony with respect to authenticity and credibility; they evaluate bookkeeping in the light of the organizations and groups that produced the documents. Descriptive historians also emphasize primary sources, whereas analytical historians often rely on secondary sources. Because the understanding of the past invariably is open to various interpretations, the historical researcher ideally should not focus on a single explanation, but instead critically evaluate and compare the relative plausibility of alternative explanations.

Researchers use content analysis to analyze the symbolic content of communication, especially verbal materials from the media. This involves selecting and defining a set of content categories, defining and then sampling the elements of the text that are described by the categories, quantifying the categories such as by counting their frequency of occurrence, and then relating category frequencies to one another or to other variables.

Key Terms

vital statistics	*analytical history*
manuscript census	*testimony*
Public Use Microdata Sample	*social bookkeeping*
data archives	*primary sources*
nonreactive measurement	*secondary sources*
selective survival	*content analysis*
selective deposit	*recording units*
descriptive history	*context units*

Review Questions and Problems

1. How does research using available data differ from the other three basic approaches to social research?

2. What are the five categories of available data described in this chapter?

3. Give three examples of public records other than those mentioned in the text that might serve as sources of data. In each case, identify a hypothesis that might be tested with the data.

4. What information is contained in birth certificates? In death certificates?

5. In what forms does the Census Bureau release information from the decennial census?

6. What is the manuscript census? When is it released to the general public? How else are individual-level data made available to the public?

7. What are private documents? Give an example of a private document available to you that might serve as a source of data. What research question might be addressed with these data?

8. How could you use the mass media to study changes in racial stereotypes? What period would you study? Which medium would you select?

9. What do the authors mean when they say that the "use of data archives is an extension of both survey research and field research"?

10. What are the principal advantages of research using available data?

11. Compare research using available data with the other three methodological approaches in terms of the problem of reactive measurement.

12. Identify two guidelines for locating appropriate sources of available data.

13. What is meant by "indirect measurement"? How is Sales's study of authoritarianism an example of indirect measurement?

14. What particular measurement problems are presented by research using available data?

15. Aside from research using survey data archives, what are the special sampling problems presented by research using available data?

16. Describe the four different forms of historical analysis outlined in the text.

17. How do users of historical documents go about determining the credibility of testimony?

18. Compare and contrast testimony and social bookkeeping with respect to (a) the populations and social processes about which they provide evidence and (b) the relevant issues for evaluating data sources.

19. What are the three interpretations of the Salem witchcraft hysteria described in the text? Is it possible for all three of these interpretations to be valid? Why or why not?

20. What is content analysis? Why is Sales's study of comic strips an example and Goffman's study of gender displays *not* an example of this method?

21. What steps are involved in doing a content analysis?

22. Identify common units of analysis in content analysis. What is the difference between a recording unit and a context unit?

23. What are the basic systems for quantifying data in content analysis?

24. Using Box 11.2 as an example, discuss the problem of using frequency counts for content analysis.

25. Describe how you would carry out a content analysis to examine some of the issues raised by Goffman's study of gender displays. (a) What materials will you select for analysis? (b) How will you sample them? (c) How will you select

and define content categories? (d) What is the recording unit? (e) What is the context unit? (f) What system of enumeration will you use?

NOTES

1. For a comprehensive listing of sources of demographic information, see Shryock et al. (1976).

2. Michael Lavin's (1996) *Understanding the Census* provides an overview of the decennial census and describes some of the many uses of census data. For an overiview of the design and implementation of the 2000 Census, including descriptions of the questionnaire, geography, available data sets, and where to go for assistance, see *Census 2000 Basics* at the World Wide Web site of the U.S. Census Bureau: http://www.census.gov.

3. To measure segregation, Farley and Frey used the index of dissimilarity, described briefly in chapter 4. The index equals a maximum of 100 if all blocks within a metropolitan area are exclusively black or exclusively white; the index equals its minimum of 0 if individuals are distributed as if they were randomly assigned. Intermediate values indicate the percentage of blacks (or whites) who would have to be shifted from one block to another to achieve an index score of 0.

4. The U.S. Bureau of the Census "Factfinder for the Nation" series is an excellent guide to census products. Also consult the "American Factfinder" on its World Wide Web site.

5. The net flow of migration to a country is equal to the number of immigrants entering minus the number of emigrants returning. The gross flow is simply the number entering.

6. For a discussion of this approach, see the special May 1992 issue (Volume 20, Number 4) of *Sociological Methods and Research*.

7. For a critique of the inductivist approach to comparative-historical sociology, see Edgar Kiser and Michael Hechter (1991); for a critique of the application of a general theoretical model to particular historical instances, see Theda Skocpol (1984:365–68).

8. Word counts have proven especially useful in content analyses designed to determine who wrote a certain document. A study of the disputed authorship of several of *The Federalist* papers showed, for example, that the disputed authors James Madison and Alexander Hamilton differed in known writings in their rate of use of noncontextual words like "by" and "to." When the papers were analyzed, the rate of use of these words corresponded closely in all but one paper to Madison's rather than Hamilton's writing (Mosteller and Wallace, 1964).

12

✓

Multiple Methods

The preceding chapters described four principal research strategies for understanding the social world: experiments, surveys, field research, and research using available data. By studying these approaches separately, you may have gotten the idea that these are entirely separate ways to proceed, that decisions about methods are necessarily of the either-or variety. However, given the limitations and biases inherent in each of the main approaches—indeed, inherent in all research procedures—the best way to study most research topics is to combine methodological approaches. This chapter begins with a discussion of a central principle called triangulation. Next we examine various "multiple methods" combinations, ranging from multiple measures of concepts within the same study to multiple tests of hypotheses across different studies. Then we compare the relative strengths and weaknesses of the four basic approaches to social research. Finally, we discuss "meta-analysis," the use of systematic procedures for summarizing the results of multiple studies.

Triangulation

In their everyday lives, people frequently use more than one means to solve a problem. Consider, for example, the simple problem of arising earlier than usual to catch a flight. Let us say a woman presented with this problem normally awakens by means of an electric clock radio set for 7 AM. To make sure that she awakened by 6:00, she might employ several methods. She might set the clock radio for 5:55, set a windup alarm clock for 6:00, and ask an early-rising friend to phone her at 6:05. She would then have three independent and somewhat dissimilar methods for solving the problem. If the electricity should go off, the windup alarm would work. If the windup alarm were defective, the friend should come through. If the friend proves unreliable, one of the other methods should work. By using multiple methods that do not share the same inherent weaknesses, we enhance our chances of solving the problem.

Social scientists have borrowed the term **triangulation** from the field of navigation to help describe how the use of multiple, independent approaches to a research question can enable an investigator to "zero in" on the answers or information sought (Campbell and Fiske, 1959). To understand the conventional meaning of triangulation, imagine that you are an employee of the Federal Communications Commission (FCC) assigned the task of determining the location of a pirate (unlicensed) radio station (P). First, using a FCC mobile receiver with directional-finder

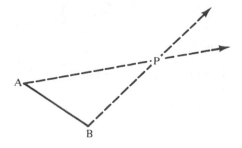

FIGURE 12.1. Triangulating a pirate radio station (P) from two points (A and B).

antenna, you measure the direction (compass bearing) to the pirate radio station from a certain point, point A, and again from a second point, point B. Knowing the distance between points A and B, you can now determine the distance AP or BP, using trigonometry, and thus the position of P (Figure 12.1).

The process of triangulation in navigation requires accurate measuring instruments. Suppose, for example, that your directional-finder antenna was off calibration (biased), so that it always gave a figure that was 15 degrees below the true figure. In that case you would fail to locate the pirate station (Figure 12.2). After failing to find the station, you might suspect that the measuring instrument (the directional antenna) was inaccurate, or you might entertain the possibility that the "concept" being measured changed between the first and second measurements (i.e., the pirate is a mobile radio station).

In social research, the logic of triangulation applies to situations in which two or more dissimilar measuring instruments or approaches are used. These approaches are analogous to the different vantage points, A and B, in the figure. The key to triangulation is the use of *dissimilar* methods or measures, which do not share the same methodological weaknesses—that is, errors and biases. The observations or "scores" produced by each method will ordinarily contain some error. But if the pattern of error varies, as it should with different methods, and if these methods independently produce or "zero-in" on the same findings, then our confidence in the result increases.

Unfortunately, social researchers rely altogether too frequently on a single method or measure when a number of approaches could be brought to bear on the

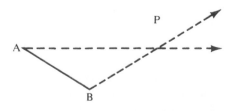

FIGURE 12.2. Triangulating a pirate radio station (P) from two points (A and B), with directional antenna off calibration by 15 degrees.

research question (Webb et al., 1981). Suppose, for example, you are investigating the hypothesis that airline disasters increase the anxiety of air travelers. Rather than rely on a single measure of anxiety, it would be better to use several. Eugene Webb and colleagues (1981) suggested the following indicators of anxiety: increased sales of alcoholic beverages at airport bars, increased sales of flight insurance policies, and decreased sales of air travel tickets following a disaster. Any one of these indicators, by itself, represents a relatively weak measure of anxiety. But note that the three measures do not share the same weaknesses: A downturn in the economy might decrease sales of tickets but would probably not affect the sales of inexpensive trip insurance policies to a great extent; publicity on insurance policy rip-offs could decrease policy sales but would not be expected to affect bar sales or ticket sales; an increase in the price of drinks might affect bar sales but would not be expected to affect the other measures, and so forth. Thus, if all three indicators of anxiety point to a relationship between airline disasters and travelers' anxiety, we can be relatively confident that such a relationship exists. As the number of dissimilar indicators increases, the likelihood that the relationship is an artifact of measurement error or spuriously created by an uncontrolled extraneous variable (such as a downturn in the economy) decreases.

Previously, we encountered the triangulation principle in terms of convergent validity assessment (chapter 4). It also applies to varied testing to eliminate rival hypotheses, as illustrated by a study of cultural differences in "susceptibility to optical illusion" (Campbell, 1969a:363–64). To rule out differences among anthropologists in the administration of visual tasks (instrumentation) as an alternative explanation for the observed cross-cultural differences, half of the researchers in one sample were purposely instructed to administer the tests in a manner deviating sharply from the standard instructions given to the remaining data collectors. By injecting this additional instrumentation variation the investigators were able to demonstrate that differences-in-administration effects were very small compared with the observed cultural differences.

Multiple methods refers here to "methods" in the broadest sense. In addition to the use of multiple indicators of a single concept and varied testing, the logic of triangulation also applies to such research activities as the use of multiple investigators in field research, cross-cultural archival research, and replications.

Jack Douglas (1976) advocates the use of a team approach in field research to obtain multiple perspectives on the setting. This is especially important when the setting contains several conflicting groups, so that it is impossible for one person simultaneously to be a member and gain the trust of more than one group. In a study of drug crisis intervention, for example, different members of an investigative team might become observers of the police, hospital staff, and drug users. Team members also might play different roles, such as we saw in David Snow and Leon Anderson's research on homelessness (chapter 10), where Anderson became an insider, or participant-observer, of the homeless street scene, while Snow for the most part remained an outsider. Similarly, mixed-gender research teams may gain access to more valid information by capitalizing on their gender identity. In a field study of a nude beach, for example, women and men team members discovered that people told them different things about the sexual dimensions of the scene (Warren and

Rasmussen, 1977). Single men told the male researcher about their sexual interests, but provided the female researcher only with the rhetoric of "naturalism and freedom." Likewise, single women revealed their real sexual interests only to the female researcher and invoked the naturalism rhetoric with the male researcher.

William Crano (1981) also holds that the principle of triangulation is implicit in studies that utilize cross-cultural archives, such as the *Ethnographic Atlas* described in chapter 11. Each society in the *Atlas* provides a different observational setting for the measurement of variables, and each ethnographer who contributed to the *Atlas* represents a different "method," subject to distinctive biases and error. Triangulation occurs when multiple methods are applied to the same setting (i.e., when a given society is investigated by two or more researchers). Since each ethnography constitutes an independent investigation, systematic biases should not accumulate in measures of the social reality experienced in any given society.

The final type of triangulation, replication, involves multiple tests of hypotheses. Each test may use a separate sample of subjects and different measures of key variables. Multiple tests also may entail either the same research strategy or a combination of strategies, such as when a researcher uses both experimentation and the analysis of available data to test the same hypothesis. Below we examine replications using the same and different approaches to social research. We begin, however, with a discussion of the most common form of triangulation: the use of multiple indicators in the same study.

Multiple Measures of Concepts within the Same Study

Suppose we want to test the hypothesis that a mother's expression of love toward her infant is directly related to the mother having a positive self-concept. In Figure 12.3, an arrow pointing from the independent variable ("self-esteem") to the dependent variable ("mother love") represents the hypothesis. "Mother love" is measured by the indicators L1 (amount of *time* a mother spends with the child), L2 (frequency of *physical contacts* such as lifting, holding, kissing, and stroking the child), and L3 (duration of *verbalizations* such as talking, singing, and cooing to the child); "self-esteem" is also measured by three distinct indicators P1, P2, and P3. There are two general ways to analyze the results of a study such as this that uses multiple measures: (1) Reduce the complexity of the data by combining all measures of each concept into a composite measure (an index or scale), and then determine whether the composite measures are related in the way hypothesized; or (2) formulate a model to represent the relationships among concepts as well as the measures of those concepts, and then test the model to see how well it fits the data. Let us examine each of these approaches in some detail.

Composite Measures: Indexes and Scales

Multiple measures are often combined into an index or scale. As we pointed out in chapter 4, it is difficult to measure a concept well with a single indicator or question. Not only do single indicators rarely capture all the meaning of a concept, but

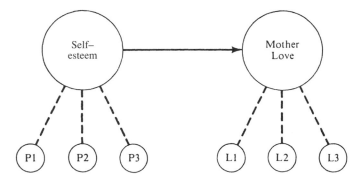

FIGURE 12.3. Diagram of the relationship between self-esteem and mother love, with three indicators per concept.

each indicator is likely to have distinctive sources of error or bias. By combining several indicators into a composite measure, we generally get a better overall representation of the concept, and the errors tend to cancel each other out, yielding a more reliable measure.

An example is provided by the questions on abortion included in the General Social Survey (Davis, Smith, and Marsden, 2002):

> Please tell me whether or not you think it should be possible for a pregnant woman to obtain a legal abortion. . . . [The interviewer then reads each of the following statements.]
>
> A. If there is a strong chance of serious defect in the baby?
> B. If she is married and does not want any more children?
> C. If the woman's own health is seriously endangered by the pregnancy?
> D. If the family has a very low income and cannot afford any more children?
> E. If she became pregnant as a result of rape?
> F. If she is not married and does not want to marry the man?

Responses to these questions may reflect attitudes unrelated to abortion per se, such as attitudes toward handicaps (A), large families (B), growing up in poverty (D), rape (E), or premarital sex (F). However, by combining these items into an index, we avoid the biases inherent in any single item. For example, if only questions A, C, or E were used as our measure, the overwhelming majority of the U.S. population in 2002 would be pro-abortion. If only question B, D, or F were used, then the majority in 2002 would be anti-abortion (Davis, Smith, and Marsden, 2002). In either case we would have a biased estimate of the general attitude toward abortion in the United States. On the other hand, if all six items were used, we would get a better overall estimate, one that is less likely than any single item to underestimate or overestimate the strength of individuals' attitudes.

How are separate measures combined or "aggregated"? The simplest and most common procedure is just to add or to take an average of the scores of the separate items; this is what we generally mean by an **index**. For example, public attitudes toward racial integration have been surveyed repeatedly with the use of the following five-question index developed by Donald J. Treiman (Taylor, Sheatsley, and Greeley, 1978).

1. Do you think white students and black students should go to the same schools or to separate schools?
2. How strongly would you object if a member of your family wanted to bring a black friend home to dinner?
3. White people have a right to keep blacks out of their neighborhoods if they want to, and blacks should respect that right. (Do you strongly agree, agree, . . . or strongly disagree?)
4. Do you think there should be laws against marriages between blacks and whites?
5. Blacks shouldn't push themselves where they're not wanted. (Do you strongly agree, agree, . . . , or strongly disagree?)

The index consists of the number of pro-integration responses to these five questions; thus, scores may range from 0 (strongly anti-integrationist) to 5 (strongly pro-integrationist). Interestingly, between 1963 and 1976 the average score for the U.S. white population increased steadily, with the sharpest rise from 1970 to 1972.

Nathan Keyfitz (1976) provides another example of an index, one that is constructed from population estimates rather than questionnaire items. To study the relationship between use of natural resources and global growth of the middle class, he needed some way to estimate the size of the world middle class in different years. He obtained this estimate by developing an index based on four separate indicators: the number of passenger cars in use, the number of telephones, the amount of electric energy produced, and the consumption of crude oil. (Each of these indicators required mathematical operations that we will not describe here.) The values yielded by the four separate estimates of the world middle class were then averaged. One of the conclusions of the study was that, if more of the poor are to enter the high-consumption middle class, ways must be found to support the middle-class standard of living with less energy and natural resources.

In both of these examples, each of the multiple measures (questionnaire items or separate population estimates) was assumed to be of equal value in determining the index score. In other words, each indicator was given the same "weight" in computing the index. One could, however, assign different weights by multiplying the separate indicators by different values (weights). Measures of socioeconomic status, for example, typically combine indicators of occupational prestige, education, and income. Because occupational prestige is thought to contribute more to socioeconomic status, it is generally weighted more heavily. Thus, in August Hollingshead's (1971) two-factor Index of Social Position, an occupation score is given a weight of 7 and an education score is given a weight of 4. To compute the index, one would first determine an individual's occupation and education scores on separate 7-point measures, multiply each score times its respective weight, and then add the score–weight products.

The advantage of indexing may be illustrated as follows. Suppose the value of each observed measure (X) is equal to a true score corresponding to the concept being measured (C) and an error score (e); thus, $X = C + e$. Now suppose that we have four different measures, and pretend we know the true and error scores for a particular respondent (see the following tabulation).

Measure	Observed score (X)	True score (C)	Error score (e)
Item 1	2	4	−2
Item 2	3	2	+1
Item 3	7	5	+2
Item 4	5	8	−3
Total	17	19	−2

For each separate item, about one-third or more of the observed score represents error. If the error tends to be random (or if systematic but in different directions for the separate items), the error scores tend to cancel out when we sum over the items. Consequently, if we form an index by summing the four items, we obtain a greatly improved measure. For the particular respondent shown above, the index score would be 17 units, only a small fraction of which represents error (2 units).

While most composite measures constitute indexes, multiple indicators may also be combined to form **scales**. The distinction between an index and a scale is rather fuzzy, and some social scientists use the terms interchangeably. But we think it is a distinction worth making. An index usually refers to the arbitrary combination of indicators, such as when we simply add together the responses to separate items without regard to what each actually contributes to the measurement of the underlying concept. The chief problem with an index is ensuring **unidimensionality**, since it may be measuring more than the intended concept (e.g., "political liberalism" as well as "attitude toward racial integration"). A scale, on the other hand, combines indicators according to nonarbitrary rules that are ordinarily designed to reflect only a single dimension of a concept.

Some scales differ from indexes by assigning scores to patterns of responses to a set of items. To illustrate the idea of patterns of responses, let us return to the Treiman index of attitudes toward racial integration referred to earlier (Taylor, Sheatsley, and Greeley, 1978:43). Suppose that two respondents, Earl and Rudolph, gave the responses shown here to the five questions (see tabulation). If the items were scored as an index and we counted pro-integration responses, Earl and Rudolph would receive the same score, even though they have very different response patterns. Can one say which of the two is more racially liberal?

Question number	Earl	Rudolph
1	Pro-integration	Anti-integration
2	Pro-integration	Anti-integration
3	Anti-integration	Anti-integration
4	Anti-integration	Pro-integration
5	Anti-integration	Pro-integration

This contrived example points out a problem with index construction, namely, an issue of validity. If the same score may be achieved with very different responses, the possibility exists that the items are measuring more than one dimension or concept. Besides attitudes toward racial integration, Earl's and Rudolph's responses may reflect other concepts, such as a concern to give socially desirable responses.

The construction of scales assumes that a concept can be understood in terms of an underlying continuum; in the case of an attitude, the continuum may range from favorable to unfavorable or positive to negative. It is further assumed that scores on individual items and composite measures represent specific points along the relevant continuum (or "scale"). Each score, in other words, should uniquely reflect the strength or degree of something—for example, an individual's degree of prejudice or a nation's level of modernization. But whereas these assumptions are implicit in an index, scaling procedures make them explicit and are designed to test their validity.

To illustrate a scaling technique, we will describe the approach developed by Louis Guttman (1950). Suppose we measure people's reading ability by testing their reading comprehension of items *ordered* in terms of difficulty, such as portions of a third-grade reader, a ninth-grade textbook, and a college textbook. Subjects would be tested on each item starting with the easiest, and the item at which someone changed from "passing" to "failing" the reading tests would indicate the subject's position on a scale of reading ability. Four response patterns are expected if the items form a perfect Guttman scale: (1) Flunk each item, (2) pass only at the third-grade level, (3) pass all but the college text, and (4) pass all reading tests. Other response patterns, such as passing the ninth-grade test and flunking the other two, are called "nonscale" or "mixed types." By selecting a set of items that minimize the proportion of "nonscale" response patterns, the Guttman approach attempts to ensure a unidimensional scale.

The actual process of **Guttman scaling** is sometimes quite elaborate. A researcher may start with a large battery of items thought to measure a concept. Then subsets of these items are tested, often with a computer program, to determine if they satisfy the expectations of a Guttman scale. Let us illustrate part of this process using the six GSS abortion items referred to earlier. Based on the proportion of 1975 GSS respondents answering "yes" to each question, Clifford Clogg and Darwin Sawyer (1981) ordered the items from the "easiest" condition under which to approve of abortion (woman's health is seriously endangered by the pregnancy) to the "most difficult" condition (woman does not want more children). Table 12.1 shows this question ordering and the seven response patterns possible if the items form a perfect Guttman scale. Each column in Table 12.1 displays a different response pattern ("Y" and "N" denote "yes" and "no" answers, respectively), and the "yes" responses are totaled to obtain a scale score for each response pattern.

In contrast to an index, a respondent's score on a *perfect* Guttman scale uniquely identifies the person's response pattern. In Table 12.1, for example, a score of 2 is always the pattern "Y Y N N N N." Note also that a score on a perfect Guttman scale indicates the point at which the respondent shifts from one response to another (e.g., those who score 3 approve of an abortion in the three "easiest" condi-

TABLE 12.1. **Response Pattern of a Perfect Guttman Scale**

Approve of an abortion if:	*Response pattern*						
The woman's own health is seriously endangered by the pregnancy.	Y	Y	Y	Y	Y	Y	N
There is a strong change of serious defect in the baby.	Y	Y	Y	Y	Y	N	N
She became pregnant as a result of rape.	Y	Y	Y	Y	N	N	N
The family has a very low income and can't afford any more children.	Y	Y	Y	N	N	N	N
She is not married and does not want to marry the man.	Y	Y	N	N	N	N	N
She is married and does not want any more chlidren.	Y	N	N	N	N	N	N
Scale Score	6	5	4	3	2	1	0

tions and then shift to disapproval). Whether a set of items is reasonably close to the ideal of a perfect Guttman scale is an empirical question. We found that 17 percent of the 2000 GSS respondents had "nonscale" response patterns (e.g., "Y N Y N N N"). Using conventional measures of scalability, this indicates that the six questions form an acceptable Guttman scale for the 2000 GSS sample. The employment of Guttman scaling to ensure unidimensionality, however, is sample dependent. A set of items may be unidimensional for one sample of respondents but not for another. Differences in scalability across samples reflect sampling and measurement error as well as population differences [see Clogg and Sawyer (1981) for details and alternatives to the Guttman approach].

Various scaling procedures have been developed. Some capitalize on the inherent pattern among a set of items, whereas others capitalize on each item's placement with regard to an underlying continuum. The construction of scales is a topic beyond the scope of the present text. For a good overview of the subject of index and scale construction, see Robin Dawes and Tom Smith (1985). (Also see Box 12.1 for a description of another popular scaling technique.)

Although we have presented composite measures from the standpoint of "triangulation," there are other good reasons for building indexes and scales. One is ease of analysis: The number of variables that must be considered is reduced. Another has to do with the variability in respondents' scores provided by the measure. Sometimes items provide very little information due to low variability (e.g., 90 percent of the respondents make the same response). By combining several items with low variability, it is possible to obtain an index with much greater variability, hence a more informative measure.

Structural Equation Modeling

Until recently, indexes and scales were almost always constructed when one had multiple measures of concepts. In part this was because most social scientists were unfa-

---

BOX 12.1

An Example of Likert Scaling: The Development of the FEM Scale

Guttman scales are designed so that each item represents a particular point on the underlying dimension. Because the set of items is ordered and cumulative, an individual's total scale score not only denotes a place on the underlying dimension but also reveals his or her responses to each and every item. Thus both the items and the individuals are scaled with respect to the underlying concept. Another scaling technique, called **Likert** or **summated ratings**, assumes that each scale item reflects the entire range of the underlying continuum to the same degree. In a measure of attitude toward feminism, for example, each item may have response categories that vary from strongly antifeminist to strongly profeminist. Each item thus constitutes a separate rating, and an individual's score consists of the sum of his or her ratings (hence, the label "summated ratings"). Unlike a Guttman scale, the items of a Likert scale are not ordered or scaled; consequently, individual scores indicate a place on the underlying continuum, but do not indicate a pattern of responses to particular items.

In developing a Likert scale, the object is to create a set of items whose combination provides the best measure of differences among respondents on the underlying concept. The construction of the FEM Scale, the validation of which we described in chapter 4 (see Box 4.2), illustrates the steps in developing a Likert scale, including the criteria for selecting constituent items.

Step 1. Eliot Smith, Myra Marx Ferree, and Frederick Miller (1975) initially developed fifty-seven items, each stating either the acceptance or rejection of a feminist belief. The sources of ideas for specific items in the Likert scale are limited only by the researcher's imagination. In this case the researchers drew many items from an earlier study by Clifford Kirkpatrick (1936); for other items they may have considered the published statements of avowed feminists and antifeminists. Below are five sample items that eventually were included in the scale.

1. Women have the right to compete with men in every sphere of activity.
2. As head of the household, the father should have final authority over his children.
3. The unmarried mother is morally a greater failure than the unmarried father.
4. A woman who refuses to give up her job to move with her husband would be to blame if the marriage broke up.
5. A woman who refuses to bear children has failed in her duty to her husband.

Step 2. The researchers asked thirty-nine students to indicate whether they agreed or disagreed with each item as they role-played a "strong profeminist" or a "strong antifeminist." The purpose of this step, not always a part of scale construction, was to eliminate items that were ambiguous—that is, items that were not clearly perceived as representing either a profeminist or antifeminist position. When there was sizeable disagreement over the direction of an item, the item was discarded. This left forty-eight items.

Step 3. The next step is to select a subset of items that best discriminates among persons who hold different attitudes. To make this selection, researchers administer an initial item set to a group of respondents who are similar to those for whom the scale is intended. Smith, Ferree, and Miller shortened their scale in two stages. First, they asked the same students who role-played to give their own opinions. From an analysis of these responses, they selected twenty-seven items. The basis of their selection was the items' variability. Greater variability generally indicates better discriminability (the ability to discriminate among individuals with different attitudes); for if an item shows low variability, meaning that it elicits similar responses from all individuals, then it does not reveal how individuals differ in their attitudes.

Next, the researchers administered the preliminary twenty-seven-item scale to 100 Harvard summer-school students. Again, they assessed the items' ability to discriminate among respondents, this time using a technique called "factor analysis." Factor analysis is one of several ways to assess an item's discriminability. A simpler approach is to calculate each individual's scale score, determine the highest and lowest 25 percent of the scores, and then identify those items that best differentiate between the high and low scores. For example, if both high and low scorers are equally likely to endorse a particular statement, that statement would have poor discriminability. On the basis of the factor analysis, Smith, Ferree, and Miller selected the twenty items with highest discriminability.

Step 4. In its final form, a Likert scale consists of a series of statements with which respondents are asked to indicate their level of agreement or disagreement. The response format permits several categories of response. For the FEM Scale there are five: "strongly agree," "agree," "undecided," "disagree," and "strongly disagree." To arrive at a scale score, these categories are assigned numbers from 1 to 5, the highest number representing strong agreement with a profeminist statement (or conversely, strong disagreement with an antifeminist statement). Adding item responses, we get a possible range of 20 to 100 for the twenty-item scale. This range corresponds to a dimension that at the low end indicates a very unfavorable attitude toward feminism and at the high end indicates a very favorable attitude toward feminism.

Step 5. At this point, the scale is ready to test for reliability and validity, a process that we have described in Box 4.2.

---

miliar with procedures for analyzing multiple measures simultaneously. However, over the past three decades, simultaneous testing has become increasingly popular as sociologists have become more knowledgeable about a technique called **structural equation modeling**. The term "structural modeling" refers to the systematic identification of the possible relationships among a set of concepts and their indicators. Each distinctive model describes a different "structure" of relationships that can be represented with a unique system of mathematical "equations." When applying this technique, one essentially checks to see how well the data fit various models. The mathematics required to do this are rather advanced. Still, one can get a sense of the value of structural equation modeling by considering the following example.

Recall the hypothetical study described earlier in this section involving the relationship between mother love and self-esteem. All the mothers in the study would have to be measured on each of the six indicators. Since measurement may be re-

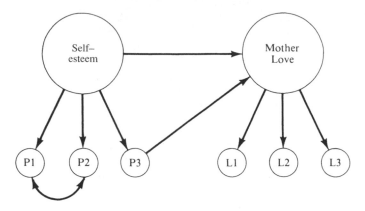

FIGURE 12.4. Diagram of a structural equation model of the relationship between self-esteem and mother love.

active, there is the possibility that measuring L1 may influence L2, L3, or even P1 or self-esteem. For example, the presence of an observer might affect the extent to which the mother touches the infant or perhaps even the mother's self-esteem. Consequently, an adequate representation of the relationships among the variables might be considerably more complicated than indicated in Figure 12.3.

Consider Figure 12.4. Notice the arrows leading from "mother love" and "self-esteem" to each of their respective indicators; these represent the assumption that the unobserved concepts "mother love" and "self-esteem" cause their measured indicators. This model also shows that P1 and P2 partly share the same methodological weaknesses (diagrammed by the curved arrow between them denoting this common bias), and that the measurement of P3 influences "mother love." Obviously, there are a large number of possible models depicting the variables in Figure 12.4. For example, deleting the arrow from P3 to "mother love" or adding a curved arrow between L1 and L3 produces a different model. It is the job of the researcher to consider the more plausible models and to test each in order to determine which "fit" the data.[1]

Structural equation modeling differs from composite measurement in that it maintains the separate identity of each indicator throughout the analysis. This requires that the researcher specify how each indicator is related to the underlying concept it measures. An advantage of this approach is that it makes it possible to test for certain kinds of measurement error. One disadvantage is that it becomes extremely difficult to consider all possible combinations of relationships as the number of indicators and concepts increases (Jacobson and Lalu, 1974). Modeling is discussed further in chapter 15.

Multiple Tests of Hypotheses across Different Studies

One of the best ways to increase our confidence in a particular finding is to repeat a study to see if we can obtain the same result. Although replications frequently aim to duplicate the original study in as much detail as possible, they can never be exactly the same. At the very least, each **replication** is conducted at a different time, and generally will involve a different sample of cases. Thus, replications are inherently dissimilar. Furthermore, the more dissimilar they are in terms of methods, time, place, and so forth, the greater the confidence that the findings support the research hypothesis rather than being an artifact of particular research conditions and procedures.

In spite of their value, replications are relatively infrequent in social research. Apparently, the cost of most studies cannot be justified solely for the purpose of replicating a finding. The one exception to this pattern is experimental research. Not only are small-scale experiments less costly to replicate than other kinds of research, but replication is the principal method of increasing the external validity of experimental results.[2] In the following example, a team of investigators carried out an initial experiment and two replications to test versions of the same basic hypothesis. The experiments used different groups of subjects as well as different manipulations and measures of the hypothesis-linked concepts.

Replications Using the Same Research Strategy: Compliance without Pressure

How are people swayed to comply with a request they would prefer to refuse? Jonathan Freedman, Sue Ann Wallington, and Evelyn Bless (1967) hypothesized that one factor that leads to increased compliance is guilt: People who feel guilty are likely to try to relieve their guilt by either doing a good deed or willingly submitting to an unpleasant experience. To test this hypothesis, they designed three experiments.

In the first experiment, the investigators manipulated guilt by inducing some subjects to tell a lie while others did not. The subjects, sixty-two high-school males, were randomly assigned to the experimental (lie) and control (nonlie) groups. A confederate of the experimenter, posing as the previous subject, introduced the manipulation while the experimenter was in another room "preparing the test." As the subject waited for the "test" to begin, the confederate struck up a conversation. In the lie condition, he described in detail the test the subject was about to be given; in the nonlie condition, he divulged no such information about the test. Before administering the test, the experimenter then asked each subject whether he had taken the test before or heard about it. Only one subject in the lie condition admitted that he had heard about the test; hence, all but one subject in this condition were induced to tell a direct lie, and it was assumed that they would experience guilt as a result. Each subject was then given the forty-minute test, after which he was thanked and paid for his participation. As the subject was leaving the room, the experimenter casually asked him if he would participate without pay as a subject in an experiment being done by someone else in the department. The study's hypothesis, that subjects who lied would be more likely to comply with the request than subjects who had not lied, was confirmed. Of the subjects in the lie condition, twenty volunteered for the additional experiment and eleven did not; the figures were exactly the opposite for the control subjects.

In the second experiment, guilt was manipulated by causing some subjects to upset "accidentally" a very large pile of carefully arranged index cards apparently containing notes for a dissertation. Sixty-seven first-year college women served as paid subjects. The subject was greeted and led by the experimenter to a room which, she explained, had been lent to her by a graduate student. In the room was a confederate (purportedly another subject), seated at a small table on which were a pile of approximately 1000 note cards separated by topic. The manipulation occurred when the experimenter left the subject and confederate alone for five minutes while she went to get the tests. One leg of the small table, hidden by the confederate's chair, was 2 inches shorter than the other three legs and was supported by a small block. In two conditions, the block was removed before the subject entered the room; in the third, the block was left in place. In the "guilt" condition, the subject inevitably touched or brushed against the table, thus tipping it and scattering the cards. In the first control condition, the confederate upset the table; in the second control condition, with the block in place, no "accident" occurred. When the table had been tipped, the confederate and subject worked together to return the index cards to the table in neat stacks (but out of order). The experimenter returned, administered the test to the subject in the same room, and led the confederate out, ostensibly to take the test in another room. Later the experimenter returned, thanked and paid the subject, and, as the subject was leaving, either asked her if she would participate as an unpaid subject in an experiment to be conducted by the graduate student in whose room the experiment had taken place (relevant request) or asked her if she would participate in an experiment to be conducted by "a graduate student in the department" (irrelevant request). Compliance was measured by the number who agreed.

The study addressed two questions: (1) Did guilt affect compliance? and (2) Was the level of compliance among the guilty affected by whether the victim or some other person would be the beneficiary of compliance? The results showed that in general, scattering the note cards did affect compliance: 75 percent of those who knocked over the cards volunteered for the future experiment, whereas less than 39 percent of those in the control conditions did so. This finding supported that of the first experiment described earlier. The results regarding the second question were more surprising. While it might seem that an opportunity to help the victim of one's guilty action might bring about compliance to a greater extent than an opportunity to help someone not associated with the guilty act, the reverse was found. The difference in compliance between guilty and nonguilty subjects showed up only when the request did not involve the injured party; no difference was found between these groups in volunteering to help the graduate student in whose office the accident took place. This perplexing finding led to the formulation of a new question: Is the guilty person under two pressures—first, to make up for the misdeed, and second, to avoid contact with the injured party? A third experiment was conceived with the dual purposes of testing this new question as well as providing additional confirmation of the hypothesis that guilt increases compliance.

The third experiment was much like the second, with the physical setting exactly the same. Subjects were seventy-four first- and second-year college women. Since there had been essentially no difference in scores of subjects in the two control conditions of the second experiment, one condition was eliminated, that in which the confederate spilled the cards. A confederate was present as before, but merely served as an assistant to answer questions the subject might have. The main difference between the second and third experiments lay in the nature of the request made at the conclusion of the experiment. While all subjects were asked to help the graduate student in whose room the experiment took place (the injured party), half were told they would be working closely with the graduate student in distributing a public opinion questionnaire (association condition), and half were told they would be working with another volunteer (nonassociation condition). As before, the number who agreed to help served as the measure of compliance.

As in the first two experiments, the hypothesis that guilt leads to compliance was confirmed, with over 55 percent of the guilty subjects acceding to the request compared with 28 percent of the controls. Results also supported the new hypothesis: Guilty subjects complied more than the nonguilty when the request did not require subjects to associate with the injured party (nonassociation condition), but there was no difference in compliance between guilty and nonguilty subjects when the request required contact with the victim (association condition).

The fact that the main hypothesis was consistently supported across three different experiments greatly strengthens our confidence in the findings. Note that across the three experiments, operational definitions of guilt and compliance varied: Guilt was manipulated in two ways (either by inducing subjects to lie or by causing subjects to scatter someone's research notes); and although the measure of compliance was always the number who agreed, the requests for the subjects' help differed somewhat (irrelevant or relevant to the victim, association or nonassociation with the victim). In addition, the populations from which subjects were drawn differed slightly in the three experiments. These differences in methods helped to eliminate rival explanations for the findings. For example, in the first experiment, a rival explanation might be that the lying subjects complied not out of guilt, but because they felt sorry for the person to whom they had lied and therefore would be more likely to comply with the request that was made (Freedman, Wallington, and Bless, 1967). However, because in experiments 2 and 3 the person making the request was not the person wronged, this explanation may be ruled out.

Replications Using Different Research Strategies: Deterrent Effects of Arrest

Two studies on the deterrent effects of arrest for domestic violence may be used to illustrate further the application of multiple methods to test hypotheses across different studies. Unlike the set of experiments just described, which entailed the same basic approach, the following two studies were carried out in different settings with different approaches.

The first study, called the Minneapolis Spouse Abuse Experiment, was designed to test the relative merits of two alternative theories of punishment. The deterrence doctrine holds that the "pains of punishment deter people from repeating the crimes for which they are punished." Labeling theory, alternatively, holds that "punishment often makes individuals more likely to commit crimes" because it changes their self-image and social interaction patterns and forecloses certain life options (Sherman and Berk, 1984:261). To test these theories, Lawrence Sherman and Richard Berk (1984) carried out a field experiment in the city of Minneapolis over an eighteen-month period, between March 1981 and August 1982. The experimental design called for police to apply randomly one of three intervention strategies when confronting incidents of simple (misdemeanor) domestic assault: Arrest the offender, force the offender to leave the premises, or give advice and/or mediate the dispute.[3] The effects of these three responses were assessed by determining whether an offender repeated an incident of domestic assault within a six-month follow-up period. The investigators measured this outcome in two ways: (1) through police records indicating whether an offense or arrest report had been filed and (2) through interviews with victims, who were asked to indicate if there had been an actual or threatened assault or property damage. On both measures, the results showed that arrested offenders were least likely to commit another act of domestic violence.[4] Thus the study tends to support the efficacy of deterrence.

Sherman and Berk considered several potential sources of error or bias that might have influenced their findings. For example, the official outcome measure—police reports—might be affected by the reluctance of victims to call the police. This effect would be confounded with the arrest intervention strategy if the arrest were seen as "an undesirable intervention, and rather than face the prospect of another arrest from a new incident, these victims [decided] not to invoke police sanctions" (p. 269). Sherman and Berk note, however, that identical results were obtained with the interview self-report data, which should not have been subject to the same source of bias. Hence, a triangulation of the dependent measure effectively eliminated this interpretation. In a similar fashion, the researchers considered other potentially problematic features of the study, and they argued in each case against the likelihood of a contaminating effect. The one limitation that they did not minimize was the external validity of the study. It is possible that special features of the site, the police department, and the officers who volunteered to take part in the study might have affected the findings. The effects of arrest, in other words, might not be the same in other jurisdictions with different characteristics.

Despite this qualification, the Minneapolis Spouse Abuse Experiment received enormous publicity and apparently began to affect police policy around the country (Berk and Newton, 1985). It became especially important, therefore, to test the generalizability of the findings. To this end, Richard Berk and Phyllis Newton (1985) conducted a second study in which they tested the same hypothesis, with the same official outcome measure, but in a different setting with a different research approach involving the analysis of existing data.

The data consisted of "783 wife-battery incidents coming to the attention of police over a 28-month period in a county in California" (p. 253). Over one-fourth of the incidents had resulted in arrest, and it was possible from police records to identify subsequent cases of police intervention as well as when the new incidents occurred. Unlike the previous study, however, where cases were randomly assigned to intervention strategies, differences between arrested and nonarrested offenders were not randomized. Therefore, the investigators statistically controlled for these differences by using other information from police records about offender characteristics (e.g., age, number of previous convictions, employment status) and situational features of the incident (e.g., time of day, presence of witness). The control amounted to a measure of the propensity of the police to arrest. With this control, the most general finding was consistent with the Minneapolis results: Arrests deter new incidents of domestic assault. Berk and Newton also found that arrests were most effective with batterers whom police would ordinarily be inclined to arrest. That is, there was a direct relationship between propensity to arrest and the deterrent effect of arrest. Although the investigators were cautious about the study's implications for policy recommendations (they noted, for example, that little is known about how the arrest process deters domestic assault), they concluded that "our study places the burden of proof heavily on those who believe that wife batterers should not be arrested" (p. 262).

Separately, each of these studies has major limitations that undermine the credibility of the findings. The setting and other unique features of the Minneapolis experiment limit its external validity. Without random assignment of offenders to treatments, the second study has relatively low internal validity. Together, however, they greatly increase our confidence in the principal finding. Not only do they represent independent confirmations of the same hypothesis, but the strengths in one study offset the weaknesses in the other. The second study enhances the generalizability of the experimental results insofar as it involves a different police department in a different setting, with a natural rather than manipulated measure of the independent variable. By the same token, we gain confidence in the findings of the second study by virtue of obtaining the same basic result in another study with high internal validity.

Although the two studies, taken together, increased the credibility of the arrest intervention strategy, research conclusions are always tentative and subject to change or reinterpretation as new evidence accumulates. Indeed, subsequent replications of the Minneapolis Domestic Violence Experiment failed to consistently replicate the original findings (Berk and associates, 1992; Pate and Hamilton, 1992; Sherman and Smith, 1992; Sherman, 1992, 1993). These replications indicated that the effect of arrest varied across jurisdictions, with a deterrent effect in some areas, no discernible effect in others, and an escalating effect in still others. Furthermore, the deterrent effects of arrest appear to depend on the length of the follow-up period, the length of detention, the background of the offender, and whether the offender perceives that he has been treated fairly (Paternoster et al., 1997). For example, arrest seems to be more effective for the employed than for the unemployed; it also is more effective when the arrested suspect perceives that he has been treated in a procedurally fair manner.

A Comparison of the Four Basic Approaches to Social Research

The principle of triangulation emphasizes the value of testing hypotheses with different methods that do not share the same methodological weaknesses. In this way, we build confidence in our assertions about the social world. This position has two related implications. First, as Joel Smith (1991:2) asserts in an article entitled "A methodology for twenty-first century sociology," social research "should be shaped by the nature of the question, the phenomena being considered, and the sort of answer that will satisfy us." Too often in social research, methods are not chosen or created to fit the task, but "have become ideologies that define what to study and how." Qualitative research is valued over quantitative (or vice versa); comparative historical methods are valued over survey research; field research is valued over experimentation. These dogmatic positions, however, obscure the fact that all conclusions in social research rest on the resolution of the same basic issues. According to Smith (1991:11–13), these are encompassed by the following five questions:

1. What does one want to know and why? (Any study should have a clear and specific purpose guided by a clear theoretical interest.)
2. What is to be observed? (Choices must be made about time and place, unit of analysis, relevant characteristics, and the processes in which units are embedded.)
3. Which and how many objects are to be examined? (Because any study provides a limited set of observations, one should be aware of what the observations represent and how many cases should be selected in light of theory, desired reliability of estimates, and available resources.)
4. How are the phenomena of interest to be observed? (The method of observing—by asking questions, noting appearance and behavior, recording physical traces, and so forth—should depend on theory and the relative advantages and disadvantages of each approach.)
5. How are answers to be decided? (The analysis should indicate what can be asserted with what certainty about what has been found.)

In short, the focus of social research should be on what one wants to know and why rather than on how to apply a particular approach. We must be capable of applying particular techniques and methods, to be sure, but these should not be treated dogmatically lest their application become an end in itself.

The second implication of triangulation is that social researchers need to know the relative strengths and weaknesses of each approach in order to decide which methods to select and how best to combine them when possible. Table 12.2 summarizes these strengths and weaknesses by identifying the vulnerability of the four main approaches to seven limitations or sources of error. To compare general strengths and weaknesses, the table focuses attention on particular ideal forms of these strategies: laboratory experiments, structured surveys, participant observation, and documentary evidence. It is important to recall, however, the variations within each basic strategy. Experiments may be conducted in the field as well as in the laboratory; survey interviews and questionnaires vary in their degree of structure and in the quality of the sample; field research differs in terms of the investigator's level of involvement in the observational setting; and available data come in myriad forms subject to distinctive methodological problems. Furthermore, there are other research strategies that do not fit neatly into this fourfold typology, which we have ignored or touched on only lightly in this book, such as structured observation, ethnographic interviews, and life histories.

The entries in the table summarize the degree of vulnerability of each approach to each limitation or source of error. "H" means that the approach is highly vulnerable, "M" means that it is moderately vulnerable, and "L" indicates low vulnerability. As the table shows, none of the basic strategies is highly flexible with regard to

TABLE 12.2. **Vulnerability of Approaches to Limitations and Sources of Error**

	Vulnerability			
Limitation/source of error	LABORATORY EXPERIMENT	SURVEY*	FIELD RESEARCH†	ARCHIVAL RECORDS‡
Content restrictions: What is and is not feasible or practical to study	H (high)	M (moderate)	M	H
Internal invalidity: Lack of control for extraneous variables	L (low)	M	H	M
Measurement difficulty: Lack of ability to measure or perform checks on reliability and validity	L	L	H	M
Reactive measurement: Effects of awareness of being tested or observed	H	H	M	L
Investigator error: Effects of researcher characteristics and behavior	H	H	M	L
Sampling error and bias	H	L	H	M
Inability to replicate	L	L	H	M

*Structured questionnaire or interview with probability sampling.
†Participant observation.
‡Available data research excluding private documents and survey and ethnographic archives.

the kinds of problems that it may address. The relative inflexibility of experiments and archival records stems from analogous limitations: experimentation depends on what it is practically and ethically possible to manipulate; available-data research depends on the availability of the data. Beyond their general accessibility to research problems, each approach is uniquely suited to obtaining particular kinds of information. Thus, surveys are best for estimating population characteristics and describing the distribution of attitudes and opinions; field research affords access to actors' definitions of complex situations and events; and the analysis of available data often provides the best and/or only means of studying the past and larger social units.

Experiments are least vulnerable to problems of internal validity, because they provide the strongest inferences about cause and effect. Statistical controls possible in surveys and some available-data research allow for partial control of extraneous variables (hence the "M" in the table); however, the absence of such formal controls generally makes field research least acceptable for testing causal hypotheses.

Although it is easier to replicate measures and assess reliability and validity in experiments and surveys, these approaches are most vulnerable to methodological artifacts stemming from subjects' awareness of being tested and experimenter or interviewer effects. Nonreactive measurement is a major strength of much available-data research. On the other hand, the extent to which field research is vulnerable to these artifacts depends on how well the investigator becomes accepted by others in the field setting and on how well he or she is able to perform simultaneously the roles of participant and observer. The greater the trust the investigator is able to develop, the less the likelihood of reactive measurement; the more adept he or she is at managing the participant and observer roles, the less the likelihood of investigator error.

Survey research affords the greatest control over error and bias associated with sampling. The susceptibility of documents to selective deposit makes the available-data approach moderately vulnerable to sampling limitations. By contrast, this is a major deficiency of experiments insofar as they typically take place in highly restricted settings with small, nonrandom samples of subjects. And while the quality of sampling is generally better in field research than in experiments, field studies are nonetheless based on isolated settings and nonrandom, albeit more systematic sampling procedures.

Experiments and survey studies are the easiest to replicate. Indeed, replication is fairly common in experiments, and surveys such as the GSS and various polls repeatedly ask the same questions to measure trends. The time-consuming nature of and lack of standardization in field research make this approach very difficult to replicate. Replication with alternative measures or with respect to different time periods is sometimes possible with available-data research, but this depends again on the availability of the data.

As Table 12.2 shows, the pattern of vulnerability varies across the four main approaches; that is, no two research strategies share the same strengths and weaknesses. Indeed, this is what makes the approaches complementary and strengthens inferences based on a triangulation of methods.

A splendid example of a research design comprising complementary methods is the **ethnosurvey**, so named because it blends ethnographic fieldwork with survey sampling methods. In a study we mentioned briefly in chapter 8, Douglas Massey and associates (1987) analyzed the social process of Mexican migration to the United States using an ethnosurvey of four different migrant "sending" communities in Mexico. The traditional weaknesses of field research (limited internal, external, and measurement validity) were offset by augmenting the fieldwork with probability sample surveys of the four communities and snowball sampling of former residents living permanently in the United States. Similarly, the ethnographic fieldwork, which included in-depth interviews, family case studies, genealogies, and historical documents, provided cultural richness and historical breadth to the interpretation and confirmation of the survey results. Furthermore, the international and interdisciplinary research team imposed a strict triangulation criterion on the findings: No conclusions were reported unless they were confirmed by both the anthropological fieldwork and the survey research.

Besides triangulation (*multiple* approaches to a research question), a variety of strategies and measures may be combined within a *single* approach to exploit the relative strengths and weaknesses of complementary methods. For example, compared with face-to-face interviews, mail questionnaires are relatively inexpensive but tend to have relatively large nonresponse rates. The advantages of both survey methods may be attained within one study by (a) mailing questionnaires to a probability sample of the target population and (b) conducting face-to-face interviews with a smaller sample of those not responding to the mail questionnaire in order to estimate the nonresponse bias (Hansen and Hurwitz, 1946). Other examples of harmonious combinations of methods within single studies include face-to-face interviewing in pretesting and debriefing experimental subjects, vignette experimental designs in survey research, preliminary interviews with open-ended questions to develop closed questions, use of archival records to identify groups for field research, field research to determine survey instrument content and to resolve ambiguous survey findings, and probability sampling in field and available data research.

Meta-Analysis

A logical extension of triangulation is a method of research synthesis called **meta-analysis**. Coined by Gene Glass (1976), the term meta-analysis refers to the application of statistical techniques to summarize the results of multiple studies that address the same research question. Prior to its development, literature reviews in the social sciences consisted of verbal descriptions of previous research in which investigators relied on their personal judgments to summarize and synthesize the basic findings. Investigators still conduct such reviews, but if the studies in an area have quantitative outcome measures, meta-analysis offers a more systematic assessment of the literature.

Performing a meta-analysis is somewhat like doing a content analysis (chapter 11), except that the observations (units of analysis) are primary research reports rather than communications produced for purposes other than research. After investigators identify reports of empirical studies in a particular area, they code their basic findings and other study features. Then they calculate summary statistics to estimate the overall strength of the relationship between the independent and dependent variable as well as the effect of other features of the study on this relationship.

Meta-analyses offer several advantages. In contrast to traditional literature reviews, which tend to generate general impressions of the strength and reliability of findings, a meta-analysis can provide summary statistics that estimate the size and significance of effects. By combining (or triangulating) the results of several studies, they also provide evidence of the reliability and external validity of a research finding. Meta-analysis is particularly useful and powerful in the experimental literature, where internal validity is strong and external validity weak. Demonstrating that an effect is consistent across experiments with varying procedures, research settings, and samples greatly increases its generalizability. Finally, meta-analysis can be applied to test hypotheses about research findings. This was the object of an interesting analysis of teacher expectancy effects by Stephen Raudenbush (1984).

Raudenbush reasoned that the mixed results of experiments testing the effects of teacher expectancy on elementary students' IQ gains might be explained by between-study differences in how well the teachers knew the pupils before the expectancy manipulation. The basic teacher-expectancy design (see Rosenthal and Jacobson, 1968) involves manipulating teacher expectations by feeding teachers bogus IQ "aptitude" test results that randomly selected pupils—the experimental group—will "bloom" during the school year. This manipulation is followed by retesting IQ at year end to determine if the "bloomers" gained more than the control group. Raudenbush hypothesized that the impact of the bogus information is inversely related to the length of teacher–pupil contact before the expectancy manipulation. Testing his hypothesis in a factorial design (manipulation of prior teacher–pupil contact as well as expectancy) would be logistically difficult in a school setting. Instead, by doing a meta-analysis of eighteen experiments that naturally varied in prior teacher–pupil contact time, Raudenbush was able to demonstrate strong support for his hypothesis.

Let us now take a closer look at the steps in carrying out a meta-analysis: defining a research problem, searching for relevant research studies, coding the studies, carrying out the analysis, and presenting the results (Cooper, 1982).[5]

Problem Formulation

Whether the impetus for a meta-analytic study is to assess the reliability and generality of a finding or to test a new hypothesis, the starting point is to identify a research question that can be answered by examining previous studies. Consider, for example, the questions addressed in the following studies and the meta-analytic results:

1. Do juvenile delinquency programs prevent recidivism? Mark Lipsey (1994) found, on the average, a small positive effect in 443 delinquency treatment studies.

2. Why do boys and girls differ in science achievement? Betsy Jane Becker and associates (1994) tested a complex causal model of the relationship of gender and achievement. One important policy-related finding was that the same factors were relevant for predicting science achievement for males and for females, which suggests that programs to foster science achievement should be the same for both sexes.

3. How does the presence of children affect marital satisfaction? Although the effects were small, Jean Twenge, W. Keith Campbell, and Craig Foster (2003) found that parents reported lower marital satisfaction than nonparents and that marital satisfaction was inversely related to number of children. The effect of parenthood on children was greater for women, especially mothers with infants, than for men, and also larger for high socioeconomic groups and younger birth cohorts. Overall, the findings suggest that role conflict and restricted freedom may explain why marital satisfaction decreases after the birth of a child.

4. Is there a positive association between the quality of marital relations and the quality of parent–child relations? In a meta-analytic review of sixty-eight studies, Osnat Erel and Bonnie Burman (1995) found a moderate positive relationship. Their findings support the spillover hypothesis (the mood of the marriage spills over to parent–child relations) in contrast to the compensatory hypothesis (parents seek satisfaction in either parent–child or marital relationships to compensate for deficiencies in the other).

5. How well does the College Board Scholastic Aptitude Test (SAT) predict college grades? Winton Manning and Rex Jackson (1984) found the average (median)

correlation between SAT scores and grades to be only 0.41 in a meta-analysis of 827 prior studies.

A research question that is amenable to meta-analysis is one that can be answered from previous studies. Raudenbush could not have tested his hypothesis if the teacher–pupil contact time before the expectancy manipulation had not varied (0–24 weeks) in the eighteen experiments. As in other available-data research, an investigator may settle for a less than satisfactory research question because of data limitations. Suppose, for example, we are interested in the criterion-related validity of the SAT for predicting aptitude for higher education. Alas, the available studies generally exclude those with lower SAT scores who are not admitted to or do not enroll in college. Consequently, we settle for a research question for which data are available: How well does the SAT predict the grades of enrolled college students?

Data Collection

The research question leads directly to consideration of the target population to which the meta-analytic results are to be generalized. Ideally, we would like to include, or sample, all studies bearing upon the research question. In actual practice, however, the data obtained will be a biased sample of the targeted research. Raudenbush (1984), for example, used published literature reviews and a computerized database to locate teacher expectancy studies using children in grades 1 through 7 and IQ as the outcome. His sample is biased to the extent that it underrepresents unpublished research and studies too recent to be included in literature reviews or databases.

The absence of unpublished research in literature searches is called the "file drawer" problem (Rosenthal, 1991:103) because results of such research are likely to be hidden away in file drawers. The suspicion is that the findings of "file drawer" studies were not statistically significant or were otherwise lacking in merit to warrant publication. Consequently, published studies may be a biased sample of all studies ever conducted.

The best approach to data collection in meta-analysis is to use multiple, complementary information channels (triangulation) that do not share the same biases (Cooper and Hedges, 1994:10,41–94). Contacting researchers working in the field, for example, is a means of locating new and unpublished studies that are unavailable through literature reviews and databases. Thomas Cook and associates (1994:289–94) suggest starting with keyword computerized literature searches (for books, articles, unpublished dissertations, research and technical reports, and conference papers), followed by cross-checking the references in each item, and finally contacting scholars who have been identified as working in the field.

A thorough search, however, may produce too many candidate studies, which then must be pared through probability sampling, or culled using eligibility criteria. Lipsey (1994:87–88) employed detailed criteria to cull over 8000 delinquency studies to 443 for his meta-analysis. Included in his eligibility criteria were requirements that the study was conducted in an English-speaking country after World War II, that a majority of the subjects were age 21 or younger, that at least one outcome variable measured delinquency for treatment and control groups, and that random assignment or other means were used to assess the similarity of treatment and control groups before treatment.

Data Evaluation

The evaluation and coding of each included study is similar to the defining and coding of categories for content analysis. The investigator determines relevant questions to ask about the studies and ways to extract answers (measures and codes) from each study. For example, in addition to outcome measures of marital and parent–child relationships, Erel and Burman (1995) abstracted such information as the study design (cross-sectional or longitudinal) and source (journal article, book chapter, or dissertation), sample size and type (families dealing with stressful life circumstances, clinical, community, or other), the child's age and birth order, and the sex of parent and child. For each juvenile delinquency study, Lipsey (1994:101–12) coded ninety-two variables about the methodological design, subjects, treatments, outcomes, and context (author's discipline, affiliation, funding source, type, and year of publication).

Decisions on what to code may emerge from the research literature, relevant theory, or the researcher's insights. Raudenbush's (1984:87) hypothesis that previous teacher–pupil contact time is inversely related to experimentally induced teacher expectancy effects was derived from cognitive dissonance theory. He also coded information relevant to published critiques of methodological shortcomings in teacher-expectancy studies, and he was able to demonstrate analytically a lack of support for rival hypotheses that variations in study findings were due to uncontrolled measurement (individual versus group-administered IQ tests) or to tester bias (blind versus aware of bogus "bloomer" information).

Cook and associates (1994:297) mention that critics have assailed meta-analysis for "camouflaging a 'garbage in-garbage out' process by using fancy statistical techniques" and allowing the more numerous poorer studies to crowd out the results of exemplary studies. Actually, variation in study quality can be used to advantage in meta-analysis, because it may explain differences in study results. Some very poor studies, of course, are unusable. Lipsey (1994) rejected many delinquency treatment studies for design shortcomings (e.g., the absence of a control group). By coding various methodological design features and technical quality ratings of the remaining 443 studies, Lipsey found that slightly over one-fourth of the variability in the delinquency study outcomes was methodological related.

Analysis and Interpretation

Meta-analyses use various statistical indices to indicate the size of a research outcome. In addition, two general statistical frameworks are used to account for study-to-study variability in the outcome of interest (for example, the mean effect, the correlation between two variables, or a complex causal model). The **fixed-effects** framework assumes that the included studies are essentially identical except for the sampling of cases. Hence, between-study variability is treated as arising from sampling and other chance processes. In the **random-effects** framework, outcome results may be shaped by between-study variability in methods, conditions, and settings as well as by sampling. The issues involved in choosing between fixed- and random-effects frameworks are complex and beyond the scope of this book (see Cooper and Hedges, 1994:525–27).

As an illustration of the main distinction between the two frameworks, let us reconsider the teacher-expectancy experiments. If one posits that the expectancy manipulation will produce the same (fixed) effect for all teachers in all studies, the variation in results from study to study is attributed to randomization and other chance processes. Meta-analysis may then be used to estimate the common (fixed) effect apart from the chance disturbances (noise). Now suppose, instead, that the teacher expectancy effect is expected to vary by teacher's sex. This would still yield a fixed-effects formulation since the expectancy effects are assumed to be the same for all male teachers and for all female teachers.

The effectiveness of the expectancy manipulation, of course, depends on both (a) successful deception of the teachers and (b) teachers behaving toward the "bloomers" in such a manner as to fulfill their expectancy for unusual intellectual development. It seems unlikely that both circumstances (deception and conveyance of expectancy) would be identical for all teachers. Therefore, using a random-effects framework would allow the expectancy effect to vary across teachers (low for some, higher for others). Within a classroom, however, the expectancy effect of a particular teacher would be the same (fixed) for all pupils. The random-effects analysis would then be used to estimate the average and the variability of expectancy effects among the teachers. A similar random-effects approach was used by Lipsey (1994) because the delinquency studies were too diverse (treatment program, subjects, methodological design, and outcomes) to justify the assumption of identical (fixed) program effects.

Public Presentation

Preparing a meta-analysis review is similar to writing a research report, which is discussed in chapter 17 [for specific meta-analysis advice, see Rosenthal (1995)]. The author must inform the reader of the purpose (research question), the data collection (literature search, eligibility criteria), the data evaluation (measures and coding, handling of incomplete or missing data), the analysis (statistical framework, presentation of findings), and the author's interpretation of the results. The latter is especially important, since potential readers differ in their ability to follow the numerical results of a meta-analysis (Cooper and Hedges, 1994:12–13).

The audience must be given specific details on procedures (operational definitions, training of coders, and so forth), the handling of difficult problems (for example, missing data), and checks on quality (reliability and validity assessments), so that they can understand and judge the merit of the meta-analysis. Erel and Burman (1995:115), for example, inform the reader that their eligibility criteria included the restriction that the marital and parent–child relations studies had to be available in a Los Angeles university library. By clearly spelling out their eligibility criteria, Erel and Burman allow the audience to evaluate the extent to which generalizations may be drawn from their meta-analysis.

Since meta-analysis is research on top of research, sometimes there is confusion about the methodological underpinnings of a conclusion. When the primary studies are true experimental designs and the research purpose is to summarize the average effect of the experimental variable, the meta-analysis results share the advantages of an experimental design (Table 12.2) plus a likely, substantial boost in external validity. However, if coded features of experiments are used to explain variations in study results, the design becomes "correlational" and more vulnerable to problems of internal validity. Hence, the evidence for Raudenbush's hypothesis that prior teacher–pupil contact reduces or mutes the teacher expectancy manipulation is weaker than if it had been derived from an experimental design.

Summary

The logic of a multiple-methods approach is best conveyed by the process of triangulation in navigation. To locate a point in space, navigators take sightings to that point from different positions. Similarly, the key to triangulation in social research is the selection of different research strategies and measures that do not share the same methodological weaknesses. If different methods produce similar findings, our confidence in the results increases.

Triangulation in social research may occur through such activities as the use of multiple measures of concepts, the deployment of investigator teams in field research, the use of cross-cultural data archives, and replications of studies. Traditionally, the use of multiple indicators has involved the construction of indexes and scales. Indexes combine indicators more or less arbitrarily in the absence of checks to see how well the indicators correspond to the underlying concept; scales combine indicators according to procedures designed to determine the degree of correspondence between indicators and a single underlying dimension. The primary benefit of indexes and scales is the reduction of measurement error. An alternative approach called structural equation modeling retains the identity of each indicator by incorporating all variables—observed indicators and their underlying unobserved concepts—into causal models. Unlike index measurement, this approach allows one to test for certain kinds of measurement error.

The most frequent replications in social research are of small-scale, low-cost experiments. Rather than duplicating an experiment exactly, investigators usually vary certain features, such as the subject population, the manipulation of the independent variable, and the measurement of the dependent variable. Less frequent, yet rendering even more confidence in research findings, are replications involving different research strategies.

The principle of triangulation implies that (1) methods should be selected to fit the particular research problem and (2) the relative strengths and weaknesses of alternative research strategies should be weighed in selecting an approach and in combining approaches.

Meta-analysis is a systematic procedure for synthesizing the results of replications or of multiple, related studies. Researchers often use meta-analysis to determine if the variability in the results of previous studies is associated with between-study differences in sampling (size and design), in methods (inherent biases), or in conditions and settings (external validity). Conducting a meta-analysis involves defining a suitable research problem, searching for and then selecting relevant research studies, coding pertinent aspects of the studies, carrying out a statistical analysis, and presenting an interpretation of the results.

Key Terms

triangulation	*structural equation modeling*
index	*replication*
scale	*ethnosurvey*
unidimensionality	*meta-analysis*
Guttman scaling	*fixed-effects model*
Likert scaling	*random-effects model*

Review Questions and Problems

1. What is the principle of triangulation? Explain how this principle applies to convergent validity assessment, discussed in chapter 4.

2. What is a composite measure? From the standpoint of triangulation, why are such measures better than single-item indicators? What are some other reasons for creating composite measures?

3. How does an index differ from a scale?

4. Although we describe the use of Guttman scaling to measure individual attitudes, social scientists also have used Guttman scaling techniques to measure characteristics of whole societies. For example, Richard Schwartz and James Miller (1964) proposed that the changes in societies' legal systems parallel changes in societal complexity (or, in Durkheim's terms, the societal "division of labor"). Fully developed legal systems were seen to have the following three characteristics:

    a. *Mediation*: regular use of third parties to settle disputes

    b. *Police*: use of specialized, armed force to enforce laws

    c. *Counsel*: regular use of specialized, nonkin advocates (e.g., lawyers)

Assuming that these three characteristics, in order, represent a progression of complexity, present a table that shows the response pattern of a perfect Guttman scale. Then give an example of a "nonscale" response pattern. How would you test these three items for Guttman scalability?

5. Describe the differences between a Guttman scale and a Likert scale (Box 12.1).

6. How does structural equation modeling differ from composite measurement?

7. How do replications constitute triangulation?

8. Each of the four basic approaches to social research examined in this book applies the principle of triangulation in various ways. Explain how triangulation typically is applied in: experiments, surveys, field studies, and research using available data.

9. Compare the relative strengths and weaknesses of the four basic approaches to social research.

10. Why is it preferable to use more than one of the four basic research strategies whenever possible?

11. How does a meta-analysis differ from a content analysis?

12. Explain how meta-analysis constitutes triangulation.

13. Discuss the advantages and disadvantages of meta-analysis from the standpoint of internal and external validity.

14. What steps are involved in doing a meta-analysis?

15. What is the "file drawer" problem? Why is it important?

16. Explain the difference between a fixed-effects and a random-effects meta-analysis.

NOTES

1. For an introduction to social science applications as well as to some of the technical details involved in structural equation modeling, see Bollen (1989), Bollen and Long (1993), and Hoyle (1995).

2. According to Howard Bahr, Theodore Caplow, and Bruce Chadwick's analysis (1983) of 300 replicative studies between 1973 and 1981, over half of the studies appeared in psychology journals. We suspect, however, that this substantially underestimates the proportion of experimental replications. Their analysis was based on a search of the *Social Sciences Citation Index* "for journal articles whose titles included the words 'replication,' 'replicating,' 'replicated,' or 'replicate.' " Yet the word "replication" is seldom used in article titles reporting experiments because of the common practice of reporting two or more experiments, often involving some form of replication, in a single article. This indeed was true of the experimental replication reported below.

3. In simple (misdemeanor) assault, both the suspect and the victim are present when the police arrive. According to Sherman and Berk (1984:262), "the experiment included only those cases in which police were empowered (but not required) to make arrests under . . . Minnesota state law." For ethical reasons, the investigators excluded "cases of life-threatening or severe injury, usually labeled as a felony (aggravated assault)."

4. The ordering of the three intervention strategies differed on the two dependent measures: arrested suspects differed significantly from those who were forced to leave with the official data, and from those given advice on the victim report data.

5. For a thorough discussion of meta-analytic research practices, see Cook and associates (1994) and Cooper and Hedges (1994).

13

✔

Evaluation Research

The goal of conventional or **basic social research** is to understand the social world. Such understanding is manifested in a discipline's theoretical knowledge; hence, basic social research is (or should be) guided by theoretical interests and directed to and evaluated by an audience of peers within a scientific discipline. In contrast, the immediate purpose of **applied social research** is to provide information for solving an existing problem; the primary audience is a client who ordinarily finances the work in the hope of gaining valued information (Rossi and Whyte, 1983). (Box 13.1 outlines other differences between these two research traditions.)

In this chapter we are concerned with a specific form of applied social research called **evaluation research**. Evaluation research consists of the application of social research methods for the purpose of assessing social intervention programs and policies. Evaluation researchers apply the same repertoire of methods as basic researchers do to address the same fundamental issues. And so, we discuss familiar issues of research design, internal validity, measurement, and external validity. What differentiates evaluation research from basic social research is the social context in which the methods are applied. As you will see, the political agenda and administrative realities to which evaluation studies are linked present unique methodological problems.

Framework and Sample Studies

Evaluation is a crucial phase in the process of rational decision making or problem solving (Cook, Leviton, and Shadish, 1985:700). First a problem is identified; second, options for its solution are considered; third, one or more options is implemented; fourth, the implemented option is evaluated; and finally, a decision is made about whether the option is worth adopting. All sorts of problems may be identified and evaluated. In the private sector, companies enlist management consultants, research and development specialists, and marketing professionals to study policies, personnel, and products. As the term is used in social research, however, evaluation research usually pertains to the analysis of social programs instituted by federal, state, and local governments to help solve social problems.

The application of scientific procedures to the solution of social problems is hardly new. Measures to assess social conditions and social experiments to test interventions can be traced to the beginnings of modern science in the 1600s (Rossi, Lipsey, and Freeman, 2004).[1] Moreover, the establishment of American sociology in the late nineteenth and early twentieth century is associated with the Progressive

BOX 13.1

Characteristics of Basic and Applied Research

The table below contrasts the characteristics of the basic and applied research traditions. As the table shows, the impetus for basic research comes from the individual investigator's intellectual curiosity and desire to advance theoretical knowledge, whereas applied researchers take their lead from a sponsor's need to test the efficacy of some program in addressing a particular problem. The public's role, therefore, is very different; basic researchers tend to regard the public as patrons, while applied researchers are more likely to envision their work as directed toward improving the general public welfare. Basic researchers adhere, so far as possible, to absolute norms regarding rigor and scholarship that emphasize laboratory-type control and internal validity; applied researchers do what is necessary to address the sponsor's needs, and the utility of their research depends crucially on its applicability in the field. Finally, basic researchers succeed insofar as they publish their work in learned journals, but the success of applied researchers depends on their ability to communicate their findings clearly to sponsors so as to facilitate rational decision making.

	Basic research	*Applied research*
Problem selection determined by:	Individual researcher	Employer or sponsor
Researcher intrinsically motivated by:	Intellectual curiosity and satisfaction in advancing knowledge	Commitment to promote the public welfare
The goal is:	Generalized theoretical understanding	Cost-effective reduction of social problems
Rigor of methods based on:	Disciplinary norms of scholarship	Uses to which results may be put
Preoccupied with:	Internal validity	External validity
Research arena tends to be the:	Laboratory	Real-world setting
Dissemination of knowledge by:	Publication in learned, technical journals	Communication with lay decision makers

Source: Adapted from Fishman and Neigher (1982) and Freeman and Rossi (1984).

and social reform movements (Oberschall, 1972). To many early sociologists, who envisioned the discipline as a means of bettering society and promoting social justice, applying the scientific method to social problems and social policy interventions was central to the discipline's mission.

From the beginnings of the discipline, however, there were tensions between "academic" and applied sociologists. By the second and third decades of the twentieth century, many academic sociologists began to distance themselves from the social reform tradition in an effort to legitimate the scientific status of sociology

(Gollin, 1983). Eventually they created a professional ideology that at first rejected the objective of social amelioration in favor of value neutrality and eventually assigned lower status to all forms of applied work. Consequently, while there always have been some sociologists engaged in applied research, evaluation research did not flourish—indeed the term was not even invented—until the federal War on Poverty and Great Society programs of the 1960s (Haveman, 1987; Weiss, 1987). Written into virtually all this social legislation was the requirement for program evaluation. As the demand for evaluation grew at an enormous rate in the 1960s and 1970s, evaluation research emerged as a distinct field of study. Numerous articles and books on the practice of evaluation research were published, journals were established, and professional associations were formed (Rossi, Lipsey, and Freeman, 2004:9).

Evaluation studies have been used to investigate literally thousands of problems and intervention strategies: for example, the extent of homelessness, child and spouse abuse, and racial discrimination in the availability of educational opportunities; the effects of increased police presence on crime rates, financial aid on ex-prisoners' adjustment to civilian life, and compensatory educational programs such as Head Start on cognitive development. Evaluation studies mentioned in previous chapters include the Chicago Homeless Survey (Rossi, 1989; chapter 5), field experiments on the television series "Sesame Street" (Ball and Bogatz, 1970; chapter 6) and on police patrol staffing in San Diego (Boydstun, Sherry, and Moelter, 1978; chapter 6), the time-series analysis of the Connecticut crackdown on speeding (Campbell and Ross, 1968; chapter 7), the Great Books and small groups study (Davis, 1964b, chapter 8), and the Minneapolis Spouse Abuse Experiment (Sherman and Berk, 1984, chapter 12). We now summarize three studies to illustrate the types and special problems of evaluation research.

Example 1: Feeding the Homeless

According to sociologist Peter Rossi (1989:14), "a societal condition becomes a social problem when it draws the attention of a significant portion of the public." By this definition, homelessness became a social problem in the United States in the 1980s. Increased public concern, in turn, gave rise to various efforts to help the homeless, including private and public shelters and soup kitchens. One legislative response to the plight of homeless people was the Homeless Eligibility Clarification Act, passed by Congress in 1986.

The general purpose of this legislation was to improve the nutrition of the homeless by expanding the food stamp program. Ordinarily food stamps are issued to low-income individuals to purchase food at a store for home preparation; however, this Act, referred to as the "prepared meals provision," allowed homeless individuals to exchange food stamps for meals prepared by nonprofit organizations, such as soup kitchens and shelters, that feed the homeless. In addition, it extended eligibility for food stamps to homeless persons living in shelters where meals were served. To assess the extent to which the Act achieved its goals, Congress mandated an evaluation study. Researchers at the Urban Institute carried out the study under contracts from the U.S. Department of Agriculture, Food and Nutrition Service, Office of Analysis and Evaluation. Our summary is based on the report prepared by the primary researchers Martha Burt and Barbara Cohen (1988).

To determine the impact of the prepared meals provision, Burt and Cohen conducted two sets of interviews, one in March 1987, immediately before the provision took effect, and the other one year later. The first survey was intended to describe the operations, procedures, and meal services available from providers of meals and shelter for the homeless and the eating patterns and other characteristics of the homeless individuals who used these services. The second survey assessed participation in and perceptions of the program among providers who had become authorized under the prepared meals provision.

The investigators devised a complex sampling design for the initial interviews consisting of a three-stage probability sample, stratified at the first two stages. First the investigators selected twenty U.S. cities with a population of 100,000 or more. Next they selected 400 providers—soup kitchens, shelters without meals, and shelters with meals—from among all providers in the twenty cities. Then they selected 1800 homeless individuals from among those who used the services offered by the sampled providers. Face-to-face interviews were conducted with both providers and homeless individuals; in addition, to analyze the nutritional value of meals, persons who interviewed providers observed and recorded information on the meals available. Finally, for comparison purposes, at various sites where the homeless congregate (e.g., parks, bus stations, certain street corners), the investigators interviewed a nonrandom sample of 142 homeless individuals who did not use the provider services.

Besides a demographic profile of the service-using homeless, Burt and Cohen provided detailed information on their eating patterns. Compared with the average American, the diet of homeless people is inadequate in frequency and nutritional value. Whereas the average low-income American eats three or more meals a day, the service-using sample of homeless averaged fewer than two meals; 37 percent reported eating one meal a day or less, and 36 percent reported that they went one day or more per week without eating anything. On an average day, moreover, homeless people consumed food from only 2.7 of the five food groups; for example, 65 percent consumed no milk or milk products, compared with 19 percent for the average American. (Eating patterns were worse on every measure for the sample of homeless persons who did not use shelter and meal services.)

Although virtually all of the service-using homeless qualified for food stamps, Burt and Cohen found that only 18 percent were receiving food stamps when interviewed and that 40 percent had never used them at all. Almost all meal providers do not charge their clients; so the homeless receiving food stamps are able to supplement their meager diets. The prepared meals provision presumably would expand the general use of food stamps among the homeless. It also would give providers an additional source of revenue with which to purchase food. Unfortunately, the evaluation showed that the provision did little to encourage the use of food stamps.

Perhaps the principal reason that the prepared meals provision failed was that very few providers—only 40 of the estimated 3000—chose to become authorized to receive food stamps from their clients. The majority of the providers, many of whom felt morally committed to a policy of making meals available at no charge, simply were not interested in using the provision. Moreover, nearly half of the forty authorized providers either never activated the program or tried and dropped it. Among this group, some clients were unwilling to pay for meals with food stamps; some providers were reluctant to collect stamps given their clients' limited resources; and some providers had problems with a nonuniform policy that required certified clients to pay while others did not. The two authorized providers for whom the system seemed to work were unique in that they charged clients, in the form of cash or work, for every meal.

Example 2: Aid to Released Prisoners

The second evaluation study we consider was concerned with the social problem of crime. More specifically, the study evaluated a policy designed to reduce recidivism, the tendency of convicted felons to return to a life of crime after release from prison. It is estimated that somewhere between 30 and 60 percent of persons released from prison in a given year are ultimately re-arrested, convicted, and returned to prison (Rossi, Berk, and Lenihan, 1980). Two factors that seem to reduce recidivism are age and employment: "Older men and ex-felons who find jobs and retain them are less likely to be returned to prison" (Rossi, Berk, and Lenihan, 1980:6). Whereas little in the way of social policy can be done about the aging process, various social programs have been tried to improve the employment chances of ex-felons. Peter Rossi, Richard Berk, and Kenneth Lenihan (1980) investigated the effects of one such program in a $3.4-million, large-scale field experiment sponsored by the Department of Labor.

Over the years the Department of Labor has supported several different efforts to help prisoners find productive employment. Without much success, the Department has tried skills training, special job-placement services, and small amounts of financial aid. Government officials were encouraged, however, when an experiment conducted in Maryland in the early 1970s showed that modest payments in the form of unemployment insurance benefits lowered arrest rates for property crimes. On the basis of these findings, the Department of Labor commissioned a larger study, called the Transitional Aid Research Project (TARP), to test the external validity of the policy.

The TARP experiment was carried out in two states, Georgia and Texas, beginning in January 1976. Over a six-month period approximately 2000 released prisoners were randomly assigned to one of six conditions: three treatment groups that varied in the number of weeks financial aid was offered and the amount the benefit was taxed when the recipient was employed; a treatment group that consisted of special job-placement services; and two control groups. Payments were made through the state unemployment-benefit system at minimum benefit levels, $63 per week in Georgia and $70 per week in Texas. Except for one control group, all participants were interviewed before release from prison and periodically throughout the first year after release. Finally, all participants were tracked through computer files for information on arrests and earnings.

The main purpose of the TARP experiment was to test whether modest financial support would lower recidivism rates for released prisoners. When the investigators examined arrest rates, they found no overall differences between those re-

ceiving payments and the controls; hence, the payments clearly failed as administered. Additional bad news was that the payments acted as a disincentive to work,
since those in the payment groups generally worked fewer weeks and earned less
than those in the control conditions.

To understand why the experiment ostensibly failed, Rossi, Berk, and Lenihan
reexamined the theoretical model underlying the experiment. As they note (Rossi,
Berk, and Lenihan, 1980:101):

> TARP assumes that for released felons property crimes are an important source of
> income, a source that competes quite favorably with legitimate jobs, in the sense
> of being more available than such jobs and more attractive than many available
> jobs. Hence, the provision of funds may help released felons to get through a pe-
> riod of postrelease unemployment without resorting to property theft.

The designers of the experiment failed to anticipate, however, that quite modest payments could compete easily with the kinds of jobs typically available, thereby creating a strong work-disincentive effect. Furthermore, the theoretical model underlying
TARP ignores the full impact of employment on recidivism. TARP assumes that employment is a source of income that eliminates the need to resort to crime. But employment also "occupies time and reduces opportunities to commit crimes."

On the basis of such reasoning, Rossi, Berk, and Lenhihan proposed a "counterbalancing model" of TARP effects: TARP payments reduced arrests by lowering
financial need, but increased arrests by increasing unemployment. This explains, at
once, why there was no difference between treatment groups and controls in arrest
rates but there was a significant difference in employment. When this more complex model was tested, essentially examining the effect of TARP payments on arrests while controlling for length of employment, it was found that payments did
indeed reduce recidivism. Rossi, Berk, and Lenihan concluded that modest financial aid to released prisoners, by lowering arrests and thereby reducing the costs of
crime, is likely to be cost effective, provided that work disincentives are somehow
detached from the payments.

Example 3: Curbing Drunk Driving

Another social problem that has drawn considerable media attention in the United
States in recent years is drunk driving. According to H. Laurence Ross (1994:2),
"national press coverage of drunk driving increased more than tenfold between
1980 and 1983, and television networks ran stories about it on an average of more
than one every three weeks in the mid-1980s." This attention was accompanied nationwide by numerous police crackdowns, new drunk driving laws and other countermeasures to reduce drunk driving, and ultimately evaluation studies of these in-
novative policies.

Several countermeasures have been targeted at young persons who drink. Traffic accidents are the leading cause of death of young people, and in about half these
cases alcohol is involved (Ross, 1992:82). Concern about this age group was height-

ened when crash-related fatalities among young people increased after the legal drinking age was lowered in many states during the early 1970s.[2] Indeed, evidence of this relationship from early evaluation studies led to the Federal Uniform Drinking Act of 1984, which effectively established a 21-year national minimum drinking age.

The 21-year minimum drinking age, according to Ross (1992:83), "is one of the most thoroughly evaluated social interventions of our time." A review of thirty-nine studies found that raising the drinking age reduced alcohol-related traffic accidents, just as earlier evaluations showed that lowering the drinking age increased traffic accidents (General Accounting Office, 1987). Typically, these studies used interrupted time-series or multiple time-series designs (see chapter 7) that traced motor-vehicle accident rates before and after changes in the state drinking-age law. Assuming the minimum drinking age was raised to 21 in a given state, automotive crashes among the affected age group—18- to 20-year-olds—were compared with other age groups, such as 16- to 17- and 21- to 45-year-olds. Also, crash data for the affected group were compared with data for the same age group in states that did *not* change the drinking age during the same time period. For example, Alexander Wagenaar (1983), whose research was partially funded by the U.S. National Institute on Alcohol Abuse and Alcoholism, examined crash data in four states: Michigan and Maine, which raised the drinking age in the late 1970s, and New York and Pennsylvania, where the drinking age remained the same (18 and 21, respectively). He found a sudden decline in the number of 18- to 20-year-old drivers involved in injury crashes in Michigan and Maine after these states raised the drinking age to 21, but no change in injury crashes among this age group in New York and Pennsylvania.

Types of Evaluation Research

These three studies illustrate a range of evaluation activities. We can clarify these activities by considering how each phase of policymaking requires answers to different evaluative questions. Figure 13.1 illustrates this linkage in two columns: The first column presents a heuristic model of the policymaking process (adapted from Mark and Shotland, 1985; also see Pancer and Westhues, 1989); the second column identifies key evaluation activities at each stage of the process. The word "heuristic" emphasizes that this is a useful, albeit simplified, idealized model. Policymaking seldom proceeds precisely along these lines, and policies rarely involve all possible forms of evaluation. Even the development of new policies and programs seldom entails a comprehensive, staged evaluation; and evaluation research often analyzes long-established programs and past interventions.

Figure 13.1 identifies six phases of policymaking: (1) identification of a problem that requires amelioration; (2) policy planning—the consideration of alternative intervention strategies for addressing the problem; (3) development of a specific policy action or program; (4) implementation of the policy or program; (5) analysis of the program's impact; and (6) feedback on the problem and policy and administrative action. Although evaluation research is identified most often with the fifth stage, social research can contribute at all stages.

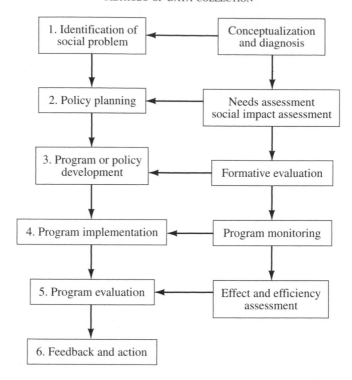

FIGURE 13.1. Stages of policymaking and associated evaluation activities.

Problem Identification: Conceptualization and Diagnosis

Social programs and policies address social problems. This begs the question, How does a social condition become identified as a social problem? It is partly a matter of objective criteria and, as Peter Rossi, Martin Lipsey, and Howard Freeman (2004:107) point out, partly a social construction. Consider homelessness. There always have been homeless people in the United States, but they have not always been considered a social problem. During the Great Depression, homelessness became an object of concern when the number of homeless people swelled to roughly 1 percent of the population (Burt, 1992). For the next four decades, however, the homeless population did not receive much media attention. In 1975, not a single article about the homeless was listed in the *Readers' Guide to Periodical Literature* (Rossi, 1989:14). In the early 1980s, homeless people became more visible on the streets of major cities, and emergency shelters and soup kitchens experienced an increased demand for their services. Still, while the homeless population increased, the best estimates of its size—about 0.2 percent of the population (Burt, 1992:4)—indicated that homelessness in the 1980s was nowhere near the problem it was in the 1930s. Suddenly, however, the plight of the homeless began to receive a great deal of media attention. Public consciousness was raised by the appearance of numerous articles and several television documentaries on the homeless and by the creation of the National Coalition for the Homeless.

In short, problems are not revealed directly by statistical patterns and trends. Rather, problem identification depends on how data are interpreted and whether the interpretation becomes a matter of public concern, which depends upon the values and influence of various parties, especially political elites. Social scientists may contribute to problem definition, but they generally have played a lesser role than investigative reporters, advocacy groups, and political and moral leaders in bringing problems to public attention.

Once a problem has been identified, government officials appear to be relying more and more on social research to inform their decisions (Chelimsky, 1991). Social science input may begin with conceptualization and analysis, indicating what is known and unknown about the problem and providing insights into its nature and causes. For example, when called upon by the superintendent to help solve racial problems in the Austin, Texas, schools, social psychologist Elliot Aronson (Aronson et al., 1975, 1978) drew upon his knowledge of the scientific literature for clues about why desegregation was increasing rather than decreasing racial tension. Research and theory suggested that equal-status contact—presumably created by desegregation—should increase interracial interaction and reduce prejudice. This should occur, however, only when members of different racial groups were in pursuit of common goals. The problem, as Aronson saw it, was that children in the typical American classroom rarely rely on one another to pursue common goals. Systematic observations of numerous elementary school classrooms led him to conclude that the educational process is highly competitive, with children vying with one another for the attention of the teacher and the respect of their classmates. And, this competitive environment accentuates prejudices and differences in ability that existed prior to desegregation. For desegregation to work, therefore, we need to change the process of education so that children will learn to use one another as resources.

Social science data also may be used to document the extent of the problem: to specify when and where the problem takes place and who is affected. The prepared meals provision evaluation study performed this important diagnostic function. As one of the first surveys of the homeless based on a national sample, it yielded detailed information on the eating patterns of homeless people and on the food services (e.g., number of meals served, sources of food, meal variety) available from providers of food and shelter for the homeless.

Unfortunately, this information was collected in the process of evaluating a policy that already had been enacted. It would have been more valuable had the data been gathered before legislation was passed. In that way, more appropriate solutions might have been considered or, at the least, a program such as the prepared meals provision, based on erroneous assumptions about the organization of soup kitchens and shelters, might have been rejected. Now, after a decade and a half of intensive research, we know much more: the forces behind the growth of homelessness in the 1980s, basic characteristics of the homeless population, the relation of homelessness to poverty, mental illness, and chemical dependency, and so forth (see Burt, 1992). Any policy initiatives, therefore, should be informed by this literature.

In many instances, social scientists use existing data to estimate the extent of and historical trends in social problems. A particularly useful type of data for identifying trends is a **social indicator**. Social indicators are broad, aggregate measures of important social conditions that are relevant to policy decisions. Examples include measures of crime, family life, health, job satisfaction, satisfaction with government services, schools and public transportation, and so forth; these indicators may be contrasted with familiar economic indicators such as the consumer price index, the gross national product, and the unemployment rate.

Like economic indicators, social indicators may be measured at repeated intervals to identify societal trends. One large household survey conducted monthly by the Bureau of the Census, known as the Current Population Survey (CPS), is the primary source of information on labor force characteristics of the U.S. population. The interview survey includes questions on employment, earnings, hours of work, and other characteristics. The Bureau of Labor Statistics uses these data to compile statistics, chart trends, and make projections, which serve as important indicators of the nation's economic situation for government policymakers and legislators. From the CPS, for example, we know that the labor force participation of married women with children under 6 years old increased from 30.3 percent in 1970 to 62.5 percent in 2001; and in the next decade the three fastest growing occupations are projected to be computer software engineers and support specialists, personal and home care aides, and computer systems analysts (U.S. Bureau of the Census, 2002:373, 384).

Social indicators can greatly facilitate problem identification and policy planning (Rossi, Lipsey, and Freeman, 2004:110). Trends may reveal whether particular problems are improving, remaining the same, or getting worse. The data also may provide information on the size of the problem and its geographic and social distribution. For many social problems, however, no social indicators exist. For others, the national data are of little or no use in tracking the problem at the state or local level. When the data do not exist, local sample surveys usually provide the most accurate information on the extent and distribution of social problems, although they often require considerable resources.

Policy Planning: Needs and Social Impact Assessments

Having defined the problem, the second stage in rational decision making is to conceive alternative solutions. Rational decision making also implies that numerous feasible options will be considered. Policymakers, however, tend to examine a restricted range of alternatives, often dictated by ideological and pragmatic considerations. Richard Berk and Peter Rossi (1976) point out, for example, that policymakers are rather conservative, and new policies rarely amount to bold reforms. Moreover, the urgency of a problem and the pace at which new programs are sometimes legislated simply may not allow enough time for empirical evaluation. Consequently, social scientists typically have had little input into policy formulation prior to the proposal of a new program (Chelimsky, 1987).

Still, two forms of evaluation research have proven useful at the stage of policy formation and program planning: needs assessment and social impact assessment. **Needs assessment** refers to several different kinds of appraisals. It may be undertaken to identify and forecast problems that need attention, to establish perceived priorities among problem areas in communities and organizations, to study the scope of a problem, and to estimate the extent to which a program will be used or otherwise address appropriate needs. A good example of this last form of needs assessment is Rossi's survey of the Chicago homeless (1989), described in chapter 5. The survey was sponsored by the Robert Wood Johnson Foundation and the Pew Memorial Trust, which were financing medical clinics for the homeless in nineteen U.S. cities. To assess the coverage and adequacy of these clinics, the foundations needed precise, reliable estimates of the size of the homeless population and the nature and extent of their medical problems.

Another example of needs assessment is Royce Singleton's (1994) Senior Center Survey of Worcester, Massachusetts, residents 60 years of age and older. Despite its relatively large older population at the time, Worcester did not have a senior center, while many surrounding, much smaller towns did. The telephone survey was designed to aid a committee of the Commission on Elder Affairs as it sought to establish a senior center. Among the questions addressed were whether residents would be likely to use a center, what locations they favored for the center, and what kinds of programs and services they preferred.

A second aid to program planning is impact assessment. Once policy alternatives have been proposed, social research may be conducted to assess the potential consequences, or impact, of the alternatives. Since 1969, federal law has required **environmental impact studies** (EISs) for all public works projects receiving federal funds except minor projects that are deemed to have no significant impact on the environment. An important part of all EISs is a **social impact assessment** (SIA): an assessment of the consequences of a policy or project on individuals, groups and organizations, and communities or neighborhoods (Finsterbusch and Motz, 1980:94).

Projects for which SIAs would be appropriate include the expansion or relocation of a hospital, various forms of urban renewal, the construction of alternative highway routes, and the closing of military bases. Such projects may have myriad consequences. They can affect individuals biologically (e.g., putting them more or less at risk to health and safety hazards), psychologically (e.g., increasing levels of stress), economically (e.g., increasing or decreasing the availability of jobs, goods, and services), and socially and personally (e.g., affecting people's social networks or accessibility to social institutions) (Finsterbusch and Motz, 1980:94–110). Although a major concern is potential negative consequences, EISs ideally should present a balanced picture so that conflicting interests as well as costs and benefits can be weighed in judging alternatives. Kurt Finsterbusch and Annabelle Bende Motz (1980) cite an EIS of the proposed expansion of New York's Kennedy Airport as an example. The study pointed out costs of the expansion, such as damage to the natural environment of Jamaica Bay, the negative effect on the recreational use of the bay, and the pervasive problem of aircraft noise; but it also detailed the benefits of airport convenience and recommended alternative means of expanding airport service.

Program Development: Formative Evaluation

After a specific program or policy intervention has been proposed, the next step is development and preparation of the intervention for implementation. As this occurs, a **formative evaluation** may be conducted to help improve the program design. Formative evaluation is much like experimental pretesting. Experimental pretests provide feedback on how well the components of the experiment—the cover story, randomization process, manipulation, and so forth—are working. Similarly, formative studies provide feedback on specific program components to determine whether they are consistent with program objectives.

One of the best examples of a successful formative evaluation occurred during the creation of the television program "Sesame Street" (Reeves, 1970). The planners of the program did eighteen months of formative research before they went on the air. The research staff first translated the general goals of the program into highly specific objectives. They also tested the general level of competence of the targeted audience—economically disadvantaged children. Then they developed technical strategies for achieving objectives and reaching this audience. Filmed segments under development were tested repeatedly in relatively simple experiments. Since audience appeal was vital to the program's success, a key dependent variable was level of attention, which was measured by the distractor method. As children watched the program on a television monitor, slides were projected on a wall at an angle to the child. Attention was operationalized as the proportion of time a child viewed the program instead of the slide. Through this method, program content was related to attention, and generalizations about the relative effectiveness of various filmed segments and their elements (e.g., animation, animals, children, adults) were developed.

Like experimental pretests, formative studies are less rigorous and sophisticated than tests of effects after the program has been fully implemented. The emphasis is on speed of feedback rather than on generalizability or precise estimates of effects. Therefore, formative research typically uses unstructured interviews and observation with small nonrandom samples of the target population, observed at one or a few sites. Data of this sort can be especially important in the design of educational programs. Catherine Matthews and colleagues (1995), for example, used semistructured and unstructured interviewing techniques with students and teachers to help develop an AIDS education program for secondary students in South Africa. By providing an in-depth understanding of students' sexual experiences and sexual health needs and teachers' concerns and by exploring the impact of cultural values and religious beliefs on AIDS education, the researchers could develop a culturally appropriate educational program. And as important, through the interview process the researchers were able to gain the trust and support of the teachers who would implement it.

Program Implementation: Program Monitoring

When it comes time to assess the impact of a program, it is essential to know whether the program was carried out as designed. If implemented fully and appropriately, observed outcomes can be attributed confidently to the program; but if the implementation is incomplete or faulty, interpretations are ambiguous. To assess the fit between the design and implementation of a program, evaluation researchers resort to **program monitoring**. Also called "implementation research" and "process evaluation," program monitoring consists of the systematic evaluation of (1) program coverage, or the extent to which the program is reaching its target population; (2) program delivery, or whether the services provided by the program are, in fact, consistent with design specifications; and (3) the resources expended to conduct the program (Rossi, Lipsey, and Freeman, 2004:171). Program monitoring may be as basic as checking to see that a particular service or program was implemented as planned or as elaborate as a detailed description of program activities, administrative staff, and program participants.

Our first and second sample evaluation studies involved extensive program monitoring. A major part of the evaluation of the prepared meals provision assessed the experience of providers who became authorized to accept food stamps during the provision's first year of implementation. Through telephone interviews with authorized providers, Burt and Cohen described characteristics of providers, their reasons for applying for authorization, the ease of the application process, and whether and how providers had clients actually exchange food stamps for meals. This information, together with the larger, pre-implementation provider survey, offered crucial insights into why the program failed. The evidence indicated that relatively few nonprofit organizations that fed the homeless heard about the provision, the majority were not interested in applying, and only about half of those that became authorized ever activated the program. In short, a major problem was coverage; the program did not reach the homeless population or organizations it was intended to help.

The investigation of the implementation process also was a critical feature of the TARP evaluation study. To assess whether the experimental design was carried out properly, the experimenters gathered evidence on the success of the randomization procedure, the delivery of payment benefits, and TARP participants' understanding of the terms of their eligibility. If random assignment were successful, experimental and control groups should differ only within the range of chance variation. Consistent with this expectation, in each state where the experiment was conducted the experimenters found no significant differences across the treatment and control groups on a dozen variables (e.g., age, percent female, years of education, length of sentence).

When they inspected agency records to audit payment delivery, TARP investigators found that the substantial majority of subjects used up all their payment eligibility by the end of the postrelease year. On the other hand, interviews with TARP participants indicated a less than satisfactory understanding of the details of the benefit plans. Almost all participants knew the amounts of the weekly payments for which they were eligible, but only one-third to one-half knew the number of weeks of eligibility. Even more problematic was knowledge of benefit loss due to earned income. Two treatment groups were "taxed" at 100 percent—their benefit was reduced one dollar for each dollar earned. A third treatment group had a 25-percent tax rate, with benefits reduced 25 cents for each dollar earned. The purpose of this generous tax rate was to encourage participants to work; however, most participants in this treatment group either were unaware of the favorable tax rate or did not understand how it operated. Thus, the program's failure to reduce recidivism appears to have been masked not only by conceptual limitations of the experimental design, noted earlier, but also by deficiencies in its implementation. Because participants did not understand the terms of their eligibility for benefits in the event of employment, a clear work incentive (the favorable tax rate) had no chance of offsetting the work disincentive created by the benefit payment.

As these studies illustrate, when evaluating social programs it is vitally important to know whether the program or treatment is delivered appropriately and is attracting or reaching its target population. Ineffectiveness of a program may not be due to the nature of the program or treatment as planned but to how well the plan was implemented. Implementation problems, unfortunately, are fairly common. Rossi, Lipsey, and Freeman (2004:183–195) document cases in which services or treatments were never delivered, most eligible participants were never reached, and program delivery was incomplete or inconsistent across sites. By the same token, when a program achieves positive results, a detailed knowledge of how it was implemented can enable the researcher to explain more fully why it worked.

Program Evaluation: Effect and Efficiency Assessment

For new or ongoing programs or any sort of social intervention, the ultimate issue is whether they are effective. Has the program achieved the desired outcomes, goals, and objectives? Is it worth continuing in light of benefits and costs? The type of evaluation study that addresses these questions is called a **summative** or **outcome evaluation**. Outcome evaluations focus on two issues: Has the program produced its intended effects? What are its benefits in relation to its costs? We will refer to the former as **effect assessment** and to the latter as **efficiency assessment**.

Effect assessment was the primary objective of the TARP experiment and the drinking-age studies. The TARP experimenters assessed effects by applying statistical tests to determine whether the TARP payments lowered recidivism. As noted above, TARP payments did lower arrest rates, but only when the effect of the payments on employment was removed. Many studies analyzed differences among age groups in traffic accidents before and after the raising of the legal drinking age. On the basis of this research, Wagenaar (1983) estimated that raising the drinking age reduced the number of alcohol-related automobile crashes involving young drivers by approximately 20 percent.

The principal method of assessing effects in basic research are tests of statistical significance, which determine the probability that research findings are due to chance factors. Statistical tests assume, however, either random sampling or random assignment of subjects, both of which may be missing in an evaluation study. Although social statisticians disagree over the use and meaning of significance tests (see Morrison and Henkel, 1970), we share David Gold's position (1969) that results that easily could have occurred by a chance process (i.e., "nonsignificant" results) should not be taken seriously. Consequently, as a minimal but not sufficient condition for attributing importance to a program, the results should be statistically significant.

On the other hand, discovery that a program has had a statistically significant effect does not have the same meaning or importance in evaluation research that it would have in basic hypothesis-testing research. Whereas in basic research the researcher is most interested in whether a predicted effect is present, the evaluation researcher is more interested in the magnitude of the effect and its practical significance. Consider, for example, a new, expensive program for the vocational rehabilitation of disabled persons. If this program were found to have statistically significant effects, but resulted in only a few more persons being placed in permanent jobs, the program most likely would be abandoned.

In addition to estimating a program's impact on targets, evaluation researchers are interested in the program's efficiency. If a progam is ineffective, it makes no sense to undertake an efficiency analysis. But if a program has estimable effects, an efficiency assessment can reveal whether it is worth the cost to continue or to fund on a larger scale. Efficiency assessment generally takes two forms: **cost-effectiveness analysis** and **cost–benefit analysis**. The difference lies in how the outcomes of a program are measured; in cost-effectiveness analyses, outcomes are measured in substantive terms; in cost–benefit analyses, outcomes are measured in monetary terms (Rossi, Lipsey, and Freeman, 2004:333).

The TARP experiment was designed to reduce recidivism; therefore, the relevant outcome was the percentage of released felons who returned to prison. A cost-effectiveness analysis of TARP might have calculated the costs of payments to released prisoners per 1-percent reduction in the percentage of released prisoners who were re-incarcerated. Or one could carry out a cost–benefit analysis by comparing the costs of the payments with the costs of imprisonment and processing persons through the criminal justice system. When the TARP investigators did this, they found that "it is cheaper to provide payments of between $800 and $1200 to 100 released prisoners than to process about five additional persons through the criminal justice system, provide prison space for them for periods of 2 and 3 years, and cover other associated costs of imprisonment as well as welfare payments for dependents" (Rossi, Berk, and Lenihan, 1980:112).

Methodological Issues in Evaluation Research

Each type of evaluation presents distinct methodological problems that require different research procedures. In-depth interviews and participant observation, for example, can be particularly effective in formative evaluation. Implementation studies, being chiefly concerned with *describing* the operation of a program, use questionnaires and interviews, field observation, and the analysis of program records—in short, every major approach except experimentation. For determining when, how, and in what combination to use these approaches in implementation studies, evaluation researchers have devised many useful guidelines [see, for example, King, Morris, and Fitz-Gibbon (1987)]. Space does not allow us to examine the application of methods in all types of evaluation. In the remainder of the chapter, therefore, we focus on methodological issues pertinent to effect assessment.

Theory as a Guide to Research

Like basic explanatory research, effect assessments are concerned with cause and effect. A useful paradigm for thinking about cause and effect is the "black box model." The black box consists of organisms or situations; inputs to and outputs from the black box can be observed, but the connecting processes within the box are not readily visible. According to Martin Lipsey (1993), this model aptly depicts the research paradigm in most evaluation studies. The black box is the situation in which a social program is applied; the input is the program, treatment, or intervention; and the output is its effects. Thus, in the TARP experiments, benefit payments (the input) were given to released prisoners (the black box of interest) to try to reduce their postrelease arrest rates (the output of interest).

Lipsey uses the black box model to draw attention to a major shortcoming of many evaluation studies: the lack of an adequate "treatment" theory of program effects. While theory building is the primary objective in basic research, the value of theory in applied research has not always been appreciated. Thus, evaluation researchers, like behaviorists who treat the mind as a black box, often ignore what goes on inside the black box; that is, they fail to describe the causal process through which a program or intervention is expected to affect a specified target population. Without a theory of this process, effect assessment amounts to a trial-and-error, "let's try this and see if it works" approach (Lipsey, 1993). This may prove useful at times, but often it oversimplifies a complex reality. The TARP experiment illustrates this problem. The anticipated effects and research design were based on the relatively simple principle that financial aid to released prisoners would reduce their need to resort to property crime as a source of income. A more complete description of the causal process, however, would have accounted fully for the work disincentive of the payment benefit and the impact of employment on recidivism.

The problem of unspecified or oversimplified theories of the causal process applies to input and output as well as to the forces operating within the black box. On the input side, intervention programs often are treated as singular "molar" categories when in fact they are complex and multidimensional. Moreover, contextual and environmental factors may interact with and significantly affect the impact of a program. On the output side, effects frequently are assessed in terms of "a narrow range of dependent variables to the neglect of unexpected side effects, the interrelationships among effects, and the timing, magnitude, and durability of those effects" (Lipsey, 1993:8).

Consider, for example, the Head Start program. Begun in 1965 as part of the federal War on Poverty, Head Start was designed to prepare disadvantaged preschool children for school, so that they would have a better chance to succeed. To accomplish this objective, the program was multifaceted, involving efforts to improve the child's physical and emotional health as well as cognitive skills, to provide social services, and to involve parents in their children's education. As it developed, Head Start included both summer and year-round programs; in addition, it was arranged into more or less autonomous local centers, which varied considerably in activities, services, and organization. This variability in input and expected outcomes made Head Start exceedingly difficult to evaluate: No matter what the results, an investigator would be hard-pressed to identify the program's critical components. Both the success of the program and its evaluability would be enhanced greatly if a treatment theory were developed to explain precisely what practices were necessary to achieve specific results, such as giving children a "head start" intellectually.

Lipsey's critique of the atheoretical nature of much evaluation research heeds a familiar theme in social research: the mutual dependence of theory and research. For effect assessment to be most fruitful, its methods must be integrated with a treatment theory, which will determine the research design capable of detecting effects, the operationalization of the treatment, and the selection of appropriate output measures. Having identified this general problem, we now address problems of research design and internal validity, measurement validity, and external validity.

Research Design and Internal Validity

As in basic research, the ideal design strategy in effect assessment is a true experiment, with units of analysis randomly assigned to at least two conditions, one with the intervention present and the other with the intervention absent. Whether this strategy may be implemented depends on whether the intervention is (a) existing or new and (b) delivered to all or only some members of a target population. Indeed, the crucial distinction for determining available design strategies is among programs or interventions that (1) provide full coverage, whether existing or new; (2) are existing and provide partial coverage; and (3) are new and provide partial coverage. Only with this last type of program is it possible to use a true or randomized experimental design.

Existing and new programs/interventions that provide full coverage. For ongoing and new programs that reach or are designed to reach virtually all of the population (called "full-coverage" programs), the primary research design is a time-series analysis. This consists of repeated measures of effects before and after the time when the program or intervention was introduced. Rossi, Freeman, and Lipsey (1999:268) point out that while time-series analyses are technically complex, the underlying logic is quite simple:

> The researcher analyzes the trend before a treatment was enacted in order to obtain a projection of what would have happened without the intervention. This projection is then compared with the actual trend after the intervention. Statistical tests are used to determine whether or not the observed postintervention trend is sufficiently different from the projection to justify the conclusion that the treatment had an effect.

For example, Wagenaar (1983) used a time-series analysis to study the effects of raising the legal drinking age to 21 in the state of Michigan. On the basis of an analysis of alcohol-related crashes before the age was raised in 1978, he projected the number of such accidents in 1979 and then compared this figure with the actual number. The comparison showed that 18- to 20-year old drivers in Michigan had 22 percent fewer alcohol-related crashes in 1979 than were predicted.

Wagenaar's time-series analysis used aggregate archival data. When full-coverage interventions and programs are not delivered uniformly, it may be possible to assess effects by conducting a panel study, a survey design with repeated measurements of the same *individuals*. For example, whereas exposure to television is almost universal among young children, there is variation from child to child and over time in exposure to programs containing episodes of violence and aggression. Therefore, by repeatedly measuring aggressiveness and the viewing of violent TV programs, one could determine if aggressiveness at one time is a function of viewing patterns at an earlier time. Several studies incorporating this design have found a modest over-time correlation between exposure to TV violence (measured by viewing frequency weighted for program violence) and interpersonal aggression (generally measured by peer ratings) (Comstock and Paik, 1991:253).

Finally, variation in the intensity of full-coverage treatments may also permit cross-sectional surveys and other intergroup comparisons. For example, Phillips Cutright and Frederick Jaffe (1977) studied the impact of family planning clinic programs by examining fertility rates and level of clinic activity (as measured, for example, by clinic enrollment) in different regions. Holding constant many factors known to be related to fertility, they found that heightened activity was associated with lower fertility rates.

The major weakness of cross-sectional designs, discussed in chapter 8, is that the investigator must be aware of and be able to control statistically for factors that might be confounded with program effects. Time-series and panel designs, therefore, generally are preferable. On the other hand, panel studies are rarely feasible; they cannot be used to analyze existing programs, and they are also expensive and time-consuming. The feasibility of time-series designs depends on the availability of appropriate statistics; and a serious limitation is that they require a relatively large number of measurements before the program or intervention went into effect (at least thirty points in time are recommended) in order to model pre-intervention trends accurately. In addition, history may be a major threat to internal validity. In the Michigan drinking-age study, for example, any reduction in the number of accidents after the drinking age was raised may have been due to other forces acting at that time, such as highway improvements, less hazardous weather conditions, or a police crackdown on speeding.

Despite these weaknesses, survey designs and time-series analyses are superior to the alternatives—either no evaluation or expert judgment.

Existing programs/interventions that provide partial coverage. When evaluating programs that are delivered to part of the population and are in place before the evaluation is undertaken, the general approach is to compare those who are exposed to or participate in the program (participants) with those who are not or do not (nonparticipants). Because random assignment is not possible, the evaluator must find alternative means of creating equivalent groups. Two general strategies are used, often in combination: statistical control and matching.

Statistical control, discussed at length in chapter 15, is the method of establishing causality (or nonspuriousness) in cross-sectional survey designs. Suppose, for example, you were asked to evaluate the impact of a study-skills training program for first-year college students in which half of the first-year class participated. The object of the program was to improve academic performance. Thus, if it worked, participants should have achieved higher grades than nonparticipants at the end of their first year. Any difference in grades between these two groups might be due, however, to initial differences in their verbal aptitude. To make the two groups equivalent on this variable, you could analyze the program's effect on grades while holding verbal aptitude constant; for example, you could examine this relationship separately for students with verbal Scholastic Aptitude Test (SAT) scores below 500 and for students with verbal SATs above 500. Now, if program participants in each case have higher first-year grades than nonparticipants, you have strengthened the inference that it is the program and not verbal aptitude that accounts for participants' higher grades.

Andrew Greeley and Peter Rossi (1966) used statistical control in a cross-sectional survey on the effects of Catholic schooling. As federal support for elementary and secondary schools was expanding in the 1960s, a policy debate arose over whether these funds should be extended to private schools, the largest group being Catholic-sponsored schools. One concern was whether Catholic-school attendance would have a divisive effect, so that adults who had attended Catholic schools would be, for instance, less tolerant of others. To obtain a national random sample of Catholics, Greeley and Rossi reinterviewed persons from a large national sample who had classified themselves as having been raised as or currently practicing Catholics. They then identified the type of schools that the respondents had attended and also obtained measures of their political attitudes as well as numerous social and demographic characteristics. By controlling for a broad range of selection factors, Greeley and Rossi found no evidence of a divisive effect of Catholic education.[3]

Another method of control is to construct or find a comparison group that is similar to the treatment group in crucial respects. This may be achieved either through individual or aggregate matching (Rossi, Lipsey, and Freeman, 2004:276). Individual matching, described in chapter 6, pairs each participant with a nonparticipant who is the same on one or more variables. Aggregate matching consists of finding treatment and control groups that correspond to one another in the overall distribution of matching variables. For example, if one is evaluating a secondary school multiculturalism program, one may select nonparticipant schools for comparison that are similar to the participant schools in the proportion of minority students.

An interesting example of a quasi-experimental design that used aggregate matching was a study of interracial housing conducted fifty years ago. As a result of a housing shortage, public housing expanded rapidly after World War II. At this time, racial segregation was still the rule in the United States, and most of the newly constructed housing projects either were racially segregated or contained a very low percentage of blacks. In this context, Morton Deutsch and Mary Evans Collins (1951) studied the impact of integrated versus segregated housing on interracial attitudes. More specifically, they decided to compare tenants' attitudes in projects with two different occupancy patterns: an integrated interracial occupancy pattern (families were assigned to apartments without consideration of race) and a segregated biracial pattern (black and white families resided in the same project but were assigned to different buildings). The study design was thus a static-group comparison. To control for selection bias, the principal source of invalidity in this design, Deutsch and Collins matched the projects on key variables. First, they obtained the cooperation of two neighboring cities, one (New York) with an integrated and the other (Newark) with a segregated housing policy. Next, they carefully matched housing projects in terms of their racial ratio, selecting one project in each city that was about two-thirds black and one project in each city with a 50:50 black/white ratio. Finally, they noted that approximate matching occurred on several other variables. For example, the two cities were similar in important ways, such as in their racial and ethnic composition; residents of the two cities were exposed to similar cultural influences, such as the same media; all the housing projects began at about the same time, were subject to the same federal regulations, had similar administrative setups, and were located in similar neighborhoods.

In addition to matching, Deutsch and Collins controlled statistically for some variables; they also argued against selection on the basis of racial attitudes because of the desperate need for housing and the low rate of refusals. Still, the principal weakness of this quasi-experimental design as well as cross-sectional surveys is their vulnerability to selection bias. Since statistical control is logically equivalent to matching but usually easier to carry out, the use of cross-sectional surveys with statistical controls has supplanted quasi-experimental matching designs to a considerable extent in recent years (Rossi, Lipsey, and Freeman, 2004:279). Cross-sectional surveys can provide quick, cost-effective estimates of program effects; however, the validity of such assessments depends heavily on how well the investigator has conceptualized possible selection effects and has measured characteristics of participants and nonparticipants that permit the statistical control of these potential effects.

One other quasi-experimental design, the multiple-time series, combines statistical control and matching with the analysis of available data to enable particularly strong causal inferences about program effects. The major validity threat to the single time-series design is history. Adding a control group time series permits tests for the threat of history (as well as other validity threats such as instrumentation). Recall, for example, Wagenaar's study of the impact of raising the legal drinking age in Michigan. We described this study as testing a full-coverage program since *all* 18- to 20-year-olds in the state were affected. With a single time-series design, Wagenaar showed that alcohol-related accidents among 18- to 20-year-olds in the state of Michigan decreased after the drinking age was raised. That was only part of the study, however. The Michigan law also could be construed as a partial-coverage intervention insofar as it did not affect all age groups nor did it apply in other states. In fact, as we described earlier in the chapter, Wagenaar analyzed time-series data in two kinds of control groups. First, he compared accident trends for older age groups in Michigan who were unaffected by the law; second, he compared accident trends among 18- to 20-year-olds in two other states, New York and Pennsylvania, where the drinking age remained the same during the same time period. Neither the older age groups nor the control states showed the same decrease in alcohol-related accidents, thereby strengthening the causal inference that raising the drinking age reduced accidents among 18- to 20-year-olds.

New programs/interventions that provide partial coverage. Any of the designs mentioned above may be used to assess new, partial-coverage programs. Studies of such programs permit far greater control, however, than studies of ongoing and/or full-coverage programs. Indeed, it may be possible to meet the requirements of a true experiment, with random assignment to treatment and control groups whose experiences are comparable except for exposure to the new program or intervention. As scientific opinion has shifted more strongly in favor of randomized experiments and away from quasi-experimental and nonexperimental designs in recent years (Cook and Shadish, 1994), evaluation researchers have sought ways to circumvent the obstacles to conducting true experiments. The implementation problem that has received the most attention is how to plan and carry out random assignment (Boruch and Wothke, 1985).

If we assume that random assignment is feasible, the decision to implement it usually boils down to matters of practicality and ethics. Randomized experiments are time-consuming and often very costly. The TARP experiment cost $3.4 million and took over two years to plan and carry out; experiments of other government programs have cost upward of $100 million at today's dollar value and have taken seven or more years to complete (Rossi, Lipsey, and Freeman, 2004:261).

Project sponsors, administrators, and staff also may resist randomization for ethical reasons. They may argue that it is unfair, harmful, or illegal to deprive some people of a treatment or program that is believed to be beneficial. To counter this objection, evaluation researchers offer two principal arguments. First, they point out that the effectiveness of the program is unknown and will remain so until a scientific test of it is performed. Second, they argue that, since the effects of the program are unproven and since there might even be undesirable effects in some cases, randomization is the only fair way to assign persons to treatment and control groups.

Ultimately, such costs and objections must be weighed against the cost of weaker causal inferences that are likely to be drawn from nonexperimental studies (Cook and Campbell, 1979:346). Evaluation researchers who investigate the effects of social programs may draw support from scientists who have studied medical experiments. John Gilbert, Bucknam McPeek, and Frederick Mosteller (1977), for example, have concluded that the social costs of being wrong about the effectiveness of a treatment or drug outweigh the costs of randomization. Imagine the social costs, for example, of continuing for years to use a less desirable treatment or program.

Even when program administrators are convinced of the value of random assignment and it is incorporated into the research design, other problems frequently arise. Commonly, the researcher designs the randomization process, but must depend on various other officials to make the actual assignments. In the TARP experiments, for example, the state Department of Corrections was responsible for subject selection and random assignment (Rossi, Berk, and Lenihan, 1980:50). Problems occur when staff misunderstand what they are supposed to do or when they let professional judgment override random assignment because of a client's perceived need or merit. To prevent this from occurring, Thomas Cook and William Shadish (1994:559) recommend

> giving better explanations of the necessity of random assignment, having local research staff carry out the assignment rather than service professionals, instituting earlier and more rigorous monitoring of the selection process, and providing professionals with the chance to discuss special cases they think should be excluded from the assignment process.

Finally, the randomization process is far more likely to break down in an evaluation study than in basic research once the study has begun. The biggest problem here is treatment-related loss of participants, which would lead to dissimilarity of the treatment and control groups. This may occur either when individuals who have been assigned to a treatment or control group refuse to participate in the assigned group (selection bias) or when individuals drop out of the treatment and control groups at different rates (differential attrition). Treatment-related refusals to participate may be minimized by restricting the subject population to persons who agree at the outset to participate in any condition to which they are assigned. Solutions for minimizing treatment-related attrition include: paying subjects to remain in the experiment or paying controls to provide outcome data that can be compared with those who participated; monitoring attrition cases to determine their causes and reduce their occurrence; and omitting the control group and creating different treatment groups that are approximately equal in attractiveness (Cook and Shadish, 1994:560–61). (See Box 13.2 for a case study of randomization in an evaluation experiment.)

Randomization, in short, is far more problematic in evaluation experiments than in laboratory experiments. In the laboratory, the researcher usually assigns subjects to conditions, and the success of the randomization procedure is taken for granted. Similarly, the laboratory experimenter has a high degree of control over the knowledge that subjects have about various treatment conditions, including the ability of subjects to communicate information to one another about treatments. Not so in evaluation studies. In fact, Thomas Cook and Donald Campbell (1979:54–55) have outlined four novel threats to validity that derive from the **diffusion of information** from one treatment to another. All four threats have been observed in evaluation studies (Cook and Shadish, 1994:555).

The validity threat of "resentful demoralization" occurs when members of control groups become resentful and demoralized upon learning that they are receiving a less desirable treatment. As a consequence, they lower their performance or productivity, so that their resentful reaction rather than the putative cause—the treatment or program—accounts for the difference between treatment and control groups. Upon learning of their less desirable treatment, members of control groups also may react with "compensatory rivalry." This occurs when the control group, perceiving itself as an underdog in a social competition, is motivated to reduce or reverse the expected difference. The expected difference between unequally treated groups also may be lowered when administrators engage in "compensatory equalization." In this case, administrators may try to reduce treatment–control inequities, such as by providing equal funds to control groups not receiving a new program. The problem is that this additional resource may generate effects that equal the effects of the new program. Finally, "treatment imitation or diffusion" "occurs when treatment providers or recipients learn what other treatment groups are doing and, impressed by the new practices, copy them" (Cook and Shadish, 1994:555).

Elliot Aronson (Aronson et al., 1975) discovered treatment diffusion in his evaluation of a cooperative learning technique. Earlier in the chapter we described how Aronson was asked to evaluate and propose solutions for reducing racial tensions in the Austin, Texas, schools. Having concluded that the competitive classroom was the root of the problem, Aronson devised a new structured method of in-

BOX 13.2

Randomization in the Minneapolis Spouse Abuse Experiment

Unfortunately, evaluation researchers rarely present detailed information on the practical problems of implementing and maintaining randomization. One instructive exception is Lawrence Sherman and Richard Berk's (Sherman and Berk, 1985; Berk and Sherman, 1988; Berk, Smyth, and Sherman, 1988) discussion of randomization in the Minneapolis Spouse Abuse Experiment. Planning for this study began with a research design submitted to the National Institute of Justice (NIJ) by Lawrence Sherman. The design called for random assignment of some 300 misdemeanor domestic assault cases to one of three interventions: arrest, mediation, or separation. Before Sherman could implement this design, he had to gain the cooperation of the chief of police of a major city, convince the NIJ of the ethical and legal justifications for randomization, and persuade a group of officers to "voluntarily give up their discretion in domestic assault cases for a year or more" (Sherman and Berk, 1985). To the NIJ, Sherman argued that because there was no empirical evidence on the deterrent effects of arrest, the study would provide important information to help police effectively reduce repeat violence; moreover, police were making few arrests in domestic assault cases and were doing so on "an arbitrary and capricious basis." Having obtained the cooperation of a "free-thinking police chief," Sherman met some resistance from officers in the upper echelons of the chain of command; however, after a three-day conference with thirty-four patrol officers, he was able to convince all but one of them to volunteer for the experiment.

To minimize implementation problems, the investigators used several strategies. They gave the officers extensive information and training, including role-playing exercises and practice in applying the experimental procedures; met monthly with officers during the course of the experiment; had research staff periodically ride along when the officers were on patrol; and devised a randomization procedure that was easy to implement and to monitor (Berk, Smyth, and Sherman, 1988). According to this procedure, police officers participating in the experiment carried

> a special pad of report forms, color coded for the three treatments. Each time officers encountered a situation meeting the experimental criteria, they were to apply the treatment indicated by the color of the report form on the top of the pad. . . .
>
> All of the color-coded forms were arranged in random order, stapled together in sets of 25, and numbered sequentially. The colors were meant to assist officers who might have to apply a random treatment rapidly under difficult circumstances. The stapling and numbering were meant to discourage even well-intentioned efforts by officers to match particular treatments to particular incidents. The numbering also provided [a] check on whether the treatments were being implemented as designed (Berk and Sherman, 1988:71).

Because the police faced potentially volatile situations, the researchers knew there would be circumstances where random assignment could and should be avoided.

Consequently, they anticipated and clearly defined those situations in which "upgrading" to arrest from the mediation and separation interventions would be permitted (e.g., if the officers were assaulted or the offender would not leave the premises when ordered).

Still, despite their efforts to ensure proper implementation, the investigators knew that random assignment would not be perfectly executed. There would be occasions when police would make errors, forget their forms, or "place law enforcement concerns ahead of the research design" (Berk, Smyth, and Sherman, 1988:213). The low volume of cases of domestic assault made it impossible to monitor through observation whether the officers were following the randomization procedure. This not only placed a premium on the officers' cooperation and commitment to the study but also made it necessary to analyze the assignment process.

To analyze randomization, the investigators relied on information the police were instructed to record as part of the experiment. The first important evidence that the experiment was implemented validly was that there were no significant differences in the characteristics of the treatment groups (Sherman and Berk, 1985). Moreover, when the investigators compared the designed treatments with the treatment actually delivered in the field, they found that these were the same in 82 percent of the cases; virtually all of the discrepant cases consisted of the assignment of arrest when the advice or separation treatment was called for, a pattern readily explicable in terms of the special allowances for upgrading.

Although the investigators were satisfied that compliance with the randomization procedure was quite high, they performed one final analysis. They analyzed the results of the experiment on the basis of both design and actual assignment of treatments, and they also attempted "to adjust for potential biases that could result from the nonrandom assignment of arrest" (Berk, Smyth, and Sherman, 1988:217). These analyses all pointed to the same positive effect of arrest in cases of misdemeanor assault.

terdependent learning called the jigsaw method.[4] His first experimental evaluation of this method showed several significant differences between children in classrooms with jigsaw-learning groups and children in traditional classrooms. After a six-week period, children in the jigsaw groups liked their peers more, showed more positive attitudes toward school, had more positive self-concepts, and showed an improvement in grades. When Aronson and his associates attempted to replicate this study, however, they failed to obtain the expected, significant differences between experimental and traditional classrooms. Instead, children in both conditions showed the same increase in liking for peers, satisfaction with school, and so forth. The reason for the failure was a classic case of treatment diffusion. During the course of the experiment, Aronson's trained observers discovered that

> the control classrooms were anything but traditional. Virtually all of the control teachers were using some form of group interaction with their students—not as systematically or as extensively as the experimental teachers, but enough to have an impact on the children. These control groups produced changes in the kids' liking for school and each other that were greater than the original control groups, but not so large as the experimental ones.

. . . part of the reason for [the contaminated controls] was that many of the teachers, pleased and enthused over the earlier studies, told their colleagues about the new method, and word-of-mouth reports traveled across the school system. (Aronson et al., 1975:50)

Measurement Validity

The utility of evaluation research depends not only on an adequate design strategy but also on the conceptualization and reliability and validity of the measures of cause (the treatment or program) and effect (the expected outcome). Special measurement problems arise, however, because of the political context of evaluation research. Social programs and program objectives are political statements. "They are not meant to be precise explications of how a program might reduce the severity of a social problem or to provide evaluators with explicit program rationales that can be easily translated into evaluation objectives or criteria" (Cook, Leviton, and Shadish, 1985:703). Consequently, measurement may be made more difficult in several ways: Policymakers and program administrators may present vague conceptual and operational definitions of both the treatment and desired goals; the treatment program may be nonuniform; the treatment program may be relatively clear but the goals are stated very broadly for political reasons (e.g., to attract or keep support of a government agency or sponsor); different interest groups (e.g., administrators, staff, clients) may have conflicting or unrelated goals for the program.

In the case of nonuniform treatment programs, the best means of determining the nature of the "cause" is a thorough implementation study of the program as it operates at various sites and times. With regard to ill-defined and multiple program goals, the adequacy of evaluation research depends on the evaluator's ability to perform the delicate task of translating politically acceptable goals into measurable outcomes without losing the support of the program administrators and other interested parties.

Assuming a well-defined program with clear objectives, the measurement problem amounts to finding or creating valid indicators of program outcomes. For research on existing programs or past interventions, evaluation researchers often use government statistics, as in the drinking-age studies. But, unfortunately, these are frequently inadequate for addressing policy questions (Mark and Shotland, 1985).

Another measurement problem relates to the timing of outcome measurement. Social research has shown that the effects of a treatment may be immediate or may occur later in time, and that effects may be gradual and continuous or occur all at once (Bernstein, Bohrnstedt, and Borgatta, 1975). The problem this presents in evaluation studies is that the time between program implementation and measurement might not correspond to the time it takes for the program to manifest its effects. Indeed, Melvin Mark and R. Lance Shotland (1985) argue that the time frame of evaluation studies may restrict the researcher's ability to assess potentially more important or relevant long-term effects.

In the long run, perhaps the best solution to all these problems is multiple measurement. As we argued in chapter 12, the use of multiple indicators can increase reliability and validity insofar as they contain offsetting biases and errors.

If independent measures produce convergent findings, we become even more confident when the indicators derive from different sources, such as archival records, questionnaire surveys, and observation. And if different indicators produce conflicting results, this may lead policymakers appropriately to exercise caution and recognize the complexity of the issue.[5] In addition, diverse measures of outcomes will permit the analysis of possible unplanned and unanticipated effects, the assessment of program goals held by different constituencies, and, if outcomes are measured at different points in time, the assessment of longer-term as well as short-term effects.

External Validity

Basic researchers tend to believe that internal validity should take precedence over external validity. Before one explores the generalizability of a causal connection, they reason, one should establish the validity of the connection. Some evaluation researchers maintain, however, that more emphasis should be placed on external validity (Cronbach, 1982). In either case, the issue of external validity is particularly important in evaluation research. The purpose of undertaking evaluation studies is to make informed decisions about whether to extend a program to other participants or beneficiaries. Yet generalizing results may be hazardous for several reasons.

With regard to the sampling of units, the target population often is too difficult or too expensive to enumerate, thereby precluding probability sampling. If enumeration is possible, it still may not be feasible to draw a probability sample. Cook and Shadish (1994:571) point out the "enormous practical difficulties" of implementing a high-quality program with a random sample of a dispersed population. Experiments also are likely to be restricted to those individuals who agree to be randomly assigned, a group that may not be representative of the whole target population.

When evaluation researchers must rely on nonprobability samples, several selection biases may threaten external validity. Sometimes subjects self-select themselves into a treatment; sometimes program participants are selected because they are most likely to generate positive results; and sometimes units are chosen because of their availability (Bernstein, Bohrnstedt, and Borgatta, 1975). As long as a program is designed only for volunteers who seek treatment, self-selection should permit reasonable generalizations to the target population. Otherwise, self-selection, as well as selection for availability and presumed excellence, is likely to produce samples that differ systematically from the target population.

The social context of evaluation research also may threaten external validity in various ways (Bernstein, Bohrnstedt, and Borgatta, 1977:119–25).

1. The effectiveness of a social program may depend on the personal qualities of the staff who administer it. Thus, results would not be generalizable to later, widespread implementation by staff who are less able, committed, or enthusiastic about the program's success.
2. Knowledge that one is a participant in the evaluation of a social program can affect results. The Hawthorne effect, described in Box 2.1, suggests that program participants may increase their effort when they know that they are being

evaluated. Or, they may perform better because of the excitement of participating in a new program. Such effects raise the question of whether findings are generalizable to settings where the program is no longer experimental or being evaluated.

3. The program may be effective only at the historical time in which it takes place and/or in the particular geographic setting where it takes place. This seems especially likely when an experimental program takes place at a location far removed from the setting where it ultimately will be administered.

There are no easy solutions to these external validity problems. To begin, one should draw a probability sample of the target population if possible. Whether or not this is done, one should also attempt to vary those factors—time, setting, staff, and so on—that are likely to limit the generality of study results. Another approach is to attempt to make the conditions of the experimental program (e.g., sample, setting, staff) representative of the conditions under which the program ultimately would be implemented. Robert St. Pierre and Thomas Cook (1984) refer to this as **modal instance sampling**. It requires first that one describe the manner in which the program would be carried out if it became formal policy (the modal setting). Then one selects or creates a research setting in which the program is implemented in a manner very similar to that of the modal setting. If, for example, a modal program involved health education services directed to the urban poor, then the test program should involve urban poor. One would not choose to evaluate a program located in a small town or one directed to a wider range of socioeconomic groups.

Finally, because a delivered intervention can rarely be separated from its context, Rossi, Lipsey, and Freeman (2004:58) see program monitoring evaluations as an "indispensable adjunct" to effect assessments. Through monitoring, one can carefully identify aspects of the program or intervention, such as the geographic setting, physical plant, rules and regulations, characteristics and training of staff, and so forth, that might affect the outcome of the intervention.

The Social and Political Context of Evaluation Research

As we have seen, issues of design, measurement, and sampling are as germane to evaluation research as they are to basic research. The peculiar social context of evaluation research, however, creates unique problems in resolving these technical issues. Thus we have alluded to the validity threat posed by the diffusion of information across treatments; the difficulties in applying randomization procedures when program staff must be enlisted to carry them out; the measurement problems created by ambiguous program means and goals; and the impact of staff, locale, and time on the generalizability of program effects. Let us take a closer look now at the social and political contexts of evaluation research.

In contrast to basic researchers who exercise considerable freedom in selecting research topics and in conducting their research, evaluation researchers are constrained by and beholden to various stakeholders. **Stakeholders** are "the individuals, groups, or organizations that have a significant interest in how well a program functions" (Rossi, Lipsey, and Freeman, 2004:18). In any evaluation study, there are numerous potential stakeholders. The most obvious is the program sponsor—the government agency, private organization, or community group—that initiates and funds the program. This may or may not be the same as the evaluation sponsor who mandates and funds the study. The Food and Nutrition Service of the Department of Agriculture funded Burt and Cohen's (1988) study of the prepared meals provision for the homeless and also sponsored the program. Another stakeholder is the policymaker or decision maker who ultimately determines the fate of the program. For Burt and Cohen, this was the U.S. Congress. Then there are program participants, program management and staff, the evaluators, and other interested parties. For Burt and Cohen, such stakeholders included the homeless individuals affected by the program, the staff of the soup kitchens and shelters where meals were delivered, and groups acting on behalf of the homeless, such as the National Coalition for the Homeless. Finally, Rossi, Lipsey, and Freeman (2004:374) note that, "in an abstract sense, every citizen who should be concerned with the efficacy and efficiency of efforts to improve social conditions has a stake in the outcome of an evaluation."

Evaluation researchers must be aware of the various stakeholders as they design and conduct their research and communicate their findings. Because stakeholders have conflicting interests, the researcher should clearly identify the perspective from which the research is being undertaken, while acknowledging the legitimacy of other perspectives. Sometimes the policymaking stage (see Figure 13.1) will dictate the relevant perspective; for example, program staff will have the primary stake in formative research designed to fine-tune programs, whereas policymakers would be primarily interested in needs assessment.

Evaluation researchers also should be aware of possible difficulties in communicating with different stakeholders. This applies both to the intelligibility of the communication, which must eschew technical vocabulary, and to the form of the communication. While most evaluation studies culminate in a detailed, technical report that describes the research design, methods, and results, Rossi, Lipsey, and Freeman (2004:380) point out that these are "rarely read by the stakeholders who count. Many of these stakeholders simply are not accustomed to reading voluminous documents, do not have the time to do so, and might not be able to understand them." Therefore, evaluation researchers must be prepared to issue executive summaries, memos, and especially oral reports geared to the needs of specific stakeholders.

Because evaluation research takes place in the context of policymaking, with different types of evaluation linked to each policymaking phase, it is part of a political process. To be effective, therefore, the evaluation researcher must understand his or her role in this process. Speaking of program evaluation at the federal level, Eleanor Chelimsky (1987) maintains that evaluation research is likely to be maximally useful when the purpose of evaluation is to provide the highest quality information in addressing policy questions determined by the policymaker. The researcher undertaking an evaluation thus should not act as an advocate, but rather should serve as a handmaiden of the policymaker. Similarly, Rossi, Lipsey, and Freeman (2004:382) liken the

> evaluator's role to that of expert witness, testifying to the degree of a program's effectiveness and bolstering that testimony with empirically based information. A jury of decisionmakers and other stakeholders may give such testimony more weight than uninformed opinion or shrewd guessing, but they, not the witness, are the ones who must reach a verdict.[6]

So, how much use is made of the evaluator's expert testimony? Unfortunately, there is very little systematic evidence and general disappointment regarding the extent of the use of evaluation studies (Rossi, Lipsey, and Freeman, 2004; Sechrest and Figueredo, 1993). Much of the time the information is simply ignored by policymakers. This seems to have been the case, for example, with regard to the TARP experiments on the effect of short-term financial support on reducing recidivism. Still, Chelimsky (1991) cites several instances in which evaluation research provided critical knowledge for policy development in the federal government, including forecasting the likely impact of new immigration policy and obtaining precise counts of homeless populations. She contends (Chelimsky, 1987:32) that the use of evaluation in policymaking "is real, measurable, and growing dramatically."

Others (Weiss, 1987; Rossi, Lipsey, and Freeman, 2004) contend that while few evaluation studies lead to direct and immediate changes in policy and practice, they do influence thinking in a more indirect, general way. "The generalizations and ideas that [these studies] produce percolate into the consciousness of informed publics, and over time they can alter the terms of policy discourse" (Weiss, 1987:44). Given the expansion of the evaluation enterprise, the steady development of technical knowledge, and the increasing awareness of the political context in which evaluation takes place, we expect the partnership between research and policymaking to continue to grow.

Summary

Evaluation research is a form of applied social research that gained impetus from federally mandated evaluations of social programs enacted in the 1960s. Its basic aim is to apply social research methods to the assessment of social intervention programs. Evaluation is integral to rational decision making and can be linked to the various stages of policymaking. At the stage of problem identification, evaluation researchers draw upon existing social scientific knowledge to help conceptualize problems and solutions; and they use social indicators to estimate the prevalence of and trends in social problems. To aid in policy formulation and program planning, evaluation researchers assess perceived priorities among problem areas, called needs assessment, and assess the impact of proposed programs on the social environment. Evaluation researchers also conduct formative evaluations to assist in the development of programs; do program monitoring to determine how well the implementation of a program matches its design; and conduct summative or outcome evaluations to determine the impact and efficiency of a program.

While each type of evaluation encounters different methodological problems, this chapter focused on the application of methods to summative evaluations of program effects. A general problem with such evaluation studies is the absence of an adequate theory that specifies the relationship between program elements and presumed outcomes. The ideal design strategy depends on the stage and coverage of the program. For existing and new programs and interventions that affect the entire population, time-series analyses work best, although their feasibility depends on the existence of appropriate data. Without such data, surveys may suffice. For existing programs that reach part of the population, the design usually involves a survey and comparison of affected and unaffected groups, with some form of control for selection bias. In the case of partial-coverage new programs, the ideal design is a true experiment. Because of the real-world setting of the evaluation, however, implementing experiments often is highly problematic. For example, various stakeholders must be convinced of the value and ethics of randomization, which must be carefully monitored; also, the possible diffusion of information from one treatment to another may threaten internal validity.

The political context of evaluation research creates special measurement problems, such as vaguely defined program means and ends, nonuniform programs across sites, and an indeterminate time lag between treatments and effects. An implementation study of the program provides one means of identifying causes, but multiple measurement offers the best overall solution to these measurement problems. Because the usefulness of evaluation findings depends on their applicability to real-world settings, evaluation researchers place a premium on external validity. Yet external validity may be threatened by self-selection, the Hawthorne effect, the special qualities of the staff, and the limited locales and times in which a program is tested. One solution to such problems is modal instance sampling, in which the evaluation setting is selected for its similarity to conditions under which the program is likely to be enacted.

Throughout the research process, evaluation researchers must be aware of relevant stakeholders. Ultimately, the utility of evaluation studies depends on the researcher's ability to address the needs and interests of stakeholders and to successfully carry out his or her role in the political process to which evaluation is linked.

Key Terms

basic social research
applied social research
evaluation research
social indicator
needs assessment
environmental impact studies
social impact assessment
formative evaluation
program monitoring

summative evaluation
effect assessment
efficiency assessment
    cost effectiveness analysis
    cost–benefit analysis
treatment diffusion of information
modal instance sampling
stakeholders

Review Questions and Problems

1. Differentiate between basic and applied social research with regard to (a) goal or purpose and (b) primary audience.

2. Explain how evaluation is related to rational decision making.

3. When did evaluation research emerge as a distinct field of study?

4. Match the type of evaluation in column B with the appropriate policy-making phase in column A.

Column A	*Column B*
policy planning	conceptualization and diagnosis
program development	formative evaluation
program evaluation	needs assessment
program implementation	program monitoring
policy problem formulation	summative evaluation

5. What type(s) of evaluation was (were) carried out in the (a) study of the prepared meals provision for the homeless, (b) the TARP experiment on the effect of financial aid to released prisoners on recidivism, and (c) the time-series analysis of the effect of raising the minimum drinking age on alcohol-related traffic accidents?

6. How does a social condition become identified as a social problem?

7. How can evaluation provide a conceptual foundation for the formulation of policy problems?

8. Give an example of a social indicator. What purposes do social indicators serve for the policymaker?

9. Explain how needs assessment and social impact assessment assist the policymaker.

10. How is formative evaluation analogous to experimental pretesting?

11. What are the purposes of program monitoring? Using the TARP experiment as an example, explain how this form of evaluation can facilitate the interpretation of program effects.

12. What is the difference between effect assessment and efficiency assessment?

13. Why do evaluation researchers place less emphasis on statistical significance than basic researchers do?

14. Explain how the atheoretical nature of much evaluation research creates problems in investigating program or treatment effects.

15. What are the optimum research strategies or designs for assessing the effects of (a) existing and new full-coverage programs, (b) existing partial-coverage programs, and (c) new partial-coverage programs?

16. Describe three methods of control that are used when estimating the impact of existing partial-coverage programs.

17. How is the implementation of randomized experiments more problematic for the evaluation researcher than for the basic researcher?

18. Why are program sponsors and staff likely to resist random assignment to programs and treatments? What are evaluation researchers' counterarguments to these objections?

19. How can the diffusion of information from one treatment group to another threaten the internal validity of evaluation studies?

20. What peculiar measurement problems arise in evaluation studies? How are these generally resolved?

21. What factors inhibit the ability to use probability sampling in evaluation studies?

22. How does the social context of evaluation threaten external validity?

23. What is modal instance sampling?

24. Describe five potential stakeholders in an evaluation study. How does the existence of these stakeholders affect evaluation research?

25. Suppose your college is initiating a new policy of assigning first-year students to the same residence halls, thereby segregating the residence halls into first-year versus upper-class. They have asked you to advise them on how to evaluate the impact of this policy.

    a. Who are the relevant stakeholders in this study?

    b. Explain how you will identify the relevant and potential effects of this new living arrangement.

    c. Carefully describe the general research strategy that you would recommend.

NOTES

1. Frederick Mosteller (1981) describes a "nutrition experiment" carried out in 1601 to test the effects of lemon juice on scurvy among sailors on four British ships sailing from England to India. Among those on the largest ship in the fleet, who drank three teaspoons of lemon juice every day, few became ill. But over a third of those on the three smaller ships died before they reached the Cape of Good Hope. Despite this evidence and another successful experiment done 150 years later, it was not until 1795 that "the British Navy began using citrus juice on a regular basis and wiped out scurvy in the service." (p. 882)

2. Throughout the first half of the twentieth century, individuals in most states did not gain either the right to vote or the right to purchase alcoholic beverages until they reached the age of 21. During the late 1960s, however, popular support for lowering the voting age grew as large numbers of 18- to 20-year-olds were sent to Vietnam. "The central argument was that someone old enough to die for his country should be old enough to vote" (Clark, 1992:228). This reasoning led ultimately to a Constitutional amendment in 1971 that gave 18-year-olds the right to vote in federal elections. When most states followed suit by lowering the local and state voting age to 18, they adopted the same rationale for lowering the legal drinking age. In fact, between 1970 and 1975, twenty-nine states lowered their drinking ages, usually from 21 to 18 or 19 (Saffer and Grossman, 1989).

3. In the Greeley and Rossi study, the outcome variable was tolerance; they controlled statistically for various demographic variables that might have created selection bias. This statistical procedure, called outcome modeling, works by estimating the effects of the treatment variable (Catholic-school attendance) beyond the effects of other predictors (possible selection factors) of the outcome variable. An alternative approach, called selection modeling, is to carry out the analysis in two stages: first, predict membership in the treatment or comparison group on the basis of the selection factors; then use this information to create a

proxy variable for selection effects in predicting the outcome measure (see Heckman, 1979; Stolzenberg and Relles, 1997).

4. The jigsaw method begins by placing students in six-person learning groups. Each group is given a lesson that is divided into six paragraphs, and each paragraph is assigned to one member of the group. To learn the entire lesson, group members must put together the six paragraphs, like the pieces of a jigsaw puzzle, to get the whole picture. But to do so, each individual group member must learn his or her own segment and teach it to the other members of the group. [See Aronson et al. (1978), for a more complete description.]

5. According to Shotland and Mark (1985:354), however, divergent results may induce less salutary reactions. Instead of producing uncertainty, contradictory findings may strengthen the beliefs of partisans on both sides; or they may reduce policymakers' confidence in social scientists' ability to provide useful information.

6. Alternatively, Irwin Deutscher and Margaret Gold (1979) argue that maintaining a position of scientific objectivity may limit the usefulness of evaluation research. They believe that the proper role of evaluators is that of a "sympathetic skeptic," whose "partisanship . . . is essential for a sympathetic grasp of the intentions and the problems posed by the program."

III

■ ■

DATA PROCESSING, ANALYSIS, AND INTERPRETATION

As with other facets of research, data analysis is very much tied to the researcher's basic methodological approach. In the chapters on field and available data research, we discussed certain data-analytic techniques at length, but in the case of experiments and surveys we alluded only briefly to this stage of research. The first two chapters in this section take up where our discussions in chapters 6 and 8 left off. Having collected data in a study, the researcher must quantify it, put it in computer-readable form, and analyze the data statistically. Chapter 14 charts this process for survey research, outlining the key steps in processing data prior to analysis and describing elementary statistical analyses. Chapter 15 then considers some more advanced statistical techniques for assessing the causal relations among sets of variables.

Even though our attention in these two chapters is focused mostly on the analysis of survey data, the underlying logic and flow of the analysis described is basically the same as it is in other approaches. There is, for example, always a constant interplay between theory and data. The stage for data analysis is set by the researcher's theoretical model of anticipated relationships, because this limits and guides the kinds of analyses that can be carried out. The analysis, in turn, assays and elaborates this model and invariably suggests new models for further analysis. The first rule in all this is that "facts (data) never speak for themselves." Rather, they must be interpreted. Ultimately, that interpretation takes the form of a research report, book, or article that will be read and interpreted by others. Thus, in chapter 17, we examine the writing of research. All research also must be interpreted in terms of standards of research ethics, examined in chapter 16.

443

14

✓

Data Processing and Elementary Data Analysis

As we consider the later stages of research, it is valuable to recall the broader process of scientific inquiry. Science is a means to understanding that involves a repetitive interplay between theoretical ideas and empirical evidence. Data analysis takes place whenever theory and data are compared. This comparison occurs in field research when an investigator struggles to bring order to, or to make sense of, his or her observations. In surveys and experiments, the researcher typically brings theory and data together when testing a hypothesis once the data have been gathered and processed. In any case, initial data analyses set the stage for a continued interaction between theory and data.

This chapter and the next chapter focus on data processing, analysis, and interpretation. Together the two chapters follow the typical development of a survey study following data collection: from handling the data and putting them in computer-readable form to preliminary analyses involving one and two variables (chapter 14) to more advanced statistical analyses (chapter 15). Both chapters are oriented toward the reader more as consumer than producer of research and in no way can substitute for a course in statistics. In fact, we eschew computational formulas in favor of verbal presentations. What we want to do is give the reader a sense of the *process* of data analysis—a learning process achieved through comparing empirical evidence with theoretical expectations.

Preview of Analysis Steps

In a sense, data analysis begins with a statement of hypotheses, the construction of a theoretical model, or, at the very least, implicitly anticipated relationships among a set of variables; for these models guide the collection of data and thereby determine the alternative relationships or models that may be analyzed. In chapter 3, for example, we discussed Beckett Broh's (2002) study of the impact of extracurricular involvement on academic achievement. In examining this relationship, Broh considered the impact of gender, race-ethnicity, parent's educational attainment, family income, and other antecedent variables. Each of these variables, she reasoned, could either independently affect academic achievement or possibly create a spurious causal relationship between extracurricular involvement and academic achievement. She also identified various intervening variables intended to capture theoretical links between sports participation and educational achievement, which

445

she derived from developmental theory, the leading crowd hypothesis, and social capital theory. As in all social research, these theoretical expectations guided Broh's selection and measurement of variables and ultimately her analysis of the data.

Chapter 15 focuses on statistical techniques for assessing the causal relations among sets of variables. This is where we see how Broh tested her various theoretical models. Following data collection, however, several steps are necessary to prepare for this final stage of hypothesis testing. Let us preview the basic analysis steps that we cover in this chapter: (1) placing relevant information in computer-readable form, (2) inspecting and transforming the data for the intended statistical analyses, and (3) preliminary hypothesis testing.

In survey research, the first step includes editing and summarizing the responses (coding), data entry, and error checking (cleaning). Some of this **data processing** occurs during data collection in computer-assisted surveys. Researchers performing secondary analysis, as in Broh's analysis of data from the National Educational Longitudinal Survey (NELS), begin their analysis at the second, data inspection and modification, step. The goal of inspection is to get a clear picture of the data in order to determine appropriate statistical analyses and necessary data modifications. Usually one examines each variable singly (univariate analysis), especially for insufficient variation in responses, missing information, abnormalities, and other weaknesses that may be mitigated prior to the analysis. The reasons for **data modification** are many: For example, a researcher may want to combine the responses to several items in order to create an index or scale, change one or more of the values for a variable, or collapse categories for purposes of analysis. In chapter 4 we described how Beckett Broh created measures of interscholastic sports participation and time spent on homework by combining variables in the NELS dataset.

The analysis then turns to empirical testing of the theorized relationships. For simple two-variable (bivariate) hypotheses, the analyst determines if the association between the independent and dependent variables confirms theoretical expectations. Broh, for example, found that participation in interscholastic sports was positively associated with students' math and English grades, as predicted. In a true experiment, assessing the relationship between the independent and dependent variables is the final analysis step because an adequate design effectively controls extraneous variables. But in non-experimental designs, extraneous variables may pose serious rival explanations that require statistical control. Broh had to explore the possibility, for example, that higher-performing students were more likely than their peers to play interscholastic sports.

Some researchers skip the previous step (preliminary hypothesis testing) in favor of a full-blown multivariate model containing all relevant independent, dependent, antecedent, intervening, and other variables. We prefer to conceptually describe the process as having two interrelated stages. If preliminary hypothesis testing supports theoretical expectations, the analyst formulates multivariate models to rule out, to the extent possible, that the initial results were a spurious consequence of uncontrolled antecedent variables. Conversely, if hypothesized relationships are not supported in preliminary testing, the researcher designs multivariate models to determine if uncontrolled extraneous variables are blocking or distorting the initial results. The preliminary testing step also may reveal unanticipated (serendipitous) findings that suggest alternative multivariate models.

Data Processing

According to James Davis and Tom Smith (1992:60), data preparation (or process-ing) is "the least glamorous aspect of survey research." Yet, as they also point out, "probably at no other stage . . . is there a greater chance of a really horrible error be-ing made. . . . To avoid such errors, many checks and safeguards must be built into the system." In survey data processing, four essential steps constitute the process of checking the data and making them serviceable for analysis: editing, coding, data en-try, and cleaning. Some of these procedures have been taken over by software in com-puter-assisted interviewing (CATI, CAPI) or self-interviewing (CASI).

Editing

Editing is a quality control process applied mostly to paper-and-pencil surveys. Its purpose is to ensure that the information on a questionnaire or interview schedule is ready to be transferred to the computer for analysis (Sonquist and Dunkelberg, 1977). "Ready" means that the data are as complete, error-free, and readable as possible.

Editing is carried out both during and after the process of data collection, and much of it occurs simultaneously with coding (see below). In interview studies, the editing process begins in the field. Interviewers should check over their completed forms for errors and omissions soon after each interview is conducted. Respondents should be recontacted if necessary, or corrections should be made from memory. Field supervisors may also do some editing at this point, such as determining whether the interviews have been properly conducted from the standpoint of using the cor-rect forms, legibly recording answers, and interviewing the correct respondents.

Most of the editing in large-scale surveys is done in a central office. Here an editor or coder, who serves much the same function as a copy editor for a writer, goes over each completed form (1) to evaluate interviewers and detect interview-ing problems (e.g., inadequate use of probes to obtain answers to open-ended ques-tions); (2) to check for multiple answers to single items, vague answers, response inconsistencies (e.g., reporting zero hours of television watched in one section and the viewing of a specific TV program in another section), and the like; and (3) to make sure that the interview schedule or questionnaire is complete—that all items, especially those with "missing" responses, have coded values. The editor may bring glaring errors to the attention of the principal investigator or the field supervisor, who provides feedback to interviewers, but mostly he or she simply will make cor-rections directly on the form.

The NELS involved both on-site and centralized follow-up editing and data re-trieval. Students, teachers, and parents completed questionnaires, which were sup-plemented with data from school officials. Field interviewers checked the student questionnaires at the schools, giving special attention to items designated as "criti-cal," such as a student's sex, race, and date of birth, household composition, and parents' employment status and education. If they found missing or undecipherable responses to these critical items, they privately contacted the respondents. For the other questionnaires and data, similarly designated critical items were checked in the central office and retrieval took place by telephone.

Some editing activities can be programmed into computer-assisted interviewing (CAI) and self-interviewing (CASI) software. CAI or CASI programs can prompt an interviewer or respondent to answer certain questions, to skip others, to use appropriate response codes, and to review obviously inconsistent responses to related questions. But lacking the intelligence of a human editor, CAI and CASI software cannot determine fully if interviewers and respondents are recording consistent and adequate answers. A web-based or laptop CASI program, for example, may accept "none of your business" as an adequate answer to an open-ended question.

Coding

Coding for computer analysis consists of assigning numbers or symbols to variable categories. In surveys such as the NELS, the categories are answers to questions; and the common practice, which simplifies data entry and analysis, is to use numerical codes only. For the variable gender or sex in the NELS, a code of 1 was used for males and 2 for females. The particular numbers used are arbitrary; a code of 2 might just as well have been used for males and a code of 1 for females. These numerical codes generally are specified directly on the questionnaire or interview schedule. For example, in the NELS second follow-up survey, students were asked if they had participated in (a) a team sport (baseball, basketball, football, soccer, hockey, etc.), (b) an individual sport (cross-country, gymnastics, golf, tennis, track, wrestling, etc.), and (c) cheerleading, pompon, or drill team. For each question, they circled the highest number that applied among five response alternatives: (1) school does not have, (2) did not participate, (3) participated on a junior varsity team, (4) participated on a varsity team, and (5) participated as a captain/co-captain on any team.

For closed-ended questions, coding is straightforward: There are relatively few categories, and you simply need to assign a different code to each category. For open-ended questions, however, the number of unique responses may number in the hundreds. Coding for this type of question is very much like coding in content analysis (see chapter 11). The researcher tries to develop a coding scheme that does not require a separate code for every respondent or case but that adequately reflects the full range of responses. The idea is to put the data in manageable form while retaining as much information as practical. (See Box 14.1 for an example of coding open-ended questions.)

If anything, the tendency for novice researchers is to use too few categories, which gloss over potentially meaningful differences. Once the data are coded and data analysis is under way, it is easy to combine code categories for purposes of analysis, but it is impossible to recover lost detail. Consider a questionnaire study that needed a count of respondents' siblings: Instead of asking for that number, respondents were asked to list the ages of any brothers and sisters. Now, one could code only the number of siblings. But consider what happens when all the available information is retained—when the age and gender of each sibling are coded and entered separately into the database. Doing this makes it possible, by computer manipulation, not only to count the number of siblings but also to generate measures of number of brothers, sisters, older brothers, younger sisters, respondent's spacing from next sibling, and so on.

BOX 14.1

Reasons for Giving Up Cigarette Smoking: An Example of Coding Responses to Open-Ended Questions

Developing coding categories for open-ended questions, like many other research activities, involves an interplay between theory and data. Let us follow the procedure used by Bruce Straits (1967) in a study based on personal interviews of ex-smokers ("quitters"), current smokers who tried but were unable to quit smoking ("unables"), and current smokers who have never made a serious attempt to stop smoking ("smokers"). Hypothesizing that specific factors precipitate and support smoking cessation, Straits asked quitters and unables the open-ended question: Why did you want to stop smoking? (Smokers were asked, What reasons might you have for giving up smoking?) Individual responses to the question were too diverse and numerous to manage and analyze without grouping them into a smaller number of categories.

Both theory and data guided Straits's development of coding categories. Theoretical considerations included the hypothesis that current physical ailments (especially those easily connected with smoking) play a more important role in the discontinuation of smoking than health fears for the future (e.g., incurring lung cancer). The coding procedure involved first listing each reason given by the 200 respondents. (Typically studies use a sample of about 50 to 100 respondents to build codes.) Tally marks were used to note identical reasons. Here is part of the listing:

"I couldn't get over a bad cough" |||| |||| ||||

"Job requirements" |||| |

"Not good for health" |||| |||| |||| |||

"It is too expensive" |||| |||| |||

"Live longer" |||| |

"Sore throat" |||| |||| |

"To see if I could" |||| ||||

"Heart attack" |

"Quit for Lent and didn't return" |

"Doctor's advice" |||| |||| |||

"Sinus condition" |||| |||| |

"Causes lung cancer" |||| |||| |||| |||

"My wife hates it" |||

Next, coding categories were formed by grouping together reasons that seemed similar from the research perspective. For example, people with bad coughs were placed in the same category as those reporting sore throats. Although the distinction between a cough and a sore throat is important from a medical standpoint, it was not pertinent to Straits's hypothesis.

Empirical considerations also influenced construction of the coding categories. Some reasons had to be lumped together in "other" categories, because they occurred too infrequently. An unanticipated category had to be established for quitters who had not made a conscious decision to quit, but instead found themselves in situations where they were unable to smoke for a temporary period, such as while recovering from an operation.

The final coding scheme, which was used to code *each* reason given, was as follows.

Current health reasons

  1. Didn't feel well (unspecified illness)
  2. Nasal congestion (bad cold, sinus, etc.)
  3. Cough, sore throat (smoker's cough, dry throat, etc.)
  4. Shortness of breath (cutting down on wind, etc.)
  5. Poor appetite, loss of weight
  6. Other ailments (headaches, nervous condition, nausea, dizziness, etc.)

Advised by doctor

  7. Unspecified (ordered by doctor, etc.)
  8. Because of specific ailment (heart trouble, palsy, etc.)
  9. Doctor said smoking harmful

Future health reasons

10. Smoking is harmful (unspecified)
11. Live longer
12. Fear of cancer (lung cancer, etc.)

Other

13. Sensory dislike (bad taste in mouth, smell, dirty house, etc.)
14. Pressure from close associates (wife, co-worker, etc.)
15. Financial reasons (waste of money, etc.)
16. Test of willpower (to see if could, control life, etc.)
17. Work requirement (smoking not allowed)
18. Quit temporarily (because of operation, illness, Lent, etc., and didn't return to smoking)
19. Other reasons
20. Don't know
21. No answer

The coding scheme represents a balance between too much and too little detail. The classification preserves possibly relevant distinctions such as identifying those who specifically mentioned cancer. The detailed categories are easily collapsed (recoded) when the analysis requires broader groupings. For example, Straits (1967:75) reports that a higher proportion (82 percent) of quitters mentioned current health ailments and/or advice from a doctor than did the unables (60 percent) or smokers (37 percent), who mentioned less immediate health threats or weaker reasons such as "waste of money" or "test of willpower" more frequently.

Entering the Data

One can think of the data as a matrix or spreadsheet, with observations as rows and variables as columns, which has been entered into a computer file and stored on a disk, tape, CD, or other media.[1] In a data matrix for a survey, the coded responses to each question occupy a designated column in the rows for each respondent. There are several options for data entry. One can type information from paper-and-pencil surveys into a computer file using data-entry software programmed to detect some kinds of erroneous entries, called computer-assisted data entry (CADE). The NELS used this method to enter data obtained from school administrators and school records. An optical scanner or reader is another option. One device reads pencil-marked "bubbles" adjacent to question response categories on survey instruments or on response sheets, such as the answer forms to the Scholastic Aptitude Test (SAT), and then enters this information into a computer file. The NELS optically scanned the questionnaire data from students, parents, and teachers. Finally, in computer-assisted surveys, interviewers (CATI and CAPI) or respondents (CASI) simply type the answers directly into a computer laptop or terminal.

Before the development of CAI and CASI direct data entry, optical scanners, and data-entry monitoring software, clerical staff would enter the data by hand using a computer terminal or keypunch machine. This introduced various errors as entry operators misread edits and codes on the survey forms, skipped over or repeated responses to questions, transposed numbers, and so on. The standard procedure for minimizing such data entry errors is to enter the information on each survey twice (ideally by a different person each time) and then compare the two entries for errors. When punched cards were the means of recording and storing data, this was done on a machine called a verifier. Nowadays, two persons can independently enter the data into separate computer files, and a software program then compares the two files for noncomparable entries. The same verification strategy can reduce coding errors if each file is independently coded by a different person.

Cleaning

After the data have been entered into a computer file, the researcher should check them over thoroughly for errors. Detecting and resolving errors in coding and in transmitting the data to the computer is referred to as **cleaning** the data. This is an essential process that may also identify respondent-related errors. Researchers who have invested a great deal of time and energy in collecting their data do not want their work undermined by avoidable mistakes made at the stage of data processing, because, unlike sampling error and certain kinds of measurement error, data-processing errors *are* avoidable. The way to avoid them is to be exceedingly careful about entering the data and to use every possible method of checking for mistakes. Here are a few ways to clean your data.

First, data entry should be verified whenever feasible. When verification is not possible, as in CAI or CASI direct data entry, the error rate may be minimized by careful training and monitoring of the data entry persons (interviewers or respondents) and extensive field pretesting of the computer-assisted survey procedure.

Beyond training, monitoring, and verification, two cleaning techniques generally are applied. The first of these is sometimes called **wild-code checking** (Sonquist and Dunkelberg, 1977:211). Every variable has a specified set of legitimate codes. The aforementioned NELS questions on sport participation, for example, had possible codes of 1 (for "school does not have") to 5 ("participated as a captain/cocaptain"); in addition, a code of 6 was used for "multiple response" and 8 for "missing." Wild codes are any codes that are not legitimate. Wild-code checking consists of examining the values recorded for each item to see whether there are any out-of-range codes, such as 7, 9, and 0 for the sport participation questions. Some CAI, CASI, and data-entry software can be programmed to do this kind of cleaning automatically by refusing to accept wild-code values. Alternatively, one can run a frequency distribution for the variable, check to see if there are any erroneous codes, and then computer search the data file to find the errors. Of course, one should keep in mind that wild-code checking does not detect typographical or other errors involving legitimate codes.

Third, most large-scale surveys use a process called **consistency checking** (Sonquist and Dunkelberg, 1977:215). The idea here is to see whether responses to certain questions are related in reasonable ways to responses to particular other questions. For example, it would be unreasonable, and therefore an indication of coding error, to find a respondent who is married and age 5, or a medical doctor with three years of formal schooling.

One common type of consistency checking involves contingency questions. As you may recall from chapter 9, these are questions designed for a subset of the respondents. The GSS, for example, first asks people about their employment status last week. If the respondent is working full or part time, he or she is asked the following contingency question: "How many hours did you work last week, at all jobs?" Consistency checking determines if a question such as this was answered only by those for whom the question was intended. We would not expect an answer to this question if the respondent was unemployed, retired, or in school. To identify such erroneous responses, one must break down the frequency distribution for the contingency question by pertinent subsamples of the population. One might check to see, for example, if any of the subsample of nonworking respondents answered the question on number of hours worked last week.

Ideally, a suspected error can be resolved by retracing the process from the survey interview through to the dubious data entry. One may resolve errors by examining the original questionnaires or survey schedules, by listening to taped telephone interviews, or by contacting the original respondents. When this is not possible, researchers may flag the dubious entries as suspicious or reclassify them as missing data.

One can get an idea of the importance of editing and data cleaning by considering the measures taken to edit and clean the GSS data (Davis and Smith, 1992). Before the data are entered, interviewers in the field go over their interview schedules after each interview to check for errors; field supervisors review the first two forms submitted by each interviewer to check for completeness, clarity, and following of proper coding procedures, and then they check a sample of forms submitted thereafter; and coders or editors at NORC's central office carry out various checks and prepare the completed forms for data entry. The latter includes coding responses to open-ended questions and other responses that are not precoded (e.g., "not applicable" or "no answer") on the form; attempting to obtain missing data on crucial questions; and selecting random cases for validation checks. The data are entered into the computer with the aid of a data-entry program, which automatically alerts the investigator to wild-code errors at the time of entry. Once data from all of the forms have been entered, data from a proportion of the forms are entered a second time to ensure that data entry errors are minimal. Next, cleaning programs are run, first to check again for wild-code errors and then to do consistency checking for certain questions. When errors are detected, corrections are made and the cleaning process is "repeated until all questions on all cases come up as 'clean'." Finally, the coders turn this "clean" file over to the researchers, who generate frequency distributions for another round of consistency checking.

Data Matrices and Documentation

Once you have entered all the data into a computer file, you are ready to inspect, modify, and analyze the data. Before we discuss these steps, however, let us examine the typical form of data storage, the technical terms, and the documentation required to describe a dataset. Imagine that you are preparing the data for secondary analysis. What would others need to know to analyze your data? What documentation accompanies the NELS and other processed archived data?

Two types of information are necessary to adequately describe study data: a matrix of variable values or codes for each observation, and supporting documentation. The spreadsheet view in Figure 14.1 illustrates a partial **data matrix** of selected variables (columns) for over two hundred countries of the world (rows) gathered from *The World Factbook 2002* and other online sources.[2] The countries are in alphabetical order, and only the first 14 observations (the A's) are shown. The number in each cell of the data matrix represents the value of a particular variable (column) for a particular country (row). The first coded cell value of "27.8" indicates that the 2002 population size (first column) of Afghanistan (first row) is estimated as approximately 27,800,000 persons. One can read down a column to inspect the distribution of values for each variable. The literacy rate in the 14 countries, for example, ranges from 100 percent (Andorra and Australia) to 36 percent (Afghanistan).

The accompanying online documentation explains variable definitions and important data limitations. The Total Fertility Rate (second column), for example, is defined as " . . . a figure for the average number of children that would be born per woman if all women lived to the end of their childbearing years and bore children according to [current birth rates] at each age" (*The World Factbook 2002*). Thus if Angola's 2002 age-specific birth rates do not change over time, women will average 6.4 children during their lifetime. Andorra and Austria, in contrast, currently have very low fertility rates. Perusal of the data for the first 14 countries suggests

Country	Population Mid-2002 (millions)	Total Fertility Rate	Life Expectancy at Birth (years)			Percent Urban	Literacy Rate (% ages 15 and above)		
			Total	Male	Female		Total	Male	Female
Afghanistan	27.8	5.7	46.6	47.3	45.9	22	36	51	21
Albania	3.5	2.3	72.1	69.3	75.1	43	93	NA	NA
Algeria	32.3	2.6	70.2	68.9	71.7	58	62	74	49
America Samoa	0.1	3.4	75.5	71.1	80.2	53	97	98	97
Andorra	0.1	1.3	83.5	80.6	86.6	92	100	NA	NA
Angola	10.6	6.4	38.9	37.6	40.2	35	42	56	28
Anguilla	0.01	1.8	76.5	73.6	79.5	100	95	95	95
Antigua, Barbuda	0.1	2.3	71.0	68.7	73.4	37	89	90	88
Argentina	37.8	2.4	75.5	72.1	79.0	88	96	96	96
Armenia	3.3	1.5	66.6	62.3	71.1	67	99	99	98
Aruba	0.1	1.8	78.7	75.3	82.2	51	97	NA	NA
Australia	19.6	1.8	80.0	77.2	83.0	91	100	100	100
Austria	8.2	1.4	78.0	74.8	81.3	67	98	NA	NA
Azerbaijan	7.8	2.3	63.1	58.8	67.5	52	97	99	96

FIGURE 14.1. Partial data matrix for countries (main source: *The World Factbook 2002*).

research questions for exploring the full dataset: Do high fertility countries tend to have low female literacy? Is there a positive relationship between country literacy levels and life expectancy at birth? Do more urbanized countries have lower birth rates?

Before one tests hypotheses, however, it is important to carefully examine the documentation ("the fine print") for data inconsistencies and other limitations. Even though the *World Factbook 2002* is based on information available on January 1, 2002, some of the data were collected much earlier in time. The literacy rate for Algeria females, for example, is based on a 1995 estimate. Besides data collection dates, variable definitions may vary by country. The *Factbook* reports that there "are no universal definitions and standards of literacy. Unless otherwise specified, all rates are based on the most common definition—the ability to read and write at a specified age." For the first 14 countries the specific age was 15, except for Albania (age 9) and Anguilla (age 12). Finally, invariably some of the information is unavailable (missing). For the country data, the missing cells are coded NA (not available) in Figure 14.1.

Figure 14.2 presents a partial data matrix for 10 of the 12,578 NELS student respondents in Broh's study. The rows represent respondents, who are identified by unique id codes (first column). The remaining columns represent variables, whose names may identify time frames (e.g., "by" = base year) and question numbers (e.g., "36a" = question 36a), or abbreviated variable names (e.g., "pared" = parental education). Numerical codes in the matrix cells identify ques-

Id	bys36a	bys36b	bys36c	sex	race	bypared	byfcomp
124902	3	2	2	1	4	3	1
124915	3	2	2	1	4	3	1
124916	2	3	3	2	4	3	1
124932	2	3	3	2	4	3	1
124939	3	2	2	1	4	3	4
124944	3	3	3	2	4	2	1
124947	2	3	2	2	4	2	1
124966	3	3	3	2	4	3	1
124968	3	3	3	1	4	3	1
124970	1	2	3	1	4	4	1

FIGURE 14.2. Partial data matrix for NELS:88.

tion responses or summary variable categories. For respondent's sex (fifth column), recall that a code of 1 was used for males and 2 for females. Thus the first two listed respondents are males, and the next two are females. For race, a code of 1 was used for "Asian or Pacific Islander," 2 for "Hispanic, regardless of race," 3 for "Black, not of Hispanic origin," 4 for "White, not of Hispanic origin," 5 for "American Indian or Alaskan Native," and 8 for "Missing" (no answer or multiple race categories were chosen by the respondents). Although Figure 14.2 lists only whites (sixth column), about a third of the students were members of the other race-ethnicity categories.

Once study results are entered into a data matrix or equivalent computer-readable format, the researcher should prepare the **codebook** documentation. A codebook is like a dictionary in that it defines the meaning of the numerical codes for each named variable, such as the NELS codes for sex and race. Codebooks also may contain question wording, interviewer directions, and coding and editing decision rules, such as how to handle two answers circled to a single-response question. Originally, survey codebooks were single physical documents, but now this information may be scattered across various sources and media. In addition to an electronic codebook accompanying NELS datasets on CDs, numerous technical and methodological reports are available online from the National Center for Education Statistics.[3] The NELS electronic codebook reports, for example, that sex was coded from the "Your Background" section of the base year student questionnaire, or, when unavailable from this source, from school rosters. If sex was missing from both the student questionnaire and the school roster, it was imputed from the student's name if this could be done unambiguously. Extremely complex coding rules are given for parental education (seventh column of Figure 14.2) and family composition (eighth column), which are composite variables based on relevant responses from student and parent questionnaires.

When variables are coded directly from a questionnaire, the codebook entries look very much like the survey instrument with the addition of response and nonresponse codes. The entry for Broh's parent–child social capital variables (columns 2–4 of Figure 14.2) includes:

> 36. Since the beginning of the school year, how often have you discussed the following with either or both of your parents or guardians?
>
> {bys36a} Selecting courses or programs at school
> {bys36b} School activities or events of particular interest to you
> {bys36c} Things you studied in class

Code	Label
1	NOT AT ALL
2	ONCE OR TWICE
3	THREE OR MORE TIMES
6	{MULTIPLE RESPONSE}
8	{MISSING}

A code of 6 indicates students who marked more than one response on the optical scan questionnaire. If they failed to respond at all, a code of 8 was used to indicate missing information. In many surveys, missing data for a variable are divided into three categories of those who "don't know" (DK), who provide "no answer" (NA), or for whom the question is not applicable (NAP).

An excellent online site for viewing codebook documentation for the General Social Survey (GSS) is maintained by the National Opinion Research Center (NORC).[4] The GSS surveys, which we described in chapter 8, consisted of interviews administered to national samples using a standard interview schedule (Davis and Smith, 1992). Among the items covered were (1) requests for standard background information on gender, race, occupation, religion, and so on; (2) questions about the quality of the respondent's life in various areas (e.g., health, family, social relations); (3) requests for evaluations of government programs; and (4) questions covering opinions and attitudes about a wide range of issues, such as drug usage, abortion, religious freedom, and racial equality. One can search the online codebook for all GSS variables, either by alphabetically-arranged variable name ("abany" to "zodiac") or by subject ("abortion" to "world view"). Information for each GSS variable includes question wording, response codes, response trends over time, links to related appendices and methodological reports, and an annotated bibliography of previous usage.

The Functions of Statistics in Social Research

Starting with a cleaned dataset, the next analysis step would be to inspect the data to decide on subsequent statistical analyses. But how do you decide what kind of analysis to do? Naturally, that decision depends on what you want to know. Broh wanted to know if playing interscholastic sports (the independent variable) promotes academic achievement (the dependent variable). Of course, to establish a causal relation such as this, she would need to show that the two variables are associated (that changes in one variable accompany changes in the other), that the direction of influence is from the independent variable to the dependent variable, and that the association between the variables is nonspurious. To begin her analysis, Broh could have examined the NELS data respondent by respondent to see if playing interscholastic sports was associated with academic achievement. But with over 12,000 respondents, this task would be incredibly tedious and probably not very reliable. Therefore, what she needed was a fast and efficient means of summarizing the association between these variables for the entire sample of respondents. This is precisely where statistics (and computers) enters in. A *statistic* is a summary statement about a set of data; statistics as a discipline provides techniques for organizing and analyzing data.

Traditionally, statistics has been divided according to two functions—descriptive and inferential. **Descriptive statistics** is concerned with organizing and summarizing the data at hand to make them more intelligible. The high and low scores and average score on an exam are descriptive statistics that readily summarize a class's performance. Broh needed a descriptive statistic that would summarize the degree of association between playing interscholastic sports and academic achievement in the NELS sample. **Inferential statistics** deals with the kinds of inferences that can be made when generalizing from data, as from sample data to the entire population. Broh needed this form of analysis as a means of determining what the NELS sample of observations indicated about the effects of playing interscholastic sports on academic achievement in the target population of American secondary students.

Based on probability theory, inferential statistics may be used for two distinct purposes: to estimate population characteristics from sample data (discussed in chapter 5) and to test hypotheses.[5] Traditionally, hypothesis testing is employed to rule out the rival explanation that observed data patterns, relationships, or differences are due to chance processes arising from random assignment (in the case of experiments), sampling error (in the case of probability sampling), random measurement error, or other sources.[6] In experiments (discussed in chapter 6), such testing determines if the differences between experimental conditions are "statistically significant"—that is, not attributable to random assignment. The appropriate role of significance tests in the analysis of nonexperimental data is a longstanding controversy (see Morrison and Henkel, 1970). Following David Gold's argument (1969) that results that easily could have occurred by a chance process should not be taken seriously, we view tests of significance as an effective means of screening out trivialities and chance mishaps.

Inspecting and Modifying the Data

At this stage, the researcher is ready to give the computer instructions for inspecting and transforming the data.[7] Some of these operations may occur during earlier data cleaning and coding processes. The goal of inspection is to get a clear picture of the data by examining one variable at a time. The data "pictures" generated by univariate analysis come in various forms—tables, graphs, charts, and statistical measures. The nature of the techniques depends on whether one is analyzing variables measured at the nominal/ordinal level or variables measured at the interval/ratio level (discussed in chapter 4). Following data inspection, the researcher may want to change one or more variable codes, rearrange the numerical order of variable codes, collapse variable categories, impute estimated values for missing data, add together the codes for several variables to create an index or scale, and otherwise modify the data for analysis.

Nominal- and Ordinal-Scale Variables

Broh might have done univariate analyses simply to get a sense of the nature of the variation in the variables to be analyzed. It is generally a good idea, for example, to see if there is sufficient variation in responses to warrant including the variable in the analysis. As a rule, the less variation, the more difficult it is to detect how differences in one variable are related to differences in another variable. To take the extreme case, if all students scored the same on self-esteem, then it would be impossible to determine how *differences* in this variable were related to differences in academic achievement. Fortunately, there was sufficient variation in Broh's main independent variable as nearly a third of the students reported participating in interscholastic sports during both the tenth and twelfth grades.

A core GSS question asks, "Would you say that most of the time people try to be helpful, or that they are mostly just looking out for themselves?" Suppose that we wanted to inspect the responses to this question in the 2000 GSS. One means is to organize responses into a table called a **frequency distribution**. A frequency distribution is created by first listing all the response categories and then adding up the number of cases that occur in each category. If we instruct the computer to do this, our output might look like that in Table 14.1, which gives the 2000 distribution of responses to the helpfulness question. This certainly presents a clearer picture than does a case-by-case listing of responses. However, this sort of table generally would serve as a preliminary organization of the data, because more readable formats can be derived from it. In particular, researchers often compute the percentage of re-

TABLE 14.1. **Frequency Distribution of Belief in the Helpfulness of People,* 2000 General Social Survey**

Code	Label	Frequency
1	Try to be helpful	866
2	Just look out for themselves	851
3	Depends (volunteered)	166
7	Don't know	10
8	No answer	3
9	Not applicable	921
TOTAL		2817

*Question: "Would you say that most of the time people try to be helpful, or that they are mostly just looking out for themselves?

spondents in each category. To see how this might create a still clearer picture, examine the raw figures in Table 14.1.

Notice that the number of "try to be helpful" responses in the sample is 866. This number by itself is meaningless unless we provide a standard or reference point with which to interpret it. More than likely as you peruse the table you will see the figures in relation to one another, invoking implicit points of comparison. You may note, for example, that there are slightly more "try to be helpful" than "just look out for themselves" answers or that 166 respondents volunteered a qualified response ("it depends"). **Percentage distributions** provide an explicit comparative framework for interpreting distributions. They tell you the size of a category relative to the size of the sample. To create a percentage distribution, you divide the number of cases in each category by the total number of cases and multiply by 100. This is what we have done in Table 14.2. Now you can see more clearly the relative difference in responses. Now we see, for example, that fewer than 9 percent of the respondents volunteered a qualified response.

It should be noted that the percentages in Table 14.2 are based on the total number of responses, excluding "missing data"—those in the "no answer" and "not applicable" categories. About one-third (921) of the respondents were in a random subsample that were not asked the helpfulness question, and three others (the "no answers") either were not asked the question (interviewer error) or did not respond. Since these are not meaningful variable categories (i.e., they say nothing about belief in the helpfulness of people), it would be misleading to include them in the percentage distribution. The total number of missing responses is important information. If this information is not placed in the main body of a table, then it at least should be reported in a footnote to the relevant table or in the text of the research report. Also notice that the base upon which percentages are computed (1893) is given in parentheses below the percentage total of 100 percent. It is customary to indicate in tables the total number of observations from which the statistics are computed. This information may be found elsewhere—at the end of the table title or in a headnote or footnote to the table; often it is signified with the letter *N*.

Univariate analysis is seldom conducted as an end in itself, especially in explanatory research. One important function mentioned earlier is to determine how

TABLE **14.2. Percentage Distribution**
of Helpfulness of People for the
Distribution in Table 14.1

Response	%
Try to be helpful	45.7
Just look out for themselves	45.0
Depends (volunteered)	8.8
Don't know	0.5
TOTAL	100.0
(Number of responses)	(1893)
(Missing data)	(924)

to collapse or recode categories for further analysis. For the helpfulness variable, one might limit the analysis to those who directly answered the question (codes 1 and 2 in Table 14.1), but this would result in the loss of 176 "depends" and "don't know" responses that then would be recoded as "missing" for analysis purposes. Instead, one might retain the "depends" and "don't know" responses by recoding them as middle responses in a three-category ordinal scale:

1   Try to be helpful
2   Depends, Don't Know
3   Just look out for themselves

Alternatively, one could collapse the responses into a dichotomy by comparing either of the extreme categories with all others. Respondents definitely expressing low faith in people, for example, could be contrasted with the less pessimistic or uncertain responses:

1   Just look out for themselves
2   Depends, Don't Know, Try to be helpful

Either of the above recodes achieves the practical objective of minimizing the "missing" observations. The choice of one of these, or an alternative recoding, should be guided primarily by theoretical considerations.

A univariate inspection also can inform decisions about how to collapse the categories of a variable for further analysis. Collapsing decisions may be based on theoretical criteria and/or may hinge on the empirical variation in responses. Thus, years of education might be collapsed into "theoretically" meaningful categories (grade 8 or lower, some high school, high school graduate, some college, college graduate) on the basis of the years of schooling deemed appropriate over time in the United States for leaving school and qualifying for certain occupations. Alternatively, one might collapse categories according to how many respondents fall into each category. If the sample contains only a handful of respondents with less than a college education, these respondents may be placed in one category for purposes of analysis.

In the absence of theoretical criteria for collapsing, the best strategy is to try to obtain an approximately equal proportion of cases in each category. If the distribution is to be dichotomized, this would mean a 50:50 split. Achieving such a split for a nominal variable is a matter of combining conceptually similar categories. For example, if we wanted to compare students with different majors on some relevant variable and we found that 50 percent majored in mathematics or natural science, 30 percent in sociology, and 20 percent in psychology, then we might combine the latter two categories. At the ordinal, interval, and ratio levels, a variable is typically collapsed into about five to eight categories in order to preserve essential information from the original distribution.

Information is invariably lost when the original categories of a variable are collapsed. Ideally, the information lost should not be pertinent to the intended research. One might dichotomize the age of Cuban respondents into those older than or younger than age 55, for example, if the only research purpose was to compare older Cubans with those too young to have experienced pre-Castro Cuba. Similarly, respondents with 9, 10, or 11 years of education may be viewed as essentially equivalent ("some high school") in studying occupational attainment. For other purposes, such as health conditions and practices, dichotomizing age or collapsing education into a few categories would result in a serious loss of vital information.

Interval- and Ratio-Scale Variables

Creating frequency or percentage distributions is about as far as the univariate analysis of nominal- and ordinal-scale variables usually goes. On the other hand, data on interval and ratio variables may be summarized not only in tables (or graphs) but also in terms of various statistics. Consider a 2002 GSS question measuring television viewing, which asks respondents "On the average day, about how many hours do you personally watch television?" Since respondents' answers were recorded in number of hours (the range was 0–24), this variable may be considered a ratio scale measure. We could get a picture of the number of hours watched, as we did with the helpfulness variable, by generating a distribution of the responses. Table 14.3 presents a computer-like output for this variable. Though not a problem here, the relatively large number of values for most interval and ratio variables

TABLE 14.3. **Number of Hours of Television Watched on Average Day, 2002 General Social Survey**

Code	Label	Frequency	Percentage
00	0 HOURS	32	3.5
01	1 HOUR	200	22.1
02	2 HOURS	233	25.7
03	3 HOURS	170	18.8
04	4 HOURS	105	11.6
05	5 HOURS	76	8.4
06	6 HOURS	39	4.3
07	7 HOURS	6	0.7
08	8 HOURS	23	2.5
09	9 HOURS	2	0.2
10	10 HOURS	7	0.8
11	11 HOURS	2	0.2
12	12 HOURS	6	0.7
16	16 HOURS	1	0.1
20	20 HOURS	1	0.1
22	22 HOURS	1	0.1
24	24 HOURS	1	0.1
98	DON'T KNOW	3	MISSING
TOTAL		908	100.0
(VALID CASES)	(905)	(MISSING CASES)	(3)

makes it necessary to collapse categories to get a compact, readable table. Had we generated the distribution for the variable of age, for example, we would have had so many values—over seventy—that they might not have fit on a single page of computer output. In this case, we might lump together respondents according to the first age digit—those under 20, between 20 and 29, 30 and 39, and so on.

Notice that Table 14.3 presents two kinds of distributions: frequency and percentage. Can you tell from the table what percentage of respondents report that they do not watch any television at all on the average day? We also could get a picture of a distribution by looking at its various statistical properties. Three properties may be examined. The first consists of measures of central tendency—the mean, median, and mode. These indicate various "averages" or points of concentration in a set of values. The **mean** is the arithmetical average, calculated by adding up all of the responses and dividing by the total number of respondents. It is the "balancing" point in a distribution, because the sum of the differences of all values from the mean is exactly equal to zero. The **median** is the midpoint in a distribution—the value of the middle response; half of the responses are above it and half are below. You find the median by ordering the values from low to high and then counting up until you find the middle value. The **mode** is the value or category with the highest frequency. The modal value in Table 14.3 is 2 hours. With the aid of a computer program we calculated a mean of 2.98 hours and a median of 2.45 hours.

A second property that we can summarize statistically is the degree of variability or dispersion among a set of values. The simplest dispersion measure is the **range**. Statistically, this is the difference between the lowest and highest values, but it is usually reported by identifying these endpoints, such as "the number of hours of television watched ranged from 0 to 24 hours." Of several other measures of dispersion, the most commonly reported is the **standard deviation**. As we saw in chapter 5, this is a measure of the "average" spread of observations around the mean. One of its important uses in statistics involves the calculation of "standard scores." A standard score is calculated by dividing the standard deviation into the difference between a given value and the mean of the distribution. This converts the value from a "nonstandard" measurement (e.g., hours, years) specific to the variable and sample to a "standardized" measure expressed in terms of standard deviations from the mean. Similar in some ways to "percentaging" a table, standardizing provides a reference point for comparing individual responses in the same or different distributions.

With respect to the variable of television viewing, the standard deviation is perhaps best interpreted as an index of heterogeneity, which could be used to compare the degree of variability in hours watched among different subsamples or in samples from different populations. The standard deviation of the foregoing distribution of all GSS respondents was 2.22. Among respondents with less than a high school education, the standard deviation in hours watched was 3.30, revealing more variability in this group than among those respondents with at least some college, for whom the standard deviation was 2.42. As a further example, the ages of GSS respondents in 2002 ranged from 18 to 89, with a standard deviation of 17.4 years. By comparison, the standard deviation for age in a sample of college undergraduates would be around 1.5 years.

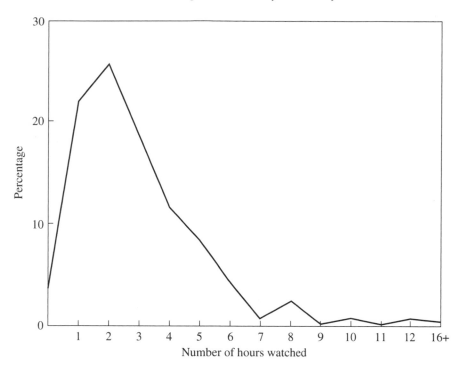

FIGURE 14.3. Percentage polygon for the distribution in Table 14.3.

A third statistical property of univariate distributions is their shape. This property is most readily apparent from a graphic presentation called a **frequency** or **percentage polygon**. Figure 14.3 presents the percentage polygon for the data in Table 14.3. The figure reveals that the distribution has a single high point (or mode), with the data lopsided or "skewed" mostly to the right (or positive side) of this point. This shape also is typical of income distributions. Many variables in social research have "bell-shaped" distributions, so-called because they form the general shape of a bell. In a bell-shaped distribution, the three measures of central tendency are identical, whereas in a positively skewed distribution like Figure 14.3 the mode has the lowest value (2), followed by the median and then the mean. One particular type of bell-shaped distribution, called the **normal distribution**, describes the shape of many variables and statistics, such as the sampling distribution of the mean. The normal distribution is a very important concept in inferential statistics.

Collectively, these three statistical properties—central tendency, dispersion, and shape—provide such a good picture of quantitative data that they often obviate the need for tabular presentations. Many investigators, in fact, describe their data simply in terms of a mean or median, an index of dispersion, and occasionally the overall form (for which there are also statistical indices). Other researchers prefer to be as "close" as possible to the data, and use various graphical procedures to inspect the data for unexpected patterns and other anomalies (see Box 14.2). If a researcher, for example, computes only the mean and standard deviation of reported

BOX 14.2

Television Viewing and Labor Force Status:
An Example of Graphing Data

Developments in graphic procedures for data analysis (Cleveland, 1985:1), when implemented in computer software, offer an attractive alternative to strictly numerical analysis of data. One useful tool is the *box-and-whisker* or *box plot* (Tukey, 1977:39–41). Figure A presents box plots that summarize television viewing reported by the 1985 GSS female respondents grouped according to their current labor force status. (The personal computer program Stata produced these examples.)

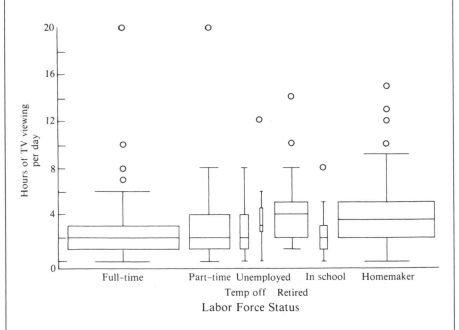

FIGURE A. Average daily television viewing by labor force status, female, 1985 General Social Survey.

The box plots aptly display key aspects of each frequency distribution. The top and bottom of each box indicates respectively the seventy-fifth and twenty-fifth percentiles of television viewing, and the crossbar within each box shows the median (fiftieth percentile). The height of a box is one measure of dispersion, showing the spread of television viewing among the middle 50 percent of the respondents (e.g., 1–3 hours for full-time female workers). An off-center position of the crossbar (median) within the box reflects skewness in the central 50 percent of the distribution (e.g., positive skewness for part-time workers). The width of each box is proportional to the number of respondents; this serves to flag patterns in the data that must be ignored or cautiously interpreted because of small sample sizes (e.g., the unemployed).

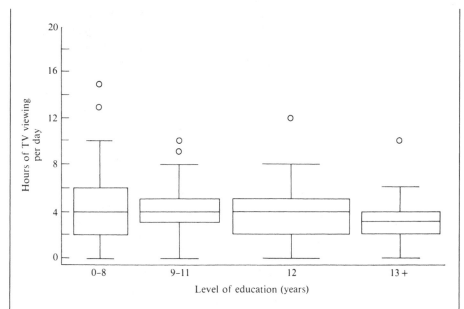

FIGURE B. Average daily television viewing by education, female homemakers, 1985 General Social Survey.

The vertical lines (or "whiskers") extending above and below each box include all but the most extreme data values, which are plotted separately as circles.* The whiskers serve to fence out stray values, which are possibly *outliers* requiring special attention. Sometimes outliers result from measurement error, which seems likely here for the full-time worker who watches television twenty hours a day. Conversely, the reports of watching television eight hours daily by a few full-time workers are not overly suspicious. Extreme outliers are usually excluded from the data analysis (especially if measurement error is suspected) or analyzed separately from the main data, since some statistical procedures may be adversely affected by a few unusual values.

Now you should be able to intepret the box plots in the figure. Which groups report the lowest median television viewing? Which has the lowest variation (dispersion) in viewing habits? How do the retired differ from those keeping house?

Box plots are one of a set of tools designed for exploratory data analysis, which has applications ranging from preparing data for testing prior hypotheses to dredging data for theoretically unexpected patterns. Because of their exploratory purpose, these techniques are relatively resistant to outliers and other data anomalies. And with an appropriate computer program it is quite easy to explore a data domain. When you studied the box plots in the figure, for example, you may have wondered about the large variation in television viewing among women working at home. Perhaps the viewing differences among the homemakers reflect, in part, educational differences. This hunch is easily checked by requesting the computer program to draw box plots for various educational groups (8 years or fewer of completed schooling, 9–11, 12, and 13 years or more), which is shown in Figure B. What do these box plots show?

*Each whisker extends 1.5 times the height of the box or to the most extreme value if that distance is shorter.

television viewing and fails to inspect the entire distribution (Table 14.3), he or she would miss the possibly exaggerated reports of 20-, 22-, and 24-hour daily television watching. It is important to spot extreme values or **outliers** as they can adversely affect some statistical procedures, and may have to be excluded from the data analysis.

One important function of data inspection is to determine the prevalence of missing values. The simplest way to handle cases with missing values, which we did in percentaging Table 14.2, is to remove them from the statistical calculations. This method, called **listwise deletion**, often is used when there are relatively few missing cases. Excluding cases with missing data on *any* of the variables in a planned multivariate analysis, however, can lead to a much smaller, biased sample that is unrepresentative of the target population. Paul Allison (2002) relates a hypothetical illustration of a sample of 1000 that shrinks to only 360 respondents after excluding the 5 percent of missing values on each of the 20 variables.[8] Consequently, researchers typically use various ad hoc or formal procedures for replacing or otherwise handling missing data.

When missing data result from the respondents' uncertainty ("don't know") or refusal to answer the question ("no answer"), a recoding operation, as previously described for the GSS helpfulness question, may eliminate the missing values. Alternatively, researchers with in-depth knowledge of the data may use their expertise to replace missing values with "educated guesses." Suppose that one wanted to study the male literacy rates for the countries illustrated in Figure 14.1. One might replace the missing values for males with the country's total literacy rate, or with a corresponding male rate for a similar, neighboring country. In like manner, other responses within a survey interview, or from a similar respondent, may be used on an ad hoc basis to replace missing data.

Besides these ad hoc procedures, many formal statistical solutions, called **imputation**, have been devised to replace missing values with a typical value calculated from the available ("non-missing") data. Broh simply replaced her NELS missing values with variable sample means. According to Allison (2002), however, this method often produces biased statistics and generally should be avoided. Consider, for example, replacing missing data on respondents' ages with the sample mean for the available data. Although the replacements will not change the calculated mean age, they will bias downward the estimated standard deviation, as all imputed values are zero distance from the mean. The most sophisticated imputation procedures for handling missing data predict missing values from the known values of other variables. These computer-intensive methods, which are beyond the scope of this textbook, are difficult to learn and implement and are underutilized in survey research; nonetheless, they offer the best solutions for the missing data problem.

Another important function of data modification is to reduce data complexity by combining variables into indexes, scales, or other composite measures. We discussed this process in relation to both measurement and the use of multiple methods in earlier chapters. The simplest composite measure would consist of combining two "yes/no" questions. This would produce four distinct response categories: (1) yes, yes; (2) yes, no; (3) no, yes; and (4) no, no. An index based on the number of "yes" responses reduces the category total from four to three (0, 1, or 2 yes's). Similarly, the 16 possible response patterns for four "yes/no" questions reduces to five by indexing the affirmative responses (0, 1, 2, 3, or 4 yes's). Paul Lazarsfeld (1972) describes this data reduction approach as "arbitrary numerical" as formerly distinct categories (e.g., "yes, no" and "no, yes") are combined.

Beckett Broh used this approach to create measures of several concepts. For example, she measured social capital between students and parents by combining responses to three questions (see p. 456), which asked how frequently students talked with their parents about course selection, school activities, and studies. Possible responses included "not at all," "once or twice" and "three or more times," which she coded as 0, 1, and 2 respectively. Thus, when these questions were summed, the composite measure of "student-parent talk" had a possible range of 0 to 6.

Finally, the assignment of numerical values to the categories of nominal-scale variables may be used to transform them into ordinal or interval scales for some purposes. In the GSS, for example, the occupations of respondents and their relatives (mother, father, spouse) are coded into 503 U.S. Census occupational categories. Numerical values representing occupational characteristics, such as prestige ratings or gender composition, may be used to convert the 503 nominal categories into simpler, continuous variables for studying, say, occupational mobility or gender segregation. Each coded occupation in the GSS is assigned a prestige score, which ranges from 86 (physicians) to 17 (miscellaneous food preparation occupations).[9] Occupational complexity is substantially reduced as formerly distinct occupations receive the same prestige ratings, such as prestige scores of 73 (architects, chemical engineers, and chemists), 49 (funeral directors, real estate sales occupations), and 22 (messengers, janitors and cleaners, hand packers and packagers). Similarly, the percentage female in each Census occupational category may be used to transform the 503 categories into a continuum ranging from about 2% (e.g., mechanical engineers) to 96% (kindergarten teachers) for studying gender-based occupational segregation (Straits, 1998).

Preliminary Hypothesis Testing

Following data inspection and necessary modifications, researchers turn to empirical testing of bivariate relationships. The object of bivariate analysis is to assess the relationship between two variables, such as that between extracurricular involvement and academic performance. In general, this amounts to determining, first, whether the relationship is likely to exist (or whether it might be a product of random error) and, second, how much effect or influence one variable has on the other. As with univariate analysis, the way in which this is done depends on the level of measurement.

Nominal- and Ordinal-Scale Variables

When the variables analyzed have only a few categories, as in most nominal- and ordinal-scale measurement, bivariate data are presented in tables. The tables constructed are known as cross-tabulations, cross-classifications, or contingency tables.

A cross-tabulation requires a table with rows representing the categories of one variable and columns representing the categories of another. When a dependent variable can be identified, it is customary to make this the row variable and to treat the independent variable as the column variable, although this arbitrary convention is often broken for formatting considerations.

Let us first consider the cross-tabulation of the two nominal-scale variables from the 2000 GSS shown in Table 14.4. The row variable consists of "attitude toward capital punishment" or, more precisely, whether the respondent favors or opposes the death penalty for persons convicted of murder. The column variable is "gender." Gender is the independent variable simply because, in one's lifetime, one's gender is determined earlier than one's attitude toward capital punishment. What sort of information does this table convey?

First, notice that the last column and the bottom row, each labeled "Total," show the total number of respondents with each single characteristic, for example, 1149 men. Because these four numbers (1764, 801, 1149, 1416) are along the right side and the bottom margin of the table, they are called **marginal frequencies**, or *marginals*. The row marginals (1764, 801) are the univariate frequency distribution for the variable "attitude toward capital punishment"; the column marginals (1149, 1416) are the univariate frequency distribution for the variable "gender." Also, the number at the lower right-hand corner (2565) is N, the total sample size excluding missing cases. N equals the sum of either the row or column marginals, or the sum of the four numbers (865 + 899 + 284 + 514) in the body of the table.

The body of the table where the categories of the two variables intersect contains the bivariate frequency distribution. Each intersection is called a *cell* and the number in each cell is called a **cell frequency**. Cell frequencies in a *bi*variate table indicate the numbers of cases with each possible combination of *two* characteristics; for example, there were 865 *men* who *favored capital punishment*. Because Table 14.4 has two rows and two columns, it is referred to as a *2 × 2 table*.

Now that we know the meaning of the numbers in a cross-tabulation, how do we analyze these numbers to assess the relationship between the variables? What comparisons should we make? With gender the independent variable in Table 14.4, the relevant substantive questions are: Does gender influence attitude toward capital punishment? If so, how much influence does it have? If a relationship exists, then a change in gender should produce a change of "favor"/"oppose" responses in

TABLE 14.4. **Attitude toward Capital Punishment by Gender, 2000 General Social Survey**

Attitude toward capital punishment*	Gender		Total
	MALE	FEMALE	
Favor	865	899	1764
Oppose	284	517	801
Total	1149	1416	2565

*Question: "Do you favor or oppose the death penalty for persons convicted of murder?"

the distribution on the dependent variable. Either men will be more likely to favor and less likely to oppose than women, or women will be more likely to favor and less likely to oppose than men. Notice, however, that when we compare cell frequencies there are more women than men who both favor (899 versus 865) and oppose (517 versus 284).

Obviously, there is a problem here. Although we are comparing the proper cells, the comparison is invalid because the cell frequencies for men and women are based on different total frequencies. To be valid, the cell numbers compared must be expressed as parts of the same total. This is accomplished by creating separate percentage distributions for men and women, thereby converting each total to 100 percent. The result is a bivariate percentage distribution, presented as Table 14.5. Now when we compare responses across gender, we see clearly that men are more likely to favor capital punishment by a percentage of 75.3 to 63.5 and, conversely, less likely to oppose (24.7 percent to 36.5 percent).

A bivariate percentage distribution enables one to compare the distribution of one variable across the categories of the other. In Table 14.5, we created such a distribution by percentaging *down* so that the column totals, corresponding to the categories of the independent variable, equaled 100 percent. The rule that we followed in deriving this table is to *compute percentages in the direction of the independent variable* (i.e., based on the categories of the independent variable). If gender had been the row variable and attitude toward capital punishment the column variable, we would have run the percentages in the other direction—across rather than down. To interpret the relationship in Table 14.5, we compared percentages by reading *across* the table. In so doing, we followed a second rule: *make comparisons in the opposite direction from the way percentages are run*. Having percentaged down, we compared across; had we percentaged across, we would have compared down.

These are extremely important rules to follow, because cross-tabulations may be percentaged in either direction and are easily misinterpreted.[10] If we percentage Table 14.4 in the direction of the attitude variable, the results would indicate whether those who favor capital punishment are more likely to be men than those who oppose, which is indeed an odd and unlikely research question.

Broh might have done bivariate analyses to see if there were gender differences on her key variables. Table 14.6 presents the percentage distribution of student reports of school discussions with their parents by gender.[11] What does this table re-

TABLE 14.5. Attitude toward Capital Punishment by Gender (%), 2000 General Social Survey

Attitude toward capital punishment	Gender	
	MALE	FEMALE
Favor	75.3%	63.5%
Oppose	24.7	36.5
Total	100.0%	100.0%
(*N*)	(1149)	(1416)

TABLE 14.6. Discuss Programs at School* with
Parents by Gender (%), NELS:88 Base-Year

Discuss selecting courses or programs at school with parents	Gender	
	MALE	FEMALE
Not at all	14.8%	8.7%
Once or twice	48.7%	44.9%
Three or more times	36.5%	46.4%
Total	100.0%	100.0%
(N)	(5661)	(5819)

*Question 36a: "Since the beginning of the school year, how
often have you discussed the following with either or both of
your parents or guardians?—Selecting courses or programs at
school."

veal about the relationship between these variables? It clearly shows that in this sample of students, girls report more school discussions with their parents than do boys. But does this necessarily mean that the relationship holds for the population from which the sample was drawn?

As you read across Table 14.6, you see that there is a small difference of 9.9 (46.4 − 36.5) in the percentage of girls as opposed to boys who report three or more school discussions with their parents. This "percentage difference" indicates that a relationship exists for these data; if there were no difference between the percentages, we would conclude that no relationship exists. Remember, however, that these are *sample* data. The important question is not whether a relationship exists in these data; rather, do the observed cell frequencies reveal a true relationship between the variables in the *population*, or are they simply the result of sampling and other random error?

The latter judgment is made by means of *tests of statistical significance*. For cross-tabulations, the most commonly used statistic is the **chi-square (*or* χ^2) test for independence**. The chi-square test is based on a comparison of the observed cell frequencies with the cell frequencies one would expect if there were no relationship between the variables. Table 14.7A shows the expected cell frequencies, assuming no relationship, and Table 14.7B shows the derived bivariate percentage distribution. Notice that the cell percentages in Table 14.7B (reading across) are the same as the marginals; this indicates that knowing whether a respondent is male or female is of no help in predicting school discussions with parents, precisely the meaning of "no relationship" between variables. The larger the differences between the actual cell frequencies and those expected assuming no relationship, the larger the value of chi-square and the more likely that the relationship exists in the population. Chi-square values for the data in Tables 14.5 and 14.6 are both statistically significant.[12] This suggests that in the American population, women are less likely than men to favor capital punishment (Table 14.5), and high school girls are more likely than high school boys to discuss school courses or programs with their parents (Table 14.6).

TABLE 14.7. Discuss Programs at School with Parents by Gender, Assuming No Relationship

Discuss selecting courses or programs at school with parents	A. Frequencies			B. Percentages		
	Gender			Gender		
	MALE	FEMALE	TOTAL	MALE	FEMALE	TOTAL
Not at all	663	682	1,345	11.7%	11.7%	11.7%
Once or twice	2,647	2,720	5,367	46.8%	46.8%	46.8%
Three or more times	2,351	2,417	4,768	41.5%	41.5%	41.5%
Total	5,661	5,819	11,480	100.0%	100.0%	100.0%
(N)				(5,661)	(5,819)	(11,480)

Knowing that these relationships exist in the population, however, does not tell us how much effect the independent variable has on the dependent variable. It is possible for a relationship to exist when changes in one variable correspond only slightly to changes in the other. The degree of this correspondence is a second measurable property of bivariate distributions. In a 2×2 table, the percentage difference provides one indicator, albeit a poor one, of the strength of the relationship: The larger the difference, the stronger the relationship. However, researchers prefer to use one of several other statistics to measure the size of this effect. These **measures of association** are standardized to vary between 0 (no association) and plus or minus 1.0 (perfect association). One such measure, commonly used for 2×2 tables, is Yule's Q, which equals .27 for the data in Table 14.4.[13] Although the choice of labels is somewhat arbitrary, the magnitude of Q suggests a "low" association between gender and attitude toward capital punishment (see Davis, 1971:49). (For variables with nominal categories, the sign, + or −, does not reveal anything meaningful about the nature of the relationship.)

A third property—the *direction* of the relationship—may be measured when the categories of both variables can be ordered, that is, when both have at least ordinal-level measurement. Direction refers to the tendency for increases in the values of one variable to be associated with systematic increases, or decreases, in the values of another variable. Both variables may change in the same direction (a positive relationship) or in opposite directions (a negative relationship). In a positive relationship, lower values of one variable tend to be associated with lower values of the other variable, and higher values of one variable tend to go along with higher values of the other. The categories of the variables of education and income, for example, can be ordered from low to high. When we examine the association between these variables we expect it to be positive, with lower educated persons tending to have lower incomes and persons of higher education tending to have higher incomes.

Table 14.8 shows a positive relationship between two 2000 GSS ordinal variables, level of education (highest degree obtained) and self-reported happiness. Carefully examine this table before reading further. We will consider happiness and highest degree as dependent and independent variables respectively, since educational

**TABLE 14.8. General Happiness by Highest Degree Received,
2000 General Social Survey**

	Highest degree				
Happiness*	LESS THAN HIGH SCHOOL	HIGH SCHOOL	ASSOCIATE/JUNIOR COLLEGE	BACHELOR DEGREE	GRADUATE DEGREE
Not too happy	19.8%	10.1%	8.9%	6.0%	6.1%
Pretty happy	54.6%	60.3%	56.2%	55.3%	51.9%
Very happy	25.6%	29.6%	35.0%	38.7%	42.0%
Total	100.0%	100.0%	100.0%	100.0%	100.0%
(N)	(425)	(1487)	(203)	(432)	(212)

*Question: "Taken all together, how would you say things are these days—would you say that you are very happy, pretty happy, or not too happy"

attainment occurs earlier in time and is a much more permanent condition than the expression of happiness given during the interview. Notice that, as in the previous examples, Table 14.8 is percentaged down for each category of the independent variable, highest degree; thus comparisons should be made across. The percentage of persons "not too happy" (first row) generally falls with increasing education: 19.8 to 10.1 to 8.9 to 6.0 to 6.1 percent. Similarly, the percentage claiming that they are "very happy" (third row) consistently rises as educational attainment increases: 25.6 to 29.6 to 35.0 to 38.7 to 42.0 percent. It is this sort of pattern (greater happiness associated with higher education) that suggests a clearly positive relationship.

In a negative (inverse) relationship, there is a tendency for *lower* values of one variable to be associated with *higher* values of the other variable. Table 14.9 reveals such a relationship between education and the number of hours of television watched on an average day: as education increases, television viewing time decreases. (There are many possible explanations here: Perhaps higher income persons are more apt to be exposed to and can better afford other, more expensive forms of entertainment, or perhaps higher educated people have less leisure time, or maybe they read more.)

The statistical significance of a relationship between two ordinal-scale variables also may be tested with the chi-square statistic. Ordinal measures of the strength of association, while differing in name from nominal measures of association, are similar in concept. The magnitude of such statistics, ignoring the sign, indicates the strength of the relationship; and the sign (+ or −) indicates the direction of the association (positive or negative). One such statistic, gamma, equals .20 for the data in Table 14.8 and −.38 for the data in Table 14.9.[14] Thus, there is a low positive association between happiness and educational attainment and a moderate negative association between television hours and years of schooling.

Armed with the knowledge of how to interpret cross-tabulations, you are ready to test a bivariate hypothesis. We will illustrate hypothesis testing first with the results from a split-ballot wording experiment from the 2002 General Social Survey. The GSS uses a series of questions about spending priorities in key policy areas to track trends in public support for various government spending programs. Respon-

TABLE 14.9. **Number of Hours per Day Watching TV by**
Highest Degree Received, 2002 General Social Survey

	Highest degree				
Number of *TV hours*	LESS THAN HIGH SCHOOL	HIGH SCHOOL	ASSOCIATE/JUNIOR COLLEGE	BACHELOR DEGREE	GRADUATE DEGREE
0–1	16.4%	20.6%	38.2%	35.0%	51.4%
2–3	38.8%	44.7%	43.6%	52.1%	40.0%
4 or more	44.8%	34.8%	18.2%	12.9%	8.6%
Total	100.0%	100.0%	100.0%	100.0%	100.0%
(*N*)	(134)	(506)	(55)	(140)	(70)

dents are asked whether they think "we're spending too much money on it, too little money, or about the right amount" on various labeled problems (crime, welfare,
national defense, education, etc.). Since the "welfare" label may convey unfavorable connotations, it was paired with an alternative "assistance to the poor" label in
one of several wording experiments. Respondents were randomly assigned to either
the "welfare" or to the "assistance to the poor" question version. Table 14.10 reveals that the wording manipulation (independent variable) produced dramatic differences in support for government spending (dependent variable). Only 20.6 percent in the "welfare" condition thought too little money was being spent, compared
to 65.6 percent in the "assistance to the poor" condition. Similarly, the percentage
responding that government spending was too much increased from 7.8 percent for
the "poor" to 39.3 percent for the "welfare" label. Since the split-ballot was a true
experimental design, the only rival explanation for the wording results is that they
were created by prior subject differences uncontrolled by random assignment. This
is ruled out by a statistically significant chi-square test result.[15]

TABLE 14.10. **Split-Ballot Wording Experiment,**
2002 General Social Survey

	Experimental wording	
Response	"ASSISTANCE TO THE POOR"	"WELFARE"
Too little	65.6%	20.6%
About right	24.5%	37.0%
Too much	7.8%	39.3%
Don't know	2.1%	3.0%
Total	100.0%	100.0%
(*N*)	(1405)	(1355)

*Question: We are faced with many problems in this country, none of
which can be solved easily or inexpensively. I'm going to name some of
these problems, and for each one I'd like you to tell me whether you
think we're spending too much money on it, too little money, or about
the right amount. Are we spending too much money, too little money, or
about the right amount on . . . [assistance to the poor/welfare]

In a true experiment, the analysis usually begins and ends with an empirical examination of the hypothesized relationship between the dependent variable and the independent variable (experimental treatment). In surveys and other non-experimental designs, the bivariate association between the dependent and independent variables is only the first step toward a multivariate analysis as extraneous variables may pose rival explanations for the results. Next, we present two non-experimental examples of preliminary hypothesis testing, and we introduce statistical techniques that are the foundation for the advanced multivariate techniques discussed in chapter 15.

So far we have restricted ourselves to variables having only two to five categories and to tables with four to fifteen cells. This is not unusual, because most cross-tabulation analyses in social research are limited to variables with relatively few categories. There are three important reasons for this. First, the size of the table increases geometrically as the number of categories for each variable increases. And the larger the table, the more difficult it is to discern the pattern of the relationship, which can be much more complex than the positive or negative relationships we have described. Second, as we pointed out in our discussion of sampling, the finer the breakdown of one's sample into various categories, the fewer cases there will be for any given breakdown (or cell of the table). Hence, larger tables may require impractically large samples for reliable assessments. Finally, variables with a relatively large number of categories either constitute or tend to approximate interval-scale measurement. With interval-scale variables, we can use a more precise and more powerful form of statistical analysis known as correlation and regression.

Interval- and Ratio-Scale Variables

In chapter 3 we showed how relationships between two quantitative variables are depicted by plotting the values of each variable in a graphic coordinate system. In conjunction with this form of presentation, social researchers use a statistical method called **regression analysis** to analyze the effect of one interval/ratio variable on another. This is done by finding the mathematical equation that most closely describes the data.

We will use previously described variables from the country dataset (Figure 14.1) to explore the hypothesis that countries with low rates of female literacy tend to have high rates of fertility. Let us begin our analysis by looking at a **scatterplot** of total fertility rates and female literacy rates for 178 countries (Figure 14.4).[16] Each plot or point in the graph represents the values of one of the 178 countries on two variables. With the vertical axis as our reference, we can read the value of the dependent variable (total fertility rate); and with the horizontal axis as our reference, we can read the value of the independent variable (female literacy rate). The country of Niger, for example, has the highest fertility rate (7.1) and the lowest female literacy rate (10%). The lowest total fertility rates belong to Hong Kong (1.0) and Georgia (1.1), which have high female literacy rates (90% and 98%, respectively).

The scatterplot gives the researcher a rough sense of the form of the relationship: whether it is positive or negative, and whether it is best characterized with a straight or curved line. This is crucial information because regression analysis as-

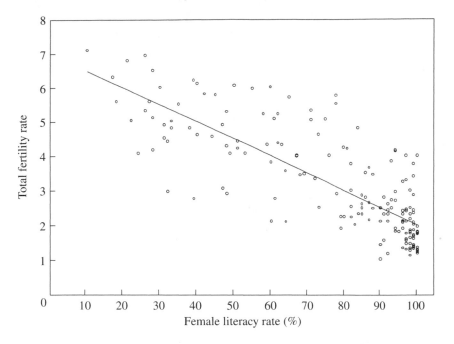

FIGURE 14.4. Scatterplot of total fertility rate by female literacy, 178 countries.

sumes that the data have a particular form. If a straight line provides the best fit with the data, one should do linear regression; if a curve provides the best fit, one should use special techniques for fitting curvilinear relationships (which are beyond the scope of this book). As a first step in our analysis, we will examine the scatterplot to make a judgment about form. The overall form of the data in Figure 14.4 is somewhat difficult to discern; however, since the relationship does not appear to be sharply curvilinear, we can assume that a straight line offers as good a fit as a curved line. The trend of the data also suggests that fertility decreases as literacy increases.

Having decided to fit a straight line to the data, and therefore to do *linear* regression analysis, we need to know two things: (1) the mathematical equation for a straight line and (2) the criterion for selecting a line to represent the data.

The general form of the equation for a straight line is $Y = a + bX$, where Y is the predicted value of the dependent variable and X is the corresponding value of the independent variable. Thus, an equation for a straight line relating female fertility and literacy is

$$\text{Total fertility rate} = a + b \text{ (Female literacy rate)}$$

The value a, called the **Y-intercept**, is the point where the line crosses the vertical axis (where literacy = 0). The value b, called the **slope** or **regression coefficient**, indicates how much Y increases (or decreases) for every change of one unit in X—in other words, how much increase (or decrease) occurs in the total fertility rate (number of children) for every change of one percent in female literacy. To get the line of best fit, then, we could simply draw a line on the scatterplot that seems to reflect best the trend in the data and then determine the values of a and b from the graph. Of course, there are many lines that we could draw—a and b can take on an infinite number of values. How, then, do we know when we have obtained the best fit?

Regression analysis uses the method of least squares as the criterion for selecting the line that best describes the data. According to this method, the best-fitting line minimizes the sum of the squared vertical distances from the data points to the line. We have drawn the **regression line**, also called the **least squares line**, on the scatterplot. Now imagine a dashed line showing the vertical distance, as measured by the fertility number of children, between a specific data point, say Niger, and the regression line. The regression line represents the equation for predicting Y from X; the vertical distances between data points and this line represent prediction errors (also called **residuals**). Thus, by finding the line that minimizes the sum of the squared distances from it we are, in effect, finding the best linear predictor of the fertility rate from knowledge of a country's rate of female literacy.

The precise equation generated by the method of least squares can be found via a mathematical formula with the aid of a computer program. When we applied this formula to the data in Figure 14.4, we got the following equation:

$$\text{Total fertility rate} = 6.98 - .05 \,(\text{Female literacy rate})$$

In other words, women in a hypothetical country with zero percent literacy would be predicted to average about 7 children during their lifetime; and, for every ten-unit increase in literacy (10%), a decrease of about a half a child (.50) is expected in birth rates. The regression equation gives the best linear prediction of the dependent variable based on the data at hand. Niger, for example, has a predicted fertility rate of 6.48 ($6.98 - .05 \times 10$), which is 0.62 less (the residual) than its current 7.1 fertility rate. Can you spot the largest residuals in Figure 14.4? They belong to the Republic of Congo (5.76 TFR, 78% literacy) and Bangladesh (2.95 TFR, 32% literacy).

The strength of the association between two variables measured at the interval/ratio level is frequently measured by the **correlation coefficient** (symbolized as r), which may vary between -1 and $+1$. The sign of the coefficient, which is always the same as the sign of the regression coefficient, indicates the direction of the relationship. The magnitude of its value depends on two factors: (1) the steepness of the regression line and (2) the variation or scatter of the data points around this line. If the line is not very steep, so that it is nearly parallel to the X-axis, then we might as well predict the same value of Y for every unit change in X, as there is very little change in our prediction (as indicated by b in the equation) for every unit change in the independent variable. By the same token, the greater the spread of values about the regression line, regardless of the steepness of the slope, the less accurate are predictions based on the linear regression. The scatterplot for the regression of fertility on literacy shows that the line is fairly steep in relation to the horizontal axis and that the data points (countries) cluster fairly close to the line. Not surprisingly, therefore, the correlation coefficient indicates a strong negative association of -0.80. Statistics also exist for testing whether the correlation coefficient and the regression coefficient are significantly different from zero. These may be found in most statistics textbooks. Both of these coefficients are significant ($p < .001$) for the data in Figure 14.4.

The strong negative association between countries' fertility and female literacy rates, by itself, however, does not tell us whether there is a causal connection between the two. To establish this, we need to show that the direction of influence is from literacy to fertility (the presumed independent and dependent variables respectively) and that the association between the variables is not spurious. This, in turn, requires a country-level theoretical model of fertility determinants, along with a multivariate analysis to rule out rival explanations of the negative association. At the country (aggregate data) level, both high fertility and low female literacy may reflect discrimination against women in traditional societies, as well as low income levels, high infant mortality rates, government opposition to family planning, poor health care, and so forth.

Our second example of regression analysis is from Broh's (2002) study of extracurricular activities and academic achievement. In a preliminary analysis, she explored the hypothesis that playing high school interscholastic sports (independent variable) improves students' math grades (dependent variable). Since the NELS longitudinal (panel) study collected information from eighth graders in 1988 (baseline) with follow-ups when most were in the tenth (1990) and twelfth (1992) grades, she examined if the interscholastic sports participants during both the tenth and twelfth grades ("athletes") had higher twelfth-grade math grades than those who did not participate in the tenth and twelfth grades ("nonathletes").

Regression analysis can be applied to independent variables with only two categories, such as Broh's comparison of "athletes" and "nonathletes," by creating what is called a **dummy variable**. This is a variable that has been recoded so that one of its categories has a value of 1 and the other category has a value of 0. Dummy coding enables the researcher to manipulate the variable numerically and to use certain kinds of statistical analysis that would not be possible otherwise. We could, for example, code women as 1 and men as 0 and proceed to regress an interval-/ratio-level variable, such as number of television hours watched, on gender. The horizontal axis would have only two values, 0 and 1, and the regression coefficient would indicate the difference between men and women in the mean number of television hours watched. Broh used dummy-coding to measure interscholastic sports performance during both the tenth and twelfth grades (1 = participated in both years, 0 = did not participate in both years).

Because the scaling of some NELS measures differed in baseline and follow-up years, Broh put them on equal footing by reexpressing them in standard score form (mean = 0, standard deviation = 1).[17] A student with 1990 math grades right at the mean for all NELS students and 1.5 standard deviation below the mean in 1992, for example, would have standardized scores of 0 and -1.5, respectively.

When Broh regressed interscholastic sports participation on twelfth-grade (1992) math grades for 10,379 students, she got the following equation:

$$1992 \text{ math grades} = .005 + .230 \text{ (athlete in 10th \& 12th grade)}$$

In other words, the regression equation estimates that athletes in both the tenth and twelfth grades will have math grades in 1992 about one-quarter (.230) of a standard deviation higher than students not playing interscholastic sports.[18] Although the higher math grades for interscholastic athletes was statistically significant ($p < .001$), the observed association between playing sports and math grades may be spurious. Better math students, for example, might be more likely than their peers to play interscholastic sports. In the next chapter we describe how Broh used multivariate statistical techniques to test for spuriousness and to model theorized causal links between high school sports participation and educational achievement.

Summary

Data analysis involves an iterative comparison of theory and data. Data analysis begins and ends with the researcher's hypotheses or theoretical model. Such models guide the collection and analysis of data, indicating what variables should be measured and statistically controlled. The analyses, in turn, suggest new theoretical formulations and new directions for research.

Before quantitative analysis can begin, the data are processed and put in computer-readable form. In survey research, this entails four steps: editing, coding, data entry, and cleaning. Some of these procedures occur during data collection in computer-assisted surveys. Editing is designed to ensure that the data to be entered into the computer are as complete, error free, and readable as possible. Coding consists of assigning numbers to the categories of each variable. Most coding in survey research is done before data collection, since answer codes for fixed choice questions appear directly on the survey form. Codes for open-ended questions are developed after the data are collected.

After editing is complete, the data are entered into the computer and stored in a data file. Typically, a dataset is organized as a matrix or spreadsheet with observations as rows and variables as columns. After entry, the data are cleaned for errors in coding and transmitting the data to the computer. This is a multi-step process, sometimes beginning with a verification procedure whereby all data are entered into the computer a second time and each dual entry is checked for noncomparable codes. Wild-code checking consists of checking for "illegal" codes among the values recorded for each variable. Consistency checking consists of checking for reasonable patterns of responses, such as whether contingency questions are answered only by those for whom the questions are intended.

With the data cleaned, the researcher usually prepares a codebook, which gives the answers that correspond to each numerical code, the location of each variable in the data file, and coding and decision rules. At this point, the researcher is ready to inspect and modify the data for the planned analysis. The goal of inspection is to get a clear picture of the data by examining each variable singly (univariate analysis). Data modifications include changing one or more variable codes, rearranging the numerical order of variable codes, collapsing variable categories, imputing estimated values for missing data, and adding together the codes for several variables to create an index or scale.

The primary functions of statistics are descriptive and inferential. Descriptive statistics are designed to summarize the data at hand; inferential statistics indicate the extent to which one may generalize beyond the data at hand. In univariate analysis the categories or values of each variable first are organized into frequency and percentage distributions. If the data constitute interval-level measurement, the researcher will also compute statistics that define various properties of the distribution. Statistical measures of central tendency reveal various points of concentration: the most typical value (mode), the middle value (median), and the average (mean). Common measures of dispersion are the difference between the lowest and highest values (range) and an index of the spread of the values around the mean (standard deviation). Distributions also may be described in terms of their shape, such as their skewness.

Bivariate analysis examines the nature of the relationship between two variables. For relationships involving exclusively nominal- or ordinal-scale variables, such analysis begins with the construction of cross-tabulations, with table cells containing the bivariate distribution. The rule for percentaging cross-tabulations is to percentage in the direction of the independent variable; the rule for reading such tables is to make comparisons in the direction opposite the way the percentages are run. For relationships involving interval- or ratio-scale variables, the data are plotted in a scatterplot and characterized in terms of a mathematical function. Linear regression analysis identifies the straight-line function that provides the best fit with the data by virtue of minimizing the sum of the squared deviations from the line. The slope of the line reveals the predicted change in the dependent variable per unit change in the independent variable. Nominal-/ordinal-scale variables may be included in regression analyses as independent variables by dummy-coding categories 0 and 1, in which case the slope indicates the mean difference between categories on the dependent variable.

Regardless of measurement level, bivariate analysis assesses both the likelihood that the observed relationship is the product of random error and the strength of the association between the variables. The first task usually is accomplished for cross-tabulations by means of the chi-square test for independence. Statistical measures of association generally vary from $+1$ to -1, with the sign indicating the direction of the relationship and the magnitude indicating the strength of the association.

Bivariate analysis may be used to test simple two-variable hypotheses, which is the final analysis step in true experiments since an adequate design effectively controls extraneous variables as rival explanations for the results. But in non-experimental designs, extraneous variables may pose serious rival explanations that require statistical control in a multivariate model, which we discuss in the next chapter.

Key Terms

data processing
data modification
editing
coding
data cleaning
    wild-code checking
    consistency checking
data matrix
codebook
descriptive statistics
inferential statistics
univariate analysis
    frequency distribution
    percentage distribution
    mean
    median
    mode
    range
    standard deviation

frequency/percentage polygon
normal distribution
outliers
listwise deletion
imputation
bivariate analysis
    marginal frequencies
    cell frequencies
    chi-square test for independence
    measures of association
    regression analysis
      scatterplot
      Y-intercept
      slope/regression coefficient
      regression (least squares) line
      residuals
      correlation coefficient
      dummy variable

Review Questions and Problems

1. What are the four basic analysis steps following data collection?

2. When and how is coding generally carried out in survey research?

3. Why is it a good idea to include as much information as practical when coding data for analysis?

4. What information generally is contained in a codebook?

5. What is the purpose of editing?

6. Describe the general structure of a data matrix? Where would you place an additional observation? Where would you place additional variables?

7. What are some reasons for inspecting the data prior to analysis?

8. Carefully state Broh's hypothesis regarding interscholastic sports participation and academic achievement. How might the variables of gender, parent's educational attainment, and family income each create a spurious association between playing sports and high school grades?

9. Imagine that you have collected data from 100 students using a four-page questionnaire containing about thirty-five questions. Describe how you would go about cleaning your data once you have entered them into the computer.

10. What is the difference between wild-code checking and consistency checking?

11. Give an example of data transformation other than one mentioned in this chapter.

12. What are the functions of descriptive and of inferential statistics? Are these the same as the scientific goals of description and explanation? Briefly explain.

13. How may univariate analyses of variables aid multivariate analyses?

14. Why do data analysts compute percentage distributions? What do these distributions tell you that frequency distributions do not?

15. Why is it sometimes necessary to collapse or combine categories when presenting the frequency distribution of an interval-/ratio-scale variable?

16. What are the three statistical properties of frequency distributions of interval-/ratio-scale variables?

17. Identify the three measures of central tendency. What does each tell you about the distribution?

18. What does the standard deviation describe about a distribution?

19. What was the general shape of the distribution of the hours of television watched for the 2002 GSS?

20. How can an examination of the frequency distribution inform researcher decisions about collapsing variable categories?

21. What do bivariate analyses in general tell you about the relationships between two variables?

22. What is the rule for percentaging bivariate tables? What is the rule for comparing percentages in such tables?

23. What does the chi-square test for independence tell you about the association between variables?

24. Consider the following values of Yule's Q for three different sets of variables: (a) $-.82$, (b) $+.04$, (c) $+.35$. Which association is strongest? Which association is negligible?

25. Explain some options for handling missing data.

26. Dummy-code the following variables: gender; attitude toward capital punishment (favor/oppose); race (white/black, treating "other" as missing). What does the mean value of a dummy variable indicate?

27. Why do data analysts examine the form of the relationship before doing a regression analysis?

28. Consider the following equation based on 2002 GSS data:

Respondent's years of education $= 10.42 + .294$ (Father's years of education)

Describe the predicted relationship in this equation. How much change in respondent's education is associated with each increase of one year in father's education? What are the predicted years of education of a respondent whose father has completed sixteen years of education? (This will require some calculation.)

29. Describe the difference between a regression coefficient and a correlation coefficient.

30. What does the regression coefficient indicate when an interval-/ratio-variable is regressed on a dummy variable?

NOTES

1. There are other database options for organizing complex data sets. In contextual analysis, a single data file may contain, for example, both student-level and school-level variables. Or there could be a hierarchical arrangement of separate data files (e.g., neighborhoods, schools, classrooms, and students) with links identifying the students in a particular classroom, the class-

rooms in a particular school, and the schools in a particular neighborhood. In one social network design, the social actors are listed in both the rows and the columns of a data matrix, with the cell entries representing relationships or connections among pairs of actors.

2. Sources: *The World Factbook* (http://www.cia.gov/cia/publications/factbook/index.html); Population Division of the Department of Economic and Social Affairs of the United Nations Secretariat, *World Population Prospects: The 2002 Revision and World Urbanization Prospects: The 2001 Revision*, (http://esa.un.org/unpp).

3. http://www.nces.ed.gov/surveys/nels88/

4. http://www.icpsr.umich.edu:8080/GSS/homepage.htm

5. The distinction between descriptive and inferential statistics should not be confused with the scientific goals of description and explanation. Both forms of statistical analysis may be used to accomplish both goals. The first purpose of inferential statistics identified here is description, and the second purpose is explanation. Similarly, descriptive statistics may provide a summary measure of some characteristic of the sample data (description) or may indicate the strength of a hypothesized association between two variables (explanation).

6. Chance may enter into theoretical explanations, which has important implications for popular statistical techniques (Berk, 1983).

7. Social scientists today rarely write their own programs of instructions to the computer. Instead, they rely on "canned" or "packaged" programs stored in the computer and specially written to perform statistical analyses of social science data. To use these programs, you must (1) give the computer a command that accesses the particular package, (2) using the rules for that package, describe the format and location of the data file, and (3) indicate the specific analyses you want done. Thorough discussions of these procedures can be found in the manuals for SPSS, Stata, SAS, or any other packages available for your computer.

8. Allison assumes that the chance of missing data on one variable is independent of the chance of missing data on any other variable.

9. See GSS online site (note 4 above), Appendices F (Occupational Classification Distributions) and G (Prestige Scores).

10. Sometimes these rules are broken for descriptive reasons (e.g., to ascertain the educational background of different income groups), or because the data are unrepresentative of the population with respect to the dependent variable (see Zeisel, 1968:30–36).

11. For pedagogical purposes, Tables 14.6 and 14.7 are based on unweighted frequencies. A more appropriate analysis would require adjustments for a complex sampling design (stratification, disproportionate sampling, students clustered by school).

12. For Table 14.5, Pearson's chi-square statistic = 41.08, 1 df ($p < .001$); for Table 14.6, chi-square = 167.78, 2 df ($p < .001$).

13. For an explanation of Yule's Q and other popular measures of association, see chapter 5 in Bohrnstedt and Knoke (1994).

14. See Bohrnstedt and Knoke (1994:168–75) for a discussion of gamma.

15. For Table 14.10, excluding the "don't know" responses, chi-square = 653, df = 2, $P < .001$.

16. Sources: *The World Factbook* (http://www.cia.gov/cia/publications/factbook/index.html) and World Bank Developmental Data (http://devdata.worldbank.org/dataonline/). Missing female literacy values for 15 high-literacy countries were replaced with the country's total literacy rate. Countries with missing values for total literacy and/or for fertility were excluded from the analysis.

17. Variables are standardized by subtracting the variable mean from each original score, and then dividing by the standard deviation of the original scores.

18. The equation for athletes is $.005 + .230(1) = .235$; for non-athletes, $.005 + .230(0) = .005$.

15

✔

Multivariate Analysis

In the last chapter we examined bivariate relationships; statistically, this amounted to calculating the degree of association or correlation between two variables. Bivariate analysis provides a basis, as exemplified by regression slope coefficients, for predicting the values of one variable from values of another. However, if our goal goes beyond prediction to testing causal hypotheses, then calculating bivariate associations is never sufficient. As we have emphasized repeatedly, causal inferences are based not only on association but also on theoretical assumptions and empirical evidence about direction of influence and nonspuriousness.

In a cross-sectional survey, for example, a correlation between X and Y may imply that X causes Y, that Y causes X, that X and Y mutually cause each other, or that X and Y are causally unrelated (spurious association). The statistical techniques introduced in this chapter help the researcher to choose among such possible interpretations. But it is important to realize that statistical analyses by themselves do not provide a basis for inferring causal relationships. Instead, a researcher starts with a theoretical model of the causal process linking X and Y and then determines if the data are consistent with the theory.

Direction of influence, in particular, is usually based on theoretical or practical knowledge. In experiments, of course, the direction is set by the manipulation of the independent variable, which always precedes measurement of the dependent variable. Similarly, the natural time order of many non-experimental variables indisputably determines causal direction. In relating high school students' occupational aspirations to their parents' education, for example, the latter occurs earlier in time and may be a cause but not an effect of students' occupational aspirations. When time order is indeterminate, causal direction often is determined on the basis that one variable is more fixed, permanent, or less alterable than the other (Rosenberg, 1968:11–12; Davis, 1985:14–15). Gender, a fixed variable, may influence sport participation, but not vice versa. Religious affiliation may influence happiness if we theorize that the former is relatively unchangeable compared with the latter.

Theoretical knowledge sometimes dictates treating direction of influence as mutual or reciprocal. Reviewing explanations of the inverse correlation between American women's employment and childbearing, Linda Waite and Ross Stolzenberg (1976) found strong arguments for mutual causation. Young women may be having fewer children because they want to work more outside the home (career aspirations influence fertility). And women may be working more because they want fewer children (fertility plans influence employment). Using a statistical method appropriate for studying mutual causation, Waite and Stolzenberg concluded that employment plans dominate fertility expectations.[1]

The misguided self-esteem enhancement movement underscores the importance of causal direction. Acting on the "obvious" supposition that low self-esteem (independent variable) is a cause of poor performance (dependent variable) in school and elsewhere, a flourishing cottage industry in the last 30 years has been churning out intervention programs to raise the self-esteem of students, workers, cigarette smokers, underage drinkers, drug addicts, and even tax payers.[2] An extensive review of the self-esteem literature by psychologist Roy Baumeister and his colleagues (2003), however, found little evidence for the efficacy of self-esteem interventions. Indeed, some experiments and longitudinal studies with objective measures of school performance suggest that self-esteem is an effect (dependent variable) rather than a cause (independent variable) of good school performance. Doing well in school may make students feel good about themselves (i.e., boosts self-esteem).

Theory also guides tests for spuriousness. Through theory, for example, we identify antecedent variables that might produce spurious statistical associations. Utilizing such theoretical knowledge, we can apply statistical techniques that go a long way toward demonstrating nonspuriousness. In principle, these techniques have the same effect as randomization in experiments. The main difference is that whereas randomization is assumed to control for *all* antecedent variables, statistical control in non-experimental studies can be applied only to measured variables. Obviously, this places a premium on identifying and measuring relevant variables and on specifying their causal relations. Thus it is easy to see why modeling has become so important, because modeling is a way of specifying various possible causal relations among a set of variables. It is now time to take a closer look at the data analyst's conception of a model.

Modeling Relationships

A statistical model is a simplified picture of reality, a representation of the theorized relations among the variables that generated the observed data. The translation of a theory into a statistical model ordinarily takes the form of one or more mathematical equations. However, to convey the logic of modeling and analysis, we will use easily understood arrow diagrams, which often serve as a modeling visualization aid.

Arrow Diagrams

Arrow diagrams represent the causal ordering of a set of variables. Each arrow indicates causal direction. Thus, the arrow pointing from X to Y in Figure 15.1A means that X is hypothesized to be a cause of Y. Two arrows pointing in opposite directions (Figure 15.1B) indicate **reciprocal causation**—that X and Y are thought to influence each other. A single line (often curved) with arrows on both ends (Figure 15.1C) indicates that there may be a statistical association between the variables, but that a causal explanation of the association is not part of the model (**noncausal** association). Finally, the absence of an arrow connecting two variables means that no causal relationship is hypothesized.

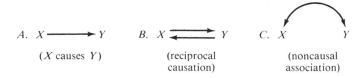

FIGURE 15.1. Arrow diagrams for different causal relationships.

Besides causal order, arrow diagrams can indicate the direction of a relationship. This is generally signified with a sign, + or −, above the arrow. A plus sign indicates a presumed positive relationship: As X increases in value, Y increases. A minus sign indicates a presumed negative (inverse) relationship: As X increases in value, Y decreases.[3] Thus the arrows in Figure 15.2 pointing from X to Y in models A and B indicate predicted positive and negative relationships, respectively. Adding an antecedent variable, T, to the picture creates alternative theoretical models positing that the original relationship is spurious. Models C and E also predict a positive association between X and Y as antecedent T causes both variables to move in the same direction even though there is no direct causal link (arrow) between X and Y. As T increases in model C (or model E), both X and Y increase (or decrease), thus creating a spurious positive association. Similarly, a decrease in T causes both X and Y to move in the same direction (downward for model C, upward for model E).

Note that models C and E represent rival explanations for model A, but not for model B, because they predict a positive rather than a negative statistical associa-

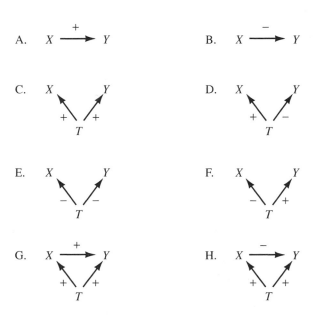

FIGURE 15.2. Two-variable relationships and alternative antecedent variable models.

tion between X and Y. Antecedent variable T in models D and F generates a spurious negative relationship (X and Y move in opposite directions), which is a rival explanation for the negative association predicted by model B. Finally, model G illustrates another theoretical possibility in which both X and T causally produce a positive association between X and Y. In Beckett Broh's study (2002), for example, a positive association between students' extracurricular involvement (X) and academic achievement (Y) may be spurious, or partially spurious, if antecedent parent's income (T) positively influenced both variables (models C or G). On the other hand, if parent's income is inversely related to extracurricular involvement (model F), parental income could not produce a spurious *positive* association between extracurricular involvement and academic achievement.

Figure 15.3 shows arrow diagrams of an intervening variable (T) causally positioned between an independent (X) and a dependent (Y) variable. Model I predicts a positive association between X and Y: When X increases, T decreases; when T decreases, Y increases—thus X and Y move in the same direction (positive relationship). The intervening variable in model K produces a negative relationship: When X goes up, T goes up; when T goes up, Y goes down. The predicted relationship between X and Y can be determined by simply multiplying the signs of the arrows along the path connecting the two variables (Davis, 1985:29). The predicted relationship will be positive (models I and J) unless there is an odd number of negative arrows (models K, L, and M) intervening between X and Y. In Broh's study, an intervening mechanism producing a positive association between students extracurricular involvement (X) and academic achievement (Y) might be time spent on

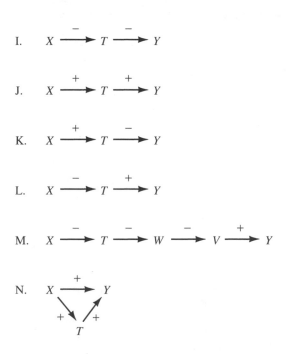

FIGURE 15.3. Alternative intervening variable models.

homework (*T*) if both causal arrows are positive (model J). But if extracurricular involvement (*X*) decreases time spent on homework (*T*) as in model L, then homework could not represent the intervening causal process by which extracurricular involvement promotes academic achievement.

Model N in Figure 15.3 posits that an independent variable (*X*) positively affects the dependent variable (*Y*) by having a **direct effect** (the positive arrow from *X* to *Y*) and an **indirect effect** via a positive path involving a causally intervening variable (*T*). That is, theoretical model N identifies part of the causal process, the indirect effect, by which *X* affects *Y*. Model J, in contrast, theorizes that the only causal mechanism linking *X* and *Y* is intervening variable *T*. For the previous Broh example, model N proposes that homework (*T*) is responsible for only part of the positive association between extracurricular involvement (*X*) and academic achievement (*Y*).

These alternative models have different implications for the original hypothesis of a *positive* relationship between academic achievement and extracurricular involvement: models A and G support it; models B, C, D, E, F, H, K, L and M do not support it; and models I, J and N, in addition to supporting the basic hypothesis, provide a more thorough understanding of the causal sequence. And these three-variable models do not exhaust the possibilities. For example, time spent on homework and extracurricular activities may interact in promoting academic achievement.

Stochastic and Systematic Components

Besides specifying hypothesized relationships among the explanatory variables, statistical models posit that some variability in phenomena occurs randomly or by chance. Thus models contain both **systematic** (theorized relationships as represented by arrow diagrams) and **stochastic** (chance processes) **components** (King, 1989:8–12). To clarify this distinction, we will consider a simple example.

Suppose that the midterm exam (50 true–false questions) for a social research class was given to a physics class by mistake! The physics students duly completed the test without raising any questions about the content, but some scored better than others. How can we explain this distribution (variability) of exam scores? One simple hypothesis is that the students merely guessed the answers, which could be translated into a statistical model corresponding to flipping a fair coin fifty times and marking the question as true for "heads" outcomes (statistically this would be modeled as a binomial distribution). The model (and its underlying theory) would then be judged by comparing the model-predicted distribution of exam scores with the actual class results. A good fit between the model and the observed data would provide support for the hypothesis that the physics students were merely guessing the answers.

The foregoing model contained only a stochastic component: The only theorized basis for differences in exam scores was a chance process. Systematic components could be included in the model by adding independent variables. For example, we might hypothesize that (1) men would guess more often than women and (2) lower-division students would guess more frequently than upper-class students on the midterm. This would translate into a model that explains the exam scores as a combination of stochastic (chance) and systematic (hypothesized sex and class-standing differences) components.

Earlier we discussed simple models containing stochastic and systematic components in conjunction with experimental designs and probability sampling. In the former, the stochastic component is introduced by random assignment of subjects to experimental conditions. A test of statistical significance is then used to rule out the rival hypothesis that the experimental outcome is due to chance (stochastic component produced by randomization) rather than by the experimental manipulation (systematic component). Similarly, a stochastic component is introduced by probability sampling. Significance tests or confidence intervals are then used to distinguish sample results due to systematic differences in the population from those due to chance (sampling error).

In addition to being produced by randomization, probability sampling, and measurement errors, the stochastic or chance component may be produced during the process theorized to have generated the data, as in the above midterm example of guessing answers (Berk, 1983; King, 1989:3–13). For example, a theory might specify that actions by nations, voting decisions of the electorate, or people's friendship ties may be explained by stochastic (chance) as well as by systematic components.

The Process of Modeling

Since they are derived from tentative theories, models are never "correct" about social processes. Instead, they serve as an economical and informed means of getting on with the data analysis. Research then becomes a learning process as the analysis reveals discrepancies between model predictions and the data; these discrepancies, in turn, lead the analyst to modify or replace the model that will be used for further or new data analysis; and so forth (Box, 1976). To illustrate this learning process, suppose you hypothesize that cynicism (dependent variable) is positively related to educational attainment (independent variable). The data, unfortunately, reveal a negative correlation between education and cynicism, an explanation of which requires a new theoretical model. One possibility is that better educated people are more trusting of human nature because they have experienced a better life (jobs, health, etc.) and have been less victimized than those with less schooling— a new model that yields a number of testable predictions.

How does one determine if the data support a model? In the last chapter we did a bivariate analysis of the effect of interscholastic sports participation on math grades, finding a statistically significant positive relationship consistent with Broh's original hypothesis (model A in Figure 15.2). But as you can see, to draw conclusions from this analysis alone could be very misleading. The question now is, how do we analyze the data to estimate effects represented by other, more complex models involving three or more variables, such as models C, E, G, I, J, and N in Figures 15.2 and 15.3?

Multivariate analysis of non-experimental data is basically a matter of statistical control. Statistical control is analogous to randomization in experiments; both procedures are designed to eliminate the possibility that prior (antecedent) variables have created a spurious association. Randomization does this by creating random variation across experimental conditions in all extraneous variables; statistical control does it by examining the relationship between an independent and a dependent variable with specified antecedent variables held constant. As we have noted, statistical controls cannot be applied to unmeasured antecedent variables. Also, the presence of measurement error in control variables reduces the effectiveness of statistical control procedures. Despite these limitations, however, this form of analysis does have one major advantage over experimental randomization: It enables us to test for indirect as well as direct effects and to analyze much more complex models than is possible with experimental designs.

Among the several strategies for multivariate analysis, we now introduce elaboration of contingency tables and multiple-regression analysis.

Elaboration: Tables and Beyond

Throughout the 1950s and 1960s, **multivariate analysis** with contingency tables usually involved a simple technique known as **elaboration** (Lazarsfeld, 1955). This technique introduces a third (and sometimes additional) control variables into the analysis to enhance or "elaborate" our understanding of a bivariate relationship. We start with an illustration of elaboration using contingency tables. Then we discuss the logic of three-variable elaboration and describe various meaningful outcomes. Our main purpose is to introduce a general modeling strategy, focusing on antecedent and intervening variables, that may be used with simple, three-variable tables as well as with the more complex, multivariate procedures that we introduce later in this chapter.

George Gerbner and associates (1978) used questions on television viewing and fear of violence from the 1977 GSS to test the hypothesis that heavy television viewing cultivates perceptions of reality that are consistent with television content. Because of the excessive violence on television, heavy viewers will tend to see the world as more violent that it really is. The question they used as a measure of fear of violence was, "Is there any area right around here—that is, within a mile—where you would be afraid to walk alone at night?" Responses to the GSS television viewing question ("On the average day, about how many hours do you personally watch television?") were collapsed into three groups: those who watched two hours or less ("light" viewers), those who watched three hours ("medium" viewers), and those who watched four hours or more ("heavy" viewers). Both of these questions were also included in the 1985 GSS, which we now use to replicate part of the Gerbner analysis.

Table 15.1 replicates their bivariate analysis for the 1985 GSS data. Notice that the biggest difference is between "heavy" viewers and the other two categories: "Heavy" viewers are most fearful, as predicted. This is what Gerbner and associates found in the 1977 data that they analyzed. In 1985, however, "medium" viewers were less fearful than "light" viewers, although this difference was not statistically significant.[4] Gerbner and associates realized that heavy television viewing tends to be associated with lower education and other socioeconomic variables that might also distort one's view of the world.

To explore the possibility that education is creating a spurious causal relationship between television viewing and fear of violence, we introduce education into the analysis by holding it constant. In contingency table elaboration, third variables are held constant by means of subgroup classification. Each category of the third

TABLE 15.1. Fear of Walking Alone at
Night by Television Viewing (%),
1985 General Social Survey

| Afraid | Television viewing | | |
	LIGHT	MEDIUM	HEAVY
Yes	39.3%	37.4%	45.4%
No	60.7	62.6	54.5
Total	100.0%	100.0%	100.0%
(N)	(737)	(310)	(462)

variable constitutes a distinct subgroup, and the original two-variable relationship is recomputed separately for each subgroup. Table 15.2 does this for the variables of fear of violence, television viewing, and education. The table gives the actual marginal frequencies for the 1985 GSS with hypothetical percentages.

Notice that we now have three "tables," one for each category of the variable "education." These are called **partial tables** or **partials**, because each shows the association between television viewing and fear of violence for part of the total number of observations. Education is held constant, because in each partial table all respondents are alike with respect to their level of education. Look over the partial tables carefully. What do they reveal about the relationship between television viewing and fear of violence when education is controlled?

Reading across each partial table, we find virtually no association between television viewing and fear of violence. In other words, the original relationship (shown in Table 15.1), which indicated that heavy viewers were more fearful than light or medium viewers, has disappeared when education is controlled. These hypothetical data, therefore, support model E in Figure 15.2: The relationship is spurious, produced by a common association with education. We draw this inference not only on the basis of the data, however, but also on the basis of prior theoretical assumptions about the causal ordering of these variables. These same data might just as well have been generated by the following model:

Television viewing ⎯⎯⎯▶ Education ⎯⎯⎯▶ Fear of violence

TABLE 15.2. Percentage of Persons Afraid of Walking Alone at Night, by Television Viewing and Education (Hypothetical Data)

| Afraid | Low education | | | Medium education | | | High education | | |
	LIGHT	MEDIUM	HEAVY	LIGHT	MEDIUM	HEAVY	LIGHT	MEDIUM	HEAVY
Yes	50.0%	50.0%	49.7%	38.2%	38.6%	38.2%	36.6%	36.4%	37.2%
No	50.0%	50.0%	50.3%	61.8%	61.4%	61.8%	63.4%	63.6%	62.8%
Total	100.0%	100.0%	100.0%	100.0%	100.0%	100.0%	100.0%	100.0%	100.0%
(N)	(154)	(78)	(179)	(217)	(114)	(170)	(366)	(118)	(113)

Here "education" is an *intervening variable* between "television viewing" and "fear of violence," whereas in model E education is an *antecedent variable* with respect to these variables. We prefer model E as an interpretation because it is unreasonable to believe that the daily number of hours that adults watched television in 1985 determined the years of education that they had completed. But it is crucial to realize that this interpretation rests on theory; the data in Table 15.2 are consistent with either model.

The outcomes of elaboration analysis are seldom this tidy; indeed, the actual data for the 1985 GSS reveal a much more complex relationship among these three variables. As Table 15.3 shows, the relationship between television viewing and fear of violence reduces to near zero for respondents with low and medium education, but remains essentially the same for those with high education. (Compare the latter partial relationship with that shown in Table 15.1.) That is, there is no association between these variables for respondents of low and medium education, but among those of high education, heavy viewers are more fearful than other viewers. This particular outcome, an interaction effect, is known as **specification**: The control variable has *specified* the conditions under which the original relationship holds, namely, among highly educated respondents.

In their analysis of the 1977 GSS data, Gerbner and associates (1978) found a similar pattern of specification when education was controlled. However, they emphasized the tendency for heavy viewers to be more fearful than light viewers when separate controls for age, gender, and education were introduced. This conclusion opened them to three criticisms that pertain to much analysis of contingency tables: (1) They may have lost important information or distorted the results by collapsing television viewing and the control variables into a few categories; (2) they failed to control for several other variables (e.g., race, income, hours worked per week) that might produce a spurious association between television viewing and fear of violence; and (3) they controlled for extraneous variables separately rather than simultaneously. We can never be absolutely certain that television viewing causes fear of violence. But our confidence in this causal relationship depends on our holding constant all antecedent variables that might reasonably be expected to produce a spurious relationship. Moreover, we should not introduce controls one at a time, since spuriousness may be created by the simultaneous action of two or more extraneous variables.

TABLE 15.3. **Percentage of Persons Afraid of Walking Alone at Night, by Television Viewing and Education (Actual Data), 1985 General Social Survey**

Afraid	*Low education*			*Medium education*			*High education*		
	LIGHT	MEDIUM	HEAVY	LIGHT	MEDIUM	HEAVY	LIGHT	MEDIUM	HEAVY
Yes	48.1%	51.3%	50.8%	39.2%	33.3%	40.6%	35.8%	32.2%	44.2%
No	51.9%	48.7%	49.2%	60.8%	66.7%	59.4%	64.2%	67.8%	55.8%
Total	100.0%	100.0%	100.0%	100.0%	100.0%	100.0%	100.0%	100.0%	100.0%
(*N*)	(154)	(78)	(179)	(217)	(114)	(170)	(366)	(118)	(113)

Multiple regression, a technique described later, is generally better when we want to analyze the simultaneous effects of several independent variables on a dependent variable. Still, because of its simplicity and clarity, elaboration of contingency tables will continue to be used when there are a limited number of control variables and the variables have relatively few categories.

Although the elaboration scheme was originally developed for analyzing contingency tables, the general logic of three-variable elaboration is easily extended to multiple regression and other forms of multivariate analysis involving many variables. Figure 15.4 presents a logical guide to using a third variable (T) to elaborate the relationship between and an independent variable (X) and a dependent (Y) variable (adapted from Lazarsfeld, 1955; Rosenberg, 1968). The original association between X and Y is called a **zero-order relationship** because there are zero variables being controlled. If T is introduced as a control variable, then the association between X and Y becomes a **first-order relationship** or simply a "partial."[5] The columns of Figure 15.4 are arranged in the logical order of elaboration steps: (1) Formulate a three-variable theoretical model, (2) confirm that the three-variable model is consistent with the initial zero-order association, (3) control for the third variable, and (4) interpret the results. The first step requires a theoretical decision on the causal position of the third variable: Should T be antecedent to, intervening after, or unrelated to variable X? In the preceding example, educational attainment was modeled to be antecedent to television viewing and fear of violence.

In the following steps, brackets denote the statistical association between two variables. For example, $[XT] = +$ (or $-$, or 0, or $\neq$ 0) indicates a positive (or negative, or zero, or nonzero) association between variables X and T. The necessary empirical prerequisites for the three-variable models are outlined in column two of Figure 15.4. For example if $[XY] = +$, then $[TX]$ and $[TY]$ would have to be both positively or both negatively associated for an antecedent model to predict a positive, albeit spurious, zero-order association between X and Y. In our earlier discussion of Figure 15.2 arrow diagrams, models C and E, but not models D and F, are consistent with a positive association between X and Y. Thus for education to qualify as a possible explanation for a spurious relationship between television viewing and fear of violence, it must have either a positive or a negative association with both variables. The marginal frequencies of Table 15.3 confirm that education is negatively associated with both television viewing and fear of violence.[6]

Provided that the empirical requirements (column two) are satisfied, the next step is to examine the relationship between X and Y when the third variable (T) is controlled. If the data are consistent with the first model in Figure 15.4, for example, then the association between X and Y in the partials should vanish or become very small (≈ 0) since only variable T produces the zero-order association. This ideal type of outcome is called **explanation** as the third variable "explains" away the zero-order association. Conversely, if the zero-order relationship is also being produced by other antecedent variables besides T, or by a causal link between X and Y (model G in Figure 15.2), the first-order partials may be smaller than the zero-order relationship but not vanish. Something of this sort happened when we controlled for education in Table 15.3.

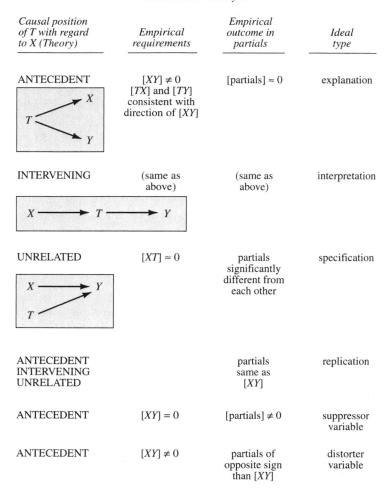

Causal position of T with regard to X (Theory)	Empirical requirements	Empirical outcome in partials	Ideal type
ANTECEDENT	$[XY] \neq 0$ $[TX]$ and $[TY]$ consistent with direction of $[XY]$	[partials] ≈ 0	explanation
INTERVENING	(same as above)	(same as above)	interpretation
UNRELATED	$[XT] \approx 0$	partials significantly different from each other	specification
ANTECEDENT INTERVENING UNRELATED		partials same as $[XY]$	replication
ANTECEDENT	$[XY] = 0$	[partials] $\neq 0$	suppressor variable
ANTECEDENT	$[XY] \neq 0$	partials of opposite sign than $[XY]$	distorter variable

FIGURE 15.4. Ideal types of elaboration.

The second ideal elaboration outcome, **interpretation**, has the same empirical requirements and outcomes as explanation. The only difference between the two is the causal position of the third variable. If the partials vanish when an intervening variable T is controlled, the model provides an "interpretation" of the causal process or mechanism by which X influences Y (Lazarsfeld, 1955). On the other hand, if T does not completely account for the causal process linking X and Y (e.g., model N in Figure 15.3), the zero-order partials will not completely disappear. Mollie Orshansky and Judith Bretz (1976) provide an interesting example of an intervening variable that interprets the relationship between family size and poverty. First, they show that the prevalence of poverty increases as the household head's number of siblings increases. Then they show that this relationship disappears when the household head's level of education is controlled. Thus, the larger one's family of origin, the lower one's level of education, and as a consequence, the more likely that one will experience poverty (model I in Figure 15.3).

Even when T is causally unrelated to X, the first-order partials may be significantly different from each other if T and X interact in affecting Y. Although Paul Lazarsfeld (1955) reserved the term "specification" for a strong form of interaction *when* T was unrelated to X, generally the term is applied also whenever an antecedent or intervening control variable specifies the conditions under which the initial zero-order relationship varies (our previous interpretation of Table 15.3). In a 1952 study of college students' values, Morris Rosenberg (1968:140–42) found that students with low faith in people (general attitude toward humanity) placed more emphasis on the importance of getting ahead in life (success-orientation). When gender was controlled, Rosenberg discovered that the initial relationship between faith in people and success-orientation became stronger in the partial table for females and weaker in the partial table for males. He concluded that the initial relationship is weaker among males because males at that time were under more "general social pressure" to be successful, irrespective of their faith in people, than were females.

Replication is just the opposite of specification: the partials are not significantly different from the initial zero-order relationship (Hirschi and Selvin, 1967:99). The causal position of the control variable in replication may be antecedent, intervening, or unrelated to the original independent variable. Although, at first glance, replications appear to be undesirable or boring outcomes, they often represent favorable evidence in support of the initial zero-order hypothesis. To show that the initial relationship holds when critical antecedent variables are controlled, or that it remains essentially unchanged within categories of various control variables (gender, race, education, age, and so forth), strengthens one's confidence that the relationship is nonspurious and has high external validity.

The final ideal types of elaboration shown in Figure 15.4, **suppressor** and **distorter variables**, are really the mirror image of explanation. In the latter, the zero-order association supports the initial hypothesis, and an antecedent variable is introduced to test for a possible spurious relationship. In the former, the hypothesis is not supported, and an antecedent variable is controlled to determine if it is suppressing, or distorting the direction, of the zero-order association. An uncontrolled suppressor variable may reduce or cancel out the true relationship between two variables, whereas an uncontrolled distorter variable may reverse the true direction of the relationship (Rosenberg, 1968). As an illustration, let us return to our chapter 3 example of a positive zero-order correlation between the number of firefighters at a fire (X) and the amount of damage suffered (Y). Model H (Figure 15.2) reveals how an antecedent variable, size of fire (T), can distort the apparent effectiveness of firefighters in reducing damage. As the size of the fire (T) increases, so do the number of firefighters (X) called up and also the amount of fire damage (Y), thus producing a positive association between X and Y. If the positive relationship produced by T is stronger than the negative causal link between X and Y, the resultant zero-order association will be positive. When T is controlled, the first-order relationship changes to a negative direction, confirming that having more firefighters will reduce the amount of damage. A suppressor variable is very similar to a distorter variable in that by operating in the opposite direction than the causal link between X and Y, it may weaken or even eliminate the zero-order association. The relationship between X and Y is revealed when the suppressor variable is controlled.

The elaboration labels in the fourth column of Figure 15.4 describe ideal types of expected outcomes provided that (1) the social phenomenon can be adequately represented by a three-variable model and (2) the data are free of measurement error. Since these assumptions are never satisfied with real data, actual outcomes fall short of the ideal types. In a typical "explanation" outcome, for example, the partials may weaken but not disappear. Establishing spuriousness (i.e., vanishing partials) is likely to require controlling additional antecedent variables simultaneously in a multivariate model, and possibly better measurement. Similarly, teasing out the intervening mechanism causally linking two variables may require a more elaborate model than a simple three-variable representation.

In a multivariate analysis, it is important to consider carefully all antecedent variables that reasonably might be expected to produce a spurious association, as well as theorized intervening variables, interaction effects, and other predictions. For example, using a representative sample of 21,204 U.S. adults from the 1987 National Health Interview Survey, demographer Robert Hummer and associates (1999) found a strong inverse relationship between religious involvement, as measured by reported church attendance, and the risk of dying over a nine-year follow-up period. Compared to those who attend church "more than once a week," the risk of dying between 1987 and 1995 was 87 percent higher for those who "never attend," 31 percent higher for the "less than weekly" attendees, and 15 percent higher for the "weekly" church goers. To explore the possibility that the relationship was spuriously produced by uncontrolled antecedent variables linked to church attendance and mortality, Hummer and associates simultaneously controlled for selected background factors (age, sex, race, region, income, and education) and baseline measures of health (self-reported health status, activity limitations, and bed-sick days). Controlling for background factors, or for interaction effects between background and church attendance, did not explain away the initial relationship between religious involvement and the risk of dying ("replication"). Controlling for health factors, however, did slightly reduce the zero-order association between church attendance and mortality (limited "explanation").

Besides demonstrating that likely antecedent variables are not spuriously producing the strong zero-order association, Hummer and associates identified two sets of intervening variables, social ties (marital status, social activity, friends and relatives to call upon in times of need) and harmful behaviors (cigarette smoking, alcohol use, and obesity), that link religious attendance to mortality. Frequent church attendance may promote social ties and discourage harmful behaviors, which in turn may affect mortality. Not only did the social ties and harmful behaviors account for a portion of the association between religious attendance and mortality ("interpretation"), the intervening variables varied in a meaningful way for various causes of death. For example, controlling on social ties substantially reduced the association between religious attendance and diabetic mortality; diabetics often need to rely heavily on social ties to maintain adequate care.

Now we will introduce multiple regression analysis, and provide three illustrations of its use in multivariate modeling.

Multiple-Regression Analysis

Multiple regression is simply an extension of bivariate regression (chapter 14) to include two or more independent variables. Like the partial tables of elaboration analysis, it provides information on the impact of an independent variable on the dependent variable while simultaneously controlling for the effects of other independent variables. Unlike the case with partial tables, control is not limited to a few variables nor is information lost from collapsing variables into fewer categories. Here we present a cursory exposition of this very powerful and popular linear-modeling technique. Our main purpose is to make it easier for you to read and understand research employing multiple-regression analysis.

Example 1: The Moral Integration of American Cities

Let us start with an early application of multiple regression in sociology—Robert Angell's 1951 study "The Moral Integration of American Cities." Angell was interested in understanding why the populations of various cities differ in their conformity to certain social mores ("moral integration"). As an operational definition of moral integration, he constructed an elaborate index combining information on crime rates (negative integration) with local contributions to community charity funds (positive integration) for forty-three cities with a population over 100,000. Angell theorized that moral integration is more easily maintained in homogeneous populations and in those with a low turnover of members. Two measures were constructed to test these hypotheses: (1) a heterogeneity index based on the relative number of nonwhites and foreign-born whites in each city and (2) a mobility index based on the relative number of persons moving into and out of each city.

An arrow diagram representing Angell's model is shown in Figure 15.5. The arrows pointing from mobility and from heterogeneity to moral integration indicate the hypothesized negative relationships. The curved arrow indicates that mobility and heterogeneity may be correlated, which is taken as given and not to be explained in the model. An incorrect approach to testing Angell's theory would be to test each hypothesis separately using bivariate regression. The results from such an approach show that each of these variables is significantly related to moral integration in the predicted direction; for ethnic heterogeneity, $b = -.1027$, and for residential mobility, $b = -.1789$.

Thus, on the basis of bivariate regressions, Angell appears to be right: Moral integration decreases with increasing heterogeneity and with increasing mobility. Unfortunately, this is not a proper test of his model. Study Figure 15.5 again. First, since the theory signifies that both independent variables *simultaneously* influence moral integration, they should be analyzed accordingly. Second, since heterogene-

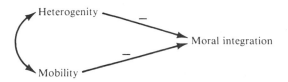

FIGURE 15.5. Angell's moral integration model.

ity and mobility may be strongly correlated (curved arrow), some or all of the apparent contribution of one to a bivariate prediction of moral integration actually may be due to the other. Suppose, for example, that heterogeneity but not mobility is causally related to moral integration and that mobility and heterogeneity are strongly correlated. Then a bivariate regression of moral integration on mobility could produce a significant regression coefficient, which would be entirely a consequence of the correlation between mobility and heterogeneity. Leaving out important variables from a model, which may produce misleading results, is called a **specification error**. Clearly, therefore, bivariate regressions represent misspecification of Angell's theory.

Now that we are convinced that a multivariate test is in order, how do we proceed? The general formula for a multiple-regression equation is

$$Y = a + b_1X_1 + b_2X_2 + b_3X_3 + \ldots e$$

where Y is the dependent variable, each X represents an independent variable, the b values are **partial-regression coefficients** or **partial slopes**, a is the Y-intercept (the predicted value of Y when all of the X values are equal to zero), and e represents the prediction error or residual (the stochastic component). This, of course, is the linear equation for bivariate regression (chapter 14), augmented to include additional independent variables. For Angell's data, the equation reduces to

Moral integration $= a + b_1$ heterogeneity $+ b_2$ mobility $+ e$

Estimation of the coefficients in a multiple-regression equation follows the same logic as bivariate regression. In the case of two independent variables, the approach is easy to visualize geometrically. Imagine constructing a three-dimensional scatterplot of Angell's data within a large room. The forty-three cities will appear as a "swarm" of points within the room, with the location of each point determined by that city's score for moral integration (using the room height as the axis of measurement), heterogeneity (room length), and mobility (room width). The multiple-regression solution appears as a (two-dimensional) plane in this three-dimensional space. (The bivariate-regression solution was also a geometric figure, a line, in a two-dimensional space.) Now, if we mentally position the regression plane in the room so as to minimize the sum of the squared residuals (vertical distances from the city points to the regression plane), we have found the multiple-regression solution.

A computer program, of course, is a more practical approach to multiple-regression estimation. Computing estimated coefficients for Angell's data gives the following prediction equation:

$$\text{Moral integration} = 19.993 - .108(\text{heterogeneity}) - .193(\text{mobility})$$

These results are consistent with Angell's model and are statistically significant. The multiple-regression or partial coefficients reveal the amount by which the dependent variable is expected to change with a one-unit change in the independent variable *when* the other independent variables are held constant (controlled). Thus the moral integration index for a city is expected to fall by .193 unit for every unit increase in the residential mobility index. What is predicted when ethnic heterogeneity decreases by ten units?

The partial coefficients address questions like the following: If several cities have the same degree of residential mobility but differ on ethnic heterogeneity, how will these differences in heterogeneity affect moral integration? A geometric interpretation of partial coefficients for the case of two independent variables is provided in Figure 15.6. As discussed, this regression equation represents a plane positioned to minimize the sum of the squared vertical distances (Y axis) of the observations (not shown) from the plane. Now if we construct a plane perpendicular to the X_1 axis, we are in effect holding X_1 constant, since any observation lying on this plane has the same X_1 value. This plane intersects the regression plane in a straight line (heavy line in the figure), the slope of which is the partial coefficient for independent variable X_2. That is, this partial slope indicates the amount by which the dependent variable (Y) is expected to change with each unit change in X_2 when the other independent variables (only X_1 in this case) are controlled.

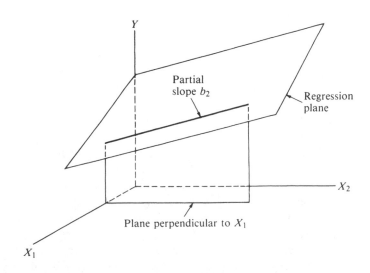

FIGURE 15.6. The multiple regression plane.

The basic principle underlying partial coefficients and partial tables is the same expounded for good experimental design (chapter 7): "doing only one thing at a time"—that is, allowing only one independent variable to vary while controlling all other variables. Sometimes this is difficult to achieve in regression analysis because of high correlations among the independent variables. Consider the extreme case of a **collinear**, or perfect, **association** between two independent variables. Suppose that we inadvertently included two collinear predictors in a regression equation: age and year of birth. Then it would be impossible to estimate the regression equation, since age could not be varied while year of birth was held constant. Perfect collinearity is easily handled by dropping one of the collinear variables from the regression equation. A far more difficult problem is high **multicollinearity**, which arises when combinations of two or more independent variables are highly correlated with each other. The presence of high multicollinearity requires great care in interpreting the regression results, since estimates of the coefficients will be quite unstable (varying greatly from sample to sample) and it will be difficult to distinguish significant from nonsignificant independent variables.

Example 2: Interscholastic Sports and Academic Achievement

Throughout the book we have been describing Broh's study of extracurricular involvement and academic achievement. We now present a series of Broh's analyses that are intended to give you a feel for the modeling enterprise and to show you how to read and interpret regression results. Our discussion will be limited to only one of her four outcome measures (math grades) and to only one of her three sets of intervening variables (the developmental model).

In the last chapter, standardized math grades in the twelfth grade was regressed on interscholastic sports participation during both the tenth and twelfth grades, which supported the hypothesized positive relationship between athletic performance (independent variable) and classroom performance (dependent variable). Could the positive zero-order relationship between math grades and sports participation be a spurious result of uncontrolled antecedent variables? To explore the possibility that higher-performing students were more likely than their peers to play interscholastic sports, Broh added as controls a prior measure of the dependent variable, tenth-grade math grades, and various family and social characteristics found in previous studies to predict academic achievement.

Broh's bivariate (model 1) and multivariate (model 2) regression results are summarized in Table 15.4, which is typical of the format used in research articles. Model 1 coefficient estimates (discussed in the last chapter) for the Y-intercept (.005) and playing sports (.230) are listed in the first column. The third column displays partial-regression coefficient estimates for the additional variables included in model 2. The second and fourth columns display estimated standard errors for each regression coefficient. These are used to compute significance tests (**t-tests**), which indicate whether a regression coefficient is significantly different from zero when the other independent variables are taken into account. All **t-values** large enough to be significant at some predetermined probability level are flagged by a marker (asterisks in Table 15.4) or otherwise noted.[7] Consequently, for model 1 the likelihood

TABLE 15.4. **Standardized Twelfth-Grade Math Grades
Regressed on Selected Independent Variables, NELS:88**

Independent variables	Model 1 (N = 10,379)		Model 2 (N = 10,379)	
	COEFFICIENT ESTIMATE	STANDARD ERROR	COEFFICIENT ESTIMATE	STANDARD ERROR
Athlete, tenth and twelfth grades	.230***	.021	.044**	.017
Tenth-grade math grades	—	—	.608***	.007
Female	—	—	.172***	.014
African American	—	—	−.373***	.024
Asian American	—	—	.057	.036
Hispanic	—	—	−.138***	.026
American Indian	—	—	−.339***	.077
Family income (in $10,000s)	—	—	.004*	.002
Parental education	—	—	.091***	.007
Two-parent household	—	—	.074***	.016
Public school	—	—	−.066*	.028
Suburban school	—	—	−.047*	.019
Rural school	—	—	−.010	.022
School size	—	—	−.045***	.007
Intercept	.005		−.114	
R^2	.011		.481	

*$p < .05$, **$p < .01$, ***$p < .001$ (two-tailed tests).
Source: Table 1 of Broh (2002). Used by permission of the author and the American Sociological Association.

is less than 1 in 1000 ($p < .001$) that the observed coefficient for playing inter-scholastic sports could have occurred by chance.[8]

To interpret model 2, one must start with an understanding of the variable coding, which is specified in Table 15.5. The variables described in column 3 ("Metric") as "standard units" were transformed to standard scores (mean = 0, standard deviation = 1) to facilitate comparisons of measures collected during both the tenth- and twelfth-grade follow-ups. The range, mean, and standard deviation are reported in Table 15.5 for NELS-coded variables family income, parents' education, and school size.[9] The remaining variables are dummy (0/1) coded. Broh represents the five-category classification of race (discussed in chapter 14) by four dummy variables in her regression models:

Black   = 1 if the respondent identifies his or her race as black; 0 if not.
Hispanic   = 1 if the respondent identifies his or her race as Hispanic; 0 if not.
Asian   = 1 if the respondent identifies his or her race as Asian American ; 0 if not.
American Indian = 1 if the respondent identifies his or her race as American Indian; 0 if not.

TABLE **15.5.** **Variable Descriptions, Means and Standard Deviations**

Variable name	Description	Metric	Mean	SD
Athlete	Interscholastic sport participant in tenth and twelfth grades	0 = did not participate both years	.32	.47
Math grades (tenth, twelfth grades)	Standardized scores of math grades	Standard units	.00	1.0
Female	Sex of student	0 = male, 1 = female	.49	.50
Black	Respondent identifies as black	0 = no, 1 = yes	.11	.31
Hispanic	Respondent identifies as Hispanic	0 = no, 1 = yes	.09	.29
Asian	Respondent identifies as Asian American	0 = no, 1 = yes	.04	.19
American Indian	Respondent identifies as American Indian	0 = no, 1 = yes	.01	.09
White	Respondent identifies as white	0 = no, 1 = yes	.75	.43
Family income	Total annual family income in $10,000s	Range: 0–29.6285	4.24	4.07
Parents' education	Highest educational level attained by either parent	1 = didn't finish high school 6 = Ph.D., MD, or other	3.11	1.22
Parent structure	Student lives in a dual, biological parent household	0 = no, 1 = yes	.69	.46
Public school	Student's school is public	0 = private, 1 = public	.91	.29
Urban school	School is located in an urban area	0 = no, 1 = yes	.25	.44
Suburban school	School is located in a suburban area	0 = no, 1 = yes	.41	.49
Rural school	School is located in a rural area	0 = no, 1 = yes	.34	.47
School size	Number of students in respondent's school	1 = under 400 students 5 = over 2000 students	3.02	1.21
Self-esteem (tenth, twelfth grades)	Standardized scale (lower scores represent lower self-esteem)	Standard units	.00	1.00
Locus of control (tenth, twelfth grades)	Standardized scale (lower scores represent less internal control)	Standard units	.00	1.00
Homework (tenth, twelfth grades)	Number of hours student spends on homework per week	Standard units	.00	1.00

Source: Appendix of Broh (2002). Used by permission of the author and the American Sociological Association.

The key to the use of dummy variables is that one category of the original variable must be omitted from the dummy-variable set. Gender, for example, is represented by the dummy "female" and the male category is left out. The excluded race category consists of students identifying themselves as "white." What to exclude is an arbitrary decision. Broh could just as easily have included a dummy variable for whites and excluded some other racial category. Similarly, school location is represented by two dummy variables (suburban school, rural school) with urban schools as the omitted category.

Broh also constructed two dummy athlete "controls" to represent students who played interscholastic sports in the tenth but not in the twelfth grade, or in the twelfth but not in the tenth grade. All of her regression models include three dummies for sports participation: (1) in the tenth grade only, (2) in the twelfth grade only, and (3) in both years ("athletes"). The omitted category represents "non-athletes" who did not play sports in either year. Broh did not, however, report the values of the estimated coefficients for the two dummy "controls" (sports participant in only one year) for any of her regression models. Apparently, she used the "controls" to ensure a pure comparison between "athletes" and "non-athletes" that was not obscured by students who played sports in only the tenth or only the twelfth grades.

Armed with an understanding of the variable coding, one next looks for significant regression coefficients. That is, the significance tests may be used to screen out results in the sample that easily could have happened by chance. Only two variables in model 2, Asian American and Rural School, are not significant (Table 15.4). Since both are members of dummy sets, they have to be compared to the omitted categories: That is, Asian Americans (or rural school students) are not significantly different from whites (or urban school residents) when all other variables in model 2 are held constant. The significant dummy coefficient for female students ($p <$ .001), in contrast, indicates that modeled math grades are expected to be .172 standard deviation higher if the student is female rather than male (omitted category).

With such a large sample of over 10,000 students, most coefficients are likely to be statistically significant. After screening for significance, one can examine the sign and size of the partial coefficients to determine the separate contribution of each variable in predicting twelfth-grade (1992) math grades. Not surprisingly, the best predictor is math grades in the tenth grade (1990): For every unit change of one standard deviation in 1990 math grades, an increase of .608 standard deviation in 1992 math grades is expected according to model 2 (Table 15.4). Similarly, 1992 math grades is positively associated with being female ($b = $ .172), family income ($b = $ .004), parental education ($b = $ .091), and living in a two-parent household ($b = $ .074). Each slope coefficient should be interpreted in terms of the variable coding (metric) shown in Table 15.5. The coefficient for family income in model 2, for example, predicts a .004 standard deviation increase in 1992 math grades for every one unit ($10,000) increase in family income. Larger schools ($b = -$.045), public schools ($b = -$.066), suburban schools ($b = -$.047), and racial minorities (except Asian Americans) are negatively associated with math grades (i.e., associated with lower math grades) when the other variables in model 2 are held constant (controlled).

Table 15.4 also lists for each model a popular but flawed measure of fit, R^2, which indicates approximately the proportion of the variance in the dependent variable (spread of observations around the mean) predicted or "explained" by the independent variable(s). R^2 is not always useful because it mechanically focuses on prediction instead of the theory under investigation and because it is subject to other weaknesses (Berk, 1983:526–27). Moreover, an unknown amount of the variance in the dependent variable is attributable to the stochastic component (King, 1989:24). Consequently, it is impossible to judge the performance of the independent variables from R^2, since it is not based exclusively on the systematic variance that may be "explained." For example, an R^2 of .02 (2%) would be excellent if only 3 percent of the variance is systematic. Nevertheless, R^2 can be useful for comparing models based on the same dependent variable that differ on included independent variables, such as baseline model 1 ($R^2 = .011$) compared to model 2 ($R^2 = .481$).

A comparison of models 1 and 2 suggests that a substantial portion of the positive association between 1992 math grades and interscholastic sports performance is due to antecedent variables. The value of the regression coefficient for sports participation drops from .230 (model 1) to .044 (model 2) with the inclusion of the control variables. Taken together, the set of independent variables in model 2 explain nearly half (48%) of the variance in twelfth-grade math grades. But even with this excellent set of math performance predictors, interscholastic sports performance still showed a small positive relationship to improved math grades ($b = .044, p < .01$).[10] Consequently, even after controlling the available NELS:88 variables in model 2, Broh was unable to explain away the higher math grades of student athletes as a spurious relationship. Since it is impossible in a nonexperimental study to *control* for *all* antecedent variables, the possibility exists that future research, employing different model specifications, may reveal the athlete-grade relationship to be spurious.

Another way to buttress the inference that playing sports fosters academic achievement is to identify the intervening mechanism linking the two activities. According to one explanation, developmental theory, sports participation increases students' self-esteem, feeling of control over their lives, and their work ethic. That is, the theory predicts a positive association between playing sports (independent variable) and the intervening developmental variables, which in turn are predicted to be positively associated with academic performance (dependent variable).

To explore the possibility that "character development" explains the positive effect of sports on grades, Broh constructed measures of self-esteem, locus of control, and time spent on homework.[11] First, to determine if the developmental indicators *could* be intervening variables between sports participation and math achievement, she regressed each on sports participation, individual background, and school characteristics. Table 15.6 reveals that after controlling for the tenth grade (1990) measure of each developmental variable and the background and school variables, interscholastic sports participation is positively associated, as hypothesized, with significant 1990–92 increases in self-esteem ($b = .085, p < .001$), feeling of self-control ($b = .076, p < .001$), and time spent on homework ($b = .162, p < .001$) between the tenth (1990) and twelfth (1992) grades.

Having established that the developmental indicators are positively associated with sports participation, Broth then needed to demonstrate that they promote academic achievement in math. Her results are summarized in Table 15.7. The first regression, model 3, is essentially her previous set of independent variables from model 2, but limited to slightly fewer cases (9,777 instead of 10,379 students) due

TABLE 15.6. **Standardized 12th-Grade Developmental Model Variables Regressed on Selected Independent Variables**

Independent variables	Developmental model		
	SELF-ESTEEM (N = 10,188)	LOCUS OF CONTROL (N = 10,177)	HOMEWORK (N = 9,985)
Athlete, tenth and twelfth grades	.085*** (.020)	.076*** (.021)	.162*** (.022)
Tenth-grade measure of dependent variable	.529*** (.008)	.454*** (.009)	.316*** (.010)
Female	−.067*** (.017)	.155*** (.018)	.107*** (.019)
African American	.159*** (.030)	−.047 (.031)	.019 (.033)
Asian American	−.079 (.043)	−.096* (.045)	−.018 (.049)
Hispanic	.112*** (.032)	.038 (.033)	.156*** (.036)
American Indian	−.036 (.089)	−.056 (.094)	.321*** (.107)
Family Income (in $10,000s)	.008*** (.002)	.012*** (.002)	.004 (.003)
Parental education	.021** (.008)	.004 (.008)	.053*** (.009)
Two-parent household	−.009 (.019)	.055** (.020)	−.000 (.021)
Public school	.002 (.033)	−.039 (.035)	−.001 (.038)
Suburban school	−.010 (.023)	−.115*** (.024)	−.006 (.026)
Rural school	.023 (.026)	−.051 (.027)	.040 (.030)
School size	.012 (.008)	−.003 (.009)	−.008 (.009)
Intercept	−.162	−.088	−.305
R^2	.310	.229	.124

Note: Standard errors are shown in parentheses. $*p < .05$, $**p < .01$, $***p < .001$ (two-tailed tests).
Source: Table 2 of Broh (2002). Used by permission of the author and the American Sociological Association.

to missing information for some of the developmental variables. In the second regression equation, model 4, she adds the three developmental indicators to her previous set of independent variables. A comparison of models 3 and 4 reveals that interscholastic sports participation no longer has a significant impact ($b = .031$, $p > .05$) when the developmental indicators are controlled. Increases in students' math grades between the tenth and twelfth grades is positively associated with gains in internal control ($b = .091$, $p < .001$), time spent on homework ($b = .032$, $p < .001$), but not self-esteem ($b = −.009$, $p > .05$).

TABLE 15.7. **Standardized Twelfth-Grade Math Grades Regressed on Developmental and Control Variables**

Independent variables	Model 3 (N = 9777)		Model 4 (N = 9777)	
	COEFFICIENT ESTIMATE	STANDARD ERROR	COEFFICIENT ESTIMATE	STANDARD ERROR
Athlete, tenth and twelfth grades	.049**	.017	.031	.017
Self-esteem	—	—	−.009	.009
Locus of control	—	—	.091***	.009
Homework	—	—	.032***	.007
Intercept	−.142		−.117	
R^2	.485		.493	

Note: Both models also include the independent variables of model 2 in Table 15.4.
$*p < .05$, $**p < .01$, $***p < .001$ (two-tailed tests).
Source: Table 3 of Broh (2002). Used by permission of the author and the American Sociological Association.

Broh's findings support the developmental explanation of how sports participation promotes academic achievement in mathematics. High school athletes develop a greater work ethic and a sense of control over their lives than do non-athletes, which has a positive effect on math grades. In a separate analysis that included all intervening variables (developmental, leading crowd, and social capital models), Broh identified an additional intervening variable, student discussions with teachers outside of class ($b = .202$, $p < .001$), which further reduced the effect of sports performance on 1992 math grades to a nonsignificant association ($b = .019$, $p > .05$). Consequently, the three intervening variables (locus of control, homework, and student-teacher discussions) provide an interpretation of the process linking sports participation to math achievement. The role of the self-esteem variable, on the other hand, may be misspecified in Broh's model because it may be an effect rather than a cause of student achievement.

For pedagogical purposes, we described only part of Beckett Broh's study. You might be wondering if her findings would generalize to other academic achievements besides math grades, to other extracurricular activities besides interscholastic sports, and to other intervening processes besides the developmental variables. Please see Box 15.1 for answers to these questions and a summary of her complete study.

Example 3: Textile Workers and Union Sentiment

In the previous example, Broh estimated two separate regression equations by employing the developmental variables first as dependent variables (Table 15.6) and then as independent variables (Table 15.7). A useful statistical technique for pictorially representing and analyzing a complex model comprising a series of equations is **path analysis**. A major advantage of path analysis is that it forces researchers to be explicit about the cause-and-effect relationships among the study variables. One

BOX 15.1

Extracurricular Activities and High School Achievement

In the last two chapters we have described a part of Beckett Broh's analysis of the academic benefits of participating in high school extracurricular activities. Whereas we have restricted ourselves to the impact of playing interscholastic sports on math grades, Broh examined participating in a range of extracurricular activities, and she also included grades in English and scores on math and reading ability tests as outcome measures.

In analyses identical to the aforementioned modeling of math grade (see Table 15.4), Broh separately regressed each of the other twelfth-grade outcome measures (English grades, math and reading test scores) on corresponding tenth-grade measures of the dependent variable, on interscholastic sports participation in the tenth and twelfth grades, and on the same set of antecedent social, family, and school characteristics. Similar to the small positive relationship between playing sports and math grades ($b = .044$, $p < .01$) found after controlling for the antecedent variables, interscholastic sports participation was related to improved English grades ($b = .073$, $p < .001$), to higher math test scores ($b = .034$, $p < .001$), but to lower reading test scores ($p = -.042$, $p < .01$). Thus, her finding that playing sports positively influences math grades also generalizes to English grades and math achievement scores.

The thesis that participation in interscholastic sports has real academic benefits was strengthened by Broh's analysis of theorized intervening variables. Two developmental variables, locus of control and time spent on homework, accounted for about "one-third of the effect of sports on grades and test scores" (Broh, 2002:78). The "leading crowd hypothesis" did not fare as well: Having more academically oriented peers did not appreciably improve athlete's academic performance. Increases in social capital associated with interscholastic sports participation, on the other hand, accounted for "almost half the effect of sports participation on math grades and over a third of the effect on English grades, but only one-fifth of the effect on scores on math tests." (Broh, 2002:81). The social capital effects were largely due to two variables: (1) whether students talk to teachers outside of class and (2) the frequency of talking to parents about school studies, programs, and classes. When the intervening and antecedent variables were simultaneously controlled, the effects of sports participation was substantially lower for English grades ($b = .037$, $p < .05$) and vanished to nonsignificant levels for math grades ($b = .019$, $p > .05$) and math test scores ($b = .014$, $p > .05$). Consequently, Broh identified much of the intervening mechanisms linking sports to academic performance in her NELS:88 data.

Do the apparent academic benefits of participating in interscholastic sports also extend to other extracurricular activities? Broh expanded her regression analyses to include variables representing tenth- and twelfth-grade involvement in intramural sports, cheerleading, music groups, school drama, student council, yearbook or journalism club, and vocational clubs. When these other extracurricular activities were controlled simultaneously, the positive effects of playing interscholastic sports increased for math grades ($b = .111$, $p < .001$), English grades ($b = .141$, $p < .001$), math tests ($b = .055$, $p < .001$), and the previous negative effect on reading tests changed to a nonsignificant association ($b = .005$, $p > .05$). Participation in music groups yielded similar, but smaller, gains in math grades, English grades, and math test scores. Student council participation was linked to improved grades but not to higher test scores. In marked contrast to interscholastic athletes, students participating in intramural sports, and to a lesser extent vocational clubs, had consistently lower grades and test scores over the two-year period. Finally, involvement in cheerleading. school drama, or the yearbook did not produce consistent grade and test score benefits for the student participants.

By and large, Broh presents an impressive set of analyses demonstrating the academic benefits of playing interscholastic sports. Of all the extracurricular activities studied, playing school sports produced the strongest and most consistent positive effects on grades and test scores. An ostensibly similar activity, playing intramural sports, produced an even stronger, but negative, effect on academic performance. Broh then shows that the intramural athletes do not gain the developmental and social capital advantages associated with extramural sports and linked to academic achievement. In fact, over the two-year period, intramural athletes' sense of control over their lives significantly decreased, and their time spent on homework and relationships with teachers and parents were no different than peers who did not participate in extracurricular activities.

It is unlikely that Broh's recent research will be the conclusive study on the academic consequences of involvement in high school extracurricular activities, since her findings may be reinterpreted or contradicted by future studies involving different model specifications, better statistical procedures, or new datasets. One problem is her failure to use statistical software appropriate for the NELS:88 multistage sampling design: students clustered by school, stratification, and disproportionate sampling of certain strata (e.g., oversampling of Hispanics). Although she did use NELS:88 sampling weights to adjust for disproportionate sampling, clustering and stratification information is also needed to produce adequate standard error estimates and significance tests.[16] Ignoring clustering and stratification will generally produce standard error estimates that are too small.

Another potential problem is multicollinearity because the estimated academic effects of playing interscholastic sports are quite small after simultaneously controlling for as many as 15 or more antecedent variables.[17] Broh makes no mention of using regression diagnostic procedures to assess if collinearity among the control variables is adversely affecting the estimated effects of playing sports. Also, by creating two dummy control variables for playing interscholastic sports in only one year (tenth but not twelfth grade, or vice versa), which was intended to allow a pure comparison between "athletes" and "non-athletes," Broh may have inadvertently removed some of the poorer students from the group of athletes (tenth and twelfth-grade participants). That is, academic difficulties may explain why some of these students played sports in only one of the two years.[18]

On the other hand, future research may support Broh's pioneering study and may provide answers to important questions raised by her findings. Are the academic benefits of playing interscholastic sports similar for male and female students? Do the effects of participating in various extracurricular activities vary by race-ethnicity, as well as by parental education and income? Are there school-level effects besides the individual effects of students' family and social background? Does extracurricular participation reduce the time spent on recreational reading, and thus explain the absence of reading test improvement relative to math tests, math grades, and English grades? How does talking to teachers after class and to parents about school promote academic benefits to student athletes?

can perform a regression analysis, on the other hand, without specifying the theorized causal processes linking any of the variables. Broh performed her analyses, for example, without having to specify if there were any causal links between the developmental variables (self-esteem, locus of control, and time spent on homework) aside from their separate links to sports performance and math achievement. A second advantage of path analysis is that it provides quantitative estimates of the direct, indirect, and total effects of one variable on another.

An example of a path analysis model from a study of union sentiment among southern nonunion textile workers by Joseph McDonald and Donald Clelland (1984) is shown in Figure 15.7. The measures used were union sentiment (a higher score is more pro-union), activism (willingness to support strikes), deference (submissiveness to authority), mill size, type of ownership (coded 1 if absentee, 2 if local), wage level (hourly wages), years in mill (seniority), skill level (a higher score equals more skilled), age, and gender (coded 1 if male, 2 if female).

The arrows in Figure 15.7 represent the theorized causal paths between the variables. Activism, for example, is a cause of union sentiment but not vice versa. Although all variables are causally prior to union sentiment, only two of them (years in mill, gender) have direct effects. Seniority (years in mill) and gender also have indirect effects via paths leading to wages, deference, and activism. McDonald and Clelland estimated the path effects by regressing each of four dependent variables (union sentiment, activism, deference, and wage level) on all causally antecedent variables. Deference, for example, was regressed on all variables but activism and union sentiment.

McDonald and Clelland put the various regression coefficients on a common footing by standardizing them.[12] A **standardized regression coefficient** may be computed by multiplying an unstandardized coefficient (which we have been using)

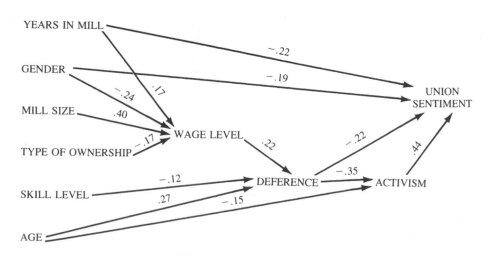

FIGURE 15.7. Path analytic model showing various effects on union sentiment. *Source:* Page 513 of McDonald and Clelland (1984). Used by permission of the authors and the University of North Carolina Press

by the ratio of the standard deviation of the independent variable to the standard deviation of the dependent variable (Pindyck and Rubinfeld, 1981:90). Standardized regression coefficients are easily interpreted as slopes in standard deviation units; a standardized coefficient of −.50, for example, indicates that the dependent variable decreases by a unit of 1/2 standard deviation for every standard deviation increase in the independent variable.[13] Only statistically significant partial-regression coefficients are shown in Figure 15.7. For example, the direct effect of mill size on wage level, a standardized coefficient of .40, indicates that wages increase by .40 standard deviation for every standard deviation increase in mill size.

The path analysis results show, for example, that seniority (years in mill) negatively affects pro-union sentiment both by direct and indirect paths (via higher wages, greater deference, and less activism). Indirect effects are measured by taking the product of the path coefficients along a causal path and summing the products over all indirect paths (see Davis, 1985:48–64). In Figure 15.7, age has only one indirect path leading to activism, for an indirect effect of $(.27) \times (−.35) = −.095$. The total effect of age on activism is the sum of the direct and indirect effects: $(−.15) + (−.095) = −.245$. Thus activism is estimated to decrease by about 1/4 standard deviation for every standard deviation increase in age.

Other Modeling Techniques

This discussion has just scratched the surface of multivariate modeling. There are special techniques for modeling various types of dependent variables (e.g., dichotomous, nominal, and ordinal measures), for straightening or transforming nonlinear relationships into a form suitable for linear modeling, for including interaction effects, for modeling mutual causation and measurement error, for multilevel modeling (hierarchical analysis), for social network analysis, and for modeling processes over time (longitudinal analysis) and space.[14]

Although statistically different from multiple regression, these techniques are similar in that they share the assumption that social phenomena are generated by both systematic and stochastic components. The systematic impact of the independent variables is represented by coefficient estimates of effect direction (positive or negative) and strength. However, interpretation of coefficient strength usually is not as straightforward as interpretation of regression slopes (see Stolzenberg and Land, 1983). The stochastic component in multiple regression is assumed to have a normal distribution, which may arise from the cumulative effect of a large number of unmeasured (extraneous) variables or from sampling error. Thus in our Figure 15.6 geometric portrayal of multiple regression, the residuals about the regression surface (plane) are assumed to be normally distributed. When the normality assumption is unwarranted, a multiple-regression model misspecifies the data and a different stochastic component is needed.[15]

Again, we must warn that our exposition of modeling is quite superficial and cannot be substituted for formal course work in statistics. Our emphasis has been on interpreting modeling results to the neglect of describing the iterative process of testing various model specifications. We essentially presented the end result of modeling moral integration, academic achievement, and union sentiment. Before reaching a "final" model, researchers typically test a series of models of increasing or decreasing complexity, such as comparing two specifications that differ on the presence or absence of a hypothesized causal path. During this iterative process, predicted effects that are statistically insignificant or otherwise inconsistent with the data are dropped from the modeling. The resultant "final" model is always a tentative conclusion; subsequent research may disclose alternative models that provide just as good, if not better, fit to the data.

Summary

Causal understanding—the goal of much social research—ultimately rests on comparisons of theory and data. Data alone cannot establish causal relationships. Rather, researchers construct theory-based models of relationships and then determine statistically the fit between data and model. Researchers base assumptions about direction of influence, which are built into their models, on theoretical knowledge. Likewise, theory guides statistical tests for nonspuriousness by suggesting potential causes of spurious relationships (antecedent variables), and it guides tests for mediating causal processes by suggesting potential intervening variables. Leaving out important variables from a model is called a specification error.

The models for data analysis include both systematic (theorized relationships) and stochastic (chance processes) components. The former very often are represented by arrow diagrams. Arrows indicate causal order; the signs above the arrows indicate the direction of the relationship—positive or negative.

Very often a series of alternative models are compared to analyze the data. Model testing occurs through multivariate analysis, which enables one to (a) examine the effects of an independent variable on a dependent variable while controlling for relevant antecedent or intervening variables and (b) examine interactions among variables.

A traditional technique for the multivariate analysis of contingency tables is elaboration. This approach begins with a two-variable relationship, and then it systematically reassesses this relationship when controls are introduced for third (and sometimes additional) variables. Variables are controlled, or held constant, by computing partial tables—that is, computing the original two-variable relationship separately for each category of the control variable. If the model specifies the control variable as causally antecedent to the other two variables, and the original relationship disappears in each partial table, then the original relationship is explained away as spurious (explanation). If the control variable is modeled as intervening, and the original relationship disappears in the partials, then the intervening causal process linking the two original variables is explicated (interpretation). Other possible outcomes include specification (an interaction effect involving the increase, reduction, or disappearance of the original relationship in some partials but not in others) and replication (the partials are essentially the same as the original relationship). Finally, an uncontrolled antecedent variable may suppress or distort the true causal relationship between the original two variables.

A better technique for analyzing the simultaneous effects of several independent variables on a dependent variable is multiple regression. The partial-regression coefficients in a multiple-regression equation show the effects of each independent variable on the dependent variable when all other variables in the equation are held constant. Holding variables constant may prove difficult and result in unstable coefficients when some of the independent variables are highly correlated with each other, a problem known as multicollinearity. Nominal- and ordinal-scale variables may be incorporated into multiple regressions by means of dummy-coding.

Comparison of partial-regression coefficients may be facilitated by standardizing them to the same metric of standard deviation units. A standardized coefficient indicates the number of standard deviation units the dependent variable changes for every unit change of 1 standard deviation in an independent variable. Standardized coefficients are used in path analysis to estimate the various indirect and direct effects between any two connected variables in a complex causal model.

Key Terms

modeling/causal modeling
    reciprocal causation
    noncausal association
    direct effects
    indirect effects
    systematic component
    stochastic component
multivariate analysis
elaboration
    partial tables, partials
    zero-order relationship
    first-order relationship
    explanation
    interpretation

    specification
    replication
    suppressor variable
    distorter variable
multiple regression
    specification error
    partial-regression coefficients/partial slopes
    collinear association
    multicollinearity
    t-tests/t values
    R^2
path analysis
standardized regression coefficient

Review Questions and Problems

1. For each of the following pairs of variables, state a "theory" of the causal process linking the two variables and indicate the likely direction of influence: (a) marital adjustment and length of the engagement period; (b) educational attainment and occupational achievement; (c) place of residence (rural, urban) and happiness; and (d) amount of interaction with and liking of others.

2. Draw an arrow diagram representing a causal ordering and likely direction of relationship (positive or negative) among the following sets of variables: (a) respondent's occupational prestige; family income when respondent was a teenager; respondent's educational attainment; (b) respondent's newspaper readership (frequency), educational attainment, and age.

3. What are the differences among antecedent, intervening, suppressor, and distorter variables in causal modeling?

4. Explain the differences between the ideal elaboration outcomes of explanation, interpretation, specification, and replication.

5. Surveys typically report that residents of large cities are more tolerant of deviant behavior than are residents of smaller cities and rural areas. Suppose that data are available for three variables: (1) respondent's tolerance of deviant behavior, (2) size of current place of residence, and (3) size of place in which the respondent was living at age 16. For each of the following hypotheses, draw arrow diagrams to specify a causal model incorporating the hypothesis: (a) the social environment of the current residence renders people more or less tolerant; (b) tolerance is learned during adolescence and remains relatively constant thereafter; (c) both age-16 and current residential environments affect tolerance of deviant behavior.

6. What is a specification error? Is it likely to occur in a true experimental design? Why or why not?

7. Explain the difference between the regression coefficient in bivariate regression and the partial-regression coefficients in multiple regression. Why are they called "slopes"?

8. In a multiple-regression analysis of grade-point average (range 0–4.0) for the first year in college, the partial coefficients for gender (dummy variable = 1 for females, 0 for males), high school grade-point average (range 0–4.0), and employment during the school year (range 0–50 hours) were, respectively, +0.30, +0.50, and −0.01. Given that the three partial coefficients were statistically significant, explain the meaning of each. Hint: Explain as partial slopes.

9. Which of the following variables are collinear: (a) respondent's education, (b) annual family income, (c) respondent's age, (d) respondent's income, (e) weekly family income, (f) respondent's year of birth, (g) family size? Why?

10. What is meant by high multicollinearity? Why is it a problem in multiple regression?

11. Consider the following results of t-tests for three different regression coefficients: (a) t-value = $-1.77, p = .430$; (b) t-value = $2.70, p = .007$; (c) t-value = $-0.01, p = .746$. Which are statistically significant—that is, not likely to have occurred by chance?

12. What is R^2? Why is it called a measure of fit?

13. The General Social Survey (GSS) codes age-16 place of residence as a six-category variable: rural farm, rural nonfarm, small city, medium-size city, suburb near a large city, and large city. Show how this information could be represented by a set of dummy variables.

14. Interpret the following standardized regression coefficients: (a) +0.40, (b) −1.5, (c) 0.0, and (d) −0.02.

15. Summarize the results from Broh's multiple regression of selected independent variables on the time spent on homework by twelfth-grade students (see Table 15.6). Interpret the statistically significant coefficients.

16. Calculate the indirect effects and total effects of seniority (years in mills) on union sentiment in McDonald and Clelland's path model (Figure 15.7).

NOTES

1. For related studies, see Smith-Lovin and Tickamyer (1978) and Cramer (1980).

2. California State Assemblyman John Vasconcellos, supporting an annual $245,000 task force to increase the self-esteem of state residents, "argued that raising self-esteem would help solve many of the state's problems, including crime, teen pregnancy, drug abuse, school underachievement . . . and would help balance the state's budget because people with high self-esteem earn more money than people with low self-esteem and therefore pay more taxes" (Baumeister et al., 2003:3).

3. See Davis (1985) for a discussion of arrow diagrams as these apply to the logical rules for causal ordering among a set of variables.

4. For Table 15.1, chi-square $= 6.25$ ($p < .05$).

5. A second-order partial has two control variables, a third-order relationship has three controls, and so forth.

6. Collapsing Table 15.3 on television viewing reveals that fear of walking alone falls with increasing education: 49.9% with low education, 38.8% with medium education, and 36.7% with high education are afraid of walking alone. Similarly, heavy television viewing drops with increasing education: 43.5% with low education, 33.9% with medium education, and 18.9% with high education are heavy viewers.

7. These *t-value* statistics are computed by dividing each sample regression coefficient by its estimated standard error. In testing the null hypothesis that a coefficient has zero slope in the population [against an alternative hypothesis of a positive or negative slope (two-tail test) or a directional alternative (one-tail test) that the slope is positive (or negative)], the significance level (p value) is obtained from a t (sampling) distribution.

8. Strictly speaking, the probability level is a crude approximation, since it depends on the extent to which the assumptions underlying the regression model are met and on proper specification of the process being modeled.

9. Apparently, Broh treats parents' education (coded 1–6) and school size (coded 1–5) as interval scale variables in her regression analyses.

10. This was also true for two other of Broh's four outcome measures (English grades and math test scores).

11. Broh's measures of self-esteem and time spent on homework were discussed in Chapter 4. She reports that locus of control is also a "composite measure in the NELS data . . . comprised of multiple measures of students' . . . sense of control" (Broh, 2002:75).

12. Path analysis may also be performed with unstandardized coefficients.

13. Broh obtained a similar interpretation by standardizing the metric coding of some variables.

14. Raftery (2001) provides an excellent overview of 1950–2000 modeling developments in sociology. Introductory treatments of these topics may be found in Fienberg (1980), Maddala (1983), Tuma and Hannan (1984), Bollen (1989), King (1998), and Raudenbush and Bryk (2002).

15. See McCullagh and Nelder (1989) and Gill (2001) for ways to model the stochastic component with Poisson, binomial, gamma, inverse Gaussian, and other probability distributions.

16. The statistical packages STATA and SUDAAN, for example, provide estimates of standard errors for complex sampling designs.

17. For example, the interscholastic athlete coefficient for math grades (Table 15.4) is only .044 after controlling for 13 social, family, or school characteristics and for the two dummy variables for sports participation in only one year. The total count of independent vari-

ables increases by about eight with the inclusion of all intervening variables, and by about seven when all forms of extracurricular activities are included in the regression analysis.

18. Although Broh does not report any of the estimated coefficients for the two athlete dummy controls, there is indirect evidence that one or both have negative effects in the baseline modeling of math grades (model 1, Table 15.4) since the other two coefficient estimates are positive (.230 for athletes, .005 for intercept) and the weighted total effects across all students should sum to zero (the mean of the standardized math grades).

16

✔

Research Ethics

Thus far we have dealt with the technical side of social research—with issues of research design, data collection and analysis. Besides these technical aspects, there is another dimension to social science that must be considered—the moral dimension. When we think about how to conduct research, we must think not only of using the *right* techniques but also of *rightly* using the techniques we have learned. We must think about **research ethics**.

Ethics is a branch of philosophy and theology. Both theological ethicists, who define the field in terms of religious tradition and sacred texts, and philosophical ethicists, who define it strictly on the basis of reasoning independent of religious faith, are concerned with the same fundamental question: What ought to be done? Ethics is the study of "right behavior." For the social scientist, ethics poses questions concerning how to proceed in moral and responsible ways.

Ethical considerations underlie many decisions about research methods. Just as practical considerations can prevent researchers from implementing the ideal research design or obtaining as large or diverse a sample as desired, so too can ethical concerns constrain scientific inquiry. Ethics may prohibit researchers from using experimental treatments that could harm research participants, from asking questions that would prove extremely embarrassing or threatening, from making observations that would deceive or place subjects under duress, and from reporting information that would constitute an invasion of privacy.

There are three broad areas of ethical concern in scientific research: the ethics of data collection and analysis, the ethics of treatment of participants, and the ethics of responsibility to society (Reese and Fremouw, 1984). First, researchers are expected to be careful and forthright in observing, analyzing, and reporting findings. Being ethical in this sense is synonymous with being a good research scientist. Second, scientists have ethical obligations regarding the treatment of human subjects. Basic ethical principles accepted in our cultural and legal tradition demand that research participants be treated with respect and protected from harm. Finally, ethical concerns arise from the relationship between science and society, especially regarding the uses of scientific knowledge. Many social scientists believe that researchers have a responsibility to assess the possible uses of scientific findings, to promote their beneficial application, and to speak out against their destructive application.

In this chapter, we consider each of these areas of ethical concern; however, we give the greatest attention to the treatment of research participants. Historically, the most controversial studies, many of which are described below, have involved clashes between scientific practice and the rights and welfare of research participants. Concern about potential harm to subjects led to the codification and adoption of federal regulations regarding research practices (Singer and Levine, 2003). It also is a major focus of the ethical codes developed by professional societies such as the American Sociological Association and the American Psychological Association.

Data Collection and Analysis

Conducting ethical social research involves, first, researchers' obligations to one another and to their discipline to make sure that their data are sound and trustworthy. Because scientific progress rests upon the trustworthiness of findings from the work of many investigators, dishonesty and inaccuracy in reporting and conducting research undermine science itself. Scientific norms therefore demand intellectual integrity. Scientists are expected to be "unremittingly honest" in their observations and analyses, to be tolerant, questioning, and willing to admit error, and to place the pursuit of knowledge and understanding above personal gain or the promotion of a particular philosophy or ideology (Cournand, 1977). Violations of this ethical code vary from manipulating data in order to obtain a desired result to the complete fabrication of data.

Unethical data manipulation can occur in many ways. A researcher may exclude certain cases from the analysis to achieve a significant difference between experimental conditions; fail to report results that contradict a favored hypothesis; and search for statistical tests, however inappropriate, that improve the appearance of the data by yielding significant results or larger effect sizes [for an example, see Berry (1991)]. The extent to which data are obscured in these ways is unknown; however, more extreme ethical violations involving the complete fabrication of data are thought to be exceedingly rare in science (Marshall, 2000). When, in 2001, social psychologist Karen Ruggiero retracted articles in two journals because she had fabricated the data, the editor of one journal remarked that he had never seen a retraction of this sort in the social psychology literature (Biernat and Crandall, 2001).

The Ruggiero case reveals the gravity of scientific fraud. Ruggeiro's work, published in some leading psychology journals between 1995 and 2000, drew a great deal of attention. One 1995 paper was cited in over 50 studies. Her provocative central thesis—that racial and sexual discrimination are more widespread than most people think—also had important policy implications. Before the revelation of fraud, Ruggiero was a rising star in the discipline. After completing her PhD at McGill University in 1996, she became an assistant professor at Harvard, then moved to the University of Texas in 2000, where she quickly gained a reputation as an excellent teacher and colleague (Biernat and Crandall, 2001). Apparently, suspicions about the validity of her research arose when others could not replicate her findings. When a former research assistant asked Harvard to investigate, she admitted to using "invalid data" in her research studies at Harvard (Holden, 2001).

The impact of scientific fraud is far-reaching. For the scientist who is discovered to have published false data, the consequences are severe. Ruggiero was subjected to professional disgrace and to public humiliation from media coverage of the incident. She resigned her faculty position and almost certainly ended her career as a research scientist. "The ripple effect on the field," as Chris Crandall (2001:20) points out, "can be even worse." Because scientists build their research on the work of others, false leads can result in the loss of considerable time, money, and energy for those who pursue them. Similarly, the publication of fraudulent data harms everyone associated with it: Graduate students working in the researcher's lab lose time and the trust of colleagues; the institution where the fraud took place must investigate the case and, if the research was supported by external funding, possibly return the funds; the image of the discipline may be tarnished; and the validity of the work of everyone who cites the invalid articles may be questioned.

Science is a public activity, carried out by a community of scholars who constantly evaluate each other's work. In the end, it was this scrutiny, specifically the inability of others to replicate her findings, that called into question Ruggiero's research. So, in one sense, the case shows that science's system of checks is working. Still, incidents of data manipulation and fabrication may be difficult to uncover. Even though fraud would seem most likely to surface when the research gains prominence, as did Ruggiero's, fraudulent data may remain undetected for years. It was well over a decade before it was discovered that Cyril Burt's data on twins (see Box 2.2), which were highly influential in research on the heritability of intelligence, were fabricated. Furthermore, replication may not be the most effective means of preventing or detecting fraud. Exact replications are not highly valued as scholarly work; they are expensive; and varying conditions may confound the interpretation of failures to replicate. Therefore, social researchers must resort to other methods to prevent scientific fraud.

Part of the fallout from the Ruggiero case was a discussion of the measures that should be taken by social scientists to prevent scientific misconduct. Among the recommendations were the following (Murray, 2002):

- Research institutions should educate students about scientific misconduct. Ethics training is mandatory for professional psychology programs accredited by the American Psychological Association, and is required for students working on NIH (National Institutes of Health) research grants. The topic of research ethics also should be an integral part of all courses in social research methods.
- Institutions, funding agencies, and individual researchers should periodically check data. The NIH conducts regular research audits. But because universities do not have the resources for intensive audits that the NIH has, we recommend at least random quality checks by principal investigators. Survey researchers, for example, should validate a sample of interviews for every interviewer.
- Investigators should prescribe specific criteria for the inclusion or exclusion of certain data, such as outliers, before data are collected and analyzed.
- In papers submitted for publication, researchers should provide detailed information on how they collected, processed, and analyzed their data, and journal editors should insist on such detailed accounting.

We cannot overemphasize the importance of carefully conducting research and honestly reporting findings. For the scientist, this is the most fundamental ethical dictum.

Treatment of Human Subjects

Four problem areas have been identified most often regarding the ethical treatment of human subjects: potential harm, lack of informed consent, deception, and privacy invasion (Diener and Crandall, 1978). Each of these problems arises when research practices violate basic human rights. It is considered a violation of basic rights to harm others, to force people to perform actions against their will, to lie to or mislead them, and to invade their privacy. While most social research poses no threat to these individual rights, there have been some ethically questionable studies in the social sciences. A review of these four issues will sensitize the reader to research situations that are potentially unethical as well as to strategies and guidelines that help to ensure subjects' rights.

Harm

All new physicians take an oath of ethical, professional behavior attributed to the Greek physician Hippocrates (460–377 BC). One of the first provisions of the Hippocratic oath is that the doctor "abstain from whatever is deleterious. . . ." These words of Hippocrates, advising that the physician do no harm, offer sound ethical advice for research scientists as well. The first right of any participant in a research project is the right to personal safety. Ethical researchers recognize this right and are careful to respect it. Research that would endanger the life or physical health of a human subject is simply not acceptable in the social science community. Even research that harms animals, although it might directly benefit humans, has been the focus of contemporary ethical concern [see, for example, Plous (1996) and Rowan (1997)].

The issue of harm is not quite so simple and straightforward as it may appear, however. For one thing, harm is sometimes difficult to define and predict. Given the nature of social science research projects, physical harm to subjects is highly unlikely. Yet, not all harm is of a physical nature. People can be harmed personally (by being humiliated or embarrassed), psychologically (by losing their self-esteem), and socially (by losing their trust in others) through their participation in research that might never threaten their physical well-being (Diener and Crandall, 1978:17f). Moreover, it is often difficult to predict whether, or the extent to which, one's investigative procedures will be harmful to research participants. The prison simulation study of Philip Zimbardo and colleagues (1973) is a good example. These investigators created a mock prison in the basement of a Stanford University building in which subjects role-played prisoners and guards. The study was scheduled to run two weeks but had to be terminated after only six days because of its unanticipated adverse effects on subjects. Guards physically and psychologically abused prisoners, and prisoners broke down, rebelled, or became servile and apathetic. The subjects got so caught up in the situation, became so absorbed in their roles, that they began to confuse role-playing and self-identity. While Zimbardo and colleagues intended to study how the roles of "guard" and "prisoner" influenced subjects' reactions, they never anticipated such extreme effects.

Besides the difficulty of predicting harm, most scientists would not adhere to the dictum that no harm whatsoever should ever come to research participants. Some researchers take the position that potential harm should be weighed against the benefits that might be derived from the research. This stance is implied by one criterion for approval of research in the Code of Federal Regulations (1995:116): "Risks to subjects are reasonable in relation to anticipated benefits. . . ." If there is little or no scientific value from a study that knowingly exposes subjects to harm, the study should not be done, no matter how small the harm. But if a study has considerable scientific merit, some degree of potential harm may be justified. For example, although some research on hypothermia requires subjecting informed volunteers to physical harm, such as by immersing them in cold water, this is justified by the potential scientific benefit of such an investigation.

A major difficulty with this approach lies in being able to assess the full extent of costs and benefits. Costs and benefits may be impossible to predict or to measure; and a **cost–benefit analysis** ignores individual rights, or at least makes them subservient to societal benefits and to pragmatic considerations. Research seems most justifiable when the person exposed to the risks will also receive the benefits of potentially harmful procedures. However, the benefits of much scientific research accrue not to the individual research participant but to the investigator, to science, or to the general public, and it is more questionable to justify costs to an individual solely on these grounds (Diener and Crandall, 1978).

In spite of these problems, a cost–benefit analysis can be a helpful first step in examining the ethics of a proposed study. One should also be sensitive to areas of study and to research procedures that pose the greatest risk of harm. The potential for doing harm to subjects may be highest in social research that investigates negative aspects of human behavior (e.g., aggression, obedience to malevolent authority, cheating). The principal arena for such research is in laboratory and field experiments. Through experimental manipulation, subjects may suffer a temporary loss of self-esteem or experience a high degree of stress, and as a result they may be embarrassed or may become angry about their involvement in research.

Consider, for example, the work of Stanley Milgram (1974) on obedience to authority. Under the guise of a teacher–learner experiment, Milgram asked subjects playing the role of teacher to deliver to learners what the subjects thought were dangerously high levels of electric shock. It goes without saying that the learner, a confederate of the experimenter, was not actually being shocked. But to the subjects this was a highly stressful conflict situation: Should they obey the experimenter in administering the shocks or should they refuse to continue in the experiment? The subjects showed many obvious signs of stress; indeed, one subject had a convulsive seizure that made it necessary to terminate his participation. Milgram, in turn, was severely criticized for not protecting his subjects from potential harm. For example, he made no effort to determine before their participation whether subjects should be excluded from the experiment for physical or psychological reasons. Some researchers also questioned the long-term effects that the experiment might have had on subjects' self-concepts. What would subjects think of themselves knowing that they were capable of inflicting pain on another person?

Field experiments present even greater problems. In these settings the researcher may find it virtually impossible to intervene when subjects are about to experience harm. The laboratory setting guarantees a certain amount of control over subjects' behavior, allowing for intervention if necessary, but that control may be altogether absent in a field setting. Bibb Latané and John Darley (1970), for example, staged a crime (looting of a liquor store) to explore the conditions under which bystanders intervene to help. One bystander in their field experiment telephoned the police, who showed up with guns drawn to arrest the researchers. This was a situation in which considerable harm could have come to both subjects and researchers.

The ethical issue of harm is much less a problem for survey researchers and participant observers than it is for experimentalists, but even they must be alert to the potential for doing harm. Survey researchers can harm people by asking threatening questions. Participant observers can harm people by their own active involvement as participants. William Foote Whyte (1981:313), for example, reports that during the course of his study of Cornerville, he voted four different times in the fall 1937 congressional election. Whatever damage might have been done to the opposition candidate by Whyte's illegal actions, while probably insignificant, is not irrelevant.

Aside from assessing the risk of harm to research participants and designing one's research to minimize such risks, the researcher needs to be aware of several widely adopted ethical principles that are designed to protect participants from harm (see Diener and Crandall, 1978).

1. Researchers should inform subjects of any reasonable or foreseeable risks or discomforts before the study begins and should give subjects sufficient opportunity to consider whether to participate. Indeed, federal regulations mandate such "informed consent," discussed below, for all federally funded research. A major criticism of Milgram's experiment, which predates the latter regulation, is that he did not obtain prior permission from subjects to allow him to place them in a highly stressful conflict situation.

2. Where appropriate, researchers should screen out research participants who might be harmed by the research procedures. In their prison simulation study, Zimbardo and associates (Zimbardo, 1973) gave several personality tests to volunteers in order to select subjects with "normal" personality profiles and thereby minimize the possibility of destructive effects. Another criticism of Milgram's experiment is that he failed to administer examinations before the experiment to determine whether subjects suffered from psychological or physical problems that might have excluded their participation.

3. If stress or potential harm is possible, measures should be taken to assess harm after the study, and research participants should be informed of procedures for contacting the investigator. The debriefing session in experiments can help to assess as well as ameliorate negative reactions. But if long-lasting effects are possible, the researcher has a special obligation to conduct follow-up interviews and possibly to provide counseling. Zimbardo (1973) held an encounter session after his study to allow subjects to express their feelings. He also conducted follow-up interviews to assess the impact of the experience and found no evidence of long-

lasting negative effects. Indeed, most subjects regarded the experiment as a valuable learning experience. Milgram (1974) also carefully questioned his subjects, interviewing all of them immediately after the experiment and sending them reports of the study and follow-up questionnaires asking for their reactions to their participation in his research. His ultimate ethical justification for this research was that it was judged acceptable by those who took part in it.

Informed Consent

The second ethical issue arises from the value placed on freedom of choice in Western societies. For moral and legal reasons, subjects should not be coerced into participating in social research. Not only must subjects understand that their participation is voluntary, they must also be given enough information about the research to make an informed decision about whether to participate. In other words, researchers should obtain the explicit or implicit **informed consent** of their subjects to take part in an investigation.

Just how much information about the research must be conveyed to subjects for them to exercise their *informed* consent is not always clear and depends largely on the nature of the research. Full disclosure of the research purpose and procedures is usually not necessary, although subjects generally should be given some explanation of the general purpose of the research and who is sponsoring it. Minimally, they should be told that their participation is voluntary and that they are free to withdraw from the study at any time; moreover, they must be given a clear description of the risk of harm involved and of personal rights that might be jeopardized by their participation. Milgram's subjects, for example, should have been told that they would feel stress and that this stress conceivably could have harmful effects.

Ethical regulations for federally funded research dictate that a written consent form, signed by the subject or the subject's legal guardian, must be used when more than "minimal risk" of harm is anticipated. Minimal risks refer to risks that are no greater than those ordinarily encountered in daily life (Code of Federal Regulations, 1995). In such cases, informed consent protects both subjects and researchers. Subjects are protected from harm by being able to make up their own minds about the risks of participation; researchers are legally protected by subjects' explicit voluntary agreement. However, although written informed consent is accepted practice in biomedical research, it has several limitations as an ethical safeguard and is not always desirable in social research.

As Edward Diener and Rick Crandall (1978) point out, it is often difficult, even in biomedical research, truly to inform subjects about all the risks of research, since these are not always known. Moreover, the subject's consent to participate does not remove the researcher's responsibility to minimize danger to the subject, and it should never be used to justify other unethical practices. Finally, the use of informed-consent procedures presents methodological problems for several kinds of studies. Research by Eleanor Singer (1978) has shown that requiring a signature on a consent form reduces the response rate and elicits more socially desirable responses in surveys. And in laboratory experiments, the provision of full information about the study can completely undermine its validity. As the concept of demand characteristics implies, subjects who are told the true purpose of the study may not behave naturally. It is not surprising, then, that studies that convey hypothesis-related information in their informed-consent procedures have failed to replicate findings of studies not containing such information (Adair, Dushenko, and Lindsay, 1985).

While it is clear that documentation of consent and full disclosure of research purposes and procedures can present methodological problems, there are ways of circumventing these problems while following the doctrine of informed consent. In survey research, obtaining a signature to document consent "seems unnecessarily burdensome," as Singer (1978:159) has noted, given that the "same protection is afforded respondents by the right to refuse the interview, or to refuse to answer particular questions within the interview." In fact, the Code of Federal Regulations (1995:110) does not require written consent for surveys unless (1) the information collected is recorded so that respondents can be identified and (2) disclosure of the information could place respondents at risk for criminal or civil liability or damage respondents' reputation (e.g., if respondents are asked about sensitive topics such as sexual behavior, drug abuse, illegal conduct). Federal regulations also provide for a waiver of documentation or an alteration of some of the elements of informed consent when these would adversely affect the study. However, the waiver of documentation can only be made when the research involves minimal risk to subjects. Finally, it is common in medical and experimental research today to forewarn subjects that a full disclosure of the purposes of the research is not possible until after their participation. They might be told, in addition, that they may be in one of several treatment conditions, but that the study results would be invalid if they knew their assigned condition prior to the conclusion of the research.

Field experiments and disguised or covert participant observation present the greatest ethical risk from the standpoint of informed consent. In both types of studies, the researcher's desire to observe subjects' spontaneous and natural behavior is incompatible with the acquisition of consent: To obtain informed consent destroys subjects' naivete and defeats the purpose of the study. Whether such research is regarded as unethical depends, for some people, on other ethical considerations, such as invasion of privacy, risk of harm, and the costs incurred in terms of time and money. If the research does not invade the subjects' privacy, is harmless, and is not costly to the subjects, informed consent may be ethically unnecessary. In this sense, testing the effects of different appeals when soliciting donations for a charitable organization, such as Robert Cialdini and David Schroeder (1976) did in a field experiment, would not be considered ethically questionable, because subjects were not at risk and their rights were not violated. However, Latané and Darley's 1970 field experiment involving the staging of a crime would be ethically questionable because subjects were exposed to considerable stress and risk of harm.

One of the most controversial studies involving covert participant observation was Laud Humphreys's study (1975), mentioned in chapter 10, of sexual encounters in public restrooms. Humphreys posed as a voyeur and "watchqueen," whose job was to warn homosexuals of intruders as they engaged in fellatio. He also recorded the license numbers of these men, traced their identities through the Department of Motor Vehicles by misrepresenting himself as a market researcher, and later interviewed them in their homes after changing his appearance so that he would not be recognized. Despite the fact that Humphreys carefully guarded the confidentiality of his subjects, this study now is considered ethically indefensible by many social scientists. Among several other problems, Humphreys failed to obtain his subjects' informed consent and risked doing serious damage to their psyches and reputations.

Disguised participant observation studies such as the one by Humphreys are relatively rare and do not always pose such dangers. No matter what the apparent risk of harm, however, this kind of research is invariably controversial. In contrast to the relativist ethical judgments about field experiments, some social scientists take the absolutist position that research simply should not be done where investigators deliberately misrepresent their identity in order to enter an otherwise inaccessible social situation. Sociologist Kai Erikson (1967:368), for example, argues that this kind of research "can injure people in ways we can neither anticipate in advance nor compensate for afterward"; that it "may be painful to the people who are . . . misled; and even if that were not the case, there are countless ways in which a stranger who pretends to be something else can disturb others by failing to understand the conditions of intimacy that prevail in the groups he has tried to invade." In regard to this kind of research, Erikson (1967:368) also reiterates one of the most basic assumptions of informed consent:

> If we happen to harm people who have agreed to act as subjects, we can at least argue that they knew something of the risks involved and were willing to contribute to that vague program called the "advance of knowledge." But when we do so with people who have expressed no readiness to participate in our researches (indeed, people who presumably would have refused if asked directly), we are in very much the same ethical position as a physician who carries out medical experiments on human subjects without their consent.

Deception

Deception, the third area of ethical concern, in some ways is the most controversial. On the one hand, deception is a widely used and accepted practice in social research, especially in experiments; one study found that, in 1983, 58 percent of the empirical studies reported in three major social psychology journals used some form of deception (Adair, Dushenko, and Lindsay, 1985). The most common deception involves misleading subjects or respondents about the purpose of the study. A cover letter for a survey, for example, might indicate that the study's objective is to examine general beliefs about health when, in fact, the investigators are interested specifically in their respondents' knowledge of and beliefs about the relationship between smoking and lung cancer.

In their epileptic seizure experiment, described in chapter 6, Darley and Latané (1968) told subjects that they were interested in the kinds of personal problems faced by college students when in reality they were testing subjects' willingness to intervene in an emergency. They also deceived subjects about the reasons for the experimental setup, explaining that it was necessary to separate subjects to avoid the embarrassment of face-to-face interaction and that the experimenter would not be present lest they feel inhibited by his presence. The actual reasons for these conditions were to allow the experimenters to simulate the discussion of other subjects and to remove the experimenter from the scene of the emergency. Other frequent forms of deception in experiments are using confederates to mislead subjects about research purposes and tasks, as well as providing false feedback about subjects' own behavior as a way of manipulating their feelings and thoughts.

The basic rationale for deception is that it is necessary in order to place research participants in a mental state where they will behave naturally. If subjects know the true purpose of a study, the results are meaningless. As we have seen, subjects typically will act so as to present the most favorable impression of themselves or to help out the researcher by confirming the hypothesis. Deceiving subjects about the true purpose of a study diverts their attention from the hypothesis and enhances experimental realism by giving subjects a believable and engrossing explanation for what they are doing. Defenders of deception also maintain that without it one simply could not effectively study behavior that people normally find objectionable, such as aggression, conformity, cheating, or failing to aid others in an emergency.

On the other hand, there are strong and vocal opponents of deception. Perhaps the most vocal is psychologist Diana Baumrind (1985:165), who argues that "intentional deception in the research setting is unethical, imprudent, and unwarranted scientifically." Deception is unethical, according to Baumrind, because it violates a subject's right to informed consent (i.e., consent obtained by deceit, by definition, cannot be informed) and violates the trust implicit in the investigator–subject relationship. It is imprudent because it ultimately damages the credibility of behavioral scientists as well as trust in other expert authorities. And it is unwarranted scientifically because deceptive practices do not accomplish the scientific objectives that justify their use. Baumrind claims that the almost routine use of deception in experiments is common knowledge among some groups of subjects (presumably college students), which makes them suspicious and unlikely to accept the experimenter's cover story. Because of this, deception may not produce the naive and spontaneous behavior that it is designed to elicit, thereby making experimental results inherently ambiguous.

Despite these objections, the prevailing sentiment among social scientists is not to rule out deception entirely. The codes of ethics of both the American Psychological Association (APA) and American Sociological Association (ASA) allow for deception. Since describing the whole purpose of the study beforehand invalidates most social research, omitting such information is considered a mild and acceptable form of deception as long as none of the omitted information concerns serious risks. However, because of the legitimate concerns expressed by Baumrind and others, deceptions of greater magnitude, such as telling direct lies to subjects, using confederates, or deliberating misrepresenting oneself, warrant special attention. The ASA code (1997) also states that

(a) Sociologists do not use deceptive techniques (1) unless they have determined that [its] use will not be harmful to research participants; [and] is justified by the study's prospective scientific, educational, or applied value. . . .

(b) Sociologists should never deceive research participants about significant aspects of the research that would affect their willingness to participate, such as physical risks, discomfort, or unpleasant emotional experiences.

(c) When deception is an integral feature of the design and conduct of research, sociologists attempt to correct any misconception that research participants may have no later than at the conclusion of the research.

John Adair and colleagues (1985) point out that the negative consequences in deception research are usually minimal and that there is a lack of viable alternative methodologies. Therefore, the deception dilemma may be rectified best by the ASA's point (c)—adequate debriefing.

Debriefing. Debriefing serves methodological and educational as well as ethical purposes; ideally, it should occur in all studies with human participants, not just those studies involving deception. By interviewing subjects after their participation, researchers may gain valuable information about subjects' interpretations of research procedures; furthermore, by understanding the nature of the study, subjects can gain a greater appreciation for their research experience. If subjects are deceived, however, then the debriefing session becomes critically important. Not only must the researcher explain the true purpose of the study and the reasons for the deception, he or she must do so with great care and sensitivity.

Researchers must be alert to the fact that, when exposed to the truth, subjects may feel embarrassed or angered about having been "fooled" and may harbor resentment toward the investigator and toward social research in general. To obviate such feelings, investigators have developed elaborate debriefing techniques (see Carlsmith, Ellsworth, and Aronson, 1976; Mills, 1976). While we will not describe these techniques in detail, certain common aspects deserve mention. First, it is best to debrief subjects as soon after their participation as possible, especially if the deception or its revelation is likely to cause discomfort. Second, the debriefing should be carried out slowly and deliberately, first eliciting subjects' reactions and then gradually explaining the nature of the experiment until subjects fully understand every point. Third, since negative feelings about being deceived are worsened when the deceiver is smug about it, researchers can relieve some of their subjects' discomfort by expressing their own discomfort about the necessity of using deception in order to arrive at the "truth." Fourth, researchers should point out to subjects that if the experiment works well—if the cover story is convincing—then virtually *everyone* gets fooled. Finally, above all, researchers should follow Herbert Kelman's (1968:222) guideline "that a subject ought not to leave the laboratory with greater anxiety or lower self-esteem than he [or she] came in with."

Research on the effects of deception and debriefing indicates that, in general, carefully administered debriefing is effective. Stevens Smith and Deborah Richardson (1983) found that subjects who were deceived and subsequently debriefed reported more positive experiences—for example, greater enjoyment and greater educational benefit—from their research participation than did subjects who were not deceived and, as a consequence, received less adequate debriefing. Indeed, the final word on deception may be the finding of another study of subjects' reactions:

"[i]t appears that subjects are willing to accept or tolerate certain discomfitures or unpleasantries if they are viewed as necessary elements of a scientific enterprise. Thus, learning that they had been deceived . . . *enhanced* the subject's assessment of the experiment's scientific value; elaborate deceptions are apparently viewed as good social science methodology!" (Straits, Wuebben, and Majka, 1972:515)

Privacy

The idea of the right to privacy goes back to antiquity. For example, Hippocrates' oath promises: "Whatever . . . I see or hear, in the life of men, which ought not to be spoken of abroad, I will not divulge as reckoning that all such should be kept secret." Despite its ancient origins, however, the moral claim to privacy was not widely respected as a fundamental right until the last few centuries. The Industrial Revolution made physical privacy possible, and political democracies granted and increasingly protected the privacy of individual belief and opinion (Ruebhausen and Brim, 1966). Today, invasion of privacy remains a public concern as a result of widely publicized accounts of government wiretapping, police entrapment, and corporate drug testing.

The right to privacy is the individual's right to decide when, where, to whom, and to what extent his or her attitudes, beliefs, and behavior will be revealed. Social research presents many possibilities for invading the privacy of research participants, and it is essential that researchers be sensitive to the ways in which their actions can violate this basic right.

The dramatic case of the Wichita Jury Study in 1954 shows how social research can come into direct conflict with the value of privacy (Vaughan, 1967). In an effort to understand and perhaps even improve the operations of juries, researchers secured the permission of judges to record six actual jury deliberations in Wichita, Kansas, without the knowledge of the jurors. When news of the study became known, it was roundly criticized by columnists and commentators across the country, was investigated by a Senate subcommittee, and led ultimately to the passage of a law prohibiting the recording of jury deliberations. The argument against this study was that jury deliberations must be sacrosanct to protect the inalienable right to trial by impartial jury. Surveillance "threatens impartiality to the extent that it introduces any question of possible embarrassment, coercion, or other such considerations into the minds of actual jurors" (Vaughan, 1967:72).

As this study shows, one way in which subjects' privacy can be invaded is through the use of concealed devices such as one-way mirrors, microphones, and cameras. If such devices are used with subjects' knowledge and consent, they pose no problem. If they are used without subject's knowledge to record behavior in public places (e.g., restaurants and waiting rooms), they also are acceptable to many researchers so long as subjects remain anonymous and are not at risk. But when hidden recording devices are used to observe behavior in private settings to which the research participant would not ordinarily allow the researcher access, an invasion of privacy occurs. Besides juries, other settings that are considered private are homes, personal offices, closed meetings, and physicians' examining rooms (Diener and Crandall, 1978).

Closely related to the use of concealed recording devices is the use of a false cover to gain information that subjects would not reveal if their informed consent were obtained. This became a major problem in the second phase of Laud Humphreys's study, mentioned above, when he got the names of men he had observed performing homosexual acts and interviewed them in their homes. When Humphreys observed these men in public restrooms, he did not know their names or other details of their private lives. But the identifying information he subsequently obtained intruded on his subjects' privacy and, in the worst of circumstances, could have led to legal difficulties or even blackmail. (Unlike physicians, lawyers, and the clergy, social scientists are subject to subpoena and cannot promise their respondents legal immunity.)

Whether we define access to information as an invasion of privacy will depend on how private that information is. Humphreys's research drew attention not just because he used questionable means to procure information, but also because he was investigating a sensitive area—sexual behavior. Clearly, some information is considered more private or sensitive than others. Among the most sensitive and threatening areas are sexual behavior and illegal activities. Researchers investigating these areas have a special obligation to protect the privacy of their informants.

Anonymity and confidentiality. No matter how sensitive the information, however, ethical investigators protect the right to privacy by guaranteeing anonymity or confidentiality. Obviously, information given anonymously secures the privacy of individuals, but this safeguard is usually possible only in surveys using self-administered questionnaires without names attached or in some available data studies. Most often the investigator can identify each individual's responses; therefore, the principal means of protecting research participants' privacy is to ensure confidentiality. The researcher can do this in a variety of ways: by removing names and other identifying information from the data as soon as possible, by not disclosing individuals' identities in any reports of the study, and by not divulging the information to persons or organizations requesting it without the research participant's permission.

Laud Humphreys defended his research partly in terms of the steps he took to ensure confidentiality, such as destroying all data containing personally identifying information after the completion of his study. Likewise, the researchers in the Wichita Jury Study acted to protect privacy by destroying the original recording of each jury deliberation after transcribing the recording and editing the transcript so as to avoid the identification of any of the persons involved. The Census Bureau protects confidentiality in a variety of ways, for example, by not releasing individual responses to the census of population and housing for seventy-two years—a person's average lifetime—and, when releasing the Public Use Microdata Sample, suppressing identifying information.

Field research usually requires more ingenuity to safeguard anonymity and confidentiality. The traditional approach is to use fictitious names for individuals, groups, and locations, although this alone may not be sufficient to prevent people from recognizing themselves and others. For example, in a study of the community of "Springdale," a small town in upstate New York, the researchers promised their informants that no individuals would be identified in printed reports. However, when Arthur Vidich and Joseph Bensman (1958) published their research in a book, the people of the town could clearly identify each character in spite of the authors' use of pseudonyms. The townspeople were so outraged by the transparency of their characterizations and the consequent invasion of their privacy that they featured a float in the annual Fourth of July parade with a large-scale copy of the jacket of the book, *Small Town in Mass Society*. This was followed first by residents "riding masked in cars labeled with the fictitious names given them in the book" and then by a manure spreader, with an effigy of the author Vidich bending over the manure (Whyte, 1958).

Because Vidich and Bensman reported private material without protecting the anonymity or obtaining the consent of their informants, they were severely criticized by other social scientists. To remove the possibility of recognition, the authors might have altered some of the information about people, such as their family background, occupation, or other intimate details of their lives, or they might have developed composite characters based on more than one informant. Perhaps the best solution, however, is to ask the subjects themselves if the material considered for presentation or publication is acceptable to them. This is the strategy adopted by Bettylou Valentine in her study of a community called "Blackston."

Valentine (1978:166) believed that some intimate details of people's lives involving family size, family structure, and interrelationships were relevant to important points she wanted to make. She "did not see how it would be possible to disguise the people enough to make them unrecognizable even to themselves and at the same time accurately illustrative of the Blackston community." Therefore, after she had completed a draft of her manuscript, she sent copies to all the major characters. She explained that her story might be published in the future, and she asked each person (1) whether her account was accurate and fair; (2) whether any material would be embarrassing to anyone; and (3) whether they had any comments, corrections, or other reactions. Finally, she subsequently returned to Blackston to talk to several of the persons involved. As a result of these contacts, Valentine not only worked out additional disguises that protected the privacy of her informants but also gained valuable insights and suggestions for her book.

Making Ethical Decisions

Ethical issues arise in social research when conflicts occur between societal values such as freedom and privacy and scientific methods aimed at obtaining the highest quality data. In the preceding sections we have identified some areas of potential conflict—harm to participants, involuntary participation, intentional deception, and an invasion of privacy. We also have examined some current resolutions of these ethical issues. It should be clear from our discussion that there are no easy answers; indeed, frequently there is considerable disagreement among reviewers about the ethicality of research proposals that raise ethical issues (Ceci, Peters, and Plotkin, 1985). With this in mind, how does the researcher decide what to do?

Some social scientists, such as Diana Baumrind (1971:890), take the position that "scientific ends, however laudable they may be," should never justify the use of means, such as lying to subjects, that violate fundamental moral principles or sacrifice the welfare of research participants. In philosophy, this ethical position is known as *deontology*: Basic moral principles should allow no exceptions, no matter what the consequences. By contrast, the operating ethical philosophy of most social scientists today—the philosophy behind professional ethical codes and federal ethical guidelines for research—is basically *teleological*: The morality of acts should be judged in relation to the ends they serve. The overall guiding principle is that "the potential benefits of the research (e.g., advancement of scientific knowledge, beneficial technological applications, advantages to subjects) must be weighed against the potential costs (e.g., harm to subjects, detrimental technological applications)" (Schlenker and Forsyth, 1977:371–72). As we saw in our discussion of harm, cost–benefit analyses do not always help to resolve ethical dilemmas. Nonetheless, it is from this guiding cost–benefit principle that other rules for the conduct of social research have been derived:

> These include obtaining informed consent; remaining open and honest with the participants; respecting the participants' freedom to decline participation; insuring the confidentiality of the participants' data; protecting the participants from physical and mental discomfort, harm, and danger; completely debriefing the participants; and removing any undesirable effects of the research. (Schlenker and Forsyth, 1977:371)

Although exceptions sometimes are made to these rules, these exceptions must be based on a careful analysis of the possible benefits and costs of the study.

Initially, the individual researcher is responsible for examining the ethics of a study and its prospective benefits and costs. Of course, when attempting to make difficult ethical decisions, it is always a good idea to solicit others' opinions. Celia Fisher and Denise Fryberg (1994) argue that this should include the opinions of participants, especially in deception research. To assess the potential impact of deception as well as enhance the protection of subjects, they propose that researchers survey prospective participants on ethical issues at the initial stages of planning a study. Subjects could be asked, for example, about the scientific value of the study, the relative advantage of deception and alternative procedures, their psychological reactions to experimental manipulations, and the efficacy of debriefing procedures in alleviating psychological discomfort. In this way, research participants become partners in the process of ethical decision making.

Increasingly, however, the ultimate decision about whether a given study will be conducted rests not with the researcher but with a committee responsible for reviewing research proposals involving the use of human (and animal) subjects. The Department of Health and Human Services (DHHS), as well as most other federal agencies, institutes, and foundations, requires the approval of all research proposals by a human subjects committee (called an **institutional review board**, or **IRB**) as a precondition for the release of its funds. Virtually every college and university in the United States and most tax-exempt private research foundations have IRBs. And, in recent years, these institutions increasingly have mandated the IRB approval of *all* research involving human participants, not just research funded by the federal government (Singer and Levine, 2003).

According to federal regulations (Code of Federal Regulations, 1995), each IRB has at least five members, with varying backgrounds that ensure the adequate review of research proposals. To provide a diversity of expertise, the members must include at least one nonscientist (such as a lawyer, ethicist, or member of the clergy) and at least one member not affiliated with the research institution, as well as persons competent to review specific research activities (such as a social scientist in the case of social research). Investigators submit written documents to the IRB that describe the proposed research and specifically outline how research participants' rights are to be protected, such as provisions for informed consent and measures to ensure confidentiality. IRBs then approve, modify, or disapprove the research according to their interpretation of federal regulations outlined by DHHS.

Besides federal regulations, social scientists are guided by ethical codes for the treatment of research participants developed by professional societies. Box 16.1 provides excerpts from the ethical codes of three such societies: the American Anthropological Association (1998), the American Psychological Association (2002), and the American Sociological Association (1997). These codes cover ethical responsibilities not only to those studied, but also to the profession, the public, and students. In the next section, we examine ethical responsibilities to society.

BOX 16.1

Codes of Professional Ethics

The following statements are excerpts from the professional codes of ethics of three national organizations: the American Anthropological Association (AAA), the American Psychological Association (APA), and the American Sociological Association (ASA). You can read the complete codes of ethics by visiting their Web sites.

Professional Practice in the Conduct of Research

Anthropological researchers bear responsibility for the integrity and reputation of their discipline, of scholarship, and of science. Thus anthropological researchers are subject to the general moral rules of scientific and scholarly conduct: They should not deceive or knowingly misrepresent (i.e., fabricate evidence, falsify, plagiarize), or attempt to prevent reporting of misconduct, or obstruct the scientific/scholarly research of others. (AAA)

Psychologists seek to promote accuracy, honesty, and truthfulness in the science . . . of psychology. In these activities psychologists do not steal, cheat, or engage in fraud, subterfuge, or intentional misrepresentation of fact.

Psychologists do not fabricate data.

If psychologists discover significant errors in their published data, they take reasonable steps to correct such errors in a correction, retraction, erratum, or other appropriate publication means.

Psychologists do not present portions of another's work or data as their own. . . . (APA)

Sociologists adhere to the highest scientific and professional standards and accept responsibility for their work. . . .

In planning and implementing research, sociologists minimize the possibility that results will be misleading.

Sociologists do not fabricate data or falsify results in their publications or presentations.

In presenting their work, sociologists report their findings fully and do not omit relevant data. They report results whether they support or contradict the expected outcomes.

Sociologists take particular care to state all relevant qualifications on the findings and interpretation of their research. Sociologists disclose underlying assumptions, theories, methods, measures, and research designs that might bear upon findings and interpretations of their work. (ASA)

Treatment of Research Participants

Anthropological researchers must do everything in their power to ensure that their research does not harm the safety, dignity, or privacy of the people with whom they work, conduct research, or perform other professional activities.

Anthropological researchers must determine in advance whether their hosts/providers of information wish to remain anonymous or receive recognition, and make every effort to comply with those wishes. Researchers must present to their research participants the possible impacts of the choices, and make clear that despite their best efforts, anonymity may be comprised or recognition fail to materialize.

Anthropological researchers should obtain in advance the informed consent of persons being studied. . . . (AAA)

When psychologists conduct research . . . they obtain the informed consent of the individual or individuals using language that is reasonably understandable to that person or persons except when conducting such activities without consent is mandated by law or governmental regulation or as otherwise provided in this Ethical Code.

Psychologists discuss with persons . . . and organizations with whom they establish a scientific . . . relationship the relevant limits of confidentiality and the foreseeable uses of the information generated through their psychological activities.

Psychologists do not conduct a study involving deception unless they have determined that the use of deceptive techniques is justified by the study's significant prospective scientific, educational, or applied value and that effective nondeceptive alternative procedures are not feasible.

Psychologists do not deceive prospective participants about research that is reasonably expected to cause physical pain or severe emotional distress.

Psychologists explain any deception that is an integral feature of the design and conduct of an experiment to participants as early as is feasible, preferably at the conclusion of their participation, but no later than at the conclusion of the data collection, and permit participants to withdraw their data. (APA)

Sociologists have an obligation to ensure that confidential information is protected.

Informed consent is a basic ethical tenet of scientific research on human populations.

Sociologists take steps to implement protections for the rights and welfare of research participants and other persons affected by the research.

In their research, sociologists do not encourage activities or themselves behave in ways that are health- or life-threatening to research participants or
others. (ASA)

Responsibility to the Public

Anthropological researchers should make the results of their research appropriately
available to sponsors, students, decision makers, and other nonanthropologists. In
doing so, they must be truthful; they are not only responsible for the factual content of their statements but also must consider carefully the social and political implications of the information they disseminate. They must do everything in their
power to insure that such information is well understood, properly contextualized,
and responsibly utilized. They should make clear the empirical bases upon which
their reports stand, be candid about their qualifications and philosophical or political biases, and recognize and make clear the limits of anthropological expertise.
At the same time, they must be alert to possible harm their information may cause
people with whom they work or colleagues. (AAA)

Psychologists are committed to increasing scientific and professional knowledge of behavior and people's understanding of themselves and others and to the
use of such knowledge to improve the condition of individuals, organizations,
and society. . . . They strive to help the public in developing informed judgments
and choices concerning human behavior.

If psychologists learn of misuse or misrepresentation of their work, they take
reasonable steps to correct or minimize the misuse or misrepresentation. (APA)

Sociologists are aware of their professional and scientific responsibility to
the communities and societies in which they live and work. They apply and make
public their knowledge in order to contribute to the public good. When undertaking research, they strive to advance the science of sociology and to serve the
public good. (ASA)

Source: American Anthropological Association (1998), American Psychological Association
(2002), copyright © 2002 by the American Psychological Association, and American Sociological Association (1997). Reproduced by permission. Not for further reproduction.

The Uses of Research: Science and Society

The Issue of Value-Neutrality

Social scientists have become increasingly sensitive not only to the ethical implications of their work for research participants but also to its moral and ideological
implications for the larger society. In the interest of promoting the scientific side of
social research, some people once held that social science should be "value-free."
According to this position (Lundberg, 1961), we can and should make a sharp distinction between the roles of scientist and citizen. Science is nonmoral. The methods of science are designed to eliminate personal preferences and values; and "there
is nothing in scientific work, as such, which dictates to what ends the products of
science shall be used" (Lundberg, 1961:32). Scientists' only imperative is "to say
what they know"—to present relevant findings and theoretical interpretations. In

their capacity as citizens, scientists may take moral positions, campaigning, for example, against nuclear weapons, acid rain, or racial oppression. But if social scientists are to be taken seriously as scientists, they should not confuse this role with that of citizen and should not let their personal values affect their research.

This value-free ideology is no longer tenable for two main reasons. First, it is now clear that values have a substantial influence on the research process. Personal values and political beliefs inevitably affect how scientists select and conceptualize problems and how they interpret their findings. As we noted in chapter 3, many nonscientific factors affect problem selection: personal interests and ideologies, the availability of funding, the climate of opinion in society, research fads and fashions. Similar factors affect the perspective that researchers take and the kinds of questions they ask, which in turn determine the kinds of answers they will find. When IQ tests were first administered on a large scale during World War I, the prevailing belief in both scientific and nonscientific circles was that ethnic groups migrating from southern and eastern Europe were inferior to earlier immigrant groups. Consequently, when the former groups scored consistently lower than Americans of northern and western European ancestry, this was seen not only as proof of existing beliefs about ethnic differences but also as a validation of the tests as measures of innate intelligence. Of course, neither of these interpretations is acceptable today because social scientists, whose perspective led them to focus on the social environment, have demonstrated conclusively the effects of language, culture, and socioeconomic factors on test scores.

The value-free ideology alleges that as scientists, social researchers can remain neutral in accumulating facts about social life that are of equal utility to Democrats and Republicans, liberals and conservatives. The second problem with this position is that while claiming to be value-neutral seemingly protects the scientist's self-interest and autonomy, in effect it places researchers in the service of others' values, such as those of research sponsors or anyone else who chooses to use their findings. Those who advocated complete value neutrality took physical scientists as their model, claiming that these "real" scientists could serve equally well under fascistic or democratic political regimes (Lundberg, 1961). But the moral bankruptcy of this position comes into sharpest focus when we consider such "real" scientists under the Nazi regime. German physicians, apparently operating out of a value-free model of science, "systematically froze human beings in tubs of ice and, in the conduct of sterilization experiments, sent electrical charges through female ovaries" (Gray, 1968). This example is extreme; no one today would argue that value neutrality justifies harming others. More to the point, scientists have come to realize that they bear some responsibility for applications of their research. Physicists who worked on the atomic bomb did not do so out of a value-free ideology, but out of patriotism and a belief that Japan and Germany had to be stopped. However, many of them had second thoughts about helping to build the bomb, especially after they saw its destructive effects.

Both of these problems of maintaining value neutrality are exacerbated for social scientists, who typically study problems that have immediate relevance to people's lives. Indeed, more often than the astronomer or chemist or physicist, the social researcher is drawn to the study of particular phenomena for their social as well as their scientific significance. The nature of the problems selected and the motivation to study them are inherently value laden in social research. Social scientists, therefore, must be aware not only of the influence of personal values and political preferences on their own work, but also of the implications of their findings for constructive or destructive use by others.

Among social scientists, anthropologists probably have been most keenly aware of the impact of values on the research process. They developed the sensitizing concept of "cultural relativity" to guard against the tendency to judge other cultures in relation to one's own cultural world view. **Cultural relativity** is the idea that cultural values—standards of truth, morality, beauty, correct behavior, and so forth—vary widely and must be judged in relation to a given society. In addition, anthropologists also have pointed out the importance of language—that Western scientific language may not be appropriate for "translating" the behavior of another culture and that it is therefore necessary to understand how subjects perceive the world in their own terms.

In a similar vein, sociologist Howard Becker (1967) pointed out that research is always contaminated by personal and political sympathies, but that the way to deal with this is not to forsake the standards of good scientific work and take sides, but rather to consider carefully "whose side we are on." Becker had in mind field researchers, who often study the "underdog"—the deviant, oppressed, or subordinate. In trying to understand reality from the subjects' perspective, field researchers may become sympathetic with that point of view, which usually is contrary to the accepted view of the conventional, economically well-off, or superordinate. However, this does not mean that one should always present all sides or should avoid taking sides. These options are seldom, if ever, possible. What we should do, according to Becker, is admit to whose side we are on, use our theories and techniques impartially—taking precautionary measures designed to guard against bias—and make "clear the limits of what we have studied, marking the boundaries beyond which our findings cannot be safely applied" (Becker, 1967:247). Part of this "sociological disclaimer," Becker believes, should be a statement

> in which we say, for instance, that we have studied the prison through the eyes of the inmates and not through the eyes of the guards or other involved parties. We warn people, thus, that our study tells us only how things look from that vantage point—what kinds of objects guards are in the prisoners' world—and does not attempt to explain why guards do what they do or to absolve the guards of what may seem, from the prisoners' side, morally unacceptable behavior. (p. 247)

Becker does not argue that social scientists should stand pat with their "one-sided" views of reality. In fact, he sees the long-term solution to an enlarged understanding of institutions as the accumulation of many one-sided but different views of reality. This position is analogous to the methodological principle of triangulation introduced in chapter 12. However, whereas before we suggested various triangulation techniques as ways of eliminating methodological biases and errors, here we suggest that these techniques also might be used to shed light on personal values that may be embedded in a particular methodological approach or view of reality.

The Application of Research Findings

For many social scientists, guarding against the intrusion of values in research and carefully noting the limitations of conclusions are not the extent of one's ethical responsibility to society. We also must be aware of and, some believe, provide direction to how others use social science findings. There is little question that the products of social science will be used by others. They already have had and will continue to have a major impact on social policy. To cite one prominent example, the Supreme Court decision of 1954 (*Brown* v. *Board of Education of Topeka*), which declared that separate educational facilities for blacks and whites were inherently unequal, was based in large part on social science findings. The unanimous opinion cited several studies showing that segregation had a detrimental psychological effect on black children.

Since this decision, social scientists have continued to be among the staunchest and most vocal supporters of integration and civil rights, with many testifying in cases involving school desegregation, busing, and affirmative action. These scholars have taken the initiative in offering their expert advice in areas of social policy. For the most part, they have attempted to show how social science findings supported positions that most of their colleagues favored, and their political involvement is noncontroversial. The hard ethical debate concerns how much responsibility researchers bear for applications that are destructive or contrary to prevailing scientific and public sentiment. That is the question that physicists debated after the bomb. Should one try to foresee possible misuses and abuses of scientific findings? If one can foresee misuse or abuse, should the research be conducted at all? And if such research is conducted, how active a role should the researcher play in the dissemination of the findings? Is the researcher responsible for the way information is presented and for assessing the public's reaction?

The most controversial studies in the annals of social science raise just these issues. For example, Project Camelot, a multimillion-dollar research study funded by the U.S. Army, was designed to measure and forecast the causes of revolution and insurgency in underdeveloped areas of the world (Horowitz, 1967). Because of its huge scope, the project drew a large team of respected social scientists. Some, seeing the project as an unprecedented opportunity to do fundamental research on a grand scale, may not have inquired too deeply into the ultimate purpose of the project. Others believed for various reasons that they were, in no sense, "selling out" to the military. They believed that they would have great freedom in handling the project, that there was a possibility of improving conditions in underdeveloped nations, and that they could have an enlightening influence on the military (Horowitz, 1967). What they failed to envision was the "uses to which the United States Army or Central Intelligence Agency could have put the information, such as fostering revolutions against regimes hostile to the United States. They failed to recognize the grave concern those in other countries would have over such potential uses" (Diener and Crandall, 1978:108). Indeed, in July of 1965, seven months after the project began, after its revelation made it a cause célèbre in Chile, Project Camelot was canceled by the Defense Department.

It is precisely this potential (and actual) abuse of findings that led many social scientists to condemn the research of educational psychologist Arthur Jensen. In

1969, Arthur Jensen (1969) published an article in the *Harvard Educational Review* entitled "How Can We Boost IQ and Scholastic Achievement?" In arguing that IQ was determined largely by heredity, Jensen concluded that genetic differences accounted for the higher scores of whites than blacks on IQ tests, and that no amount of compensatory education could undo this difference. Such a view had not been propounded in respectable academic circles for many years prior to Jensen's article; as a result, the article created a furor. Many scholars severely criticized Jensen's conclusions on methodological grounds. But the point here is that Jensen apparently failed to consider the uses to which his article might be put. Although he himself was opposed to segregation and argued that his research suggested the need for educational programs tailored to individual differences (Edson, 1970), others seized upon Jensen's research to oppose integration. Less than a week after a report of his article made headlines in Virginia newspapers, defense attorneys quoted heavily from Jensen's article in a suit in federal district court to integrate schools in two Virginia counties (Brazziel, 1969). Their main argument was that differences in intelligence between whites and blacks were innate; that white teachers could not understand blacks; and that black children should be admitted to white schools strictly on the basis of standardized tests.

Still another, more recent study demonstrates the ethical tightrope that researchers traverse when their research concerns an important policy issue. Lawrence Sherman and Richard Berk (1984) were duly circumspect about the policy implications of their domestic violence experiment, reported in chapters 12 and 13, which showed that arrest reduced the likelihood of a repeat offense. The clearest implication was that police should no longer be reluctant to make arrests in domestic assault cases. But Sherman and Berk also cautioned against routinely requiring arrests in such cases. They noted the unique features of the jurisdiction of the study and concluded that, even if their findings were replicated in other jurisdictions, arrest may work better for certain types of offenders and in certain types of situations. Still, many activists, law professors, and others who favored mandatory arrest laws attacked Sherman and Berk's position on the policy implications of their study (Sherman, 1993). At the same time, others were critical of Sherman in particular because they perceived his dissemination of the study's results to the media as an effort to influence policy toward mandatory arrest (Binder and Meeker, 1993). The latter critics became especially vocal when replication experiments failed to show consistent beneficial effects of arrest. [See Sherman (1993) and Berk (1993) for rejoinders to this criticism.]

What are the ethical implications of such controversies? First, social scientists have an obligation to consider how their findings will be used. Research that is clearly intended to be exploitative, such as management-sponsored research intended to quiet labor unions, should not be done (Diener and Crandall, 1978). Second, given that eventual applications usually are unknown, scientists should disseminate knowledge to the widest possible audience, to increase public knowledge and encourage debate, so that no one group can exploit the knowledge for its own welfare (Diener and Crandall, 1978). Third, when research has obvious and immediate applications, as in applied and evaluation research, scientists have a special obligation to promote actively appropriate uses and to prevent misuses of their findings. (From this standpoint, we believe that Sherman and Berk were ethically responsible.) Finally, scientists can assume responsibility collectively for the application of research through organizations that communicate on their behalf and provide a forum for the discussion of policy-related issues (Diener and Crandall, 1978). One such organization is the Society for the Psychological Study of Social Issues (SPSSI); another is the Society for the Scientific Study of Social Problems (SSSP).

Summary

Ethics is not something one simply accedes to or ignores. Research ethics is a set of moral principles against which the actions of scientists are judged. They are not hard and fast do's and don'ts; rather, they pose dilemmas for researchers, pressing them to weigh the costs and benefits of actions and decisions. Each stage in the research process presents its own problems for the investigator who would do the "right" thing. This interaction of ethics and science repeated throughout the research process should be a part of every social scientist's consciousness.

The three major areas of ethical concern are the ethics of data collection and analysis, the ethics of the treatment of human subjects, and the ethics of responsibility to society. The first set of ethics prescribes that scientists carry out their research and report their findings honestly and accurately; violations of these principles undermine science as a body of knowledge. The second area of ethics consists of a set of rules that are designed to protect the rights of research participants. The third area, which deals with the relationship between societal values and the dissemination and use of scientific findings, generally advises scientists to promote the general welfare.

Ethical considerations regarding the effects of research on participants are a major part of any research design. Presently, it is common practice for institutional review boards to pass judgment on the ethics of proposed research. Before and after institutional approval, researchers are guided in their decisions by federal regulations and professional ethical codes. While the various codes in use differ in language and specificity and while some social scientists take issue with current practice, certain rules of conduct are fairly standard.

1. Foremost, the researcher should not expose participants to substantial risk of physical or psychological harm, unless the benefits of participation exceed the risks and subjects knowingly choose to participate.
2. Participants should be informed that their participation is voluntary and should be told about any aspects of the research that might influence their willingness to participate.
3. If deception is deemed necessary, the researcher must gently and fully inform subjects of the deception as soon after their participation as possible.
4. Researchers should use all possible means to protect the confidentiality of information provided by research participants.

The overall guiding principle is that the potential benefits of research must be weighed against the potential costs.

Researchers also must consider the ethical implications of their research for the larger society. It is now widely recognized that values—personal and societal—are implicated throughout the research process. With this in mind, researchers should be conscious of the ways in which their decisions constitute ethical judgments. They should be aware of the potential uses and abuses of the knowledge they seek, guard against the intrusion of personal values in the conduct of research, and carefully point out the limitations of their research. Finally, where appropriate, they should promote beneficial applications and fight against harmful applications of research findings.

Key Terms

research ethics	*anonymity*
ethics	*confidentiality*
cost–benefit analysis	*institutional review board (IRB)*
informed consent	*cultural relativity*
debriefing	

Review Questions and Problems

1. Why is it so important for scientists to be completely honest and accurate in conducting and reporting their research?

2. In what ways can research participants in social research be harmed?

3. Is it ever considered ethical to use procedures that might expose research participants to physical or mental discomfort, harm, or danger? Explain.

4. What are the limitations of a cost–benefit analysis of proposed research?

5. What safeguards do social scientists use to protect research participants from harm?

6. What are the basic ingredients of informed consent? How did Stanley Milgram violate this principle in his research on obedience to authority?

7. Which research approaches present the most serious problems from the standpoint of informed consent?

8. Why do researchers use deception? What are the arguments against its use in social research?

9. What is the most basic safeguard against the potentially harmful effects of deception? Is it effective? Explain.

10. When is social research likely to invade people's privacy?

11. How is research participants' right to privacy typically secured in (a) surveys and (b) field research?

12. What are institutional review boards (IRBs)? What part do they play in evaluating the ethics of research?

13. What is meant by value-free sociology? Identify the major challenges to this position.

14. Explain Howard Becker's position that social scientists should declare "whose side they are on." What purposes does this declaration serve?

15. What obligations do social scientists have regarding the use of the knowledge they generate?

16. Discuss the ethical problems raised by the following research examples.

    a. (Hypothetical) A criminologist meets a professional fence through an ex-convict he knows. As part of a study, the researcher convinces the fence to talk about his work—why he sticks with this kind of work, what kind of people he deals with, how he meets them, and so forth. To gain the fence's cooperation, the researcher promises not to disclose any personal details that would get the fence in trouble. However, when subpoenaed, he agrees to reveal his informant rather than go to jail. Has the researcher violated an ethical principle in agreeing to talk?

    b. (Hypothetical) A researcher gains access to a clinic serving AIDS patients by responding to a call for volunteers. While working at the clinic, she makes a record of patients' names and later approaches them, identifies herself as a social scientist, fully explains the nature of her research, and asks for their cooperation in her in-depth survey of AIDS victims. Most patients agree, although some react negatively to the request. What aspects of the researcher's strategy are ethically problematic?

    c. Stephen West, Steven Gunn, and Paul Chernicky (1975) tested a proposition from attribution theory in social psychology regarding the way people perceive reprehensible acts. To do this they tempted subjects to participate in a burglary and then tested whether those agreeing to participate differed from those refusing and from subjects not approached with regard to their perceptions (attributions) about this illegal act. One of the experimenters, posing as a local private detective, contacted students and presented an elaborate plan for burglarizing a local advertising firm. In two of the conditions, subjects were told that the burglary was to be committed for a government agency; in another condition, subjects were promised $2000 for their participation. The subject's agreement or refusal to take part in the burglary and his or her reasons for the decision were the major dependent variables. The researchers did not, of course, carry out the crime. What ethical problems does this study pose? Describe how you would debrief subjects in this study.

17

✔

Writing Research Reports

Scientific research is a social activity, even when done by a solitary researcher. Without communication with others, one cannot participate in or contribute to the shared, cumulative body of knowledge that defines each scientific discipline. Much scientific communication takes place orally, but the advancement of science is not based on the oral tradition; it ultimately depends on writing. Through written research reports, books, and articles, researchers communicate with others, who learn about, apply, replicate, and extend their work. The purpose of this chapter is to enhance the development of research writing skills. We will consider not only how to write about research, but also how to locate materials that can inform your research and writing.

The audience and forms of research reports vary. For the professional researcher the audience is most often peers in his or her field; the vehicle is generally an article in a scholarly journal. For the student researcher, the audience may be a class and the vehicle an oral seminar presentation, or a professor and a term paper. The task in each case is to communicate precisely and accurately what questions framed the research, what literature informed it, what the researcher did, what was found, and what conclusions might be drawn. When this is done well, the researcher clearly conveys what he or she has learned, and others are able to make an informed evaluation of the study.

Virtually all research is grounded in an existing literature, and research reports should document the relationship of the present work to this literature. However, many students come to the tasks of doing social research and of writing a research paper with no notion of where to begin. Therefore, before discussing the mechanics of research writing, we will address this issue. Where do research ideas come from? How are topics narrowed and informed by previous research? Where does research actually begin?

The Internet

When you initiate a literature search, you should have at least a general idea of what you want to study. You need not and probably should not have narrowed down the topic at the outset—although eventually it will be essential to do so. To start, it is enough to know the broad area you are interested in—for example, "sex roles," "altruism," "white-collar crime," or "social capital." So, where should you begin your information search? According to a 2001–2002 national survey, most college students nowadays search the Internet: Nearly three-quarters reported that they use the

Internet more than the library, and they tend to search the "Web" prior to going to the library to find information (Jones et al., 2002).

For reasons we will explain shortly, the library is better than the Internet for locating relevant academic resources. Still, the Internet is not a bad place to begin. Resources on the Internet for social research include data archives, government documents, newspaper publications, and library catalogs. Numerous social science datasets are available on the Internet. One of the largest depositories of social science data, the Inter-university Consortium for Political and Social Research (ICPSR), has a Web site. So does the General Social Survey, where you can find data files, codebooks, and other documentation available to download or order. You also can obtain census data from the Web site of the U.S. Census Bureau as well as data from numerous other government agencies. In fact, every major agency of the U.S. government has a Web site that provides extensive information about the agency and its publications. Some newspapers, such as *The New York Times* and *The Los Angeles Times*, also may be browsed on the Internet. Finally, numerous library catalogs, including the Library of Congress, are online.

This short list of resources suggests the scope and utility of the Internet. Some resources are accessible only on the Internet (e.g., remote library catalogs), and others may not be in your library (e.g., government documents). Additional advantages of the Internet are that it contains a vast storehouse of information, which often is more up-to-date than library resources; it can be accessed quickly; and, of course, it offers the convenience of remote access. On the other hand, the fluid and unstructured nature of information on the Web makes it a challenge to use. Search results must be evaluated carefully, since authorship can range from grade-school students to government agencies to political interest groups. The researcher must determine who has authored a document, when it was written, and whether the site at which it was found is reliable.

Every Web site is identified by an address, called a **URL**, which stands for **Uniform Resource Locator**. Researchers may find information on the Internet by either entering the URL for a particular Web site or using available search engines. The problem with using URLs, and the Internet in general, is that Web sites appear and disappear constantly, addresses change without warning, and contents are added and deleted. With this caveat, we provide a very short list of current URLs that may be of use to social scientists:

- http://www.icpsr.umich.edu: Inter-University Consortium for Political and Social Research (ICPSR). Provides information on ICPSR and links to data archives.
- http://www.icpsr.umich.edu/gss: The General Social Survey. Contains data files, codebooks, and other documentation.
- http://www.census.gov: The U.S. Census Bureau. Contains news and information about the census and access to its voluminous statistics.
- http://lcweb.loc.gov: The Library of Congress. Contains catalogs, databases, collections, and links to other Internet resources.

The second way to locate information on the Internet is to use **search engines**. Currently available search engines include Google, Alta Vista, AlltheWeb, and

Look Smart. Search engines provide subject directories and indexes of information on the Internet. The user may choose among listed categories and subcategories from subject directories or introduce his or her own search terms. Using these search utilities is complicated, however. It often is hard to find the right terms to match your research interest, and keyword searches can yield literally thousands of documents, many of which are irrelevant. When we entered the terms " 'social cap-

---

BOX 17.1

The Logic of Keyword Searching

Whether you are searching the Internet, a library catalog, or an index, a few strategies can be employed to make keyword searches more productive. Each strategy applies functions from Boolean logic. Named for Irish mathematician George Boole, Boolean logic is based on three logical operators—AND, OR and NOT. Skilled use of these operators will enable you to narrow or expand searches more effectively and thus get better search results.

- AND searches for records in which two or more terms are present, as in "sociology AND anthropology." A particular phrase, such as "social capital," can be searched using quotation marks to indicate the phrase.
- OR expands a search by entering two or more terms that are often partly or wholly synonymous, such as "colleges OR universities."
- If you were looking for information about colleges but not universities, you could use the NOT operator, as in "colleges NOT universities," to limit the search.
- Mathematical symbols also can be used to perform searches: Putting a minus sign before a term performs the NOT function; putting a plus sign before a term performs the AND function; and typing two terms into a search engine without any operators performs the OR function.
- More complicated searches can be performed by combining operators. For example, you would type "(colleges OR universities) NOT public" to find private colleges and universities only. This will first perform the function in parentheses, finding all sites related to colleges and universities, then perform the NOT function, which limits the results of the search to sites that do not contain the word "public."
- Search terms can be truncated by putting an asterisk at the end of the term. For example, typing "sport*" will yield articles about sportsmanship and sporting as well as sports. Terms created this way are called wildcards.

For a fuller treatment of Boolean keyword searching with additional examples, an excellent guide is "Boolean Searching on the Internet: A Primer of Boolean Logic." *http://library.albany.edu/internet/boolean.html.*

ital' and 'sports',", a relatively narrow topic in social research, on nine different search engines, the number of hits ranged from 74 to over 28,000. Among the Web pages identified were an article about a Northern Kentucky charity, a World Bank site on social capital and crime, and a *Cincinnati Post* editorial and *Pittsburgh Post-Gazette* article on Robert Putnam's book *Bowling Alone*. (For guidelines on the logical relationship among search terms in keyword searching, see Box 17.1.)

The Internet is potentially a very valuable research tool. But it should be approached with caution. For researchers wanting to find scholarly articles in academic journals, where social scientific research is most likely to be found, the place to search is the library. If you do begin online, go first to the online resources at your library. And if you use information sources found on the Internet, a useful reference on citing electronic information is Xia Li and Nancy Crane (1996).

Using the Library for Research

The library has many different resources with which you can begin a literature search; identifying those resources that will most effectively research a topic is an important first step. Some students are in the habit of going first to the online catalog. Others use indexes such as the *Reader's Guide to Periodical Literature* or abstracting services such as *Sociological Abstracts*. Although these are not necessarily bad ways to begin, books in the catalog rarely represent the most current thinking or the most recently published sources of literature on a given topic; the *Reader's Guide* usually provides information only from popular publications (e.g., *Time*, *Newsweek*) as opposed to scholarly ones; and *Sociological Abstracts*, although the best of these options, contains many references to unpublished papers and theses that may prove difficult to obtain.

Many library resources that were traditionally print-based began to be supplemented with CD-ROM versions in the early 1990s. In more recent years, as the Internet has become an integral part of library research and scholarship, these resources have become Web-based. Libraries subscribe to services that provide several databases and the interface with which to search them, in some cases allowing you to search multiple databases at once. Examples of such services include HW Wilson, JSTOR, FirstSearch, Elsevier Science, the ISI Web of Knowledge, and Cambridge Scientific Abstracts. Most databases and library catalogs can now be found online, although a password is often required to access these resources.

It is important to know the limits of online resources, because it is unlikely that all research could be accomplished outside the library. Although computerized databases are more dynamic than print versions, allowing for more complex searches and interconnectivity, they may be deficient in several ways. For example, many databases are not fully retrospective; they rarely cover the lifetime of a journal and usually only go back to the 1970s or 1980s (the *American Journal of Sociology*, the first in the field, was first published in 1895). Conversely, the most recent articles often are not available, depending on whether a database is updated monthly, quarterly, or yearly. And while many subscription services provide downloadable and printable articles, many articles are not available in electronic form.

Indexes and Abstracts

We recommend starting library research with an index or abstract. Many libraries have both print and electronic versions of frequently used indexes. An advantage of print indexes is that they are organized under controlled headings. The headings bring together all material on the subject and typically include cross-references, which can help in identifying related topics. Examining a few pages of headings and citations often can help you to focus your topic. On the other hand, you can only search through print indexes one topic or term at a time, you must search each year separately, and you must write down or photocopy the citations.

The electronic version can facilitate a search in several ways. Electronic indexes are more dynamic than print resources, allowing you to search more than one term at a time within a long span of years, and you can usually get a printed copy of the citations. It is often possible to save, download, and e-mail abstracts, a citation list, and even entire articles. As with conducting Web searches, the value of these resources depends on your ability to identify relevant terms. Keyword searches may yield very large lists of citations, or "hits," many of which may be irrelevant to your interests. The danger is that you may come away from the search with an unfocused citation list and a false belief that you have done sufficient library research.

Libraries generally group their online indexes by subject. If you cannot find them online, your reference librarian can tell you which resources are available and help you with your search. Three frequently used indexes in the social sciences are the *Sociological Abstracts*, *Social Sciences Index*, and the *Social Sciences Citation Index*. Each of these sources is available in both print and electronic form. To illustrate their value as well as their key features, we searched the same terms in each electronic index in December 2003.

Social Sciences Index (SSI). SSI was known as the *Social Sciences and Humanities Index* until 1974 when the social sciences and humanities parted company. It indexes over 500 scholarly, English-language social and behavioral science journals. One of its advantages is that the indexing is done by a human being who determines the subject of each article, in contrast to computer-generated indexes based only on words appearing in titles. In print form, SSI is published four times each year, is indexed by subject and author in one alphabet, and under each subject heading contains a list of articles that have appeared recently. In addition to an electronic database that offers the same indexing as the print SSI, the publisher HW Wilson offers two other databases that augment the indexing, one with abstracts (called *Social Sciences Abstracts*), the other with links to full text (called *Social Sciences Full Text*). The electronic databases go back to 1983; however, abstracts and full-text links are only available from 1995. For the following search, we used *Social Sciences Abstracts*.

Suppose you are interested in "social capital" but have yet to narrow your topic for research purposes. A search of SSI for citations under "social capital" would yield a whopping 2002 entries. Putting "social capital" in quotes narrows the list to 666. Although this is still a relatively large number of hits, searches of other topics may yield hits numbering from zero to the thousands. The number of hits is important information by itself, because it indicates that the subject of social capital is too broad for defining a research problem. However, the citations are in reverse chronological order, which should prove useful since you generally would want to read the most recent literature first and then work backward. Also, by looking at a few of the initial screens, you can quickly see what kinds of research are being done and then choose a term to add to the search in order to narrow the results.

The search can be narrowed down in many different ways. Advanced search functions allow you to search several terms at once. The citation list also can be sorted by date, relevance, or a custom field such as document type or language. If you only want the most recent articles, the searches can be limited by year or by a range of years. The list should indicate if the library owns the journal in which the article appears and whether the article is available for download. It also should indicate whether a journal is "peer-reviewed," that is, subject to the review of fellow academics and researchers, an important distinction between scholarly and popular publications. Articles of interest can then be marked, then saved, printed, and/or sent to an e-mail address.

After reviewing the list of citations, you might decide to focus on social capital and sports. When we typed "social capital" "and sports," we generated 3 hits. Below are the citations, as they appear on the screen.

1. Langbein, L., et. al., <u>Sports in school: source of amity or antipathy?</u>. Social Science Quarterly v. 83 no. 2 (June 2002) p. 436–54 3980e276.jpg
2. Eitle, T.M., et. al., <u>Race, cultural capital, and the educational effects of participation in sports</u>. Sociology of Education v. 75 no. 2 (April 2002) p. 123–46
3. <u>Confronting the Past to Build the Future</u> [Special issue]. Journal of Urban Affairs v. 24 no. 3 (2002) p. 241–368 3980e29e.jpg

SSI provides several links to other information. For example, it allows you to view all publications by each author of the article and all articles in the particular volume of the journal in which the article appeared. You also can review the subject(s) the article is classified under; for the Eitle et al. article, these were "social capital," "race differences," "high school sports," and "high school students/social conditions."

Sociological Abstracts (SA). SA is primarily a collection of abstracts—brief summaries of articles—of journals in sociology and related disciplines. SA abstracts about 1700 journals, both English-language and foreign. The print version arranges entries by subject, with author, title, and subject indexes in each bi-monthly issue and an annual cumulative issue. The electronic version is updated monthly; the abstracts go back to 1974.

Searching SA can complement an SSI research in several ways. In addition to journal articles, SA abstracts books and book chapters, and it contains listings of dissertations and a bibliography of book reviews. Its major advantage, however, is the abstracts, which provide a great deal more information than the mere title of an article as found in SSI. The abstracts are written or adapted from the source journal by SA staff members.

One might begin the search of SA by checking the SA *Sociological Thesaurus*, in which the subject headings, or "descriptors," are organized. A check of the thesaurus indicates that the term "cultural capital," introduced in 1992, has replaced "social capital" as a descriptor. You also can browse, as with the print document, lists of authors or journals, to check a name or see if a certain journal is covered. You can browse by type of publication as well, perhaps searching only journal articles, to narrow the search further. Individual citations list all relevant descriptors, which also can be used to narrow the topic and/or find related terms.

Doing a keyword "exact phrase" search for "cultural capital" produced 1520 hits. Had we found few or no references, we could have broadened the search by clicking on "any of the words." Or, in the event of a large number of hits such as we got, subject cross-references can provide useful leads to narrow the topic by searching some combination of terms. As with SSI, SA provides many options for limiting and sorting searches, as by year or journal article only. Finally, you can choose to view results by citation alone or with the abstract, or by the full record, with or without references (when available).

Looking up "cultural capital and sports" produced 21 hits. Among them were one dissertation, two books, two chapters in books, four papers presented at professional meetings, and a dozen journal articles, including the first two articles identified in the SSI search. This is how the first record, minus the list of references, appears on the screen:

Record 1 of 21
DN: Database Name
       Sociological Abstracts
TI: Title
       Race, Cultural Capital, and the Educational Effects of
       Participation in Sports
AU: Author
       Eitle, Tamela McNulty; Eitle, David J
AF: Affiliation
       Dept Sociology, U Miami, Coral Gables, FL
EA: Email Address
       [mailto:teitle@miami.edu]
SO: Source
       Sociology of Education, 2002, 75, 2, Apr, 123-146
IS: ISSN
       0038-0407
CD: CODEN
       SCYEB7
AB: Abstract
       The relationship between participation in sports & academic
       achievement is examined by exploring both the factors that predict
       participation in different sports & the influence that
       participation in specific sports has on academic achievement.
       While previous studies analyzed the effects of participation in
       sports on achievement, little research has explored whether
       students who have fewer academic resources are more likely to play
       sports. Using data from the National Educational Longitudinal

Survey, this study considers whether cultural capital, household educational resources, family structure, & race are related to participation in football, basketball, or other sports, & whether the effects of participation on several measures of academic achievement differ by race & sport. The findings suggest that cultural disadvantage contributes to an increased interest in & perhaps dependence on basketball & football as a means of social capital. In addition, playing particular sports may not have the achievement returns for either black or white students that some have previously suggested. 6 Tables, 58 References. Adapted from the source document.

LA: Language
English

PY: Publication Year
2002

PT: Publication Type
Journal Article (aja)

CP: Country of Publication
United States

DE: Descriptors
*Sports Participation (D826200); *Academic Achievement (D001500); *Cultural Capital (D190100); *Sports (D825900); *Black White Differences (D084900); *Family Structure (D288600); High School Students (D357900); Males (D484200); United States of America (D890700)

CL: Classification
1432 sociology of education; sociology of education

UD: Update
200212

AN: Accession Number
200211672

In addition to providing abstracts, articles published in key journals since 2001 include cited references, and the number of times the article has been cited, which could be very useful information, as it might indicate the significance of the reported study. If the full text is available online, citations in the text are often hyperlinked. This also is a useful function; for by examining these additional articles and books for further references, you can "reference-hop" your way through the literature. This should enable you quickly to gain a command of the literature and think of how to narrow the topic appropriately. A list of records then can be marked and collected.

Social Sciences Citation Index (SSCI). Another valuable reference source is the SSCI, which covers over 1700 journals in the social sciences and selected articles from approximately 3300 other journals. It is more comprehensive in journal coverage than either SSI or SA, and it contains more recent citations. Its currency is made possible because articles are indexed by computer processing of keywords in the article titles. In print form, the SSCI is published three times a year, with each publication divided into three separate parts: the Permuterm Subject Index (which lists topics based on keywords in the titles of articles), the Corporate and Source Index (which contains complete reference listings from recent articles), and the Citation Index (which lists organizations or authors who have been cited as well as the sources of the citation). The electronic version goes back to 1973, and is updated weekly.

Many of SSCI's functions are similar to those of SSI and SA, though several are distinctive. Perhaps its most valuable feature is the cited reference search, which allows you to discover if a particular author or article has been cited by other scholars in the field. Thus you can find the latest journal articles that have cited articles or books known to you. By identifying other relevant studies in this way, you can trace the line of inquiry forward in time. This search capacity is particularly valuable when you are researching a relatively narrow topic for which only a few relevant sources have been found in other indexes. Cross-checking articles through the various sections of the SSCI can often yield a current and quite comprehensive set of references.

The general search page allows you to search by topic, author, source title, or address and also limit the search by language or document type. Typing "social capital" in the source field produced 1226 hits; narrowing the search by adding "and sports" yielded 7 hits. Five of these were unique to SSCI; the other two were found in both the SSI and SA searches. The Eitle and Eitle article appeared as follows:

Eitle TM, Eitle DJ

Race, cultural capital, and the educational effects of participation in **sports**
SOCIOL EDUC 75 (2): 123–146 APR 2002

Like SA, SSCI provides the complete list of references in this article, a total of 58. But cited references in SSCI date back much further, and the citation list is more dynamic. For example, SSCI has a "related records" function, which searches for records that contain the most shared references with the parent record, sorted from most to least relevant. Among these records is the article by Beckett Broh (2002), which we have cited in several previous chapters. SSCI saves all searches that are run within a session, and these searches can be combined. Search histories also can be saved to be used later by using the "Open History" function. By saving searches you can keep a citation list up-to-date by calling up and repeating the searches after the index has been updated.

Outlining and Preparing to Write

Before you begin to write, you should have a conception of the overall organization of the research report. We recommend writing an outline that organizes the paper in terms of the following sections typically found in articles reporting empirical research.

- An *introduction* that includes a statement of the problem under investigation
- A *literature review* that summarizes and places the problem in the context of related theory and research
- A description of the *design and execution of the study* that indicates how the research was done in sufficient detail to allow a reasonable replication of it

- A presentation of the *data analysis and findings* that identifies the method of analysis and the specific results of the study
- A *discussion* of the findings that offers a broad interpretation of the results

Within each of these major headings you should list subtopics and important points. As you may discover, outlining frequently brings out the recognition of new ideas and the necessity for transition topics that lead from one point to the next. You should ask continually as the outline becomes detailed: How can I move logically from this point to that point? Does the organization make sense? Have I left out anything essential? A report-length paper of fifteen to twenty pages requires an outline of at least one and possibly two or more single-spaced pages.

When the outline is complete, you are ready to begin the actual report. At this point it is critical for you to have a clear grasp of the audience's level of knowledge and sources of interest. This does not mean that you should "talk down" or "write down" to the consumers of your work. But you should keep in mind who is going to read it. For the social science reader familiar with the area of study, the report may include technical language, an abbreviated presentation of previous research, and a detailed presentation of methods and findings. For lay readers it should omit technical terms and should provide a more detailed presentation of the background of the research and a more general presentation of methods and findings. Since it seems more common to err in providing too little information about research methods and using too many technical terms, we recommend that students write for intelligent and educated peers.

Of course, only you the researcher are fully aware of why the study was done; how it is related to previous research; what decisions in design, operations, and measurement were made; and why. And the overriding concern should be to communicate these points as accurately and clearly as possible. As in all good writing, this requires proper grammar, punctuation, and style. The principles of being concise and direct, of avoiding unnecessary jargon, of providing examples to clarify points, and so forth, apply just as strongly to technical as to any other form of writing.

With these points in mind, let us consider in some detail the topical outline suggested above. It is important to note that this is only one of many possible outlines. It applies best to explanatory studies involving experimentation and survey research and least to exploratory and descriptive studies, especially field research. Moreover, considerations of length, subject matter, purpose, and audience may influence the organization and elaboration of this outline in the actual paper. A paper may emphasize measurement, or sampling, or something else depending on the study. No perfect outline exists ready to be adopted for every research paper. The important point is that the outline be functional and that it facilitate the writing.

Major Headings

In the social sciences, numerous professional journals report current research. The journals encountered during a literature review provide models for the research report. These models vary according to the field, but in general contain the following or similar components.

The Abstract

Generally the first portion of a scientific paper is the abstract, a capsule version of the full report written after the report is completed. Abstracts do not describe what takes place in the report (e.g., "after a review of the literature, we formulated and tested the hypothesis that . . ."), but rather summarize the content. They act as a prose table of contents. They typically use the same words as the report and, in fact, may be pieced together by "abstracting" phrases from the finished report.

Abstracts rarely exceed half a page and frequently are limited to 150 to 200 words. The purpose of the abstract is to help potential readers decide if they are sufficiently interested in the topic to read the full report. Keeping this in mind will help in the formulation of a concise abstract. Authors should include only the information they themselves would want to know if they were unfamiliar with the study and wished to assess its utility for themselves. In many ways the title of a report serves the same purpose and may be regarded as an abstract of the abstract.

Introduction

This section sets up the rest of the paper. It should contain a clear statement of the problem and why it is of general interest and importance. General interest and importance may be demonstrated by relating the problem briefly to the theoretical context of the study or by pointing to its social and practical significance. For example, Bruce Straits (1985) opens his article in the *Journal of Marriage and the Family* (see chapter 6) by briefly describing current *theoretical* explanations for low U.S. birthrates, each of which emphasizes a different set of factors influencing childbearing plans. The point of his research, he then explains, is to disentangle and determine the relative importance of these factors among a sample of young college women.

In the introduction to their article on execution publicity and homicide in the *American Sociological Review* (see chapter 11), William Bailey and Ruth Peterson (1989:722) emphasize the social significance of the problem. They begin by noting that "the United States is the only Western nation retaining capital punishment for civil homicide," and "the death penalty is authorized in 37 of 50 states." They go on to say that the "courts have ruled that capital punishment is constitutionally acceptable as long as it is practiced properly." Since the mid-1970s, persons have been sentenced to death in thirty-four states, with over 2000 persons now on death row; and the annual number of executions has increased steadily throughout the 1980s, as 106 persons have been executed. Having established the social significance of the problem, Bailey and Peterson then point out that one empirically testable argument in favor of the death penalty is that it "discourages would-be killers." Their analysis, the introduction concludes, "examines an important deterrence and death penalty issue: the impact of execution publicity on homicides in the United States, 1940–1986."

Literature Review

The literature review must make clear the theoretical context of the problem under investigation and how it has been studied by others. The idea is to cite relevant literature in the process of presenting the underlying theoretical and methodological rationale for the research. This means citing key studies and emphasizing major findings rather than trying to report every study ever done on the problem or providing unnecessary detail.

In studies designed to test specific hypotheses, the aim of this section should be to show, if possible, how the hypotheses derive from theory or previous research. When this is not possible—for example, because the hypothesis is based on everyday observations and experiences—one should still show the relevance of the study to previous research and theory, if only to show how it contradicts existing evidence or fills a gap in scientific knowledge. Indeed, even when there are no clearly formulated hypotheses or the research is basically descriptive or exploratory, it is still appropriate to place the research in some theoretical context.

Finally, it is a good idea, especially for lengthy literature reviews, to end this section with (1) a concise restatement of hypotheses, (2) a presentation of the theoretical model in a figure, such as an arrow diagram, or (3) a brief overview of the study.

Methods

In this section you should state clearly and accurately how the study was done, providing enough information to permit replication by others. The following subtopics may help you to accomplish this objective.

Design. First you must tell what type of study you have done: experiment, survey, field research, or available-data analysis. The particular approach determines the primary design and procedural issues that must be addressed: (1) In the case of an experiment, the key issues will include the type of experimental design and the procedures of its implementation; (2) in a survey, the type of survey instrument, its length, and the sampling design; (3) in field research, the nature of the setting(s) and the researcher's relationship to informants; (4) in research using available data, the sources of data and their completeness.

Subjects. This section should make clear who participated in the study, how many cases were sampled, how they were selected, and whom or what they represent. It is necessary to discuss sampling procedures as well as the generalizability of the sample data.

Measurement. Here operational definitions are described. No matter what approach was used, you should clarify the way in which your observations were translated into variables and concepts. In an experiment, this means specifying the procedures for manipulating the independent variable and measuring the dependent variable. In a survey, this should include the specific questions that were asked as measures of each variable in the theoretical model. In field research, this means noting the kinds of observations that were made and, if relevant, other sources of information such as documents and in-depth interviewing. Longer reports may contain appendixes with some of these materials, such as copies of the complete questionnaire or transcripts of selected interviews.

Procedures. This section, which may be a part of the description of sampling and measurement, presents a summary of the various steps in the conduct of the research. This is especially important for an experiment or in field research. Experiments should include a step-by-step account of the study from the subject's point of view. Field researchers should give a chronological account of the research, telling how they selected and gained entry into the setting, how they met and developed relationships with informants, and how long they were in the setting. In fact, the research report of a field researcher often follows a narrative, from either the researcher's or informant's point of view, which begins with a discussion of these methodological issues.

Findings

The heart of the research paper is the findings section, toward which the entire report should be aimed. This is where the problems, questions, or hypotheses that framed the research are answered. Before presenting the main results, however, the researcher should first provide any evidence on reliability and validity that was not presented in the methods section. For example, it is at the beginning of the results section that one ordinarily finds the outcome of manipulation checks, survey response rates, and tests for measurement reliability and validity. Once this is done, the researcher presenting a quantitative analysis should describe what sort of statistical analyses were performed on the data. This description should be very specific with regard to the kind of analysis (e.g., "three-way analysis of variance," "paired *t*-tests," "ordinary least squares regression"), and it may include (which we recommend for the student researcher) references to descriptions of the statistical techniques or to the computer software package used to carry out the analysis.

In quantitative analyses, the researcher often constructs tables, charts, and graphs to facilitate the presentation of findings. Here we have several recommendations. First, use tables and figures sparingly, to summarize large amounts of information. During the course of research, investigators usually generate many more tables than they can possibly present in the research report. These interim tables guide the researcher in determining the course of the analysis, but more often than not they contain single facts that can be reported in the text of the report. Second, organize this section around the major hypotheses or theoretical questions and/or major findings. If there is a single main hypothesis, then a single table may suffice to summarize the findings. Third, discuss the data in terms of what they show about the research problem or hypothesis. Do not let the data speak for themselves, and do not discuss the data merely in terms of the variables or the numbers in a table. In other words, subordinate the data to your argument and use the data and tables to help tell a story.

This last point also applies to "qualitative" research. The data in such studies are usually not numbers but quotations, concrete observations, and historical events. Still, the data should be used in the same way: organized around the thesis of the report and presented to support arguments.

Discussion

This section may begin or end with a brief summary. The summary serves as a sort of "caboose abstract," reviewing the highlights of the report. This is particularly useful in cases in which the paper is long or necessarily complex. One should try not to be too repetitious here; in other words, do not lift passages from earlier parts of the paper, but rather restate the basic problem and basic findings.

The discussion section, however, generally has more lofty goals. First, it provides a place to point out the shortcomings of the research. For example, the data may be drawn from populations or under conditions that limit the generalizability of the findings. Honesty regarding such limitations is important in preventing readers from making more from the research than is warranted. Second, it provides a chance to point out inconsistencies, account for anomalies, and suggest improvements in the research design. Finally, the discussion section allows the writer an opportunity to place the whole project into broader perspective, to mention the theoretical and practical implications of the study, and to discuss possible future work.

References

Finally, some sort of bibliography must be included. Although the usual practice is to list only works cited in the body of the report, uncited works that were important in the development of the study may also be included. The format of the references varies slightly from one discipline to another. This book uses the University of Chicago Press's *A Manual of Style*.

Other Considerations

The Writing–Reading Interface

All good writers are careful to structure their material in accordance with readership patterns, and research writing is no different. Thus the "tell them what you are going to say–say it–tell them what you said" structure is a good one for readers who are interested in skimming an article quickly to assess its relevance to their interests. Writing done for other purposes may be structured differently. For example, newspaper readers normally peruse articles in a top-downward fashion (headline, first paragraph, etc.) and often do not complete every article they start because of limitations of interest or time. Journalists, therefore, like to pack as much information as possible into the headline. They often like to tell the whole story in the first paragraph (Who? What? Where? When? Why?), then elaborate and provide details in subsequent paragraphs. If you think about the way you read newspaper articles, you may recognize the truth of the observation. This kind of reading has a purpose, but the purpose differs from that of research reading and, as a consequence, so does the writing.

Many busy readers of research reports usually follow a different pattern. They begin at the title and, if they are interested, they study the abstract. Only if the abstract is relevant is the busy reader likely to go on. You may also recognize this pattern of reading from your own experiences developing research bibliographies. If the abstract is deemed immediately relevant, you may hurry through the "introduction," skim through the "methods" for keys to the author's perspective, then dwell on the "findings" and their implications. It should be noted, however, that while such skimming and racing may be useful when you are trying to assess the relevance of an article for your research interests, it is not the best practice when you really are trying to digest a piece of research.

Revisions

Many students believe that the first draft is the only draft. Most professional writers, on the other hand, assume that the first draft will be one in a series of drafts designed to sharpen and improve the final product. The advent of word-processing computers has greatly facilitated the production of subsequent drafts. The purpose of a first draft is to transfer ideas, thoughts, and facts from the mind of the writer into some material form that can be reflected on by the author. We cannot put a number on how many subsequent drafts should be written; however, it is hard to imagine a polished report that is not the product of numerous drafts. Good writing requires attention to detail; it means writing as if every word and sentence should be taken seriously. And that requires extensive rewriting.

For many people the best time to revise a paper is after taking some time away from the work. Writers who wait until the last few hours or days to write a paper will not produce a good paper. Authors' judgments about the quality of their work may vary directly with the recency of the effort. The passage of time tends to bring perspective and also a renewed energy to tackle a job that perhaps did not seem necessary earlier. Much revision, of course, can be of the "cut and paste" variety. This job usually involves the revision of what is unclear, the deletion of what is extraneous, and the addition of what had been omitted. Again, word-processing technology makes this sort of revision relatively painless.

Finally, at some point in the successive drafting of a report, a "working" draft should be shown to others who can provide critical feedback. We realize that much of the writing students do, with its rigid time constraints, does not allow for this. But there is no better way of judging the clarity of your writing than asking others if they understand what you are saying. Professionals know this and often develop a circle of friends who will read their work. We encourage students to do the same.

Length

Probably the most frequently asked question regarding student papers is, How long should they be? The most appropriate but usually unsatisfying answer is, As long as they need to be. Many students make the mistake of underestimating the length that thoroughness demands, often through one or more serious omissions. On the other hand, some students make the mistake of thinking that the longer a report is, the better it is. The techniques of "padding" a paper through overuse of citations, excessive use of full quotations when paraphrasing would be preferable, and reliance on vocabulary and jargon intended to impress the audience are mistakes that experienced readers usually see through. Jeffrey Katzer, Kenneth Cook, and Wayne Crouch (1991) refer to these smoke screens as "paraphernalia of pedantry" and conclude that they are more likely to be distracting than to facilitate communication. And it is communication that is the essence of the research process.

Summary

Doing social research demands that one not only be a careful producer of research but also clearly and accurately communicate the products of the research to others. Useful models for such communication can be found in professional social science journals; indeed, library searches of the professional literature is where most research ideas come from and where research writing essentially begins.

Most bibliographic searches should begin with an index or abstract. By providing subject headings to browse, print indexes may help to narrow a topic and focus searches on electronic indexes. Three frequently used indexes, each available in print and electronic form, are *Social Sciences Index* (SSI), *Sociological Abstracts* (SA), and *Social Sciences Citation Index* (SSCI). SSI indexes articles from core journals in the social sciences; SA provides abstracts of articles *and* books; and SSCI provides lists of bibliographies in indexed articles and lists of citations to published articles and books. Some of the most up-to-date information can be found on the Internet. The Internet may provide access to much information unavailable in the local library; however, its instability and sheer volume of information make bibliographic searches problematic.

Most research reports contain the following components: (1) an abstract or short summary placed at the beginning of the paper; (2) an introduction to the problem pointing out its theoretical, practical, and/or social significance; (3) a literature review relating the research problem to previous theory and research; (4) a methods section outlining precisely how the research was done, including the overall approach and design and methods of sampling and measurement; (5) a findings section; (6) a discussion of the limitations and anomalies as well as the broader theoretical and practical implications of the research; and (7) a list of references cited in the report.

Writing the research report is facilitated greatly by preparing an outline, keeping in mind the intended audience and how they will read the report, and writing several drafts as well as soliciting others' critical comments on early drafts.

Key Terms

Uniform Resource Locator (URL)   *search engine*

Review Questions and Problems

1. Locate the *Social Sciences Index* in your library and, using the most recent issue, find one reference held by the library for each of the following topics: (a) aged or aging, (b) homeless, (c) homicide, and (d) race differences. Locate each reference in the library and write down the library call number of the article or book as well as complete bibliographic information.

2. If possible, conduct a computerized search using the electronic version of SSI. (a) Search for one of the topics in question 1, and record the number of references indexed. (b) Combine two of the topics in question 1, again search and record the number of references, and then record or print the first entry.

3. Repeat problem 1 using *Sociological Abstracts*.

4. Look up the list of citations to an article published before 1995 in the Citation Index of *Social Sciences Citation Index*. How many times has the article been cited in the most recent Cumulative SSCI?

5. Search the Internet for reference materials on one of the topics in problem 1.

6. Read through one of the articles found in problem 1 and write down the major topical headings. How do these headings differ from those outlined in this chapter?

GLOSSARY

acquiescence response set a response bias whereby respondents tend to answer in the direction of agreement, regardless of item content. (chapter 9)

active membership role a type of participant role in field research in which the researcher assumes a functional role in the group or organization he or she is studying; *see also* complete and peripheral membership roles. (chapter 10)

aggregate data information about one set of units that is statistically combined to describe a larger social unit. For example, information about students (gender, race, college board scores, etc.) might be aggregated to describe characteristics of their colleges (sex ratio, ethnic composition, average college board score, etc.). (chapter 3)

analytical history the use of historical events and evidence to develop a generalized understanding of the social world; *see also* descriptive history. (chapter 11)

anonymity an ethical safeguard against invasion of privacy; the condition wherein researchers are unable to identify data with particular research participants. (chapter 16)

antecedent variable a variable causally antecedent to others in a theoretical model. Two variables may be spuriously associated because both are affected by an antecedent variable. (chapters 3, 14)

applied social research research undertaken for the explicit purpose of providing information to solve an existing social problem; *see also* basic social research. (chapter 13)

association the strength of the observed relationship between two variables. (chapter 3)

attrition a threat to internal validity; the loss of subjects during the course of a study (also called mortality); *see also* differential attrition. (chapter 7)

available data existing sources of information that were not produced directly by the social researcher who uses them; this includes public and private documents, products of the mass media, physical evidence, and data archives; the use of available data is one of the four major approaches to social research. (chapters 1, 11, 12)

basic social research research undertaken to advance a discipline's theoretical understanding, which may or may not address an existing social problem; *see also* applied social research. (chapter 13)

behavioral coding a field pretest technique in which live or taped interviewer-respondent interactions are systematically coded to identify the frequency of problematic respondent and interviewer behaviors on each question. (chapter 9)

between-subject designs true experimental designs in which each subject is assigned to one of two or more conditions, such as treatment and control; *see also* within-subject designs. (chapter 7)

bivariate analysis statistical analysis of the relationship between two variables. (chapter 14)

causal relationship a theoretical notion that change in one variable forces, produces, or brings about a change in another. Although the concept of "cause" is unobservable and philosophically controversial, causal theorizing is commonly and productively used in scientific investigations. (chapters 2, 3)

cell frequency the number of cases in a cell of a cross-tabulation table. (chapter 14)

chi-square test for independence a test of statistical significance used to assess the likelihood that an observed bivariate relationship differs significantly from that which easily could have occurred by chance. (chapter 14)

closed-ended questions survey questions that require respondents to choose responses from those provided; also called "fixed-choice questions." (chapter 9)

cluster sampling a probability sampling procedure in which the population is broken down into natural groupings or areas, called clusters, and a random sample of clusters is drawn. Cluster sampling may occur in a series of stages, moving from larger to smaller clusters, with individual cases sampled at the last stage; *see* multistage cluster sampling. (chapter 5)

codebook a "dictionary" for a survey study, which lists the answers or categories that correspond to each numerical code, the location of each variable in the data file, and coding and decision rules. (chapter 14)

coding (1) the sorting of raw data, such as field observations or responses to open-ended questions, into categories; (2) for computer analysis, coding consists of assigning numbers or symbols to variable categories (chapters 9, 10, 14)

cognitive interviewing verbal reports from respondents, collected during ("thinkalouds") or after (follow-up probes, paraphrasing requests) responding to pretest questions, and used to diagnose question wording, ordering, and formatting problems. (chapter 9)

cohort persons (or other units) who experience the same significant life event (e.g., birth, marriage, high school graduation) within a specified period of time; *see* cohort study. (chapter 8)

cohort study a longitudinal research design that attempts to assess the relative effects of age (life-course changes), period (current history), and cohort ("generations" who share the same past history) on attitudes and behavior. (chapter 8)

collinear association a perfect linear relationship between two variables. (chapter 15)

complete membership role a type of participant role in field research in which the researcher assumes full-member status in the organization or group he or she is studying; *see also* active and peripheral membership roles. (chapter 10)

computer-assisted personal interviewing (CAPI) a software program, usually on a portable computer, that aids interviewers by providing appropriate instructions, question wording, and data-entry supervision. (chapter 8)

computer-assisted self-interviewing (CASI) an electronic survey in which a questionnaire is transmitted on a computer disk mailed to the respondent or on a laptop computer provided by the researcher. (chapter 8)

computer-assisted telephone interviewing (CATI) a set of computerized tools that aid telephone interviewers and supervisors by automating various data collection tasks. (chapter 8)

concept abstractions communicated by words or other signs that refer to common properties among phenomena (e.g., the concept "extroversion" represents a broad range of specific behaviors); concepts developed for scientific purposes are sometimes called "constructs." (chapters 2, 4)

conceptualization the development and clarification of concepts. (chapter 4)

conditional a statement (the antecedent) introduced by an "if" followed by a second statement (the consequent) preceded by a "then." For example, "If this is a conditional proposition, then it should have an antecedent and a consequent." (chapter 3)

confidence interval a range (interval) within which a population value is estimated to lie at a specific level of confidence; used to qualify sample estimates to take into account sampling error. For example, a researcher might report that she is 99 percent confident (confidence level) that the mean personal income for a population lies within plus or minus $359 of the sample mean of $18,325 (i.e., confidence interval of $18,684–$17,966). (chapter 5)

confidentiality an ethical safeguard against invasion of privacy; the assumption that all data on research participants is given to the researcher in strict confidence, not to be divulged to anyone without the participants' permission. (chapter 16)

consistency checking a data-cleaning procedure involving checking for unreasonable patterns of responses, such as a 12-year-old who voted in the last presidential election. (chapter 14)

construct validation measurement validation based on an accumulation of research evidence, which may include evidence that the measure in question (1) relates to other variables in a theoretically expected manner, (2) correlates highly with other measures of the same concept (convergent validity), (3) correlates not too highly with measures of other concepts (discriminant validity), and (4) varies among groups known to differ on the characteristic being measured. (chapter 4)

content analysis a set of methods for analyzing the symbolic content of communications, which typically entails (1) defining a set of content categories, (2) sampling elements of the communication that are described by the categories, (3) quantifying the categories such as by counting their frequency of occurrence, and (4) relating category frequencies to one another or to other variables. (chapter 11)

content validity a subjective judgment of whether a measure adequately represents all facets (the domain) of a concept. (chapter 4)

contextual design a survey design in which information about respondents and their social environments (contexts) is collected for the purpose of studying the separate and joint effects on individuals of personal characteristics and of social contexts. (chapter 8)

context units larger units in which the recording units of content analysis are embedded, which provide the "context" necessary to classify the recording units. For example, the meaning of words (recording units) might be determined from the sentences (context units) in which they appear. (chapter 11)

contingency question a survey question intended for a subset of the respondents, addressing only those persons for whom the question is relevant; *see also* filter question. (chapter 9)

control a procedure (or procedures) that eliminates, as far as possible, unwanted variation, such as sources of bias and error that may distort study results. A common approach is to control potentially confounding variables by holding them constant or preventing them from varying. (chapters 2, 3)

control variable a variable that is held constant during the course of observation or statistical analysis. (chapter 3)

convenience sampling a form of nonprobability sampling in which the researcher simply selects cases that are conveniently available; also called "haphazard," "fortuitous," and "accidental" sampling. (chapter 5)

convergent validity the extent to which independent measures of the same concept correlate with each other; the higher the correlation, the greater the convergent validity. (chapter 4)

correlation coefficient a measure of association, symbolized as r (Pearson's), that describes the direction and strength of a linear relationship between two variables measured at the interval or ratio level; the square of Pearson's r represents the proportion of variance in one variable that may be predicted from the other using linear regression. (chapters 3, 14).

cost–benefit analysis (1) in evaluation research, an assessment of the economic efficiency of a program in terms of its monetary costs and benefits; *see also* cost-effectiveness analysis; (2) an examination of the potential costs (e.g., harm to subjects) and benefits (e.g., knowledge gained, beneficial applications) of a study as a way of assessing the ethics of the study. (chapters 13, 16)

cost-effectiveness analysis in evaluation research, an assessment of the efficiency of a program by measuring intervention outcomes in terms of program costs; *see also* cost–benefit analysis. (chapter 13)

counterbalancing a technique used to control for order effects in within-subject experimental designs; the sequence of treatment and control conditions are reversed, so that different groups of subjects experience each sequence. (chapter 7)

cover letter in a survey, a letter designed to obtain cooperation from persons in the sample. The cover letter is sent before the interviewer calls on the respondent, or, in mail surveys, it accompanies the questionnaire. (chapter 8)

cover story an introduction provided to experimental subjects to obtain their cooperation while disguising the research hypothesis. (chapter 6)

coverage error in sampling, the error that occurs when the sampling frame does not match the intended target population. (chapters 5, 8)

covert research a type of field research in which the investigator conducts research in private settings while concealing his or her identity as a researcher. (chapter 10)

criterion-related validation a method of assessing the validity of a measure in terms of the degree to which it correlates with an objective current or future criterion. (chapter 4)

cross-national surveys studies in which equivalent-sample surveys are conducted in different countries; also called "comparative studies." (chapter 8)

cross-sectional design the most common survey design, in which data on a cross section of respondents chosen to represent a larger population of interest are gathered at essentially one point in time; *see also* longitudinal design. (chapters 8, 13)

cultural relativity the principle that the cultural standards of a given society must be examined on their own terms and that researchers should be nonjudgmental regarding the society or group that is being studied. (chapter 16)

data archives repositories of precollected survey or ethnographic data collected by various agencies and researchers that are accessible to the public. (chapter 11)

data cleaning the detection and correction of errors that occur during data collection, coding, and data entry. (chapter 14)

data matrix the form of a computer data file, with rows as cases and columns as variables; each cell represents the value of a particular variable (column) for a particular case (row). (chapter 14)

data modification the process of transforming raw data for analysis, such as by collapsing the categories of a variable or imputing values for missing cases. (chapter 14)

data processing the preparation of data for analysis; in survey research it entails five steps: coding, editing, entry, cleaning, and modification. (chapter 14)

debriefing a session at the end of an experiment in which the experimenter discusses with the subject what has taken place, the real purpose of the study, the need for confidentiality, the subject's responses and feelings, and so on. (chapters 6, 16)

deductive reasoning a process of reasoning in which the conclusion necessarily follows if the evidence is true. (chapter 2)

demand characteristics cues in an experiment that convey to subjects the experimenter's hypothesis or what is expected of them. (chapter 6)

dependent variable a variable that the researcher tries to explain or predict; the presumed effect of one or more independent variables. (chapter 3)

descriptive history type of historical analysis that emphasizes the complete and accurate description of past events; *see also* analytical history. (chapter 11)

descriptive research studies undertaken to collect facts about a specified population or sample, for example, a public opinion poll. (chapters 3, 8)

descriptive statistics procedures for organizing and summarizing data. (chapter 14)

differential attrition a threat to internal validity; the existence of varying dropout rates among conditions of an experiment, which tends to make the conditions nonequivalent in composition; also called "differential mortality." (chapter 7)

direct effects when one variable is hypothesized to affect another directly in a causal model; there may also be "indirect effects" in which the impact of one variable on another is transmitted through one or a series of causally intervening variables. The total impact of one variable on another is the sum of the direct and indirect effects. (chapter 15)

direct questions survey questions in which there is a direct, clear link between what is asked and what the researcher wants to know; *see also* indirect questions. (chapter 9)

direction of influence for a presumed asymmetric causal relationship, the identification of which variable is the cause (independent) and which the effect (dependent). (chapter 3)

discriminant validity the extent to which a measure of a particular concept differentiates that concept from other concepts from which it is intended to differ. Discriminant validity is lacking if measures of supposedly different concepts correlate too highly. (chapter 4)

disproportionate stratified sampling a sampling procedure in which strata are sampled disproportionately to population composition. For example, a study of religious leaders might sample female pastors at a much higher rate than male pastors to ensure a sufficient number of the former for analysis purposes. (chapter 5)

distorter variable in elaboration analysis, a test variable that reverses the direction of the original bivariate relationship, as from a positive zero-order association to a negative association in the partial tables. (chapter 15)

double-barreled question a survey question in which two separate ideas are erroneously presented together in one question. (chapter 9)

double-blind technique a method of preventing both subjects and research personnel from knowing the subjects' treatment conditions during the running of an experiment. (chapter 6)

dummy variable a data-modification procedure that involves recoding the categories of nominal- or ordinal-scale variables for the purpose of regression or other numerical analysis. For example, gender categories may be represented by a single dummy variable having a value of 1 if the respondent is female and a value of 0 if male. (chapters 14, 15)

ecological fallacy erroneous use of information pertaining to an aggregate (e.g., organizations) to draw inferences about the units of analysis that comprise the aggregate (e.g., individual members of organizations). (chapter 3)

editing a quality control process designed to ensure that survey or other data to be read into the computer are as complete, error free, and readable as possible. (chapter 14)

effect assessment the most basic type of evaluation research, undertaken to assess the impact of a social program on program participants; also called summative or outcome evaluation; *see also* efficiency assessment. (chapter 13)

efficiency assessment a type of evaluation research in which a program's outcomes are weighed against its costs; may take the form of cost–benefit or cost-effectiveness analysis; *see also* effect assessment. (chapter 13)

elaboration a traditional technique for the multivariate analysis of contingency tables that "elaborates" the relationship between two variables by introducing a third (and sometimes additional) variable and testing the resultant causal models. (chapter 15)

empirical/empiricism a way of knowing or understanding the world that relies directly or indirectly on what we experience thorough our senses—sight, hearing, taste, smell, and touch; admissible evidence in science is limited to empirical phenomena. (chapter 2)

empirical generalization a generalization or hypothesis inductively derived from observations. (chapter 2)

environmental impact study a study undertaken, usually as required by law, to assess the impact of a public works project on the social and physical environment; *see also* social impact assessment. (chapter 13)

ethics guidelines or standards for moral conduct. In research, ethical codes prescribe principles for upholding the values of science and for resolving conflicts between scientific ideals and societal values. (chapter 16)

ethnosurvey a multiple-methods research design that blends ethnographic fieldwork with survey sampling methods. (chapter 12)

evaluation apprehension subjects' anxiety about being evaluated by the experimenter, typically a psychologist, which may make them overly concerned with producing "normal" behavior. (chapter 6)

evaluation research an area of social science research, often linked to policymaking, concerned with analyzing social policies, programs, and interventions. (chapter 13)

exhaustive the measurement requirement that a measure includes all possible values or attributes of a variable, so that every case can be classified. (chapter 4)

experiment a major approach to social research that entails the manipulation of the independent variable and researcher control over the events to which research participants are exposed. (chapters 1, 6, 12)

experimental realism when subjects become involved in or are affected by the procedures of an experiment rather than remaining detached. (chapter 6)

experimenter expectancy effect effect on subject's behavior due to the experimenter's expectations about how the experiment will turn out. (chapter 6)

explanation (1) in science, abstract statements that relate changes in one class of events to changes in another; (2) in elaboration analysis, an outcome in which, upon controlling for an antecedent test variable, the original bivariate relationship reduces to zero or near zero in each partial table. (chapters 2, 15)

explanatory research studies that investigate relationships between two or more variables, attempting to explain them in cause-and-effect terms. (chapters 3, 8)

explanatory variables those variables that are the focus of the research—the independent and dependent variables in a hypothesized relationship; *see also* extraneous variables. (chapter 3)

exploratory research studies undertaken to explore a phenomenon or topic about which very little is known. (chapter 3)

external validity the extent to which experimental findings are generalizable to other settings, subject populations, and time periods. (chapter 6, 14)

extraneous variables all variables other than the independent and dependent variables in a hypothesized relationship; *see also* explanatory variables. (chapter 3)

face validity a personal judgment that an operational definition appears, on the face of it, to measure the concept it is intended to measure. (chapter 4)

face-to-face interview a type of interview in which the interviewer interacts face-to-face with the respondent; also called in-person interview; *see also* telephone interview. (chapters 8, 12)

factorial experimental designs an extension of the basic experimental design in which two or more independent variables (factors) are manipulated; information is provided about the separate (main) effects and joint (interaction) effects of the independent variables. (chapter 7)

field experiment a "true" experimental design conducted in a natural setting. (chapter 6)

field interviewing interviewing in field research; the researcher may question others through either casual conversation or formal, in-depth interviews; *see also* in-depth interviews. (chapter 10)

field jottings short phrases, quotes, key words, and the like recorded by field researchers while in the field; *see also* field notes. (chapter 10)

field notes thorough account of field observations recorded by field researchers as soon after each period of observation as possible, preferably at the end of each day. (chapter 10)

field pretesting the evaluation of the survey instrument and personnel under realistic field conditions with respondents similar to those for whom the survey is designed. (chapter 9)

field research a major approach to social research that involves directly observing and often interacting with others, usually for an extended period, in a natural setting. (chapters 1, 10, 12)

filter question a type of survey question, the responses to which determine which subjects are to answer which of subsequent contingency questions. (chapter 9)

first-order relationship a relationship between two variables in which a third variable is controlled; *see also* zero-order relationship. (chapter 15)

fixed-effects model a statistical framework that assumes, in meta-analysis, that between-study variability arises from sampling and other chance processes; *see also* random-effects model. (chapter 12)

focus group unstructured discussions among a small group of participants, focused on a general topic and guided by a skilled interviewer. (chapter 9)

formative evaluation research undertaken in the developmental stages of a social program to guide program design; *see* evaluation research. (chapter 13)

frequency distribution a tabulation of the number of cases falling into each category of a variable. (chapter 14)

frequency polygon the graphic presentation of an interval/ratio-scale variable in which the X-axis consists of the values of the variable and the Y-axis consists of the number of cases (or frequency); a line connects the frequency for each value of the variable; in a percentage polygon, the Y-axis consists of percentages. (chapter 14)

funnel sequence a sequence of survey questions that progresses from a very general question to gradually more specific questions. (chapter 9)

gatekeepers authorities whose permission is needed to conduct research in their setting. (chapter 10)

going native a condition in field research that occurs when a participant observer loses sight of the observer role and identifies wholly with the group or culture that he or she is studying. (chapter 10)

grounded theory theory developed inductively from firsthand observations, in contrast to theories generated by other means. (chapter 10)

Guttman scaling a scaling procedure that attempts to ensure a unidimensional scale by selecting a set of items that, when *ordered* in terms of their "strength," will *order* individuals or other relevant units on the concept being measured. (chapter 12)

heterogeneity the degree of dissimilarity among cases with respect to a particular characteristic. For example, the gender composition of groups might vary from 100 percent female (maximum homogeneity) to 50 percent female (maximum heterogeneity). (chapter 5)

history a threat to internal validity; events in the subjects' environment, other than the intended experimental manipulation, that occur during the course of an experiment and that may affect the outcome. (chapter 7)

hypothesis an expected but unconfirmed relationship among two or more variables. (chapters 2, 3)

imputation a procedure for handling missing data in which missing values are imputed from other information, such as the sample mean or known values of other variables. (chapter 14)

independent variable a presumed cause of a dependent variable. (chapter 3)

in-depth interviews intensive interviews that in field research are much less structured than in survey research and are much longer, often requiring several sessions. (chapter 10)

index a composite measure of a concept constructed by adding or averaging the scores of separate indicators; differs from a scale, which uses less arbitrary procedures for combining indicators. (chapters 4, 12)

indicator an empirical manifestation of a concept. For example, the indicator "years of schooling" often represents the concept "education." (chapter 4)

indirect effects in a causal model, when one variable is hypothesized to affect another indirectly through one or a series of intervening variables; *see also* direct effects. (chapter 15)

indirect questions questions in which the relationship between the researcher's objectives and the questions asked is not obvious; a technique usually based on the psychological concept of projection; *see also* direct questions. (chapter 9)

inductive reasoning a reasoning process in which the conclusion goes beyond the evidence; unlike in a deductive argument, the evidence may be true and the conclusion false. (chapter 2)

inferential statistics procedures for determining the extent to which one may generalize beyond the data at hand. (chapter 14)

informant a person from whom field researchers acquire information in the field. (chapter 10)

informed consent an ethical practice of providing research participants with enough information about a study, especially its potential risks, to enable them to make an informed decision about whether to participate. (chapter 16)

institutional review board (IRB) a committee formed at nearly all research institutions (e.g., universities) that is responsible for reviewing research proposals in order to assess provisions for the ethical treatment of human (and animal) subjects; IRB approval is required for federally funded research. (chapter 16)

instrumentation a threat to internal validity; unwanted changes in characteristics of the measuring instrument or measurement procedure. (chapter 7)

interaction effect an outcome in which the effect of one independent variable on the dependent variable varies according to the value or level of another independent variable. That is, the effects of the variables together differ from the effects of either alone. (chapter 7)

intercoder reliability an "equivalence" method for assessing reliability that examines the extent to which different interviewers, observers, or coders get equivalent results using the same instrument or measure. (chapter 4)

internal-consistency reliability an "equivalence" method of assessing reliability in which a statistical procedure is used to examine the consistency of "scores" across all the items constituting a measure. (chapter 4)

internal validity sound evidence in an experiment that rules out the possibility that extraneous variables, rather than the manipulated independent variable, are responsible for the observed outcome. (chapters 6, 7)

interpretation an outcome in elaboration analysis in which, upon controlling for an intervening test variable, the original bivariate relationship reduces to zero or near zero in each partial table. (chapter 15)

interrupted time-series design a quasi-experimental design resembling the one-group pretest–posttest design but with a series of observations (measurements) before and after the treatment manipulation. (chapter 7)

intersubjective testability a condition wherein two or more scientists can agree on the results of observations. (chapter 2)

interval measurement a level of measurement that has the qualities of the ordinal level plus the requirement that equal distances (intervals) between assigned "numbers" represent equal distances in the variable being measured; consequently, with interval measurement it is possible to perform basic mathematical operations such as addition and subtraction. (chapter 4)

intervening variable a variable that is intermediate between two other variables in a causal chain. For example, if the model specifies that X affects W, which in turn affects Y, then W is an intervening variable that interprets the causal process by which X affects Y. (chapters 3, 15)

interview guide an outline of topics and questions used in in-depth interviewing; unlike the interview schedule in a structured inteview, the exact wording and order of the questions may vary. (chapter 10)

interview schedule a survey form used by interviewers that consists of instructions, the questions to be asked, and, if they are used, response options. (chapter 8)

interviewer debriefings a field pretest technique, usually involving focus group discussions, used to identify instrument problems from the interviewer's perspective. (chapter 9)

inverted-funnel sequence a sequence of survey questions that begins with the most specific questions on a topic and ends with the most general. (chapter 9)

key informant a contact who helps a field researcher gain entry to, acceptance within, and information about the research setting. (chapter 10)

law a proposition that has been repeatedly verified scientifically and is widely accepted. (chapter 2)

leading question a survey question that suggests a possible answer or makes some responses seem more acceptable than others. (chapter 9)

Likert response format the ordered responses (usually "strongly agree," "agree," "neutral," "disagree," and "strongly disagree") to individual items; *see* Likert scaling. (chapter 9)

Likert scaling a scaling approach commonly used to measure attitudes in which respondents choose from an ordered series of responses (e.g., ranging from "strongly approve" to "strongly disapprove") to indicate their reaction to each of a set of statements. (chapter 12)

listwise deletion a common procedure for handling missing values in multivariate analysis that excludes cases which have missing values on any of the variables in the analysis. (chapter 14)

longitudinal design survey designs in which data are collected at more than one point in time; *see* trend study, panel study, and cohort study. (chapter 8)

main effect in a factorial experimental design, the effect of a single independent variable (factor) by itself. (chapter 7)

manipulation check evidence collected in an experiment that the manipulation of the independent variable was experienced or interpreted by the subject in the way intended. (chapter 6)

manuscript census the original schedules on which census enumerators record their data, which are released to the public after a period of seventy-two years. (chapter 11)

marginal frequencies row and column totals in a contingency table (cross-tabulation) that represent the univariate frequency distributions for the row and column variables. (chapter 14)

matching a technique for assigning subjects to experimental groups so that the composition of each group matches that of the others on one or more characteristics thought to be related to the dependent variable; should be used in conjunction with but not as a substitute for randomization. (chapters 6, 13)

maturation a threat to internal validity; any psychological or physiological changes taking place within subjects that occur over time, regardless of experimental manipulations. (chapter 7)

mean a measure of central tendency that indicates the average value of a univariate distribution of interval- or ratio-scale data; calculated by adding up the individual values and dividing by the total number of cases. (chapter 14)

measures of association descriptive statistics used to measure the strength and direction of an observed bivariate relationship. (chapter 14)

median a measure of central tendency indicating the midpoint in a univariate distribution of interval- or ratio-scale data; indicates the point below and above which 50 percent of the values fall. (chapter 14)

membership role the participant role adopted by the researcher in participant observation studies; *see* active, complete, and peripheral membership roles. (chapter 10)

memos an adjunct to field notes in field research that consists of brief, recorded analyses that come to mind in going over notes and observations. (chapter 10)

meta-analysis systematic procedures for synthesizing and summarizing the results from previous, related studies. (chapter 12)

methodological empathy a fundamental approach to field research that attempts to understand behavior as it is perceived and interpreted by those under study. (chapter 10)

mixed mode survey a survey which uses more than one mode (questionnaires, personal interviews, telephone interviews) to sample and/or collect the data. (chapter 8)

modal instance sampling a sampling procedure recommended in evaluation research in which sites for program assessment are selected for their similarity to the setting in which the program will be implemented. (chapter 13)

mode a measure of central tendency representing the value or category of a frequency distribution having the highest frequency; the most typical value. (chapter 14)

modeling in statistical analysis, formal representations of hypothesized, or theoretical, relations among two or more variables. Usually alternative models are compared to determine their fit to the observed data. (chapter 15)

multicollinearity a problem that arises in multiple regression when combinations of two or more independent variables are highly correlated with each other, and that renders regression results (estimates of the coefficients) difficult to interpret. (chapter 15)

multiple regression a statistical method for studying the simultaneous effects of several independent variables on a dependent variable. (chapter 15)

multiple time-series design a quasi-experimental design in which a series of pretreatment and posttreatment observations (measurements) are made on a treatment group as well as on nonequivalent control groups. (chapters 7, 13)

multistage cluster sampling a sampling procedure in which sampling occurs at two or more steps or stages (e.g., a sample of school districts, then a sample of schools from the selected school districts, and then a sample of pupils from the selected schools). (chapter 5)

multivariate analysis statistical analysis of the simultaneous relationships among three or more variables. (chapter 15)

mundane realism when the events in an experiment are similar to everyday experiences. (chapter 6)

mutually exclusive the measurement requirement that each case can be placed in only one category of a variable; *see also* exhaustive. (chapter 4)

N an abbreviation representing the number of observations on which a statistic is based (e.g., $N = 279$). (chapter 14)

needs assessment the systematic assessment of the needs and problems of a community or agency and the ability of a program to meet appropriate needs. (chapter 13)

negative (inverse) relationship a relationship in which an increase in the value of one variable is accompanied by a decrease in the value of the other; that is, changes in one variable are opposite in direction to changes in the other. (chapter 3)

network sampling a sampling procedure in which respondents initially contacted in screening a probability sample are asked to identify other members of the target population who are socially linked to the respondent (e.g., relative, neighbor, co-worker). (chapter 5)

nominal measurement the lowest level of measurement, in which numbers serve only to label category membership; categories are not ranked but must be exhaustive and mutually exclusive. (chapter 4)

noncausal association when two variables are allowed to be statistically associated in a model, but a causal explanation of the association is not part of the model. (chapter 15)

nonequivalent control group design a quasi-experimental design that resembles a true experiment (the pretest-posttest control group design), except that random assignment of subjects to treatment and control groups is lacking. (chapter 7)

nonparticipant observation an approach to field research in which the researcher attempts to observe people without interacting with them and, typically, without their knowing that they are being observed. (chapter 10)

nonprobability sampling processes of case selection other than random selection. (chapter 5)

nonreactive measurement any process of measurement that by itself does not bring about changes in what is being measured. In contrast, reactive measures may produce changes in behavior because of people's awareness that they are being studied or observed. (chapter 11)

nonresponse bias in survey sampling, when nonrespondents (sampled individuals who subsequently do not respond or cannot be contacted) differ in important ways from respondents. (chapter 5)

nonspuriousness a criterion for inferring causality that requires that an association or correlation between two variables cannot be explained away by the action of extraneous variables. (chapter 3)

normal distribution a bell-shaped distribution of data that characterizes many variables and statistics, such as the sampling distribution of the mean. (chapter 14)

objectivity in science, the methological condition that makes it possible for two or more people to agree on the results of an observation; *see also* intersubjective testability. (chapter 2)

one-group pretest–posttest design a pre-experimental design in which a group of subjects is observed or measured (the pretest), a treatment is introduced, and the subjects are measured again (the posttest); threats to internal validity include maturation, history, testing, instrumentation, and sometimes statistical regression. (chapter 7)

one-shot case study a pre-experimental design in which a treatment is administered to a group, after which the group is observed or tested to determine the treatment effects; threats to internal validity include attrition, maturation, and history. (chapter 7)

open-ended questions survey questions that require respondents to answer in their own words; also called "free-response questions." (chapter 9)

operationalization the detailed description of the research operations or procedures necessary to assign units of analysis to the categories of a variable in order to represent conceptual properties. (chapter 4)

ordinal measurement a level of measurement in which different "numbers" indicate the rank order of cases on some variable. (chapter 4)

outliers unusual or suspicious values that are far removed from the preponderance of observations for a variable. (chapters 14, 15)

panel study a longitudinal design in which the same individuals are surveyed more than once, permitting the study of individual and group change. (chapters 8, 13)

parameter a characteristic of a population, such as the percentage of women or average age. (chapter 5)

partial-regression coefficients/partial slopes coefficients in a multiple-regression equation that estimate the effects of each independent variable on the dependent variable when all other variables in the equation are held constant. (chapter 15)

partial tables a control procedure used in elaboration that involves recomputing the original two-variable relationship separately for each category of the control variable. Each partial table displays the association between the two original variables when the control variable is held constant. (chapter 15)

participant observation an approach to field research in which the researcher actively participates, for an extended period of time, in the daily lives of the people and situations under study. (chapter 10)

path analysis a form of causal modeling utilizing standardized regression coefficients that provides, among other things, quantitative estimates of the total direct and indirect effects of one variable on another. (chapter 15)

percentage distribution a norming operation that facilitates interpreting and comparing frequency distributions by transforming each to a common yardstick of 100 units (percentage points) in length; the number of cases in each category is divided by the total and multiplied by 100. (chapter 14)

percentage polygon *see* frequency polygon. (chapter 14)

peripheral membership role a type of participant role in field research in which the researcher is only marginally involved in the setting or group under study; *see also* active and complete membership roles. (chapter 10)

population the total membership of a defined class of people, objects, or events; *see also* target population. (chapter 5)

position response set a tendency of some respondents to mark options located in a certain position, such as the first choice in a series. (chapter 9)

positive (direct) relationship a relationship in which an increase in the value of one variable is accompanied by an increase in the value of the other, or a decrease in one is accompanied by a decrease in the other; that is, the two variables consistently change in the same direction. (chapter 3)

posttest-only control group design the simplest of the true experimental designs, which incorporates these features: random assignment to treatment and control groups, introduction of the independent variable to the treatment group, and a posttreatment measure of both groups. (chapter 7)

pre-experimental designs designs that lack one or more features of true experiments, such as a comparison group or random assignment. (chapter 7)

pretesting a trial run of an experiment or survey instrument with a small number of preliminary subjects or respondents to evaluate and rehearse the study procedures and personnel; *see also* field pretesting. (chapters 6, 8, 9)

pretest–posttest control group design a true experimental design in which subjects are randomly assigned to (1) a treatment group measured before (the pretest) and after (the posttest) the experimental treatment and (2) a no-treatment control group measured at the same times (chapter 7)

primary sampling unit the sampling units in the first stage of a multistage sample. (chapter 5)

primary source a historical document, such as a diary or autobiography, that contains the testimony of an eyewitness; *see also* secondary source. (chapter 11)

probability proportionate to size sampling the selection of cases in cluster sampling so that the probability of selection is proportionate to the size of (i.e., the number of cases in) the cluster. (chapter 5)

probability sampling sampling based on a process of random selection that gives each case in the population an equal or known chance of being included in the sample; *see* random selection. (chapter 5)

program monitoring a type of evaluation research undertaken to determine whether a program is being carried out as designed and is reaching its intended target population; *see* evaluation research. (chapter 13)

Public Use Microdata Sample a computer-based sample of individual census returns with certain information excluded to ensure confidentiality. (chapter 11)

purposive sampling a form of nonprobability sampling that involves the careful selection of typical cases or of cases that represent relevant dimensions of the population. (chapter 5)

qualitative variable a variable that has discrete categories, usually designated by words or labels, and nonnumerical differences between categories (i.e., nominal level of measurement); *see also* quantitative variable. (chapter 3)

quantitative variable a variable that has categories that express numerical distinctions (ratio, interval, and ordinal levels of measurement); *see also* qualitative variable. (chapter 3)

quasi-experimental designs designs that lack some features (usually randomization) of true experiments, but permit stronger inferences about cause and effect than do pre-experimental designs, by means of special design features and supplementary data testing. (chapters 7, 13)

quota sampling a form of nonprobability sampling that involves the allocation of quotas of cases for various strata (usually proportionate to representation in the population) and the nonrandom selection of cases to fill the quotas. (chapter 5)

R^2 a measure of fit in multiple regression that indicates approximately the proportion of the variance in the dependent variable (spread of observations about the mean) predicted or "explained" by the independent variables. (chapter 15)

random assignment the assignment of subjects to experimental conditions by means of a random device, such as a coin toss or use of a table of random numbers, thus ensuring that each subject has an equal chance of being in any of the treatment and control conditions; also called "randomization." (chapters 6, 13)

random-digit dialing a sampling-frame technique for resolving the problem in telephone surveys of missing those with unlisted numbers: dialable telephone numbers are generated (sampled) from a table of random numbers or from a computer random-number program. (chapter 8)

random-effects model a statistical framework that assumes, in meta-analysis, that results may be shaped by between-study differences in methods (inherent biases), conditions and settings (external validity), as well as by sampling (size and design); *see also* fixed-effects model. (chapter 12)

random measurement error an error unrelated to the concept being measured that is the result of temporary, chance factors. Random errors are inconsistent across measurements (unpredictably varying in extent and direction) and affect reliability; *see also* systematic measurement error. (chapter 4)

random selection a process that gives each case in the population an equal chance of being included in the sample. (chapter 5)

range a univariate measure of variability or dispersion indicating the difference between the lowest and highest values, which is usually reported by identifying these two extreme values. (chapter 14)

ratio measurement the highest level of measurement, which has the features of the other levels plus an absolute (nonarbitrary) zero point; consequently, it is possible to form ratios of the numbers assigned to categories. (chapter 4)

reactive measurement effect an effect whereby the process of measurement itself, due to people's awareness of being studied, produces changes in what is being measured. (chapters 4, 6)

reason analysis the development of an accounting scheme outlining the categories of reasons for decisions, which serves as a model for formulating a series of questions in survey instrumentation. (chapter 9)

reciprocal causation when two variables are hypothesized to be causally linked in terms of their mutual influence on each other; also called "mutual causation." (chapter 15)

recording units units of analysis in content analysis, such as words, sentences, paragraphs, or plots. (chapter 11)

referral sampling *see* network sampling and snowball sampling. (chapter 5)

regression analysis a statistical method for studying bivariate (simple-regression) and multivariate (multiple-regression) relationships among interval- or ratio-scale variables. (chapters 14, 15)

regression line a geometric representation of a bivariate regression equation that provides the best linear fit to the observed data by virtue of minimizing the sum of the squared deviations from the line; also called the "least squares line." (chapter 14)

reliability the stability or consistency of an operational definition. (chapter 4)

replication (1) a repetition of a previous study, using a different sample of cases and often different settings and methods, for the purpose of exploring the possibility that the original findings were an artifact of particular research conditions and procedures; (2) an outcome in elaboration analysis in which the original relationship is essentially repeated in each partial table. (chapters 6, 12, 15)

research design the overall plan of an empirical study including the basic approach, sampling design, and measurement of key variables. (chapter 3)

research ethics *see* ethics.

residuals the difference between observed values of the dependent variable and those predicted by a regression equation. (chapters 14, 15)

respondent debriefings a field pretest technique in which structured follow-up questions at the end of pretest interviews are used to identify instrument problems from the respondent's perspective. (chapter 9)

response analysis a field pretest technique in which the responses of pretest respondents are tabulated and examined for problematic response patterns. (chapter 9)

response bias tendency a tendency of a respondent to answer in a certain biased direction (such as in the direction of social desirability) as a function of the content or form of survey questions. (chapter 9)

response effect in survey research, a general term for systematic errors due to such factors as biased or confusing questions, response bias tendencies (e.g., social desirability effects), the effects of interviewer's physical characteristics, and so on. (chapter 8)

response format the form of the response categories in closed-ended questions. (chapter 9)

response rate in a survey, the proportion of people in the sample from whom completed interviews or questionnaires are obtained. (chapter 8)

sample a subset of cases selected from a population. (chapter 5)

sample bias systematic error or bias in sample results due to problems in executing the sampling plan, such as incomplete sampling frames and incomplete data collection (not-at-home respondents, refusals, etc.). (chapter 5)

sampling design that part of the research plan that specifies how as well as how many cases are to be selected. (chapter 5)

sampling distribution a theoretical distribution of sample results (means, proportions, etc.) that would result from drawing all possible samples of a fixed size from a particular population. (chapter 5)

sampling error the difference between an actual population value (e.g., a mean) and the population value estimated from a sample. (chapter 5)

sampling fraction the proportion of the population included in the sample. (chapter 5)

sampling frame an operational definition of the population that provides the basis for drawing a sample; a sampling frame is constructed by either (1) listing all cases from which a sample may be selected or (2) defining population membership by a rule that provides a basis for case selection. (chapter 5)

sampling interval the ratio of the number of cases in the population to the desired sample size, which is used to select every *K*th (the interval) case in systematic sampling. (chapter 5)

scale a composite measure of a concept constructed by combining separate indicators according to procedures designed to ensure unidimensionality or other desirable qualities. (chapters 4, 12)

scatterplot a graph plotting the values of two variables for each observation. (chapter 14)

search engine an Internet (or Web) program that enables the user to search documents using directories and key words. (chapter 17)

secondary analysis analysis of survey or other data originally collected by another researcher, ordinarily for a different purpose. (chapters 8, 11)

secondary source a document, such as a written history, that contains indirect evidence of past events; that is, an account of anyone who was not an eyewitness; *see also* primary source. (see chapter 11)

selection a threat to internal validity; systematic differences in the composition of control and experimental groups. (chapter 7)

selective deposit systematic biases in the content of available historical data due to actions such as selective destruction or editing of written records. (chapter 11)

selective survival incompleteness of available historical data due to the fact that some objects survive longer than others. (chapter 11)

self-administered questionnaire a survey form filled out by respondents. When an interviewer records survey responses, the form is called an "interview schedule." (chapter 8)

semistructured interview a type of interview that, while having specific objectives, permits the interviewer some freedom in meeting them; *see also* structured interview and unstructured interview. (chapter 8)

separate-sample pretest–posttest design a quasi-experimental design having two groups that receive the treatment, one group randomly selected for pretreatment measurement and the other randomly selected for posttreatment measurement. (chapter 7)

serendipity pattern unanticipated findings that cannot be interpreted meaningfully in terms of prevailing theories and that give rise to new theories. (chapter 2)

simple random sampling a probability sampling procedure in which every possible combination of cases has an equal chance of being included in the sample. (chapter 5)

slope/regression coefficient a bivariate regression statistic indicating how much the dependent variable increases (or decreases) for every unit change in the independent variable; the slope of a regression line. (chapter 14)

snowball sampling a sampling procedure that uses a process of chain referral, whereby each contact is asked to identify additional members of the target population, who are asked to name others, and so on. (chapters 5, 10)

social bookkeeping documents, such as court records and vital statistics, that contain recorded information produced by groups or organizations. (chapter 11)

social desirability bias/effect a tendency of some respondents to bias their answers in the direction of socially desirable traits or attitudes, thereby endeavoring to enhance their self-esteem or make a favorable impression on the interviewer or researcher. (chapters 4, 9)

social impact assessment the systematic assessment of the consequences of a policy or project on individuals, groups, and communities; *see also* environmental impact assessment. (chapter 13)

social indicators broad measures of important social conditions, such as measures of crime, family life, health, schools, or job satisfaction, applied periodically to track trends. (chapter 13)

social network design a survey design in which data are collected on relationships or connections among social actors (people, organizations, countries, etc.) and the transaction flows (processes) occurring along the connecting links. (chapter 8)

Solomon four-group design a true experimental design requiring four groups: a treatment and a control group that are pretested as well as a treatment and a control group that are not pretested. This design provides information regarding the effect of the treatment, the effect of pretesting alone, the possible interaction of pretesting and treatment, and the effectiveness of the randomization procedure. (chapter 7)

specification (1) an outcome in elaboration analysis involving the increase, reduction, or disappearance of the original relationship in some partial tables but not in others (i.e., an interaction effect); (2) the formulation of a formal theoretical model. (chapter 15)

specification error the fitting of a false model to data, such as omission of an important variable, which may produce misleading results. (chapter 15)

split-half reliability an "equivalence" method for assessing reliability in which scores on half of the items of a scale or index are correlated with scores on the other half. (chapter 4)

split-panel tests experimental manipulations of question ordering, wording, or formats, used occasionally in field pretests to compare instrument versions. (chapter 9)

spurious relationship a statistical association between two variables produced by antecedent variables rather than by a causal link between the original variables. (chapter 3)

stakeholders of particular concern to evaluation researchers, the individuals or groups affected by the implementation and outcome of a social program; *see* evaluation research. (chapter 13)

standard deviation a univariate measure of variability or dispersion that indicates the average "spread" of observations about the mean; the square root of the variance, which is calculated by subtracting each value from the mean and squaring the result, then taking the arithmetic average of the squared differences. (chapters 5, 14)

standard error a statistical measure of the "average" sampling error for a particular sampling distribution; the standard deviation of a sampling distribution and thus a measure of how much sample results will vary from sample to sample. (chapter 5)

standardized regression coefficients coefficients obtained from a norming operation that puts the various partial-regression coefficients on common footing by standardizing them to the same metric of standard deviation units; consequently, indicates the number of standard deviation units the dependent variable changes for every unit change of 1 standard deviation in an independent variable. (chapter 15)

static-group comparison a preexperimental design in which a treatment group and a no-treatment group are both measured following the treatment; threats to internal validity include selection, differential attrition, and sometimes maturation. (chapter 7)

statistic a characteristic of a sample; statistics estimate population parameters; *see also* parameter. (chapter 5)

statistical regression a threat to internal validity; the tendency for extreme scorers on one measurement to move (regress) closer to the mean score on a later measurement; also known as "regression toward the mean." (chapter 7)

statistical significance *see* test of statistical significance.

stochastic component the variability in a statistical model that is attributable to random or chance factors; *see also* systematic component. (see chapter 15)

stratified random sampling a probability sampling procedure in which the population is divided into strata and independent random samples are drawn from each stratum. (chapter 5)

stratum the variable categories (e.g., male and female) into which a population is divided in selecting a stratified random sample; *see also* stratified random sampling. (chapter 5)

structural equation modeling a statistical technique for testing different theorized models, including "structures" of relationships among *observed* indicators and their underlying *unobserved* concepts. (chapter 12)

structured interview a type of standardized interview in which the objectives are highly specific, all questions are written beforehand and asked in the same order for all respondents, and the interviewer's remarks are standardized; the preferred interviewing approach when the research purpose is to test hypotheses; *see also* unstructured interview. (chapter 8)

structured observation a type of direct observation with explicit and preset procedures for deciding when, where, how, and what to observe; *see also* unstructured observation. (chapter 10)

subjective validation validity assessment based on the researcher's judgments; *see* face validity and content validity. (chapter 4)

summative evaluation a type of evaluation research that assesses the overall outcome of a social program in terms of meeting program goals and/or efficiency; *see* effect assessment and efficiency assessment. (chapter 13)

suppressor variable in elaboration analysis, a test variable that weakens or conceals a relationship, so that when it is uncontrolled, there may be little or no zero-order association. (chapter 15)

survey a major approach to social research that involves asking a relatively large sample of people direct questions through interviews or questionnaires. (chapters 1, 8, 12)

systematic component the variability in a statistical model that is attributable to hypothesized relations among variables; *see also* stochastic component. (chapter 15)

systematic measurement error error from factors that systematically influence (bias) either the process of measurement or the concept being measured. Systematic errors are consistent across measurements taken at different times or are systematically related to characteristics of the cases being measured (e.g., the cultural bias of IQ tests) and thereby affect validity; *see also* random measurement error. (chapter 4)

systematic sampling a probability sampling procedure in which cases are selected from an available list at a fixed interval after a random start. (chapter 5)

target population in sampling, the population to which the researcher would like to generalize his or her results. (chapter 5)

telephone interview a type of interview in which interviewers interact with respondents by telephone; *see also* face-to-face interview. (chapter 8)

testimony documents, such as depositions and private letters, containing individual eyewitness accounts of events. (chapter 11)

testing a threat to internal validity; changes in what is being measured that are brought about by reactions to the process of measurement; the effects of being measured once on being measured a second time. (chapter 7)

test of statistical significance a statistical procedure used to assess the likelihood that the results of an experiment or other study could have occurred by chance. (chapters 3, 6, 14, 15)

test–retest reliability a "stability" method for assessing reliability that involves calculating the correlation between outcomes of repeated applications of a measure. (chapter 4)

theoretical sampling a field-research sampling strategy in which broad analytical categories are sampled in order to facilitate the development of theoretical insights. (chapter 10)

theory a logically interconnected set of propositions that show how or why a relationship occurs. (chapter 2)

treatment the manipulated conditions comprising an independent variable in an experiment. (chapter 6)

treatment diffusion of information a threat to the internal validity, most problematic in evaluation studies, in which subjects' actions are affected by their knowledge of conditions in other treatment conditions. (chapter 13)

trend study a longitudinal design in which a research question is investigated by repeated surveys of independently selected samples of the same population. (chapter 8)

triangulation the addressing of a social research question with multiple methods or measures that do not share the same methodological weaknesses; if different approaches produce similar findings, confidence in the results increases. (chapter 12)

true experimental designs an experimental design that affords strong evidence of cause and effect by means of meeting five requirements: (1) manipulation of the independent variable, (2) measurement of the dependent variable, (3) randomization, (4) at least one comparison group, and (5) constancy of conditions. (chapters 6, 7)

*t***-test** in multiple regression a test of significance that tests the hypothesis that a regression coefficient is significantly different from zero when the other independent variables are taken into account. (chapter 15)

*t***-value** the outcome (statistic) computed from a *t*-test of significance. (chapter 15)

unidimensionality evidence that a scale or index is measuring only a single dimension of a concept. (chapter 12)

Uniform Resource Locator (URL) a standardized address code, consisting of a string of characters, used to identify and link computer files on the Internet. (chapter 17)

unit of analysis the entity about whom or which the researcher gathers information; the unit may be people, social roles and relationships, groups, organizations, communities, nations, and social artifacts. (chapter 3)

univariate analysis statistical analysis of one variable at a time; *see also* bivariate and multivariate analysis. (chapter 14)

unstructured interview a type of nonstandardized interview in which the objectives may be very general and the questions developed as the interview proceeds; preferred when the purpose is to acquire preliminary data or understandings; *see also* structured interview. (chapter 8)

unstructured observation a type of direct observation without preestablished procedures for determining when, where, and what to observe; *see also* structured observation. (chapter 10)

validity the congruence or "goodness of fit" between an operational definition and the concept it is purported to measure. (chapter 4)

variance *see* standard deviation.

verbal (self-) report the form of measurement typical of survey research consisting of people's replies to direct questions. (chapter 4)

vital statistics demographic data collected from the registration of "vital" life events, such as births, deaths, marriages, and divorces. (chapter 11)

wild-code checking a data-cleaning procedure involving checking for out-of-range and other "illegal" codes among the values recorded for each variable. (chapter 14)

within-subject designs experimental designs in which each subject experiences all experimental conditions, such as both treatment and control; *see also* between-subject designs. (chapter 7)

*Y***-intercept** the predicted value of the dependent variable in bivariate regression when the independent variable has a value of zero; graphically, the point at which the regression line crosses the *Y*-axis. (chapter 14)

zero-order relationship a bivariate correlation or the relationship in a bivariate table; zero-order means that there are no ("zero") control variables; *see also* first-order relationship. (chapter 15)

REFERENCES

Adair, J. G., T. W. Dushenko, and R. C. L. Lindsay. 1985. Ethical regulations and their impact on research practice. *American Psychologist* 40:59–72.

Adler, P. A. 1985. *Wheeling and Dealing: An Ethnography of an Upper-Level Drug Dealing and Smuggling Community*. New York: Columbia University Press.

Adler, P. A., and P. Adler. 1987. *Membership Roles in Field Research*. Newbury Park, CA: Sage.

Agger, B. 1991. Critical theory, poststructuralism, postmodernism: Their sociological relevance. *Annual Review of Sociology* 17:105–31.

Ainlay, S. C., and J. D. Hunter. 1984. Religious participation among older Mennonites. *The Mennonite Quarterly Review* 58:70–79.

Ainlay, S. C., R. A. Singleton, Jr., and V. L. Swigert. 1992. Aging and religious participation: Reconsidering the effects of health. *Journal for the Scientific Study of Religion* 31:175–88.

Alexander, C. S., and H. J. Becker. 1978. The use of vignettes in survey research. *Public Opinion Quarterly* 42:93–104.

Allison, P. D. 2002. *Missing Data*. Thousand Oaks, CA: Sage.

Alwin, D. F. 1992. Information transmission in the survey interview: Number of response categories and the reliability of attitude measurement. In *Sociological Methodology 1992* (ed. P. V. Marsden), pp. 83–118. Oxford: Basil Blackwell.

Alwin, D. F. 1997. Feeling thermometers versus 7-point scales: Which are better? *Sociological Methods and Research* 25:318–40.

Alwin, D. F., R. L. Cohen, and T. M. Newcomb. 1991. *Political Attitudes Over the Life Span: The Bennington Women After 50 Years*. Madison, WI: University of Wisconsin.

American Anthropological Association. 1998. *Code of Ethics of the American Anthropological Association*. Arlington, VA: Author.

American Psychological Association. 2002. Ethical principles of psychologists and code of conduct. *American Psychologist* 57:1060–73.

American Sociological Association. 1997. *Code of Ethics*. Washington, D.C.: Author.

Andrews, F. M., and S. B. Withey. 1976. *Social Indicators of Well-Being*. New York: Plenum.

Angell, R. C. 1951. The moral integration of American cities. *American Journal of Sociology* 57(Part 2):1–140.

Appelbaum, R. P. 1990. Counting the homeless. In *Homelessness in the United States*. Vol. II: *Data and Issues* (ed. J. A. Momeni), pp. 1–16. New York: Praeger.

Aquilino, W. S. 1994. Interview mode effects in surveys of drug and alcohol use. *Public Opinion Quarterly* 58:210–40.

Archer, D., B. Iritani, D. D. Kimes, and M. Barrios. 1983. Face-ism: Five studies of sex differences in facial prominence. *Journal of Personality and Social Psychology* 45:725–35.

Argyris, C. 1968. Some unintended consequences of rigorous research. *Psychological Bulletin* 70:185–97.

Armer, M., and A. Schnaiberg. 1972. Measuring individual modernity: A near myth. *American Sociological Review* 37:301–16.

Aronson, E., and J. M. Carlsmith. 1968. Experimentation in social psychology. In *The Hand-*

book of Social Psychology, 2nd ed., vol. II (eds. G. Lindzey and E. Aronson), pp. 1–79. Reading, MA: Addison-Wesley.

Aronson, E., N. Blaney, J. Sikes, C. Stephan, and M. Snapp. 1975. Busing and racial tension: The jigsaw route to learning and liking. *Psychology Today* 8(February):43–50.

Aronson, E., N. Blaney, C. Stephan, J. Sikes, and M. Snapp. 1978. *The Jigsaw Classroom.* Beverly Hills, CA: Sage.

Aronson, E., M. Brewer, and J. M. Carlsmith. 1985. Experimentation in social psychology. In *The Handbook of Social Psychology,* 3rd ed., vol. I (eds. G. Lindzey and E. Aronson), pp. 441–86. New York: Random House.

Asimov, I. 1980. Science must be understood and understanding. *The Evening Gazette* (Worcester, MA), 19 August, 19.

Babbie, E. 1995. *The Practice of Social Research.* 7th ed. Belmont, Calif.: Wadsworth.

Babbie, E., F. Halley, and J. Zaino. 2003. *Adventures in Social Research: Data Analysis Using SPSS for 11.0/11.5 Windows,* 5th ed. Thousand Oaks, CA: Pine Forge.

Bahr, H. M., T. Caplow, and B. A. Chadwick. 1983. Middletown III. Problems of replication, longitudinal measurement, and triangulation. *Annual Review of Sociology* 9:243–64.

Bailey, K. D. 1982. *Methods of Social Research,* 2nd ed. New York: Free Press.

Bailey, W. C. 1990. Murder, capital punishment, and television: Execution publicity and homicide rates. *American Sociological Review* 55:628–33.

Bailey, W. C., and R. D. Peterson. 1989. Murder and capital punishment: A monthly time-series analysis of execution publicity. *American Sociological Review* 54:722–43.

Bainbridge, W. S. 1982. Shaker demographics 1840–1900: An example of the use of U.S. Census enumeration schedules. *Journal for the Scientific Study of Religion* 21:352–65.

Ball, S., and G. A. Bogatz. 1970. *The First Year of Sesame Street: An Evaluation.* Princeton, NJ: Educational Testing Service.

Bass, B. M. 1955. Authoritarianism or acquiescence. *The Journal of Abnormal and Social Psychology* 51:616–23.

Batten, T. F. 1971. *Reasoning and Research: A Guide for Social Science Methods.* Boston: Little, Brown.

Baumeister, R. F., J. D. Campbell, J. I. Krueger, and K. D. Vohs. 2003. Does high self-esteem cause better performance, interpersonal success, happiness, or healthier lifestyles? *Psychological Science in the Public Interest* 4:1–44.

Baumrind, D. 1971. Principles of ethical conduct in the treatment of subjects: Reaction to the draft report of the Committee on Ethical Standards in Psychological Research. *American Psychologist* 26:887–96.

Baumrind, D. 1985. Research using intentional deception: Ethical issues revisited. *American Psychologist* 40:165–74.

Beatty, P. 1995. Understanding the standardized/non-standardized interviewing controversy. *Journal of Official Statistics* 11:147–60.

Becker, B. J., C. M. Schram, L. Chang, M. M. Kino, and M. Quintieri. 1994. Models of science achievement: Forces affecting male and female performance in school science. In *Meta-Analysis for Explanation: A Casebook* (eds. T. D. Cook, H. Cooper, D. S. Cordray, H. Hartmann, L. V. Hedges, R. J. Light, T. A. Louis, and F. Mosteller), pp. 209–81. New York: Russell Sage Foundation.

Becker, H. S. 1967. Whose side are we on? *Social Problems* 14:239–47.

Becker, H. S., and B. Geer. 1957. Participant observation and interviewing: A comparison. *Human Organization* 16:28–32.

Becker, H. S., B. Geer, E. C. Hughes, and A. Strauss. 1961. *Boys in White: Student Culture in Medical School.* Chicago: University of Chicago Press.

Berelson, B., and R. Freedman. 1964. A study in fertility control. *Scientific American* 210(5):29–37.

Berglund, E., D. A. Bernstein, R. A. Eisinger, G. M. Hochbaum, E. Lichtenstein, J. L. Schwartz, and B. C. Straits. 1974. *Guideline for Research on the Effectiveness of Smoking Cessation Programs: A Committee Report*. National Interagency Council on Smoking and Health. Chicago: American Dental Association.

Berk, R. A. 1983. Applications of the general linear model to survey data. In *Handbook of Survey Research* (eds. P. H. Rossi, J. D. Wright, and A. B. Anderson), pp. 495–546. New York: Academic Press.

Berk, R. A. 1993. Policy correctness in the ASR. *American Sociological Review* 58:889–90.

Berk, R. A., A. Campbell, R. Klap, and B. Western. 1992. The deterrent effect of arrest: A Bayesian analysis of four field experiments. *American Sociological Review* 57:698–708.

Berk, R. A., and P. J. Newton. 1985. Does arrest really deter wife battery? An effort to replicate the findings of the Minneapolis Spouse Abuse Experiment. *American Sociological Review* 50:253–62.

Berk, R. A., and P. H. Rossi. 1976. Doing good or worse: Evaluation research politically re-examined. *Social Problems* 23:337–49.

Berk, R. A., and L. W. Sherman. 1988. Police responses to family violence incidents: An analysis of an experimental design with incomplete randomization. *Journal of the American Statistical Association* 83:70–76.

Berk, R. A., G. K. Smyth, and L. W. Sherman. 1988. When random assignment fails: Some lessons from the Minneapolis Spouse Abuse Experiment. *Journal of Quantitative Criminology* 4:209–23.

Berkowitz, L., and E. Donnerstein. 1982. External validity is more than skin deep: Some answers to criticisms of laboratory experiments. *American Psychologist* 37:245–57.

Bernard, H. R. 1994. *Research Methods in Anthropology: Qualitative and Quantitative Approaches*, 2d ed. Thousand Oaks, CA: Sage.

Bernstein, I. N., G. W. Bohrnstedt, and E. F. Borgatta. 1975. External validity and evaluation research: A codification of problems. *Sociological Methods and Research* 4:101–28.

Berry, Bonnie. 1991. An account of a professional ethics violation in sociology. *The American Sociologist* 22:261–66.

Beveridge, W. I. B. 1957. *The Art of Scientific Investigation*, 3rd ed. London: Heinemann.

Biernacki, P., and D. Waldorf. 1981. Snowball sampling: Problems and techniques of chain referral sampling. *Sociological Methods and Research* 10:141–63.

Biernat, M., and C. Crandall. 2001. Two journal articles retracted, professor resigns. *Dialogue* 16, 2 (Fall):17.

Binder, A., and J. W. Meeker. 1993. Implications of the failure to replicate the Minneapolis experimental findings. *American Sociological Review* 58:886–88.

Blalock, H. M., Jr. 1964. *Causal Inferences in Nonexperimental Research*. Chapel Hill: University of North Carolina Press.

Bogdan, R., and S. J. Taylor. 1975. *Introduction to Qualitative Research Methods: A Phenomenological Approach to the Social Sciences*. New York: Wiley.

Bohrnstedt, G. W., and D. Knoke. 1994. *Statistics for Social Data analysis*, 3rd ed. Itasca, IL: F. E. Peacock.

Bollen, K. A. 1989. *Structural Equations with Latent Variables*. New York: Wiley.

Bollen, K. A., and J. S. Long. 1993. *Testing Structural Equation Models*. Newbury Park, CA: Sage.

Boruch, R. F., and W. Wothke, eds. 1985. *Randomization and Field Experimentation, New Directions for Program Evaluation*, No. 28. San Francisco: Jossey-Bass.

Box, G. E. P. 1976. Science and statistics. *Journal of the American Statistical Association* 71:791–99.

Boydstun, J. E., M. E. Sherry, and N. P. Moelter. 1978. Patrol staffing in San Diego: One- or two-officer units. In *Evaluation Studies Review Annual 3* (eds. T. D. Cook, M. L. Del Rosario, K. M. Hennigan, M. M. Mark, and W. M. K. Trochim), pp. 455–72. Beverly Hills, CA: Sage.

Boyer, P., and S. Nissenbaum. 1974. *Salem Possessed: The Social Origins of Witchcraft.* Cambridge, MA: Harvard University Press.

Bradburn, N. M., and S. Sudman. 1988. *Polls and Surveys: Understanding What They Tell Us.* San Francisco: Jossey-Bass.

Brandon, L., R. M. Gritz, and M. R. Pergamit. 1995. The effect of interview length and attrition in the National Longitudinal Survey of Youth. NLS Discussion Paper, Report NLS 95-28. Washington, D.C.: U.S. Department of Labor, Bureau of Labor Statistics.

Brazziel, W. F. 1969. A letter from the South. *Harvard Educational Review* 39:348–56.

Breault, K. D. 1994. Was Durkheim right? A critical survey of the empirical literature on *Le Suicide*. In *Emile Durkheim Le Suicide: 100 Years Later* (ed. David Lester), pp. 11–29. Philadelphia: The Charles Press.

Broh, B. A. 2002. Linking extracurricular programming and academic achievement: Who benefits and why? *Sociology of Education* 75:69–91.

Bromley, D. G., and A. D. Shupe, Jr. 1979. *Moonies in America: Cult, Church and Crusade.* Beverly Hills, CA: Sage.

Browne, J. 1976a. Personal journal: Fieldwork for fun and profit. In *The Research Experience* (ed. M. P. Golden), pp. 71–84. Itasca, IL: F. E. Peacock.

Browne, J. 1976b. The used car game. In *The Research Experience* (ed. M. P. Golden), pp. 60–71. Itasca, IL: F. E. Peacock.

Bruner, E. M., and J. P. Kelso. 1980. Gender differences in graffiti: A semiotic perspective. *Women's Studies International Quarterly* 3:239–52.

Bruyn, S. T. 1966. *The Human Perspective in Sociology: The Methodology of Participant Observation.* Englewood Cliffs, NJ: Prentice-Hall.

Bryan, J. H., and M. A. Test. 1967. Models and helping: Naturalistic studies in aiding behavior. *Journal of Personality and Social Psychology* 6:400–407.

Burt, M. R. 1992. *Over the Edge: The Growth of Homelessness in the 1980s.* New York: Russell Sage Foundation.

Burt, M. R., and B. E. Cohen. 1988. *Feeding the Homeless: Does the Prepared Meals Provision Help?* Report to Congress on the Prepared Meal Provision, vols. 1 and 2. Washington, D.C.: The Urban Institute.

Bushman, R. L. 1967. *From Puritan to Yankee: Character and the Social Order in Connecticut, 1690–1765.* Cambridge, MA: Harvard University Press.

Campbell, D. T. 1969a. Prospective: Artifact and control. In *Artifact in Behavioral Research* (eds. R. Rosenthal and R. L. Rosnow), pp. 351–82. New York: Academic Press.

Campbell, D. T. 1969b. Reforms as experiments. *American Psychologist* 24:409–29.

Campbell, D. T., and D. W. Fiske. 1959. Convergent and discriminant validation by the multitrait–multimethod matrix. *Psychological Bulletin* 56:81–105.

Campbell, D. T., and H. L. Ross. 1968. The Connecticut crackdown on speeding: Time series data in quasi-experimental analysis. *Law and Society Review* 3:33–53.

Campbell, D. T., and J. C. Stanley. 1963. *Experimental and Quasi-experimental Designs for Research.* Chicago: Rand McNally.

Cannell, C. F., and R. L. Kahn. 1968. Interviewing. In *The Handbook of Social Psychology,*

2nd ed., vol. II (eds. G. Lindzey and E. Aronson), pp. 526–71. Reading, MA: Addison-Wesley.

Cannell, C. F., K. H. Marquis, and A. Laurent. 1977. *A Summary of Studies of Interviewing Methodology. Vital and Health Statistics.* Series 2, Data evaluation and methods research. No. 69. DHEW Publ. No. (HRA) 77-1343, Health Resources Administration, National Center for Health Statistics, U.S. Department of Health, Education and Welfare. Washington, D.C.: U.S. Government Printing Office.

Carey, A. 1967. The Hawthorne studies: A radical criticism. *American Sociological Review* 32:403–16.

Carlsmith, J. M., P. C. Ellsworth, and E. Aronson. 1976. *Methods of Research in Social Psychology.* Reading, MA: Addison-Wesley.

Carlson, R. 1971. Where is the person in personality research? *Psychological Bulletin* 75:203–19.

Carnap, R. 1966. *Philosophical Foundations of Physics.* New York: Basic Books.

Carter, R. E., Jr., V. C. Troldahl, and R. S. Schuneman. 1963. Interviewer bias in selecting households. *Journal of Marketing* 27:27–34.

Cavan, S. 1966. *Liquor License: An Ethnography of Bar Behavior.* Chicago: Aldine.

Ceci, S. J., D. Peters, and J. Plotkin. 1985. Human subjects review, personal values, and regulation of social science research. *American Psychologist* 40:994–1002.

Chambliss, W. J. 1976. Functional and conflict theories of crime: The heritage of Emile Durkheim and Karl Marx. In *Whose Law What Order? A Conflict Approach to Criminology* (eds. W. J. Chambliss and M. Mankoff), pp. 1–28. New York: Wiley.

Charmaz, K. 1991. *Good Days, Bad Days: The Self in Chronic Illness and Time.* New Brunswick, NJ: Rutgers University.

Chein, I. 1981. An introduction to sampling. In *Research Methods in Social Relations,* 4th ed., (ed. L. H. Kidder), pp. 418–44. New York: Holt, Rinehart and Winston.

Chelimsky, E. 1987. The politics of program evaluation. *Society* 25, 1(Nov./Dec.):24–32.

Chelimsky, E. 1991. On the social science contribution to governmental decision-making. *Science* 254:226–31.

Choi, I., R. E. Nisbett, and A. Norenzayan. 1999. Causal attribution across cultures: Variation and universality. *Psychological Bulletin* 125:47–63.

Cialdini, R. B. 1980. Full-cycle social psychology. In *Applied Social Psychology Annual,* vol. 1 (ed. L. Bickman), pp. 21–47. Beverly Hills, Calif.: Sage.

Cialdini, R. B., and D. A. Schroeder. 1976. Increasing compliance by legitimizing paltry contributions: When even a penny helps. *Journal of Personality and Social Psychology* 34:599–604.

Clark, C. S. 1992. Underage drinking. *The CQ Researcher* 2:219–32.

Cleveland, W. S. 1985. *The Elements of Graphing Data.* Monterey, CA: Wadsworth.

Clogg, C. C., and D. O. Sawyer. 1981. A comparison of alternative models for analyzing the scalability of response patterns. In *Sociological Methodology 1981* (ed. S. Leinhardt), pp. 240–80. San Francisco: Jossey-Bass.

Clore, G. L., R. M. Bray, S. M. Itkin, and P. Murphy. 1978. Interracial attitudes and behavior at a summer camp. *Journal of Personality and Social Psychology* 35:107–16.

Code of Federal Regulations. 1995. *Title 45—Public Welfare.* Office of the Federal Register. Washington, D.C.: U.S. Government Printing Office.

Cole, S. 1994. Introduction: What's wrong with sociology? *Sociological Forum* 9:129–31.

Coleman, J. S. 1964. Research chronicle: *The Adolescent Society.* In *Sociologists at Work* (ed. P. E. Hammond), pp. 184–211. New York: Basic Books.

Coleman, J. S. 1988. Social capital in the creation of human capital. *American Journal of Sociology* 94:S95–S120.

Coleman, J. S. 1990. *Foundations of Social Theory*. Cambridge, MA: Belknap Press of Harvard University Press.

Collins, R. 1987. Looking forward or looking back: A reply to Denzin. *American Journal of Sociology* 93:180–4.

Collins, R. 1989. Sociology: Proscience or antiscience? *American Sociological Review* 54:124–39.

Comstock, G., with H. Paik. 1991. *Television and the American Child*. San Diego: Academic Press.

Converse, J. M., and S. Presser. 1986. *Survey Questions: Handcrafting the Standardized Questionnaire*. Newbury Park, CA: Sage.

Cook, T. D., and D. T. Campbell. 1976. The design and conduct of quasi-experiments and true experiments in field settings. In *Handbook of Industrial and Organizational Psychology* (ed. M. D. Dunnette), pp. 223–326. Chicago: Rand McNally.

Cook, T. D., and D. T. Campbell. 1979. *Quasi-experimentation: Design and Analysis Issues for Field Settings*. Chicago: Rand McNally.

Cook, T. D., and R. F. Conner. 1976. The educational impact. *Journal of Communication* 26(2):155–64.

Cook, T. D., F. L. Cook, M. M. Mark. 1977. Randomized and quasi-experimental designs in evaluation research: An introduction. In *Evaluation Research Methods: A Basic Guide* (ed. L. Rutman), pp. 103–39. Beverly Hills, CA: Sage.

Cook, T. D., H. Cooper, D. S. Cordray, H. Hartmann, L. V. Hedges, R. J. Light, T. A. Louis, and F. Mosteller. 1994. *Meta-analysis for Explanation: A Casebook*. New York: Russell Sage Foundation.

Cook, T. D., L. C. Leviton, and W. R. Shadish, Jr. 1985. Program evaluation. In *The Handbook of Social Psychology*, 3rd ed., vol. 1 (eds. G. Lindzey and E. Aronson), pp. 699–777. New York: Random House.

Cook, T. D., and W. R. Shadish. 1994. Social experiments: Some developments over the past fifteen years. *Annual Review of Psychology* 45:545–80.

Cooper, H. M. 1982. Scientific guidelines for conducting integrative research reviews. *Review of Educational Research* 52:291–302.

Cooper, H., and L. V. Hedges (eds.). 1994. *Handbook of Research Synthesis*. New York: Russell Sage Foundation.

Couper, M. P. 2000. Web surveys: A review of issues and approaches. *Public Opinion Quarterly* 64:464–94.

Couper, M. P., and S. E. Hansen. 2002. Computer-assisted interviewing. In *Handbook of Interview Research: Context and Method* (eds. J. F. Gubrium and J. A. Holstein), pp. 557–75. Thousand Oaks, CA: Sage.

Couper, M. P., M. W. Traugott, and M. J. Lamias. 2001. Web survey design and administration. *Public Opinion Quarterly* 65:230–53.

Cournand, A. 1977. The code of the scientist and its relationship to ethics. *Science* 198:699–705.

Crain, R. L., E. Katz, and D. B. Rosenthal. 1969. *The Politics of Community Conflict*. Indianapolis: Bobbs-Merrill.

Cramer, J. C. 1980. Fertility and female employment: Problems of causal direction. *American Sociological Review* 45:167–90.

Crandall, C. 2001. Scientific progress: A need for trust, a need for skepticism. *Dialogue* 16, 2 (Fall):20–21.

Crano, W. D. 1981. Triangulation and cross-cultural research. In *Scientific Inquiry in the Social Sciences* (eds. M. B. Brewer and B. E. Collins), pp. 317–44. San Francisco: Jossey-Bass.

Cronbach, L. J. 1982. *Designing Evaluations of Educational and Social Programs.* San Francisco: Jossey-Bass.

Crosby, F., S. Bromley, and L. Saxe. 1980. Recent unobtrusive studies of black and white discrimination and prejudice: A literature review. *Psychological Bulletin* 87:546–63.

Crossen, C. 1994. *Tainted Truth: The Manipulation of Face in America.* New York: Simon and Schuster.

Cutright, P., and F. S. Jaffe. 1977. *Impact of Family Planning Programs on Fertility: The U.S. Experience.* New York: Praeger.

Dane, F. C. 1981. *Student Workbook for Selltiz, Wrightsman, and Cook's Research Methods in Social Relations.* New York: Holt, Rinehart and Winston.

Danziger, S. K. 1979. On doctor watching: Fieldwork in medical settings. *Urban Life* 7:513–32.

Darley, J. M., and B. Latané. 1968. Bystander intervention in emergencies: Diffusion of responsibility. *Journal of Personality and Social Psychology* 8:377–83.

David, P. A. 1985. Clio and the economics of QWERTY. *American Economic Review* 75:332–37.

Davis, F. 1959. The cabdriver and his fare: Facets of a fleeting relationship. *American Journal of Sociology* 65:158–65.

Davis, J. A. 1964a. *Great Aspirations.* Chicago: Aldine.

Davis, J. A. 1964b. Great books and small groups: An informal history of a national survey. In *Sociologists at Work* (ed. P. E. Hammond), pp. 212–34. New York: Basic Books.

Davis, J. A. 1966. The campus as a frog pond: An application of the theory of relative deprivation to career decisions of college men. *American Journal of Sociology* 72:17–31.

Davis, J. A. 1971. *Elementary Survey Analysis.* Englewood Cliffs, NJ: Prentice-Hall.

Davis, J. A. 1985. *The Logic of Causal Order.* Beverly Hills, CA: Sage.

Davis, J. A., and T. W. Smith. 1992. *The NORC General Social Survey: A User's Guide.* Newbury Park, CA: Sage.

Davis, J. A., T. W. Smith, and P. V. Marsden. 2002. *General Social Surveys, 1972–2002* [machine-readable data file]. Principal Investigator, J. A. Davis; Director and Co-Principal Investigator, T. W. Smith; Co-Principal Investigator, P. V. Marsden; Sponsored by the National Science Foundation. NORC ed. Chicago: National Opinion Research Center (producer). Storrs, CT: Roper Center for Public Opinion Research, University of Connecticut (distributor).

Dawes, R. M., and T. W. Smith. 1985. Attitude and opinion measurement. In *Handbook of Social Psychology*, 3rd ed., vol. I (eds. G. Lindzey and E. Aronson), pp. 509–66. New York: Random House.

Deleire, T., and A. Kalil. 2002. Good things come in threes: Single-parent multigenerational family structure and adolescent adjustment. *Demography* 39:393–413.

DeMaio, T. J. 1984. Social desirability and survey measurement: A review. In *Surveying Subjective Phenomena*, vol. 2 (eds. C. F. Turner and E. Martin), pp. 257–82. New York: Russell Sage Foundation.

DeMaio, T. J., and J. M. Rothgeb. 1996. Cognitive interviewing techniques in the lab and in the field. In *Answering Questions: Methodology for Determining Cognitive and Communicative Processes in Survey Research* (eds. N. Schwarz and S. Sudman), pp. 177–95. San Francisco: Jossey-Bass.

Denzin, N. 1987. The death of sociology in the 1980s: Comment on Collins. *American Journal of Sociology* 93:175–80.

Deutsch, M., and M. E. Collins. 1951. *Interracial Housing: A Psychological Evaluation of a Social Experiment.* Minneapolis: University of Minnesota.

Deutsch, S. J., and F. B. Alt. 1977. The effects of Massachusetts' gun control law on gun-related crimes in the city of Boston. *Evaluation Quarterly* 1:543–68.

Deutscher, I., and M. Gold. 1979. Traditions and rules as obstructions to useful program evaluation. *Studies in Symbolic Interaction* 2:107–40.

Deutscher, I., F. P. Pestello, and H. F. G. Pestello. 1993. *Sentiments and Acts*. New York: Aldine DeGruyter.

Dibble, V. K. 1963. Four types of inference from documents to events. *History and Theory* 3:201–21.

Diener, E., and R. Crandall. 1978. *Ethics in Social and Behavioral Research*. Chicago: University of Chicago Press.

Dillman, D. A. 1978. *Mail and Telephone Surveys: The Total Design Method*. New York: Wiley.

Dillman, D. A. 2000. *Mail and Internet Surveys: The Tailored Design Method*. New York: Wiley.

Dillman, D. A., M. D. Sinclair, and J. R. Clark. 1993. Effects of questionnaire length, respondent-friendly design, and a difficult question on response rates for occupant-addressed census mail surveys. *Public Opinion Quarterly* 57:289–304.

Doherty, M. E., and K. M. Shemberg. 1978. *Asking Questions about Behavior: An Introduction to What Psychologists Do*. 2nd ed. Glenview, IL: Scott, Foresman.

Doob, A. N., and A. E. Gross. 1968. Status of frustrator as an inhibitor of horn-honking responses. *Journal of Social Psychology* 76:213–18.

Dorfman, D. D. 1978. The Cyril Burt question: New findings. *Science* 201:1177–86.

Dornbusch, S. M., and L. C. Hickman. 1959. Other-directedness in consumer-goods advertising: A test of Riesman's historical theory. *Social Forces* 38:99–102.

Douglas, J. D. 1967. *The Social Meanings of Suicide*. Princeton, NJ: Princeton University.

Douglas, J. D. 1976. *Investigative Social Research: Individual and Team Field Research*. Beverly Hills, CA: Sage.

Duncan, G. J. 2001. Panel surveys: Uses and applications. In *International Encyclopedia of the Social and Behavioral Sciences*, vol. 16, pp. 11009–15. Amsterdam: Elsevier.

Duneier, M. 1992. *Slim's Table: Race, Respectability, and Masculinity*. Chicago: University of Chicago.

Durkheim, E. 1951. *Suicide: A Study in Sociology*. Trans. J. A. Spaulding and G. Simpson. Glencoe, IL: Free Press.

Eagly, A. H. 1987. *Sex Differences in Social Behavior: A Social-Role Interpretation*. Hillsdale, NJ: Erlbaum.

Edson, L. 1970. Jensenism, *n*.—the theory that IQ is largely determined by the genes. In *Prejudice and Race Relations* (ed. R. W. Mack), pp. 35–55. Chicago: Quadrangle.

Eichler, M. 1988. *Nonsexist Research Methods: A Practical Guide*. Boston: Allen and Unwin.

Elder, G. H., Jr. 1999. *Children of the Great Depression: Social Change in Life Experience*, 25th Anniversary Edition. Boulder, CO: Westview.

Emerson, R. M. 1981. Observational field work. *Annual Review of Sociology* 7:351–78.

Emerson, R. M., ed. 1983. *Contemporary Field Research: A Collection of Readings*. Boston: Little, Brown.

Entwisle, D. R., K. L. Alexander, and L. S. Olson. 1994. The gender gap in math: Its possible origins in neighborhood effects. *American Sociological Review* 59:822–38.

Erel, O., and B. Burman. 1995. Interrelatedness of marital relations and parent-child relations: A meta-analytic review. *Psychological Bulletin* 118:108–32.

Erikson, K. T. 1966. *Wayward Puritans: A Study in the Sociology of Deviance*. New York: Wiley.

Erikson, K. T. 1967. A comment on disguised observation in sociology. *Social Problems* 14:366–73.

Erikson, K. T. 1970. Sociology and the historical perspective. *American Sociologist* 5:331–38.

Esposito, J. L., and J. M. Rothgeb. 1997. Evaluating survey data: Making the transition from pretesting to quality assessment. In *Survey Measurement and Process Quality* (eds. L. Lyberg, P. Biemer, M. Collins, E. de Leeuw, C. Dippo, N. Schwarz, and D. Trewin), pp. 541–71. New York: Wiley.

Evans, R. I. 1976. *The Making of Psychology: Discussions with Creative Contributors*. New York: Knopf.

Farley, R., and W. R. Allen. 1987. *The Color Line and the Quality of Life in America*. New York: Russell Sage Foundation.

Farley, R., and W. H. Frey. 1994. Changes in the segregation of whites from blacks during the 1980s: Small steps toward a more integrated society. *American Sociological Review* 59:23–45.

Faulkner, J. E., and G. F. DeJong. 1966. Religiosity in 5-D: An empirical analysis. *Social Forces* 45:246–54.

Feagin, J. R. 1964. Prejudice and religious types: A focused study of Southern fundamentalists. *Journal for the Scientific Study of Religion* 4:3–13.

Feagin, J. R., A. N. Orum, and G. Sjoberg, eds. 1991. *A Case for the Case Study*. Chapel Hill: University of North Carolina Press.

Felson, M. 1983. Unobtrusive indicators of cultural change: Neckties, girdles, marijuana, garbage, magazines, and urban sprawl. *American Behavioral Scientist* 26:534–42.

Ferraro, K. F., and R. LaGrange. 1987. The measurement of fear of crime. *Sociological Inquiry* 57:70–101.

Festinger, L. 1959. Sampling and related problems in research methodology. *American Journal of Mental Deficiency* 64:358–66.

Fienberg, S. E. 1971. Randomization and social affairs: The 1970 draft lottery. *Science* 171:255–61.

Fienberg, S. E. 1980. *The Analysis of Cross-classified Data*. 2nd ed. Cambridge, MA: MIT Press.

Filstead, W. J., ed. 1970. *Qualitative Methodology: Firsthand Involvement with the Social World*. Chicago: Markham.

Fine, G. A. 1987. *With the Boys: Little League Baseball and Preadolescent Culture*. Chicago: University of Chicago Press.

Finkel, S. E., T. M. Guterbock, and M. J. Borg. 1991. Race-of-interviewer effects in a pre-election poll: Virginia 1989. *Public Opinion Quarterly* 55:313–30.

Finsterbusch, K., and A. B. Motz. 1980. *Social Research for Policy Decisions*. Belmont, CA: Wadsworth.

Firebaugh, G. 1978. A rule for inferring individual-level relationships from aggregate data. *American Sociological Review* 43:557–72.

Fish, J, M. 2000. What anthropology can do for psychology: Facing physics envy, ethnocentrism, and a belief in 'race.' *American Anthropologist* 102:552–63.

Fisher, C. B., and D. Fryberg. 1994. Participant partners: College students weigh the costs and benefits of deception research. *American Psychologist* 49:417–27.

Fishman, D. B., and W. D. Neigher. 1982. American psychology in the eighties. Who will buy? *American Psychologist* 37:533–46.

Forsyth, B. H., and J. T. Lessler. 1991. Cognitive laboratory methods: A taxonomy. In *Measurement Errors in Surveys* (eds. P. P. Biemer, R. M. Groves, L. E. Lyberg, N. A. Mathiowetz, and S. Sudman), pp. 393–418. New York: Wiley.

Fowler, F. J., Jr. 1991. Reducing interviewer-related error through interviewer training, supervision, and other means. In *Measurement Errors in Surveys* (eds. P.P. Biemer, R. M. Groves, L. E. Lyberg, N. A. Mathiowetz, and S. Sudman), pp. 259–78. New York: Wiley.

Fowler, F. J., Jr. 1993. *Survey Research Methods*. 2nd ed. Thousand Oaks, CA: Sage.

Fowler, F. J., Jr. 1995. *Improving Survey Questions*. Thousand Oaks, Calif.: Sage.

Fowler, F. J., Jr., and C. F. Cannell. 1996. Using behavioral coding to identify cognitive problems with survey questions. In *Answering Questions: Methodology for Determining Cognitive and Communicative Processes in Survey Research* (eds. N. Schwarz and S. Sudman), pp. 15–36. San Francisco: Jossey-Bass.

Fowler, F. J., Jr. and T. W. Mangione. 1990. *Standardized Survey Interviewing: Minimizing Interviewer-Related Error*. Newbury Park, CA: Sage.

Fox, G. L., M. Colombo, W. F. Clevenger, and C. Ferguson. 1988. Parental division of labor in adolescent sexual socialization. *Journal of Contemporary Ethnography* 17:349–371.

Fox, W. 2003. *Social Statistics: A Text Using MicroCase*, 4th ed. Belmont, CA: Thomson/Wadsworth.

Freedman, J. L., S. A. Wallington, and E. Bless. 1967. Compliance without pressure: The effect of guilt. *Journal of Personality and Social Psychology* 7:117–24.

Freeman, H. E., and P. H. Rossi. 1984. Furthering the applied side of sociology. *American Sociological Review* 49:571–80.

Galle, O. R., W. R. Gove, and J. M. McPherson. 1972. Population density and pathology: What are the relations for man? *Science* 176:23–30.

Gallupe, R. B., A. R. Dennis, W. H. Cooper, J. S. Valacich, L. A. Bastianutti, and J. F. Nunamaker, Jr. 1992. Electronic brainstorming and group size. *Academy of Management Journal* 35:350–69.

Gans, H. 1967. *Levittowners: Ways of Life and Politics in a New Suburban Community*. New York: Pantheon.

Geer, B. 1964. First days in the field. In *Sociologists at Work* (ed. P. E. Hammond), pp. 322–44. New York: Basic Books.

General Accounting Office. 1987. *Drinking-Age Laws: An Evaluation Synthesis of Their Impact on Highway Safety*. Report to the Chairman, Subcommittee on Investigations and Oversight, Committee on Public Works and Transportation, House of Representatives. Washington, D.C.: United States General Accounting Office.

General Accounting Office, United States. 2001a. *2000 Census: Better Productivity Data Needed for Future Planning and Budgeting*. GAO-02-4. Washington, D.C.: U.S. General Accounting Office.

General Accounting Office, United States. 2001b. *2000 Census: Significant Increase in Cost Per Housing Unit Compared to 1990 Census*. GAO-02-31. Washington, D.C.: U.S. General Accounting Office.

Gerbner, G., L. Gross, M. Jackson-Beeck, S. Jeffries-Fox, and N. Signorielli. 1978. Cultural indicators: Violence profile no. 9. *Journal of Communication* 28(3):176–207.

Gergen, K. J. 1973. Social psychology as history. *Journal of Personality and Social Psychology* 26:309–20.

Giddens, A. 1965. The suicide problem in French sociology. *The British Journal of Sociology* 16:1–18.

Gilbert, J. P., B. McPeek, and F. Mosteller. 1977. Statistics and ethics in surgery and anesthesia. *Science* 198:684–89.

Gill, J. 2001. *Generalized Linear Models*. Thousand Oaks, CA: Sage.

Glaser, B. G., and A. L. Strauss. 1967. *The Discovery of Grounded Theory: Strategies for Qualitative Research*. Chicago: Aldine.

Glass, G. V. 1976. Primary, secondary, and meta-analysis of research. *Educational Researcher* 5:3–8.

Glazer, M. 1972. *The Research Adventure: Promise and Problems of Field Work*. New York: Random House.

Gleick, J. 1990. The Census: Why we can't count. *New York Times Magazine*, 15 July, 22–26, 54.

Glenn, N. D. 1977. *Cohort Analysis*. Beverly Hills, CA: Sage.

Glenn, N. D. 1978. The General Social Surveys: Editorial introduction to a symposium. *Contemporary Sociology* 7:532–34.

Glenn, N. D., and W. P. Frisbie. 1977. Trend studies with survey sample and census data. *Annual Review of Sociology* 3:79–104.

Glock, C. Y. 1962. On the study of religious commitment. *Religious Education*, Research Supplement, 42:98–110.

Glock, C. Y. 1967. Survey design and analysis in sociology. In *Survey Research in the Social Sciences* (ed. C. Y. Glock), pp. 1–62. New York: Russell Sage Foundation.

Glock, C. Y., and R. Stark. 1966. *Christian Beliefs and Anti-semitism*. New York: Harper & Row.

Goffman, E. 1979. *Gender Advertisements*. Cambridge, MA: Harvard University Press.

Gold, D. 1969. Statistical tests and substantive significance. *American Sociologist* 4:42–46.

Gold, R. L. 1958. Roles in sociological field observations. *Social Forces* 36:217–23.

Gollin, A. E. 1983. The course of applied sociology: Past and future. In *Applied Sociology* (eds. H. E. Freeman et al.), pp. 442–66. San Francisco: Jossey-Bass.

Goodman, L. A. 1961. Snowball sampling. *Annals of Mathematical Statistics* 32:148–70.

Gorden, R. L. 1975. *Interviewing: Strategy, Techniques, and Tactics*, Rev. ed. Homewood, Ill.: Dorsey.

Gordon, R. A., J. F. Short, Jr., D. S. Cartwright, and F. L. Strodtbeck. 1963. Values and gang delinquency: A study of street-corner groups. *American Journal of Sociology* 69:109–28.

Gottlieb, J., and C. S. Carver. 1980. Anticipation of future interaction and the bystander effect. *Journal of Experimental Social Psychology* 16:253–60.

Gottschalk, L. 1969. *Understanding History: A Primer of Historical Method*, 2nd ed. New York: Knopf.

Gray, D. J. 1968. Value-free sociology: A doctrine of hypocrisy and irresponsibility. *Sociological Quarterly* 9:176–85.

Gray-Little, B., V. S. L. Williams, and T. D. Hancock. 1997. An item response theory analysis of the Rosenberg Self-Esteem Scale. *Personality and Social Psychology Bulletin* 23:443–51.

Greeley, A. M., and P. H. Rossi. 1966. *The Education of Catholic Americans*. Chicago: Aldine.

Grice, H. P. 1989. *Studies in the Way of Words*. Cambridge, MA: Harvard University Press.

Griswold, W. 1981. American character and the American novel: An expansion of reflection theory in the sociology of literature. *American Journal of Sociology* 86:740–65.

Groves, R. M. 1979. Actors and questions in telephone and personal interview surveys. *Public Opinion Quarterly* 43:190–205.

Groves, R. M. 1989. *Survey Errors and Survey Costs*. New York: Wiley.

Groves, R. M., R. B. Cialdini, and M. P. Couper. 1992. Understanding the decision to participate in a survey." *Public Opinion Quarterly* 56:475–95.

Groves, R. M., and M. P. Couper. 1996. Contact-level influences on cooperation in face-to-face surveys. *Journal of Official Statistics* 12:63–83.

Groves, R. M., and M. P. Couper. 1998. *Nonresponse in Household Interview Surveys*. New York: Wiley.

Groves, R. M., and R. L. Kahn. 1979. *Surveys by Telephone: A National Comparison with Personal Interviews*. New York: Academic Press.

Groves, R. M., and K. A. McGonagle. 2001. A theory-guided interviewer training protocol regarding survey participation. *Journal of Official Statistics* 17:249–65.

Guest, A., and B. Schneider. 2003. Adolescents' extracurricular participation in context: The mediating effects of schools, communities, and identity. *Sociology of Education* 76:89–109.

Gurwitsch, A. 1974. *Phenomenology and the Theory of Science* (ed. L. Embree). Evanston, IL: Northwestern University Press.

Guttman, L. 1950. The basis for scalogram analysis. In *Measurement and Prediction* (eds. S. A. Stouffer, L. Guttman, E. A. Suchman, P. F. Lazarsfeld, S. A. Star, and J. A. Clausen), pp. 60–90. Princeton, NJ: Princeton University Press.

Haire, M. 1950. Projective techniques in marketing research. *Journal of Marketing* 14:649–56.

Hall, C. S., and G. Lindzey. 1970. *Theories of Personality*. 2nd ed. New York: Wiley.

Hall, J. A. 1984. *Nonverbal Sex Differences: Communication Accuracy and Expressive Style*. Baltimore: Johns Hopkins University Press.

Hansen, C. 1969. *Witchcraft at Salem*. New York: Braziller.

Hansen, M. H., and W. N. Hurwitz. 1946. The problem of non-response in sample surveys. *Journal of the American Statistical Association* 41:517–29.

Harding, D. J., and C. Jencks. 2003. Changing attitudes toward premarital sex. *Public Opinion Quarterly* 67:211–26.

Haveman, R. H. 1987. Policy analysis and evaluation research after twenty years. *Policy Studies Journal* 16:191–218.

Heberlein, T. A., and R. Baumgartner. 1978. Factors affecting response rates to mailed questionnaires: A quantitative analysis of the published literature. *American Sociological Review* 43:447–62.

Heckman, J. 1979. Sample selection bias as a specification error. *Econometrica* 45:153–61.

Heer, D. M. 1979. What is the annual net flow of undocumented Mexican immigrants to the U.S.? *Demography* 16:417–23.

Heilman, S. C. 1976. *Synagogue Life: A Study in Symbolic Interaction*. Chicago: University of Chicago Press.

Helmke, A., and F.-W. Schrader. 2001. School achievement: Cognitive and motivational determinants. In *International Encyclopedia of the Social and Behavioral Sciences*, vol. 20, pp. 13552–56. Amsterdam: Elsevier.

Henderson, M. R. 1975. Acquiring privacy in public life. *Urban Life and Culture* 3:446–55.

Henretta, J. A. 1965. Economic development and social structure in colonial Boston. *William and Mary Quarterly* 22:75–92.

Higbee, K. L., R. J. Millard, and J. R. Folkman. 1982. Social psychology research during the 1970's: Predominance of experimentation and college students. *Personality and Social Psychology Bulletin* 8:180–83.

Hirschi, T., and H. C. Selvin. 1967. *Delinquency Research: An Appraisal of Analytic Methods*. New York: Free Press.

Holbrook, A. L., M. C. Green, and J. A. Krosnick. 2003. Telephone versus face-to-face interviewing of national probability samples with long questionnaires: Comparisons of respondent satisficing and social desirability response bias. *Public Opinion Quarterly* 67:79–125.

Holden, C. 2001. Psychologist made up sex bias results. *Science* 294:2457.

Hollingshead, A. B. 1971. Commentary on "the indiscriminate state of social class measurement." *Social Forces* 49:563–67.

Holloway, M. 1966. Shaker societies. In *Heavens on Earth: Utopian Communities in America, 1680–1880*, 2nd ed. (ed. M. Holloway), pp. 64–79. New York: Dover.

Holsti, O. R. 1969. *Content Analysis for the Social Sciences and Humanities*. Reading, MA: Addison-Wesley.

Horowitz, I. L., ed. 1967. *The Rise and Fall of Project Camelot: Studies in the Relationship between Social Science and Practical Politics*. Cambridge, MA: MIT Press.

Horowitz, R. 1986. Remaining an outsider: Membership as a threat to research rapport. *Urban Life* 14:409–30.

Howell, J. T. 1973. *Hard Living on Clay Street: Portraits of Blue Collar Families*. Garden City, NY: Anchor/Doubleday.

Hoyle, R. H. (ed.). 1995. *Structural Equation Modeling: Concepts, Issues and Applications*. Thousand Oaks, CA: Sage.

Huck, S. W., and H. M. Sandler. 1979. *Rival Hypotheses: Alternative Interpretations of Data Based Conclusions*. New York: Harper & Row.

Hughes, E. C. 1960. Introduction: The place of field work in social science. In *Field Work: An Introduction to the Social Sciences* (ed. B. H. Junker), pp. iii–xiii. Chicago: University of Chicago Press.

Hume, D. 1748 (1951). An inquiry concerning human understanding. In *Theory of Knowledge* (ed. D. C. Yalden-Thomson). Edinburgh: Nelson.

Hummer, R. A., R. G. Rogers, C. B. Nam, and C. G. Ellison. 1999. Religious involvement and U.S. adult mortality. *Demography* 36:273–85.

Hummon, D. H. 1990. *Commonplaces: Community Ideology and Identity in American Culture*. Albany: State University of New York Press.

Humphreys, L. 1975. *Tearoom Trade: Impersonal Sex in Public Places*, Enl. ed. Chicago: Aldine.

Hyman, H. H. 1955. *Survey Design and Analysis*. Glencoe, IL: Free Press.

Hyman, H. H. 1972. *Secondary Analysis of Sample Surveys: Principles, Procedures, and Potentialities*. New York: Wiley.

Hyman, H. H., C. R. Wright, and J. S. Reed. 1975. *The Enduring Effects of Education*. Chicago: University of Chicago Press.

Ibarra, H. 1992. Homophily and differential returns: Sex differences in network structure and access in an advertising firm. *Administrative Science Quarterly* 37:422–47.

Isen, A. M., and P. F. Levin. 1972. Effect of feeling good on helping: Cookies and kindness. *Journal of Personality and Social Psychology* 21:384–88.

Jacob, H. 1984. *Using Published Data: Errors and Remedies*. Beverly Hills, CA: Sage.

Jacobs, J. 1967. A phenomenological study of suicide notes. *Social Problems* 15:60–72.

Jacobson, A. L., and N. M. Lalu. 1974. An empirical and algebraic analysis of alternative techniques for measuring unobserved variables. In *Measurement in the Social Sciences* (ed. H. M. Blalock, Jr.), pp. 215–42. Chicago: Aldine.

Jensen, A. R. 1969. How much can we boost IQ and scholastic achievement? *Harvard Educational Review* 39:1–123.

Jobe, J. B., D. M. Keller, and A. F. Smith. 1996. Cognitive techniques in interviewing older people. In *Answering Questions: Methodology for Determining Cognitive and Communicative Processes in Survey Research* (eds. N. Schwarz and S. Sudman), pp. 197–219. San Francisco: Jossey-Bass.

Johnson, J. M. 1975. *Doing Field Research*. New York: Free Press.

Johnson, R. C. 1978. A procedure for sampling the manuscript census schedules. *Journal of Interdisciplinary History* 8:515–30.

Johnstone, R. L. 1983. *Religion in Society: A Sociology of Religion*. 2nd ed. Englewood Cliffs, NJ: Prentice-Hall.

Jones, S., et al. 2002. *The Internet Goes to College: How Students are Living in the Future with Today's Technology*. Pew Internet & American Life Project. http://www.pweinternet.org

Joy, L. A., M. M. Kimball, and M. L. Zabrack. 1986. Television and children's aggressive behavior. In *The Impact of Television: A Natural Experiment in Three Communities* (ed. T. M. Williams), pp. 303–60. Orlando, Fl: Academic Press.

Junker, B. H. 1960. *Fieldwork: An Introduction to the Social Sciences*. Chicago: University of Chicago Press.

Kahn, R. L., and C. F. Cannell. 1957. *The Dynamics of Interviewing: Theory, Technique, and Cases*. New York: Wiley.

Kalton, G. 1983. *Introduction to Survey Sampling*. Beverly Hills, CA: Sage.

Kalton, G. 2000. Developments in survey research in the past 25 years. *Survey Methodology* 26:3–10.

Kalton, G., and C. F. Citro. 1993. Panel surveys: Adding the fourth dimension. *Survey Methodology* 19:205–15.

Kamin, L. J. 1974. *The Science and Politics of IQ*. Potomac, MD: Erlbaum.

Kane, E. W., and L. J. Macaulay. 1993. Interviewer gender and gender attitudes. *Public Opinion Quarterly* 57:1–28.

Kanter, R. M. 1977. *Men and Women of the Corporation*. New York: Basic Books.

Katz, D. 1949. An analysis of the 1948 polling predictions. *Journal of Applied Psychology* 33:15–28.

Katzer, J., K. H. Cook, and W. W. Crouch. 1991. *Evaluating Information: A Guide for Users of Social Science Research*, 3rd ed. New York: McGraw-Hill.

Kelman, H. C. 1968. *A Time to Speak: On Human Values and Social Research*. San Francisco: Jossey-Bass.

Kemeny, J. G. 1959. *A Philosopher Looks at Science*. Princeton, NJ: Van Nostrand.

Kephart, W. M. 1982. *Extraordinary Groups: The Sociology of Unconventional Life-styles*, 2nd ed. New York: St. Martin's Press.

Kerlinger, F. N. 1973. *Foundations of Behavioral Research*, 2nd ed. New York: Holt, Rinehart and Winston.

Keyfitz, N. 1976. World resources and the world middle class. *Scientific American* 235:28–35.

Kidder, L. H., and D. T. Campbell. 1970. The indirect testing of social attitudes. In *Attitude Measurement* (ed. G. F. Summers), pp. 333–85. Chicago: Rand McNally.

King, G. 1989. *Unifying Political Methodology: A Likelihood Theory of Statistical Inference*. Cambridge: Cambridge University Press.

King, G. 1998. *Unifying Political Methodology: The Likelihood Theory of Statistical Inference*. Ann Arbor, MI: University of Michigan.

King, G., R. O. Keohane, and S. Verba. 1994. *Designing Social Inquiry: Scientific Inference in Qualitative Research*. Princeton, NJ: Princeton University Press.

King, J. A., L. L. Morris, and C. T. Fitz-Gibbon. 1987. *How to Assess Program Implementation*. Newbury Park, CA: Sage.

Kirkpatrick, C. 1936. The construction of a belief-pattern scale for measuring attitudes toward feminism. *Journal of Social Psychology* 7:421–37.

Kiser, E., and M. Hechter. 1991. The role of general theory in comparative-historical sociology. *American Journal of Sociology* 97:1–30.

Kish, L. 1959. Some statistical problems in research design. *American Sociological Review* 24:328–38.

Kish, L. 1965. *Survey Sampling*. New York: Wiley.

Kleinman, S., B. Stenross, and M. McMahon. 1994. Privileging fieldwork over interviews: Consequences for identity and practice. *Symbolic Interaction* 17:37–50.

Kohler Riessman, C. 1990. *Divorce Talk: Women and Men Make Sense of Personal Relationships*. New Brunswick, NJ: Rutgers University Press.

Kotarba, J. A. 1977. The chronic pain experience. In *Existential Sociology* (eds. J. D. Douglas and J. M. Johnson), pp. 257–72. New York: Cambridge University Press.

Kotarba, J. A. 1980. Discovering amorphous social experience: The case of chronic pain. In

Fieldwork Experience: Qualitative Approaches to Social Research (eds. W. B. Shaffir, R. A. Stebbins, and A. Turowetz), pp. 57–67. New York: St. Martin's Press.

Kovar, M. G., and P. Royston. 1990. Comment. *Journal of the American Statistical Association* 85:246–47.

Krosnick, J. A. 1991. Response strategies for coping with the cognitive demands of attitude measures in surveys. *Applied Cognitive Psychology* 5:213–36.

Krosnick, J. A. 1999. Survey research. *Annual Review of Psychology* 50:537–67.

Krueger, R. A., and M. A. Casey. 2000. *Focus Groups: A Practical Guide for Applied Research*, 3rd ed. Thousand Oaks, CA: Sage.

Krysan, M., and Farley, R. 2002. The residential preferences of blacks: Do they explain persistent segregation? *Social Forces* 80:937–80.

Kuhn, T. S. 1962. *The Structure of Scientific Revolutions.* Chicago: University of Chicago Press.

Kunkel, D., B. Wilson, E. Donnerstein, D. Linz, S. Smith, T. Gray, E. Blumenthal, and W. J. Potter. 1995. Measuring television violence: The importance of context. *Journal of Broadcasting and Electronic Media* 39:284–91.

Kvale, S. 1996. *InterViews: An Introduction to Qualitative Research Interviewing.* Thousand Oaks, CA: Sage.

Kwak, N., and B. Radler. 2002. A comparison between mail and Web surveys: Response pattern, respondent profile, and data quality. *Journal of Official Statistics* 18:257–73.

Labov, W. 1973. The linguistic consequences of being a lame. *Language in Society* 2:81–115.

Labovitz, S., and R. Hagedorn. 1981. *Introduction to Social Research*, 3rd ed. New York: McGraw-Hill.

Latané, B., and J. M. Dabbs, Jr. 1975. Sex, group size and helping in three cities. *Sociometry* 38:180–94.

Latané, B., and J. M. Darley. 1970. *The Unresponsive Bystander: Why Doesn't He Help?* Englewood Cliffs, NJ: Prentice-Hall.

Latané, B., and S. Nida. 1981. Ten years of research on group size and helping. *Psychological Bulletin* 89:308–24.

Laumann, E. O., J. H. Gagnon, R. T. Michael, and S. Michaels. 1994. The *Social Organization of Sexuality: Sexual Practices in the United States.* Chicago: University of Chicago Press.

Lavin, M. R. 1996. *Understanding the Census: A Guide for Marketers, Planners, Grant Writers, and Other Data Users.* Kenmore, NY: Epoch Books.

Lavrakas, P. J. 1993. *Telephone Survey Methods: Sampling, Selection, and Supervision*, 2nd ed. Newbury Park, CA: Sage.

Lazarsfeld, P. F. 1955. Interpretation of statistical relations as a research operation. In *Language of Social Research* (eds. P. F. Lazarsfeld and M. Rosenberg), pp. 115–25. Glencoe, IL: Free Press.

Lazarsfeld, P. F. 1972. Some remarks on typological procedures in social research. In *Continuities in the Language of Social Research* (eds. P. F. Lazarsfeld, A. K. Pasanella, and M. Rosenberg), pp. 99–106. New York: Free Press.

Lazarsfeld, P. F., B. Berelson, and H. Gaudet. 1948. *The People's Choice.* New York: Columbia University Press.

Lee, G. R. 1984. The utility of cross-cultural data: Potentials and limitations for family sociology. *Journal of Family Issues* 5:519–41.

Leik, R. K. 1972. *Methods, Logic, and Research of Sociology.* Indianapolis: Bobbs-Merrill.

Lever, J. 1978. Sex differences in the complexity of children's play and games. *American Sociological Review* 43:471–83.

Lever, J., and S. Wheeler. 1984. *The Chicago Tribune* sports page, 1900–1975. *Sociology of Sport Journal* 1:299–313.

Levine, R. V., T. S. Martinez, G. Brase, and K. Sorenson. 1994. Helping in 36 U.S. cities. *Journal of Personality and Social Psychology* 67:69–82.

Lewontin, R. C., S. Rose, and L. J. Kamin. 1984. *Not in Our Genes: Biology, Ideology, and Human Nature*. New York: Pantheon.

Li, X., and N. B. Crane. 1996. *Electronic Styles: A Handbook for Citing Information*, 2nd ed. Medford, NJ: Information Today.

Liebert, R. M. 1976. Evaluating the evaluators. *Journal of Communication* 26(2):165–71.

Lincoln, J. R., and G. Zeitz. 1980. Organizational properties from aggregate data: Separating individual and structural effects. *American Sociological Review* 45:391–408.

Lincoln, Y. S., and E. G. Guba. 1985. *Naturalistic Inquiry*. Beverly Hills, CA: Sage.

Lipset, S. M., M. Trow, and J. Coleman. 1956. *Union Democracy*. Garden City, NY: Doubleday.

Lipsey, M. W. 1993. Theory as method: Small theories of treatments. In *Understanding Causes and Generalizing about Them, New Directions for Program Evaluation*, no. 57 (eds. L. B. Sechrest and A. G. Scott), pp. 5–38. San Francisco: Jossey-Bass.

Lipsey, M. W. 1994. Juvenile delinquency treatment: A meta-analytic inquiry into the variable of effects. In *Meta-Analysis for Explanation: A Casebook* (eds. T. D. Cook, H. Cooper, D. S. Cordray, H. Hartmann, L. V. Hedges, R. J. Light, T. A. Louis, and F. Mosteller), pp. 83–127. New York: Russell Sage Foundation.

Lofland, J., and L. H. Lofland. 1995. *Analyzing Social Settings: A Guide to Qualitative Observation and Analysis*, 3rd ed. Belmont, CA: Wadsworth.

Lofland, L. H. 1971. *A World of Strangers: Order and Action in Urban Public Space*. Unpublished doctoral dissertation, University of California, San Francisco.

Lofland, L. H. 1973. *A World of Strangers: Order and Action in Urban Public Space*. New York: Basic Books.

Loomis, W. F. 1970. Rickets. *Scientific American* 223:76–82.

Lucy, J. A., and R. A. Shweder. 1979. Whorf and his critics: Linguistic and nonlinguistic influences on color memory. *American Anthropologist* 81:581–615.

Luker, K. 1975. *Taking Chances: Abortion and the Decision Not to Contracept*. Berkeley: University of California Press.

Lundberg, G. A. 1961. *Can Science Save Us?* New York: Longmans, Green.

Maddala, G. S. 1983. *Limited-dependent and Qualitative Variables in Econometrics*. Cambridge: Cambridge University Press.

Mangione, T. W. 1995. *Mail Surveys: Improving the Quality*. Thousand Oaks, CA: Sage.

Mann, C., and F. Stewart. 2002. Internet interviewing. In *Handbook of Interview Research: Context and Method* (eds. J. F. Gubrium and J. A. Holstein), pp. 603–27. Thousand Oaks, CA: Sage.

Manning, P. K. 1987. *Semiotics and Fieldwork*. Newbury Park, CA: Sage.

Manning, W. H., and R. Jackson. 1984. College entrance examinations. In *Perspectives on Bias in Mental Testing* (eds. C. R. Reynolds and R. T. Brown), pp. 189–220. New York: Plenum Press.

Marcoux, M. 1982. *Cursillo: Anatomy of a Movement*. New York: Lambeth Press.

Mark, M. M., and R. L. Shotland. 1985. Toward more useful social science. In *Social Science and Social Policy* (eds. R. L. Shotland and M. M. Mark), pp. 335–70. Beverly Hills, CA: Sage.

Marshall, E. 2000. How prevalent is fraud? That's a million-dollar question. *Science* 290:1662.

Marx, G. T. 1988. *Undercover: Police Surveillance in America*. Berkeley: University of California Press.

Massey, D. S., R. Alarcon, J. Durand, and H. Gonzalez. 1987. *Return to Aztlan: The Social Process of International Migration from Western Mexico*. Berkeley: University of California Press.

Matthews, C., K. Everett, J. Binedell, and M. Steinberg. 1995. Learning to listen: Formative research in the development of AIDS education for secondary school students. *Social Science and Medicine* 41:1715–24.

Mazur, A. 1968. The littlest science. *The American Sociologist* 3:195–200.

McCabe, S. E., C. J. Boyd, M. P. Couper, S. Crawford, and H. D'Arcy. 2002. Mode effects for collecting alcohol and other drug use data: Web and U.S. Mail. *Journal of Studies on Alcohol* 63:755–61.

McCain, G., and E. M. Segal. 1977. *The Game of Science*, 3rd ed. Belmont, CA: Brooks/Cole.

McCall, G. J. 1984. Systematic field observation. *Annual Review of Sociology* 10:263–82.

McCall, G. J., and J. L. Simmons, eds. 1969. *Issues in Participant Observation: A Text and Reader*. Reading, MA: Addison-Wesley.

McConahay. J. B. 1986. Modern racism, ambivalence, and the modern racism scale. In *Prejudice, Discrimination, and Racism* (eds. J. F. Dovidio and S. L. Gaertner), pp. 91–125. Orlando, FL: Academic Press.

McCullagh, J. A., and J. A. Nelder. 1989. *Generalized Linear Models*. London: Chapman and Hall.

McDonald, J. A., and D. A. Clelland. 1984. Textile workers and union sentiment. *Social Forces* 63:502–21.

McFarland, S. G. 1981. Effects of question order on survey responses. *Public Opinion Quarterly* 45:208–15.

McGuigan, F. J. 1993. *Experimental Psychology: Methods of Research*. 6th ed. Englewood Cliffs, NJ: Prentice-Hall.

McGuire, M. B. 1982. *Pentecostal Catholics: Power, Charisma, and Order in a Religious Movement*. Philadelphia: Temple University Press.

McKinney, J. C. 1966. *Constructive Typology and Social Theory*. New York: Appleton-Century-Crofts.

Melbin, M. 1969. Behavior rhythms in mental hospitals. *American Journal of Sociology* 74:650–65.

Merton, R. K. 1957. *Social Theory and Social Structure*, Rev. and enl. ed. Glencoe, IL: Free Press.

Miles, M. B., and A. M. Huberman. 1994. *Qualitative Data Analysis*, 2nd ed. Thousand Oaks, CA: Sage.

Milgram, S. 1974. *Obedience to Authority: An Experimental View*. New York: Harper & Row.

Mills, J. 1976. A procedure for explaining experiments involving deception. *Personality and Social Psychology Bulletin* 2:3–13.

Mook, D. G. 1983. In defense of external validity. *American Psychologist* 38:379–87.

Morrill, C. 1995. *The Executive Way: Conflict Management in Corporations*. Chicago: The University of Chicago.

Morrison, D. E., and R. E. Henkel, eds. 1970. *The Significance Test Controversy*. Chicago: Aldine.

Mosteller, F. 1981. Innovation and evaluation. *Science* 211:881–86.

Mosteller, F., and D. L. Wallace. 1964. *Inference and Disputed Authorship: The Federalist*. Reading, MA: Addison-Wesley.

Murdock, G. P. 1967. Ethnographic atlas: A summary. *Ethnology* 6:109–236.

Murdock, G. P., and D. R. White. 1969. Standard cross-cultural sample. *Ethnology* 8:329–69.

Murray, B. 2002. Research fraud needn't happen at all. *Monitor on Psychology* 33, 2(February):27–28.

Myers, D. G. 1983. *Social Psychology*. New York: McGraw-Hill.

Nagel, E. 1967. The nature and aim of science. In *Philosophy of Science Today* (ed. S. Morgenbesser), pp. 3–13. New York: Basic Books.

Namenwirth, J. Z. 1969. Marks of distinction: An analysis of British mass and prestige newspaper editorials. *American Journal of Sociology* 74:343–60.

Nathan, G. 2001. Telesurvey methodologies for household surveys—A review and some thoughts for the future. *Survey Methodology* 27:7–31.

Navazio, R. 1977. An experimental approach to bandwagon research. *Public Opinion Quarterly* 41:217–25.

Neale, J. M., and R. M. Liebert. 1986. *Science and Behavior: An Introduction to Methods of Research*, 3rd ed. Englewood Cliffs, NJ: Prentice-Hall.

Nettler, G. 1970. *Explanations*. New York: McGraw-Hill.

Nunn, C. Z., H. J. Crockett, and J. A. Williams, Jr. 1978. *Tolerance for Nonconformity: A National Survey of Americans' Changing Commitment to Civil Liberties*. San Francisco: Jossey-Bass.

Nunnally, J. C., Jr. 1970. *Introduction to Psychological Measurement*. New York: McGraw-Hill.

Oakes, W. 1972. External validity and the use of real people as subjects. *American Psychologist* 27:959–62.

Oberschall, A. 1972. The institutionalization of American sociology. In *The Establishment of Empirical Sociology: Studies in Continuity, Discontinuity, and Institutionalization* (ed. A. Oberschall), pp. 187–251. New York: Harper and Row.

Orne, M. T. 1962. On the social psychology of the psychological experiment: With particular reference to demand characteristics and their implications. *American Psychologist* 17:776–83.

Orne, M. T. 1969. Demand characteristics and the concept of quasi-controls. In *Artifact in Behavioral Research* (eds. R. Rosenthal and R. L. Rosnow), pp. 147–79. New York: Academic Press.

Orne, M. T., and F. J. Evans. 1965. Social control in the psychological experiment: Antisocial behavior and hypnosis. *Journal of Personality and Social Psychology* 1:189–200.

Orshansky, M. and J. S. Bretz. 1976. Born to be poor: Birthplace and number of brothers and sisters as factors in adult poverty. *Social Security Bulletin* 39 (1):21–37.

Osgood, C. E., C. J. Suci, and P. H. Tannenbaum. 1957. *The Measurement of Meaning*. Urbana: University of Illinois Press.

Ostrander, S. 1993. "Surely you're not in this just to be helpful": Access, rapport, and interviews in three studies of elites. *Journal of Contemporary Ethnography* 22:7–27.

Padgett, V. R., and D. O. Jorgenson. 1982. Superstitution and economic threat: Germany, 1918–1940. *Personality and Social Psychology Bulletin* 8:736–41.

Page, E. B. 1958. Teacher comments and student performance: A seventy-four classroom experiment in school motivation. *Journal of Educational Psychology* 49:173–81.

Pancer, S. M., and A. Westhues. 1989. A developmental stage approach to program planning and evaluation. *Evaluation Review* 13:56–77.

Parade Magazine. 1993. The high cost of law and order. *Parade Magazine*, 13 June, 12.

Pate, A. M., and E. E. Hamilton. 1992. Formal and informal deterrents to domestic violence: The Dade County Spouse Assault Experiment. *American Sociological Review* 57:691–97.

Paternoster, R., R. Bachman, R. Brame, and L. W. Sherman. 1997. Do fair procedures matter? The effect of procedural justice on spouse assault. *Law and Society Review* 31:163–204.

Payne, S. L. 1951. *The Art of Asking Questions*. Princeton, N.J.: Princeton University Press.

Pearson, W., Jr., and L. Hendrix. 1979. Divorce and the status of women. *Journal of Marriage and the Family* 41:375–85.

Phillips, D. L. 1971. *Knowledge from What?* Chicago: Rand McNally.

Phillips, D. P., T. E. Ruth, and S. MacNamara. 1994. There are more things in heaven and earth: Missing features in Durkheim's theory of suicide. In *Emile Durkheim: Le Suicide One Hundred Years Later* (ed. D. Lester), pp. 90–100. Philadelphia: Charles Press.

Pierce, A. 1967. The economic cycle and the social suicide rate. *American Sociological Review* 32:457–62.

Piliavin, J. A., P. L. Callero, and D. E. Evans. 1982. Addiction to altruism? Opponent-process theory and habitual blood donation. *Journal of Personality and Social Psychology* 43:1200–13.

Piliavin, J. A., and I. M. Piliavin. 1972. Effect of blood on reactions to a victim. *Journal of Personality and Social Psychology* 23:353–61.

Pindyck, R. S., and D. L. Rubinfeld. 1981. *Econometric Models and Economic Forecasts.* New York: McGraw-Hill.

Plous, S. 1996. Attitudes toward the use of animals in psychological research and education: Results from a national survey of psychologists. *American Psychologist* 51:1167–80.

Polkinghorne, D. 1983. *Methodology for the Social Sciences: Systems of Inquiry.* Albany: State University of New York Press.

Pope, W. 1976. *Durkheim's Suicide: A Classic Analyzed.* Chicago: University of Chicago.

Portes, A. 1998. Social capital: Its origins and applications in modern sociology. *Annual Review of Sociology* 24:1–24.

Presser, S. 1984. The use of survey data in basic research in the social sciences. In *Surveying Subjective Phenomena*, vol. 2 (eds. C. F. Turner and E. Martin), pp. 93–114. New York: Russell Sage Foundation.

Presser, S., and J. Blair. 1994. Survey pretesting: Do different methods produce different results? In *Sociological Methodology 1994* (ed. P. Marsden), pp. 73–104. San Francisco: Jossey-Bass.

Rabinow, P., and W. M. Sullivan, eds. 1987. *Interpretive Social Science: A Second Look.* Berkeley: University of California Press.

Raftery, A. E. 2001. Statistics in sociology, 1950–2000: A selective review. *Sociological Methodology* 31:1–45.

Raudenbush, S. W. 1984. Magnitude of teacher expectancy effects on pupil IQ as a function of the credibility of expectancy induction: A synthesis of findings from 18 experiments. *Journal of Educational Psychology* 76:85–97.

Raudenbush, S. W., and A. S. Bryk. 2002. *Hierarchical Linear Models*, 2nd ed. Thousand Oaks, CA: Sage

Reese, H. W., and W. J. Fremouw. 1984. Normal and normative ethics in behavioral science. *American Psychologist* 39:863–76.

Reeves, B. F. 1970. *The First Year of Sesame Street: The Formative Research.* New York: Children's Television Workshop.

Reiss, A. J., Jr. 1967. *Studies in Crime and Law Enforcement in Major Metropolitan Areas.* Field Studies III, vol. II, Section I. Washington, D.C.: U.S. Government Printing Office.

Reiss, A. J., Jr. 1968. Stuff and nonsense about social surveys and observation. In *Institutions and the Person* (eds. H. S. Becker, B. Geer, D. Riesman, and R. S. Weiss), pp. 351–67. Chicago: Aldine.

Reynolds, P. D. 1971. *A Primer in Theory Construction.* Indianapolis: Bobbs-Merrill.

Riesman, D., with N. Glazer and R. Denney. 1950. *The Lonely Crowd.* New Haven, CT: Yale University Press.

Riley, M. W. 1963. *Sociological Research I. A Case Approach.* New York: Harcourt, Brace & World.

Robinson, W. S. 1950. Ecological correlations and the behavior of individuals. *American Sociological Review* 15:351–57.

Roethlisberger, F. J., and W. J. Dickson. 1939. *Management and the Worker: An Account of a Research Program Conducted by the Western Electric Co. Hawthorne Works, Chicago.* Cambridge, MA: Harvard University Press.

Rokeach, M. 1960. *The Open and Closed Mind*. New York: Basic Books.

Rosenau, P. V. 1992. *Post-Modernism and the Social Sciences: Insights, Inroads, and Intrusions*. Princeton, NJ: Princeton University.

Rosenberg, M. 1965. *Society and the Adolescent Self-Image*. Princeton, NJ: Princeton University Press.

Rosenberg, M. 1968. *The Logic of Survey Analysis*. New York: Basic Books.

Rosenberg, M. 1979. *Conceiving the Self*. New York: Basic Books.

Rosenberg, M. J. 1965. When dissonance fails: On eliminating evaluation apprehension from attitude measurement. *Journal of Personality and Social Psychology* 1:28–42.

Rosenberg, M. J. 1969. The conditions and consequences of evaluation apprehension. In *Artifact in Behavioral Research* (eds. R. Rosenthal and R. L. Rosow), pp. 279–349. New York: Academic Press.

Rosenthal, R. 1966. *Experimenter Effects in Behavioral Research*. New York: Appleton-Century-Crofts.

Rosenthal, R. 1967. Covert communication in the psychological experiment. *Psychological Bulletin* 67:356–67.

Rosenthal, R. 1969. Interpersonal expectations: Effects of the experimenter's hypothesis. In *Artifact in Behavioral Research* (eds. R. Rosenthal and R. L. Rosnow), pp. 187–227. New York: Academic Press.

Rosenthal, R. 1991. *Meta-Analytic Procedures for Social Research*. Newbury Park, CA: Sage.

Rosenthal, R. 1995. Writing meta-analytic reviews. *Psychological Bulletin* 118:183–92.

Rosenthal, R., and K. L. Fode. 1963. Psychology of the scientist: V. Three experiments in experimentor bias. *Psychological Reports* 12:491–511.

Rosenthal, R., and L. Jacobson. 1968. *Pygmalion in the Classroom: Teacher Expectation and Pupils' Intellectual Development*. New York: Holt, Rinehart and Winston.

Rosenthal, R., and R. L. Rosnow, eds. 1969. *Artifact in Behavioral Research*. New York: Academic Press.

Ross, H. L. 1992. *Confronting Drunk Driving: Social Policy for Saving Lives*. New Haven, CT: Yale University Press.

Ross, H. L. 1994. Drunk driving. Primis Books. New York: McGraw-Hill.

Rossi, P. H. 1989. *Down and Out in America: The Origins of Homelessness*. Chicago: University of Chicago Press.

Rossi, P. H., R. A. Berk, and K. J. Lenihan. 1980. *Money, Work, and Crime: Experimental Evidence*. New York: Academic Press.

Rossi, P. H., H. W. Freeman, and M. W. Lipsey. 1999. *Evaluation: A Systematic Approach*, 6th ed. Thousand Oaks, CA: Sage.

Rossi, P. H., M. W. Lipsey, and H. E. Freeman. 2004. *Evaluation: A Systematic Approach*, 7th ed. Thousand Oaks, CA: Sage.

Rossi, P. H., and W. F. Whyte. 1983. The applied side of sociology. In *Applied Sociology* (eds. H. E. Freeman et al.), pp. 5–31. San Francisco: Jossey-Bass.

Rossi, P. H., J. D. Wright, G. A. Fisher, and G. Willis. 1987. The urban homeless: Estimating size and composition. *Science* 235:1336–41.

Roth, J. 1963. *Timetables: Structuring the Passage of Time in Hospital Treatment and Other Careers*. Indianapolis: Bobbs-Merrill.

Rothbart, G. S., M. Fine, and S. Sudman. 1982. On finding and interviewing the needles in the haystack: The use of multiplicity sampling. *Public Opinion Quarterly* 46:408–21.

Rowan, A. N. 1997. The benefits and ethics of animal research. *Scientific American* 276, 2(February):79.

Ruan, D., L. C. Freeman, X. Dai, Y. Pan, and W. Zhang. 1997. On the changing structure of social networks in urban China. *Social Networks* 19:75–89.

Rubin, H. J., and I. S. Rubin. 1995. *Qualitative Interviewing: The Art of Hearing Data*. Thousand Oaks, CA: Sage.

Rubin, Z. 1970. Measurement of romantic love. *Journal of Personality and Social Psychology* 16:265–73.

Rubin, Z. 1976. On studying love: Notes on the researcher-subject relationship. In *The Research Experience* (ed. M. P. Golden), pp. 508–13. Itasca, IL: F. E. Peacock.

Ruebhausen, O. M., and O. G. Brim, Jr. 1966. Privacy and behavioral research. *American Psychologist* 21:423–37.

Rugg, D. 1941. Experiments in wording questions: II. *Public Opinion Quarterly* 5:91–92.

Saffer, H., and M. Grossman. 1989. Drinking age laws and highway mortality rates: Cause and effect. *Economic Inquiry* 25:403–17.

Sales, S. M. 1973. Threat as a factor in authoritarianism: An analysis of archival data. *Journal of Personality and Social Psychology* 28:44–57.

Sales, S. M., and K. E. Friend. 1973. Success and failure as determinants of level of authoritarianism. *Behavioral Science* 18:163–72.

Salmon, W. C. 1973. *Logic*, 2nd ed. Englewood Cliffs, NJ: Prentice-Hall.

Schaeffer, N. C. 1991. Conversation with a purpose—or conversation? Interaction in the standardized interview. In *Measurement Errors in Surveys* (eds. P. P. Biemer, R. M. Groves, L. E. Lyberg, N. A. Mathiowetz, and S. Sudman), pp. 367–91. New York: Wiley.

Schlenker, B. R., and D. R. Forsyth. 1977. On the ethics of psychological research. *Journal of Experimental Social Psychology* 13:369–96.

Schmitt, E. 2001. Count of 2000 Census said to err by millions. *New York Times*, 15 March, 12.

Schuman, H., and G. Kalton. 1985. Survey methods. In *Handbook of Social Psychology*, 3d ed., vol. I (eds. G. Lindzey and E. Aronson), pp. 635–97. New York: Random House.

Schuman, H., J. Ludwig, and J. A. Krosnick. 1986. The perceived threat of nuclear war, salience, and open questions. *Public Opinion Quarterly* 50:519–36.

Schuman, H., and S. Presser. 1981. *Questions and Answers in Attitude Surveys: Experiments on Question Form, Wording, and Context*. New York: Academic Press.

Schuman, H., and J. Scott. 1987. Problems in the use of survey questions to measure public opinion. *Science* 236:957–59.

Schwartz, H., and J. Jacobs. 1979. *Qualitative Methodology: A Method to the Madness*. New York: Free Press.

Schwartz, R. D., and J. C. Miller. 1964. Legal evolution and societal complexity. *American Journal of Sociology* 70:159–69.

Schwartz, S. H., and A. Gottlieb. 1981. Participants' postexperimental reactions and the ethics of bystander research. *Journal of Experimental Social Psychology* 17:396–407.

Schwarz, N. 1996. *Cognition and Communication: Judgmental Biases, Research Methods, and the Logic of Conversation*. Mahwah, NJ: Lawrence Erlbaum.

Schwarz, N., R. M. Groves, and H. Schuman. 1998. Survey methods. In *The Handbook of Social Psychology*, 4th ed., vol. I (eds. D. T. Gilbert, S. T. Fiske, and G. Lindzey) pp. 143–79. Boston: McGraw-Hill.

Schwarz, N., B. Knauper, H. J. Hippler, E. Noelle-Neumann, and L. Clark. 1991. Rating scales: Numeric values may change the meaning of scale labels. *Public Opinion Quarterly* 55:570–82.

Schwarz, N., F. Strack, and H. P. Mai. 1991. Assimilation and contrast effects in part-whole question sequences: A conversational logic analysis. *Public Opinion Quarterly* 55:3–23.

Sears, D. O. 1986. College sophomores in the laboratory: Influences of a narrow data base on social psychology's view of human nature. *Journal of Personality and Social Psychology* 51:515–30.

Sechrest, L., and A. J. Figueredo. 1993. Program evaluation. *Annual Review of Psychology* 44:645–74.

Seider, M. S. 1974. American big business ideology: A content analysis of executive speeches. *American Sociological Review* 39:802–15.

Selltiz, C., L. S. Wrightsman, and S. W. Cook. 1976. *Research Methods in Social Relations*, 3rd ed. New York: Holt, Rinehart and Winston.

Selvin, H. C. 1965. Durkheim's *Suicide*: Further thoughts on a methodological classic. In *Emile Durkheim* (ed. R. A. Nisbet), pp. 113–36. Englewood Cliffs, NJ: Prentice-Hall.

Shafer, R. J., ed. 1980. *A Guide to Historical Method*, 3rd ed. Belmont, CA: Wadsworth.

Shaffir, W. B., R. A. Stebbins, and A. Turowetz, eds. 1980. *Fieldwork Experience: Qualitative Approaches to Social Research*. New York: St. Martin's Press.

Shapiro, A. K. 1960. A contribution to a history of the placebo effect. *Behavioral Science* 5:109–35.

Sherman, L. W. 1992. *Policing Domestic Violence: Experiments and Dilemmas*. New York: Free Press.

Sherman, L. W. 1993. Implications of a failure to read the literature. *American Sociological Review* 58:888–89.

Sherman, L. W., and R. A. Berk. 1984. The specific deterrent effects of arrest for domestic assault. *American Sociological Review* 49:261–72.

Sherman, L. W., and R. A. Berk. 1985. The randomization of arrest. In *Randomization and Field Experimentation: New Directions in Program Evaluation*, no. 28 (eds. R. F. Boruch and W. Wothke), pp. 15–25. San Francisco: Jossey-Bass.

Sherman, L. W., and D. A. Smith. 1992. Crime, punishment, and state in conformity: Legal and informal control of domestic violence. *American Sociological Review* 57:680–90.

Shosteck, H., and W. R. Fairweather. 1979. Physician response rates to mail and personal interview surveys. *Public Opinion Quarterly* 43:206–17.

Shotland, R. L., and C. A. Stebbins. 1983. Emergency and cost as determinants of helping behavior and the slow accumulation of social psychological knowledge. *Social Psychology Quarterly* 46:36–46.

Shryock, H., J. S. Siegel, et al. 1976. *The Methods and Materials of Demography*, Condensed ed. (ed. E. G. Stockwell). New York: Academic Press.

Sigall, H., E. Aronson, and T. Van Hoose. 1970. The cooperative subject: Myth or reality. *Journal of Experimental Social Psychology* 6:1–10.

Sigall, H., and N. Ostrove. 1975. Beautiful but dangerous: Effects of offender attractiveness and nature of the crime on juridic judgment. *Journal of Personality and Social Psychology* 31:410–14.

Silverman, I. 1968. Role-related behavior of subjects in laboratory studies of attitude change. *Journal of Personality and Social Psychology* 4:343–48.

Simon, J. L. 1978. *Basic Research Methods in Social Science: The Art of Empirical Investigation*, 2nd ed. New York: Random House.

Singer, E. 1978. Informed consent: Consequences for response rate and response quality in social surveys. *American Sociological Review* 43:144–62.

Singer, E., and F. J. Levine. 2003. Protection of human subjects of research: Recent developments and future prospects for the social sciences. *Public Opinion Quarterly* 67:148–64.

Singleton, R. A., Jr. 1994. Worcester senior center survey: Summary of findings. Unpublished report.

Singleton, R., Jr., and J. B. Christiansen. 1977. The construct validation of a short-form attitudes towards feminism scale. *Sociology and Social Research* 61:294–303.

Sirken, M. G., D. Herrmann, S. Schechter, N. Schwarz, J. M. Tanur, and R. Tourangeau, eds. 1999. *Cognition and Survey Research*. New York: John Wiley & Sons.

Skinner, B. F. 1953. *Science and Human Behavior*. Toronto: Macmillan.

Skocpol, T. 1979. *States and Social Revolutions: A Comparative Analysis of France, Russia, and China*. Cambridge: Cambridge University Press.

Skocpol, T. 1984. Emerging agendas and recurrent strategies in historical sociology. In *Vision and Method in Historical Sociology* (ed. T. Skocpol), pp. 356–91. Cambridge: Cambridge University Press.

Slonim, M. J. 1957. Sampling in a nutshell. *Journal of the American Statistical Association* 152:143–61.

Slonim, M. J. 1960. *Sampling in a Nutshell*. New York: Simon and Schuster.

Smit, J. H., W. Dijkstra, and J. van der Zouwen. 1997. Suggestive interviewer behaviour in surveys: An experimental study. *Journal of Official Statistics* 13:19–28.

Smith, E. R., M. M. Ferree, and F. D. Miller. 1975. A short scale of attitudes toward feminism. *Representative Research in Social Psychology* 6:51–56.

Smith, H. W. 1975. *Strategies of Social Research: The Methodological Imagination*. Englewood Cliffs, N.J.: Prentice-Hall.

Smith, J. 1991. A methodology for twenty-first century sociology. *Social Forces* 70:1–17.

Smith, S. S., and D. Richardson. 1983. Amelioration of deception and harm in psychological research: The important role of debriefing. *Journal of Personality and Social Psychology* 44:1075–82.

Smith, T. W. 1990. The International Social Survey Program. *ICPSR Bulletin* (December):1–2.

Smith-Lovin, L., and A. R. Tickamyer. 1978. Nonrecursive models of labor force participation, fertility behavior, and sex role attitudes. *American Sociological Review* 43:541–57.

Snow, D. A., and L. Anderson. 1987. Identity work among the homeless: The verbal construction and avowal of personal identities. *American Journal of Sociology* 92:1336–71.

Snow, D. A., and L. Anderson. 1991. Researching the homeless: The characteristic features and virtues of the case study. In *A Case for the Case Study* (eds. J. R. Feagin, A. M. Orum, and G. Sjoberg), pp. 148–73. Chapel Hill: University of North Carolina Press.

Snow, D. A., and L. Anderson. 1993. *Down on Their Luck: A Study of Homeless Street People*. Berkeley: University of California Press.

Snow, D. A., S. G. Baker, and L. Anderson. 1989. Criminality and homeless men: An empirical assessment. *Social Problems* 36:532–47.

Snow, D. A., S. G. Baker, L. Anderson, and M. Martin. 1986. The myth of pervasive mental illness among the homeless. *Social Problems* 33:409–23.

Snow, D. A., R. D. Benford, and L. Anderson. 1986. Fieldwork roles and information yield: A comparison of alternative settings and roles. *Urban Life* 14:377–408.

Snow, D. A., C. Robinson, and P. L. McCall. 1991. "Cooling out" men in singles bars and nightclubs: Observations on the interpersonal survival strategies of women in public places. *Urban Life* 19:423–49.

Snow, D. A., L. A. Zurcher, and G. Sjoberg. 1982. Interviewing by comment: An adjunct to the direct question. *Qualitative Sociology* 5:285–311.

Sonquist, J. A., and W. C. Dunkelberg. 1977. *Survey and Opinion Research: Procedures for Processing and Analysis*. Englewood Cliffs, NJ: Prentice-Hall.

Sorokin, P. A.. 1937. *Social and Cultural Dynamics*, vol. II. New York: American Book Company.

Sorokin, P. A. 1950. *Altruistic Love: A Study of American "Good Neighbors" and Christian Saints*. Boston: Beacon Press.

Spencer, B. D., M. R. Frankel, S. J. Ingels, K. A. Rasinski, R. Tourangeau, and J. A. Owings. 1990. *National Education Longitudinal Study of 1988: Base Year Sample Design Report*. Washington, D.C.: U.S. Department of Education, Office of Educational Research and Improvement.

Spradley, J. P. 1980. *Participant Observation*. New York: Holt, Rinehart and Winston.

Sprague, J., and M. K. Zimmerman. 1989. Quality and quantity: Reconstructing feminist methodology. *American Sociologist* 20:71–86.

Squire, P. 1988. Why the 1936 *Literary Digest* poll failed. *Public Opinion Quarterly* 52:125–33.

St. Pierre, R. G., and T. D. Cook. 1984. Sampling strategy in the design of program evaluation. *Evaluation Studies Review Annual* 9:459–84.

Stannard, D. E. 1977. *The Puritan Way of Death: A Study in Religion, Culture, and Social Change*. New York: Oxford University Press.

Stark, R., and W. S. Bainbridge. 1996. *Religion, Deviance, and Social Control*. New York: Routledge.

Stephan, F., Jr., and P. J. McCarthy. 1958. *Sampling Opinions: An Analysis of Survey Procedure*. New York: Wiley.

Stevens, S. S. 1951. Mathematics, measurement, and psychophysics. In *Handbook of Experimental Psychology* (ed. S. S. Stevens), pp. 1–49. New York: Wiley.

Stier, H., and N. Lewis-Epstein. 2003. Time to work: A comparative analysis of preferences for working hours. *Work and Occupations* 30:302–26.

Stinchcombe, A. L. 1968. *Constructing Social Theories*. New York: Harcourt, Brace & World.

Stolzenberg, R. M., and K. C. Land. 1983 Causal modeling and survey research. In *Handbook of Survey Research* (eds. P. H. Rossi, J. D. Wright, and A. B. Anderson) pp. 613–75. New York: Academic Press.

Stolzenberg, R. M., and D. A. Relles. 1997. Tools for intuition about sample selection bias and its correction. *American Sociological Review* 62:494–507.

Stouffer, S. 1966. *Communism, Conformity, and Civil Liberties*. New York: Wiley.

Strack, F., L. L. Martin, and N. Schwarz. 1988. Priming and communication: The social determinants of information use in judgments of life-satisfaction. *European Journal of Social Psychology* 18:429–42.

Strack, F., N. Schwarz, and M. Wänke. 1991. Semantic and pragmatic aspects of context effects in social and psychological research. *Social Cognition* 9:111–25.

Straits, B. C. 1967. Resume of the Chicago study of smoking behavior. In *Studies and Issues in Smoking Behavior* (ed. S. V. Zagona), pp. 73–78. Tucson: University of Arizona Press.

Straits, B. C. 1985. Factors influencing college women's responses to fertility decision-making vignettes. *Journal of Marriage and the Family* 47:585–96.

Straits, B. C. 1998. Occupational sex segregation: the role of personal ties. *Journal of Vocational Behavior* 52:191–207.

Straits, B. C., and P. L. Wuebben. 1973. College students' reactions to social scientific experimentation. *Sociological Methods and Research* 1:355–86.

Straits, B. C., P. L. Wuebben, and T. J. Majka. 1972. Influences on subjects' perceptions of experimental research situations. *Sociometry* 35:499–518.

Suchman, L., and B. Jordan. 1990. Interactional troubles in face-to-face survey interviews. *Journal of the American Statistical Association* 85:232–41.

Sudman, S. 1976. *Applied Sampling*. New York: Academic Press.

Sudman, S., and N. M. Bradburn. 1974. *Response Effects in Surveys: A Review and Synthesis*. Chicago: Aldine.

Sudman, S., and N. M. Bradburn. 1982. *Asking Questions: A Practical Guide to Questionnaire Design*. San Francisco: Jossey-Bass.

Sudman, S., N. M. Bradburn, and N. Schwarz. 1996. *Thinking about Answers: The Application of Cognitive Processes to Survey Methodology*. San Francisco: Jossey-Bass.

Sudman, S., and G. Kalton. 1986. New developments in the sampling of special populations. *Annual Review of Sociology* 12:401–29.

Sudman, S., M. G. Sirken, and C. D. Cowan. 1988. Sampling rare and elusive populations. *Science* 240:991–96.

Survey Research Center. 1976. *Interviewer's Manual*, Rev. ed. Ann Arbor, MI: Institute for Social Research.

Sutton, J. R. 1991. The political economy of madness: The expansion of the asylum in progressive America. *American Sociological Review* 56:665–78.

Swigert, V. L., and R. A. Farrell. 1977. Normal homicides and the law. *American Sociological Review* 42:16–32.

Tanur, J. M., ed. 1992. *Questions about Questions: Inquiries into the Cognitive Bases of Surveys*. New York: Russell Sage Foundation.

Taylor, C. J. 1998. Factors affecting behavior toward people with disabilities. *The Journal of Social Psychology* 138:766–71.

Taylor, D. G., P. B. Sheatsley, and A. Greeley. 1978. Attitudes toward racial integration. *Scientific American* 238:42–49.

Taylor, S. J., and R. Bogdan. 1984. *Introduction to Qualitative Research Methods: The Search for Meanings*, 2nd ed. New York: Wiley.

Thomas, W. I., and F. Znaniecki. 1918. *The Polish Peasant in Europe and America*. Boston: Gorham Press.

Tilly, C. 1981. *As Sociology Meets History*. New York: Academic Press.

Titmuss, R. M. 1971. *The Gift Relationship: From Human Blood to Social Policy*. New York: Random House.

Tittle, C. R. 1980. *Sanctions and Social Deviance: The Question of Deterrence*. New York: Praeger.

Tourangeau, R., L. J. Rips, and K. Rasinski. 2000. *The Psychology of Survey Response*. Cambridge: Cambridge University.

Tourangeau, R., and T. W. Smith. 1996. Asking sensitive questions: The impact of data collection mode, question format, and question context. *Public Opinion Quarterly* 60:275–304.

Trachtman, L. E., and R. Perrucci. 2000. *Science Under Siege? Interests Groups and the Science Wars*. Lanham, MD: Rowman and Littlefield.

Traugott, M. W., and J. P. Katosh. 1979. Response validity in surveys of voting behavior. *Public Opinion Quarterly* 43:359–77.

Tuckel, P. S., and B. M. Feinberg. 1991. The answering machine poses many questions for telephone survey researchers. *Public Opinion Quarterly* 55:200–17.

Tukey, J. W. 1977. *Exploratory Data Analysis*. Reading, Mass.: Addison-Wesley.

Tuma, N. B., and M. T. Hannan. 1984. *Social Dynamics*. Orlando, FL: Academic Press.

Turner, C.F., and E. Martin, eds. 1984. *Surveying Subjective Phenomena*, vol. 1. New York: Russell Sage Foundation.

Twenge, J. M., W. K. Campbell, and C. A. Foster. 2003. Parenthood and marital satisfaction: A meta-analytic review. *Journal of Marriage and the Family* 65:574–83.

U.S. Bureau of the Census. 2002. *Statistical Abstract of the United States: 2002*, 122nd ed. Washington, D.C.: U.S. Government Printing Office.

Useem, B. 1980. Solidarity model, breakdown model, and the Boston anti-busing movement. *American Sociological Review* 45:357–69.

Valentine, B. 1978. *Hustling and Other Hard Work: Life Styles in the Ghetto*. New York: Free Press.

Van Poppel, F., and L. H. Day. 1996. A test of Durkheim's theory of suicide—without committing the "ecological fallacy." *American Sociological Review* 61:500–7.

Vaughan, T. R. 1967. Governmental intervention in social research: Political and ethical dimensions in the Wichita jury recordings. In *Ethics, Politics, and Social Research* (ed. G. Sjoberg), pp. 50–77. Cambridge, MA: Schenkman.

Vidich, A. J., and J. Bensman. 1958. *Small Town in Mass Society*. Princeton, NJ: Princeton University Press.

Wagenaar, A. C. 1983. *Alcohol, Young Drivers, and Traffic Accidents: Effects of Minimum Age Laws*. Lexington, MA: D.C. Heath.

Waite, L. J., and R. M. Stolzenberg. 1976. Intended childbearing and labor force participation of young women: Insights from nonrecursive models. *American Sociological Review* 41:235–52.

Wallace, W. L. 1971. *The Logic of Science in Sociology*. Chicago: Aldine-Atherton.

Wallis, W. A., and H. V. Roberts. 1956. *Statistics: A New Approach*. New York: Free Press.

Warden, G. B. 1976. Inequality and instability in eighteenth-century Boston: A reappraisal. *Journal of Interdisciplinary History* 6:585–620.

Warr, Mark. 1995. The polls poll trends: Public opinion on crime and punishment. *Public Opinion Quarterly* 59:296–310.

Warren, C. A. B. 2002. Qualitative interviewing. In *Handbook of Interview Research: Context and Method* (eds. J. F. Gubrium and J. A. Holstein), pp. 83–101. Thousand Oaks, CA: Sage.

Warren, C. A. B., and P. K. Rasmussen. 1977. Sex and gender in field research. *Urban Life* 6:349–69.

Warringer, K., J. Goyder, H. Gjertsen, P. Hohner, and K. McSpurren. 1996. Charities, no; lotteries, no; cash, yes: Main effects and interactions in a Canadian incentives experiment. *Public Opinion Quarterly* 60:542–59.

Wasserman, S., and K. Faust. 1994. *Social Network Analysis*. Cambridge: Cambridge University Press.

Watters, J. K., and P. Biernacki. 1989. Targeted sampling: Options for the study of hidden populations. *Social Problems* 36:416–30.

Wax, R. H. 1971. *Doing Fieldwork: Warnings and Advice*. Chicago: University of Chicago Press.

Webb, E. J., D. T. Campbell, R. D. Schwartz, and L. Sechrest. 1966. *Unobtrusive Measures: Nonreactive Research in the Social Sciences*. Chicago: Rand McNally.

Webb, E. J., D. T. Campbell, R. D. Schwartz, L. Sechrest, and J. B. Grove. 1981. *Nonreactive Measures in the Social Sciences*, 2nd ed. Boston: Houghton-Mifflin.

Weber, R. P. 1990. *Basic Content Analysis*, 2nd ed. Beverly Hills, CA: Sage.

Weber, S. J., and T. D. Cook. 1972. Subject effects in laboratory research: An examination of subject roles, demand characteristics, and valid inference. *Psychological Bulletin* 77:273–95.

Webster, F. E., Jr., and F. von Pechmann. 1970. A replication of the "shopping list" study. *Journal of Marketing* 34:61–63.

Wechsler, H., A. Davenport, G. Dowdall, B. Moeykens, and S. Castillo. 1994. Health and behavioral consequences of binge drinking in college: A national survey of students at 140 campuses. *Journal of the American Medical Association* 272:1672–77.

Weick, K. E. 1968. Systematic observational methods. In *The Handbook of Social Psychology*, 2nd ed., vol. II (eds. G. Lindzey and E. Aronson), pp. 357–451. Reading, MA: Addison-Wesley.

Weinberg, E. 1983. Data collection: Planning and management. In *Handbook of Survey Research* (eds. P. H. Rossi, J. D. Wright, and A. B. Anderson), pp. 329–58. New York: Academic Press.

Weinberg, M., and C. J. Williams. 1972. Fieldwork among deviants: Social relations with subjects and others. In *Research on Deviance* (ed. J. D. Douglas), pp. 165–86. New York: Random House.

Weiss, C. H. 1987. Evaluating social programs: What have we learned? *Society* 25, 1(November/December):40–45.

Weiss, R. S. 1966. Alternative approaches in the study of complex situations. *Human Organization* 25:198–206.

West, K. K, and D. J. Fein. 1990. Census undercount: An historical and contemporary sociological issue. *Sociological Inquiry* 60:127–41.

West, S. G., S. P. Gunn, and P. Chernicky. 1975. Ubiquitous Watergate: An attributional analysis. *Journal of Personality and Social Psychology* 32:55–65.

Whyte, W. F. 1958. Editorial. Freedom and responsibility in research: The "Springdale" case. *Human Organization* 17(Summer):1–2.

Whyte, W. F. 1981. *Street Corner Society: The Social Structure of an Italian Slum*. 3rd ed., rev. and enl. Chicago: University of Chicago Press.

Willard, J. C., and C. A. Schoenborn. 1995. Relationship between cigarette smoking and other unhealthy behaviors among our nation's youth: United States, 1992. Advance Data from Vital and Health Statistics, No. 263. Hyattsville, MD: National Center for Health Statistics.

Willimack, D. K., H. Schuman, B. Pennell, and J. M. Lepkowski. 1995. Effects of a prepaid nonmonetary incentive on response rates and response quality in a face-to-face survey. *Public Opinion Quarterly* 59:78–92.

Winston, S. 1932. Birth control and the sex-ratio at birth. *American Journal of Sociology* 38:225–31.

Wiseman, J. P., and M. S. Aron. 1970. *Field Projects for Sociology Students*. Cambridge, MA: Schenkman.

Xu, M., B. J. Bates, and J. C. Schweitzer. 1993. The impact of messages on survey participation in answering machine households. *Public Opinion Quarterly* 57:232–37.

Yammarino, F. J., S. J. Skinner, and T. L. Childers. 1991. Understanding mail survey response behavior: A meta-analysis. *Public Opinion Quarterly* 55:613–39.

Young, G., and W. Dowling. 1987. Dimensions of religiosity in old age: Accounting for variation in types of participation. *Journal of Gerontology* 42:376–80.

Young, R. L. 1991. Race, conceptions of crime and justice, and support for the death penalty. *Social Psychology Quarterly* 54:67–75.

Zanes, A., and E. Matsoukas. 1979. Different settings, different results? A comparison of school and home responses. *Public Opinion Quarterly* 43:550–57.

Zeisel, H. 1968. *Say It with Figures*. New York: Harper & Row.

Zelditch, M., Jr. 1962. Some methodological problems of field studies. *American Journal of Sociology* 67:566–76.

Zeller, R. A., and E. G. Carmines. 1980. *Measurement in the Social Sciences: The Link between Theory and Data*. New York: Cambridge University Press.

Zimbardo, P. G. 1973. On the ethics of intervention in human psychological research: With special reference to the Stanford prison study. *Cognition* 2:243–56.

Zimbardo, P. G., C. Haney, W. C. Banks, and D. Jaffe. 1973. The mind is a formidable jailer: A pirandellian prison. *New York Times Magazine* 122(April 8):38–60.

Zipp, J. F., and J. Toth. 2002. She said, he said, they said: The impact of spousal presence in survey research. *Public Opinion Quarterly* 66:177–208.

Zito, G. V. 1975. *Methodology and Meanings: Varieties of Sociological Inquiry*. New York: Praeger.

Zoble, E. J., and R. S. Lehman. 1969. Interaction of subject-experimenter expectancy effects in a tone length discrimination task. *Behavioral Science* 14:357–63.

Zurcher, L. A. 1968. Social psychological functions of ephemeral roles: A disaster work crew. *Human Organization* 27:281–97.

NAME INDEX

SUBJECT INDEX